Gaming and Cognition:
Theories and Practice from the Learning Sciences

Richard Van Eck
University of North Dakota, USA

INFORMATION SCIENCE REFERENCE

Hershey · New York

Director of Editorial Content:	Kristin Klinger
Director of Book Publications:	Julia Mosemann
Acquisitions Editor:	Lindsay Johnston
Development Editor:	Elizabeth Ardner
Publishing Assistant:	Deanna Zombro
Typesetter:	Deanna Zombro
Production Editor:	Jamie Snavely
Cover Design:	Lisa Tosheff
Printed at:	Yurchak Printing Inc.

Published in the United States of America by
Information Science Reference (an imprint of IGI Global)
701 E. Chocolate Avenue
Hershey PA 17033
Tel: 717-533-8845
Fax: 717-533-8661
E-mail: cust@igi-global.com
Web site: http://www.igi-global.com/reference

Library of Congress Cataloging-in-Publication Data

Gaming and cognition : theories and practice from the learning sciences / Richard Van Eck, editor.
    p. cm.
  Includes bibliographical references and index.
  Summary: "This book applies the principles of research in the study of human cognition to games, with chapters representing 15 different disciplines in the learning sciences (psychology, serious game design, educational technology, applied linguistics, instructional design, eLearning, computer engineering, educational psychology, cognitive science, digital media, human-computer interaction, artificial intelligence, computer science, anthropology, education)"--Provided by publisher.
  ISBN 978-1-61520-717-6 (hardcover) -- ISBN 978-1-61520-718-3 (ebook) 1. Video games--Psychological aspects. 2. Computer games--Psychological aspects. 3. Cognitive learning. 4. Learning, Psychology of. 5. Learning--Social aspects. I. Van Eck, Richard, 1964-
  GV1469.3.G425 2010
  794.801'9--dc22
                    2009044468

British Cataloguing in Publication Data
A Cataloguing in Publication record for this book is available from the British Library.

Table of Contents

Section 1
Historical Perspectives

Section 2
New Theories and Models

Section 3
Theory Into Practice

Section 4
Research and Design

Section 5
Practitioner Perspectives

Detailed Table of Contents

Section 1
Historical Perspectives

Chapter 1
Video Games Revisited 1
Patricia M. Greenfield, University of California - Los Angeles, USA

When Greenfield wrote her chapter on video games in her 1984 landmark book *Mind and Media*, video games were played primarily in arcades, and popular opinion held that they were at best a waste of time and at worst dangerous technology sure to lead to increased aggression. As a cognitive psychologist and media scholar, she was interested in what was really going on in these games and brought the theoretical rigor and research tools of her discipline to bear on games and their cognitive effects on game players. Part anthropologist and part stranger in a strange land, she studied games and game players and played games herself. Her conclusions at the time were both surprising and prescient; research failed to support the common sense connection of games and violent behavior, and games in fact appeared to have cognitive benefits unseen by those who did not play them. Her conclusions both provided a glimpse of then-current research and laid the foundation for a rigorous empirical study of games and cognition. What is shocking upon rereading this chapter today is how relevant it remains and how many of the research possibilities remain largely unexplored. Her chapter is reprinted here along with her current analysis and thoughts about her original ideas, 25 years later. Its placement as the first chapter in a book dedicated to cognitive perspectives on games is appropriate, both as a reminder of where we come from and of how far we have yet to go.

Chapter 2
Distinctions Between Games and Learning: A Review of Current Literature on
Games in Education 22
Katrin Becker, Simon Fraser University, Canada

One of the challenges we face in serious games lies in being aware of the work that has come before us (e.g., Greenfield's chapter at the beginning of this volume) and building on it as we generate new research. In the early years, it was possible (if not always done) to survey the entire landscape of serious games literature. With the explosion of research in this field over the last 5 years, it has become much harder to remain aware of all the research, let alone to sift through it for the most salient and coherent strands for future research. In this chapter, Becker presents an overview of some of the most significant research in serious games. While a complete, comprehensive literature review of the field is impossible, the work she presents is arguably a core research canon of which any serious games researcher today should be aware.

Chapter 3

Massive multiplayer online role-playing games (MMORPGs) are among the most popular games world-wide and may also be the best games for addressing 21st-century learning skills like distributed problem solving and social negotiation and collaboration. Anderson provides an overview of MMORPGs and how they differ from other game formats; generates a theoretical framework for their educational potential drawn from the fields of education, psychology, and linguistics; and provides an analysis of current research trends and needs with MMORPGs. He closes with a discussion of some of the implications for future research on MMORPGs and serious games.

Section 2
New Theories and Models

While most would agree that any instruction, be it a game or classroom lesson plan, is unlikely to succeed without a clear understanding of the desired outcomes, Dempsey notes that instructional taxonomies are rarely used explicitly by serious game designers. An experienced researcher and game designer himself, Dempsey combines research on simulations, games, and instructional design with his experience as an educational game designer to propose an integrated framework (the Pyramid of Fidelity) for the design of serious games. This framework, which comprises five major cognitive learning outcomes, focuses on fidelity to learning outcomes rather than on instructional taxonomies, making the framework easier to apply and more accessible to a wider audience. Because the design process focuses on iterative re-finement of learning outcomes, it is more compatible with the emergent, bottom-up processes typically associated with game design. He uses the framework to generate design propositions that can be used in serious game design and provides an example of each one in a gaming context.

Chapter 5

One of the essential characteristics of good game design is engagement, but this remains one of the most challenging aspects to design. This chapter sets out to examine the potential for design theory to provide heuristics for designing engaging games. In describing operational principles (the essential description of how something functions) of engagement, Swan identifies the core components of engagement (meaningful challenge, self-consistent setting, core performance, and embedded helps) and the active principle that animates the process of engagement. He also uncovers fundamental misconceptions of feedback and proposes a new concept called feedforward that is essential to engagement. He closes with suggestions for further research and design to extend and validate this approach to designing serious games.

Chapter 6

    Wen-Hao David Huang, University of Illinois, Urban-Champaign, USA
    Sharon Tettegah, University of Illinois, Urban-Champaign, USA

Empathy may be a precondition for attitude change in persuasive games. The authors in this chapter suggest that if one does not empathize with nonplayer characters and player characters in games like *Darfur is Dying*, it is less likely that attitudes will change. Because persuasive games have different learning outcomes from educational games (changes in affective states rather than knowledge schemas), some may assume that educational theory and instructional design research have little to offer designers of persuasive games. The authors of this chapter, however, suggest that empathy may have its own cognitive requirements and effects, and that cognitive load theory may have important applications to the study and design of persuasive games. Using research on empathy development and cognitive load theory, the authors propose a conceptual framework to guide future research and design.

Section 3
Theory Into Practice

Chapter 7

    Amy B. Adcock, Old Dominion University, USA
    Ginger S. Watson, Old Dominion University, USA
    Gary R. Morrison Old Dominion University, USA
    Lee A. Belfore, Old Dominion University, USA

Games are, the authors of this chapter contend, essentially exploratory learning environments designed to promote expertise in a given domain. As such, they are amenable to research and design principles from the study of expertise development in technology-based environments such as simulations. They begin with an overview of the research on expertise development, including the need for adaptive instructional strategies to support different levels of expertise on the part of learners in general and within learners as their domain expertise develops during instruction. They then pull from existing research on simulation design and interface affordances to generate a set of heuristics for serious game design to support the development of expertise in different domains.

Chapter 8

Cognitive load theory is arguably one the most important contributions of cognitive science to the design of serious games. The addition of learning outcomes to a game environment, regardless of design methodology, creates an additional load on player cognition independent of that associated with normal gameplay. Some of what must be learned when playing a game relates to the navigation of the interface (tools and processes within the game, game controller functions, etc.). This is referred to as extraneous cognitive load, which should be minimized when possible to leave sufficient cognitive resources for players to deal with the complexity of the content (intrinsic cognitive load) and while processing new information into knowledge via metacognitive activities (germane cognitive load). The authors of this chapter, recognized experts in cognitive load theory, provide a detailed description of cognitive load theory and several design heuristics for managing cognitive load in serious games that are backed by extensive empirical evidence.

Chapter 9

Constructivist principles, because they focus on socially negotiated and/or constructed knowledge as a result of an individual's interaction with the environment, have often been cited as particularly suited to describing learning in games. But it is a significant leap from such assertions to the kinds of design heuristics we need for creating serious games. In this chapter, Charsky outlines constructivist teaching structures, which include environments such as open learning environments, cognitive apprenticeship, and anchored instruction. Each of these structures provides the potential for guiding the design of serious game environments. Charsky then maps these teaching structures to specific gameplay characteristics and game genres to illustrate how they are amenable to games and how game design can rely on them to address educational outcomes.

Chapter 10

We often discuss scenarios as convenient ways of capturing design and player experiences within games. Closer inspection of this familiar term, however, reveals little in the way of design heuristics. What makes a good scenario? What is the relationship of scenario to narrative? If we all define the term "scenario" differently, its value for design and analysis is diminished. Marsh examines the use and definition of this term in different fields, including film, human–computer interaction, and activity theory, to see what commonalities and gaps exist and to identify core design characteristics that may inform serious game design. What emerges in the process is an interdisciplinary framework that bridges the design, development, and implementation processes, preserves the flexibility of the concept, and provides a common set of tools for designers to use that also accounts for learning objectives and the need for assessment.

Section 4
Research and Design

Chapter 11

The literature is rife with claims that games induce flow, but nothing in regard to what flow looks like, how it is measured, what design propositions promote flow, or how learning is both measured and related to flow. The apparent reluctance of our field to engage in the development of conceptual models of constructs such as flow and engagement, and to then to then validate those models validate those models via rigorous empirical testing, may present our most significant challenge to becoming a true discipline. In this chapter, we see perhaps a model for future studies. Reese and colleagues have developed a research program they call Cyberlearning through Game-based, Metaphor Enhanced Learning Objects, or CyGaMEs. As part of this research program, they have further developed a suite of assessment tools for measuring learning and related cognitive constructs. Reese describes their approach to research using a game they have developed as a case study. She then describes one assessment tool in particular, the Flowometer, which they use to measure flow. After describing the tool within the context of its application within a game, she suggests that the tool and research CyGaMEs platform be adopted by others looking to do similar forms of research.

Chapter 12

Because commercial games are designed to entertain and serious educational games are designed to teach first and entertain second, we often focus on how to blend learning and engagement seamlessly within educational games. But one of the underlying assumptions of this approach is that all learners do play games already and that they will want to play all games equally. After all, if we are going to invest in building a learning game, our assumption is that all students will participate. The authors of this chapter point out that while children who play games self-select this activity, game-based learning will often be a required activity in which all students must participate. This means that designers should account for game experience, game preferences, and other individual learning differences when designing educational games. In this chapter, they identify four key issues backed by research, game literacy, motivation, goal orientation, and mindset, and describe how all can be accommodated within a single game experience if included in the design parameters up front.

Section 5
Practitioner Perspectives

Chapter 13

Artificial intelligence in games is usually discussed in the context of nonplayer character behavior and game adaptation to ongoing events in commercial games, rather than as a pedagogical component of serious games. Designers at Alelo make it a key component of their approach to teaching language, along with principles of situated learning and cognition. By situating learning within a meaningful context, including cultural components of learning as part of that context and using artificial intelligence to adjust the real-time conversations players engage in, they have created a successful model of language learning that has been used with more than 50,000 people to date. In this chapter, the authors describe their approach and the theory that drives pedagogical and game design and development, including the way they address the need for prior knowledge (blended online training and games, and game affordances), how they address the resulting instructional design challenges (e.g., rapid prototyping and iterative design processes), and what the end results look like (by describing several of the games they have developed). What emerges is a rare, seamless, and transparent description that is equal parts theory, instructional design, and game development.

Chapter 14

Game design and development is a resource-intensive process that few of us have engaged in fully from start to finish, and when we do, the result is often intended as much for research as it is for integrated instructional use. The game designers at the Worldwide Web Instructional Committee at North Dakota State University have developed many games over the last decade, each for a specific instructional need and each exhibiting the same core design features. This "signature" is the result of theoretical, philosophical, and practical research and experience, resulting in a suite of empirically tested and validated instructional games. In this chapter, the authors describe the theoretical and practical origins of their approach, the empirical testing they have done for the key components of their design signature, and some of the games they have developed. They suggest that this approach, while certainly not the only way to make games, is nonetheless a replicable, established approach to designing serious games that others may adopt, adapt, and validate further.

Foreword

More than two millennia ago on the shores of what we now call Turkey, Heraclitus of Ephesus wrote: "You cannot step twice into the same river."

Heraclitus was a philosopher, and although the city in which he lived remained relatively unchanged for 500 years, he argued that existence is a state of constant flux. Nothing remains constant.

How much more apt, then, is Heraclitus' epigram today, when in less than three decades, computers more powerful than those that once sent the first humans to the moon are available in the pocket of any teenager with a cell phone?

Not all changes are equal, however. A river is different from moment to moment, but each molecule of water is much the same as the next, even if their exact position and velocity change. The shape of the river shifts over time, but its motion still obeys the same basic laws of physics. On the other hand, a car is not just a horse-drawn carriage that goes faster, and the printing press did more than just make copies of the Bible.

The central question behind the essays in this volume is thus critical, urgent, and enduring. In the face of dramatic technological change, few doubt that computers have a role to play in preparing young people for a future where the norm is continual change: in how we work, how we entertain ourselves, how we make civic decisions, and how we take care of our own bodies.

But do computers fundamentally change how we think about education? Is the psychology of computer games a new field or merely an extension of existing ideas into a new medium? What lessons of the past should we carry forward as we face the future?

The field of the Learning Sciences is relatively new, but it builds on a long tradition of research in education. The remit of the learning scientist is to understand the particular forms of cognition that take place when people develop skills, capacities, and habits of mind that matter in the world—when they grow to be more full participants in the world around them. The Learning Sciences exist at the intersection of individual development, social interaction, and the technologies and systems in which and through which learning takes place.

The study of games and simulations has an even longer pedigree, perhaps because of the close association between game theory and economics, war, and politics. Film and popular media more generally have similarly been subjected to extensive examination, again because of their commercial and cultural impact. We understand a great deal about the mechanics of the cinema and of games.

With all of this knowledge of the pieces, though, we have yet to solve the equation:

Learning Theory + Game Theory + Media Theory = ??

At this early stage in the development of a framework for thinking about games and cognition, the discussion and debate are lively. Questions of definition abound: What is a game? What is a computer game? What is the difference—or is there a difference—between a learning game and an entertaining game? Are games just interactive movies? Are computer games just board games played on a screen? Is learning with a computer just learning with a particularly smart—or particularly literal-minded, or particularly patient—teacher or peer?

Different authors in the chapters that follow come at these questions from different directions, from different perspectives and theoretical backgrounds. The answers they suggest point to different paths of development, different hypotheses to explore, different implications for the future of games and of learning. That is the nature of science and of scholarship, where theoretical concerns and frameworks generate empirical examinations that show which lines of reasoning are the most productive.

Perhaps computer games are a new kind of cognitive activity, best understood as a novel and unique cultural form requiring new theories of cognition. Or, perhaps they are better understood in terms of existing ideas about learning, games, or media.

The value in investigating such issues, ultimately, is to ask: What next? What does each perspective imply for future research? How can we continue the discussion in a more informed way as the field moves forward?

In grappling with the relationship between games and cognition, this volume captures a moment in time when a field collectively pauses to take stock, and individual researchers and practitioners reflect on the decisions they will make moving forward.

It is a moment to ask whether we are stepping again into a river—and if so, which one?—or whether we are leaping into truly uncharted seas.

David Williamson Shaffer
University of Wisconsin, USA

David Williamson Shaffer *is a Professor at the University of Wisconsin - Madison in the departments of Educational Psychology and Curriculum and Instruction and also a Game Scientist at the Wisconsin Center for Education Research. Before coming to the University of Wisconsin, Dr. Shaffer taught grades 4-12 in the United States and abroad, including 2 years working with the Asian Development Bank and US Peace Corps in Nepal. His M.S. and Ph.D. are from the Media Laboratory at the Massachusetts Institute of Technology, and he taught in the Technology and Education Program at the Harvard Graduate School of Education. Dr. Shaffer studies how new technologies change the way people think and learn. His particular area of interest is in the development of epistemic games: computer and video games in which players become professionals to develop innovative and creative ways of thinking.*

Preface

INTRODUCTION

Twenty-five years ago, the idea that playing video games would lead to significant cognitive benefits flew in the face of conventional wisdom. Video games were seen as a frivolous waste of time, if not an insidious medium that promoted violence and signaled a decline in the work ethic and intelligence of our youth. Today, of course, playing video games is far less controversial, and the idea that games can have positive impacts is widely accepted.[1]

While game researchers and designers might feel encouraged by the changes over the last quarter-century, a careful examination of the scholarship on games and cognition during this time is in many ways discouraging. Quantity is not quality, and while we can point to a vast number of authors and publications that now make up the games and learning landscape, closer inspection reveals a highly fragmented field that is at times surprisingly unaware of prior research, theories, and models. The popularity of games as an area of study has attracted many people from multiple disciplines and perspectives, which is good. But the value of diversity lies in the synergies that result from shared perspectives, and the literature in the emerging field of serious games has not always been characterized by this. Much of our scholarship has failed to build on existing research in related areas, with many assuming that as a new medium, serious games have no antecedents in prior research. Where and when scholars do look to prior research in areas like psychology, education, communication, and anthropology, they are often unaware of parallel research efforts by others who study games. This has resulted in a highly diverse but somewhat incoherent body of research in which we have unwittingly reinvented the wheel and failed to follow up on important avenues of research.

The diverse approach to research we all bring to this emerging field has generated a rich body of theory and practice. But a field only matures through periods of expansion *and* contraction, on the one hand generating enough theory and practice to build upon, yet on the other pausing at strategic times for critical examination of that base. The origins of this book are in this latter process.

WHY GAMING AND COGNITION?

While there are many aspects of this field worth studying, one could argue that the effects of digital game play on human cognition (in its broadest sense, human thinking and behavior) is the sin qua non of what we most commonly refer to as serious games. Yet this seemingly obvious conclusion often gets lost in practice and research. The number of people interested in designing and writing about games seems to be greater than the number of those interested in conducting the necessary research. Digital game researchers have been discussing flow and engagement in games for at least 20 years, for example, so why don't we have meaningful models that have been validated through empirical testing? Games are routinely cited for their ability to promote critical thinking and problem solving, yet the majority of our research in this area consists of thought experiments and convenience sample studies using unvalidated, inconsistent measures of these constructs. If we don't conduct the research we need to validate and define these constructs, the field can never hope to evolve into a coherent discipline.

Like the gold rush of the 19th century in the United States, it is almost as if once the idea that games *could* have cognitive benefits caught on, the rush to design those games was on. To be sure, we learn a lot from the design process itself, and the theory that emerges is often unique and critical to refining our understanding of a phenomenon. But it is only one half of the research cycle: the "cool" half. We must also look to theory across disciplines to determine which are relevant to games and cognition, to propose and validate our own theories and models through empirical research, and to then use those theories to design games.

THE LEARNING SCIENCES

Cognition is studied across many different disciplines, including psychology, education, instructional design, and communication. While each of these fields brings critical theoretical and practical perspectives to bear on the study of cognition, perhaps none sufficiently captures the full range of theory as it relates to human cognition in the digital age. The need for cross-disciplinary approaches to the study of cognition, coupled with the increasing role of technology in human culture has led to a new field of studies referred to as the learning sciences. The learning sciences, which also include computer science and anthropology, emphasize a rigorous, empirical approach to theory and practice in the study of cognition in general and more specifically in learning and technology. As such, they may represent the best lens for studying the cognitive effects of digital games.

I come to the study of games via English, psychology, and instructional design, the latter two having the most to do with my interest in cognition. As someone interested in developing multimedia, I spent a lot of time looking for guidance on effective design rather than on the tools themselves. My search led me to the field of instructional design, where I spent the majority of my time reading work in what is now called the learning sciences but which at the time was cognitive psychology, education, communication, and instructional design. While everything I read was valuable, it was the studies that focused on empirical testing of well-established theories of cognition as they applied to learning and technology that had the greatest impact on my understanding and later design of games for learning. I attributed the small number of such studies to the relative immaturity of the field. It was not until 8 years later in 2003, when I read Shawn Green and Daphne Bavalier's study of the effects of gameplay on visual processing that I realized how rare such studies had become. While there was no shortage of claims in the literature about how games could improve processing of visual and other forms of information, the majority of these claims relied solely on anecdotal and thought experiment evidence.

Green and Bavalier actually set out to test these assumptions. They employed rigorous, empirical protocols with eye-tracking equipment and meticulous operational definitions of separate visual processing skills to compare video game players (VGPs) to nonvideo game players (NVGPs). They found that VGPs outperformed NVGPs on a variety of skills. What made this stand out was not their conclusion, which many had asserted before, but their rigorous methodology in establishing it. This alone, for me, would have put them in the top 10% of research in this area, but it is what they did next that truly made the study unique among video game research. They followed up their research with a study that exposed NVGPs to 10 hours of gameplay to see if the observed differences were the result of self-selection (correlation) or video game play itself (causation). They found that indeed it was video game play itself that resulted in visual processing improvement. The finding itself is among the most important research we've seen in this field for the last 20 years, but what made it really resonate for me was how much it was *unlike* most video game research published during this time period. Why has this kind of research been more the exception than the rule?

The answer is that it is harder to do. It takes expertise in the cognitive and learning sciences, knowledge of rigorous, empirical methodologies, specialized equipment, funding, and participants. Of course, this is only one kind of research, and I do not mean to suggest that it is the only approach with merit. Grounded theory, design theory, qualitative research, and philosophical approaches to the study of cultural, social, and anthropological effects are all important to the long-term success of the serious game field. Likewise, we cannot conduct experimental research without the theoretical and practical work that derives from these other approaches. But focusing on cognitive research theories, models, and methodologies is critical and too often ignored in video game studies, irrespective of the approach used. This book arises out of that belief, and it is my hope that you either already agree (by virtue of having selected this book for reading) or that you will come to see the value of the approaches the authors in this volume have taken to answer important questions about video games and cognition.

ABOUT THE BOOK

The chapters represent 15 different disciplines in the learning sciences (psychology, serious game design, educational technology, applied linguistics, instructional design, eLearning, computer engineering, educational psychology, cognitive science, digital media, human–computer interaction, artificial intelligence, computer science, anthropology, education), by authors from four countries (Australia, Canada, Singapore, and the United States).

Each chapter is the result of an original proposal, each of which was reviewed by three peers in a double-blind review process, with the exception of the first chapter which is an invited, updated version of Patricia Greenfield's chapter on video games from 1984 (more on this shortly). In doing so, I assigned reviewers chapters based on interest, expertise, and in the case of reviewers who were also authors, on the potential of the authors to benefit from a different disciplinary perspective on work similar to their own. Based on these reviews, some authors were invited to submit full chapters, which were again reviewed using the same double-blind process as before.

Based on my readings and that of the reviewers, I organized these chapters into five sections: Historical Perspectives, New Theories and Models, Theory Into Practice, Research and Design, and Practitioner Perspectives. Like all good scholarship, each chapter in this volume focuses on theory past and present, and all have practical implications, so the classification of chapters into these different sections is somewhat artificial. The first section discusses past video game research in the learning sciences to help establish where we have been. The second section presents works by four learning sciences researchers who rely on existing theory and models to propose new frameworks, theories, and models for understanding learning and cognition in video games. The third section presents work that synthesizes across multiple disciplines and theories to propose specific heuristics for the design of video games for learning. The fourth section presents significant research studies that are as valuable for their methodologies and approaches as for their findings. The fifth section presents research by educational game developers that has both been informed by theories and models in cognitive science and which proposes new hybrid models for cognition in educational games.

Each author was also asked to generate a list of "must-reads" on their chapter topic for those who want to understand more about the theory and approach behind each chapter. In addition, they were also asked to identify what they would consider to be the most important texts for interdisciplinary studies of serious games. Both of these lists can be found at the end of each chapter, immediately after the references. I have collated all of the authors' interdisciplinary texts across this book and a companion volume that collected the same information[2]. I present this composite list sorted by rank and author at the end of the book.

You will find both a short and long version of the table of contents, the latter of which provides my own summary of what each chapter is about, so I will confine my comments here in the preface to a discussion of each section of the book and how I think each chapter contributes to that section.

HISTORICAL PERSPECTIVES

Patricia Greenfield's original chapter on video games in 1984 ("Video Games," in *Mind and Media*) is a seminal example of research on the cognitive benefits of video games. It is fitting, then, that this volume begins with a chapter in which she revisits her work 25 years later. Given the speed with which games and their study change from year to year, I was surprised to see how relevant her findings and suggestions from 1984 are today and dismayed by how many of the research avenues she suggested there remain, for the most part, unexplored. If the dates were changed, this chapter could for the most part be read as a contemporary contribution to the field, which is a testament to her foresight as well as a depressing commentary on our progress as scholars in this field. Dr. Greenfield provides an analysis and running commentary on this work from her perspective today, identifying what has changed and what has not as well as providing suggestions for current research (graduate students take note!).

As I described earlier, one of the weaknesses of research by new scholars in video games today is the failure to account for, build on, or refine existing research. While we are certain to need new theory to fully account for games and cognition, that theory must begin with prior research. Games may be a new medium, but cognition is the oldest game of them all, and unless video games have turned thousands of years of evolutionary process on its head, it stands to reason that some of what we know already about cognition will be useful in the study of games. In this spirit, Katrin Becker provides a literature review of games in education in this second chapter of this volume that highlights some of the most important findings of the last 50 years. While no literature review in this field can be comprehensive today, her critical analysis of some of the most significant research in our field should be required reading for new scholars and students in this field.

As fast as the literature in this field is growing, it is not necessarily representative of the full range of video games today. While massively multiplayer online role-playing games (MMORPGs) are among the fastest growing and most widely adopted type of game, the research base for them is quite sparse when it comes to empirical studies of their cognitive effects. Given the prevalence of MMORPGs and their potential to cross social, cultural, and cognitive areas of study, they are one of the most underexplored and important areas of video game research. In the final chapter in this section, Bodi Anderson provides a conceptual framework for MMORPG use in research and learning and describes current and future trends for their study.

NEW THEORIES AND MODELS

As we build on prior research across multiple disciplines in our own research, it stands to reason that new theories and models will also emerge. Whether as the result of our extension of existing theories as we apply them within this new medium or because of the unique features and applications of the medium itself, these new theories will serve as a bridge between past and future research.

In the first chapter in this section, John Dempsey weaves many strands from the past together using new concepts to propose a model for the design of learning outcomes in games. He argues persuasively that current instructional taxonomies are too unwieldy and impractical for widespread adoption and that they ignore critical differences between learning outcomes that are representative of the actual performance (elemental learning) and learning outcomes that serve a supporting cognitive role in that performance (synthetic learning). In addition to the resulting instructional implications (e.g., learning transfer vs. inert knowledge), this distinction also has game design implications (e.g., determining when contextual fidelity to the learning task is required and where and when synthetic content can be delivered didactically in or outside that game). The resulting five cognitive outcomes (two elemental and three synthetic) are unified by the overall concept of fidelity, which is manifested in a model he calls "the pyramid of fidelity." The resulting conceptual model serves the same purpose as an instructional taxonomy but does so in a way that is more reflective of learning and game design than traditional approaches.

Richard Swan also focuses on the application of existing theory and practice to the solution of one of the most pervasive challenges for game-based learning design: engagement. All the learning theory in the world will make little practical impact if it fails to account for the unique nature of gameplay experience. While we may be able to design effective learning environments using games, doing so in a way that captures the engagement of commercial games remains an elusive goal. Swan identifies principles from design theory and applies them to the concept of engagement. The principles he uncovers not only have significant implications for the design of engaging educational games but serendipitously lead to a concept he calls feed*forward*. This latter concept reflects the anticipatory cognition that players employ during engagement, and he argues it may be far more useful than its conceptually flawed cousin, feedback. Like Dempsey's chapter, the resulting framework and design heuristics make a valuable contribution to our understanding of the design of educational games.

In the final chapter in this section, Wen-Hao David Huang and Sharon Tettegah identify a gap in the literature that has important implications for the design of persuasive games, or games for change. Like Low, Jin, and Sweller's chapter in the next section, Huang and Tettegah recognize the importance of considering cognitive load in learning game environments. Persuasive games, however, often focus on attitude change and, while this is an instructional outcome in many taxonomies, little attention has been paid to the instructional and cognitive requirements for promoting attitude change via gaming environments. One of the theoretical paths to attitude change in many persuasive games, they argue, is to induce empathy for characters in the game that ostensibly represent the people involved in those real-world situations (e.g., *Darfur is Dying*). They suggest that empathy itself may have its own cognitive load requirements that should be taken into account when designing persuasive games. Their conceptual framework for examining cognitive load and empathy not only points out a promising avenue of research but suggests other related research on emotional/cognitive constructs associated with gameplay (e.g., cognitive load during flow or engagement).

THEORY INTO PRACTICE

Theory must lead to practice both as a means of validating models through research and for guiding future development of games. This section comprises chapters that connect theory to practice in the form of principles and heuristics that can be used to guide future educational game design. Amy Adcock, Ginger Watson, Gary Morrison, and Lee Belfore argue that games with designed learning outcomes are essentially another form of exploratory learning and that the empirical literature and related design principles in exploratory learning environments is therefore relevant to the design of educational games. In connecting theory to the practice of educational game design, they rely on key concepts from the learning sciences such as interface affordances, cognitive load, and the development of expertise within gameplay. They propose a grounded set of design heuristics that can be validated and used to design education games today.

Renae Low, Putai Jin, and John Sweller connect the literature base in cognitive load, arguably one of the most significant issues facing educational game designers, to educational game design. Like Dempsey, they outline a key distinction in learning outcomes based on biologically primary and secondary knowledge. The result is an extensible model for classifying types of learning and managing cognitive load through the design of the game environment. Like Adcock et al., Low, Jin, and Sweller propose a set of design heuristics, derived in this case from evidence-based cognitive load principles and suggest promising lines of research.

Dennis Charsky articulates the connection between constructivist teaching structures, which he suggests are akin to open learning environments, and game genres and characteristics. Like Adcock et al., Charsky believes that the existing research and design principles for open learning environments are relevant to the design of educational games. By describing and mapping constructivist learning theory and the corresponding teaching and learning principles to specific instances of games and gameplay, he makes it possible for even those who are novices in this field to both understand and to begin to apply theory to the practice of game design.

Tim Marsh closes this section with his framework for designing scenarios in games that both honors the diversity of the term scenario as it is currently used while also bringing some much-needed structure and theoretical rigor to bear on its definition and application to game design. Borrowing from film, human–computer interaction, and activity theory, Marsh provides an operational definition for scenarios and proposes a standardized "template" for discussing and designing game scenarios.

RESEARCH AND DESIGN

Research and design go hand in hand in business and manufacturing circles, but they are too often viewed and conducted as separate endeavors in serious games. The result is research that fails to connect to practice and practice driven not by theory but by the idiosyncrasies of the design team and the exigencies of the moment. This need not be the case, however. Whether we are conducting research to identify new theories and design heuristics or to validate theories and models such as those proposed in the previous sections, we should all be designing games to test theory and using theory to design our games. The two chapters in this section exemplify the symbiotic relationship between research and design in serious games and illustrate how these processes are in fact two sides of the same coin. Each describes theory-driven game design that serves to operationally define existing game theory, identify new theories, and provide models for future game design and research practices.

Flow is a construct that virtually every researcher and designer of educational games would agree is part of what makes games engaging and effective (optimal) learning experiences. Csikszentmihalyi himself in an article about flow and television viewing in 1981 suggested that video games may promote flow.[3] Yet in the nearly 30 years since, we have failed to operationalize flow in a way that allows for meaningful design and research or measures its impact on learning. For an idea deemed so central to our field, we have made shockingly little progress in understanding it.

In the first chapter in this section, Debbie Denise Reese describes the game system she and her colleagues have designed and the assessment toolset they use for measuring learning and engagement. The Flowometer tool for measuring flow during learning is alone a significant contribution to the field, but by describing the theoretical origins of this tool and providing data and analysis on its use in an educational game, she lays the groundwork for others to adopt and adapt the tool for research and design. More importantly, this chapter serves as a model for future research on other constructs like engagement and intrinsic motivation. By clearly articulating the theoretical basis of the games developed, describing the development of the tool within the context of a full assessment suite designed according to that model, and presenting data from a designed game that then puts their theory and tools to the test, she illustrates the full research and design cycle to which studies of games should adhere.

In the second chapter, Brian Magerko, Carrie Heeter, and Ben Medler identify a key, but often overlooked, challenge to educational games as an instructional medium: how to account for different prior experience and attitudes toward games during formal instruction with educational games. Rather than suggesting that we design alternative instructional experiences for those with little or no experience with or interest in games, they suggest we look to existing research on game literacy, motivation, goal orientation, and mindset, to design games that account for individual differences within a single game experience. Like Reese, they also report the results of a game designed using this model, which provides empirical support and points the way toward future research.

PRACTITIONER PERSPECTIVES

I have argued, here and elsewhere, that for our field to advance we must have theory and models that we test through research and design before we can establish a meaningful body of practice from which to draw conclusions. While we need hundreds, if not thousands, of learning games across a full range of content, environments, cultures, and game formats if we are to truly understand how games function in support of learning, this can only happen *after* we have done the necessary theoretical research and design. It is appropriate, then, that at the end of this volume (itself organized as a microcosm of this process), we turn to two examples of significant practice in the development of educational games.

In the first chapter, K. A. Barrett and Lewis Johnson describe the significant body of work that Alelo, Inc., has developed as a designer of games for training. The games they have developed to teach language and related tactical skills have been used by more than 50,000 people, which places them among the most robustly tested serious games today. More importantly, however, it represents the full process of educational game design. From existing learning theory to integrated theoretical models, to heuristics, to game design and project management approaches, they present a seamless picture of the game design process. Their approach, which relies on artificial intelligence, scaffolding for expertise, cultural contexts for learning, and instructional design, is also unique in that it eschews monolithic game design in favor of unified instructional environments that tap games only for the learning outcomes that they best support, relying on other instructional modalities for outcomes that do not require games (e.g., prior knowledge). In some ways, this serves as an example of the approaches suggested by Dempsey and by Low, Jin, and Sweller, earlier in this book. The end result is a set of theories that are well documented with real-world game examples that have been tested in the field.

Like Barrett and Johnson, Borchert and colleagues are also practitioners with years of experience and dozens of games to their credit, which they rely on in the final chapter in this section and the book. The games in question here, however, have been developed and tested in higher education environments rather than corporate/military environments. Like Barrett and Johnson, the authors also begin with a description of the theory that guides their practice. This theory is then tied to what they refer to as "signature elements," or hallmarks of all the games they build, which makes it clear how theory is manifest in their design. Most significantly, because each signature element has been formatively evaluated in each of the games they have designed during the last decade, what emerges is a model for educational game design that is supported by a significant body of work and which is potentially transferable.

A FINAL NOTE

I believe that the field of serious games is at a significant crossroads in its development from concept to discipline. It is critical that we remain aware of the multiple disciplines that can inform our research and practice and avoid the all-too-common academic tendency to close ranks and create research silos within our own disciplines. If we do not strive for this, we will at best end up with duplicative research that slows the advance of the field and, at worst, will become so fractured that we fail to coalesce as a discipline.

Having said that, I must also confess that the title of this book comes as much from my experience with cognitive psychology research as it does from anything else. Cognitive psychology has a long history of studying how humans think and process information. Beyond this, however, cognitive psychology also has a tradition of rigorous experimental practice in studying what goes on in that black box we call the mind. Some of the most creative and important studies have come from researchers interested in nebulous, unobservable phenomena like memory, problem solving, sensory input, attitude, and emotion. The rigor and design of the experiments run in the study of these aspects of cognition is far too rare in game research today. I believe the chapters in this volume are examples of the kinds of approaches we should be taking, and it is my hope that many who read them will be inspired to conduct similar work in applying the principles of research in the study of human cognition to games. At the same time, as an educator, I am also aware of the significant limitations of these approaches, which trade ecological validity for replicability and measurement and too often ignore qualitative and anthropological methodologies in favor of clean laboratory tests. So while I hope that those not in the learning sciences are inspired to take a more rigorous approach to the study of games and cognition, I hope too that those in the learning sciences come to see the value in other approaches. No single approach or perspective will be sufficient, but each must be aware of, and build upon, the others.

Richard Van Eck
University of North Dakota, USA

ENDNOTES

[1] The Entertainment Software Association reported that 68% of households play games and that 63% of parents believe games are a positive part of their children's lives (Entertainment Software Association. [2009]). Industry Facts. Retrieved October 18, 2009, from http://www.theesa.com/facts/index.asp).

[2] Van Eck, R. (Ed.). (2010). *Interdisciplinary models and tools for serious games: Emerging concepts and future directions*. Hershey, PA: IGI Global

[3] Csikszentmihalyi, C., & Kubey, R. (1981). Television and the rest of life: A systematic comparison of subjective experience. *Public Opinion Quarterly, 45*, 317 - 328.

Acknowledgment

Anyone who has ever watched the Academy Awards show knows there is never enough time to acknowledge everyone who has contributed to a body of work. It is also painfully clear during those acceptance speeches that the more the winner tries to be inclusive, the more inevitable it is that they leave someone out or shortchange those they list at the end. To that end, I want to first thank everyone who had a hand in making this volume a reality.

In particular, I want to thank the authors and contributors to this volume for trusting me with stewardship of their work and ideas. An edited book is only as good as its contributors, and the combined intellect, creativity, and scholarship of all the submissions made the reading and editing process both rewarding and humbling. I would also like to thank my editorial assistant at IGI, Beth Ardner, for her support in developing the book and responding to all my questions and requests as the book evolved from proposal to publication. I would also like to acknowledge the work of the editorial board and reviewers, who dedicated many hours to reviewing the submissions to help ensure that authors got the best feedback and that I benefited from the collective intelligence of the community in my selection of chapters.

I would also like to acknowledge a few people whose contributions extend beyond the book itself. I owe my mother a debt of gratitude for convincing my elementary school teachers that my performance was the result of boredom in the days before anyone really knew what ADHD was. My mother also instilled a love of reading from an early age by reading classics to us like *The Hobbit*, *Wind in the Willows*, and *The Dark Is Rising*. Reading has been fundamental to my beliefs about the power of narrative for learning, instruction, and games. I also have my grandmother, Ann, to thank for instilling that love of reading in my mother. Ann was a children's librarian for many years, and some of my best memories are of the children's books (*The Three Billy Goats Gruff*, for one) that she "read" to us by heart every time we visited.

My father is responsible for my interest in technology in general, whether from the many times I accompanied him to work as a systems analyst at the Institute for Social Research or his patient support in showing me how to using *DocuMat*, the word processing program he wrote for the CPM operating system. The day he brought home *Cave Adventure* on an 8.5-inch floppy disk may be the single most important event in terms of leading to my scholarship in games and to the book you hold in your hands now.

I want to thank two mentors in my professional life whom I am also privileged to call friends. Jack Dempsey was my committee chair during my doctoral studies at the University of South Alabama, but this does not begin to convey the influence he had and continues to have on my life. From responding to an unknown doctoral program applicant's question about games as an area of study to involving me in research well before I could be much help to him in doing so, to treating me as much as a colleague and friend as a student, his mentorship has been key to any success I have had. His is a hard example to follow in this regard, but it has served as a guide to me in my own experience as a professor in higher education.

Likewise, I have Art Graesser to thank for showing me the true value of interdisciplinary research and productivity. My experience working with him at the Institute for Intelligent Systems at the University of Memphis convinced me that the biggest questions and the best research can only be tackled with the will and perspective of a diverse group of researchers from multiple disciplines. It takes a special person to keep a group like that focused and productive while also allowing everyone to feel like an equal partner in the process.

Finally, I would like to thank my wife, Sandy, for everything she has done for me and meant to me. What a daunting sentence—there is no way I could thank her adequately even if I were to fill the rest of the pages in this book. As a collaborator in my professional life, she is an equal partner. As my partner in life, she is the reason any of it makes sense.

Section 1
Historical Perspectives

Chapter 1
Video Games Revisited

Patricia M. Greenfield
University of California—Los Angeles, USA

ABSTRACT

When Greenfield wrote her chapter on video games in her 1994 landmark book Mind and Media, video games were played primarily in arcades, and popular opinion held that they were at best a waste of time and at worst dangerous technology sure to lead to increased aggression. As a cognitive psychologist and media scholar, she was interested in what was really going on in these games and brought the theoretical rigor and research tools of her discipline to bear on games and their cognitive effects on game players. Part anthropologist and part stranger in a strange land, she studied games and game players and played games herself. Her conclusions at the time were both surprising and prescient; research failed to support the common sense connection of games and violent behavior, and games in fact appeared to have cognitive benefits unseen by those who did not play them. Her conclusions both provided a glimpse of then-current research and laid the foundation for a rigorous empirical study of games and cognition. What is shocking upon rereading this chapter today is how relevant it remains and how many of the research possibilities remain largely unexplored. Her chapter is reprinted here along with her current analysis and thoughts about her original ideas, 25 years later. Its placement as the first chapter in a book dedicated to cognitive perspectives on games is appropriate, both as a reminder of where we come from and how far we have yet to go.

PREFACE

When this chapter was published 25 years ago in *Mind and Media: The Effects of Television, Video Games, and Computers*, video games were a new phenomenon that many saw as potentially dangerous. Counter to the prevailing zeitgeist, I pointed out the complex cognitive skills required to play the games. In my own laboratory, my analysis provided the blueprint for an experimental research program over the next 10 years on the cognitive processes developed by action video games (Greenfield & Cocking, 1994). With the popularity of the book (it has been translated into nine different languages since then) and of games as a medium, I assumed that others would take up the threads of the research questions raised here and extend the study of the cognitive and social effects of video

DOI: 10.4018/978-1-61520-717-6.ch001

games. In fact, a few other researchers did take up this line of research in the years following the publication of *Mind and Media* (De Lisi & Cammarano, 1996; De Lisi & Wolford, 2002; Dorval & Pepin, 1986; Gagnon, 1985; McClurg & Chaille, 1987; Okagaki & Frensch, 1994); but this line of research—investigating the cognitive effects of video games—was definitely out of the mainstream.

Today, the prevailing zeitgeist is quite different. There currently exists a strong "serious games" movement, and my once shocking assertion that popular games develop important cognitive skills for a technological world is now taken for granted. As the zeitgeist changed, new research paradigms for studying the cognitive skills used and developed by video games began to appear and go mainstream, as the tremendous response to Green & Bavelier's (2003) study showed. Yet Green and Bavelier studied the same basic attentional issues as Greenfield, deWinstanley, Kilpatrick, and Kaye (1994) a decade earlier and found a very parallel developmental role of video games.

The history of research on social effects of video games has been a bit different from the history of research on their cognitive effects. In one area of social development, aggression, research has been more continuous and cumulative. Notably, systematic research on the impact of video game violence accelerated, to the point where the quantity of studies made meta-analysis possible (Anderson & Bushman, 2001). I attribute much of this difference in the research trajectory between cognitive and social effects to the influence of television research, where violence and aggression (the dangers) have always garnered much more attention than cognitive skills (benefits).

Another reason for the differential trajectory in these two areas of video game research may be the fact that when children first started playing video games, thematic content (notably aggression) was obvious, even to the unskilled (in video game play) observer. The cognitive domain was different in this respect: researchers, not having grown up with video games or knowing how to play, often lacked the cognitive skills that were being developed by the games. Indeed, in my video game investigations, I was an anthropologist going into a foreign culture (Greenfield, 1984; Greenfield & Cocking, 1994), a foreign culture that very few others of my generation dared to explore. In sharp contrast to the first generation of potential and actual video game researchers, Green, a graduate student in 2003 when the Green & Bavelier study was published, was an expert video game player and was studying the cognitive effects of his own cultural experience. We now have a whole new generation of researchers, gamers themselves from a young age, for whom video game research is a natural and easy extension of their own experience.

A third reason for the initial lack of interest in the cognitive effects of action video games was the emphasis on educational content rather than form. Researchers were much more interested in harnessing the capacity of gaming to teach educational content than they were in the cognitive by-products of popular action video game forms, the types of literacy skills developed by gaming. In contrast, ever since I investigated the cognitive by-products of print literacy in my dissertation in Senegal (Greenfield, 1972), I have been interested in cognitive by-products of various literacies that are independent of content. In addition, as a cultural developmental psychologist, I was interested in the effects of what children were actually doing with digital media, rather than trying to get children to do something else that would be "more educational."

As I reread my chapter today, I have been pleased to discover that the issues I identified in 1984 remain core issues in the field. Although games have developed in complexity, variety, animation, and graphic quality, the issues concerning cognitive and social development have not changed. At the same time, rereading also reveals that a number of my hypotheses concerning the cognitive and social effects of video games have yet to be explored through systematic behavioral research.

In order to point out both advances and lacunae in the field of video game research since the 1984 publication of the chapter, I have prepared new author notes. Apart from eliminating cross-references to other chapters of *Mind and Media* and the clearly marked 2009 author notes, the chapter is reprinted below exactly as it appeared in the 1984 book.

– Patricia Greenfield, 2009

INTRODUCTION

In Glendale, California, a suburb of Los Angeles, I witnessed a scene that has recently been repeated in many parts of the United States. The City Council was hearing testimony about a proposed ordinance against video game arcades. These are establishments similar to old-fashioned pool halls, but featuring action games played on TV screens. A mother of two teenagers got up and complained that children use half their lunch money to play the games. The president of the Glendale Council of Parent-Teacher Associations pursued the same theme. In the most eloquent part of her emotional plea, the first speaker said, "It reminds me of smoking. Smoking doesn't do us any bit of good. We don't depend on it to live. And yet it's addictive and it's expensive, and this is what these games are ... There are kids in there that really cannot stay away from them."

Let us go through this list of complaints and see what is known about each of them. First, are video games addictive? J. David Brooks interviewed 973 young people in video arcades in southern California. While he found some who felt compelled to play, they were in a minority. In fact, about half the kids were playing games less than half the time they were in the arcade. The rest of the time they were socializing. The arcades, like the ice cream parlor of yore, were providing a social gathering place, more than a place for compulsive play (Brooks, 1983). In terms of management and physical environment, however, some arcades,

unlike the old-fashioned ice cream parlor, are not healthy places for young people to gather. We should be concerned about regulating this aspect of the arcades in our communities.

In northern California, Edna Mitchell had twenty families keep diaries for one week each month for five months after getting a video game set. If the games were addictive (whatever that means), this should have been reflected in long hours spent playing, particularly since the games could be played at home without spending quarters. However, Mitchell found that the game sets were used an average of 42 minutes a day per *family*— and many families included more than one child, as well as parents who played (Mitchell, 1983). This is hardly an addictive pattern, especially compared with the amount of time spent watching television. According to even the most conservative estimate, preschool children in the United States spend two and a half hours a day with the television set on (Anderson, 1983).

Author's Note, 2009:*After staying rather flat for about twenty years (Christakis, Ebel, Rivara, & Zimmerman, 2004), the daily consumption of video games has risen sharply in the last five years. A survey utilizing a representative national sample published in 2009 found that boys between 8 and 18 now spend an average of two hours and 20 minutes a day gaming, while girls in this same age range spend an average of one hour and 19 minutes per day (Gentile et al., 2009).*

Second, how expensive are video games? Eighty percent of the kids interviewed by Brooks spent five dollars or less per week, the price of a movie. Only 7 percent spent lunch money. In fact, because they are better players, children put less money in the machines than adults do. In the world of video arcade games, skill is rewarded with play time, and a good player can play for an hour and a half on a quarter.

Finally, do the games "do us any bit of good"? The way to answer this question is to discover what skills are required by the games and what skills, therefore, the players might be developing. Here, I shall not limit myself to arcade games, but will also discuss other types of games that are available for home computers, as well as games that could become available in the future.

Thus, the available evidence indicates that video games are, in terms of time spent, much less addictive than television. Nor are they, in comparison with other entertainment, particularly expensive. Yet they are undeniably attractive, and there is something about that attraction that disturbs people. Before deciding that video games are bad simply because they are attractive, it makes sense to consider what features make them so attractive.

Author's Note, 2009: *In recent years, sophisticated research on video game addiction has been carried out, based on accepted psychiatric symptomatology of pathological gambling. Pathological gambling in turn shares characteristics considered core facets of addiction; these include tolerance, withdrawal symptoms, and relapse. In a national random sample of more than one thousand young people from 8 to 18 years of age, 11.9% of male video game players and 2.9% of female video game players exhibited at least six out of eleven symptoms of pathological or addictive video game use (Gentile, 2009).*

THE ATTRACTION OF VIDEO GAMES: THE TV CONNECTION

What makes computer games able to compete so successfully with the things children did before the games? As is by now common knowledge, television has in recent years been children's major waking activity. Video games have been dubbed the "marriage of television and the computer" (Gardner, 1983). At the most obvious level, what television and computers have in common is a television screen, a cathode ray tube. Both use the screen to present visual motion. There is evidence that children with a television background develop a preference for dynamic visual imagery. And we learned that visual action is an important factor in attracting the attention of young children to the television screen. The popular arcade games involve a tremendous amount of visual action, and this may be one source of their appeal.

Thomas Malone analyzed the appeal of computer games, starting with a survey of the preferences of children who had become familiar with a wide variety of computer games in computer classes at a private elementary school in Palo Alto, California. The children ranged in age from about five to thirteen, and the games spanned the range from arcade games to simulations to adventure games to learning games. Visual elements were important in the games' popularity: graphics games such as Petball (computer pinball) and Snake 2 (two players controlling motion and shooting of snakes) were more popular than word games such as Eliza (conversation with a simulated psychiatrist) and Gold (a fill-in-the-blanks story about Goldilocks). A clue as to the attraction of *moving* visual images comes from the fact that the three most unpopular graphics games—Stars, Snoopy, and Draw—have no animation at all or much less animation than more popular games (Malone, 1981).

If moving visual imagery is important in the popularity of video games, then perhaps the visual skills developed through watching television (as demonstrated especially in the research of Salomon, 1979) are the reason children of the television generation show so much talent with the games. Research has shown that children also pick up and use more information about action from seeing action on television than from hearing action described (as in radio) or from verbal description combined with static images (as in picture books). Children who watch a lot of television get a great deal of experience in taking in information about action—more so than did generations socialized with the verbal media of print and radio. Perhaps this experience with the moving visual images of television leads to skills that can be applied to playing video games. I shall return to this possibility later when I analyze the skill requirements of the various games.

Video games have the dynamic visual element of television, but they are also interactive. What happens on the screen is not entirely determined by the computer; it is also very much influenced by the player's actions. A straightforward example is the original commercial computer game, Pong, an electronic ping-pong game. Like other popular computer games, Pong involves moving imagery, as television does. But instead of merely watching an animated ping-pong match, as one might watch Wimbledon on television, the player actually plays the match, and thus has a part in creating the video display.

It is possible that, before the advent of video games, a generation brought up on film and television was in a bind: the most active medium of expression, writing, lacked the quality of visual dynamism. Television had dynamism, but could not be affected by the viewer. Video games are the first medium to combine visual dynamism with an active participatory role for the child.

What evidence exists that a desire for interaction (in contrast to mere observation) is an important part of the appeal of computer games? No systematic research exists on this subject, to my knowledge, but studies have been done in other settings in which there are both things to observe and things to interact with, such as science museums, field trips, zoos, and aquariums. These studies show a predictable pattern: children are attracted to activities that let them become personally involved. In the zoo, for example, they prefer pigeons and squirrels, with whom they can interact, to the more exotic animals isolated behind bars (Rosenfeld, 1982).

To get an idea of whether this finding applied to video games and of whether the games were displacing the one-way medium of television, I asked four children, ranging in age from eight to fourteen, what they used to do with the time they now spend on video games. In answer, three of the four mentioned television. Two of those three mentioned only television, the third a number of other activities, including playing games with friends. Information from my tiny sample is confirmed by Mitchell's larger study of families with home video game sets; the children in her sample also watched less television after getting their game machines.

I also asked my four interviewees which they liked better, TV or video games, and why. They were unanimous in preferring the games to television. They were also unanimous about the reason: active control. The meaning of control was both very concrete and very conscious. One nine-year-old girl said, "In TV, if you want to make someone die, you can't. In Pac-Man, if you want to run into a ghost you can." Another girl of the same age said, "On TV you can't say 'shoot now' or, with Popeye, 'eat your spinach now.'" She went on to say she would get frustrated sometimes watching Popeye and wanting him to eat his spinach at a certain time when he didn't.

OTHER REASONS FOR THE APPEAL OF VIDEO GAMES

One of the children I interviewed mentioned playing games with friends as an activity she used to do more before video games. If video games are in fact displacing more traditional games as well as television, then the question arises, what are the elements that make computer games more attractive than other sorts of games? Perhaps the most obvious and important comparison is between computer games and the indoor games that existed before them: board games like checkers and monopoly, card games, tic-tac-toe. (Even though these games now exist in computer form, they were not, of course, developed for the computer medium.)

Malone found that the presence of a goal was the single most important factor in determining the popularity of games. This is a quality that arcade games share with all true games. Other qualities he found to enhance the popularity of computer games were automatic scorekeeping, audio effects, randomness (the operation of chance), and the importance of speed. Of these qualities, randomness (as in games controlled by dice) and speed (as in double solitaire) are part of some conventional games. The others, automatic scorekeeping and audio effects, are essentially impossible without electronics.

THE PROBLEM OF VIOLENCE

If dynamic visual graphics, sound effects, and automatic scorekeeping are the features that account for the popularity of video games, why are parents so worried? All of these features seem quite innocent. But another source of concern is that the games available in arcades have, almost without exception, themes of physical aggression. Daniel Anderson points out the parallels with other media: "Video games have violent content; TV has violent content; comic books had violent content; movies had (have) violent content. There has long been the belief that violent content may teach violent behavior. And yet again our society finds a new medium in which to present that content, and yet again the demand is nearly insatiable" (1982). And there is evidence that violent video games breed violent behavior, just as violent television shows do: both Space Invaders and Roadrunner have been found to raise the level of aggressive play (and lower the level of prosocial play) in five-year-old children; interestingly enough, they do so to the same degree (Silvern, Williamson, & Countermine, 1983b).

The effects of video violence are less simple, however, than they at first appeared. The same group of researchers who found these negative effects of Roadrunner and Space Invaders have more recently found that two-player aggressive video games, whether cooperative or competi-

tive, reduce the level of aggression in children's play. (In this study, both the competitive and the cooperative games were violent. It is notable that playing the violent but cooperative game neither decreased nor increased subsequent cooperative behavior; Silvern, Williamson, & Countermine, 1983a).

It may be that the most harmful aspect of the violent video games is that they are solitary in nature. A two-person aggressive game (video boxing, in this study) seems to provide a cathartic or releasing effect for aggression, while a solitary aggressive game (such as Space Invaders) may stimulate further aggression. Perhaps the effects of television in stimulating aggression will also be found to stem partly from the fact that TV viewing typically involves little social interaction.

Author's Note, 2009: *Now that so many games, especially online games, can be played either cooperatively or alone, following up on this study could be an interesting line of research with great social importance.*

With or without social interaction, violent content is certainly not a necessary feature of video games. It does not even seem necessary to the games' popularity. The most popular game in Malone's survey was Petball, a version of computer pinball, a game that has no obvious aggression in it at all. (Computer pinball does, however, have all of the qualities that distinguish computer games from conventional indoor games.) Similarly, Breakout, the number three game, has a relatively mild aggressive theme (balls knocking a brick wall down); it was more popular than more violent games such as Mission, which involves bombing submarines, and Star Wars, which consists of shooting at Darth Vader's ship.

These rankings indicate that the popularity of computer games does not depend on violence, but on other features that can be used with both violent and nonviolent themes. Ironically enough, the same message comes from recent television research: action, not violence in itself, is what attracts young children to the screen (Huston & Wright, 1983). It follows that programs can present many forms of action other than violent action without sacrificing popularity. There is a clear message for the manufacturers of video games: they should forsake violence because of its undesirable social consequences; they can use other action themes without sacrificing the popularity of the games.

Indeed, some children are actually alienated from arcade games *because* of the aggressive themes. Malone analyzed the appeal of Darts, a game designed to teach fractions to elementary school children. The left side of figure 1 shows the basic display on the screen. The child must try to guess the position of the balloons by typing in a mixed number (whole number and fraction) specifying each balloon's position on the number line. If the answer is right, an arrow comes shooting across the screen and pops the balloon. If it is wrong, the arrow shoots across to the number line and remains there as permanent feedback about the error. Thus, the game has a mildly aggressive fantasy theme. Malone created several versions of this game, each one lacking one or more features of the original. Two such versions are shown in the middle and right-hand sides of figure 1. Adding the aggressive fantasy (right side of illustration) to a version without an aggressive theme (middle

of illustration) increased its popularity among boys but decreased it among girls. In short, the aggressive fantasy was a turn-on for the boys but a turn-off for the girls.

This sex difference has important social implications. In the crowds around game machines, boys far outnumber girls. This may be a serious problem, because it appears that games are the entry point into the world of computers for most children. If children's interest in computers begins with games, then the fact that the most common computer games involve aggressive and violent fantasy themes may have the effect of turning many girls away from computers in general. This would be especially unfortunate in a field that is still in rapid growth and therefore should be especially promising for women. There is an urgent need for widely available video games that make as firm contact with the fantasy life of the typical girl as with that of the typical boy. (There does seem to be a trend in this direction with the addition to arcades of less violent games, such as Donkey Kong, that are more popular with girls; Lauber, 1983).

Nothing intrinsic to video games requires one theme rather than another. The same formal features can be embodied in a myriad of themes. For example, as Tom Malone pointed out to me, the aggressive game of Space Invaders is formally similar to the basically nonviolent game of Break-

Figure 1. Three darts displays. The basic game is on the left. The version on the right differs from the one in the middle in including an element of aggressive fantasy. (Adapted from Malone, "Toward a Theory of Intrinsically Motivating Instruction.")

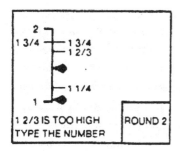 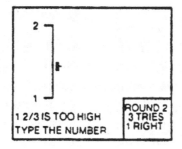 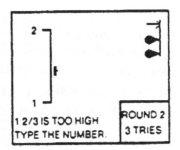

out. Children's Computer Workshop, a division of Children's Television Workshop, is creating educational software with action game formats and nonviolent themes. One that has been developed is Taxi, a game where the goal is to drive a passenger through a city as quickly and efficiently as possible, overcoming obstacles on the way. Taxi has the action and high-speed appeal of an arcade game without the violent content.

Author's Note, 2009: *In subsequent years, it has become clear that popularity does not depend on violence and that good games without violence can lead to popularity among both girls and boys. In roughly chronological order, I think of Barbie Fashion Designer (Mattel, 1996), the first game to have mass popularity with girls (Subrahmanyam & Greenfield, 1999); Where in the World Is Carmen San Diego? (Broderbund, 1985); the Sims games; and play sites for little children such as Jump Start (www.jumpstart.com) and Penguin Club (www.clubpenguin.com).*

Another important point about this and other games being developed by the Workshop is that, besides being nonviolent, they can be played cooperatively with another person. Leona Schauble, the director of Children's Computer Workshop, reports that, in play tests of Taxi, children became increasingly cooperative as they became experienced with the game and learned that cooperation paid off. Like television, the medium of video games is in itself neutral with respect to social values. Nevertheless, the choice of a game design can have an important influence on children's behavior.

Author's Note, 2009: *The prosocial potential of games has very recently been explored in systematic fashion. In a suite of three studies, each using a different method (experimental, survey, and longitudinal), each taking place in a different country (United States, Singapore, and Japan), with ages ranging from 10 to college across the three studies, researchers found that playing games with prosocial content causes players to be more helpful to others in the real world (Gentile et al., 2009).*

THE SKILLS OF VIDEO GAMES

Another concern about video games is that they are merely sensorimotor games of eye-hand coordination and that they are therefore mindless. I take issue with that proposition on two grounds. First, sensorimotor skills such as eye-hand coordination are important in themselves. They are useful in many occupations, as well as in everyday life, and according to Piaget's theory they are the foundation for later stages of cognitive development.

Second, it turns out that there is much more to the games than eye-hand coordination. In fact not only are they complex, they incorporate types of complexity that are impossible with conventional games. I am convinced that many of the people who criticize the games would not be able to play them themselves, and that their problems would be more than just those of eye-hand coordination. Let me illustrate with the game of Pac-Man.

Pac-Man

When I played Pac-Man for the first time, I had watched it played quite a number of times, and I assumed I would be able to play it myself, even if not with consummate skill. But when I started, I found I could not even distinguish Pac-Man, whom I was supposed to control, from the other blobs on the screen! A little girl of about five had to explain the game to me.

On a later play, I decided that I had so much trouble finding Pac-Man that first time because when Pac-Man first appears in the complex array of blobs and dots he does not have a wedged-shaped piece cut out of him; he is simply a yellow circle. I think that, as a person socialized into the world of static visual information, I made the unconscious assumption that Pac-Man would not change visual form. My hypothesis is that children socialized with television and film are more used to dealing with dynamic visual change and are less likely to make such a limiting assumption.

After trying the game again, I thought I had the basics. True, my score was not very good, but I assumed that was because my reflexes were not fast and I lacked sensorimotor practice. A few months later I bought The Video Master's Guide to Pac-Man in the hopes of finding out something about the psychology of video games (Sykora & Birkner, 1982). I was amazed to discover that I had missed all but the most obvious aspects of the game. Pac-Man is much more complex than I had imagined. Furthermore, most of the complexities are of a sort that cannot be incorporated in conventional board games such as checkers, chess, or monopoly. True, Pac-Man is an action game and therefore requires a certain amount of eye-hand coordination, but that is only the beginning of the game, not the end.

I am convinced that the people who criticize video games do not understand what the games involve. As I found out to my chagrin, a game like Pac-Man is not something one can pick up by standing around a machine for a few minutes, watching someone else play. I will describe Pac-Man in some detail in order to analyze the learning and cognitive processes that one must go through to become a skilled player.

When a player inserts a quarter into the Pac-Man machine, a maze filled with white dots appears on the screen (see figure 2). In the middle of the lower half of the screen appears Pac-Man, a yellow circle. The player uses the control stick to guide Pac-Man (now with open wedge-shaped mouth) through the maze. As Pac-Man encounters each white dot he "eats" it and it disappears; the object is to clear the maze of dots by having Pac-Man eat them all.

Thus far, the game seems simple enough, and it can be played at the level of this basic description. This was probably about the level at which

I played it at first. As in all games, however, there are obstacles. In Pac-Man the obstacles are not physical barriers but four monsters or ghosts, which chase Pac-Man through the maze and eat him if they catch him. Each monster has its own characteristic behavior. For example, the red monster, Shadow, is the most aggressive. The pink one, Speedy, the fastest monster, usually does not chase Pac-Man for very long at one time but does tend to come after him fairly often. The third monster, Pokey, will not cross any of the energizers. (The energizers are four large blinking dots. Each time Pac-Man eats an energizer, he is awarded fifty points and for a few seconds he becomes more powerful than the monsters, so that he can chase and eat them. For each monster he devours he gets more points; Sykora & Birkner, 1982).

This situation may sound a bit like chess, in which each piece has its own allowed behavior. But in PacMan, as in other video games, no one tells the player the rules governing each monster's behavior; these rules must be induced from observation. In this way, PacMan is more like life than like chess. The player must not only overcome the obstacles but must also perform the inductive task of figuring out the nature of the obstacles. The behavior patterns the player must discover lie in the game's computer program. Rick Sinatra, a computer programmer, may have had this aspect of the games in mind when he remarked: "Video games are revolutionary; they are the beginnings of human interaction with artificial intelligence."

As another obvious source of complexity, the arcade-style video games, unlike board games, have real-time movement in them. In chess or checkers the player moves pieces around a board, but the movement itself is not part of the game. Timing does not count. In Pac-Man, by contrast, quickness is vital as the player tries to keep Pac-Man away from the monsters.

Further complexity comes from the nature of the maze. It looks simple; there are no blind alleys or cul-de-sacs, complications of the conventional precomputer maze. However, the Pac-

Figure 2. Pac-Man game board layout. (From Sykora and Birkner, The Video Master's Guide to Pac-Man.

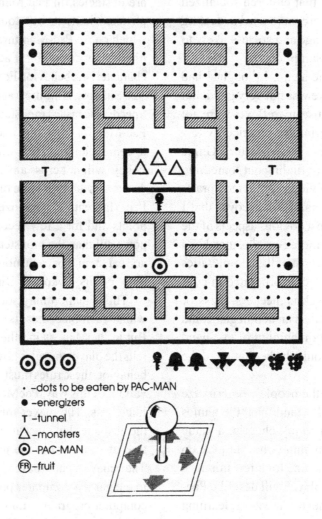

• –dots to be eaten by PAC-MAN
● –energizers
T –tunnel
△ –monsters
◉ –PAC-MAN
FR –fruit

Man maze has complications of a different sort, which would not be possible without computer technology. The possibilities for movement are not uniform throughout the maze, even though the terrain all looks the same. The relative speeds of the monsters and Pac-Man are different in different parts of the maze, so that the monsters can overtake Pac-Man in the labyrinthine parts but not on the straightaways. In addition, there are some areas of the maze where Pac-Man can enter much more easily than the monsters and which therefore provide Pac-Man with relative safety.

Such movement-related constraints simply do not exist in conventional games. These invisible complexities are programmed into the game's microcomputer.

Note that, as with the behavior of the monsters, the player does not know these spatial contingencies before starting to play. Whereas a conventional board game gives you all the rules, Pac-Man and other arcade-type computer games require the player to induce the rules from observation. Computer games therefore call up inductive skills much more than did games of the precomputer era.

Without this inductive effort, the games seem to be something like gambling games, in which a player deals with primarily random events. My son, Matthew, said of Pac-Man, "At first it was thought to be incredibly hard. Then people realized it wasn't random and figured out the patterns." Matthew also confirmed the existence of the inductive process: by watching others and then playing yourself, he said, "You just learn what things have what characteristics and what they do." An idea of the rate of learning is revealed in a saying among players: "You spend fifteen or twenty dollars on a game. Then you can play an hour and a half for a quarter." Part of the excitement of the games surely must lie in this process of transforming randomness into order through induction. (Adults may not learn as quickly; a bartender who had games in his bar estimated that it typically cost one of his customers a hundred dollars to get his name in the top five.)

Author's Note, 2009: *We subsequently followed up these ethnographic observations with a laboratory experiment that documented the inductive nature of action video game mastery through interaction with the game (Greenfield et al., 1994).*

Pac-Man also illustrates another cognitive requirement of skillful video game playing: parallel processing. This term refers to taking in information from several sources simultaneously; it contrasts with serial processing, in which the mind takes in information from one source at a time. In Pac-Man, to be a good player, you must simultaneously keep track of Pac-Man, the four monsters, where you are in the maze, and the four energizers. Many other games have even more information sources that must be dealt with simultaneously.

Here the skills and habits developed by watching much television may be very useful. Pictorial images in general tend to elicit parallel processing (Singer & Singer, 1981), while verbal media, because of the sequential nature of language (you read or hear one word at a time), tend to elicit serial processing. In television there are frequently several things happening on the screen simultaneously. For example, in the series *Hill Street Blues,* plot development uses this formal characteristic of the medium; Robert Altman's film *Nashville* provides a similar example. Consequently, a child whose main media background was television, rather than print or radio, could be more prepared for the parallel processing demanded by skillful video game playing.

Author's Note, 2009: *We subsequently carried out a laboratory experiment demonstrating that video game expertise and experience are associated with greater skill in dividing visual attention between two locations on a video screen (Greenfield, deWinstanley, Kilpatrick, & Kaye, 1994). Parallel processing or divided attention is the attentional foundation for multitasking. In 2005, Kearney published an experiment demonstrating that playing a first-person shooter game, Counterstrike, for 2 hours can improve multitasking performance on a set of four computer-based tasks—memory, mathematics, visual, and auditory—presented simultaneously. In the last couple of years, media multitasking has become a topic of great popular and scientific interest (Greenfield, 2009).*

Pac-Man embodies another cognitive complexity that was impossible in precomputer games: the interaction of two elements yields results that could not be predicted from either one separately. Thus, if you watched Pac-Man's behavior alone, you could not discover the special qualities of different parts of the maze. Nor could you by watching the monsters' behavior alone. Even inspection of the maze itself gives no clue. Only by watching the monsters interacting with Pac-Man in different parts of the maze can you detect the dynamic qualities of the maze.

This quality of interacting dynamic variables characterizes just about all computer action games.

In fact, it exists in about the simplest form possible in Pac-Man. This simplicity is handy for getting across the concept of interacting variables to people who may not be familiar with computer games, but it hardly scratches the surface of the cognitive complexity that expert players of the more difficult games (for example, Defender) have to deal with.

Tranquility Base

Let me give an example of complex interacting dynamic variables from an action game that has more educational content. The game, called Tranquility Base, is similar to Moon Lander, a computer game found in a number of children's museums and science centers around the United States. The object of the game is to land a space ship without crashing it. There are six basic variables involved: altitude, vertical speed, horizontal speed, direction, amount of fuel, and terrain (the same as horizontal location). The player controls thrust (acceleration) and horizontal direction. Each of the variables interacts with the others in complex ways. In order to land the spaceship safely, the player must take account of the variables not only one at a time but also as they influence one another. As I tried to learn the game, I found myself wanting to deal with one variable at a time. When that proved impossible, I tried dealing with them simultaneously, but as independent, rather than interacting, variables. That was no more successful. I worked for over an hour without making one successful landing. Matthew, who had taught me the game, strategy as well as basics, was frustrated with me. He could not understand why I was having so much trouble. Clearly, the strategy of integrating the interacting variables had become second nature to him. This may well be an important skill that video players are acquiring through practice with the games.

Author's Note, 2009: *Understanding the inductive process by which players integrate interacting variables in a game is an area in which, to my knowledge, little if any scientific progress has been made. This is an area that is ripe for investigation; it has great relevance to the use of complex simulations in educational settings.*

Experimental work confirms that games that require the player to induce the relations among multiple interacting variables are difficult for many people. Learning to play this type of game, furthermore, brings out important skills such as flexibility and an orientation toward independent achievement (Kahn, 1981). These skills are not called into play either by simpler games in which the variables do not interact or by games in which the player is told all the rules in advance. This is, I think, an important finding. Learning to deal with multiple interacting variables is a significant accomplishment because the world is not a simple system, but rather many complex systems of multiple interacting factors. But how much transfer can we expect from video games to other domains of knowledge and life?

The Issue of Transfer

Such transfer from the games to other domains cannot be taken for granted; it is far from automatic. As research has shown with print literacy, transfer from a medium to a skill is not just a question of basic knowledge of the medium, but depends on how the medium is used (Scribner & Cole, 1981).

Transfer of concepts to a new domain often seems to require their verbal formulation; yet the knowledge gained in playing video games is more than likely nonverbal. Research shows that verbal explanation is fostered by the dialogue between teacher and student that typically goes on in school. The transfer and generalization of the formal knowledge gained in playing video games may therefore depend on bringing the games into the school, not necessarily to play them, but to make them an object of study and discussion.

Spatial Skills

Spatial skills are another area of cognitive skills that many computer games require and therefore must promote as players become more skilled. Michael Williams first suggested this idea to me, using the example of Star Raiders. Star Raiders presents three-dimensional information in two dimensions, using conventions of perspective. Thus, in order to play the game well, the player must be skilled at interpreting these conventions. This skill is required by a number of popular games besides Star Raiders, such as Zaxxon.

Author's Note, 2009: *Subsequent to this analysis, we conducted a series of two studies to see whether skill in navigating through three-dimensional space represented on a two-dimensional screen in an action video game would transfer to mental paper-folding, a test of dynamic three-dimensional representation presented on a two-dimensional surface. We found evidence of transfer from video game expertise to skill in mental paper-folding (Greenfield, Brannon, & Lohr, 1994). In addition, an experiment demonstrating the transfer of video game experience to a whole suite of spatial skills was carried out bySubrahmanyam and Greenfield (1994).*

Many computer games require the ability to coordinate visual information coming from multiple perspectives. This is a skill emphasized in Piaget's account of intellectual development. For example, Tranquility Base involves a very simple coordination of perspectives (see figure 3). As the game begins, the player sees a long view of the space ship and the terrain where it is to land (top of illustration). As the ship gets closer to the ground, the view shifts to a close-up of the particular section of terrain that has been chosen

Figure 3. Two screens from Tranquility Base: top, long shot; bottom, close-up view

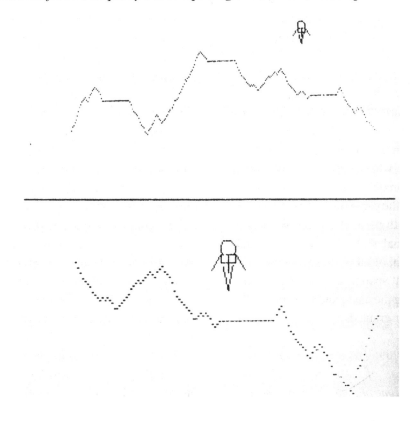

for landing (bottom of illustration). It is a bit like what a pilot would see as a plane (or spaceship) approached the earth.

Castle Wolfenstein is a game for home computers that involves a more complex coordination of perspectives. It is a chase game with an anti-Nazi theme that takes place in a series of mazes. Although the mazes are in two dimensions, they are meant to be part of a three dimensional prison. The storeys of the prison are linked by visible stairs, whose position serves as the visual cue for coordinating the individual mazes into a three-dimensional layout. In addition, each storey consists of more than one maze. Parts of a single storey are linked by doors, which, like the stairs, serve as cues for integrating individual mazes into the layout of a given storey.

When Matthew taught me how to play this game, I completely missed the aspect of spatial integration. I treated the mazes as if they were independent. I was totally unaware that the mazes were linked in the third dimension through stairs. I even missed the connections between mazes on the same level and did not realize that to leave a maze by the same door by which I entered was to go backward to an earlier maze instead of advancing to a new one. Matthew commented, "Most people realize *that* even if they are not paying attention." Apparently, the ability to integrate different spatial perspectives has become automatic in him, but not in me. This anecdote cannot tell us anything about what caused the difference, whether it is the male's greater spatial ability, practice in playing the games at a relatively young age, familiarity with particular game formats, a foundation of visual skills developed through watching television, or all of these together. But it does indicate that spatial integrative skills are involved in playing the game and that such skills cannot be taken for granted.

Author's Note, 2009: *Later we documented a player's mental map of the Castle Wolfenstein maze from the first time playing the game through* *increasing expertise. The player drew the maze a number of times during a sequence of Castle Wolfenstein games. We found that his mental map of the interlinked mazes grew and became more accurate as he gained more game experience, thus indicating the role of video game practice in spatial integration and mental mapping.*

The ability to coordinate information from more than one visual perspective is one of the skills that Israeli children developed through watching *Sesame Street*. Perhaps this skill, first developed through watching television, is later helpful to a child playing a video game such as Castle Wolfenstein.

Author's Note, 2009: *To my knowledge, there has been no research investigating the transfer of expertise in coordinating visual perspectives in video games to the use of this skill in other situations; this is another area that is ripe for experimental study.*

The suspicion that visual-spatial skills could be useful with and developed by video games was reinforced in my mind when I noticed that almost every child at the computer camp Matthew attended in the summer of 1981 came equipped with the Rubik's cube. Some of the campers had computer experience; some did not. But virtually all were experienced video game players. Not only did they have cubes, as many children did at that time, but the majority of them could solve the cube, some with amazing speed. (There were regular contests, not to see *if* you could do it, but how fast!) It seemed to me that this group of video game aficionados had more interest and skill with the cube than would be found in children with no experience with video games. My hypothesis is that Rubik's cube and video games demand and develop some of the same visual-spatial skills.

The culture gap was impressed upon me when I found that I not only was unable to do the cube but also could not understand my son's patient explanation, even accompanied by demonstration. The very terminology and frame of reference made no contact with anything familiar to me. It was as if he were speaking a foreign language. Clearly, I lacked some sort of spatial conceptualization required for the cube. Perhaps this lack of spatial skills is one element in my great difficulty with video games.

Fantasy Games

Not all computer games are action games. Another important type of game is the fantasy adventure game. Until very recently games of this type have not been available in arcades, but only as programs for home computers. Fantasy games involve complex characters with a medieval flavor who go on adventures together and meet a wide variety of circumstances and obstacles. This type of game has a number of interesting features that separate it from traditional games.

One distinguishing mark of this type of game is that there are so many more possible happenings and characters than in a traditional game. Events are constrained by rules, but the constraints are much broader than in traditional games; in this way the games are more like life. Another interesting feature is that characters are multidimensional. In the game of Wizardry, for example, the characters are composed of different combinations of six qualities—strength, IQ, luck, agility, vitality, and piety—in addition to belonging to unidimensional categories, as chess pieces do. (Rather than kings, queens, pawns, and so on, the categories in Wizardry are fighters, priests, gnomes, and so on.) The characters also have complex and varying combinations of external qualities, notably armor, weapons, gold, and spells. Thus, to play such games well, children have to understand and construct multidimensional character structure.

Another interesting feature is that the characters are created by the player. Within certain constraints, qualities are chosen rather than assigned. Thus, the games stimulate creative thinking in the players. Also, there is more character development than in conventional games. For example, characters gain "experience points" as they go through adventures, and their capabilities change as a function of this experience. Characters can be "saved" on computer disk, so that this development can continue over a period of time and continuous progress can be made. Thus, the fantasy games are not only more complex in some ways than conventional games, they are also more dynamic. The player is stimulated to develop or use concepts of character development.

Other Examples of Creativity

Eric Wanner has suggested that video games could be much more interesting if they provided for more creation, particularly the creation that comes with programming (Wanner, 1982). While it is true that arcade games are totally preprogrammed, the fantasy games, available for home computers, do involve a certain amount of creation. Even more open-ended and creative is a game like the Pinball Construction Set (see figure 4), where you first build your own pinball alley, manipulating its geometry, physics, and electrical wiring as well as the placement of its flippers, bumpers, and so on. Then you play the pinball game you have created. Thus, creative and constructive abilities, as well as the playing abilities of a traditional game, are called into play. The computer makes it possible for video games to have this creative and open-ended aspect.

Going one step further in this direction are games that incorporate programming into a game format. In Robot Wars, for example, the player first programs a robot to behave in certain ways. Each player creates his or her own robot through programming. This type of game seems to combine the excitement of control and creation (when the program works) with the motivation of a goal-oriented game.

As Wanner points out it is a shame that the more imaginative and creative types of games

Figure 4. Two screens from Pinball Construction Set. Both contain the basic alley. The top screen shows the various parts the player can use in constructing the game: flippers, bumpers, targets, and so on. The bottom screen contains dials for adjusting the physical variables of the game: the player can decrease or increase gravity, the speed of the simulation, the kicking strength of bumpers, and the elasticity (resilience) of collisions between balls and alley surfaces

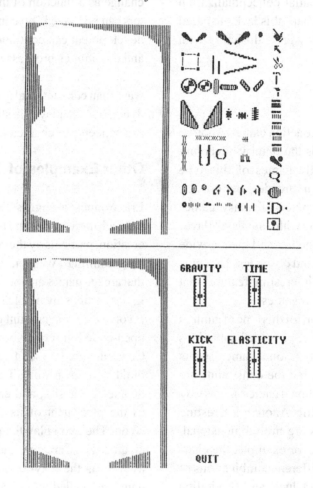

are not available to the general public, those who are able to spend quarters but not bigger money on computer technology. Perhaps the invasion of schools by computers will make these creative games available on a much broader scale. Although this is bound to happen to some extent, inequities in school ownership of computers based on social class of the school's population has already arisen, putting poorer children at a disadvantage in this area, as in others (Center for Social Organization of Schools, 1983).

A LADDER OF CHALLENGES

One more general characteristic of video games is, I believe, an important contributor to their learning potential. This is the fact that almost all the games have different levels, geared to the player's skill. In Pac-Man, after the player has cleared the dots on one maze, a new maze appears on the screen with more difficult characteristics. For example, in later stages of the game, PacMan cannot eat the monsters, even after having been "energized"; he can only force their retreat. A series of levels should have several effects. First, moving to a new level is a tangible sign of progress. Secondly, each new level presents a new challenge. And finally, having multiple levels introduces great variety into the game and creates curiosity as to what the next level will be like.

Evidence from work with learning-disabled children in an after-school educational setting emphasizes the appeal of levels of increasing difficulty. A game called Space Eggs, for instance, had such multiple levels. As they became expert players of Space Eggs, children kept moving from level to level, discovering new properties as they did so. "The day finally came, however, when one child achieved to the degree that the computer had no further response to: all that happens is that the most complex pattern repeats itself. The child's response was simple: he stopped playing the game. During future days at computer time, he chose other games, going back to Space Eggs only rarely" (Laboratory of Comparative Human Cognition, 1982). It seems that far from being lazy or seeking mindless games, children look for games that challenge them.

Video Games and Learning-Disabled Children

The same study of learning-disabled children found that the arcade games were in many ways better educational tools for learning-disabled children than "educational" games or education in general. Children who avoid instruction during reading time were willing to be instructed during computer time. Some children who refused to concentrate on conventional learning tasks concentrated very well on the arcade-style games, showing perseverance and making a great deal of progress from trial to trial. The children also began to act as teachers of their peers and of adults. They would ask one another how to get a game started or how to play, and expert players would coach novices in the game's advanced strategies. Here is a case where computer technology removes

handicaps that impede progress in other areas of education.

Multiple Levels and Addiction

According to Malone's study, the existence of multiple levels does not affect the popularity of particular games. But as the anecdote about Space Eggs shows, this characteristic may well affect *how long* a game remains interesting and popular, as well as how much is learned from it.

The existence of multiple levels may also be responsible for the addictive properties of the games claimed by the Glendale mother at the beginning of this chapter. A video game player makes visible progress in the form of improved score and reaching the next level. Yet there is always another level to master. The challenge of ever-new game conditions, added to the feeling of control that children claim computer games give them, creates a long-term appeal. As Malone has pointed out, learning situations other than computer games ought to be able to incorporate these powerful motivational features. Perhaps the most valuable thing we can learn is not how to make the games less addictive but how to make other learning experiences, particularly school, more so.

GAMES OF THE FUTURE

The motivating features of video games are beginning to be put to more explicit educational use. For example, Rocky's Boots, designed for home computers, uses a game format to teach the logic of computer circuitry. Early research findings indicate that players are engrossed by the game and learn from it. In Green Globs the player writes equations to hit randomly placed globs with a plotted curve, making progress in analytic geometry in moving from level to level (Chaffin, Maxwell, & Thompson, 1982; Linn, 1983).

James Levin and Yaakov Kareev have suggested some imaginative possibilities for future games. A video game always creates its own microworld, and they point out that game designers could structure these worlds to reflect knowledge we want the players to acquire. For example, they describe a "chemical adventure" game that could be designed to teach about the periodic table of elements:

Suppose that in a game world, we personify elements as people having characteristics analogous to their namesake elements. So we would have the muscle men Chromium, Manganese, and Iron, the attractive Chlorine, Fluorine, and Iodine, the casanovas Lithium, Sodium and Potassium, the super rich Platinum, Gold, Silver, and Copper. A goal in this game might be to rescue Silver, who is being held hostage by the seductive Chlorine (the compound silver chloride, used in photographic paper). .. the player could use a magic powder (free electrons) to sprinkle over Silver to reduce his attraction to Chlorine, so that he can be set free. .. along the way the player would have to avoid the dangerous Arsenic and Plutonium, distracting Arsenic with Gallium, or using Lead as a shield from Plutonium's rays. .. This sketch of a chemical adventure points to the ways that a computer game program could draw upon the same aspects that make current adventures entertaining, yet teach an abstract knowledge domain (Levin & Kareev, 1980, p. 40-41).

Video games are a new medium, and scientific study of them is just beginning. Most of my discussion of skills involved in the games has been based on analyses of the games themselves, plus a few observations of individual cases. Such analyses furnish but a starting point for the systematic research of the future. More important, while this type of analysis can give important clues as to the skill involved in playing the games, it cannot tell us how far these skills transfer to situations outside the game itself. Just as is the case for other media, the games may well have to be used in an instructional context, with guidance and discussion by

teachers, for the important skills to transfer very far. We should not forget, however, that knowledge and skill can be of value in themselves even if they are not transferable to new situations.

In thinking about video games, we should not think only of the shoot-'em-up space games that predominate in the arcade. There are, and there can be, a wide variety of game formats that utilize the marriage of computer and television. Because it can be programmed, the computer is a highly flexible medium, and the possibilities are endless.

As with any medium, the medium of video games has its own pattern of strengths and weaknesses. This medium may include more variation than most, however. For example, the real-time action games may foster parallel processing skills and fast reaction time but may also discourage reflection. (If you stop to think while playing Space Invaders, you're lost). By contrast, games with a verbal format (for example, some of the fantasy-adventure games) use serial processing and allow unlimited time for reflection and planning. The real danger may be in the very variety, complexity, and appeal of game worlds that are so responsive to the child's input. As Karen Sheingold has speculated, too much control over the fantasy worlds of video games could bring about impatience with the messy, uncontrollable world of real life. This possible danger must, however, be weighed against the positive effects of achievement and control for children who, for whatever reasons, lack a sense of competence and predictability in other domains of life.

REFERENCES

Anderson, C. A., & Bushman, B. J. (2001). Effects of violent games on aggressive behavior, aggressive cognition, aggressive affect, physiological arousal, and prosocial behavior: A meta-analytic review of the scientific literature. *Psychological Science, 12,* 353–359. doi:10.1111/1467-9280.00366

Anderson, D. (1982). *Informal features.*

Anderson, D. R. (1983, April). *Home television viewing by preschool children, and their families.* Paper presented at the Society for Research in Child Development.

Broderbund. (1985). *Where in the world is Carmen San Diego?* [Video game].

Brooks, J. D. (1983). *Video games and human development A research agenda for the '80s.* Cambridge, MA: Monroe C. Gutman Library, Harvard Graduate School of Education.

Center for Social Organization of Schools. (1983, April). *School uses of microcomputers: Reports from a national survey.* Center for Social Organization of Schools, John Hopkins University.

Chaffin, J. D., Maxwell, B., & Thompson, B. (1982). ARC-ED curriculum: The application of video game formats to educational software. *Exceptional Children, 49,* 173–178.

Christakis, D. A., Ebel, B. E., Rivara, F. P., & Zimmerman, F. J. (2004). Television, video, and computer game use in children under 11 years of age. *The Journal of Pediatrics, 145,* 652–656. doi:10.1016/j.jpeds.2004.06.078

De Lisi, R., & Cammarano, D. M. (1996). Computer experience and gender differences in undergraduate mental rotation performance. *Computers in Human Behavior, 12,* 351–361. doi:10.1016/0747-5632(96)00013-1

De Lisi, R., & Wolford, J. L. (2002). Improving children's mental rotation accuracy with computer game playing. *The Journal of Genetic Psychology, 163,* 272–282. doi:10.1080/00221320209598683

Dorval, M., & Pepin, M. (1986). Effect of playing a video game on a measure of spatial visualization. *Perceptual and Motor Skills, 62,* 159–162.

Gagnon, D. (1985). Video games and spatial skills: An exploratory study. *Educational Technology and Communication Journal, 33,* 263–275.

Gardner, H. (1983, March 27). When television marries computers [Review of *Pilgrim in the microworld* by Robert Sudnow]. *New York Times,* 12.

Gentile, D. A., Anderson, C. A., Yukawa, S., Ihori, N., Saleem, M., & Ming, L. K. (2009)... *Personality and Social Psychology Bulletin, 35,* 752–763. doi:10.1177/0146167209333045

Green, S., & Bavelier, D. (2003). Action video game modifies visual selective attention. *Nature, 423,* 534–537. doi:10.1038/nature01647

Greenfield, P. M. (1972). Oral or written language: The consequences for cognitive development in Africa, the United States, and England. *Language and Speech, 15,* 169–178.

Greenfield, P. M. (1984). Video games. In *Mind and media: The effects of television, video games, and computers* (pp. 97–126). Cambridge, MA: Harvard University Press.

Greenfield, P. M. (2009). Technology and informal education: What is taught, what is learned. *Science, 323,* 69–71. doi:10.1126/science.1167190

Greenfield, P. M., Brannon, C., & Lohr, D. (1994). Two-dimensional representation of movement through three-dimensional space: The role of video game expertise. *Journal of Applied Developmental Psychology, 15,* 87–103. doi:10.1016/0193-3973(94)90007-8

Greenfield, P. M., Camaioni, L., Ercolani, P., Weiss, L., Lauber, B., & Perucchini, P. (1994). Cognitive socialization by computer games in two cultures: Inductive discovery or mastery of an iconic code? *Journal of Applied Developmental Psychology, 15,* 59–85. doi:10.1016/0193-3973(94)90006-X

Greenfield, P. M., de Winstanley, P., Kilpatrick, H., & Kaye, D. (1994). Action video games and informal education: Effects on strategies for dividing visual attention. *Journal of Applied Developmental Psychology, 15,* 105–123. doi:10.1016/0193-3973(94)90008-6

Huston, A. C., & Wright, J. C. (1983). Children's processing of television: The informative functions of formal features. In Bryant, J., & Anderson, D. R. (Eds.), *Watching TV, Understanding TV: Research on children s attention and comprehension*. New York: Academic Press.

Kahn, T. M. (1981). *An analysis of strategic thinking using a computer-based game*. Ph.D. dissertation, University of California, Berkeley.

Kearney, P. R. (2005). Cognitive calisthenics: Do FPS computer games enhance the player's cognitive abilities? *Proceedings of the DIGRA World Conference.*

Laboratory of Comparative Human Cognition. (1982). A model system for the study of learning difficulties. *Quarterly Newsletter of the Laboratory of Comparative Human Cognition, 4*, 39–66.

Lauber, B. A. (1983). *Adolescent video game use*. Unpublished paper, Department of Psychology, University of California, Los Angeles.

Levin, J. A., & Kareev, Y. (1980). Problem solving in everyday situations. *Quarterly Newsletter of the Laboratory of Comparative Human Cognition, 2*, 47–52.

Malone, T. W. (1981). Toward a theory of intrinsically motivating instruction. *Cognitive Science, 4*, 333–369.

Mattel. (1996). *Barbie Fashion Designer*. [Video game].

McClurg, P. A., & Chaillé, C. (1987). Computer games: Environments for developing spatial cognition? *Journal of Educational Computing Research, 3*, 95–111.

Mitchell, E. (1983, May). *A research agenda for the '80s. Conference on video games and human development*. Cambridge, MA: Harvard Graduate School of Education.

Okagaki, L., & Frensch, P. A. (1994). Effects of video game playing on measures of spatial performance: Gender effects in late adolescence. *Journal of Applied Developmental Psychology, 15*, 33–58. doi:10.1016/0193-3973(94)90005-1

Rosenfeld, S. B. (1982, June). *Informal learning and computers*. Position paper prepared for the Atari Institute for Education-Action Research.

Salomon, G. (1979). *Interaction of media, cognition, and learning*. San Francisco: Jossey-Bass.

Scribner, S., & Cole, M. (1981). *The psychology of literacy*. Cambridge, MA: Harvard University Press.

Silvern, S. B., Williamson, P. A., & Countermine, T. A. (1983a). *Video game playing and aggression in young children*. Paper presented to the American Educational Research Association, Montreal.

Silvern, S. B., Williamson, P. A., & Countermine, T. A. (1983b). *Video game play and social behavior: Preliminary findings*. Paper presented at the International Conference on Play and Play Environments.

Singer, J. L., & Singer, D. G. (1981). *Television, imagination and aggression: A study of preschoolers*. Hillsdale, NJ: Erlbaum.

Subrahmanyam, K., & Greenfield, P. M. (1994). Effect of video game practice on spatial skills in girls and boys. *Journal of Applied Developmental Psychology, 15*, 13–32. doi:10.1016/0193-3973(94)90004-3

Subrahmanyam, K., & Greenfield, P. M. (1999). Computer games for girls: What makes them play? In Cassell, J., & Jenkins, H. (Eds.), *Barbie to Mortal Kombat: Gender and computer games* (pp. 46–71). Cambridge, MA: MIT Press.

Sykora, J., & Birkner, J. (1982). *The video master's guide to Pac-Man*. New York: Bantam.

Wanner, E. (1982, October). Computer time: The electronic Boogey-man. *Psychology Today*, 8–11.

Reprinted From: Greenfield, P. M. (1984). Video games. In Mind and media: The effects of television, video games, and computers (pp. 97–126). Cambridge, MA: Harvard University Press.

Chapter 2
Distinctions Between Games and Learning:
A Review of Current Literature on Games in Education

Katrin Becker
Simon Fraser University, Canada

ABSTRACT

Serious games are digital games designed for purposes other than pure entertainment. This category includes educational games but it also includes a great deal more. A field that was unheard of until Ben Sawyer referred to it as Serious Games in late 2002 (Sawyer, 2003) has already grown so large that one can only hope to keep track of a very small part of it. The time is rapidly coming to an end when literature surveys of even one branch of Serious Games can be considered comprehensive. This chapter will examine the current state of the part of the serious games discipline that intersects with formal education, with a particular focus on design. The chapter begins broadly by looking at games in order to define the term serious game but then narrows to a specific focus on games for education. In this way, it provides an educational context for games as learning objects, distinguishes between traditional, (i.e. non-digital; Murray, 1998) and digital games, and classifies games for education as a subcategory of serious games while at the same time still being part of a larger group of interactive digital applications.

Anyone who makes a distinction between games and learning doesn't know the first thing about either.

—Marshall McLuhan

DOI: 10.4018/978-1-61520-717-6.ch002

INTRODUCTION

Serious games are digital games designed for purposes other than pure entertainment. This includes educational games but also a great deal more, such as Games for Health, Games for Change, Military Games, Games for Politics, Advergaming, and Exergaming. While learning plays a role in many of these serious games 'genres' it is not necessarily the primary role and it most certainly is not the only one. This volume focuses on serious games whose primary purpose is education. The study of games for education, even traditional games designed for or used in that context, has no broadly accepted research or literature base, and so existing ones must be extended in new ways. Learning through play - which is closely related, but still not the same - has been given a certain amount of attention, at least in the context of early childhood development, and some of the noteworthy celebrities involved in the study of play and learning, such as Montessori, Bruner, and Papert, have influenced scholarship on games in education. The contributions of Fröbel (1912), and Piaget (1951) are also influential. This foundational work in play has helped to inform current work in games, but in spite of the fact that there are a growing number of studies involving specific games used in educational settings, as well as studies of games in specific contexts (like sports, math skills, early literacy, some areas of science), there exists no general "theory of gaming" as applied to learning, let alone a "theory of videogames." This implies that this author and others are charting what amounts to new territory, even in the mapping of the terrain itself. The connections made are almost all going to be new ones. This chapter is an examination of the current 'state of the field' of digital games in formal education. Within this subset of serious games, the focus of this review is on literature written over the last decade, with a particular emphasis on game design.

Alan Kay said that "technology is anything that was invented after you were born" (the actual wording of the quote varies from source to source, e.g., see Ceer, 2006, p. 86). A distinct challenge in the study of serious games generally and games for education specifically is that research related to modern digital games can go out of date very quickly because digital game technology is evolving at breakneck speeds. The expectations and

capabilities of our learners are changing alongside those technological advances as does (or at least should) our understanding of its potential. For the most part, comparing digital games of the 1980s and early 1990s to those of today is akin to comparing a Model-T Ford to a SmartCar. One implication of this is that conclusions based on studies conducted before about 1999 may no longer apply to current circumstances. This also means that many of the works on simulations and digital games published in the last century are of limited relevance.

SETTING THE SCENE

Definitions: What Is a Game?

"Most controversies would soon be ended, if those engaged in them would first accurately define their terms, and then adhere to their definitions."

—*Tryon Edwards (Berkeley, 1853, p. 51)*

Is a game still a game when it is not being played, and can anything become a game if we play with it? Some have argued that we cannot categorize any game because, despite its designed intent, a game is almost entirely dependent on the intentions of the user at the time of use (Leigh, 2003). From a design perspective, this position is not useful. A working definition, however flawed, is essential to designing a game (how can we know what to design if we have no concept of our goal?). The goal of this section is to provide the context for an overview of the literature on digital games in education; what follows here are the highlights of just a few of the more popular definitions.

In his classic work, *Homo Ludens,* written years before the first commercial digital game became known, Johan Huizinga (1950) states that to be a game, it must: be voluntary, have spatial and temporal limits, have rules, and a self contained goal. Roger Caillois, who wrote another of the classic works in the field entitled, *Man, Play, and Games* also claims that a game one is made to play stops being a game (Caillois, 1961). The notion of a game being voluntary poses a dilemma for games used for learning: participation is often not voluntary, especially in formal educational settings (see Magerko, Heeter, & Medler, this volume). This is one reason why it is necessary to devise a definition that fits the context being discussed here, which is that sub-category of serious games that are intended for learning.

After reviewing a number of the main definitions of game in their more recent work, Katie Salen and Eric Zimmerman (2004) say games are systems that can be considered in at least three ways: 1) as rules (closed systems), 2) as play, and 3) as culture (the way the game exchanges meaning with the culture at large). Jesper Juul devoted an entire volume to defining the videogame (2005), and in their recent book, *Understanding Video Games*, Egenfeldt-Nielsen, Smith, and Tosca said that the way we define game affects everything from methodology to funding for research and can blind us to our own biases (2008). Brian Sutton-Smith (1997) suggests that each person defines games according to his (or her) own perspectives, and Wittgenstein said that there is no one feature common to all games but that there exists a certain 'family relationship' (Wittgenstein, 1973). The remainder of this section will make the connection between media and games and explain why digital games should be singled out as distinct from other media as well as from other (non-digital) games. This will facilitate a classification for digital games and other related technology as a distinct educational technology in the next section.

Old & New Media

As a medium, digital games are unique in recent history. Games are a medium of communication and expression that requires the participation of the players. There is good reason to believe that games predate language. When we became a literate culture (with the invention of the Gutenberg printing press) we began shifting from active and participatory media to more passive ones (See Figure 1). Even performing arts and storytelling were once much more participatory than they are now (although there has been a resurgence in the popularity of participatory theater).

Digital games have two primary antecedents:

1.   traditional (pre-digital) games such as board games, card games, and live action role playing (LARP) games
2.   other communication media such as television, film, and print.

Both have had a significant impact, and yet digital games represent a Gestalt - they are more than a simple evolution. Games and game technology (which in this chapter includes digital simulations) represent a fundamental shift in how we can communicate. My generation grew up with film and television; the generation before mine grew up with print, film, and radio; the one before that primarily with print, as did the generation before it, and the one before that, ... We have been subjected to passive media (watch, read, listen) for a very long time now - it should come as no surprise that a medium as demanding of interaction as games should be met with resistance by those who have been entrained to sit quietly and pay attention.

"In a culture like ours, long accustomed to splitting and dividing all things as a means of control, it is sometimes a bit of a shock to be reminded that, in operational and practical fact, the medium is the message. This is merely to say that the personal and social consequences of any medium - that is, of any extension of ourselves - result from the new scale that is introduced into our affairs by each

Figure 1. Communication media through history

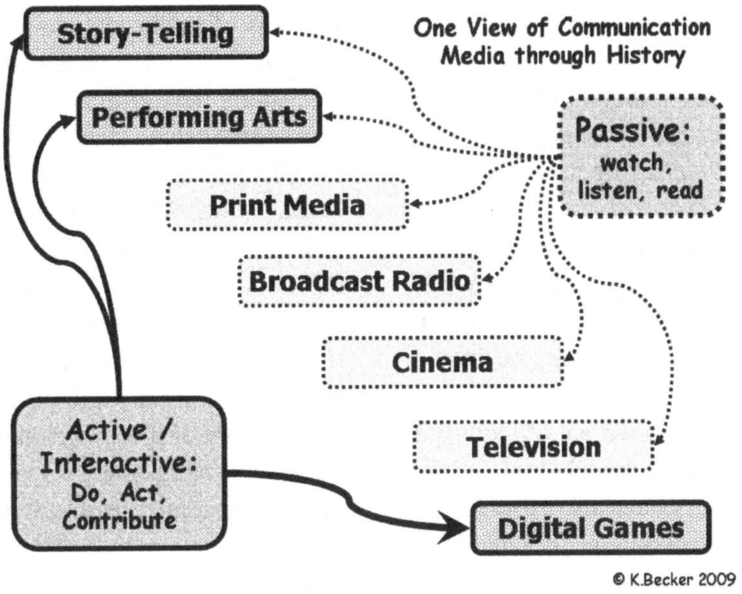

extension of ourselves, or by any new technology."
(Marshall McLuhan, 1964, p. 7)

McLuhan's now famous message reminds us that the medium inevitably affects the interpersonal dynamics of the society into which it is introduced. Although he was referring to predigital games, McLuhan described games as media of interpersonal communication. If we put these notions together, that games are interpersonal and require active engagement with the medium and that they in turn affect their users, then digital games are indeed poised to bring about a change to society. Games are an extension of ourselves, and represent a change our interpersonal dynamics—gamers come to expect to be interactive agents as opposed to passive receptacles, and this notion spreads to other aspects of their lives—including formal education. It is no wonder that there is resistance to games from the established institutions who are, by and large, still lagging far behind when it comes to appropriate or effective use of technology. "The commercial and educational interests in the old media and modes of thought have frozen

personal computing pretty much at the 'imitation of paper, recordings, film and TV' level" (Kay, 2007, p. 4). Games may be cultural constructs that have been with us since pre-literate times, but the synergy of games gone digital changes things, and we mustn't assume that what was known about old media will apply to this new medium.

Going Digital

Will Wright, creator of one of the best selling game franchises of all time–*The Sims*–discussed games as media in David Freeman's (2003) book, *Creating Emotion in Games*, claiming that games are distinct from other media like film or theatre:

"Comparing games to previous forms of media (which are, for the most part, linear experiences) can be both useful and dangerous. Useful, because by studying other forms, we get a good sense of what games are missing and how far they have to go in this important direction. Dangerous, because interactive entertainment is a fundamentally different proposition than its linear cousins, involv-

ing quite different psychological mechanisms. ... Games, on the other hand are most directly dependent on something else entirely: the concept of agency. Agency is our ability to alter the world around us, or our situation in it. ... This is the crucial distinction between interactive and linear entertainment." (p. xxxii)

The point Will is making that is of direct relevance to this chapter is that digital games, while sharing some qualities with other forms of media, are still distinctly different and cannot be treated in the same manner as other media forms. In some ways (already outlined), video games conform to a relatively classic game model (Juul, 2005), but by 'going digital' they have also evolved into something new that becomes more difficult to peg with each new development.

For the purposes of this discussion, a distinction is made between 'pure' digital games (the focus of this chapter), and digital *versions* of non-digital games. There are some games that only exist as computer games, such as the *Mario* franchise and *Katamari Damacy*, while others are merely digital versions of traditional games, such as Solitaire and Chess. *Wii Sports* is part simulation of the real sports they represent, part something else. In addition, some digital games like *Starcraft*, *Civilization* or even *Tetris* are being turned into board games. While MMOs have some similarities with both traditional paper-book-and-model RPGs as well as LARPs (live action role plays), there are also significant differences (player location, number of participants, rule structures and enforcement to name a few) so these too fall under the category of 'pure' digital games.

Also, although there is some overlap, the body of literature (and researchers) dealing with digital games differs from those who deal with traditional games. While some see this as a continuum, I would argue it is not. 'Going digital' changes things. Table 1 summarizes those differences.

These distinctions have implications for the design and use of digital as opposed to traditional

Table 1. Digital vs. non-digital games

	Digital	Traditional (board games, card games etc.)	Live Role-Play
Rule enforcement	hard-coded; can only be changed by changing the program (It is possible to create rule systems that can be player-edited, but this just moves the 'enforcement' up one level of abstraction)	on the fly; player (or facilitator) controlled; this means they CAN be bent, broken, changed	
Rule Structures	pre-determined - can be monitored apart from players and facilitators	negotiable - monitoring is by players and facilitators	
Roles	accurate placement into context (complete with sights, sounds, behaviours)	imagined, personally mediated	
Play Space /Environment	dynamic; same for all players (This can be altered, but this is not player created)	static; unchanging	imagined - each player has a different view - personal
Play space / environment resolution	can be manipulated - can be high - universal/microscopic	static - physical game (board, pieces) don't change	mediated by individual imaginations (i.e. not shared)
Game Objects	can be autonomous	either inert or mechanical	imagined
Game Interaction (what people can do with / to the game)	is consistent across all instantiations of the game	consistent	each instantiation can be different
Players	there need only be one human player	all players/participants in traditional games must be human	

games in education. While understanding that informs the design of traditional games can also inform the design of digital games, it is not a simple process of applying what is already known to this new medium.

The Edutainment Dilemma

Okie use 'ta mean you was from Oklahoma. Now it means you're scum. Don't mean nothing itself, it's the way they say it.

—John Ernst Steinbeck, The Grapes of Wrath, 1939

Alessi and Trollip (2001) claim that much elementary and middle school educational software gets marketed under the label of 'edutainment', and that it often refers to repetitive practice activities. The term 'edutainment' has become problematic, as it carries different connotations in different communities. Many discussions of 'edutainment' put forward by game scholars add value judgments to the term (Buckingham & Scanlon, 2004; Egenfeldt-Nielsen, 2005; Fabricatore, 2000; Leyland, 1996; Prensky, 2001a)—the conclusion seems to be that 'bad' educational software (by whatever measure) is far more likely to be referred to as 'edutainment' than it is if it is somehow deemed to be 'good'. Mitch Resnick, a chief proponent of active learning through the use of well-designed technology, has a similarly dim view of the term.

"So why don't I like edutainment? The problem is with the way that creators of today's edutainment products tend to think about learning and education. Too often, they view education as a bitter medicine that needs the sugar-coating of entertainment to become palatable. They provide entertainment as a reward if you are willing to suffer through a little education. Or they boast that

you will have so much fun using their products that you won't even realize that you are learning—as if learning were the most unpleasant experience in the world. (2004)

The notion that fun and learning are somehow mutually exclusive is at least part of the reason 'edutainment' has not been well accepted. Simon Egenfeldt-Nielsen (2005) executes a fairly detailed analysis of edutainment software in his 2005 dissertation and identifies seven properties of edutainment, including little intrinsic motivation, no integrated learning experience, drill-and-practice learning principles, simple gameplay, small budgets, no teacher presence, and distribution and marketing.

Clearly, a negative view of 'edutainment' has persisted since the early days of its use, but it seems quite clear that there exists no fully shared meaning for this term. Some modern scholars refer to the period from the beginning of the use of digital games in the classroom—circa 1980—to the first general rejection of the medium as a viable educational technology (which interestingly coincides with videogames achieving mainstream status as entertainment)—the early 1990s—as 'The Edutainment Era'. There is reason to believe that we are making better games now: ones that aim for higher order learning, that can be integrated into the teacher's pedagogy, and that fulfill many constructivist learning methods (e.g., Kurt Squire & Mathew Gaydos' *Citizen Science,* in press). In modern educational games, we are aiming for intrinsic motivation; we want teachers to take part in constructing the learning environment that is based around a game. We are not trying to shut them out nor are we aiming for simple game play—we are aiming for complex experiences to help facilitate complex learning.

The Clark / Kozma Debate, Revisited

As has been true with any other technology introduced into schools to assist teaching and learning, digital games have their detractors as well as their champions. The now-classic Clark/Kozma "media effects" debate, where Richard E. Clark claims that media has no effect on instruction and serves as nothing more than the 'vehicle' for delivery (Clark, 1983), and Robert B. Kozma (1994) counters by saying that the medium changes things, has moved into the serious games space as revived in an editorial by Clark in Educational Technology Magazine (2007). Clark argues that serious games have little to offer that improves upon traditional teaching methods such as lectures. He continues to invoke his 'vehicle' analogy which describes the medium as merely the vehicle of delivery for instruction - something that is not really a part of the instruction itself. What Clark fails to acknowledge is that this analogy doesn't work with games or with a great many other technologies - especially those that are interactive in some way.

Viewing games as receptacles for content rather than teaching methods does work in a select subset of games (puzzles, game show styles, etc.) but this represents a very small portion of the ways in which games can be and have been used to facilitate learning. The design of a digital game is a complex process, as is the design of instruction—one cannot simply be imposed onto the other, and the success of an educational game can only come from a successful synergy of both. Thus, if an educational game is a success or failure, the credit (or blame) cannot be attributed solely to the game (design) OR the instructional design, but must instead be placed squarely on the shoulders of both. The medium of the videogame isn't just a vehicle, like a car that gets us from one place to another. Even if we did want to stay with the vehicle analogy, a closer approximation might be to use land vehicles, planes, ships, and submarines rather than just Clark's trucks. True, they do all get us from one place to another (much like successful instruction does), and much as I like nice cars, I wouldn't want to have a Ferrari as my vehicle when what I really need is a submarine.

Further, it is interesting that Clark chose to reference the older edition of Gredler's chapter (1996) when a newer one was available (Gredler, 2004). In 1996 there was no XBox, no Gamecube, no Playstation II (as there were in 2004). In fact, the Playstation I had been released only two years earlier and almost certainly played no role in Gredler's work. Console games were just beginning to acquire some sophistication. For example, *Final Fantasy VII* had not yet been released and most console games were rendered in 2D. There were no handheld games, no cell phone or mobile games, and no technologies that a modern developer would recognize. In other words, the "technology" of educational technology was vastly different then, and discussing the effectiveness of media, potential or otherwise, in 2007 using reports from more than ten years ago is like discussing today's traffic issues using data from 1820.

The truth of the matter is that technology, in and of itself, neither improves or impoverishes instruction: "instructional technology only works for some kids, with some topics, and under some conditions—but that is true of all pedagogy. There is nothing that works for every purpose, for every learner, and all the time." (Mann, 2001, p. 241) But technology *does* affect instruction.

And Now, The Non-Definitive Definition

The difference between the almost right word and the right word is really a large matter—'tis the difference between the lightning bug and the lightning.

—Mark Twain

Many in this community argue about the meanings of several key terms important to the field.

Is this object a game or a simulation? Are digital games more like traditional board games, face-to-face play, theatre, or something else? Is "serious game" a misnomer? Does it matter? In the forward of Seels and Richey's volume defining the field of instructional technology, they say that in order "to function effectively specialists need to be able to communicate with other specialists in the field, and they need to understand how they fit into the field as a whole" (1994, p. xvi). A clear understanding of what is meant by educational game is crucial to effective communication. While the full debate is too complex to summarize here, several points should be emphasized. First, this chapter is not about 'educational simulations', which are live action scenarios played out in the classroom, but it does include digital simulations used for education. They are not the same things—'going digital' transforms the learning environment into something new. Second, all digital games are computer simulations, although the reverse is not true.

The way we delineate the borders defining what is and is not an educational game is important because it has implications for research and development. A definition that is too broad is not useful, and a definition that is too narrow excludes development choices that might otherwise be useful. A development team must be clear on what it is building and yet retain sufficient flexibility to foster innovation. The design process is likely to proceed along very different lines if one group envisions *Wheel of Fortune* as their idea of a game and another envisions *World of Warcraft*.

Margaret Gredler's (2004) definition of games distinguishes games quite clearly from simulations, which causes difficulty since her's is commonly cited in much of the educational literature on games for education. According to Gredler, simulations model complex real-world situations, must have a defined role for each participant, must include a data-rich environment, and feedback must be in the form of changes to the problem, while games are objects where the primary objective is to win, where "bells and whistles" and losing points for incorrect anserws interfere with learning, and where trying some action in order to "see what happens" is undesirable. Kurt Squire (2003) suggests that the 'accepted' definition of game (i.e. Gredler's) breaks down in light of modern digital games which has also been reiterated in other articles (Parker, Becker, & Sawyer, 2008).

Where does that leave us? A digital game is a game that requires a computer to run it. A fundamental quality of a game is that it have rules (which may be implicit or explicit), but which are enforced by the design of the computer programs that implement the game. It may have one or more goals, but must have at least one explicit goal and it must be finite in time and space. The voluntary part mentioned by both Huizinga and Caillios must be excluded from our definition because in any formal educational setting, while there should be some degree of choice, the tasks that learners are given to do are typically *not* voluntary.

Digital games and digital simulations belong to the same domain; they are far more similar to each other than they are to either traditional games or to non-digital educational simulations, and research into educational applications of these technologies as well as understanding about best practices for design all help to construct the same terrain. The field of educational game studies, therefore, must include both objects that can clearly be defined as digital games and non-game computer simulations that make use of the same technology.

Having delineated the extent and bounds of the types of objects to be considered as games in this chapter, the next section introduces the field that includes the design, use, and study of digital games.

DIGITAL GAMES IN EDUCATION

One learns by doing a thing; for though you think you know it, you have no certainty until you try.

—Sophocles

Although research on and development of computer games appeared promising a generation ago (Malone, 1981; Malone & Lepper, 1987; Papert, 1980; White, 1984), its popularity appeared to wane through the 90s as ultimately the games that were built did not live up to their promise. This situation is changing, but still relatively little scholarly work exists on the use of modern digital games for education. This section highlights the major literature reviews that have been published since the inception of the modern "serious games" movement in 2003.

Alice Mitchell and Carol Savill-Smith (2004) published a major review of the literature on the educational use of games in 2004 where they consulted eleven earlier literature reviews and examined 200 publications produced during 2000-2004. The publications they examined included various uses of games for education, including clinical practice and supporting reading and math, but they found that one of the most popular uses was as a form of experiential learning through simulations. The benefits of the use of games was not clear but it was noted that the literature base was still quite sparse. In that same year, John Kirriemuir and Angela McFarlane (2004) also conducted a review of the literature and also published a major report. They sought to explore several questions, including whether conventional games could be used in formal education, and found that identifying the potential uses of specific games, persuading stakeholders, finding time to familiarize oneself with specific games and the persistence of irrelevant content which could not be ignored were all factors that conspire to keep games out of mainstream education. On the other hand, even though they concluded that many barriers were perceptual rather than practical, they noted that there was a commonly held belief that games had the potential to become powerful learning tools because of their experiential nature. Becker and Jacobsen (2005) were able to confirm some of these findings the following year with a survey conducted with local area teachers,

where two important barriers identified were lack of time and support. These findings have been largely supported again by the more recent work of Baek (2008), who also found differences between experienced teachers who were more concerned about the inflexibility of curriculum and negative effects of gaming, and inexperienced teachers who believed that adopting games in teaching was hindered by a lack of supporting materials and by fixed class schedules.

Ellis, Heppell, Kirriemuir, Krotoski, & McFarlane (2006) published another review of the literature where they found that there had been some progress in the adaptation of games for education settings in the ensuing years. They also found more use of Commercial Off the Shelf (COTS) games than in 2004, but their use was still not widespread. A major barrier remained the time it takes to become familiar enough with a game to know how to use it. This has been a common complaint and was one of the motivating factors in several workshops the author has offered, as well as an education graduate course on digital game based learning that the author designed and delivered (Becker, 2005b; Becker & Parker, 2005). In their review, Ellis, et al. suggested that part of the solution is to open a dialogue between game developers and educators to reconcile the knowledge gaps (2006). The author's own work connecting game design to known pedagogy is partially aimed towards this end (Becker, 2005a, 2005b, 2006a, 2006b, 2008b).

Also in 2006, FutureLab and the 'Teaching with Games' project reported on a year-long study intended to offer a broad view of teachers' and learners' attitudes towards and use of COTS games (Sandford, Ulicsak, Facer, & Rudd, 2006). They conducted national surveys as well as ten detailed case studies of COTS games used in four different schools. Among the key findings were that there is a large difference between students' and teachers' game-playing habits, with 82% of students playing games and 72% of teachers NOT playing games. They also found that student motivation was positively affected by the use of familiar games and through having some autonomy when playing. Fixed-length lessons were constraining, games did not need to be highly accurate to be beneficial, and meaningful use of games "within lessons depended far more on the teacher's effective use of existing pedagogical skills than it did on the development of any new, game-related skills" (p. 4).

The following year, 2007, was a banner year for literature reviews. Sara de Freitas (2007) reported on several case studies as well as providing a review of the literature. She found that many of the cutting edge examples of games use are currently being piloted in K-12 schools rather than in HE/FE (higher or further education), and she felt that it reflected a broader uptake of game-based approaches amongst younger learners. Another explanation is that it could reflect a more conventional approach in HE/FE as compared to K-12. Punya Mishra and Aroutis Foster (2007) published an analysis of claims made in 60 different sources and found that on the whole, most claims do not take the interaction of the game's content, pedagogy, and technology into account, which results in an inability to draw clear conclusions about how games are useful. Simon Egenfeldt-Nielsen (2007) suggests that in order to achieve a real breakthrough in the use of educational games, we must realize that there is no magic to the medium, but rather that games need to be tailored far more closely to the learning content and that educators and researchers alike need to rethink their teaching and learning assumptions.

Sigmund Tobias and J.D. Fletcher (2007) also surveyed the existing research in order to suggest 13 recommendations for improving the pedagogical effectiveness of games for instruction. One noteworthy issue expressed by these authors was that assessing the use of games is complicated by a difficulty in distinguishing between simulations and games. This author agrees that the issue is an important one, but as was outlined in an earlier section, those who come from a computer science background see no need to distinguish between games and simulations at all since they are built using the same algorithms. In a similar vein to Tobias and Fletcher but somewhat later, Charsky & Mims (2008) published a paper on the integration of COTS games in school education that offers an additional set of guidelines specifically for the integration of COTS into school curricula. Also, Van Eck (2008) describes a detailed process for developing lesson plans that integrate COTS games that provides additional details.

As the body of literature on Games for Education continues to grow, it becomes more challenging to compile comprehensive reviews, and more recent reviews have tended to focus on specific sub-domains such as one commissioned by the Defense Academy within the U.K. Ministry of Defense. This study (Caspian Learning, 2008) looked at serious games specifically for use in military training and "found many compelling reasons and a growing evidence that justify a 'learning through games strategy' within this landscape" (p. 5). Another study (Mayo, 2009) reviews data on learning outcomes for video games in science, technology, engineering, and math (STEM) disciplines, and finds the results encouraging. It is unlikely that any more comprehensive literature reviews on serious games or even on educational gaming will be forthcoming. The reviews will become increasingly focused as we move to reports on Games for Health, literature reviews of Exergaming, Patient Education, or Practitioner Training. Perhaps this is a sign that the field is beginning to mature.

CURRENT RESEARCH

"The invention of new methods that are adequate to the new ways in which problems are posed requires far more than a simple modification of previously accepted methods."

—Vygotsky & Cole, 1977, p. 58

We now see that (digital) Game Studies is a field that is developing at lightning speed, at least as far as academic disciplines go. Although it may sound like an exaggeration, the rapid evolution of the field means that most works published in game studies and game technology areas prior to 2000 are no longer useful. Both *World of Warcraft* and *Second Life*, two massively multiplayer online environments with 11.5 (Gray, 2008) and 15 (Chapman, 2009) million subscribers respectively, did not exist in 2004 & 2003, respectively. Not only have gaming and game studies changed a great deal in the last few years, but academic and institutional attitudes have also evolved. As Tobias and Fletcher report in their 2007 article, "five years ago fewer than a dozen universities offered game related programs of study; that figure has now jumped to over 190 institutions in the United States and another 161 worldwide." Clearly, the landscape has changed dramatically in recent years, and serious games researchers are working furiously to keep up.

Years from now, when we look back to the beginning of this century, we will mark sometime around 1999-2000 as the point in history when information technology came of age. In his recent book, *The World is Flat*, New York Times columnist Thomas Friedman devotes considerable time to exploring the elements that came together at that time to bring about this revolution in how we communicate, work, and socialize (2006). Digital games are a part of that, and the remainder of this chapter explores the recent and current state (circa 2009) of serious game studies as they relate to games for education. It is not intended to be an exhaustive inventory of all research on game studies. Instead, sources were selected to present a broad cross section of the work being done and to highlight some of the key scholars and formative work in the field of serious games, primarily between 2000 and 2009. The main focus is on work dealing with design, as that is the author's primary area of expertise and the area in which she is best qualified to offer an analysis. Individuals

and studies were chosen either for the variety of perspectives they represent or for the influence of their work on others in the field, and in many cases both. However, should readers wish further resources, there are two substantial bibliographies of works related to game studies: 1) The Digiplay Initiative maintained by Jason Rutter and Jo Bryce, and 2) The IEEE Game Bibliography maintained by J.R. Parker and Katrin Becker.

The final sections of this chapter are organized into four categories: 1) theoretical foundations, which looks at some of the theories and models that are informing design; 2) development of games for education, which looks at development and design research involving games designed specifically for education; 3) empirical studies for learning which examines some of the recent work looking at games being used in educational settings; and finally, 4) analytical approaches, which primarily looks at studies involving commercial games in education.

Theoretical Foundations: Educational Game Design

What theories and models underpin educational game design and who is building new theories & models? Research on educational game design is a very active field and much of what we are learning about the process has just come out in the last few years, with some of it still in press as this chapter is being written. With such a dynamic field of study it is difficult to trace the development in any definitive way, but the following sections highlight, in no particular order, a few key examples of 'classic' and breaking research that is shaping how we approach the design of games for educational purposes.

Learning Through Design (i.e. Making Games)

The study of learning by making games is a somewhat separate but related category that has been studied both in theory and practice. Seymour Papert is the creator of LOGO (Papert, 1980) and along with his colleagues at M.I.T. is responsible for much of the seminal work with children and computers in learning, as well as for the concepts of "constructionism," and "microworlds" (Rieber, 1996). Papert's research has evolved with the technology, and LOGO has evolved into an open source modeling language called OpenStarLogo (Colella, Klopfer, & Resnick, 2001) that is both graphical and requires very little in the way of programming experience. In fact, Papert remains one of the most prominent champions of the use of games for education as well as using games design as a framework for improving current practices. Says Papert, "Video games teach children what computers are beginning to teach adults—that some forms of learning are fast-paced, immensely compelling, and rewarding" (Papert, 1996).

In 1996, Amy Bruckman and Mitchel Resnick reported on groundbreaking work they did on a text-based virtual environment called *MediaMOO*. It was one of the first virtual communities, a professional community constructed by members, and it adapted many of its ideas from the fan communities that surrounded video games of the time. Virtual environments have certainly evolved since 1996, and *MediaMOO* is no longer active but the idea of creating a professional online social space began there.

Yasmin Kafai, along with other researchers at M.I.T., was among the first researchers to focus on learning that happens through making games for education (constructionism) rather than playing games for education (2006). She has done fieldwork with children building games.

"With thousands of instructional computer games on the market, including popular titles such as Math Blaster, we know little about which features make an educational game good for learning. A survey of the past 20 years of educational publications reveals a rather sparse bounty, in particular if one is interested in hard-core academic benefits rather than motivational or social aspects of playing games for learning" (Kafai, 2006, p. 37)

More recently, Kafai and her colleagues have been examining the use of games and game environments (largely in a place called *Whyville*) and their application to students' understanding of a virtual infectious disease in relation to their understanding of natural infectious diseases. They found that students did not reason about the causes of virtual diseases in ways similar as natural diseases. They also found that integrating the curriculum around the simulation stimulated teacher–student discussions. (Neulight, Kafai, Kao, Foley, & Galas, 2006). As in many other situations and studies, the game may be the focal point around which learning happens, but it is not sufficient alone.

Carrie Heeter and Brian Winn (Heeter & Winn, 2008; Winn & Heeter, 2007) have been advancing the field with active playtesting and balanced approaches to addressing the gender divide in games designed for educational purposes. They suggest that while we can gain insights into the design of educational games by studying successful commercial games, we must be cautious not to borrow blindly from commercial games as there remain significant differences in the kinds of games boys and girls play as well as how much experience can be assumed. Other researchers have found similar results in terms of gameplay, game preferences, and game design (e.g., Van Eck, 2006). Through all age groups, Winn and Heeter have found that boys play more and longer than girls do. If we simply adopt the styles and strategies found in successful games, there is a real danger of incorporating gender biases, which should have no place in most educational games. Based on their research, they suggest four characteristics that should be incorporated in games intended for classroom learning:

1. they strongly engage both girls and boys;
2. they accommodate diverse play style preferences
3. they provide support where needed for learners with limited gaming experience;
4. they result in deep learning through play (Winn & Heeter, 2007).

On a more general note, Winn and Heeter (2007) have also found that a chief obstacle of educational game design is finding an optimal convergence of the perspectives of the instructional designers, game designers, and content experts for a particular content domain in order to produce a set of learning goals. This challenge is both significant and recurring.

In my own work as a computer science instructor, I have been using digital games, particularly classic arcade games, as assignments to help novice students learn how to program. I have found that, with very few exceptions, the women I have taught enjoy making games even when they have little interest in playing them (Becker, 2001; Becker & Parker, 2005). The practice of building digital games to learn programming is a fairly specialized subcategory of "learning through making games," and will not be detailed here, but if readers want to pursue that area further, they are referred to the author's works referenced above, as well as that of Mitch Resnick, Yasmin Kafai and colleagues at M.I.T. (Maloney, Peppler, Kafai, Resnick, & Rusk, 2008).

Microworlds

Although now more than a decade old (and so, by my own criteria of limited relevance), Lloyd Rieber's paper, *Seriously Considering Play* remains a key paper in education that deals with play and games (1996). In it, Rieber traces the history of play and its importance to learning. Expanding on Seymour Papert's original concept of 'microworlds' (1980), Rieber outlines a design of a hybrid interactive learning environment which he eventually implemented and studied in addition to various design projects with elementary and middle school students. He found that much of the 'data' we have on the use of games and virtual environments is anecdotal and there is still little hard evidence of the effectiveness of games and other interactive media as learning environments (Rieber, 2005). This is not to say there isn't any benefit, it's just that we still lack clear evidence. He suggests the use of design research and other mixed methods approaches. Though groundbreaking when first defined, the term 'microworld' has not gained widespread usage and is now mainly used in connection with work involving LOGO or STARLOGO programs. Perhaps the availability and ease of access to macro- or mega-worlds like Second Life has subjugated continued work in this area.

Input-Output-Process Model

Garris, Ahlers, and Driskell (2002) have offered an input-process-output model of instructional games and learning, but it does not address the perspective of game design itself. Instead, it focuses on the educational content and instructional design, as many of the earlier models do. The educational objectives in an educational game are key aspects to be sure, but the importance of the synergy between game design and instructional design cannot be overstated. This model begins with elements of instructional content and game characteristics—the 'inputs'. The middle contains the process elements which include user judgments, user behavior, and system feedback. The learning outcomes form the 'output' part of the model. Although the authors do expand on the details of the model, it still forms a fairly traditional design model that does not fully acknowledge the importance of attention to the design of the game part.

The Game Object Model (GOM)

An early educational game development model is one proposed by Alan Amory and Robert Seagram in 2003 called the Game Object Model, based on object oriented programming concepts. It is a generic game design model with several embedded conceptual models: the 'Personal Outlining Model' and the 'Game Achievement Model'. It claims to be a model that integrates education theory and game design, but it does so at an abstract level by simply placing a requirement for learning objectives as part of the model. The models were used by Amory to help design games in several workshops, but there has been no use or testing of the model beyond the authors' own. It is somewhat disconcerting that the authors talk about focus groups and evaluations without ever mentioning a game that was developed this way. There are no actual examples and there are no data. This model doesn't really do much to address how to implement learning objectives, which to my mind is at the core of all instructional design. I think a game design for an educational game must begin much like an instructional design needs to begin: with some kind of needs assessment that drives the rest of the process. Instructional game design must begin with some goal(s)—what is it we want people to learn from this game? The rest follows from there. It needs some framework to be sure, but the learning objectives are key. This model identifies the need for such an element but provides no real help in incorporating one into the design.

The conclusion of the paper mentions learning objectives several times (Amory & Seagram, 2003), but it is difficult see how they fit into the models provided. In one review by Ismael Rumzan (2002) of a later version of the same model, it was found that

"while this study is of good value in reducing the learning curve and development time for developers of similar projects, it lacks detail in the process of translating the learner outcomes to concrete and abstract interfaces as described in the Game Object Model. Furthermore, nothing is mentioned about user testing relative to the retaining of learner outcomes, which would have been valuable to evaluate the success of the implementation of this model." (p. 143)

Digital Game-Based Learning

No description of the state of educational games in the early 21st century can be complete without mentioning Marc Prensky, who deserves credit as a key mover and shaker in the field. Marc Prensky has been a vocal and tireless champion of the use of games for education and maintains that games are uniquely suited to the learning styles developed in today's youth (Prensky, 2001a, 2006). He has done much to help raise the profile of the use of games for education. He coined the now popular term 'digital natives' as a description for today's youth whereas those of us born before 1970 are 'digital immigrants'. Digital natives are those for whom most of what we (older generations) perceive as 'Technology' (as per Alan Kay's quote recounted earlier in this chapter) is a natural part of their world. He has championed the use of all sorts of games, commercial and otherwise, and suggests (among other things) that today's youth are different from the generations that came before in (at least) the following ways: comfort with technology, multi-tasking, graphical, on-demand, and active (Prensky, 2001b, 2001c). Though it is known that there is still little empirical data on the efficacy of games in formal settings (Parker, et al., 2008), Prensky's most recent book contains a great many examples of places where games have been used with positive reactions (2006).

Prensky's work is important as a layman's entry point into the world of learning with games and has many endnotes that provide references to scholarly studies and other details, but it is not a scholarly work and does not add much to the existing body of research.

Gee's 36 Principles

The work of Jim Gee is considered by many to be seminal and has been widely cited. His 36 principles (2003) have become well known for connecting notions of what is considered good practice in situated learning to what is experienced while playing games. The fact that it was written for a general audience rather than fellow educators and researchers makes it a highly accessible introduction to the positive educational potential that can be found in modern games. While some of these principles would appear to be idealized extrapolations of what commercial games have to offer, they do present a fairly comprehensive set. Gee does make some references to well-known educational theorists such as Ann Brown and Jean Lave in his book (Gee, 2003), but the weakness in this work is that he does not give adequate credit to the theories and models whose ideas he borrows. However, this list was a significant impetus for the author's own work connecting game elements explicitly with known pedagogy and in that way giving credit to those theorists and researchers who have described instructional and learning design principles that have, even if unknowingly, contributed to the success of some of the games deemed to be among the masterpieces (Becker, 2006a, 2008b). Table 2 provides a list of all 36 principles along with a brief explanation for each.

Upon careful inspection, some of these thirty-six principles appear to be variations of one another. For example, the 'Text Principle' and the 'Multimodal Principle' could arguably be included as part of the 'Situated Meaning Principle' as both

are variations of the situated meaning of symbols. Some are genuinely new, such as the semiotic principles related to Gee's original discipline of linguistics. Others appear to be reworded expressions of theories put forth by others, such as the 'Discovery Principle', credit for which should probably go to Jerome Bruner (Bruner, 1961), or the "Achievement Principle," which appears to be based on a combination of Morrison's Mastery Learning (1931), and Malone's work on Intrinsic Motivation (1981), or the 'Incremental Principle', which bears striking resemblance to Reigeluth's Elaboration Theory (Reigeluth & Stein, 1983). The principles are sound, but are presented as a fait accompli, and in terms of advancing the field; it would have been nice to see some suggestions for how these principles might be verified or even some suggestion for what kinds or percentages of games actually possess some or all of these principles.

Epistemic Games

David Shaffer has proposed the notion of epistemic games, which are games based on professional innovation as enacted by professionals. In his book (Williamson Shaffer, 2007) he also examines several hypothetical games (like 'The Debate Game', and 'The Game of School'), several custom made games (like, *'Escher's World'* and *'The Pandora Project'*) and others meant to serve as examples (like *'The Soda Constructor'*). The idea of creating a virtual environment as a semiotic domain is a good one, but in order to succeed in formal education Shaffer admits that it would require a major reshaping of the current institutional structures which is not likely to happen easily, or soon. This work is necessary and important, but is unlikely to find its way into schools in any significant way in the near future. Instead I see his approach being adopted in more informal settings—affinity groups that form out of a shared interest rather than a prescribed curriculum. Even-

Table 2. Gee's 36 principles

1	**Active, Critical Learning Principle** The learning environment is set up to encourage active and critical learning.
2	**Design Principle** Learning about and appreciating design and design principles are core to the learning experience
3	**Semiotic Principle** Using multiple sign systems (images, words, actions, symbols, artifacts, etc.)
4	**Semiotic Domains Principle** Mastering semiotic domains and participating in the affinity group or groups connected to them.
5	**Metacognitive Thinking about Semiotic Domains Principle** Active and critical thinking about the relationships of the current semiotic domain to other semiotic domains.
6	**"Psychosocial Moratorium" Principle** Learners can take risks in space where real consequences are lowered.
7	**Committed Learning Principle** Learners are engaged through a commitment to extensions of their real-world identities and virtual work that they find compelling
8	**Identity Principle** Taking on and playing with identities in such a way that the learner can explore the relationship between new identities and old ones.
9	**Self-Knowledge Principle** The virtual world is constructed in such a way that learners learn not only about the domain but about themselves and their current and potential capacities.
10	**Amplification of Input Principle** For little input, learners get a lot of output
11	**Achievement Principle** Intrinsic rewards exist for all learners, customized to each learner's level, effort, and growing mastery and signaling the learner's ongoing achievements.
12	**Practice Principle** Learners get lots of practice in a context where the practice is not boring and spend lots of time on task.
13	**Ongoing Learning Principle** The distinction between learner and master is vague. There are cycles of new learning, automatization, undoing automatization, and new reorganized automatization.
14	**"Regime of Competence" Principle** The learner gets ample opportunity to operate within, but at the edge of, his or her resources, so tasks are challenging but not "undoable."
15	**Probing Principle** Learning is a cycle of acting (probing); reflecting in and on this action, forming a hypothesis; reprobing; and then accepting or rethinking the hypothesis
16	**Multiple Routes Principle** This allows learners to make choices, rely on their own strengths and styles of learning and problem solving, while also exploring alternative styles.
17	**Situated Meaning Principle** The meanings of signs (words, actions, objects, artifacts, symbols, texts, etc.) are situated in embodied experience.
18	**Text Principle** Texts are not understood just verbally (i.e, in terms of definitions) but in terms of embodied experiences.
19	**Intertextual Principle** The learner understands texts as a family ("genre") of related texts.
20	**Multimodal Principle** Meaning and knowledge are built up through various modalities (images, texts, symbols, interactions, abstract design, sound, etc.), not just words.
21	**"Material Intelligence" Principle** Thinking, problem solving, and knowledge are "stored" in material objects in the environment.
22	**Intuitive Knowledge Principle** Intuitive or tacit knowledge built in repeated practice and experience counts and is honored. Not just verbal and conscious knowledge is rewarded.
23	**Subset Principle** Learning even at its start takes place in a (simplified_ subset of the real domain.
24	**Incremental Principle** Learning situations are ordered in the early stages so that earlier cases lead to generalizations that are fruitful for later cases.
25	**Concentrated Sample Principle** Fundamental signs and actions are concentrated in the early stages so that learners get to practice them often and learn them well.
26	**Bottom-Up Basic Skills Principle** Basic Skills are not learned in isolation or out of context.
27	**Explicit Information on-Demand and Just-in-Time Principle** The learner is given explicit information both on-demand and just-in-time.
28	**Discovery Principle** The learner is given opportunities to experiment and make discoveries.
29	**The Transfer Principle** Skills and knowledge gained in early parts of the experience are used in later parts.
30	**Cultural Models about the World Principle** Learners come to think consciously and reflectively about some of their cultural models of learning and themselves as learners, and juxtapose them to new models of learning and themselves as learners.

continued on following page

Table 2 continued.

31	**Cultural Models about Learning Principle** Learners can reflect on cultural models of learning and on themselves as learners, and juxtapose them to new models of learning and themselves as learners.
32	**Cultural Models about Semiotic Domains Principle** Learners think consciously and reflectively about the cultural models about a particular semiotic domain they are learning, and juxtapose them to new models about this domain.
33	**Distributed Principle** Meaning/Knowledge is distributed across the learner, objects, tools, symbols, technologies, and the environment
34	**Dispersed Principle** Meaning/Knowledge is dispersed and can be shared with others outside the domain/game, some of whom the learner may rarely or never see face to face
35	**Affinity Group Principle** Learners constitute a group bonded through shared endeavors, goals, and practices and not shared race, gender, nation, ethnicity, or culture.
36	**Insider Principle** The learner is an "insider," "teacher," and "producer" (not just a consumer).

tually, approaches like Shaffer's will become the norm—games and game–like environments will be used as spaces where people with a shared interest that demands considerable learning in a specialized domain can connect with each other and develop their expertise.

Activity Theory

There have been a number of people who have applied concepts of activity theory to game design, with Kurt Squire providing the opening move in suggesting that activity theory "provides a theoretical language for looking at how an educational game or resource mediates players' understandings of other phenomena while acknowledging the social and cultural contexts in which game play is situated" (2002). Oliver and Pelletier (2004) designed a framework using activity theory's concept of contradictions that would enable them to track the process of learning without disturbing the natural flow of game play. The work by Oliver and Pelletier was based on the work of Yrjö Engeström who connected learning with notions of solving contradictions. Contradictions are defined as blocks or tensions in an activity system when a subject is blocked from achieving their goal (Engeström, 1987). In a game designed using this framework, one cannot progress to the next stage in the game

without learning how to overcome a particular obstacle. Overcoming a contradiction and being able to transfer the same strategy to a similar situation is considered evidence of learning. Hence it is believed that analysing contradictions in an activity system can be used as a framework from which to study the process of learning in an RPG. Pelletier and Oliver (2006) tried out their method using two commercial games: *Harry Potter and the Chamber of Secrets*, and *Deus Ex* and concluded that their framework was useful.

Analysis and design using Activity Theory has also been advanced by Aida Hadziomerovic & Biddle (2006) who also examined humor in games using activity theoretic frameworks (Dormann & Biddle, 2006), and Mike Dobson and his colleagues at Simon Fraser University (Dobson, Ha, Mulligan, & Ciavarro, 2005) have used CHAT (cultural historical activity theory) as a framework through which to analyse activity in a multiplayer game as part of a user-centered design approach. They found that viewing parts of the game as activity systems allowed for a focused examination of interaction that was coherent for each part. While the process could become unwieldy if not carefully organized, it did allow for targeted feedback from participants asked to examine the game as it was being developed.

Lee Sherlock (2007) used activity theory and genre theory as bases for analysis to examine the activity of grouping in the massively multiplayer online role-playing game *World of Warcraft*, and Matthew Sharritt's chapter (in press) reports in part, on the use of activity theory, cultural historical activity theory (CHAT) and other approaches in attempting to understand the mediational role of artifacts in the social processes of learning in *Roller Coaster Tycoon III*, *Making History: The Calm and the Storm*, and *Civilization IV*. He found Activity Theory to be a good fit for understanding how learning occurs in social contexts in these games.

Tim Marsh (this volume) has also described a framework, tool and approach that is both flexible and standardized enough to support scenario design and development through stages of a serious games life cycle. Activity Theory and its related theories have so far proven quite fruitful in providing a framework for understanding how games facilitate learning and it is hoped that this work will continue to develop for some time.

Games for Activating Thematic Engagement (GATE)

William Watson has taken a more structured approach and has developed a design model for developing instructional games (Watson, 2007). His model is one that combines accepted approaches to both game and instructional design into a single representation. As with many other models and theories about the design of instructional games, this model is still too new for there to be a body of evidence that either supports or refutes its value. In the single case examined in the thesis, it was found to be helpful which should come as no surprise as these design steps are fairly standard ones and combine well-known best practices of both instructional and game design.

Design is a creative process that requires healthy doses of innovation, and, according to Michael Schrage (2000), "the interplay between individuals and the expression of their ideas" (p.13). Various researchers have taken different approaches in their efforts to address the design problem, some of which have been described above. Some feel we need to perfect the models we have and become more skilled at applying them—the computer field of software engineering is in large part devoted to this approach. However, the reality seems to be that in spite of the best efforts of many expert minds, we are no closer to an "ideal" software design model than we were 40 years ago. Even worse, there isn't even any real evidence that the methods thus far developed actually contribute to safer, or more error-free, or easier to maintain systems in spite of claims to the contrary like this one: "Lean Software Development helps you refocus development on value, flow and people—so you can achieve breakthrough quality, savings, speed, and business alignment" (Poppendieck & Poppendieck, 2003, back cover). The truth is that designing good software is hard. Designing good games is hard. So is designing good instruction. Designing a good digital educational game is at least one order of magnitude more difficult than either of these alone, and although it is highly unlikely that any single design approach will prove to be 'the one', there is value in continuing to try so that what we learn in the process can continue to inform our designs.

Development of Games for Education: Who is Making Educational Games?

There is a need for basic research to help quantify who is using games for education, in what ways, and with what success (Freitas, 2007). Finding reports and studies on the successes of games used for education is still difficult; however one field where considerable progress is being made is in development. No attempt is made here to offer a full accounting of who is making educational games, but there are several lists available online that attempt to keep track of who is doing what, including: SocialImpactGames.com and SuperSmartGames.com. Not surprisingly, many who are studying educational games are also making them. Prototypes are being produced, but they are often not generally available, and finding the means and locations for formal testing is far more difficult so only a small proportion have been tested in any formal way. In this sense, the field of educational game development is much like SENG (Software Engineering), where many papers are published describing new approaches that are claimed to improve productivity, reliability, etc., but where few if any comparative tests are ever completed or reported. In the case of digital games, the evaluation process is complicated by the fact that human subjects are involved, and finding formal settings where games can be tested is difficult.

The following is a list of ten educational games (sorted in alphabetical order). These do not necessarily represent the best, but have instead been chosen to show the breadth of approaches and subject-areas.

- **Add'Em** Up (BlueBugGames): Some drill and practice games can be a lot of fun, and this one qualifies as both. The goal of this simple puzzle is to clear the board of numbered tiles by finding adjacent tiles whose sum equals that of the 'target' number. Similar in style to some other well-known puzzle games like Bejeweled.
- **Booze** Cruise (Jim Parker): Driving game to show people what it's like to drive while drunk. This game has received a certain amount of media attention for its subject matter though there are, as yet no studies to indicate if this game does in fact deliver on its goal, which is to discourage people from drinking and driving.
- **Food Force** (UN's World Food Programme): A humanitarian game targeted at 13-16 year olds and has players completing food airdrops over crisis zones and driving trucks struggling up difficult roads under rebel threat with emergency food

supplies. Anecdotal evidence suggests that this game portrays an accurate perspective on the issues presented. I had a student in a graduate class where we were examining educational games who had been a refugee from Africa and he reported that he found the game to be quite compelling.
- **Global Conflict: Palestine** (Serious Games Interactive): A 3D-adventure/RPG where the player is given the role of a reporter in Jerusalem and has to write articles for a newspaper. This game has the look and feel of a commercial title, and it appears to be popular, having been sold in 50 countries.
- **Knight Elimar's Last Joust** (Richard Levy): A vocabulary building and literacy game for grades 4 and 5. The game is set in a virtual medieval village and incorporates a mystery quest that can only be solved by successfully unraveling a series of challenging written and verbal clues.
- **Real Lives** (Educational Simulations): A turn-based simulation where players live the life of some person chosen at random, but which is based on real world statistics. In other words, the chances that you would get to live the life of a child born into a middle-class family in, say, Canada are very small. This game is not animated, but requires the player to make various choices during each turn which not only affect the character that the player is playing, but their family as well. This is a game that was designed for a school setting.
- **Re-Mission** (HopeLab): A 3-D Shooter to help improve the lives of young persons living with cancer. This is a game designed to help young people with cancer to become more actively involved in their own treatment. It was investigated in a study to see if it actually could be an effective vehicle for health education in adolescents and young adults with chronic illnesses and

a specific effect was found (Beale, Kato, Marin-Bowling, Guthrie, & Cole, 2007).

- **Service Rig Trainer** (Coole Immersive, Inc.): A training simulation that is used in some technical schools to help train people who service oil wells. The oil industry tends to be a conservative bunch, and most of the approaches used for training here make little use of modern media, so this game is one of the first of its kind.

- **The Typing of the Dead** (Smilebit): Another drill and practice game, this one has now become a classic in educational game circles. It is a repurposing of the old zombie shooter, *The House of the Dead 2*. The original gameplay and sound are virtually unchanged except that the zombies now wear small black boards upon which words and short phrases are written and rather than simply shooting at them, players must type the letters of the words. I have yet to come across a teenager that did not think this game was both silly and fun, AND more fun than *Mavis Beacon Teaches Typing!*

- **Virtual Leader** (Clark Aldrich): Designed to teach interpersonal skills and used by numerous business schools, and studies of this game have suggested that learners continue to assimilate what they have learned for a longer time than they do when learning the same lessons through more traditional means (SimulLearn, 2006) which would in turn seem to imply that retention is a factor we should be looking at when studying how and what people learn in games.

With so many groups developing games, but only a few actually analysing them, there is a real danger of once again missing the mark by making unverified claims about the value of game-based education and again risking widespread institutional rejection of the medium. Hyped up claims about the ability of this new medium to solve all our educational ills was one of the prime factors that contributed to the disillusionment with game-based learning during the Edutainment Era and is an error that we can ill-afford to repeat. The fact that the vast majority of the educational games produced during the 80's were awful was of course the other reason for the failure. Had we actually looked, we might have noticed just how bad these games were; they were not only bad as games but also as instruction. Assessment is crucial, but many forms of assessment cannot proceed without institutional help or at least willing subjects. Nonetheless, one aspect that can be analysed in the absence of human subjects and formal settings is the game itself, and the author has developed several new ways of approaching such analysis. They will not be detailed here but those interested are referred to the author's thesis as a starting point (Becker, 2008a).

Empirical Studies of Games for Education: Who is Studying Games in Educational Practice?

What do we already know about the effectiveness of games in classrooms, corporate settings, or experimental settings? It is one thing to determine whether a game is fun (highly subjective) or popular (typically measured by sales or downloads) but 'fun' is not the most important aspect of an educational game—although engaging might be high on the list. The most important aspect of an educational game is whether or not it delivers on its educational goals. The problem is that there are still very little data on the effectiveness of digital games in formal or even informal educational contexts. Quite a lot of this work is being done in the private sector, but very little is formally published (Parker, et al., 2008): most developers producing games in the private sector have a vested interest in keeping details about their designs private for proprietary reasons—just like the commercial game developers. Make no mistake, game developers use play testing extensively—they do try their products out on real people. Will Wright (2004) uses something he calls 'Kleenex testing' in his company Maxis - where the tester is unfamiliar with the game (i.e. has never played it) and is only ever used once, but even Will doesn't share his data with us. The primary motivation for commercial and private sector developers is usually financial gain (or in the case of producers of training games, sales success), NOT dissemination or advancement of knowledge. In fact, they may have a justifiable interest in NOT sharing what they have learned and since they are not likely to start sharing their data anytime soon, those of us in the Academy on our own.

In spite of the difficulties involved and the relatively short time frame available for performing good studies, some data are available. The Rosas et al. study was one of the first to look at using games as a tool for teaching the regular curriculum (2003). They looked at what happens when educational video games are introduced into the classroom and all they could really conclude was that the effects tend to be more positive than negative. They suggest that the Hawthorn effect may play a role in the lack of difference between the test and control groups within the same schools, which highlights one of the major hurdles in any study attempting to measure the effectiveness of a specific intervention: the processes and actions of the 'subjects' can never be studied in isolation and the complexity of the situation makes clear results all but impossible.

Specific Sony *Playstation* games were studied by Din and Calao (2001) to see if they help with math, spelling and reading. They found no differences in math achievement over the control group but did find improvement in spelling and reading. They reported to have used over 40 different games but nowhere in the study did they say which games they used. Here, as in so many studies, especially in the early years, no attention was paid to the game itself, as if it were irrelevant. Using that same logic one could easily assume

that *Mathblaster* and *Zoo Tycoon* could be used interchangeably to study whether videogames helped people learn math.

Rieber, Davis, Matzko & Grant (2001) studied middle school students who were asked to critique educational games created by other students and found that important game characteristics for the students included story, challenge, and competition, but did not include integration of storyline with educational content or production values. Given the age of this paper (i.e. before *World of Warcraft* and the general explosion of online games) it cannot be assumed that these results are still relevant. It would be interesting to repeat this study now and see. The sophistication and learning curve required to get into many modern commercial games may well have changed the way that elementary and middle school children would critique educational games.

Heeter, et al. (2003) studied 12 space exploration games (4 educational, 8 commercial), and discovered the educational games to be less complex, shorter, easier to install and learn, and less challenging to play than the commercial games. The educational games also involved considerably less reading and typing, included fewer forms of fun, and contained less competition and fewer opponents than the commercial games did (Heeter, et al., 2003; Rieber & Matzko, 2001). One of the common laments of those developing educational games is that we simply do not have the kinds of budgets that commercial developers do, and as a result we can hardly be expected to produce games of similar quality. The results that this group found do not reflect a necessary reality so much as they reflect a need for educational game developers to find and apply creative approaches to the designs of their games. We are not likely to get our hands on the kinds of budgets that commercial developers can access any time soon, so we need to approach the challenge of making compelling games differently.

In another study that was the focus of Mansureh Kebritchi's doctoral research, the effects of a series of mathematics computer games on mathematics achievement and motivation of high school students were examined. The overall results indicated that the mathematics games used were effective teaching and learning tools to improve the mathematics skills of the students. The sample size was reasonable (n=193), but, as is so often the case it was impossible to say with confidence that the measured effect was in fact due to the game and not influenced by other factors such as the novelty of using games in the classroom or the knowledge that the subjects were, being studied (Kebritchi, 2008). Perhaps a different way of looking at such results is to note that the students who played the games did do better than the students who didn't—from the perspective of a teacher in the classroom, the reasons why may not be important.

An argument often made against the use of games in the classroom is that too much time is taken up by activities that have nothing to do with the learning goals. This study attempted to answer the question of whether unproductive learning activities in serious games falsify the hypothesis that games can promote learning and how such 'unproductive' activities could be reduced during the design. Shumin Wu developed a game for language learning called *Tactical Language & Culture Training System* (TLCTS). What he found was that less experienced game players often waste more time doing things in the game that don't help the learning objectives. He postulates that learners' incapability of formulating optimal learning plans are due to limited skill development and did some preliminary work to see if more tutoring help in the game could alleviate this problem. For a designer of educational games, it is reassuring to learn that the learners do not find that the tutoring detracts from the experience (Wu, 2008). One of the great challenges in educational game design is in striking the right balance between 'game' and 'education', which includes knowing when and how to help the learner and so increase the likelihood that the desired objectives will be met.

As has been said before there are still far too few studies that go beyond how people 'feel' about their experiences with educational games and really start to uncover how games teach. While this author wholeheartedly agrees that we should be trying to verify the effectiveness of our approaches, she also notes, with more than a little criticism that there similarly exists little evidence proving the effectiveness of traditional media. The effectiveness of textbooks, lectures and testing as a motivator are, for the most part, assumed but not proven. As Clark Aldrich has said, "Part of the trap, of course, is that any new approach to education has to pass a theoretical, ideal, and rigorous standard that no traditional approach could."

Analytical Approaches to Games for Education: Who is Studying Commercial Games in Educational Contexts?

The use of commercial games in educational contexts is also still an understudied area, due at least in part to the difficulty of finding willing participants. As with other areas in digital game-based learning, very few studies have produced any quantitative data that could be used to compare against more traditional forms of teaching. By far the majority of studies have been qualitative, ethnographic case studies. The following paragraph highlights just a few of these.

Sandford et al. (2006) conducted a yearlong study using three COTS games: *The Sims 2*, *RollerCoaster Tycoon III*, and *Knights of Honor* and found that teacher familiarity with the game was important, but not as important as familiarity with the curriculum and general teaching competence. One possible inference that can be drawn from this study, which supports findings from other studies regarding the need for active teacher involvement in the process is that while commercial games can enhance classroom experiences with learning, they cannot compensate for lack of knowledge or skill on the part of the teacher. Kurt Squire devoted his doctoral dissertation to a study of *Civilization III* in high school history, and among his conclusions were that even though the game may not have provided measurable learning when it came to historical facts, it did seem to help students learn about historical contexts and that historical choices (such as building a village by a river) can influence outcomes (Squire, 2003). In his study, Squire also found that players make up recognizable 'types', who take up the game for various reasons: achievers, explorers, socializers, game killers (Bartle, 1996), and that a key motivating factor had to do with elements often overlooked by educators: humor, style, and aesthetics (Squire, 2003). Simon Egenfeldt-Nielsen also conducted a classroom study as part of his doctoral work (2005). He used the game *Europa Universalis II* in a Danish school to teach history over an eight week period. All found that the games they used could motivate and foster information-handling and problem-solving skills, but they also highlight the constraints that occur as a result of the technical demands of the game.

FUTURE RESEARCH DIRECTIONS

Instructional designers and those designing educational games must remember that digital games share properties with games generally but also with both other interactive communication media and entertainment media, and even though the primary reason for the existence of an educational game is 'to teach something', we must adopt a balanced design approach sensitive to the true nature of the medium or our games will end up realizing Seymour Papert's fear of educational games as Shavian reversals—"offspring that keep the bad features of each parent and lose the good ones" (Papert, 1998). The work up to now has been important, encouraging and occasionally even enlightening "but most educational games to date have been produced in the absence of any coherent theory of learning or underlying body of research. We need to ask and answer important questions about this relatively new medium. We need to understand how the conventions of good commercial games create compelling virtual worlds." (David Williamson Shaffer, Squire, Halverson, & Gee, 2004).

When it comes to outlining what we should be doing next, the only appropriate answer is: more of everything. We need a better understanding of how game design can be blended with instructional design to produce effective and engaging educational games. We know that some aspects, such as the inclusion of tutorials do not in and of themselves detract from a game, but we have yet to produce a coherent set of 'best practices' that designers can use. There is plenty of room for both learning and design models and theories—we should be expanding the body of work in this area before we can begin to narrow the field. We need to study commercial games as well as games designed specifically for some serious purpose and we need to study them in formal as well as informal contexts. We need effective methodologies for studying games and people as well as for studying and analysing the games themselves. The only way to sustain the current interest in serious games for education is to be able to back up our claims with real data.

CONCLUSION

We have seen why digital games should be treated as a medium distinct from other media as well as from traditional games. We have seen that the medium used for instruction often affects the instruction itself. Modern games represent a sea change in educational technology and we must respond by doing new research rather than relying on our old favorites. We also know that teachers are not, for the most part, gamers (Sandford, et al., 2006) so their perceptions of expected learning outcomes in games may not be valid. In a recent study, Paul

Pivec (2009) was able to gather data that suggested that teachers still mostly think that games are chiefly useful in improving motor skills while gamers believe they learn social skills. Both groups believe that declarative knowledge is a strong learning outcome, but they are at opposite ends when it comes to whether games increase higher order thinking, with teachers on the 'yea' side and gamers on the 'nay' side. Clearly, we don't know enough about how game based learning works.

While there are many involved in studying games for the purposes of education, the medium is far too new and the discipline too young to become complacent and accept the existing approaches as sufficient. We will need far more theories and models, if for no other reason that to help us understand games; in other words we will need to broaden the field before we can start to look at narrowing the field.

REFERENCES

Alessi, S. M., & Trollip, S. R. (2001). *Multimedia for learning: methods and development* (3rd ed.). Boston: Allyn and Bacon.

Amory, A., & Seagram, R. (2003). Educational game models: Conceptualization and evaluation. *South African Journal of Higher Education, 17*(2), 206–217.

Baek, Y. K. (2008). What hinders teachers in using computer and video games in the classroom? Exploring factors inhibiting the uptake of computer and video games. *Cyberpsychology & Behavior, 11*(6), 665–671. doi:10.1089/cpb.2008.0127

Bartle, R. (1996). Hearts, clubs, diamonds, spades: Players who suit MUDs. *Journal of Virtual Environments* (Vol. 1). Retrieved from http://www.brandeis.edu/pubs/jove/index.html

Beale, I. L., Kato, P. M., Marin-Bowling, V. M., Guthrie, N., & Cole, S. W. (2007). Improvement in cancer-related knowledge following use of a psychoeducational video game for adolescents and young adults with cancer. *Journal of Adolescent Health, 41*(3), 263–270. doi: DOI: 10.1016/j.jadohealth.2007.04.006

Becker, K. (2001). Teaching with games: The *Minesweeper* and *Asteroids* experience. *Journal of Computing in Small Colleges, 17*(2), 23–33.

Becker, K. (2005a, July 4–6). *Games and learning styles*. Paper presented at the Special Session on Computer Games for Learning and Teaching, at the The IASTED International Conference on Education and Technology, ICET 2005, Calgary, Alberta, Canada.

Becker, K. (2005b, June 16–20). *How are games educational? Learning theories embodied in games*. Paper presented at the DiGRA 2005 2nd International Conference, "Changing Views: Worlds in Play," Vancouver, B.C.

Becker, K. (2006a). Pedagogy in commercial video games. In Gibson, D., Aldrich, C., & Prensky, M. (Eds.), *Games and Simulations in Online Learning: Research and Development Frameworks*. Hershey, PA: Idea Group.

Becker, K. (2006b, Sept 21–24). *A psycho-cultural approach to video games*. Paper presented at the Canadian Games Studies Association Symposium, York, University, Toronto, Ontario.

Becker, K. (2008a). *The invention of good games: Understanding learning design in commercial video games*. Unpublished dissertation, University of Calgary, Calgary, Canada.

Becker, K. (2008b). Video game pedagogy: Good games = good pedagogy. In Miller, C. T. (Ed.), *Games: Their purpose and potential in education*. New York: Springer Publishing.

Becker, K., & Jacobsen, D. M. (June 16–20, 2005). *Games for learning: Are schools ready for what's to come?* Paper presented at the DiGRA 2005 2nd International Conference, "Changing Views: Worlds in Play," Vancouver, B.C.

Becker, K., & Parker, J. R. (October 13–15, 2005). *All I ever needed to know about programming, I learned from re-writing classic arcade games.* Paper presented at Future Play, The International Conference on the Future of Game Design and Technology, Michigan State University, East Lansing, Michigan.

Berkeley, E. (1853). The world's laconics, or, the best thoughts of the best authors in prose and poetry. New York: M.W.Dodd.

Bruckman, A., & Resnick, M. (1996). The MediaMOO project: Constructionism and professional community. In Y. B. Kafai & M. Resnick (Eds.), Constructionism in practice: designing, thinking, and learning in a digital world (pp. xii, 339). Mahwah, NJ: Lawrence Erlbaum Associates.

Bruner, J. (1961). The act of discovery. *Harvard Educational Review, 31*(1), 21–32.

Buckingham, D., & Scanlon, M. (2004). Connecting the family? 'Edutainment' web sites and learning in the home. *Education Communication and Information, 4.*

Caillois, R. (1961). *Man, play, and games.* Glencoe, IL: Free Press of Glencoe.

Caspian Learning. (2008). *Serious Games in Defence Education.* White Paper Retrieved from http://www.caspianlearning.co.uk/MoD_Defence_Academy_Serious_games_Report_04.11.08.pdf

Ceer, D. (2006). Pervasive medical devices: less invasive, more productive. *Pervasive Computing IEEE, 5*(2), 85–87. doi:10.1109/MPRV.2006.37

Chapman, G. (2009, Mar 13, 2009). Second Life finding new life. *AFP.* Retrieved from http://www.google.com/hostednews/afp/article/ALeqM5h-HXGgsClglmLWwN2hCXGS-fqYwqQ

Charsky, D., & Mims, C. (2008). Integrating commercial off-the-shelf video games into school curriculums. *TechTrends, 52*(5), 38–44. doi:10.1007/s11528-008-0195-0

Clark, R. E. (1983). Reconsidering research on learning from media. *Review of Educational Research, 53*(4), 445–459.

Clark, R. E. (2007). Learning from serious games? Arguments, evidence, and research suggestions. *Educational Technology,* (May–June): 56–59.

Colella, V. S., Klopfer, E., & Resnick, M. (2001). *Adventures in modeling: exploring complex, dynamic systems with StarLogo.* New York: Teachers College Press.

Crawford, C. (2003). *Chris Crawford on game design.* Indianapolis, IN: New Riders.

Din, F. S., & Calao, J. (2001). The effects of playing educational video games on kindergarten achievement. *Child Study Journal, 31*(2), 95–102.

Dobson, M., Ha, D., Mulligan, D., & Ciavarro, C. (2005, June 16–20). *From real-world data to game world experience: Social analysis methods for developing plausible & engaging learning games.* Paper presented at the DiGRA 2005 2nd International Conference, "Changing Views: Worlds in Play," Vancouver, B.C.

Dormann, C., & Biddle, R. (2006). Humour in game-based learning. *Learning, Media & Technology. Special Issue: Digital Games and Learning, 31*(4), 411–424.

Egenfeldt-Nielsen, S. (2005). *Beyond edutainment: Exploring the educational potential of computer games.* Unpublished dissertation, IT University Copenhagen, Copenhagen.

Egenfeldt-Nielsen, S. (2007). *Educational potential of computer games*. New York: Continuum.

Egenfeldt-Nielsen, S., Smith, J. H., & Tosca, S. P. (2008). *Understanding video games: The essential introduction*. New York: Routledge.

Ellis, H., Heppell, S., Kirriemuir, J., Krotoski, A., & McFarlane, A. (2006). *Unlimited learning: The role of computer and video games in the learning landscape*. Retrieved from http://www.elspa.com/assets/files/u/unlimitedlearningtheroleofcomputerandvideogamesint_344.pdf

Engeström, Y. (1987). *Learning by expanding: An activity-theoretical approach to developmental research.* Paper presented at the Orienta-Konsultit, Helsinki.

Fabricatore, C. (2000). *Learning and videogames: An unexplored synergy.* Paper presented at the International Conference of the Association for Educational Communications and Technology, Denver, Colorado.

Freeman, D. (2003). *Creating emotion in games: The craft and art of emotioneering*. New Riders Games.

Freitas, S. d. (2007). Learning in immersive worlds: A review of game based learning. London: Joint Information Systems Committee (JISC).

Friedman, T. L. (2006). The world is flat: A brief history of the twenty-first century (1st Updated and Expanded ed.). New York: Farrar, Straus and Giroux.

Fröbel, F. (1912). *Froebel's chief writings on education* (Fletcher, S. S. F., & Welton, J., Trans.). London: Arnold.

Garris, R., Ahlers, R., & Driskell, J. E. (2002). Games, motivation, and learning: A research and practice model. *Simulation & Gaming, 33*(4), 441–467. doi:10.1177/1046878102238607

Gee, J. P. (2003). *What video games have to teach us about learning and literacy* (1st ed.). New York: Palgrave Macmillan.

Gray, M. (2008). World of Warcraft hits 11 million subscribers worldwide. *WoW Insider*. Retrieved from http://www.wowinsider.com/2008/10/28/world-of-warcraft-hits-11-million-subscribers-worldwide/

Gredler, M. E. (1996). Educational games and simulations: A technology in search of a research paradigm. In Jonassen, D. H. (Ed.), *Handbook of research on educational communications and technology* (pp. 521–540). New York: Simon & Schuster Macmillan.

Gredler, M. E. (2004). Games and simulations and their relationships to learning. In Jonassen, D. H. (Ed.), *Handbook of research on educational communications and technology* (2nd ed.). Mahwah, NJ: Association for Educational Communications and Technology, Lawrence Erlbaum.

Hadziomerovic, A., & Biddle, R. (2006, October 10–12). *Tracking engagement in a role play game.* Paper presented at the Future Play, The International Conference on the Future of Game Design and Technology, The University of Western Ontario, London, Ontario, Canada.

Heeter, C., Chu, C. K., Maniar, A., Winn, B., Punya, M., Egidio, R., & Portwood-Stacer, L. (2003, 4–6 November). *Comparing 14 plus 2 forms of fun (and learning and gender issues) in commercial versus educational space exploration digital games.* Paper presented at the International Digital Games Research Conference, University of Utrecht: Netherlands.

Heeter, C., & Winn, B. (2008). Implications of fender, player type and learning strategies for the design of games for learning. In Kafai, Y., Heeter, C., Denner, J., & Sun, J. (Eds.), *Beyond Barbie to Mortal Combat: New perspectives on games, gender, and computing*. Cambridge, MA: MIT Press.

Huizinga, J. (1950). *Homo Ludens: a study of the play element in culture*. New York: Roy Publishers.

Juul, J. (2005). *Half-real: Video games between real rules and fictional worlds*. Cambridge, MA: MIT Press.

Kafai, Y. B. (2006). Playing and making games for learning: Instructionist and constructionist perspectives for game studies. *Games and Culture, 1*(1), 36–40. doi:10.1177/1555412005281767

Kay, A. (2007). The real computer revolution hasn't happened yet (VPRI Memo M-2007-007-a). (Viewpoints Research Institute, Ed.).

Kebritchi, M. (2008). *Effects of a computer game on mathematics achievement and class motivation: An experimental study*. Unpublished doctoral dissertation University of Central Florida, FL, USA.

Kirriemuir, J., & McFarlane, A. (2004). *Literature review in games and learning*. Retrieved from http://www.nestafuturelab.org/research/reviews/08_01.htm

Kozma, R. B. (1994). Will media influence learning? Reframing the debate. *Educational Technology Research and Development, 42*(2), 7–19. doi:10.1007/BF02299087

Leigh, E. (2003). *A practitioner researcher perspective on facilitating an open, infinite, chaordic simulation. Learning to engage with theory while putting myself into practice*. Unpublished doctoral dissertation, University of Technology, Sydney.

Leyland, B. (1996, 2–4 December). *How can computer games offer deep learning and still be fun?* Paper presented at the ASCILITE 96, Adelaide, South Australia.

Malone, T. W. (1981). Towards a theory of intrinsically motivating instruction. *Cognitive Science, 5*(4), 333–369.

Malone, T. W., & Lepper, M. R. (1987). Making learning fun: A taxonomy of intrinsic motivations for learning. In R. E. Snow & M. J. Farr (Eds.), Aptitude, learning and instruction. Volume 3: Conative and affective process analysis (pp. 223–253). Hillsdale, NJ: Lawrence Erlbaum Associates.

Maloney, J. H., Peppler, K., Kafai, Y., Resnick, M., & Rusk, N. (2008). Programming by choice: Urban youth learning programming with scratch. In *Proceedings of the 39th SIGCSE technical symposium on computer science education* (pp. 367-371).

Mann, D. (2001). Documenting the effects of instructional technology: A fly-over of policy questions. In Heineke, W. F., & Blasi, L. (Eds.), *Research methods for educational technology: Methods of evaluating educational technology* (*Vol. 1*, pp. 239–249). Greenwich, CT: Information Age Pub.

Marsh, T. (in press). Activity-based scenario design, development and assessment in serious games. In Van Eck, R. (Ed.), *Gaming & cognition: Theories and practice from the learning sciences*. Hershey, PA: IGI Global.

Mayo, M. J. (2009). Video games: A route to large-scale STEM education? *Science, 323*(5910), 79–82. doi:10.1126/science.1166900

McLuhan, M. (1964). *Understanding media: The extensions of man* (1st ed.). New York: McGraw-Hill.

Mishra, P., & Foster, A. (2007). *The claims of games: A comprehensive review and directions for future research*. Paper presented at the Society for Information Technology and Teacher Education International Conference 2007, San Antonio, Texas, USA.

Mitchell, A., & Savill-Smith, C. (2004). *The use of computer and video games for learning*. Retrieved from http://www.lsda.org.uk/files/pdf/1529.pdf

Morrison, H. J. C. (1931). *The practice of teaching in the secondary schools*. Chicago: University of Chicago Press.

Murray, J. H. (1998). *Hamlet on the holodeck: The future of narrative in cyberspace*. Cambridge, MA: MIT Press.

Neulight, N., Kafai, Y. B., Kao, L., Foley, B., & Galas, C. (2006). Children's participation in a virtual epidemic in the science classroom: Making connections to natural infectious diseases. *Journal of Science Education and Technology, 16*(1), 47–58. doi:10.1007/s10956-006-9029-z

Oliver, M., & Pelletier, C. (2004, July). *Activity theory and learning from digital games: Implications for game design*. Paper presented at the Digital Generations: Children, young people and new media, London.

Papert, S. (1980). *Mindstorms: children, computers, and powerful ideas*. New York: Basic Books.

Papert, S. (1996). *The connected family: Bridging the digital generation gap*. Atlanta, GA: Longstreet Press.

Papert, S. (1998). Does easy do it? Children, games, and learning. [Soapbox]. *Game Developers Magazine, 88*.

Parker, J. R., & Becker, K. (n.d.). *IEEE game bibliography*. Retrieved from http://www.ucalgary.ca/~jparker/TFGT/publications.html

Parker, J. R., Becker, K., & Sawyer, B. (2008, January). Re-reconsidering research on learning from media: Comments on Richard E. Clark's point of view column on serious games. *Educational Technology Magazine*, 39–43.

Pelletier, C., & Oliver, M. (2006). Learning to play in digital games. *Learning, Media & Technology. Special Issue: Digital Games and Learning, 31*(4), 329–342.

Piaget, J. (1951). *Play, dreams, and imitation in childhood*. New York: Norton.

Pivec, P. (2009). *Game-based learning or game-based teaching?* Research report prepared for the BECTA.

Poppendieck, M., & Poppendieck, T. D. (2003). *Lean software development: An agile toolkit*. Boston: Addison-Wesley.

Prensky, M. (2001a). *Digital game-based learning*. New York: McGraw-Hill.

Prensky, M. (2001b). Digital Natives, Digital Immigrants. *Horizon, 9*(5). Retrieved from http://www.marcprensky.com/writing/Prensky%20-%20Digital%20Natives,%20Digital%20Immigrants%20-%20Part1.pdf.

Prensky, M. (2001c). Digital Natives, Digital Immigrants, Part II: Do They Really Think Differently? *Horizon, 9*(6), 1–6. Retrieved from http://www.marcprensky.com/writing/Prensky%20-%20Digital%20Natives,%20Digital%20Immigrants%20-%20Part2.pdf. doi:10.1108/10748120110424843

Prensky, M. (2006). *Don't Bother Me Mom I'm Learning!* St. Paul, MN: Continuum.

Reigeluth, C. M., & Stein, F. S. (1983). The Elaboration Theory of Instruction. In Reigeluth, C. M. (Ed.), *Instructional-Design Theories and Models: An Overview of Their Current Status* (*Vol. 1*, pp. 335–381). Hillsdale, N.J.: Erlbaum.

Resnick, M. (2004). Edutainment? No Thanks. I Prefer Playful Learning. *Associazione Civita Report on Edutainment*. Retrieved from http://www.parents-choice.org/full_abstract.cfm?art_id=172&the_page=consider_this

Rieber, L. P. (1996). Seriously Considering Play: Designing Interactive Learning Environments Based on the Blending of Microworlds, Simulations, and Games. *Educational Technology Research and Development, 44*(2), 43–58. doi:10.1007/BF02300540

Rieber, L. P. (2005). Multimedia Learning in Games, Simulations, and Microworlds. In Mayer, R. E. (Ed.), *The Cambridge Handbook of Multimedia Learning* (pp. 549–567). Cambridge, MA: Cambridge University Press.

Rieber, L. P., Davis, J., Matzko, M., & Grant, M. (2001, April 10–14). *Children as multimedia critics: Middle school students' motivation for and critical analysis of educational multimedia designed by other children.* Paper presented at the What We Know and How We Know It, Seattle, WA. Rieber, L. P., & Matzko, M. J. (2001). Serious design for serious play in physics. *Educational Technology, 41*(1), 14–24.

Rosas, R., Nussbaum, M., Cumsille, P., Marianov, V., Correa, M. n., & Flores, P. (2003). Beyond Nintendo: Design and assessment of educational video games for first and second grade students. *Computers & Education, 40*(1), 71. doi:10.1016/ S0360-1315(02)00099-4

Rumzan, I. (2002). Research report. [Review of the article Building an Educational Adventure Game: Theory, Design and Lessons, by Amory (2001)]. *Canadian Journal of Learning and Technology, 28*(3), 143–144.

Rutter, J., & Bryce, J. (n.d.). *Digiplay initiative.* Retrieved from http://digiplay.info/

Salen, K., & Zimmerman, E. (2004). *Rules of play: Game design fundamentals.* Cambridge, MA: MIT Press.

Sandford, R., Ulicsak, M., Facer, K., & Rudd, T. (2006). *Teaching with games: Using commercial off-the-shelf computer games in formal education.* Bristol, UK: FutureLab. Retreived from http:// www.futurelab.org.uk/projects/teaching-with- games/research/final-report

Sawyer, B. (2003). Serious games: Improving public policy through game-based learning and simulation. *Woodrow Wilson International Center for Scholars.* Retreived from http://wwics.si.edu/ foresight/index.htm

Schrage, M. (2000). *Serious play: How the world's best companies simulate to innovate.* Boston: Harvard Business School Press.

Seels, B., & Richey, R. (1994). *Instructional technology: The definition and domains of the field.* Washington, DC: Association for Educational Communications and Technology.

Shaffer, D. W. (2007). *How computer games help children learn.* New York: Palgrave Macmillan.

Shaffer, D. W., Squire, K. R., Halverson, R., & Gee, J. P. (2004). *Video games and the future of learning.* Madison, WI: University of Wisconsin-Madison, Academic Advanced Distributed Learning Co-Laboratory.

Sharritt, M. J. (in press). Evaluating video game design and interactivity. In Eck, R. V. (Ed.), *Interdisciplinary models and tools for serious games: Emerging concepts and future directions.* Hershey, PA: IGI Global.

Sherlock, L. M. (2007). When social networking meets online games: The activity system of grouping in *World of Warcraft.* In *Proceedings of the 25th annual ACM international conference on Design of communication* (pp. 14–20).

SimuLearn. (2006). Independent research from corporate, academic, and military institutions on the effectiveness of SimuLearn's *Virtual Leader.* Retrieved from http://www.simulearn.net/pdf/ practiceware_works.pdf

Squire, K. (2002). Cultural framing of computer/ video games. *Game Studies, 2*(1).

Squire, K. (2003). *Replaying history: Learning world history through playing Civilization III.* Unpublished dissertation, Indiana University.

Squire, K., & Gaydos, M. (in press). Citizen science: Designing a game for the 21st century. In Eck, R. V. (Ed.), *Interdisciplinary models and tools for serious games: Emerging concepts and future directions.* Hershey, PA: IGI Global.

Sutton-Smith, B. (1997). *The ambiguity of play*. Cambridge, MA: Harvard University Press.

Tobias, S., & Fletcher, J. D. (2007). What research has to say about designing computer games for learning. *Educational Technology*, (September–October): 20–29.

Van Eck, R. (2006). Using games to promote girls' positive attitudes toward technology. *Innovate Journal of Online Education, 2*(3).

Van Eck, R. (2008). COTS in the Classroom: A teachers guide to integrating commercial off- the-shelf (COTS) games. In Ferdig, R. (Ed.), *Handbook of research on effective electronic gaming in education*. Hershey, PA: Idea Group.

Vygotsky, L. S., & Cole, M. (1977). *Mind in society: The development of higher psychological processes*. Cambridge, MA: Harvard University Press.

Watson, W. R. (2007). *Formative research on an instructional design theory for educational video games*. Unpublished doctoral dissertation, Indiana University.

White, B. Y. (1984). Designing computer games to help physics students understand Newton's Laws of Motion. *Cognition and Instruction, 1*(1), 69. doi:10.1207/s1532690xci0101_4

Winn, B., & Heeter, C. (2007). Resolving conflicts in educational game design through playtesting. *Innovate Journal of Online Education, 3*(2).

Wittgenstein, L. (1973). *Philosophical investigations: The English text of the* (3rd ed.). New York: Macmillan.

Wright, W. (2003). Forward. In *Freeman, D. Creating emotion in games: The craft and art of emotioneering*. Indianapolis, IN: New Riders Games.

Wright, W. (2004). Pop quiz with Will Wright, Education Arcade. Los Angeles: E3.

Wu, S. (2008). *Reducing unproductive learning activities in serious games for second language acquisition*. CA, USA: University of Southern California.

APPENDIX: ADDITIONAL REFERENCES

"Must-Reads" for this Topic

Becker, K. (2006, October 10 - 12). *Design paradox: Instructional games*. Paper presented at the Future Play, The International Conference on the Future of Game Design and Technology, The University of Western Ontario, London, Ontario, Canada.

Ellis, H., Heppell, S., Kirriemuir, J., Krotoski, A., & McFarlane, A. (2006). *Unlimited learning: The role of computer and video games in the learning landscape*. Retrieved from http://www.elspa. com/assets/files/u/unlimitedlearningtheroleofcomputerandvideogamesint_344.pdf

Fullerton, T., Swain, C., & Hoffman, S. (2008). *Game design workshop: A playcentric approach to creating innovative games* (2nd ed.). Boston: Elsevier Morgan Kaufmann.

Gredler, M. E. (2004). Games and simulations and their relationships to learning. In D. H. Jonassen (Ed.), *Handbook of research on educational communications and technology* (2nd ed.). Mahwah, NJ: Association for Educational Communications and Technology.

Jonassen, D. H. (2004). *Learning to solve problems: an instructional design guide*. San Francisco: Pfeiffer.

Top Texts for Interdisciplinary Studies of Serious Games

Aldrich, C. (2009). *The complete guide to simulations and serious games: How the most valuable content will be created in the age beyond Gutenberg to Google*. San Francisco: Pfeiffer.

Bogost, I. (2007). *Persuasive games: The expressive power of videogames*. Cambridge, MA: MIT Press.

Crawford, C. (2003). *Chris Crawford on game design*. Indianapolis, IN: New Riders.

Egenfeldt-Nielsen, S., Smith, J. H., & Tosca, S. P. (2008). *Understanding video games: The essential introduction*. New York: Routledge.

Huizinga, J. (1950). *Homo Ludens: A study of the play element in culture*. New York: Roy Publishers.

Juul, J. (2004). *Half-real: Video games between real rules and fictional worlds*. Unpublished doctoral dissertation, IT University of Copenhagen, Copenhagen.

Koster, R. (2004). *Theory of fun for game design*. Scottsdale, AZ: Paraglyph Press.

Prensky, M. (2001). *Digital game-based learning*. New York: McGraw-Hill.

Salen, K., & Zimmerman, E. (2004). *Rules of play: Game design fundamentals*. Cambridge, MA: MIT Press.

Sutton-Smith, B. (1997). *The ambiguity of play*. Cambridge, MA: Harvard University Press.

Games Referenced

Add 'Em Up. Published by Blue Bug Games, Blue Bug Games (Developer). Game Site: http://www. bluebuggames.com/games/addemup.htm

Bejeweled. Popcap Games (Developer). Game Site: http://www.popcap.com/gamepopup. php?theGame=diamondmine

Citizen Science. (2008). Kurt Squire, Filament Games (Developer). Game Site: http://www.filament-games.com/home

Civilization III. (2001). Published by Infogrames. Game Site: http://www.civ3.com/

Civilization IV. (2005). Published by 2K Games. Game Site: http://www.2kgames.com/civ4/home.htm

Deus Ex: Invisible War. (2003). Published by Eidos Interactive. Game Site: http://www.deusex.com/

Escher's World. (1997). Published by Epistemic Games, D. W. Shaffer (Developer). Game Site: http://epistemicgames.org/ew/start.html

Europa Universalis II. (2003). Published by Virtual Programming Ltd, Paradox Entertainment AB (Developer). Game Site: http://www.ppcstudios.com/eu2prod.shtml

Final Fantasy VII Advent Children. (1997). Published by Square Co. Ltd., Game Site: http://www.square-enix-usa.com/dvd/ff7ac/

Harry Potter and the Chamber of Secrets. (2002). Published by Electronic Arts, Inc., Game Site: http://www.ea.com/

The House of the Dead 2. (1999). Published by SEGA Enterprises Ltd., Wow Entertainment Inc. (Developer)

Katamari Damacy. (2004). Published by Namco, Game Site: http://katamari.namco.com/

Knight Elimar's Last Joust. (2008). R. Levy, H. Wideman, R. Owston & A. Orich (Developers). [PC]

Knights of Honor. (2005). Published by Paradox Interactive AB, Black Sea Studios Ltd

Making History: The Calm and The Storm. (2006). Published by Muzzy Lane Software, Muzzy Lane Software (Developer). Game Site: http://www.making-history.com/home.php

Math Blaster! Master the Basics. (2005). Published by Davidson & Associates, Inc., Game Site: http://www.knowledgeadventure.com/mathblaster/preview.aspx

Mavis Beacon Teaches Typing! (1988). Published by Software Toolworks, Inc.

New Super Mario Bros. (2006). Published by Nintendo, T. Tezuka (Developer). Game Site: http://mario.nintendo.com/

Pandora Project, Published by Epistemic Games, D. W. Shaffer (Developer). Game Site: http://epistemicgames.org/ew/start.html

Real Lives. (2002). Published by Educational Simulations, Game Site: http://www.educationalsimulations.com/

Re-Mission. (2006). Published by HopeLab, HopeLab (Developer). Game Site: http://www.re-mission.net/

Roller Coaster Tycoon III. (2005). Published by Atari, Inc., Frontier Developments Ltd. (Developer). Game Site: http://www.atari.com/rollercoastertycoon/

Second Life. (2003). Published by Linden Lab, Game Site: http://www.secondlife.com

Service Rig Trainer. (2007). Coole Immersive (Developer). Game Site: http://cooleimmersive.com/

The SIMs. (2000). Published by Electronic Arts, Maxis Software Inc. (Developer). Game Site: http://thesims.ea.com/

The Sims 2. (2004). Published by EA Games, Maxis Software Inc. (Developer). Game Site: http://thesims2.ea.com/

Soda Constructor. (1996). Soda Creative Ltd. (Developer). Game Site: http://sodaplay.com/creators/soda/items/constructor

StarCraft. (1998). Published by Blizzard Entertainment Inc. Game Site: http://www.blizzard.com/starcraft/

Tetris. (1987). Published by Mirrorsoft Ltd.

The Typing of the Dead. (2000). Published by Sega, Smilebit (Developer).

Virtual Leader. (2002). Published by SimuLearn. Game Site: http://www.simulearn.net/SimuLearn/ standalone.htm

Whyville. (1999). Published by Numedeon, Inc. Game Site: http://www.whyville.net/smmk/nice

Wii Sports. (2006). Published by Nintendo, Game Site: http://wii.nintendo.com/software_wiisports.jsp

World of Warcraft. (2004). Published by Blizzard Entertainment Inc. Game Site: http://www.worldof-warcraft.com/index.xml

Zoo Tycoon 2. (2004). Published by Microsoft Game Studios. Game Site: http://www.microsoft.com/ games/zootycoon/zoo2/

Chapter 3
MMORPGs in Support of Learning:
Current Trends and Future Uses

Bodi Anderson
Northern Arizona University, USA

ABSTRACT

This chapter provides an overview of current massively multiplayer online role-playing games (MMORPG) research and creates a conceptual framework for their use in support of learning. Initially, a definition of MMORPGs in education is considered in light of research to date. Here attention is paid to how MMORPGs differ from most video games in terms of types of player–game interaction, levels of player– player interaction, environments in which interaction occurs, and the ability for MMORPGs to tap into student motivation levels. Based on this definition and considering previous theoretical and empirical studies on MMORPGs from a variety of disciplines, including education, psychology, and linguistics, a conceptual framework for the use of MMORPGs in support of learning is created. Next an overview of current research trends in MMORPGs is examined, concluding with suggestions concerning future research of the use of MMORPGs in support of learning.

INTRODUCTION

Since the late 1990s, there has been a steady increase in the number of people who play online games. Massively multiplayer online role-playing games (or MMORPGs) are a $20-billion/year industry, with the top MMORPGs comprising between 11 (United States) and 20 million (Asia) players for a global market of over $9 billion dollars (Wauters, 2008; Wei 2007). Given the popularity of this medium, and the growing use of video games in support of various learning, it was not long before educators began using MMORPGs in instructional settings. Instructors from academic disciplines such as childhood education, communication technology, psychology, and computer-assisted language learning began to experimentally investigate the use of MMORPGs in instructional settings.

While an increasing number of teachers and educational institutions are making use of MMOR-

DOI: 10.4018/978-1-61520-717-6.ch003

PGs as an instructional medium, the amount of research on MMORPGs to date is still limited. The youth of this game genre and sudden boom of popularity are significant factors when considering the currently small, yet growing amount of research on MMORPGs (Au 2007; de Freitas & Griffiths, 2007). Research on MMORPGs comes from multiple academic genres such as psychology, sociology, education and, more recently, ESL (English as a Second Language) and applied linguistics. In their meta-analysis on education technology, Waxman, Lin, and Michko (2003), contest that there is a need for consolidation of education technology research in methodology and commonly accepted frameworks. They argue that much of the problem with education technology research stems from the numerous research methods and norms of the various academic disciplines with interest in distance education as well as ever-present changes in technology, which can serve to significantly impact education technology research in terms of the longevity of generalizable findings.

Naturally, each specific academic discipline is driven by different purposes, pedagogy, and field-specific theoretical issues. Likewise, each discipline has particular needs for both instructors and students. But because serious game studies represents a large body of research across many different academic disciplines, it is important to understand and study MMORPGs from an interdisciplinary perspective. This chapter will attempt to provide an outline of current MMORPG research from an interdisciplinary perspective. First, a definition of MMORPGs will be established, particularly with regard to current research of serious game theory and concepts. Once established, this definition will be used in conjunction with current research on MMORPGS in order to propose a conceptual framework for MMORPGs in support of learning. Here a focus will be placed on combining interdisciplinary research in order to make a general theoretical model, which may hopefully serve as a foundation for further research

into the MMORPG medium. Following this, an overview will be given of current research trends in MMORPGs across disciplines, and finally, suggestions concerning future research in the medium will be proposed. It is hoped that by developing a foundational conceptual framework and providing an overview of MMORPG research to date that better planned and consolidated efforts for future research into the medium will be made.

BACKGROUND

In order to better understand modern day MMORPGs, this chapter will first look into the history and technological innovations of various types of games that served to shape and influence current MMORPGs. MMORPGs evolved out of online multi-user dungeons (MUDs), which were preceded by computer role-playing games (CRPGs) and, in turn, pencil and paper (PnP) role-playing games (RPGs) such as *Dungeons and Dragons* (D&D; Childress & Braswell, 2006). This becomes more clear when one breaks down the acronym in reverse: "RPG" stands for role-playing games, which were originally non-digital (PnP and D&D), "O" stands for online, which signifies the shift of the medium from analog to digital (primarily, CRPGs), and "MM" stands for massive multi-player, signifying the shift from a small number of players to large numbers (MUDs).

In addition to being the first RPG, D&D is often heralded as the most popular PnP RPG of all time. First developed in 1974 by Gary Gygax and David Arneson, D&D went on to develop a huge following. Unlike most board and card games, RPGs center on social interaction (which often includes elements of player teamwork) rather than player-versus-player (PvP) competition alone (Rilstone, 1994). At their core, RPGs work much like stage drama with a bare-bones script with a high degree of improvisation. In RPGs, most players assume the identity of characters, or different personas, much in the manner that an actor assumes the persona of a character in a play or movie. However, in an RPG, players create a background story for and have full control over the actions of their characters (also commonly known as the player character or PC). In addition to players assuming the roles of characters in PnP RPGs, one person must also take on the role of the dungeon master or game master (DM or GM, respectively—GM has become the more common term as games have moved beyond the setting of dungeons alone). The GM acts much like a director, producer, and storyteller and is responsible for creating a rough plot and challenges for players to interact with and overcome. As the players describe their characters' actions, it is the job of the GM to determine how these actions affect the fictional world in which the game takes place (Kim, 2008). For instance, if a player's character entered a tavern, the GM would then describe the scenery and patrons much as a novelist would. However, all RPGs also have strong rule sets which lay down everything from the more static attributes of a PC (such has how strong, intelligent, or comely they are, or how skilled they are at cooking), to the results of random events (such as the outcome of a fight, or the chances of a character slipping and falling if walking on an icy ledge). Ultimately, many of these rules are governed by chance (rolls of dice in RPGs or algorithms in today's MMORPGs) in order to represent a probability factor. The GM is also in control of the actions of all of the other individuals and creatures characters may later meet in their adventures. These GM-controlled entities are called nonplayer characters or NPCs. While PCs will usually be the protagonists of the game, the GM-controlled NPCs consist of everyone from the most minor of background characters to the most prevalent villain. It is the job of the GM to provide each NPC with a unique personality and to decide how the NPCs react to the actions of PCs.

While a typical PnP role-playing session might last a few hours, games are set across broad-arching stories called campaigns. A campaign is set across many sessions and generally details the ongoing adventures of the same set of PCs. However, much as in novels, new players and characters must also be worked in, and some characters may meet untimely ends, thus calling for their players to assume the persona of a new character. Campaigns tend to last as long as the players hold interest, with some claiming to have gone on for over 20 years across a multitude of changes in players and GMs. Again, with focus on the key element socialization involved in PnP RPGs and the aspect of interactive storytelling, despite the popularity of modern day video games, PnP RPGs still continue to enjoy popularity with both younger and veteran players today.

With the popularization of personal computer-based video games, role-playing games made a transition into the electronic medium where they continue to enjoy success. While game historians may trace a clearer path to MUDs (detailed below), there is still a lesser, though still present, connection between MMORPGs and CRPGs. Amazingly enough, the first CRPGs appeared in late 1974. However, at the time, they were limited to mainframe play and, for the most part, were not publically available (Barton, 2007). It was not until the early 1980s that the genre started to receive a popular audience, with the conception of such titles as Richard Garriott's *Ultima* franchise and the *Wizardry* series. The genre then was quick to expand with many new titles (including various attempts to recreate D&D as a solid CRPG) making use of real-time interaction and advanced graphics. Current titles such as the *Elder Scrolls* series offer players huge expansive worlds and open-ended plots.

While nearly all CRPGs have their roots in their PNP predecessors, CRPGs are for the most part a single-player experience. In fact, Barton (2007) notes that many of the earlier CRPGs were marketed as a more convenient way to role-play, without the need for having to assemble a large group of players and with the ability to start and stop when the player wishes. While PnP RPGs focused more on social interaction, CRPGs aimed to immerse the player in a fantasy world via graphics and strong storylines. The players were still free (within in the limits of the game rules and world) to make choices and decisions but for the most part, and much like reading a novel, were still tied to a main storyline. While the basic rule systems of CRPGs attempted to emulate those PnP RPGs, as technology progressed, CRPGs began to develop more complex and detailed rule systems, allowing for a progression from turn-based to real-time combat rule sets, larger virtual worlds, and 3-D gameplay. In 1985, the *Ultima* series was the also the first to popularize the term "avatar," or the player's visual on-screen in-game persona in computer gaming. The word has its etymological origins in Sanskrit, meaning an (often human) embodiment of the divine/godly (*Longman Dictionary of Contemporary English*). The hero of many installments of the *Ultima* series was often referred to as the avatar. Later, this term became a popular term in the CRPG and MMORPG world, referring to player-made, customized, and controlled characters.

Given the popularity of CRPGs and the rising number of Internet users in the 90s, multi-user dungeons (or domains), also called MUDs (or, less commonly, multi-user domain object oriented, or MOOs) were created to mix role-playing elements of PnP RPGs in an online setting. Richard Bartle and Roy Trubshaw are noted for creating the first MUD on the University of Essex's mainframe back in the early eighties. It was not until 1988 that the first popular MUD code began to gain a strong following of players. Original MUDs worked much like PnP RPGs with limited or no graphics, instead relying on text-based descriptions of events and surroundings. This was combined with real-time interaction or synchronous computer-mediated communication (CMC) as a means of relaying player communication. In this manner, MUDs kept the focus of player social interaction at the forefront of the experience (Turkle, 1995). The lack

of limited virtual space (such as in CRPGs) and the text-based medium allowed MUD players to be limited only by their imaginations as to where and how they chose to engage in role-playing. And while most MUDs had compared rule sets (albeit limited in comparison to CRPGs), some were merely chat rooms in which, through text-based descriptions, players (sometimes with the presence of a GM) interacted. As MUDs evolved, they added many new aspects such as user interface graphics and PvP combat rule sets. While a few MUDs continue today, many players and researchers note the popularity of MMORPGs for sweeping up much of the MUD player base (Childress & Braswell, 2006).

The term *massively multiplayer online RPG* was first coined by *Ultima* creator Richard Garriott. In fact, although not the first MMORPG (which was a version of D&D available to America Online users), the release of *Ultima Online* in 1996 is viewed by many as the first MMORPG to reach a high level of popularity and success (Hill, 2005). Following the success of *Ultima Online* (Mythic Entertainment, 2009), a spinoff company of Sony Online Entertainment, called Verant Interactive, launched a rival game, *Everquest* (Sony Online Entertainment, 2009). Released in 1999, *Everquest* was the first widely popular 3-D MMORPG. By 2003, *Everquest* had nearly 500,000 player subscriptions (MMOG Chart.com) and was considered the most popular game released at the time. It was also around this time that MMORPGs started to receive popular press and academic attention. This success was then followed by Blizzard Entertainment's well-known *World of Warcraft* (Blizzard Entertainment Inc., 2009), released in 2004. *World of Warcraft* is noted for popularizing the MMORPG genre to a whole new level. With current subscription numbers claimed to be over 11 million, it continues to dominate the market and continues to raise its subscription numbers (Wauters, 2008). Currently, close to 200 MMORPGs have been released or are in development with big name genre tie-ins such as the *Star Wars* franchise, Marvel and DC comics, *The Lord of the Rings*, D&D, and Disney—all proof that the genre is continuing to flourish (MMORPG.com).

In essence, the MMORPG combines the social interaction found in MUDs with the complex rule systems and graphics of CRPGs and thus can be viewed as a natural progression of the two mediums. A typical MMORPG functions much like a normal Internet chat room or MUD; however, there is an added element, in that all interaction takes place in large polygonated three-dimensional virtual world(s) wherein players are represented by virtual personifications, again called avatars or characters. Player create and assume control over their avatars and uses them as a vehicle to interact with the virtual world and to communicate with other players' avatars. This interaction occurs in a manner similar to that of many other video games and particularly CRPGs, where the player takes control of a character and uses it to interact with challenges and puzzles within the game. In the simplest of forms, MMORPGs can be seen as chat rooms with interactive tasks (Yee, 2006). However, given the progress of current technology, MMORPGs go beyond both MUDs and PnP RPGs by allowing tens of thousands of players to simultaneously inhabit and interact in the same virtual world.

. Many of the virtual worlds in which MMORPGs take place are immense in size, each with multiple virtual cities and towns and large wildernesses. Depending on the game, each virtual world can also house tens of thousands of avatars (as a result of technological restrictions that are being lifted as server technology advances, particularly scalable server hardware/software technologies), allowing for an avatar and player to interact with many others over the course of a play session. Additionally, most MMORPGs allow players to create multiple avatars (although in most cases, only one can exist in the virtual world at a time). This allows players to take on different personas and different paths for each of their avatars if they

so wish. As noted above, MMORPGs combine elements of other video games (namely CRPGs) with additional interactive social features found in CMC (and MUDs). The next section will develop a definition for MMORPGs, building upon many of the concepts discussed above as well as incorporating concepts from other video games. It will start by detailing basic frameworks used by current MMORPG designs in order to give readers a better picture of what MMORPGs look like.

WHAT ARE MMORPGS?

To develop a definition, it is best that one first understand the basic frameworks used to create and guide MMORPGs. Current MMORPGs generally follow a few basic design frameworks that have evolved out of the most successful titles in the genre. Here, some of the most prominent frameworks will be detailed; this is, however, by no means an exhaustive list, which again can be attributed to the fact that research into MMORPGs models is still relatively new in academia.

Levels and Skills

One common rule here is that almost all MMORPGs center on the advancement and progression of the avatar. Psychology studies on player motivations have found that player attachment to their avatars (along with socializing) is one of the key reasons for continued game play, something also found in MUDs (Turkle, 1995; Yee, 2006) This is often done through accomplishing specific in-game goals (such as defeating a powerful enemy or creating in-game items with one's avatar) or through a natural progression of the game's rule system (many games use the "level" system, popular to PnP RPGs to rank a character's progress and relative power, e.g., a level 10 avatar will most likely be much weaker when compared to similar level 30 avatar). It should be noted though that not all MMORPGs use level systems as a measurement of avatar progression. Some, such as *Star Wars Galaxies* (Lucasfilm Ltd., 2009), employ a skill-based system in lieu of a level system, in which by repeated successful use of skills (e.g., cooking, starship piloting) players will see a rank increase. Both systems, however, usually employ a maximum achievable level (often raised as game companies add paid expansions, with new level increases and types of skills available to avatars). It should be noted that both systems trace their roots back to PnP RPG and, in turn, CRPG character progression.

Character Classes

Another major defining feature found more often in level-based games is that they often make use of character classes (from PnP RPGs) or avatar archetypes, which guide and limit how an avatar will progress. For instance, upon avatar creation, one might choose a wizard over a priest. The wizard will be able to destroy things more quickly and may have the ability of teleportation, while the priest, on the other hand, can help to heal wounded avatars and even resuscitate dead avatars. However, avatar progression in rule-based MMORPGs is not limited to level or skill point systems alone. As noted above, even upon reaching the level cap in a game, avatars can still "progress" via the acquisition of rare items, which can make them more proportionately powerful, or special titles, which follow an avatar's in-game name and serve as a badge of success or pride in game. For instance, in the *World of Warcraft* (Blizzard Entertainment Inc., 2009), an avatar who explores every corner of the vast virtual world will receive the title "The Explorer"; thus, instead of simply being known as "Jon," other avatars will view him as "Jon the Explorer."

Goal-Based vs. Sandbox

Another major framework difference lies in the difference between "goal-based" (also sometimes

called quest-based) and "sandbox" MMORPGs. Much as with rule-based systems, goal-based MMORPGs occupy a large majority of the current market. These games follow a pattern similar to CRPGs in which there are game-generated tasks, quests, and storylines for players to complete. Such goals help serve to increase player immersion and provide a larger story to a game. Now, players are by no means limited to these goals; they can choose to simply wander the world or go off slaughtering its inhabitants (whether those characters are PCs or NPCs) However, most of the quests and tasks offer sizeable in-game rewards as an incentive to get players to undertake them (e.g., if you accept a quest to kill a powerful dragon, upon completion, the NPC who assigned the quest will reward the avatar with a powerful magic sword). Sandbox games, on the other hand, simply provide players with a virtual world (supplemented with lore and history) and rules, but beyond that, expect players to create their own adventures and experiences. This is much more akin to a MUD style of playing, where players must come up with their own motivations and ideas for how to interact with their virtual world. Players in a sandbox-based MMORPG may choose to group together and slay a dragon, but there is no in-game-based road pointing them there.

Player vs. Environment and Player vs. Player

Finally, a major distinction among rule-based systems lies in player vs. environment (PvE) and player vs. player PvP content. The former is modeled on CRPG gameplay (with the added element of multiplayer, real-time interaction), in which computer-controlled and computer-generated avatars (called NPCs, as in PnP RPGs), creatures/enemies (often referred to as "mobs," from the military slang for mobile object) and environments are the main focus of player interaction with the game. Here players will group together in numbers ranging from a one to hundreds of avatars to challenge pregenerated content (such as slaying a dragon). The primary difference between NPCs and "mobs" is that the former are generally non-aggressive to players and often serve as a means of limited social interaction between players and the game (in order to progress a storyline, provide immersion or give players quests), and the latter consist of enemy units which will actively try to harm players' avatars. PvP play, on the other hand, focuses on competing with other players. This competition is most often realized through combat (players can defeat or even kill other players; although most MMORPGs fall short of permanent avatar death, most all have some sort of in-game penalty for letting one's avatar die, such as reviving a dead player's avatar in a weakened state for a short amount of time. However, PvP can also take less violent forms such as controlling certain virtual economic markets or routes of supply, as in the complex sandbox MMORPG *EVE Online* (CCP, 2009). Unlike the above two frameworks, PvE and PvP play are not mutually exclusive. Most popular MMORPGs, such as *World of Warcraft* (Blizzard Entertainment Inc., 2009) and *Everquest2* (Sony Online Entertainment, 2009), employ both models at the same time. For instance, an avatar in combat with a computer-generated foe may suddenly find itself in even more trouble as an avatar controlled by another player takes advantage of its situation. Still, it is not uncommon for games to be marketed as primarily PvE, such as the *Everquest* series, or PvP, such as *Warhammer Online: Age of Reckoning* (Mythic Entertainment, 2009), in order to capture an audience which favors either style of gameplay. This is also partially based on the difficulty of balancing game mechanics around the two systems simultaneously. Adjusting particular aspects of PvE gameplay for challenge and balance may unintentionally adversely affect PvP gameplay, making certain archetypes of avatars (e.g., wizards) unusually powerful or weak. In games that try to employ both models equally, such as *World of Warcraft* (Blizzard Entertain-

ment Inc., 2009), the player base is often quick and vocal to point out any perceived inequalities on the game forums.

Now that basic frameworks for the different types of MMORPGs have been established, a few additional observations about how MMORPGs are and are not related to other video game genres is warranted. MMORPGs primarily differ from other video games (including many CRPGs) in that (1) they take place in a persistent (and often naturalistic) online environment which continues to exist and progress/change whether or not players are logged on, (2) interaction between players goes beyond simple cooperative and tactical play (as traditional multiplayer and LAN games), and encourages rich and collaborative social interactions, and (3) MMORPGs offer players and increasingly large and varied amount of avatar creation. (Childress & Braswell, 2006; Riegle & Matejka, 2006Yee, 2006;). Unlike other video games, MMORPGs need to account for the different play styles and times of their players; thus, the virtual world in which the games take place is a persistent world which exists whether or not a particular player is logged on and, furthermore, is modified in the form of frequent content updates by the developers of the games. MMORPGs have a dynamic model compared with standard video games, as time continues and events progress in the "persistent" world, regardless of who is (or is not) playing (Schrader & McCreery, 2007). Other players, computer-controlled avatars, and even virtual weather and day and night patterns will progress regardless of an individual player's presence. This persistent world creates many opportunities for players for different types of interaction with the world and other players.

The concept of a persistent world works on both a macro and micro level as well. Most of the popular MMORPGs (in the western world) are subscription based, although there are a number of free as well as pay-as-you-play microtransaction models. Subscription-based games involve players making an original purchase as well as paying a small monthly subscription fee to support in part the development and upkeep costs. Microtransaction MMORPGs make their income in the form of selling in-game items, clothing, and even plots of virtual land. This means that new game rules and types of interaction as well as modification or even removal of current ones is a constant in MMORPGs. New content often comes in the form of new virtual geography, new abilities granted to avatars, and expansions or variations on current rules in the game. Yang, Wu, and Wang (2007) report that this constant addition of new material and modification of current material (when done to players' satisfaction) is one of the key factors (along with socializing and quality of project) that keep MMORPG users subscribing to and playing the same game for long periods of time (even years).

Social interaction in MMORPGs also exceeds that of standard video games in that at any given time a player has the chance to interact with one or many thousands of other players in the same virtual world. Much research has shown that levels of social interaction between players in MMORPGs equals or exceeds that of traditional CMC settings (Anderson 2008; Bryant, 2008; Yee, 2006). MMORPGs also have a greater variety of possible social interaction than found in most video games. Here research shows that players can work towards a common goal, engage in competitive play such as player vs. player combat or activities (PvP) as well as socialize in much the same way found in normal CMC environments such as chat rooms. Furthermore, based on the need in many MMORPGs for players to often work together to achieve in-game goals organized social networking is often inherent to players' success and progression in the virtual word of an MMORPG (Chen, Sun, & Hsieh, 2008; Ducheneaut, Yee, Nickell, & Moore, 2006).

The creation and use of avatars in MMORPGs also goes beyond most video game models. Many players report great enjoyment derived from designing and customizing their avatars (Yee,

2005). Most MMORPGs allow highly detailed avatar customization during the creation process and throughout the game. Players can select the gender, race, hair color, and hairstyle of their avatars in most MMORPGs, with some being even more detailed, allowing players to make many subtle variations in facial structure and build. Furthermore, as avatars progress throughout the virtual world, they can often modify their roles or appearances by either specializing in certain skills and/or changing their clothes (many games have over 10 distinctly different clothing option slots, such as shoes, capes, pants, etc., which players can use to achieve individual appearances). Some games go so far as having in-game barbershops and plastic surgeons allowing players to reformulate the entire look of their avatar down to the gender. In this sense MMORPGs allow gamers to explore a large range of identities by playing a character created and customized by the player (Eatough, Davies, Griffiths, & Chappell, 2006; Hussain & Griffiths, 2008).

We have seen how MMORPGs draw on various concepts from videos games, including typical adventure and combat styles, tap into creativity and construction skills as seen in many simulation and MUD games, provide deep and varied levels of social interaction, and offer a wide range of avatar customization. This large range and variety of interaction and task type also has been found to be conducive of MMORPGs functioning as naturally occurring learning environments, and particularly so in relation to the cognitivist idea of socially constructed knowledge (Steinkuehler, 2004, 2005). Thus, MMORPGs operate on a complex level, incorporating features from both standard video games and CMC, making them unique in the study of serious gaming, yet informed by research on games and CMC. In the next section, I will attempt to create an interdisciplinary and multidimensional conceptual framework of MMORPGs as they support learning. There I will explore how research connects these primary aspects of MMORPGs to learning as well as discuss what the advantages and disadvantages are of using MMORPGs for structured learning.

A CONCEPTUAL FRAMEWORK: HOW MMORPGS SUPPORT LEARNING

MMORPGs combine elements of video game play with the high levels of social interaction found in synchronous CMC as well as the use of avatars, or virtual representations of the self as a means for interacting with the virtual world. This comes from blending the play styles and mechanics from both CRPGs and MUDs. In order to develop a conceptual framework for MMORPGs and pedagogy, three basic factors will be considered: (1) The use of video games in education and their effects on learning, cognition, and (to a lesser extent) motivation; (2) the role online social interaction plays in aiding learning; and (3) the sociopsychological research on self-projection through the use of avatars and the benefits it offers to learning and motivation. Thus, this conceptual model consists of analyzing the benefits of MMORPGs in terms of learning (cognition), social, and psychological factors.

There is a marked difference in research between games designed specifically for educational purposes and those that are not (Pivec, 2007). Nonetheless, many of the benefits MMORPGs hold for learning are shared by other forms of games, so research on other game genres will be used where relevant in addition to MMORPG-specific research to indicate features of MMORPGs that might be expected to support learning. In selecting the studies for this purpose, an emphasis was given to empirically based studies from peer-reviewed journals when at all possible.

The Cognitive Benefits of MMORPGs in Support of Learning

Space does not permit an accounting of all of the cognitive benefits of games in general, many of which apply equally or especially to MMORPGs. Several other authors in this book have addressed some of these benefits in more detail, and the reader is referred to those chapters as well as the "Must-Reads" at the end of this and other chapters. As described by O'Neil, Wainess, and Baker (2005), standard (i.e., non-education-based) games can potentially be seen as being potentially supportive of learning in four distinct ways: (1) the presence of complex and diverse approaches to learning processes and outcomes, (2) high levels of various types of interactivity, (3) the ability to address cognitive as well as affective learning issues, and (4) the ability to tap into motivation for learning. Considering the aforementioned characteristics, one outstanding feature of MMORPGs is that they expose players to a large variety of interaction and goal types (including, amongst other types, interactional features found in both standard and simulation games) when compared to most video games (Childress & Braswell, 2006; Yee, 2006). In that players can encounter a wider range of interaction when compared with traditional games, MMORPGs are theoretically suited to meet all four of the effective characteristics of games in learning.

For instance, in the *World of Warcraft* (Blizzard Entertainment Inc., 2009) and *Everquest 2* (Sony Online Entertainment, 2009), players are offered many different choices regarding how they choose to interact with the game. They can, for instance, choose to test their strategic and teamwork-based skills in tackling PvE content against challenges in the game. Many of the more difficult PvE encounters require large groups of players, (also called raids, varying in size from ten to 40 or more players), and require precise timing and teamwork to overcome a particular raid challenge, in addition to the development-specific strategies that differ from raid to raid. Players often are required to research game forums and discuss with other players effective strategies needed to successfully overcome raid encounters (Steinkuehler & Duncan, 2008). Furthermore, players are then required to put that research into action not only as part of an individual effort but also in coordination with other players. This can be further advanced by adding player vs. player (PvP) engagements which involve strategic capture of landmarks or even virtual versions of capture the flag; such as is present in *World of Warcraft* (Blizzard Entertainment Inc., 2009), wherein the added human element of competing against other players in groups and individually requires quick thinking and skill adaptation. Additional forms of interaction can be found in in-game crafting skills, which require players to assemble components and possibly barter with other players in order to craft complex in-game items.

For instance, in order to build a house in Sony's *Vanguard, Saga of Heroes* (Sigil, 2009), multiple players are required because each avatar can only focus on a particular trade skill (such as carpentry). While players can make a roof and lay down a base structure for their houses, they must also find a miner to procure ore for them and then a stone crafter to build them bricks. Such interaction builds both cognitive planning skills as well as social interaction skills (Smyth, 2007). Most MMORPGs have in-game auction houses where players can "play the market" in hopes of trading their way to virtual wealth. Crafters can also hope to corner a specialty market by attempting to be the only provider of certain rare goods. *Eve Online* (CCP, 2009) adds in elements of territorial control, thus limiting access to raw materials. The economic structure of *Eve Online* is so complex that the developers have hired professional economists to help monitor the game.

Smyth (2007) states that MMORPGs help to promote problem-solving skills and critical thinking and further creativity at levels significantly higher than standard video games. Again this can be seen in the complex strategies, various types of interaction, and often-needed teamwork described above. Similarly, Steinkuehler and Duncan (2008) note that players in MMORPGs often must collaborate to solve complex problems within the virtual world, such as determining what combination of skills, proficiencies, equipment, and strategy are needed to overcome a particular challenge, which in turn promotes naturalistic learning and helps to develop cognitive skills. Furthermore, the wide range of interaction and task types found in most MMORPGs can appeal to a broad range of learning types in promoting the development of cognitive skills (Steinkuehler, 2005). In the above examples, we can see this as players in a given game can choose to tackle PvE content alone or with friends, attempt to craft in-game items or property, or even choose to risk their avatar's virtual goods and cash on the economic market. Finally, all MMORPGs to an extent employ a nonlinear model, allowing players to either follow guided missions and quests, or simply explore their virtual world as they wish, even simply sitting around talking to friends (Wei, 2007). Unlike most other video games, this flexibility permits players much more freedom of choice in their interaction and time spent in the game world, thus allowing players to choose which types of interaction they wish to engage in and when. This can also potentially help to facilitate cognitive skills (Steinkuehler, 2004).

With specific reference to motivations for learning delineated in O'Neil et al.'s model (2005), current research notes that much of the advantage of the use of video games in support of learning comes from the fact that they can provide students with high levels of intrinsic motivation and a sense of accomplishment from conquering various aspects of the game, whether it be solving puzzles, defeating antagonists, or constructing items in a simulation (Ebner & Holzinger, 2007; Pan & Sullivan, 2008). The constantly changing nature of MMORPGs (as they are modified by the companies who make them) supplies players with constant motivation to progress in the game, which can far outlast interest in a standard video game (Yang et al., 2007). Some games go so far (with varying results) as to change some of the very basic principles of the game itself, introducing new rules and styles of play. Occasionally, game developers can go overboard and end up alienating their player base. This was seen in Sony's handling of *Star Wars Galaxies Online* (Lucasfilm Ltd., 2009) "New Game Experience" or NGE, in which an entirely new game play model was introduced without listening to enough player feedback, resulting in the loss of most of the game's player base. This infamous and often referenced move in MMORPG history has made current developers cautious about focusing much more on player feedback regarding possible changes made.

Additionally, unlike most traditional games, there is no way to beat an MMORPG; rather, they provide multiple paths and constantly changing goals to be achieved. MMORPGs have higher levels of the ability to both tap and sustain player motivation and interest. This is perhaps most evident as noted by Yee (2005), who argues that MMORPGs are so successful in tapping into player motivation that a very small number of individuals can become addicted to them. While this is a negative factor from an educational standpoint, and it suggests some active monitoring of player/learner habits is necessary, it is also evidence of the power of MMORPGs to tap and keep player interest. Finally, the highly interactive nature of MMORPGs would suggest that more in-depth levels of instructor interaction are possible and needed when compared with the use of standard video games in instructional settings, in that instructors need to take an active role in guiding their students (Childress & Braswell, 2006).

As can be seen from the studies referenced above, MMORPGs combine elements of many different types of video games and give players potential exposure to many of the different cognitive benefits video games offer in a single medium. A common misconception in the use of video games in support of learning, however, is that teachers can let their students go unmonitored and the game will take care of the learning process. Though we have seen evidence of MMORPGs promoting naturalistic learning (Steinkuehler & Duncan, 2008), it should be stressed that whenever any video game is used in support of learning, the instructor needs to take an active role in the process.[1]

The Social Benefits of MMORPGs in Support of Learning

As the interaction which occurs in MMORPGs takes place primarily though IRC (Internet relay chat, or more commonly known as simply "chat") much of the research on IRC used in educational technology in general, and distance learning in particular, is relevant to MMORPGs. While overall research points to CMC-based education as being able to provide more support for collaborative projects and encourage students to be more outspoken and in-depth in their discussions (Gunawardena & McIsaac, 2003; Rovai, 2007), one hindrance of CMC-based instruction that distance education researchers have noted is that sometimes some users feel disconnected socially, lacking solidarity. Thus, distance education classes tend to have higher dropout rates when compared to traditional classes (Instructional Technology Council, 2008). Studies on MMORPGs, however, have found both psychological (Choi & Kim, 2004; Smyth, 2007; Yee 2005, 2006) and linguistic evidence (Anderson, 2007; Weininger & Shield, 2003) pointing towards high levels of solidarity and interaction in MMORPGs. It has been suggested that explicit socialization processes are embedded into many MMORPGs and that trust and responsibility are both fostered by them.

Jakobsson and Taylor (2003), in their study of *Everquest* (Sony Online Entertainment, 2009), found that by design many of the challenges in the game required social interaction. This can be seen in the examples presented in the cognitive section detailing raids and the barter needed to progress avatar trade skills. Additionally, groups of formal player organizations frequently called "guilds" (and to a lesser extent "kinships" or "clans") in which avatars belong to a recognizable, hierarchically structured group permit advanced levels of organization often needed to complete many of the cooperative challenges faced in an MMORPG. Chen et al. (2008) note guilds as being the most social organization in online game societies, in many ways mirroring a combination of both business and family online. A high percentage of MMORPG players report that joining guilds is either highly preferable or perceived as almost necessary for game progression; sometimes the importance of guilds approaches that of the game itself (Chen et al., 2008; Ducheneaut et al., 2006). Guilds also allow for stronger and deeper social relationships to develop between players, as players in guilds will regularly interact with their guild mates more so than with other avatars, specifically with regard to completion of collaborative goals. Furthermore, guilds will often form alliances or rivalries with other guilds, allowing players more varied social interaction.

In her study of MUDs, Turkle (1995) found that players' immersion factor (or the ability to suspend belief and become absorbed in what is happening on-screen) was closely tied to social bonds made in the game and in turn had a positive effect on motivation to play. Finally, while anecdotal evidence suggests video games on the whole may be more of a male-oriented interest, Yee (2006) found that roughly 43% of the MMORPG population he examined was female, and that most female players listed the deep social relationships formed in MMORPGs as one of their top motivations for continued play. This suggests that, compared with standard video games, MMORPGs may be more likely to be positively received by female players.

Yee (2005) also found that high levels of player solidarity are due to the fact that many of the in-game goals in MMORPGs are designed around cooperative and collaborative quests, in which players need to interact with each other and develop teamwork mechanics in order to be successful. This is confirmed in a corpus-based register comparison study by Anderson (2008), who found four of six linguistic features of interaction, as operationalized by Biber, Conrad, and Leech (1999), to be more frequent in MMORPG communication when compared with traditional IRC. Features representative of collaborative and cooperative interaction were found at particularly high levels, suggesting that MMORPGs not only have greater levels of interaction but features which, according to Gunawardena and McIsaac (2003), are important in distance education settings. Additionally, Griffiths, Davies, and Chappell (2004) surveyed MMORPG players finding that socialization was one of the most important factors in players' continued engagement in MMORPGs. Hussain and Griffiths (2008) added that female players in particular often logged on simply for the sake of socialization. All of these studies would suggest strong empirical support for high levels of social interaction being present in MMORPGs.

One arguable weakness of MMORPGs in support of learning with regard to both educational and social contexts, however, lies in the frequent use of synchronous over asynchronous CMC as a primary means of communication. Most of the interaction that occurs within MMORPGs is chat-based. However, most MMORPGs also have in-game mail systems similar to e-mail. Moreover, nearly every MMORPG also has out-of-game asynchronous discussion forums that are used by players and developers to discuss issues in the game and to socialize with each other. Steinkuehler and Duncan (2008) conducted an analysis of asynchronous MMORPG discussion forums and found that players who used these forums presented complex models in their discussion of game mechanics and strategies to apply to games. When presenting comments tied to a critique of game rules or changes, and of effective in-game performance, players were often expected to supply empirical and often quantitative data in combination with complex logical arguments much in the same way academic research papers are constructed. To support these discussions, a number of second-party database and data management home pages and programs are available. For example, one such Web site that is often used in conjunction with the game *The World of Warcraft* (Blizzard Entertainment Inc., 2009) is *WoW Web Stats* (often referred to as WWS by players). This program advertises itself as "a unique tool to enhance your experience in *The World of Warcraft*. With WWS, you generate and share reports of your raids, which include a tremendous amount of information and statistics" (WoW Web Stats, 2009). Players not only use information and statistics from program sources such as WWS in order to provide logical, data-backed critiques of the game and each other but also to analyze their own performance within the game. Again, with regard to naturalistic learning, findings by Steinkuehler and Duncan (2008) on the content of forum activity point to it being highly supportive of developing logical and scientific, cognitive, and group work skills. There is, however, no published research here with regard to using game-based asynchronous forums in conjunction with MMORPGs in classroom settings and the benefits and drawbacks of their reliance on synchronous vs. asynchronous communication as the primary method of communication.

The Psychological Benefits of MMORPGs in Support of Learning

MMORPGs are seen as being cognitively and psychologically productive in terms of both collaboration and interaction (Wagner, 2008; Yee, 2005). Furthermore, the social relationships players have in MMORPGs can be just as fulfilling and deep as in traditional relationships (Yee, 2006). Over half of the players surveyed by Yee also reported that their MMORPG friendships were comparable to or better than their material world friendships. Moreover, almost all players also felt a degree of attachment to their in-game personas, or avatars. Yee (2005, 2006) found that players noted that they enjoyed the creative aspects of modifying their avatar's initial appearance and subsequent customizations, with some players even going as far as inventing fictitious background stories for their avatars. Players also reported being invested emotionally and psychologically in what happened to their avatars. Thus, successes and failures as realized through the avatar can have a psychological impact on players and, because most MMORPGs are designed to reward players regularly, this could have potential effects on long-term motivation and esteem.

To date, a growing body of psychological literature has examined the use of avatars in virtual settings. Turkle's (1995) work found that player immersion and connection to their characters was often therapeutic in allowing players to relieve real-life stress by engaging in a MUD. With the introduction of visually observable avatars, however, players seem to have grown even more attached to their characters. Rehak (2003) lists different levels of connection between players and their avatars in video games, everything from conscious and internal role-playing of avatars to players seeing the avatar as a double or an actual representation of self. Players are heavily invested in their avatars because they interact with each other primarily through their avatars.

Avatars also offer the potential for therapeutic benefits as well as a means for heightened social interaction. Hussain and Griffiths (2008) explored gender-swapping in MMORPGs and found that 56% of players surveyed, both male and female, engaged in creation and play of avatars of the opposite gender. Players surveyed stated that they enjoyed virtual gender-swapping, as it gave them insight into how the other gender perceives, and more so, is perceived, in the world. Hussain and Griffiths (2008) suggest that the possible explanations include greater anonymity online, less importance on physical appearance (still with a focus on avatar appearance though), and the greater control gamers have over the time and pace of their interaction. Additionally, they suggest that more research is warranted into the psychological and social therapeutic benefits that avatar gender-swapping may have. This idea of avatars as a means of increased social interaction is supported by Svensson (2003), who anecdotally reported that the use of avatars served to encourage shy students to interact more, as they felt safe behind the anonymity of their avatars. Bryant (2006) also observed the high levels of linguistic interaction and negotiation in MMORPGs to be conducive of second language acquisition. He notes that social motivations for communication as well as the desire to progress within the game itself helped promote a feeling of accomplishment amongst students and a social and goal-oriented environment for the classroom.

Still perhaps the greatest power avatars have to support learning lies in their potential use as pedagogical agents. Baylor (2002, 2003) and Baylor and Kim (2006) have done extensive research supporting the uses and advantages of pedagogical agents in computer-based learning, as have others (Lester et al., 1997; Moreno, Meyer, Spires, & Lester, 2001; Shaw, Johnson, & Ganeshan, 1999). Agents are described as personified computer-based teaching applications (such as the famously annoying paperclip character that often popped up in older versions of Microsoft Windows offering help). Thus, one can see a definite connection between avatars and agents. Overall, the research here suggests that pedagogical agents help learners by stimulating social interaction and socially based cognition and motivation and allow for more naturalistic learning, making them an invaluable tool in computer-based educational technology. Baylor (2003) also found that multiple pedagogical agents focusing on distinctly different roles (e.g., expert, motivator) facilitated greater learning. Furthermore, Baylor and Kim (2006) note that one great advantage of

pedagogical agents is that they can be tailored to the needs of specific learners and learning environments. MMORPGs already have a number of computer-controlled (again called NPCs) agents which are used not only to focus players on in-game tasks but also to act as in-game guides to game mechanics (thus one will tend to find a large number of NPCs in the starting or tutorial zone of an MMORPG, with many, such as those in *Everquest 2* (Sony Online Entertainment, 2009) and *World of Warcraft* (Blizzard Entertainment Inc., 2009), being able to give limited answers to player questions). Additionally, player-controlled avatars theoretically possess abilities far beyond those of any preprogrammed pedagogical agent, because as human instructors are able to quickly adapt to the needs of learners individually as well as provide deeper elements of social interaction. Thus, MMORPGs are able to facilitate computer-based learning with the presence of a wide range of potential pedagogical agents and, with the addition of instructor-controlled avatars, support and go beyond the ability of current pedagogical agents, and researchers have begun to advocate for their use in games like MMORPGs (e.g., Van Eck, 2006).

The motivation and engagement of MMORPGs does not come without potential drawbacks. Smyth (2007) purports that some players, deemed predisposed to addiction, reported that MMORPGs interfered with their homework and social life schedules to an extent. While this might be said of any game genre or entertainment source, this may be particularly true of MMORPGs, given their persistence and lack of a predetermined end-goal state. When compared to control and standard video game groups, MMORPG players displayed no loss of academic performance, and Smyth (2007) also observed that the use of avatars allowed shy or socially inhibited students to improve their social skills significantly. While the potential for addiction is an important factor to consider with any educational application, in the popular press, there have been many warnings about addiction to computer games. Additionally, limited data suggest that, when users begin playing MMORPGs in excess, social anxiety in real-world relationships can increase; however, light to moderate use is implicative of only positive gains (Lo, Wang, & Fang, 2005). As was discussed in the section on cognition, there is a need here for instructors to be closely involved with students when using MMORPGs (as with any other computer-based learning application), both for guiding instruction and to make sure students are using applications properly. This noted, blogs and other social sites such as *MySpace* and *Facebook* have also been shown to have potentially addictive features, yet are commonly used in classrooms around the world (Smith, 2008). Similarly, concerning computer games and, in particular, MUDs, Wilson (1992) reports that multiple studies have found that very few individuals actually become addicted to MUDs or computer games and that most that do have other personal or psychological problems. Additionally, given the prevalent use of other Internet and CMC-based applications in the classroom and the common theme of a shared risk of addiction, instructors need not be overly cautious of MMORPGs specifically. Altogether,

psychological research suggests that the use of avatars and pedagogical agents in MMORPGs are responsible for increased levels of socialization and motivation in players and that there are many potential benefits of their use in the classroom.

Considering all of the above factors for the potential of MMORPGs to support learning, there is strong evidence for their use as an educational medium with benefits in cognitive, social, and psychological gains. Additionally, these features overlap to an extent, such as providing intrinsic motivation for players resulting from both psychological and social factors. A summary of the points discussed above can be seen in Table 1, wherein the potential benefits and drawbacks of the use of MMORPGs discussed in this section are noted.

Finally, as is true with nearly all educational technology applications, there is no single educational theory behind the use of MMORPGS in the facilitation of learning (Conole, 2008). Again, many of the advantages MMORPGs offer over traditional games lie in their inherent social networks and the benefit of providing players with multiple types of game–based interaction. MMORPGs can be readily adapted to fit any

Table 1. Advantages and limitations of the use of MMORPGS

Discipline	Advantages	Limitations
Cognitive	• Meets all four of O'Neil, Wainess, and Baker's (2005) educational game standards. • Promote critical thinking, creativity, and problem solving. • Inspire high levels of long-term motivation. • Conducive to nontraditional and naturalistic learning.	• Require higher levels of instructor interaction than traditional games used in instructional settings.
Social	• Stronger user solidarity and interaction compared with traditional CMC. • Focuses on collaborative and cooperative tasks and strengthens social bonds. • Embedded socialization networking.	• Most MMORPGs lack developed in-game asynchronous CMC (although possess outside of game forums).
Psychological	• Inspire motivation. • Help with social and emotional development skills. • Potentially therapeutic. • Use of pedagogical agents to facilitate computer-based learning. • Useful for providing "shy" students with a communication venue.	• Potentially addictive users with addict-prone personalities, although perhaps no more than other ed. tech mediums.

combination of learning theories; however, the responsibility in this case falls on the instructor to actively control which educational theories are used to support MMORPGs as a medium to scaffold and foster learning.

This section has proposed a conceptual model of MMORPGs in support of learning aimed at covering research from across multiple academic disciplines. In this model, emphasis is placed on the versatility of the medium in terms of types of interaction, the deep levels of socialization, and intrinsic motivation MMORPGs can offer learners. However, as previously mentioned, research into MMORPGs is still relatively new in the world of academia. In this next section, an overview of current research trends to date on MMORPGs in support of learning will be discussed followed by implications for future research.

CURRENT TRENDS IN MMORPG RESEARCH

It should first be noted that one overall problem currently is the lack of published research on MMORPGs as instructional mediums. This lack of research is further compounded by the small number of empirically based studies. A majority of the published research on MMORPGs falls into either loose theoretical work or anecdotal accounts of classroom use. While such reports can be useful for direct classroom implementation, there is a definite need for a higher level of scholarly examination. This current chapter has attempted to place emphasis on empirical work; however, it is somewhat limited by the current lack of quality empirical research directly on MMORPGs. Thus it has taken studies and theoretical concepts from multimedia learning, CMC, social relationships in virtual environments, online social behaviors, and traditional serious game research into consideration. Reasons for an overall lack of research on MMORPGs are conjectured as resulting from the relative newness of the medium as well as a

perceived social stigma in academia on the study of video games (Bonk & Dennon, 2005; de Freitas & Griffiths, 2007; Riegle & Matejka, 2006). Furthermore, Wagner (2008) notes that the initial cost of setting up MMORPG research may be a factor to consider in the lack of current empirical research. This cost stems from game purchase and subscription costs, as well as the need for computers or research subjects with computer and Internet access.

MMORPG Research in Education

As was presented in the last section of this chapter, focus has been placed primarily on techniques and methods for the integration and use of MMORPGs in classroom settings (Bonk & Dennen, 2005; de Freitas & Griffiths, 2007). Numerous studies have reported that students responded well to MMORPG-based lesson models (Bonk & Dennen, 2005; Cameron & Dwyer, 2005). Cognitive skill gains, exposure to various levels of interaction, and appeal to multiple learning styles have also been noted (Childress & Braswell, 2006; Dede, 1992; O'Neil et al., 2005; Riegle & Matejka, 2008; Steinkuehler & Duncan, 2008). There is, however, a lack of *longitudinal* studies present in this body of research. Most of the studies discussed above were limited in that they employed a one-shot design and examined the use of MMORPGs over a few lessons at most. Additionally, when examining the empirically based research, there is a large amount of qualitative research when compared with quantitative studies. More empirically based studies in education might be beneficial in that they could better contribute to data sets for potential meta-analyses. Finally, Castronova et al. (2009) offer an interesting model for using virtual worlds as evaluative instruments to replicate social science experiments. They stress that although full understandings of the surroundings and mediums for interaction in virtual worlds is necessary for researchers to grasp in order to make generalizable results, virtual worlds allow researchers to more accurately manipulate and observe variables as well as offer (in the form of motivation) the potential for greater participant retention in longitudinal studies. The guidelines proposed by Castronova et al. (2009) make an excellent case and foundation for researchers interested in using MMORPGs as a method for data collection.

MMORPGs Research in Psychology

In psychology, we have seen that studies have examined the ability of MMORPGs to motivate and tap the interests of players as well as develop social and emotional skills (Smyth, 2007; Schroeder, 2002; Wagner, 2008; Yee, 2005, 2006). Results point to MMORPGs as being valuable educational tools, specifically for traditionally shy or introverted students (Smyth, 2007; Svensson, 2003). Initial research into the psychological effects of MMORPGS focused on the fact that some players might run the risk of becoming overly immersed in the virtual worlds of MMORPGs and could face the possibility of becoming addicted. A large inquiry has been presented here and has presented various results ranging from negative aspects to suggesting that MMORPGs can provide positive influences such as support for depression or socially disadvantaged players (Lo et al., 2005; Morgan & Cotten, 2003: Peris et al., 2002). More recent trends have shifted toward examining more subtle psychological factors present in MMORPGs with particular attention to the use of avatars, representations of the virtual self, life in virtual space, and potential therapeutic uses of games (Eatough et al., 2006; Hussain & Griffiths, 2008). Most all studies in the realm of psychology on MMORPGs have stuck to traditional quantitative empirically based models. Similarly, a range of populations has been studied, from classroom-sized groups to thousands of players, providing both quality one-shot and longitudinal studies. These approaches make good models for new researchers in this area. Research methods in these studies seem to be primarily questionnaire-based, however, lacking in more neuropsychological and hard science data, which represent a significant opportunity for future research.

Sociology Research on MMORPGs

Sociology-based studies on MMORPGs have focused on an investigation into social relationships and behaviors in virtual environments. This work has been both theoretical and empirical in nature. Much of the debate in this research centers on comparison studies of how virtual relationships and behaviors compare to face-to-face social encounters and off-line society in general (Hussain & Griffiths, 2008; O'Brian & Levy, 2008). Recently, however, a 3-year longitudinal study employing over 60 terabytes of data from the most popular MMORPGs and researchers from four different universities found that online gaming communities are now so massive that they can be used to mirror traditional communities (Srivastava, Williams, Contractor, & Poole, 2009). This is to say that research models used in traditional sociological studies can be applied to MMORPG communities. The full impact of this major study on sociological research into MMORPGs has not yet been seen; potentially this could help promote an increase in the number of MMORPG-based studies, as sociological research models are directly applicable to massive virtual worlds. This field promises to be interesting to watch in the years to come.

ESL Research on MMORPGs

Finally, research based in ESL and applied linguistics have in part, as with education studies, provided anecdotal models for using MMORPGs in the classroom (Weininger & Shield, 2003) as well as listed their benefits to language learners (Bryant, 2008; Svennson, 2003). In my own research (Anderson, 2007) I have found significant linguistic evidence of high levels of interaction and solidarity in MMORPG players. Additionally, levels of interaction have been found to be higher for MMORPGs than for traditional CMC (Anderson, 2008). For the most part, however, research making use of linguistic methodologies and data is lacking, despite numerous linguistics studies based on traditional CMC. It is hoped that more researchers in the field of linguistics and applied linguistics will study the use of MMORPGs as language-learning tools.

FUTURE RESEARCH DIRECTIONS

As the body of MMORPG research continues to grow, the focus needs to shift from isolated reports and anecdotal classroom models to strong theoretical models, and more specifically toward providing a greater body of empirical research to support these models. The study of the use of MMORPGs occurs across multiple academic disciplines and the standards and traditions of research in those disciplines strongly influence the studies done (Bernard et al., 2004). Thus, to date, a large amount of empirical research on the subject of MMORPGs comes from psychology. Researchers such as Yee (2005, 2006) and Steinkuehler (2004, 2005; Steinkuehler & Duncan, 2008) have led the use of empirical techniques to operationalize and measure many of the theoretical models advanced by MMORPG theorists. More empirical studies of the quality of these two researchers are needed to help provide support for the use and study of MMORPGs in educational contexts. Additionally, as research on MMORPGs is scattered across multiple disciplines and journals, the study of MMORPGs would benefit from a consolidated research journal.

Different academic disciplines need to play on their own strengths of their research traditions and methods while being aware of MMORPG research in other fields. Successful researchers here need to balance current research trends in their own academic discipline while actively seeking out research from other disciplines. This is especially true in MMORPG research, as there is still only a limited amount of peer-reviewed published research on the topic. Further empirical research here is also needed to sort out the specifics of how closely MMORPGs are linked with traditional games and educational technology models, and what implications and levels of transfer studies in these fields have on MMORPG research.

One area in which empirical research is specifically lacking is in studying the use of MMORPGs in classroom settings. Most classroom-based research to date on MMORPGs has consisted of anecdotal evidence from classroom implementation. Moreover, most of the empirical research studies examined in this chapter have focused on populations of existing players in MMORPGs. There is a definitive need for more research using subjects required to use MMORPGs for classes as opposed to existing MMORPG players. Of the studies surveyed here, only Smyth (2007) collected empirical data from students using a MMORPG in a classroom setting. Smyth determined that subjects who had encountered MMORPGs for the first time while in an instructional setting found the educational use of MMORPGs enjoyable and that roughly 28% of subjects continued to play MMORPGs even after the required play time had elapsed (nearly double that of traditional games used in classroom settings). It is believed that more classroom-based empirical research on the use of MMORPGs will serve to further confirm current theoretical and conceptual models and in turn promote continued research into using MMORPGs in educational settings. One aspect in particular here which would help provide insight into classroom-based learning would be further exploration of Baylor's (2002, 2003) work on pedagogical agents and how computer-controlled agents with the support of instructor-controlled avatars could better facilitate computer-based learning in MMORPGs.

Finally, this chapter has attempted to present the many complex reasons why currently available MMORPGs can easily be adapted to instruction and aid in learning. Although no MMORPGs specifically targeted at learning have been released as yet, Castronova et al. (2009) predict that soon we will see such products and that there is a market waiting for educationally focused MMORPGs, as the same has already proven true for MUDs (Sonstroem, 2006). Another key and much more immediate element of interest to serious game developers is that many popular MMORPGs openly allow for and even encourage player-created modifications (mods). This allows serious game developers the chance to create user interfaces and game mods that can focus on particular pedagogies, such as increasing in-game asynchronous CMC. Limited only by EULAs (*End-User License Agreements*) and terms of use, there is tremendous potential for modifying current MMORPGs to meet the specific needs of a group of students or even for using currently available free mods to aid instruction. For instance, the home page Curse.com offers thousands of readily available modifications, such as those to track trends of the in-game auction (akin to a virtual eBay), which could be used to help teach economic principles. Even more, some MMORPGs such as the superhero-themed *City of Heroes/Villains* (NCsoft, 2009) and the sandbox game *Saga of Ryzom* (Neverax, 2009) have recently given players the ability to actually modify content to the virtual world in the form of creating new virtual locales as well as designing new quests and NPCs. More so than simple interface modding, the ability to make permanent changes to the content of an MMORPG allows would-be developers (even those with limited tech skills) to more accurately shape and develop aspects of currently released MMORPGs for specific pedagogical agendas. This is one area where even a single serious game developer and programmer can (relatively) easily produce quality and accessible content.

CONCLUSION

This paper has attempted to create an overview of the dynamics and importance of MMORPGs as an instructional medium. This was achieved by creating and supporting a definition of the medium and then developing a conceptual framework for the use of MMORPGs in support of learning. When possible, this was done with direct empirical and theoretical evidence from studies to date. The proposed definition argues that MMORPGs are a melding of standard video games (with an emphasis on CRPGs) and CMC-based forms of social interaction. MMORPGs also offer players a wide range of game-based interaction and goal types that exceed elements found in any single type of video game. In support of learning and a conceptual model, it was argued that MMORPGs have much to offer potential learners and instructors in aiding cognition, motivation, and sociopsychological skills and issues. MMORPGs have also been shown to support naturalistic learning and problem-solving skills while providing entertainment and motivation for players/learners. Furthermore, as MMORPGs are highly social in nature and encourage collaborative play, they promote good communication skills and require well-thought-out coordinated strategies in order for players to be successful. Ultimately, MMORPGs have the potential to serve as an excellent medium for educational purposes. The number of instructors implementing MMORPGs into their classrooms is ever-increasing, as is the popularity of MMORPGs in everyday life. Much as is the case with all educational technology, effectively applying MMORPGs to pedagogical design requires that teachers understand the complex workings and interactions within the games.

Current research tells us that MMORPGs excel in tapping into player interests and providing a wide variety of interaction and skill types when examined through theoretical models concerning the use of games for education. MMORPGs also appear to be beneficial in aiding online social presence and motivation issues frequently reported in distance education instruction. Finally, psychological research suggests that in addition to cognitive and social skills, MMORPGS can also help in a therapeutic manner with emotional skills. MMORPGs appear to have the potential to be a useful tool in education, compounded by the growing popularity of the medium in both classroom and home settings. What is currently needed the most is more quality empirical research to test the many theoretical claims made by current MMORPG studies.

Below is a list of recommended readings in MMORPG research. These range from more generally accessible books such as Kelly (2004), Meadows (2008), Bartle (2003), and Taylor (2006) to collections of research, including Schroeder (2007) and Castronova (2005), to theoretical and anecdotal-based reports of MMORPG usage in the classroom, Childress & Braswell (2006), Svensson (2003), Jakobsson and Taylor (2003), and key empirical articles (chosen for both their ease of readability and breadth of coverage), Yee (2006), Cameron & Dwyer (2005), Schrader & McCreery (2007). However, as the medium truly needs to be experienced to be fully understood, it is recommended that readers investigate MMORPG interactions and culture first hand. Most MMORPGs offer free trials to potential players, allowing those interested to try out the virtual worlds for a week or so at no cost. This chapter would recommend a number of MMORPGs, ranging from the very popular *World of Warcraft* (Blizzard Entertainment Inc., 2009), to the expansive and detailed world of *Everquest 2* (Sony Online Entertainment, 2009), as well as the original *Everquest* (Sony Online Entertainment, 2009), which continues to hold onto a player base after 12 years and offers players a good glimpse of a classic MMORPG world. Additionally, the complex virtual economy and society of the science fiction sandbox game *Eve Online* (CCP, 2009) offers players an interesting look at a deeply immersive and intricate virtual world. Video games have become an integral

part of modern life, and with added elements of complex social networking, MMORPGs take this to the next level. As technology progresses, the popularity of the medium grows, and as player expectations increase, the future of MMORPGs promises to be interesting and worthy of detailed study and application to learning environments.

REFERENCES

Anderson, B. (2007). *The role of place deixis in massive multiplayer online games*. Retrieved from http://pine.ucc.nau.edu/boa/mmorpgdeixis/

Anderson, B. (2008). *Operationalizing online interaction in distance education: A register comparison of IRC and MMORPG corpora*. Retrieved from http://pine.ucc.nau.edu/boa/mmoircinteraction/

Au, J. (2007). *Lord of the Rings online: MMORPG meets Web 2.0*. Retrieved from http://gigaom.com/2007/10/25/lord-of-the-rings-online-mmorpg-meets-web-20/

Barton, M. (2007). *The history of computer role playing games: Parts I, II and III*. Retrieved from http://www.gamasutra.com/features/20070223b/barton_01.shtml

Baylor, A. L. (2002). Agent-based learning environments for investigating teaching and learning. *Journal of Educational Computing Research*, *26*(3), 249–270. doi:10.2190/PH2K-6P09-K8EC-KRDK

Baylor, A. L. (2003). *Evidence That Multiple Agents Facilitate Greater Learning*. Paper presented at the AI-ED. Sydney, Australia.

Baylor, A. L., & Kim, Y. (2006). A social-cognitive framework for pedagogical agents as learning companions. *Educational Technology Research and Development*, *54*(6), 569–596. doi:10.1007/s11423-006-0637-3

Bernard, R. M., Abrami, P. C., Lou, Y., Borokhovski, E., Wade, A., Wozney, L., & Wallet, P. (2004). How does distance education compare with classroom instruction? A meta-analysis of the empirical literature. *Review of Educational Research, 74*(3), 379–439. doi:10.3102/00346543074003379

Biber, D., Conrad, S., & Leech, G. (1999). *The Longman grammar of spoken and written English.* Essex, UK: Longman.

Blizzard Entertainment Inc. (2009). *World of Warcraft.* [Online game].

Bonk, C., & Dennen, V. (2005). *Massive multiplayer online gaming: A research framework for military training and education* (Technical Report No. 2005-1). Washington, DC: U.S. Department of Defense (DUSD/R), Advanced Distributed Learning (ADL) Initiative. Retrieved from http://mypage.iu.edu/cjbonk/GameReport_Bonk_final.pdf

Bryant, T. (2008). Using *World of Warcraft* and other MMORPGs to foster a targeted, social, and cooperative approach toward language learning. *Academic Commons, 12*(4), 23–35.

Cameron, B., & Dwyer, F. (2005). The effect of online gaming, cognition and feedback type in facilitating delayed achievement of different learning objectives. *Journal of Interactive Learning Research, 16*(3), 243–358.

Castronova, E., Bell, M., Cornell, R., Cummings, J., Falk, M., & Ross, T. (2009). Synthetic worlds as experimental instruments. In Wolf, M., & Perron, B. (Eds.), *The video game theory reader 2.* New York: Routledge.

CCP. (2009). *EVE Online* [Online game]. Winch Gate Property Limited.

Chen, C., Sun, C., & Hsieh, J. (2008). Player guild dynamics and evolution in massively multiplayer online games. *Cyberpsychology & Behavior, 11*(3), 293–301. doi:10.1089/cpb.2007.0066

Childress, M., & Braswell, R. (2006). Using massively multiplayer online role-playing games for online learning. *Distance Education, 27*(2), 187–196. doi:10.1080/01587910600789522

Choi, D., & Kim, J. (2004). Why people continue to play online games: In search of critical design factors to increase customer loyalty to online contents. *Cyberpsychology & Behavior, 7*(1), 11–24. doi:10.1089/109493104322820066

Conole, G. (2008). New schemas for mapping pedagogies and technologies. *Ariadine, 56.*

de Freitas, S., & Griffiths, M. (2007). Online gaming as an educational tool in learning and training. *British Journal of Educational Technology, 38*(3), 535–537. doi:10.1111/j.1467-8535.2007.00720.x

Dede, C. J. (1992). The future of multimedia: Bridging to virtual worlds. Educational Technology. *British Journal of Educational Technology, 38*(3), 535–537.

Ducheneaut, N., Yee, N., Nickell, E., & Moore, R. (2006). Building an MMO with mass appeal: A look at gameplay in *World of Warcraft. Games and Culture, 1,* 281–317. doi:10.1177/1555412006292613

Eatough, V., Davies, M. N. O., Griffiths, M. D., & Chappell, D. (2006). *Everquest*—It's just a computer game right? An interpretative phenomenological analysis of online gaming addiction. *International Journal of Mental Health and Addiction,* 4205–4216.

Ebner, M., & Holzinger, A. (2007). Successful implementation of user-centered game based learning in higher education: An example from civil engineering. *Computers & Education, 49*(3), 873–890. doi:10.1016/j.compedu.2005.11.026

Griffiths, M., Davies, N., & Chappell, D. (2004). Online computer gaming: A comparison of adolescent and adult gamers. *Journal of Adolescence, 27*, 87–96. doi:10.1016/j.adolescence.2003.10.007

Gunawardena, L., & McIsaac, M. (2003). Theory of distance education. In Jonassen, D. H. (Ed.), *Handbook of research for educational communications and technology*. New York: Simon and Schuster Macmillan.

Hill, M. (2005). *The RPG evolution*. Retrieved from http://iml.jou.ufl.edu/projects/Spring05/Hill/

Hussain, Z., & Griffiths, M. D. (2008). Gender swapping and socializing in cyberspace: An exploratory study. *Cyberpsychology & Behavior, 11*(1), 47–53. doi:10.1089/cpb.2007.0020

Instructional Technology Council. (2008). *2007 Distance education survey results* [report]. Retrieved from http://4.79.18.250/file.php?file=/1/ITCAnnualSurveyMarch2008.pdf

Jakobsson, M., & Taylor, T. (2003). *The Sopranos meets EverQuest: Social networking in massively multiplayer online games*. Melbourne International Digital Arts and Culture Conference (Melbourne-DAC). Retrieved from http://hypertext.rmit.edu.au/dac/papers/Jakobsson.pdf

Kim, J. (2008). *Narrative or tabletop RPGs*. Retrieved from http://www.darkshire.net/~jhkim/rpg/whatis/tabletop.html

Lester, J. C., Converse, S. A., Kahler, S. E., Barlow, S. T., Stone, B. A., & Bhoga, R. S. (1997). The persona effect: Affective impact of animated pedagogical agents. In *Proceedings of 1997 Conference on Human Factors in Computing Systems*. Retrieved from http://www.acm.org/sigchi/chi97/proceedings/paper/jl.htm

Lo, S., Wang, C., & Fang, W. (2005). Physical Interpersonal Relationships and Social Anxiety among Online Game Players. *Cyberpsychology & Behavior, 8*(1), 15–20. doi:10.1089/cpb.2005.8.15

Lucasfilm Ltd. (2009). *Star Wars Galaxies* [Online game]. Sony Online Entertainment.

MMOG chart.com. (n.d.). Retrieved from http://MMOGchart.com/

MMORPG. com. (n.d.). Retrieved from http://mmorpg.com/gamelist.cfm

Moreno, R., Mayer, R. E., Spires, H. A., & Lester, J. C. (2001). The case for social agency in computer-based teaching: Do students learn more deeply when they interact with animated pedagogical agents? *Cognition and Instruction, 19*, 177–213. doi:10.1207/S1532690XCI1902_02

Morgan, C., & Cotten, S. R. (2003). The relationship between Internet activities and depressive symptoms in a sample of college freshmen. *Cyberpsychology & Behavior, 6*, 133–143. doi:10.1089/109493103321640329

Mythic Entertainment. (2009). *Ultima Online* [Online game]. Electronic Arts Inc.

Mythic Entertainment. (2009). *Warhammer Online: Age of Reckoning* [Online game]. Electronic Arts Inc.

NCsoft. (2009). *City of Heroes*. [Computer game].

Neverax. (2009). *Saga of Ryzom*. [Computer game]. Winch Gate Property Limited.

O'Brian, M., & Levy, R. (2008). Exploration through virtual reality: Encounters with the target culture. *Canadian Modern Language Review, 64*(4), 663–687. doi:10.3138/cmlr.64.4.663

O'Neil, H. F., Wainess, R., & Baker, E. L. (2005). Classification of learning outcomes: Evidence from the computer games literature. *Curriculum Journal, 16*(4), 455–474. doi:10.1080/09585170500384529

Pan, C., & Sullivan, M. (2008). Game-based learning: Guidelines, challenges, recommendations. Presented at annual AETC Convention, October, 2008, Orlando, Florida.

Peris, R., Gimeno, M. A., Ibáñez, I., Ortel, G., Peris, R., Pinazo, D., & Sanchiz, M. (2002). Online chat rooms: Virtual spaces of interaction for socially oriented people. *Cyberpsychology & Behavior, 5,* 43–51. doi:10.1089/109493102753685872

Pivec, M. (2007). Play and learn: Potentials of game-based learning. *British Journal of Educational Technology, 38*(3), 387–393. doi:10.1111/j.1467-8535.2007.00722.x

Rehak, B. (2003). Playing at being: Psychoanalysis and the avatar. In Wolf, M., & Perron, B. (Eds.), *The video game theory reader.* London: Routledge.

Riegle, R., & Matejka, W. (2006). *Dying to learn: Instructional design and MMORPGs.* 21st Annual Conference on Distance Teaching and Learning. Retrieved from http://people.coe.ilstu.edu/rpriegle/mmorpg/index.htm

Rilstone, A. (1994). Role playing games: An overview. *Inter*Action, 1.* Retrieved from http://www.rpg.net/oracle/essays/rpgoverview.html

Rovai, A. P. (2007). Facilitating online discussions effectively. *The Internet and Higher Education, 10*(1), 77–88. doi:10.1016/j.iheduc.2006.10.001

Schrader, P., & McCreery, M. (2007). The acquisition of skill and expertise in massively multiplayer online games. *Educational Technology Research and Development, 56*(5), 557–574. doi:10.1007/s11423-007-9055-4

Schroeder, R. (Ed.). (2002). *The social life of avatars: Presence and interaction in shared virtual environments.* London: Springer-Verlag.

Shaw, E., Johnson, W. L., & Ganeshan, R. (1999). *Pedagogical agents on the Web.* Retrieved from http://www.isi.edu/isd/ADE/papers/agents99/agents99.htm

Sigil. (2009). *Vanguard Saga of Heroes.* [Computer game]. Sony Online Entertainment.

Smith, J. (2008). Facebook to blame for friendship addiction. *Therapy Today, 19*(9), 10–11.

Smyth, P. (2007). Beyond self-selection in video game play: An experimental examination of the consequences of massively multiplayer online role-playing game play. *Cyberpsychology & Behavior, 10*(7), 32–39.

Sonstroem, E. (2006). Do you really want a revolution? Cybertheory meets real-life pedagogical practice in Franken MOO and the conventional literature classroom. *College Literature, 33*(3), 148–170. doi:10.1353/lit.2006.0044

Sony Online Entertainment. (2009). *Everquest.* [Computer game].

Sony Online Entertainment. (2009). *Everquest 2.* [Computer game].

Srivastava, J., Williams, D., Contractor, N., & Poole, S. (2009, February 12-16 22). *The Virtual World Exploratorium Project.* American Association for the Advancement of Science (AAAS) Conference, Chicago, Illinois.

Steinkuehler, C. (2004) Learning in massively multiplayer online games. In Y. Kafai, W. Sandoval, N. Enyedy, A. Nixon, & F. Herrera (Eds.), *Proceedings of the sixth ICLS.* Mahwah, NJ: Erlbaum, 521–528.

Steinkuehler, C. (2005). *Cognition and learning in massively multiplayer online games: A critical approach.* (Unpublished dissertation.) University of Wisconsin, Madison WI.

Steinkuehler, C., & Duncan, S. (2008). Scientific habits of mind in virtual worlds. *Journal of Science Education and Technology, 17*(6), 530–543. doi:10.1007/s10956-008-9120-8

Svensson, P. (2003). Virtual worlds as arenas for language learning. *Language learning online: Towards best practice, 10*(1), 123–142.

The Longman Dictionary of Contemporary English Online. (n.d.). Retrieved from http://www.ldoceonline.com/

Turkle, S. (1995). *Life on the screen: Identity in the age of the Internet.* New York: Simon & Schuster.

Van Eck, R. (2006). Building intelligent learning games. In Gibson, D., Aldrich, C., & Prensky, M. (Eds.), *Games and simulations in online learning: Research & development frameworks.* Hershey, PA: Idea Group.

Wagner, M. (2008). *Massively multiplayer online role-playing games as constructivist learning environments in K-12 education: A Delphi study* (Doctoral thesis.) Retrieved from http://edtechlife.com/?page_id=2008

Wauters, R. (2008, October 29). *World of Warcraft* to surpass 11 million subscribers. *New York Times.*

Waxman, C., Lin, M., & Michko, G. (2003). *A meta-analysis of the effectiveness of teaching and learning with technology on student outcomes.* Naperville, IL: Learning Point Associates.

Wei, J. (2006). The role of everyday users in MMORPGs. *Driftreality.* Retrieved on August 28, 2007, from http://www.driftreality.com/london/mmorpgs.users.pdf

Weininger, M., & Shield, L. (2003). Promoting oral production in a written channel: An investigation of learner language MOO. *Computer Assisted Language Learning, 16*(4), 329–349. doi:10.1076/call.16.4.329.23414

Wilson, D. (1992). Computer games: Academic obstacle or free-speech? *The Chronicle of Higher Education,* (November): 18.

WoW Web Stats. (n.d.). Retrieved February 20, 2009, from http://wowwebstats.com/

Yang, H., Wu, C., & Wang, K. (2007). An empirical analysis of online game service satisfaction and loyality. *Expert Systems with Applications, 36*(2), 1816–1825. doi:10.1016/j.eswa.2007.12.005

Yee, N. (2005). The psychology of MMORPGs: Emotional investment, motivations, relationships, and problematic usage. In Schroeder, R., & Axelsson, A. (Eds.), *Social life of avatars II.* London: Springer-Verlag.

Yee, N. (2006). The demographics, motivations and derived experiences of users of massively-multiuser online graphical environments. *Presence (Cambridge, Mass.),* 309–329. doi:10.1162/pres.15.3.309

ENDNOTE

[1] On a side note and quite interestingly, in serious gaming research there is a decided gap in empirical studies which examine the role of self-learning and games. This is one aspect in which further research is needed and that the field of serious game study as a whole would benefit from.

APPENDIX: ADDITIONAL READINGS

"Must-Reads" for this Topic

Bartle, R. (2003). *Designing virtual worlds*. Indianapolis, IN: New Riders Games.

Cameron, B., & Dwyer, F. (2005). The effect of online gaming, cognition and feedback type in facilitating delayed achievement of different learning objectives. *Journal of Interactive Learning Research, 16*(3), 243–358.

Castronova, E. (2005). *Synthetic worlds: The business and culture of online games*. Chicago, IL: University of Chicago Press.

Childress, M., & Braswell, R. (2006). Using massively multiplayer online role-playing games for online learning. *Distance Education, 27*(2), 187–196

Jakobsson, M., & Taylor, T. (2003). *The* Sopranos *meets* EverQuest*: Social networking in massively multiplayer online games*. Presented at the Melbourne International Digital Arts and Culture Conference. Retrieved from http://hypertext.rmit.edu.au/dac/papers/Jakobsson.pdf

Kelly, R. V. (2004). *Massively multiplayer online role-playing games: The people, the addiction and the playing experience*. Jefferson, NC: McFarland & Company.

Meadows, M. S. (2008). *I, avatar: The culture and consequences of having a second life* (New Riders). Indianapolis, IN: New Riders Press.

Schrader, P., & McCreery, M. (2007). The acquisition of skill and expertise in massively multiplayer online games. *Educational Technology Research and Development, 56*(5), 557–574.

Schroeder, R. (Ed.). (2002). *The social life of avatars: Presence and interaction in shared virtual environments*. London: Springer-Verlag.

Svensson, P. (2003). Virtual worlds as arenas for language learning. *Language Learning Online: Towards Best Practice, 10*(1), 123–142.

Taylor, T. L. (2006). *Play between worlds: Exploring online game culture*. Cambridge, MA: The MIT Press.

Yee, N. (2006). The demographics, motivations and derived experiences of users of massively-multiuser online graphical environments. *PRESENCE: Teleoperators and Virtual Environments*, 309–329.

Top Texts for Interdisciplinary Studies of Serious Games

Alessi, S., & Trollip, S. (2001). *Multimedia for learning: Methods and development* (3rd ed.). Needham Heights, MA: Allyn and Bacon.

Gee, J. (2007). *Good video games and good learning: Collected essays on video games, learning and literacy* (New Literacies and Digital Epistemologies). New York: Peter Lang Pub Inc.

Gee, J. (2007). *What video games have to teach us about learning and literacy* (2nd ed.). New York: Palgrave Macmillan.

Green, S., & Bavelier, D. (2006). The cognitive neuroscience of video games. In P. Messaris & L. Humphreys (Eds.), *Digital media: Transformations in human communication*. New York: Peter Lang.

Lee, D., & Larose, R. (2007). A Socio-cognitive model of game usage. *Journal of Broadcasting and Electronic Media*, 632–647.

Mayo, M. J. (2009). Video games: A route to large-scale stem education? *Science, 323*(5910), 79–82.

Michael, D., & Chen, S. (2005). *Serious games: Games that educate, train, and inform.* Florence, KY: Course Technology PTR.

Raessens, J., & Goldstein, J. (2005). *Handbook of computer game studies.* Cambridge, MA: The MIT Press.

Rice, J. (2007). Assessing higher order thinking in video games. *Journal of Technology and Teacher Education, 15*(1), 87–100.

Wolf, M., & Perron, B. (2003). *The video game theory reader.* London: Routledge.

Section 2
New Theories and Models

Chapter 4
Elemental Learning and the Pyramid of Fidelity

J. V. Dempsey
University of South Alabama, USA

ABSTRACT

One of the emerging issues for educators who recognize the importance of digital games and virtual worlds is fidelity to learning outcomes, both intentional and incidental. In this chapter, from the perspective of an educator, the author introduces an integrated framework that emphasizes elemental learning. The model, based on learning analysis and direct measurement of learning is iterative, as opposed to a front-end-only approach, and includes five major cognitive learning outcomes: actual elements, simulated elements, procedural understanding, conceptual understanding, and related knowledge. For each of the learning outcomes, the author provides design propositions and an example.

INTRODUCTION

It is useful to look at digital games and virtual world communities as allowing individuals to have a goal-directed embodied experience (Gee, 2008) and define learning progress along a "trajectory of experience" (Greeno, 1997). How the learning experience is best aided has been argued for at least a century along a loose continuum with one end situated, beginning perhaps with Thorndike's specific transfer theory of identical elements (Thorndike & Woodworth, 1901), and the other end

of the continuum supporting the transfer of general skills and principles, characterized by Gestalt psychologists such as Wertheimer (1945) and Katona (1940). There is certainly merit in both positions and the dichotomy has been well explored (e.g., by De Corte, 1999).

Amid all these theories and arguments come the practical considerations of educators who must design learning experiences that result in learning outcomes, both intentional and incidental. The traditional approach to doing that is what instructional designers refer to as analysis of learning outcomes using taxonomies. There are many learning taxonomies—notably, Anderson et al. (2001), Bloom

DOI: 10.4018/978-1-61520-717-6.ch004

(1956), and Gagné (1985)—but most educators simply do not overtly consider them in the design of a learning environment, whether that be a serious game or a 3-hour online workshop.

One alternative to using taxonomies can be found in how we consider our outcomes in a more general sense—an integrated framework. By this I mean something more in the nature of a folk taxonomy (no relation to folksonomy tags), like one used in an indigenous culture to classify plants or even ceramics. A folk taxonomy is used as "a taxonomic hierarchy built on a core of naturally useful distinctions" (Hunn, 1982, p. 833).

The *integrated framework* in this chapter consists of a hierarchy of elemental and synthetic learning outcomes. It is less formal than a specialized educational taxonomy but potentially useful for conducting a naturally occurring iterative process of learning analysis. This framework is not specific to the design or analysis of serious games or virtual worlds, but there may be some utility in employing the approach in designing or understanding these learning experiences. Although the framework is intentionally less specific than a learning taxonomy, it lies somewhere along the situated side of the transfer continuum largely because of its emphasis on the elemental learning outcomes described below.

LEARNING OUTCOMES AND FIDELITY

Learning taxonomies such as the classics of Bloom (1956) and Gagné (1985) are important because they give us a structure for learning analysis, i.e., figuring out the rational intended learning outcomes in a particular situation or for a particular learning process. There are many other versions of learning taxonomies useful in specific situations for analyzing learning outcomes. We might want to conduct learning analysis for assessment purposes or to plan or just understand learning. Because learning outcomes are essentially a way

to analyze content, it really does not matter how an individual acquires content or, in the case of intentional learning, how the content is taught. Additionally, taxonomies are important to identify the nature of incidental, or unintended, learning outcomes. Likewise, taxonomies can be very useful in the assessment of learning outcomes. Without defining learning outcomes, it is a difficult task to accurately assess for either formative or summative purposes. As S. J. Gould (1981) famously said, "Taxonomy is always a contentious issue because the world does not come to us in neat little packages" (p. 158). Even so, there is a common sense aspect to using learning taxonomies. Human beings are born classifiers. It helps us think through problems. It helps us analyze content. It helps us understand what content is learned.

Like all conceptual schemes of representation, learning taxonomies are mental representations that for one reason or another are socially agreed upon or at least understood so that they can be used to communicate. Many, such as the Linnaean taxonomy used in biology are hierarchical. The classification of outcomes of learning taxonomies can include simple discriminations, objects, parts of motor skills, events, "isms" of all sorts, classes of processes, principles, actions, attitudes, and situations. The simplest learning taxonomy commonly in use may be the somewhat overly simplified "KSAs" (knowledge, skills, and attitudes). There are a number of more comprehensive and well-established learning taxonomies. In instructional design, the more commonly referenced (and venerable) learning taxonomies would include Bloom's taxonomy of the cognitive domain (Bloom, 1956), the first of three handbooks of educational objectives, and Gagné's taxonomy (Gagné, 1985), which was first developed in the 1960s, as well as the more recent revisions such as those by Anderson et al. (2001), Krathwohl (2002), and Marzano (2001). These taxonomies can be viewed as somewhat hierarchical with rational and conceptually understandable components.

So, if classifying learning outcomes by using learning taxonomies helps, why don't we use taxonomies more often? Simply put, they are clunky and sometimes even misleading. Sophisticated approaches to analyzing learning outcomes are very useful for artificial intelligence learning applications, adaptive computer-based testing, and expert systems-type wizards. Yet, there is limited adoption by practitioners developing digital games or virtual worlds. Learning analysis, if it takes place at all, is more likely to be a process of intuition or trial and error.

Rethinking Learning Analysis

Analysis and design of meaningful learning and assessment can be considered both elemental and synthetic. Elemental learning outcomes are the constituent components of learning. These refer to the actual, real tasks in an actual or close proximate environment in which the learning outcomes will be used. Elemental learning outcomes are context- and content-specific but may also contribute greatly to learning similar elemental outcomes by virtue of the learner's enhanced experiential schema. They are situational. They are real or as "almost real" as possible. They are, for example, steering a ship's course on the ship or via a simulation. They go beyond, but are dependent on, the synthetic foundations of knowledge, skills, or attitudes. In contrast, synthetic learning outcomes are the cognitive learning outcomes necessary to support elemental learning. Synthetic here refers to forming something new (elemental) by combining other, usually decontextualized, outcomes. These are the traditional learning outcomes. In taxonomies such as Bloom's (1956) or Gagné's (1985), these are traditionally believed to be hierarchical, i.e., learning rules requires learning concepts, some basic knowledge is required, and so forth. Synthetic learning outcomes are less context-specific, and the learner's experience is often less important in acquiring these outcomes.

Consequently, one approach to learning analysis and design would be to embody analysis only on elemental (real-life or simulating real-life) outcomes and, when these are identified, look for those synthetic outcomes that support their learning. Throughout this paper, I will refer to this as *meaningful* learning (Wenger, 1998). Learning strategies that support these outcomes in a digital game or virtual world might include some type of apprenticeship with a person or an avatar. A simulation could include an embodied experience such as suggested by Gee's (2007) Situated Meaning Principle. This conceptualization can lead us to a simpler, more direct framework useful for assessment and the design of intentional and unintentional learning.

Fidelity of Design: Elemental and Synthetic Learning Outcomes

Fidelity of learning design is the point of learning analysis *and* learning assessment. For example, the ultimate goal of a digital game or virtual world may be to produce competent electronic technicians to repair communication equipment aboard ships. A course or module of that curriculum could be aimed at trainees' ability to apply Ohm's law to DC circuitry. Another module might be aimed at troubleshooting actual communications equipment. In most electronics training approaches, the first module would be assessed (and taught) using abstract formulae or, at best, circuitry diagrams. This is a synthetic learning environment, because by teaching and measuring only the lower-level formulae and diagrams without the troubleshooting component, we decontextualized the real "on-the-job" environment. The "on-the-job" environment requires technicians to incorporate Ohm's law and knowledge of DC circuitry into troubleshooting real electronics equipment. This is true fidelity to the ultimate transfer task. This is an elemental learning environment. A greater emphasis on learning and assessing learning at the stage of actual elements holds the most promise for real fidelity and transfer of learning, especially in training environments. Analyzing learning should reflect that. If there are voids below elemental learning, their need will become obvious in practice.

I propose a personal framework that consists of elemental learning (actual and simulated elements) and synthetic learning outcomes (usually decontextualized procedures, concepts, and knowledge). In other words, actual and simulated elements involve (assessing or learning) the real-life task or a simulation of that task. Synthetic learning outcomes do not.

How does the framework connect to serious games and virtual learning environments (VLEs)? First of all, most of these environments are intended to support learning and/or the motivation to learn (Clark, 2007). As I discussed, there is a dichotomous support by educators for situated versus generalized cognition. Even so, few would deny that concentrating on learning real-life or simulated (elemental) tasks helps both learners and designers give attention to acquiring necessary and relevant schemata. That was a harder thing to do not long ago. There were some digital games, like *Oregon Trail*, that went slightly beyond the norm. Many early educational drill-and-kill digital games (e.g., *Math Blaster*), however, have had commercial success but were decontextualized and showed a lack of creativity (Rice, 2007). These games were intended to build basic prerequisite skills, and essentially, they can be considered the electronic equivalent of the worksheets that have been used in the classroom for many years. So, they "fit" into the comfortable, vacant model of classroom babysitting. They were not really bad, but they were using an outdated and disconnected approach toward learning.

As serious games and virtual worlds become more sophisticated, educators are able to implement digital games and virtual worlds that allow for the accommodation of ill-defined learning tasks (Piaget, 1985). Games and virtual worlds allow

for affordances (Gibson, 1977) with which the learner can interact in ways that reciprocate with the environment as a version of the real world, even if that world is simulated in an otherworldly way. Designing for elemental learning outcomes aids that reciprocal interaction.

A Pyramid of Learning Fidelity

Figure 1 presents a visual metaphor for how elemental and synthetic outcomes are interrelated. The top levels of the pyramid concern elemental outcomes (actual elements and simulated elements). The lower levels are the synthetic learning outcomes (procedural understanding, conceptual understanding, and related knowledge), which concentrate on building traditional cognitive skills. The term "synthetic" is not meant to disparage the importance of creating a support for elemental learning using these important foundational levels. They are critical to attain and enrich elemental learning. What is meant is that the point of learning is to perform real-life or actual tasks (actual elements) or, from a learning perspective, practical approximations of reality (simulated elements). I would like to emphasize that a serious game or virtual learning environment aimed at elemental learning does not ignore synthetic learning outcomes; rather, it integrates them naturally and iteratively based on need.

Actual Elements

The most direct level of learning is the real-life learning outcomes required by the actual environment in which the learner needs to use those learning outcomes. If you are really going to be a nurse, for example, at some point you need to actually work as a nurse with real patients and with all of the attendant repercussions for failure. Not all learning needs to be measured at this level, but many real-life tasks do—especially critical skills (e.g., conducting invasive health care procedures under supervision). In some cases, of course, teaching and assessing actual elements may be either too expensive or too dangerous.

Simulated Elements

A considerable amount of learning from digital games and virtual worlds is assessed at this level. Simulated learning outcomes embody, but do not entirely represent, the essential features of something. In many cases, simulated elements promote learning transfer; i.e., they reproduce reality or some version of reality "close enough" to actual elements for even advanced stages of learning (e.g., helicopter simulators).

Procedural Understanding

Procedural understanding can involve fairly simple rule-using processes such as those applied in arithmetic. On the other end of the spectrum, higher-order procedures like those involved in medical specialties can be ill-defined and very

complex in their scope. In other words, procedural understanding requires that learners actually perform tasks rather than merely understand how to perform them. Even though it can be very complex, in and of itself, procedural learning is not an elemental learning outcome because it is missing essential features of the context.

Conceptual Understanding

The next level of learning involves understanding concepts. These can be both concrete (e.g., snowmobile) and abstract (e.g., altruism). Conceptual understanding can benefit from but does not usually require verbal knowledge or an intelligible verbal definition. Conceptual understanding can be learned (and assessed) by novel examples and nonexamples, by metaphors, and by deductive observation and reflection. For example, we all know what "faith" is, but the concept is different for each us.

Figure 1. Elemental learning pyramid culminating in actual elements. The top two levels are elemental learning outcomes. The bottom three learning outcomes are viewed as synthetic

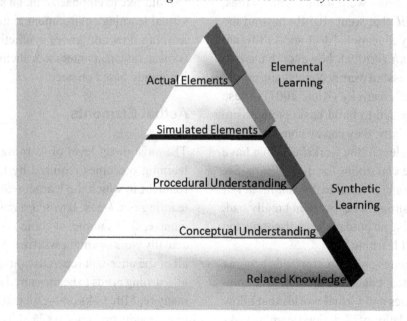

Related Knowledge

The lowest level of the pyramid is the related knowledge of the content area. This includes simple physical discriminations (e.g., matching machine screws), knowing about simple motor skills, labels, facts, and summary information (even complex summaries). Learners can acquire related information incidentally (e.g., from a television program on another subject) and intentionally (e.g., from an Internet resource accessed via a handheld mobile device). Definitions, whether memorized exactly or paraphrased, are examples of related knowledge—not concepts.

Elemental Learning: The Example of Language Learning

How might an Elemental Learning framework work in practice? Here I will offer an informal example of learning a language. Later, I will tie that to the notion of a Spiral Curriculum.

Let's imagine you are the learner, and like many Americans, you only speak English. You decide to learn Spanish. Why is that? Perhaps sometime during your life you would like to live or work in a Spanish-speaking country and converse fluently with the people there. The *actual elements* outcome could be slimmed down a bit to "*Converse fluently with the people in a Spanish-speaking country.*" That is the real-life learning outcome you need to attain. There are a number of environments where this outcome could be acquired. The best and most obvious is in a Spanish-speaking country. Second best would be to make a friend with a native Spanish-speaker in your neighborhood and speak with your friend daily using only the Spanish language. Alternately, you could converse with a friend or a "video pal" in a Spanish-speaking country via Voice over Internet Protocol (VoIP) and streaming video using a computer webcam with a software tool like Skype. All three of these situations (living in-country, conversing with a local Spanish-speaking

friend, or interacting via Skype) address the actual elements learning outcome because they maintain the highest fidelity to the real-life task. Being "in-country" is the highest fidelity environment because of all of the incidental language learning that takes place when you are immersed in a Spanish-only culture.

Now let's say these choices aren't open to you at the present time or you choose not to avail yourself of them. Your next best option would be to participate in a simulation or a simulation game that is entertaining enough to sustain your interest and designed systematically to support learning. Language simulations and simulation games promote learning outcomes at the *simulated elements* level. A friend tells you that the British Broadcasting Corporation (BBC) Internet site has an interesting interactive video simulation called Mi Vida Loca. *Mi Vida Loca* (www.bbc.co.uk/languages/spanish/mividaloca/) is a BBC immersive video mystery. Set in Spain, it uses clever narrative and structured learning situations to help you learn the basics of conversations such as getting directions, ordering a meal, shopping, interacting with a hospital, and so forth. As simulated learning environments go, it's fairly simple, but the story and characters are very engaging and the interactive story goes beyond typical tourist situations. (You make friends with a local journalist, a woman named Merche, who is stalked and eventually kidnapped by a corrupt land developer.) There is a good deal of incidental language learning beyond the topics being taught.

The elemental learning outcomes (actual and simulated) are supported by the synthetic learning outcomes of procedural understanding, conceptual understanding, and related knowledge. The Internet has countless sites with basic instruction, worksheets, and simple games (Hangman, Concentration, etc.). But, you decide to explore with *Mi Vida Loca* and see what you can find there first. That turns out to be a good decision, because the procedures, concepts, and related knowledge you learn there are situated in the video mystery simulation.

In language, the most obvious examples of *procedural understanding* involve grammar and conjugation. In *Mi Vida Loca,* initial discussion of the introductory grammar overtly taught there is communicated by a video "instructional agent," unrelated to the storyline, who appears in a booklike interface. The agent talks you through worked examples of the conjugated sentences. The Spanish text simultaneously appears on the screen on the other half of the interface as he introduces it. Where appropriate, the user can choose Spanish or English subtitles. After the introduction, you (the learner) have an opportunity to click on all the examples to hear them spoken in a native accent. Other text-based worked examples are presented and a short practice section follows. A link to worksheet material mirroring this content is available for printing. The Internet also offers a great many resources to practice grammatical rules and procedures.

Conceptual understanding can be abstract (e.g., truth) or physical (e.g., a table). One acquires understanding of concepts by classifying examples and nonexamples, by examining metaphors, or by observing "signs" in the environment. *Mi Vida Loca*, like most edutainment environments, does not overtly give attention to conceptual understanding in the sense of exercises that allow learners to classify examples and nonexamples. Nevertheless, there are a large number of concepts you can learn there by paying attention to what Gee (2007) refers to as sign systems (images, words, actions, symbols, artifacts, etc.) in the situation. Most of the conceptual understanding available to you in this situation comes from observing and interacting with the simulation videos. Therefore, much of the conceptual understanding in this particular site is closely tied to the simulated elements learning outcome.

Some of the *related knowledge* in *Mi Vida Loca* is located in the simulation as well. Parts of the video are interrupted periodically to go over the vocabulary terms and let you respond to questions presented in the video by Marche and other characters. For example, in an episode on ordering tapas, you need to decide what you want to eat and drink. Based on your choices, various food and drink come to your table as they might in real life. There is also related cultural knowledge presented throughout the video simulations. Some of this information is related to the intentional learning goals, some is incidental. There are additional vocabulary exercises in the same book like interface as the grammar exercises, As a follow-up to this site, you might play an extrinsically motivating Spanish vocabulary drill game like *Free Rice*, which is discussed later in this paper.

Other Learning Outcomes?

What about motor skills and affective learning? Aren't they important learning outcomes? Absolutely! I would argue, however, that in most cases these learning outcomes fit comfortably within the actual elements pyramid chiefly because we learn them by doing something elemental—either something real or an approximation of that reality. Otherwise, there would seem to be little point in learning motor skills or attitudes at all.

Motor Skills

When we learn a motor skill, we learn a series of physical movements. When we really learn a motor skill well, we go from an active or deliberately conscious activity to something approaching automaticity or at least fluidity. Typing and riding a bike are common examples. These activities, when learned well, can be "hard-wired" for life. Many gross motor skills (e.g., sitting up, balancing, walking) are typically learned when we are very young. Fine motor skills (e.g., operating a joystick during a digital game or using a fude to write the main characters in Japanese calligraphy) require the development of small muscle groups as well as the support of certain synthetic learning outcomes (chiefly conceptual and procedural understanding).

Another way to look at motor skill learning is that we learn them via practicing part skills and honing a calculated executive control process. Part skills are synthetic learning outcomes and often follow a particular procedure (part 1: reach for the mouse; part 2: look at the computer screen and locate the cursor; part 3: press down on the left mouse button; part 4: move the cursor to the desired location on the screen; and so on…). The executive control process that guides motor skill actions is driven by actual or simulated elements (actual tasks or their approximations). We can see that especially by considering the purpose for learning fine motor skills to any degree of control and precision. A foreigner does not learn to eat flawlessly with unfamiliar utensils according to local customs without a goal related to the local culture at the actual elements (real-life) level. It is in simulating or performing the actual task of eating in the foreign culture that the motor skills are acquired.

Attitudes

More is discussed about affective learning (and less is agreed upon) than any area in our personal lives. Consider the popular music that permeates most cultures. Almost always it is about a person's pain or joy brought about by some emotional reaction. In most circumstances, what is likely to affect those emotions or feelings the most are the attitudes that are learned. So, attitudes are very important. What are attitudes really? From a neo-behaviorist perspective, attitudes are measured simply by the choices we make. If an alcoholic (really) changes his attitude about drinking, this is illustrated by choosing not to drink. Just wanting to quit drinking does not really indicate an attitude change. From a cognitive perspective, we may be able to say that an attitude is learned based not just on the particular behavioral choices, but also on the interests and beliefs that are acquired, through experience for instance, and the influences these have on our behavior, our values, our attention, and our responses.

How do we learn our attitudes? How do we "change" an attitude? One way that we know from practical experience is by emulating a human or some humanlike entity. As very young children, we emulate our parents or those around us in a kind of mimicry. As we develop emotionally and intellectually, the sphere of "influencers" broadens greatly and will include many people or people-like entities we don't know (movies stars, avatars, sports figures, androids, or theorists). Essentially, we identify with the influencer and simulate that entity—by actions, beliefs, or interests—or we apply that influence into learning actual elements tasks. These attitudes can be either explicitly learned or implicitly learned, i.e., they are outside of a person's awareness or unacknowledged but manifest themselves by a person's response to the real or simulated environment.

Bruner and the Spiral Curriculum: Iteration, Intuition, and Structure

There are multiple underpinnings to the Elemental Learning taxonomical model, but one of the most appropriate may be Jerome Bruner's concept of the spiral curriculum presented in his famous book, *The Process of Education* (1960), framed as a Chairman's report of the landmark Wood's Hole Conference. Later formalized by Taba (1962) and Bruner (1977), spiral curricula have been practiced, or at least professed, in a number of learning environments including medicine (Harden & Stamper, 1999). According to Bruner (1960), "A curriculum as it develops should revisit basic ideas repeatedly, building upon them until the student has grasped the full formal apparatus that goes with them" (p. 13).

Bruner, as opposed to other prominent educational theorists of the period such as Gagné, Skinner, or those of Piaget's Geneva school, focused on environmental and experiential factors and culture. In referring to children, Bruner hypothesized "that any subject can be taught effectively in some intellectually honest form to any child at any stage of development" (p. 33). Intuition is a critical part of this process. Bruner often referred to intuition in relation to experts performing real tasks where they "leap intuitively into a decision or to a solution to a problem" (p. 62).

The focus on what we refer to in the present model as actual elements (forms of elemental learning) allows for intuitive leaps as step-by-step processes as our abilities in that environment are developed and our ability to perform actual elements tasks increases. Intuitive leaps are related to what has been referred to in medicine and other areas, such as physics, as the forward reasoning (from data to solution) applied by experts (Larkin, McDermott, Simon, & Simon, 1980; Norman & Schmidt, 2000) versus the backwards (rigidly algorithmic) reasoning of novices.

This intuitive, active, iterative and spiral curriculum approach toward actual elements fits enormously well with digital games and virtual worlds, both of which can be intuitive and motivating. This critical "effort" attribute of learning motivation is enhanced by the high interactivity and, in many cases, social interaction of digital games and virtual reality. "Motives for learning must be kept from going passive," Bruner (1960) argued. "They must be based as much as possible upon the arousal of interest in what there is to be learned, and they must be kept broad and diverse in expression" (p. 80).

Consistent with the notion of the spiral curriculum, *when* these elements are important is based on what is important to the situated elemental learning outcome and the learner. In my past conversations, practical considerations of efficiency always seem to arise here, especially in regard to group learning situations. We all hear from other educators (and say to ourselves) things like, "We can't have everyone doing their own thing. We'll get too 'off-track.' We've got to keep the group together." There's no question that it is more difficult to organize and assess learning situations that are guided by learning needs versus temporal learning schedules. Even so, augmented technology gives us augmented wherewithal and, in my

opinion, at least two guiding maxims. First, where it is practically necessary for the learning group to stay together, guide the group into group-based activities, such as multiuser virtual environment (MUVE) simulations, and bind the group assignments with structures such as miniconferences on issues related to elemental learning outcomes or HyperInquiry (Dempsey & Litchfield, 2001). Second, where it is practical for individuals to work on synthetic skill building, arrange for resources that assess on-task performance and encourage repetitive practice and rehearsal with feedback and available on-demand advisement and scenarios that emphasize learning motivation.

The elemental learning framework has its foundations in the spiral curriculum. Complex learning outcomes (*converse fluently with the people in a Spanish-speaking country*) can be accessible in basic situations first and revisited in more complex situations later on. This is not repetition. The learner revisits these situations iteratively and each time the learning deepens by building on prior experience. Synthetic learning outcomes are given meaning by being situated as much as possible in the actual or simulated learning outcomes. Another parallel with both the spiral curriculum and the gaming literature is that challenge (difficulty) is increased as the learner's competence increases.

DESIGN PROPOSITIONS AND EXAMPLES

In this section of the chapter, I will discuss elemental and synthetic outcomes in more detail, posit design propositions (personal statements or proposals) for digital games and virtual reality environments, and review examples of these environments that employ some of these characteristics. To use another language example, an actual elements learning outcome might be for customer representatives to become skilled in a second language and some of the cultural mores of those who use the language in order to interact in a global economy. In addition to the specifics of the actual elements goal, there are continual knowledge, skill, geographic concept, and cultural attitude learning processes that occur at multiple levels that in an iterative fashion enrich the development of elemental learning.

The examples I chose in this section are *not* following a single content theme, although it is certainly possible to do so. Instead, I have tried to share examples within my prior experience that are one of the types of strategic approaches possible for digital games or MUVEs. I know that my chosen examples may not "speak" to some readers used to riding the crest of bleeding-edge gaming technology. The first example, and probably the second, could never be considered a game at all. What I would hope is that readers will look beyond the technology and instead consider the elemental or synthetic learning outcomes as they match the instructional and learning strategies that the technology *affordances* offer. I struggled with whether I should use the term affordance, realizing that the term has taken on a life of its own since it was introduced by J. J. Gibson (1977). Unhappily, I can find no other that serves. What I mean by technology affordance is the property of action and interaction between the world, which a technology as a vehicle delivers, and a person—a learner, a player, an individual—or even a group.

Actual Elements

The most direct level of doing anything real is simply to do the thing itself. How well we can do anything at this stage requires that we gauge the real learning outcomes required by the real environment in which the learner needs to use those learning outcomes. I want to emphasize here that assessing a learning outcome does not necessarily infer that assessment is reported to anyone other than the learner. Whether or not a learning outcome is reported to an outside entity is immaterial to the learning of the outcome itself.

A classic example of a content area where actual elements are assessed is flight training. Would YOU want to be a passenger on a plane whose pilot has not been assessed actually flying the type of plane you are on? Certainly all of the less direct measures of learning are employed in training pilots. Learning and assessment at the simulated reality level is commonplace, sometimes employing sophisticated flight simulators. Even so, given the obvious life and death repercussions for incomplete training, few training organizations are willing to be liable for not assessing at the actual elements level. Unfortunately, many other organizations are less concerned about linking directness of assessment with the repercussions of incomplete training.

I use the term "actual elements" because these learning outcomes should represent true fidelity to the actual or ultimate transfer tasks. I would have preferred to use the modifier "real" instead of "actual" learning elements. Yet the notion of "real," in a milieu where virtual avatars appear to physically represent thinking flesh and blood people doing real things, becomes too much of an existential fallacy for a framework or learning framework. There is also the issue of cyber or artificial intelligence doing "real" tasks.

Actual elemental learning can (and usually does) take place in the real world. What seems more and more evident is that real people are able and desire to act virtually on some occasions when accomplishing real tasks for a variety of practical or even aesthetic reasons. If we ignore the fading technical hurdles, this is not much of a leap at all for most people. We have played virtual roles of some sort throughout our lives. Gee (2008) expresses this very well.

What I am suggesting is that when we humans act in the world (in word or deed), we are "virtual characters" (i.e., taking on specific identities such as "tough cop," "sensitive male," "hip young adult," "caring teacher," "savvy consumer," "needy friend," "nationalist African American," and so on and so forth through an indefinite list) acting in a "virtual world" (i.e., construing the world in certain ways and not others) (Gee, 2008, p. 261)

So, it isn't a great leap to have one's avatar (our virtual self) take on the role of a negotiator at a real business meeting in a virtual world like Second Life (SL), for example. It happens every day and negotiating effectively in business is a bona fide (real-life) actual elements outcome. Virtual worlds give us the opportunity in some cases to enable actual elements outcomes capably and economically. This is especially so when it is important to emphasize our *social presence* in a way that spatial proximity is emphasized. Social presence is an area that continues to be a major driver for much research and many global business development uses (Arnfalk & Kogg, 2003; Slater & Wilbur, 1997).

Can actual elements learning outcomes be experienced and assessed via digital games? Well, it is possible, but it is much less common than with virtual worlds. As part of a 2-year study of adults playing relatively unsophisticated digital games and an intensive literature review, my colleagues and I (Dempsey, Haynes, Lucassen, and Casey, 2002) offered a definition of a game. (Notice that I say "a" definition.) This is what we came up with:

A game is a set of activities involving one or more players. It has goals, constraints, payoffs, and consequences. A game is rule-guided and artificial in some respects. Finally, a game involves some aspect of competition, even if that competition is with oneself. (p. 159)

Conceptually, I have trouble rejecting this definition we worked so long to form. Yet, if I accept this definition at face value, a business meeting or a conference in Second Life could be a game. Realistically, I would not say that an actual business meeting in Second Life is considered a game these days. I'm not sure where the line is drawn, but there is a convergence of social presence and actual intent that is important to consider. On a practical level, digital games are rarely intended to be applied immediately to real-life, actual elements learning outcomes.

Actual Elements Design Propositions

Actual elements learning outcomes result from the need to learn something in real life. Educators should ask how the technological affordances in an digital game or virtual world can contribute to actual tasks. At one end of the need continuum there are very specific tasks such as learning to construct a sprinkler system at a golf course. The other end of the spectrum includes ill-defined needs such as becoming a more effective labor negotiator.

One way to approach the complexity of learning design is to begin with meaningful assessment. Meaningful assessment has to do with the process of gathering evidence of student learning outcomes. Actual elements tasks should first and foremost represent true fidelity to the actual or ultimate transfer tasks. At the same time, the actual tasks in certain "real-life" situations may be unclear (e.g., learning to interpret a trend). So, rather than thinking about designing instruction, we need to remember what we are really trying to do is to make sure that learning takes place. As all of us know, learning is often incidental anyway (i.e., it takes place outside of intentionally designed instructional environments). So, what is our essential task as designers of instruction? The common sense response to that question is to figure out how we will estimate what learners will be able to do. If we can find an effective way to estimate, or assess, what learning should take place, everything else will fall into place.

Designing for actual tasks is almost always an iterative, cyclical process. Remember Bruner's spiral curriculum and consider a relatively difficult actual task such as being able to present a short extemporaneous speech in a new foreign language. Once you are clear how that could be assessed in real life, iteration, intuition, and experience should guide the learning. Except for very simple tasks, don't look for an algorithm. Instead fill in those elemental and synthetic learning outcomes that circumstances dictate, keeping in mind the characteristics of a spiral curriculum. As you go through the course development process and get a better handle on the learning and assessment strategies you will use, the genuine goals of the course will be clearer to you. In an artfully designed course, your final course goals will be the subject of some revision. This is the natural and healthy practice of iterative course design. Good design is almost always good revision.

It makes sense to practice the actual elements task as much as possible. There is an old saying that goes something like, "In theory there is no difference between theory and practice, but in practice there is." Assessing whether someone can say something (related knowledge) or understand something (conceptual or procedural understanding) is not assessing whether someone can do something. If only to create an equitable learning environment, it just makes sense to sufficiently practice actual elements you think should be assessed. Again, I do not signify that employing the assessment of an actual task is always necessary or even possible in all learning situations (e.g., with many serious games).

Actual Elements Example: Virtual Conference in SL

Social interaction is not a sine qua non of all actual elemental learning tasks. Yet, many actual tasks require or benefit by real social interactions. Accordingly, it is not surprising that social interactions in virtual worlds have become a standard method of learning about and performing actual tasks in our real world. There are scores of examples in which the affordances of social virtual environments are becoming familiar— conferences, business meetings, office hours, sales presentations, philosophy classes, research focus groups, counseling sessions, business receptions, music concerts, speaking foreign languages, and so forth. The benefits are clear: greatly reduced costs, no time lost in travel, convenience, reduction in greenhouse gases, and relatively open access to people on a global stage.

As an example, quite recently I attended the VR Best Practices in Education conference in Second Life. It was fairly typical of other virtual conferences in many ways. There were a variety of sessions and learning outcomes addressed. Some were quite effective and others not so much. Some were aimed only at synthetic learning outcomes, but many sessions had elemental learning outcomes and hands-on practice as their goal. There were lots of problem-solving, brainstorming, and "best examples" evaluations. To accommodate global attendees, the conference went from 4:00 a.m. to 7:00 p.m. PDT.

In some of the sessions, one or more speakers or guides was brainstorming ideas, asking the attendees questions, or guiding them in performing a task of some sort. While this was going on, attendees were interacting with other speakers or attendees, primarily by text chat. Links to relevant URL (Internet locations) or SLURL (Second Life location) exemplars were recommended and posted. Note cards and educational and building tools were passed back and forth like candy. Intermittently, individuals or small groups would "rez" in or out in order to explore URL or SLURL links or try out the new virtual tools. It was the opposite of dull. What is taking place at the best types of sessions like this is brainstorming and problem solving of actual day-to-day challenges that businesses are experiencing. It is happening by social interaction with other individuals around the world, and it is happening at an almost negligible cost for the attendees.

Simulated Elements

Simulations, according to Gredler (1992, p.14), have two primary criteria. First, learners must have a bona fide role and encounter the consequence of actions made in that role. Second, participants must address the issues and problems seriously and conscientiously or in what Jones (1984; 1987) refers to as "reality of function." The traditional reasons for learning or assessment as simulated elements usually concern practical constraints. These include time or location limitations, expense, political risks, or physical danger to the learner or examinee or others affected by that individual's actions. Essentially, simulated elements are used when assessing the actual elements if the genuine curricular goals are not practical. In practice, at their best, some simulated learning environments can be as intrinsically motivating to learners as the "the real thing," perhaps in some cases, more so. What is finest about well-designed simulations is that they proximate aspects of reality and create as rich a learning (and assessment) environment as possible. It must be supposed that in some cases simulated elements environments are so rich that they are preferred to the reality of actual elements. As the technology becomes more enticing, this will also pose challenges for educators.

Simulated reality conjures up images of holodecks on *Star Trek* Federation spaceships. In some respects, that is not very far off into the future. Holodecks, which accurately portray even minute details of real situations, are very high-level simulations. Increasingly, technology is making things possible that we would not have suspected. We suppose within the next 10 years some online learning software will include the tools to project holograms into learners' living rooms, for example. But that view of simulated elements is at the high end. Most simulated reality learning and assessment activities are not nearly so high tech. A more catholic view of simulated elements includes aspects of text-based role-playing, simulations gaming, case-based learning, microworlds, and social systems scenarios among many other approaches.

What is educationally important about simulated elements? For "a simulation to be effective,"

Jacobs and Dempsey (1993) contend, "two basic issues must be addressed: (1) what aspects of the operational environment require simulation, and (2) to what extent should they be replicated?" (p. 200). At this point in my thinking, consistent with the literature (Clariana, 1989; Gagné, 1962; Jacobs and Dempsey, 1993), I would posit the following as a representation of the optimal characteristics of simulation for learning and assessment:

Simulated elements = (Reality) – (Task irrelevant elements)

Motivational aspects aside, the critical components of simulated elements are those things, events, and characteristics that allow the learner to perform in the operational environment (the real world). A longer version of the above would be the following,

[Optimal elements of simulation] = [what takes place in the real world operational environment] – [that which is not possible or not necessary to imitate or replicate in the real world operational environment].

Task irrelevant elements are two things: what is not possible and what is not necessary. What is *not possible* includes those aspects of the learning environment that are too expensive, too dangerous, too time consuming, too inconvenient, or physically not practical. What is *not necessary* is situation-dependent. It may be, for example, that in a particular learning situation, a person performing a critical skill (e.g., a medical technician) has a bad habit that has been acquired by repetition in the real-world environment. To break this habit and replace it with a good one, a simulated environment could be used to practice that particular process affected by the bad habit over and over until fluency or automaticity is attained. That process (simulated elements) is at once more efficient and corrective.

Simulated Elements
Design Propositions

Effective educational simulation and sim game design address the variables of curiosity, challenge, fantasy, and control and pay heed to gender, nationality, and culture. A seminal work by Malone (1981) called attention to the importance of including three factors into games including simulation games: challenge, curiosity, and fantasy. Later research has detailed the marked differences in the types of scenarios and games preferred by males and females (Bertozzi, 2008; Heeter, Egidio, Mishra, Winn, & Winn, 2009) and the importance of control in addition to Malone's three original factors (Dempsey et al., 2002; Westrom & Shaban, 1992).

For simulation or sim games with narrative involvement whether reality-based or fantasy-based, the importance of the backstory cannot be overstated (Calleja, 2007). Regardless of the ongoing debate (cf., Aarseth & Jenkins, 2005; Steinkuehler, 2006) on the topic of ludology (games as formal rule systems) versus narratology (games as texts), the backstory creates the reason for someone to want to be part of a simulated reality and "hooks" the learner into caring about the scenario. Designers can reveal the backstory by using narrative, recollections, flashbacks, or any number of "widgets" built into the environment that encourage to user to engage with the background story.

It is important to provide contextualized advisement or agent input for noncompetitive simulations or simulation games. Research by Van Eck and Dempsey (2002) found that learners in a video scenario-based simulation on practical mathematics skills had a higher transfer rate when advice and comments related to the task were contextualized. Those that were in a competitive condition did best when no contextualized advisement was present.

Encouraging some form of emulation or "buy-in" in a simulation helps to promote

acquiring or changing attitudes. Simulated elements are ideal for attitude learning. As discussed above, we often acquire attitudes by emulating a human or a humanlike entity. This entity becomes an "influencer," situated in our thinking.

Simulated Elements
Example: Cancerland

The example I chose for simulated elements involves affective learning regarding thyroid cancer and its effects on Rochelle Mazar, a librarian at the University of Toronto Mississauga. *Cancerland* (Cancerland, 2009) is a Second Life "personal museum" (for want of a better term) dedicated by Rochelle (SL name: Hilde Hullabaloo) to her struggle. Although well done for its environment, it is certainly on the opposite end of the continuum from most commercially produced simulations. What it does is engage "visitors" to its environment in a very unpretentious and moving way. The visitor follows a path through a smallish virtual building that metaphorically represents Hilde's journey. Rooms are marked with signs that indicate their purpose (hall of terror, operating room, scar display room, radioactive isolation, whole body scan, post-traumatic stress) sometimes with actual photos of Rochelle, in person, on the wall. You can see a video about Cancerland at http://www.youtube.com/watch?v=r2HQGxbNMNY .

Spaces, sounds, chat text, and artifacts move the visitor to feel Hilde's pain, fear, and humanity. Some of the chat either appears without warning or after the visitor (SL avatar) touches a gadget or reaches a certain location in the build, for example, the passageway that is entered through a symbolic refrigerator door.

Surgeon: The pathology revealed a 1.5-cm cancerous tumor.

Hilde whispers: I felt as though a door had slammed shut behind me.

Hilde whispers: I would never be the same again. I felt like everyone could see it flashing over my head: I HAVE CANCER.

Hilde whispers: The hardest part was telling my parents the diagnosis. The best I could do was whisper, "It is."

Hilde whispers: With a new 6-inch swollen scar across my throat, it was hard to forget that my body had betrayed me.

Hilde: My parents drove me to the hospital, waited until I was out of the operating room, and brought me back home. They housed me, fed me, washed the dishes, did the laundry, and even stripped my bed for me. They allowed me to revert; I was their little girl again, needing care and attention.

Hilde whispers: What I didn't anticipate was how difficult it would be to cope with the scar.

Hilde whispers: With no thyroid, my body temperature dropped to below 35 degrees Celsius, or 94 Fahrenheit.

Hilde whispers: I felt cold all the time.

Rochelle's voice is tripped by the visitor's movement through the simulation in a mimic of the discontinuous thoughts that must have run through her mind in a loop.

I have cancer.

I'm not strong.

It can't be—I'm only 33.

I'm so cold.

What's wrong with me?

I'm so tired.

I can't concentrate on anything.

My joints are swelling and sore.

I feel blank.

In a number of places throughout the build, the SL visitor is encouraged to take the role of Hilde (Rochelle) and physically lie on the operating table, sit in the doctor's office, get a CT scan, and so forth. At one point my avatar was laying on the surgical table listening to the voices and sounds of the operating room I thought to myself, "I feel so exposed—alone." Suddenly, I noticed some text on the surgical table that said, "The surgery lasted two and a half hours."

The interactivity of this SL build engages the learner and becomes an empathic interaction with Rochelle. The real clinical photographs of her scars placed in picture frames on virtual walls in one of the rooms become a kind of shrine to the reality of cancer. It persuades you to learn something of this disease and the individuals who struggle with it.

Procedural Understanding

Where information and conceptual understanding provide the "who, what, where, and when," procedural understanding provides the "how" of learning. Procedural understanding always involves multiple concepts and frequently knowledge (including conditional knowledge) and other procedures. Procedural understanding can involve fairly simple rule-using, such as that applied in arithmetic. On the other end of the spectrum, higher-order procedural knowledge, such as is often involved in medical specialties, can be ill defined and very complex in its scope. In assessing procedural understanding, instructors sometimes mistake a learner's ability to state a procedure with being able to perform it. Procedural understanding goes beyond knowledge. Summarizing a procedure indicates only that the learner has acquired related information. It does not demonstrate that a learner can accomplish the procedure. In other words, procedural understanding requires that learners "walk the walk," not just "talk the talk."

Curiously, considering what we now know about human learning, the predominance of learning during the first two years of many medical schools are assessed almost exclusively at the related information level. Fortunately, in the last two decades, movements such as problem-based learning (Albanese & Mitchell, 1993) and its outgrowth, evidence-based medicine (Locatis, in press; White, 2004) have addressed the need to incorporate procedural learning and often simulated elements earlier in curricula. Although there has been limited research evidence that problem-based learning curricula improve knowledge or clinical performance (Colliver, 2000; Norman & Schmidt, 2000) interactive problem-based technologies, including Internet-based games, allow for increased opportunities for learners to practice procedures and greater accuracy and flexibility in self-assessment.

Procedural Understanding Design Propositions

All procedures, processes, and rules of any sort are composed of multiple concepts (Gagné, 1985). For example, rules of the arithmetic procedure of division require that learners understand the concept (NOT the verbal definition) of dividend, divisor, quotient, whole number, and so forth. Designers concentrating on procedural understanding games or virtual activities should make sure that essential prerequisite concepts and rules are addressed adequately.

Particularly as procedures become more complex, advisement becomes a critical part of the learning process. Of course, one form of advisement involves feedback, but advisement is guidance and tutoring as well. In his classic "2 Sigma" article, Benjamin Bloom (1984)"found that the average student under tutoring was about two standard deviations above the average of the control class (the average tutored student was above 98% of the students in the control class)." (p. 4). This was and still is startling, and these studies have been replicated on multiple occasions (Chi, Siler, Jeong, Yamauchi, & Hausmann, 2001; Juel, 1991). These findings essentially indicate that tutoring is the most effective tool we know about to increase achievement and retention. Unfortunately, in many procedural-learning situations, individual or small group, tutors just are not practical—particularly for general synthetic learning outcomes. Therefore, the next best thing is to design in some form of advisement that can be solicited by the learner. This runs the gamut from pull-down menu help to intelligent agents. What has not held up well are highly intrusive or unsolicited help "agents." Remember Microsoft Bob? (http://en.wikipedia.org/wiki/Microsoft_Bob.)

What Gestalt psychologists first referred to as "insight" is important and should be interactively addressed to promote procedural understanding, or conceptual understanding in the case of complex abstract concepts. Basically, insight occurs when learners reorganize or restructure their perceptions in order to really "see" the solution (Ohlsson, 1992). According to Gredler (2009), there are three possible mechanisms for restructuring a problem: reencoding, elaboration, and constraint relaxation (p. 55). Reencoding occurs when an incorrect or somewhat inaccurate interpretation of a problem or a procedure is corrected. Elaboration involves retrieval of additional information from long-term memory or adding overlooked information to the problem. Constraint relaxation amounts to removing unnecessary boundaries or limitations that learners impose on themselves (e.g., only doing it the way they've always done it).

Procedural Understanding Example: Basic Electricity Procedures for Kids

An Internet game, *The Blobz Guide to Electric Circuits*, developed by Andy Thelwell at Staffordshire University (see www.andythelwell.com/blobz/guide.html) addresses the three design propositions above. It builds on multiple concepts and rules; it provides advisement and feedback; and it supports insight by restructuring. The game has five sections that build from the conceptual to the procedural, from what make circuits work to building circuit diagrams. Each of the sections has three highly interactive parts: useful info, activity, and quiz. The program is colorful, amusing, and (another good design feature) it never goes more than a few screens without meaningful interaction.

The advisement in this game is given in the form of elaborated feedback by a little animated character after incorrect responses only. Because this highly visual game is aimed at young children and procedural simplicity is necessary, that approach works well here. For more complex content, I would have liked to see the advisor asking questions about the learner's thought processes. The written feedback does point out the attributes that made the response incorrect and, usually, what to

look for in a correct response, thus contributing toward the *Aha!* moment (restructuring).

Conceptual Understanding

When we think in categories, at least, we think conceptually. There is simply no more important synthetic learning outcome than clear conceptual understanding. Conceptual understanding, as Gagné (1985) and others have pointed out, can be both concrete (prison) and abstract (patriotism). The primary divergence being decided by one question, "Is the concept in the physical world?" If the answer is yes, the concept is concrete, if no, it is abstract.

Conceptual understanding can benefit from but does not usually require verbal knowledge or an intelligible verbal definition(I wish someone had told that to my 4th-grade nun!). For example, if you were brave enough to ask another person to define "ecstasy," there might be a couple of jokes, but even after the laughter, few would define it the same way. Even so, during normal discussion almost everyone would have a shared understanding of "ecstasy," however it is they define it. It is that shared understanding that makes it a concept and the basis for any kind of problem solving. Abstract conceptual understanding such as the concept of "ecstasy" can involve feelings, beliefs, and other affective components.

Concrete concepts are simply of the world—trees, computers, air, Stratoloungers, and hard drives. There is a point before a concrete concept. That is the point when we are still discriminating between concrete concepts, and although we are on track, we have not yet attained a conceptual learning outcome. That is the point of discrimination. In order to learn a concrete concept, we often have to discriminate first. For example, let's say you are an average newbie on the job and your boss, Tony, asks you to go through his junked-filled desk at work and get a high-end graphics card with a Kirlian Video In/Out, LMS connectors, and support for several monitor displays. You may be able to figure it out by comparing what you understand about the structure and functions of these things. Another way, an easier way, would be for Tony to give you a physical example of what he is looking for. In that case, you would only have to *discriminate* between the referent (Tony's card) and all the other junk in Tony's desk until you found a match. After you'd done that a few times, you probably would not need the referent (Tony's card) anymore to find what you need. You've sailed past the point of discrimination (which belongs in the related knowledge category, anyway) into conceptual understanding.

Conceptual Understanding Design Propositions

A learning activity or digital game teaching concepts should in some way address three common types of error: misconception, overgeneralization, and undergeneralization. Misconception means that the learner is simply totally off track. He or she thinks the concept is one thing, when it is clearly another. This often occurs when the concept is new and usually requires examples that epitomize the concept. Overgeneralization or undergeneralization, by contrast, are more nuanced errors that require exposure to examples whose attributes diverge from the epitome, or prime example. In these cases, the examples must be novel or unfamiliar examples that can, with feedback or an Aha! moment of some sort, refine the conceptual understanding.

Conceptual understanding can be learned (and assessed) by actively classifying examples and nonexamples with feedback using the computer's dramatic ability to keep track of on-task performance (Dempsey & Driscoll, 1996; Dempsey, Driscoll, & Litchfield, 1992). This singular characteristic of the computer, its ability to capture and use variables inputted by the user is not employed nearly often enough in correcting obvious conceptual error. Combining the structure of concept learning with a rule-base

framing structure is a efficient and moderately thorough method of learning concepts ideally suited for hyperlinked environments (Dempsey, 1986; West, Farmer, & Wolff, 1991).

Conceptual understanding should be fostered with metaphors. Metaphors play a crucial role in defining our shared understanding, and in turn, our concepts. As Lakoff and Johnson (1980) put it, "Metaphors are fundamentally conceptual in nature…grounded in everyday experience," and "unavoidable, ubiquitous, and mostly unconscious." (p. 272). Clever design benefits from metaphors in which the source domain (the one in which the metaphorical reasoning takes place) provides a utilitarian vehicle to reach the target domain (the subject matter).

We educators should promote a process of inductive observation and reflection. In the right environment, learners can work through to conceptual understanding. In the right place, in the right time, acquiring conceptual understanding can be an elegant and flowing mental process. Concepts are often wide enough to use for a variety of elemental learning outcomes, whether they are new to the learning situation or they have been learned in the past. One thing actual elements do for us, however, is to focus the learner on the *meaning* of concepts as a means to perform a real-life task well.

Conceptual Understanding Example: Sink or Float with Certitude Estimates

The classic "Sink or Float" activity has been used often with children as a basis for learning buoyancy, density and, in some cases, even the scientific method. The concepts of solutions and mixtures are sometimes included in similar activities. In a digital game I developed on this topic a while ago for the CD-ROM environmental education game, *Ribbit's Big Splash* (Ribbit's Big Splash, 2009). I tried to promote concept attainment by immediate feedback and reward by putting more animated fish in an aquarium when learners classified an object as one that either sinks or floats and would mix or dissolve.

The reason I like this digital game is because of the second part of each content question. Here the game asks the player how certain she is that she classified the concept question (sink, mix, etc.) correctly. The learner estimates the degree of confidence of the response by "wagering" starfish and trying to get correct responses in order to get additional fish in the aquarium. This notion of confidence of response (or certitude) works well with concepts and rules because it encourages learners to monitor their progress as they go along. What Kulhavy (Kulhavy, 1977; Kulhavy & Stock, 1989) argues occurs is that, for each question, the learner makes a type of hierarchy of how likely each of the possible responses is to be the correct one. So, if the player didn't really know what the correct response was, she would be unlikely to invest in that response by betting many starfish. The feedback would appear, and another question would appear. If the player knew the correct answer without a doubt, she would probably bet the maximum number of starfish. Now what happens when the player believes she knows the correct response, invests four or five starfish in that response, and gets feedback that indicates the response was instead incorrect? Kulhavy and his colleagues have argued that the learner will be much more attuned to the content, because he or she will have *expectancy for success* that did not materialize. Other research has indicated that the time learners use to study feedback for these high-confidence, wrong responses is maximized (see Dempsey, Driscoll, & Swindell, 1993). These are, in effect, "the teachable moments."

Related Knowledge

At the related knowledge level there is a gargantuan jamboree of digital games, intentionally educational, and otherwise. Many of these are poorly designed drill-and-kill iterative loops of boredom. Even so, almost all of us have used flashcards or virtual flashcards of some sort to learn new vocabulary, facts and labels, parts of a thing or system, and so forth. It's perceived as effective. Is it? Can anything so tiresome be worthwhile? That depends. When there is not a lot of related knowledge to acquire or that related knowledge is acquired naturally through elemental learning activities, there simply is no reason for rehearsal activities that "drill" related knowledge into our brains. Drill is counterintuitive to the way we prefer to learn. If it feels unnatural, it is. Nevertheless, the best-educated individuals in our society often have an enormous store of verbal knowledge, and it is a virtual certainty that these individuals have recognized the need for repetitive practice in an assortment of situations. It's not the only way to learn related knowledge, but it is a common strategy when repetitive rehearsal is desired. The point is to always consider how drill aids elemental learning; because of the synthetic learning outcomes, it is the most abstract.

Drill with knowledge of correct results feedback works (Salisbury & Klein, 1988), but it doesn't work long without adequate rehearsal. In fact, after the initial exposure to related knowledge, this type of learning activity really is just a rehearsal strategy aimed at inputting and recalling information from working memory to long-term memory and vice versa (Baddeley, 2000). It's also more efficient to align what you rehearse with adequate feedback (Dempsey & Driscoll, 1996). The purpose of this feedback is simple. It informs us that what we inferred or retrieved from long-term memory are the right data or the wrong data. Rehearsal and feedback are two major components of effective verbal knowledge retention. A third component is learning motivation, which I will operationalize here as the amount of effort one expends toward learning something. Given the abstract nature of verbal knowledge symbol systems, it is often unrealistic to expect that acquiring a reasonably large amount of verbal knowledge should be intrinsically motivating (for the gratification of acquiring this knowledge itself). Therefore, some type of extrinsically rewarding game or activity makes sense.

Related knowledge may be *contextual*, (e.g., limited to a particular elemental domain such as terms related to a specific industrial machinery operation). Knowledge may also be *general* (e.g., foreign language words that are used in numerous domains). Usually, the amount of material to learn is much greater for general knowledge domains than the learner must access with fluency. This contributes to what Dewey (1910) called *passive vocabulary* (words that are understood when heard or seen). By contrast, *active vocabulary* (what he referred to as words that are "used intelligently") is contextual. Enlarging vocabulary takes place, according to Dewey, "by wider intelligent contact with things and persons, and also vicariously from the context in which they are heard or read" (p. 180). Within the framework discussed in this paper, that context is provided by focusing on elemental learning outcomes. That has associated implications discussed in the following propositions.

Related Knowledge Design Propositions

The game or activity must emphasize the knowledge that is really related to the elemental learning outcomes and should be "chunked" rationally. If the elemental learning outcomes are broad (e.g., acquiring medical terminology) the content pools can be huge, so the designer should focus on the new and prior knowledge "related" to the actual elements task. Also, chunking the material helps in connecting drill-type strategies with other strategic learning approaches such as mnemonics

An efficient corrective feedback scheme (feedback from wrong responses) should be repeated using an efficient short-term rehearsal scheme. Computer databases are adept at capturing and repeating knowledge items that were responded to incorrectly. Further, there are a number of relatively straightforward adaptive schemes that have proven effective for algorithmic presentation of drilled items (Salisbury, 1988).

The level of difficulty should be adjusted based on user response correctness. The primary purpose for this is to increase challenge, long considered a critical component of motivation and educational games (Malone, 1981).

There is no need to repeat related knowledge questions and feedback to content learners have already responded to correctly unless there are reasons to suggest that connections to that content are weak (Kulhavy, 1977). An exception to this proposition is when a high rate of fluency or automaticity is required by the actual elements task (Jacobs, Dempsey, & Salisbury, 1990).

Long-term retention can be aided by connecting the related knowledge to the actual elements task and by scheduled cumulative practice. Using himself as his only research participant, the seminal empirical work of Hermann Ebbinghaus (1885/1962) on forgetting still has a number of implications for learning design. Ebbinghaus showed that it is harder to memorize material that is not meaningful. His experiments also suggested that increasing the amount of verbal information to be learned greatly increases the amount of time needed to acquire it. (This is the famous "learning curve.") Importantly, his data also indicated that we learn more by spacing out the verbal information over time than by trying to learn it in one session.

When the related knowledge is contextual, an intrinsically motivating digital game or activity closely tied to the elemental learning outcome is ideal. This supports the immediate relevance of the content and binds the information to the real task. General related knowledge, by contrast, often benefits from extrinsically motivating activities, especially those that have some perceived reciprocal benefit to the learner.

Related Knowledge Example: An Internet Game That Feeds the Hungry

An online digital game vehicle that illustrates some of these components is *Free Rice* (see www.freerice.com/). *Free Rice* is a casual game using a multiple-choice format to drill a variety of general related knowledge and physical concept areas including language vocabulary (English, French, Spanish, Italian, and German), mathematics, chemistry, geography, and art. Simple correct answer feedback is given for each response, and levels of difficulty are based on the number of available items in the existing content pool. A few introductory questions set the player's initial level. Questions are repeated on a scheduled basis only if the player responds to them incorrectly.

What sets *Free Rice* apart from numerous other similar edu-drill games is that by playing this game and acquiring general related knowledge, the player is contributing food to the hungry. Every time the player answers a question correctly, sponsors donate 10 grains of rice to the United Nations World Food Program. The rice appears virtually in a simple wooden bowl on the right side of the screen as the game progresses; this, along with periodic "wow!" comments, provides players with immediate and tangible positive reinforcement.

The "feel-good," socially beneficial aspect of this game has contributed to its status as a "viral" Internet casual game. The site began in October 2007. In the following year, 2008, the *Free Rice* site reported donating 43,942,622,700 grains of rice. That was sensationally successful for any kind of educational activity! Think of the amount of related knowledge players acquire on a spaced-learning schedule. At the same time, learners are reminded on an interval schedule of the importance of ending world hunger.

FUTURE RESEARCH DIRECTIONS

An additional instructional design consideration that should be discussed is the relative complexity of the technology employed for elemental versus synthetic learning outcomes. There certainly is no hard and fast boundary but, in general, casual or simpler digital games have been found to be very adaptable to many purposes involving synthetic learning outcomes or limited simulated elements. During extensive observations of adults playing 40 casual digital games, Dempsey et al. (2002) recorded dozens of educational uses of these types of games proposed by the study participants.

By contrast, I would argue that more sophisticated technological environments, such as digital video games or virtual reality can be especially desirable for simulated or actual elements learning. This notion is affirmed in the writings of some educators, notably James Gee (2007). Gee and many others have personally observed the potential for learning that MUVEs offer. Others argue that there is little evidence to determine their impact. For example, consistent with his perennially contrarian stance toward new learning technologies, Richard Clark (2007) contends that "evidence clearly indicates that games do not teach anyone anything that cannot be learned more quickly and less expensively some other way" (p. 58). This emphasis on comparison treatments, cost-benefit ratios, or randomized clinical trials by some educators allows policy makers to limit investment into more sophisticated educational innovations. Meanwhile, the average number of hours people around the world spend playing digital games and exploring virtual worlds increases beyond expectations.

Perhaps culturally shaped movements, such as the natural modern human inclination to employ advanced and motivating technologies for elemental learning activities are too nuanced and immediate for randomized clinical trials. Beyond the obvious apples and oranges concerns, perhaps comparison studies under laboratory conditions simply miss the point. Innovations are rarely immediately efficient or cost-effective. Nevertheless, more rigorous approaches to studying learning outcomes in elemental learning environments will continue to challenge researchers.

CONCLUSION

The best kind of learning is aimed at achieving or supporting something actual. Actual in this sense is meaningful, purpose-driven, and useful to learners' real lives. Tourists who plan to drive in a new country are anxious to learn to identify unfamiliar road signs (conceptual understanding) because it directly affects their potential ability to safely travel (actual elements). There are also some vocabulary (related knowledge) and regulations (procedural understanding) that supports their travel. These are simple learning outcomes, but if they were more complicated, it would make sense to artificially replicate the actual travel environment (simulated elements) before attempting to drive. Amid all of the ludology vs. narratology-type theoretical debates on digital games and virtual worlds, there are the very real and practical questions about how we incorporate these delightful technologies into fascinating and consequential learning environments.

REFERENCES

Aarseth, E. (2003). *Playing research: Methodological approaches to game analysis*. Paper presented at the 5th International Digital arts and culture conference, Melbourne.

Albanese, M. A., & Mitchell, S. (1993). Problem-based learning: A review of literature on its outcomes and implementation issues. *Academic Medicine, 68*, 52–81.

Anderson, L. W. E., Krathwohl, D. R. E., Airasian, P. W., Cruikshank, K. A., Mayer, R. E., Pintrich, P., et al. (Eds.). (2001). A taxonomy for learning, teaching, and assessing: A revision of Bloom's taxonomy of educational objectives (Complete Ed.). New York: Longman.

Arnfalk, P., & Kogg, B. (2003). Service transformation—Managing a shift from business travel to virtual meetings. *Journal of Cleaner Production, 11*(8), 859–872. doi:10.1016/S0959-6526(02)00158-0

Baddeley, A. (2000). The episodic buffer: A new component of working memory? *Trends in Cognitive Sciences, 4*(11), 417–423. doi:10.1016/S1364-6613(00)01538-2

Bertozzi, E. (2008). You play like a girl!: Cross-gender competition and the uneven playing field. *Convergence, 14*(4), 473–487.

Bloom, B. S. (1956). *Taxonomy of educational objectives: The classification of educational goals, Handbook 1: Cognitive domain*. New York: David McKay.

Bloom, B. S. (1984). The 2 sigma problem: The search for methods of group instruction as effective as one-to-one tutoring. *Educational Researcher, 13*(6), 4–16.

Bruner, J. (1960). *The process of education*. Cambridge, MA: Harvard University Press.

Bruner, J. S. (1977). Structures in learning. In Hass, B. (Ed.), *Curriculum planning: A new approach* (pp. 192–194). London: Allyn & Bacon.

Calleja, G. (2007). Digital game involvement: A conceptual model. *Games and Culture, 2*(3), 236–260. doi:10.1177/1555412007306206

Cancerland. (2009). Retrieved August 1, 2009 from http://slurl.com/secondlife/Kula%20 3/197/86/21

Chi, M. T. H., Siler, S. A., Jeong, H., Yamauchi, T., & Hausmann, R. G. (2001). Learning from human tutoring. *Cognitive Science: A Multidisciplinary Journal, 25*(4), 471–533.

Clariana, R. B. (1989). Computer simulations of laboratory experiences. *Journal of Computers in Mathematics and Science Teaching, 2,* 14–19.

Clark, R. E. (2007, May–June). Learning from serious games? Arguments, evidence, and research suggestions. *Educational Technology, 47,* 56–59.

Colliver, J. A. (2000). Effectiveness of problem-based learning curricula: Research and theory. *Academic Medicine, 75,* 259–266. doi:10.1097/00001888-200003000-00017

De Corte, E. (1999). On the road to transfer: An introduction. *International Journal of Educational Research, 31*(7), 555–559. doi:10.1016/S0883-0355(99)00023-3

Dempsey, J. V. (1986). Using the rational set generator with computer-based instruction for creating concept examples: A template for instructors. *Educational Technology, 26*(4), 43–46.

Dempsey, J. V., & Driscoll, M. P. (1996). Error & feedback: The relation between content analysis and confidence of response. *Psychological Reports, 78,* 1079–1089.

Dempsey, J. V., Driscoll, M. P., & Litchfield, B. C. (1992). Feedback, retention, discrimination error, and feedback study time. *Journal of Research on Computing in Education, 25*(2), 303–326.

Dempsey, J. V., Driscoll, M. P., & Swindell, L. (1993). Text-based feedback. In Dempsey, J. V., & Sales, G. C. (Eds.), *Interactive instruction and feedback* (pp. 21–53). Englewood Cliffs, NJ: Educational Technology Publications.

Dempsey, J. V., Haynes, L. L., Lucassen, B. L., & Casey, M. A. (2002). Forty simple computer games and what they could mean to educators. *Simulation & Gaming, 33*(2), 157–168. doi:10.1177/1046878102332003

Dempsey, J. V., & Litchfield, B. C. (2001). HyperInquiry: Surfing below the surface of the Web. In Web-based training (pp. 229–234). Englewood Cliffs, NJ: Educational Technology Publications.

Dewey, J. (1910). *How we think.* Boston, D. C.: Heath. doi:10.1037/10903-000

Ebbinghaus, H. (1885/1962). *Memory: A contribution to experimental psychology.* New York: Dover. Retrieved from http://psychclassics.yorku.ca/Ebbinghaus/index.htm

Gagné, R. M. (1962). *Psychological principles in system development.* New York: Holt, Rinehart & Winston.

Gagné, R. M. (1985). *The conditions of learning and theory of instruction.* Fort Worth, TX: Holt, Rinehart and Winston.

Gee, J. P. (2007). *What video games have to teach us about learning and literacy* (2nd ed.). New York: Palgrave/Macmillan.

Gee, J. P. (2008). Video games and embodiment. *Games and Culture, 3*(3–4), 253–263. doi:10.1177/1555412008317309

Gibson, J. J. (1977). The theory of affordances. In Shaw, R., & Bransford, J. (Eds.), *Perceiving, acting, and knowing: Toward an ecological psychology* (pp. 67–82). Hillsdale, NJ: Lawrence Erlbaum.

Gould, S. J. (1981). *The mismeasure of man.* New York: W. W. Norton & Company.

Gredler, M. (1992). *Designing and evaluating games and simulations: A process approach.* London: Kogan Page.

Gredler, M. E. (2009). *Learning and instruction: Theory into practice* (6th ed.). Upper Saddle River, NJ: Pearson Education, Inc.

Greeno, J. G. (1997). On claims that answer the wrong questions. *Educational Researcher, 26*(1), 5–17.

Harden, R. M., & Stamper, N. (1999). What is a spiral curriculum? *Medical Teacher, 21*(2), 141–143. doi:10.1080/01421599979752

Heeter, C., Egidio, R., Mishra, P., Winn, B., & Winn, J. (2009). Alien games: Do girls prefer games designed by girls? *Games and Culture, 4*(1), 74–100. doi:10.1177/1555412008325481

Hunn, E. (1982). The utilitarian factor in folk biological classification. *American Anthropologist, 84*(4), 830–847. doi:10.1525/aa.1982.84.4.02a00070

Jacobs, J. W., & Dempsey, J. V. (1993). Simulation and gaming: Fidelity, feedback, and motivation. In Dempsey, J. V., & Sales, G. C. (Eds.), *Interactive instruction and feedback* (pp. 197–228). Englewood Cliffs, NJ: Educational Technology Publications.

Jacobs, J. W., Dempsey, J. V., & Salisbury, D. F. (1990). An attention reduction training model: Educational and technological applications. *Journal of Artificial Intelligence in Education, 1*(4), 41–50.

Jones, K. (1984). Simulations versus professional educators. In Jaques, D., & Tippen, E. (Eds.), *Learning for the future with games and simulations* (pp. 45–50). Loughborough, UK: SAGSET/Loughborough, University of Technology.

Jones, K. (1987). *Simulations: A handbook for teachers and trainers*. London: Kogan Page.

Juel, C. (1991). Cross-age tutoring between student athletes and at-risk children. *The Reading Teacher, 45*(3), 178–186.

Katona, G. (1940). *Organizing and memorizing*. New York: Columbia University Press.

Krathwohl, D. R. (2002). A revision of Bloom's taxonomy: An overview. *Theory into Practice, 41*(4), 212–218. doi:10.1207/s15430421tip4104_2

Kulhavy, R. W. (1977). Feedback in written instruction. *Review of Educational Research, 47*, 211–232.

Kulhavy, R. W., & Stock, W. A. (1989). Feedback in written instruction: The place of response certitude. *Educational Psychology Review, 1*(4), 279–308. doi:10.1007/BF01320096

Lakoff, G., & Johnson, M. (1980). *Metaphors we live by*. Chicago, IL: University of Chicago Press.

Larkin, J. H., McDermott, J., Simon, D. P., & Simon, H. A. (1980). Models of competence in solving physics problems. *Cognitive Science: A Multidisciplinary Journal, 4*(4), 317–345.

Locatis, C. (in press). Performance, instruction, and technology in health care education. In Reiser, R. A., & Dempsey, J. V. (Eds.), *Trends and issues in instructional design and technology* (3rd ed.). Upper Saddle River, NJ: Merrill Education/Prentice–Hall.

Malone, T. W. (1981). Toward a theory of intrinsically motivating instruction. *Cognitive Science, 4*(13), 333–369.

Marzano, R. J. (2001). *Designing a new taxonomy of educational objectives*. Thousand Oaks, CA: Corwin Press.

Norman, G. R., & Schmidt, H. G. (2000). Effectiveness of problem-based learning curricula: Theory, practice and paper darts. *Medical Education, 34*(9), 721–728. doi:10.1046/j.1365-2923.2000.00749.x

Ohlsson, S. (1992). Information processing explanations of insight and related phenomena. In Keane, M. T., & Gilhooly, K. J. (Eds.), *Advances in the psychology of thinking* (pp. 1–44). London: Harvester–Wheatsheaf.

Piaget, J. (1985). *The equilibration of cognitive structures: The central problem of intellectual development.* Chicago, IL: University of Chicago Press.

(2009). *Ribbit's Big Splash.* Mobile, AL: Educational Concepts. [computer software]

Rice, J. W. (2007). Assessing higher order thinking in video games. *Journal of Technology and Teacher Education, 15*(1), 87–100.

Salisbury, D. F. (1988). Effect drill and practice strategies. In Jonassen, D. H. (Ed.), *Instructional designs for microcomputer courseware* (pp. 103–124). Mahwah, NJ: Lawrence Erlbaum.

Salisbury, D. F., & Klein, J. D. (1988). A comparison of a microcomputer progressive state drill and flashcards for learning paired associates. *Journal of Computer-Based Instruction, 15*(4), 136–143.

Slater, M., & Wilbur, S. (1997). A framework for immersive virtual environments (FIVE)—Speculations on the role of presence in virtual environments. *Presence (Cambridge, Mass.), 6*(6), 603–616.

Steinkuehler, C. A. (2006). Why Game (Culture) Studies Now? *Games and Culture, 1*(1), 97–102. doi:10.1177/1555412005281911

Taba, H. (1962). *Curriculum development: Theory and practice.* New York: Harcourt, Brace & World.

Thorndike, E. L., & Woodworth, R. S. (1901). The influence of improvement in one mental function upon the efficiency of other functions. *Psychological Review, 9,* 374–382.

Van Eck, R., & Dempsey, J. (2002). The effect of competition and contextualized advisement on the transfer of mathematics skills in a computer-based instructional simulation game. *Educational Technology Research and Development, 50*(3), 23–41. doi:10.1007/BF02505023

Wenger, E. (1998). *Communities of practice: Learning, meaning, and identity.* New York: Cambridge University Press.

Wertheimer, M. (1945). *Productive thinking.* New York: Harper and Row.

West, C. K., Farmer, J. A., & Wolff, P. M. (1991). *Instructional design: Implications from cognitive science.* Englewood Cliffs, NJ: Prentice Hall.

Westrom, L. E., & Shaban, A. (1992). Intrinsic motivation in microcomputer games. *Journal of Research on Computing in Education, 24*(4), 433–445.

White, B. (2004). Making evidence-based medicine doable in everyday practice. *Family Practice Management, 11*(2), 51–58.

APPENDIX: ADDITIONAL READING

"Must-Reads" for This Topic

Bruner, J. (1960). *The process of education*. Cambridge, MA: Harvard University Press.

Dempsey, J. V., Haynes, L. L., Lucassen, B. L., & Casey, M. A. (2002). Forty simple computer games and what they could mean to educators. *Simulation and Gaming, 33*(2), 157–168.

Dewey, J. (1910). *How we think*. Boston: D. C. Heath.

Gagné, R. M. (1985). *The conditions of learning and theory of instruction*. Fort Worth, TX: Holt, Rinehart and Winston.

Gee, J. P. (2007). *What video games have to teach us about learning and literacy* (2nd ed.). New York: Palgrave/Macmillan.

Greeno, J. G. (1997). On claims that answer the wrong questions. *Educational Researcher, 26*(1), 5–17.

Harden, R. M., Stamper, N. (1999). What is a spiral curriculum? *Medical Teacher, 21*(2), 141–143.

Jacobs, J. W., & Dempsey, J. V. (1993). Simulation and gaming: Fidelity, feedback, and motivation. In J. V. Dempsey & G. C. Sales (Eds.), *Interactive instruction and feedback* (pp. 197–228). Englewood Cliffs, NJ: Educational Technology Publications.

Malone, T. W. (1981). Toward a theory of intrinsically motivating instruction. *Cognitive Science, 4*(13), 333–369.

Van Eck, R., & Dempsey, J. (2002). The effect of competition and contextualized advisement on the transfer of mathematics skills in a computer-based instructional simulation game. *Educational Technology Research and Development, 50*(3), 23–41.

Top Texts for Interdisciplinary Studies of Serious Games

Csikszentmihalyi, M. (1990). *Flow: The psychology of optimal experience*. New York: Harper & Row.

Gee, J. P. (2007). *What video games have to teach us about learning and literacy*. (2nd ed.) New York: Palgrave/Macmillan.

Gee, J. P. (2008). Video games and embodiment. *Games and Culture, 3*(3–4), 253–263.

Gibson, J. J. (1977). The theory of affordances. In R. Shaw & J. Bransford (Eds.), *Perceiving, acting, and knowing: Toward an ecological psychology* (pp. 67–82). Hillsdale, NJ: Lawrence Erlbaum.

Gredler, M. E. (2004). Games and simulations and their relationships to learning. In D. H. Jonassen (Ed.), *Handbook of research on educational communications and technology* (2nd ed.). Mahwah, N.J.: Association for Educational Communications and Technology, Lawrence Erlbaum.

Lakoff, G., & Johnson, M. (1980). *Metaphors we live by*. Chicago, IL: University of Chicago Press.

Lave, J., & Wenger, E. (1991). *Situated learning: Legitimate peripheral participation*. Cambridge, UK: Cambridge University Press.

Salen, K., & Zimmerman, E. (2004). *Rules of play: Game design fundamentals*. Cambridge, MA: MIT Press.

Stephenson, N. (1995). *The diamond age: Or, a young lady's illustrated primer*. New York: Bantam Spectra.

Van Eck, R. (2007). Six ideas in search of a discipline. In B. E. S. D. Wiley (Ed.), *The design and use of simulation computer games in education* (pp. 31–60). The Netherlands: Sense Publishing.

Chapter 5
Feedforward as an Essential Active Principle of Engagement in Computer Games

Richard H. Swan
BYU Center for Teaching & Learning, USA

ABSTRACT

Learner engagement is important for learning, yet the question of how to design engaging learning experiences still lingers. One of the facets of computer games is that they tend to be engaging. In addition, they are designed experiences. By examining computer games as examples of the design of engaging experiences through the lens of design theory, it may be possible to extract more fundamental principles for the design of engagement. Such principles could inform the design of serious games and other learning experiences. This chapter uses Vincenti's fundamental design concept of operational principle to identify the core components and active principle that underlie the design of engagement in games. The chapter also introduces the concept of feedforward to describe the continual elicitation of anticipatory cognition and behavior by players/learners. This feedforward effect in the context of player/learner agency is essential to the active principle of engagement in computer games.

INTRODUCTION

Learner motivation and engagement are seen as necessary conditions for learning to occur (see Blumenfeld, Kempler, & Krajcik, 2006; Buchanan, 2006; Edstrom, 2002; Katzeff, 2000). Yet learner engagement remains a persistent problem for education (Blumenfeld, et al., 2006; Buchanan, 2006; Csikszentmihalyi, 2002; Gardner, 2002). One of

the significant potential contributions of computer games to education is that they are generally successful at eliciting engagement, and thus may foster student engagement in the learning process (Aldrich, 2004; Barab, Thomas, Dodge, Carteaux, & Tuzun, 2005; Gee, 2003; Papert, 1998; Prensky, 2001; Rieber, 1996; Squire, 2005). While engagement has been addressed from psychological and phenomenological points of view, the question of engagement has not been examined sufficiently from the perspective of design (Katzeff, 2000; Kickmeier-

DOI: 10.4018/978-1-61520-717-6.ch005

Rust, et al., 2006; Kirriemuir & McFarlane, 2004; Swan, 2008; Van Eck, 2006, 2007). Katzeff (2000) notes: "The importance of motivation for the ability to learn is well documented. But with a few exceptions, this feature of learning is rarely addressed in the literature. How do we *design* for motivation, engagement and immersion?" (p. 5, emphasis added).

In addition, Kirriemuir and McFarlane (2004) suggest,

Rather than aiming for an experience that superficially resembles leisure-based "fun" activities, or one which attempts to conceal the educational purpose, it might be argued that we should understand the deep structures of the games play experience that contribute to [optimal engagement] and build these into environments designed to support learning. (p. 6)

The purpose of this chapter is to explore the "deep structures" of games from the perspective of design to generate a better understand of the design of engaging experiences. Computer games are examined as a type of experience designed for engagement in order to inform other design situations in which engagement is desirable (i.e., serious games in particular and instructional design in general).

BACKGROUND ON DESIGN THEORY

The study of the phenomenon of design has emerged as its own discipline and is most often referred to either as design studies or design science (Bayazit, 2004; Eastman, McCracken, & Newstetter, 2001; Van Aken, 2004). Practitioners in this field assert that the study of design is fundamentally different from the natural sciences (physics, chemistry, geology and biology) in the object of study, in the type of knowledge produced, and in its research methodologies (Bayazit, 2004; Eastman, et al., 2001; Simon, 1996). The distinc-

tion of the study and practice of design from traditional scientific method has also been noted in the field of instructional design (Bannan-Ritland, 2003, 2008; Gibbons, 2000; Inouye, Merrill, & Swan, 2005; Reigeluth & Frick, 1999). Some of the notable differences are that:

- Design problems are not well defined; solutions are not theoretically or procedurally predictable, but are contingent on situational conditions as well as the preferences, competence, and creativity of the designer (Gibbons, 2000; Inouye, et al., 2005; Silber, 2007; Simon, 1996). Consequently, there is no single design solution, but a variety of alternative design possibilities that offer different affordances and constraints.
- Design knowledge is testable and verifiable, but contextually and, in many respects, qualitatively rather than universally and objectively as it is in the natural sciences (Bannan-Ritland, 2003; Collins, Joseph, & Bielaczyc, 2004; Van Aken, 2004). While science may be used in the design process, and elements of a given design may be testable scientifically, design also includes inherent subjectivity, localization and novelty in its nature and thus does not lend itself to scientific inquiry (Inouye, et al., 2005; Simon, 1996; Sloane, 2006).
- Design theory is generalizable, but as heuristic principles rather than universal laws (Silber, 2007; Van Aken, 2004; Vincenti, 1990). Again, science is often used in design, but design is not reducible to an application of science; the process of design and the object of design can take a variety of forms that tend to be guided and adapted heuristically (Gibbons, 2000; Silber, 2007; Simon, 1996; Vincenti, 1990).

Computer games are designed artifacts. It follows then, that the design of computer games might employ scientific principles in part, but would also be guided by heuristic principles of design. The explication of these heuristic principles might not lend itself to a scientific approach, but would be accessible to inquiry from the perspective of design. A theoretical framework for seeking and describing design heuristics in practice is present in Vincenti's (1990) fundamental design concepts of *operational principle* and *normal configuration* (Gibbons, 2000; Rogers, Hsueh, & Gibbons, 2005; Swan, 2008; Vincenti, 1990). This chapter employs Vincenti's framework to propose higher-level principles for the design of engaging experiences.[1]

Fundamental Design Concepts: Operational Principle and Normal Configuration

One of the classes of knowledge specific to the field of design is the class of *fundamental design concepts* (Vincenti, 1990). According to Vincenti, this class is comprised of two concepts: *operational principle* and *normal configuration*. The term *operational principle* was introduced by Polanyi (1962) and later elaborated on by Vincenti (1990). Vincenti asserts that every artifact embodies an operational principle. He defines operational principle as "...the essential characterization of how the device works." (p. 208). For example, the basic operational principle of flight can be expressed as lifting a fixed wing using the resistance of air (Vincenti, 1990).

Normal configuration is defined by Vincenti (1990) as "the general shape or arrangement that are commonly agreed to best embody the operational principle" (p. 209). As the design of a device matures through iterations of design and real-world use, a consensus among designers tends to emerge about the overall shape and arrangement of the device (Murmann & Frenken, 2006). Vincenti (1990) refers to this consensus as a *normal configuration*. The *normal configuration* is the assumptive pattern or template for an artifact that instantiates the operational principle. A normal

configuration may be a *de facto* standard or it may become a codified standard. In short, the normal configuration is the designer's general preconception of how the operational principle should be expressed in the physical or virtual world.

An operational principle can generate a variety of normal configurations (Gibbons, 2000; Rogers, et al., 2005; Swan, 2008). For example, sedans, pickup truck, and sports cars are expressions of the operational principles of automobiles, yet each brings to mind a different general arrangement and shape. This example also highlights another powerful feature of these concepts—that they are relational. A given artifact may be composed of components and subcomponents each of which can be described by a corresponding operational principle and normal configuration. Thus operational principles can be expressed in varying levels of abstraction and specificity and can provide a useful framework for expressing the relationships and interactions of different structures and properties of a given design.

It is important to emphasize that operational principle and normal configuration represent *the designer's conceptualization*. They are not physical objects or blueprints; nor do they necessarily represent established theory. Rather, the operational principle and normal configuration are the *foundational assumptions of the designer*. Referring to these, Vincenti (1990) indicates, "Designers ...bring with them fundamental concepts about the device in question. These concepts may exist only implicitly in the back of the designer's mind, but they must be there. They are the givens for the project, even if unstated." (p. 208).

Another important point is that operational principles need not be understood *explicitly* in order to create functioning artifacts; they can be applied intuitively or serendipitously (Gibbons, 2000; Vincenti, 1990). However, making operational principles explicit tends to improve the quality of designs, and reveals new lines of inquiry and experimentation (Gibbons, 2000; Rogers, et al., 2005; Vincenti, 1990). Consequently, the search for a more suitable design may require the designer to reformulate the operational principle and/or configuration (Gibbons, 2000; Murmann & Frenken, 2006; Vincenti, 1990). In the development of the airplane, Vincenti (1990) notes that reconceiving the operational principle of flight as "propelling a rigid surface forward through the resisting air…freed designers from the previous impractical notion of flapping wings" (p. 208).

An operational principle can be described by identifying the *core components* and the *active principle* that interact to achieve the intended function (Gibbons, 2000; Murmann & Frenken, 2006; Swan, 2008). According to Murmann and Frenken (2006) *core components* are those components that are essential to the nature of the object. The object may have additional components beyond the core components, but Murmann and Frenken refer to these as *peripheral components*. For example, most automobiles have radios, but radios are not an essential component of an automobile. The active principle describes the forces, information, or agency that animates the entire system (Gibbons, 2000; Swan, 2008). For example, the operational principle of flight mentioned above has a core component of a "rigid surface" (or fixed wing) and an active principle of the "resistance of air."

In summary, computer games can be viewed as a type of normal configuration that can be investigated in order to specify a higher-level operational principle for the design of engaging experiences. One of the methods of uncovering operational principles is to "reverse engineer" them from existing sources (Gibbons, 2000; Swan, 2008). Chu, Lu, Chang, & Chung (2002) define reverse engineering as "the process of analyzing a subject system to identify the system's components and their interrelationships, and to create representations of the system in another form or at a higher level of abstraction" (p. 2). One of the purposes of reverse engineering is to generate design theory or principles that are applicable to multiple design situations (Canfora & Di Penta, 2007; Chu, et al., 2001; Chu, et al., 2002).

One of the possible methods of reverse engineering is to analyze the works and writings of designers (Canfora & Di Penta, 2007; Chu, et al., 2001; Chu, et al., 2002). This is especially appropriate in this context as an operational principle represents the designer's conceptualization (Vincenti, 1990). Consequently, this chapter analyzes the writings of several influential game designers and game theorists (Elliot Avedon and Brian Sutton-Smith, Greg Costikyan, Chris Crawford, Johan Huizinga, Jesper Juul, Andrew Rollings and Ernest Adams, and Katie Salen and Eric Zimmerman) to identify possible core components, and to identify or infer an active principle that drives engagement in computer games.

CORE COMPONENTS OF COMPUTER GAMES

The analysis of the selected authors revealed a variety of possible core components (see Table 1). It is not feasible to discuss all the possible core components here, but the entries in Table 1 provide an idea of the level of agreement and the areas of difference in the discussion of game design. (For a more complete discussion of the analysis see Swan, 2008.)

In reviewing these authors, some terms and ideas were discussed as if they were competing. For example, is the best term "goal," "outcome," or "challenge?" However, the construct of operational principle provided a framework that allowed these elements to be related as subcomponents or properties within a larger component. Thus, although many of the terms and ideas may still appear familiar, I submit that the result provides a more coherent, structural and organized view of the elements of game design and provides a basis for continued definition and development of subcomponents and properties. In consequence of this approach, virtually all of the elements from these authors are accounted for as constituent parts or properties of four proposed core components of computer games: (a) meaningful challenge, (b)

Table 1. Comparison of potential core components of games by author*

Crawford	Costikyan	Rollings & Adams	Salen & Zimmerman	Huizinga	Avedon & Sutton-Smith	Juul
Rules	Rules	Rules	Operational rules Constituative rules	Rules	Rules	Rules
Focused Fantasy	Represen-tation	Game World	Artificial Reality	Temporary World	Setting	
Inter-player Conflict	Struggle	Challenge	Conflict	Test of Prow-ess	Opposition	Player Effort
Elegant controls	Interactivity	User Interface	Narrow Input			
Key element		Player's Role	Core Mechanic		Procedure	
Organic Re-sponse		Presentation	Immediate Feed-back			
			Quantifiable Outcome		Disequilibrial Outcome	Variable, Quantifiable Outcome
		Dramatic Tension	Uncertainty	Tension		
			Rewards and Punishments		Pay-off	
		Storytelling	Narrative descrip-tors			
	Goals				Goal	
	Endogenous Meaning					Valorization of Outcome
	Resources				Equipment	
					Role	
Safety						

* Terms in the same row indicate similar meanings

self-consistent setting, (c) core performance, and (d) embedded helps.

Meaningful Challenge

The idea of challenge is not new to games. However, I submit that the following provides a better structural definition of challenge and successfully relates ideas from different authors as subcomponents or properties of challenge. A *meaningful challenge* is defined as an *attainable goal of endogenous value that entails conflict constrained by operational rules and limited resources*.

Attainable Goal

According to Crawford (2003), "the point is the challenge, not the goal" (p. 38). Going to the grocery story is a goal, but it is not normally a challenge. However, going to the grocery store could be a challenge if the other elements were present. Yet it also seems reasonable to say that a challenge cannot exist without a goal.

The goal is the desired future outcome or end state of the game. Until the end state is achieved it is a goal. Once the goal is achieved, it is an outcome; however, at that point, the challenge ceases, and the game is over. It is the goal that entices the player forward. Therefore, the most appropriate term is *goal* rather than *outcome*. Thus, *goal* is a necessary subcomponent of *meaningful challenge*.

The property of being *attainable* applies both to the game structure and to player perception. For the game it means that the challenge is scaled, or scaleable to the ability level of the player. Ideally, as player ability increases, the level of challenge also increases correspondingly (Crawford, 1984; Rollings & Adams, 2003; Salen & Zimmerman, 2004).

For the player, *attainable* is the perception that it is possible to accomplish the goal. Crawford (1984) refers to this as the "illusion of winnability" (Chapter 6). It is an illusion because the game does not have to be literally "winnable." According to Crawford (1984), "if the player believes failures to be attributable to correctable errors on his own part, he believes the game to be winnable and plays on in an effort to master the game" (Chapter 6). If the goal is not perceived as attainable, the probability of engagement is minimal (Crawford, 1984; Csikszentmihalyi, 1990).[2] Thus, perceived attainability is a necessary property of a meaningful challenge.

Endogenous Value

Costikyan (2002) introduces the idea of *endogenous meaning* which he defines as having meaning within the system of the game. To illustrate, Costikyan (2002) provides the following example:

Monopoly money has no meaning in the real world. ...Yet when you're playing Monopoly, Monopoly money has value. In Monopoly, the gaily colored little bills that come with the game are the determinant of success or failure. Monopoly money has meaning endogenous to the game of Monopoly. (p. 22)

While *endogenous meaning* from Costikyan (2002) is adequate; the term *meaning* does not necessarily connote desirability. The idea of

valorization (Juul, 2003), or *value*, does imply desirability or esteem. Salen and Zimmerman (2004) also maintain that when players enter the game, they temporarily adopt the value system of the game (see also Huizinga, 1944/1970). These congruent ideas can be successfully combined as *endogenous value*.

Therefore, I will define *endogenous value* as desirability or esteem within the game system. Endogenous value is a designable property of the goal and contributes significantly to the meaningfulness of the challenge.[3]

Conflict

Conflict was one of the two possible components that all authors mentioned. Conflict is the component that makes a goal a challenge. Conflict need not be limited to interplayer conflict. Conflict can result from players' own lack of knowledge and/or ability within the game (internal conflict), or from active opposition from other players. From the game, conflict can come from passive obstacles such as terrain, unpredictable equipment such as dice, and/or from active opposition by game agents (often called non-player characters, or NPCs). Thus, conflict is active/passive, internal/external opposition to the player's goals and behaviors.

Endogenous value also relates to conflict. It can be assumed that if the goal is valuable, then other agents will value its attainment as well. The amount of value tends to increase the amount of conflict players will expect. At the same time, it can be true that the amount of conflict increases the perceived value. If these are out of balance however, players can become disappointed and disengage (Crawford, 2003; Rollings & Adams, 2003; Salen & Zimmerman, 2004).

Other authors mention uncertainty, tension, and dramatic tension as elements of games (see Table 1). I would argue that these may be viewed reasonably as synonymous for conflict, and thus constitute a property of conflict. It is the presence of conflict that produces the possibility of alternative outcomes. By manipulating conflict, you manipulate tension or uncertainty. Conflict is manipulated through the *operational rules* and the availability and quality of *resources*.

Operational Rules

All authors also mentioned rules as a part of games. Salen and Zimmerman, however, separate rules into the "rules of the game," or *operational rules*, and the "rules of the game world," or *constituative rules* (2004). Crawford (2003) makes a similar distinction although not as explicitly. This separation is structurally helpful. The operational rules apply to the design of conflict, where the constituative rules apply to the design of the game world.

Operational rules define player actions and interactions (Avedon, 1971; Crawford, 2003; Salen & Zimmerman, 2004); they can also change situationally. In football, for example, there are different rules for the situation of punting, and different rules for the situation of the kick-off. Operational rules fit as a subcomponent of *meaningful challenge* because it is through the operational rules that you can manage and manipulate conflict.

Operational rules manage conflict by allowing or encouraging certain behaviors while discouraging or prohibiting other behaviors. Operational rules are enforced through a system of rewards and punishments or other social consequences. Rewards and punishments are essential to games but as a subcomponent in support of operational rules.[4]

Limited Resources

Costikyan (1994) asserts that limited resources are part of games. Salen & Zimmerman (2004) also note that games employ sub-optimal means. *Limited resources* is a subcomponent of *meaningful challenge* because resources are necessary to meet the challenge, and acquiring and/or mastering the use of the resources is part of the challenge. Further, the structuring of resources (by type,

timing, quality and quantity) also manipulates conflict. The limitation of resources presents a possible barrier to the player's progress in the game. It introduces another element of risk or uncertainty in the game. For example, players may wonder whether to use the resource now, whether they will need the resource later, or whether they will find more of the resource when they need it. Thus, the judicious design of resources is another way to shape challenge and conflict.

In summary, the components of *meaningful challenge* can be represented hierarchically as follows:

- Meaningful challenge is composed of
- Attainable goal of endogenous value
- Conflict (which is manipulated by)
- Pperational rules
- (rewards and punishments)
- Limited resources

This structural definition of *meaningful challenge* resolves the ambiguities and overlap of the individual definitions while maintaining and interrelating the essential components. This definition provides a framework to develop and discuss additional subcomponents and properties that may be essential to games. Therefore, I submit that *meaningful challenge* is a core component of computer games.

Self-Consistent Setting

The term *self-consistent setting* is more drab than *focused fantasy* as defined by Crawford (1984) or even the term *game world*. However, it may be possible to misconstrue *fantasy* as implying something unrealistic and *world* as implying a 3-D realistic environment. S*etting* is a more general term that can apply to both the simple or abstract context as well as the richly detailed representation. The term *self-consistent* indicates that everything necessary for the experience is present in the setting, and that the elements that comprise the setting are internally congruent. Therefore, I will use the term *self-consistent setting* as the second core component of games. *Self-consistent setting* is defined as a *coconstructed alternate reality defined by constitutive rules represented thematically.*

Coconstructed Alternate Reality

The *self-consistent setting* is coconstructed in that the game designer cannot deliver "reality;" therefore, the designer constructs a subset of reality (Crawford, 1984). The player, through imagination, supplies whatever else is necessary to complete the "construction" of the setting (Crawford, 1984; Salen & Zimmerman, 2004). The notion of *alternate reality* acknowledges that the game is outside of "real life" yet the game is treated for its duration as reality (Huizinga, 1944/1970; Salen & Zimmerman, 2004).

Constituative Rules

Constituative rules are the rules that *constitute*, or formally establish, the game world. According to Salen & Zimmerman (2004), the constitutive rules "are the underlying formal structures" (p. 130) that govern the existing reality of the game setting. Essentially, the constitutive rules are the "natural laws" and the established rules and roles of societies and non-player characters that are immutable for the purposes of the game. By way of contrast, the operational rules might be considered the "rules of engagement." Thus, the constitutive rules govern the universe in which the challenge is placed and the operational rules govern the players' actions and associated consequences within the challenge itself.

Thematic Representation

It is an important distinction that the constitutive rules are not the representation (Costikyan, 2002; Rollings & Adams, 2003; Salen & Zimmerman, 2004) just as the broadcast signal is not the television show. The rules must be represented in a form that is sensible to the player. Thus, to the extent possible, the constitutive rules are communicated by representing them *thematically* (Rollings & Adams, 2003; Salen & Zimmerman, 2004). The notion of theme is chosen because it connotes both the topic, as well as a consistent style of representation.

Thematic representation relies on *narrative descriptors* as discussed by Salen & Zimmerman (2004). Narrative descriptors are elements in the game that communicate a sense of story without being a story (Salen & Zimmerman, 2004; Swan, 2008). Narrative descriptors can be images, music, sound effects, text, etc. Salen & Zimmerman (2004) indicate,

Representations in games do not exist in isolation from the rest of culture. They rely on conventions drawn from narrative genres in other media. Although the playgrounds of games may offer fictive and fantastical spaces, these spaces are almost always familiar in some way to players. The deep space of Asteroids is not something any of us have experienced directly, but it is part of a genre-based universe found in the stories of science fiction writers and astrophysicists. Players can appreciate the narrative of the game even if they have never piloted a space ship in a field of asteroids, because of the familiar conventions of its representation. (p. 401)

The chosen theme dictates, or should dictate, the narrative descriptors that represent the *self-consistent setting*. Not simply for artistic unity, although that is desirable as well (Crawford, 1984), but because the theme communicates or suggests the constitutive rules on many levels (Salen & Zimmerman, 2004). For example, the iconic "Jolly Roger," the black flag with a skull and crossbones, communicates a time in history, a general location, manners of dress and speech and other social roles and rules from the world of piracy quickly and wordlessly.

It stands to reason that to introduce extraneous narrative descriptors is to communicate another set of possibly contradictory rules, and therefore confuse the player. Certainly, themes can and have been mixed successfully; however, there is usually an additional constituative rule (such as time travel, magic, or the holodeck, for example) that explains or rationalizes the combination of themes. In other words, the players infer the rules from the representation they experience; these inferences are part of the coconstruction of the alternate reality. As Crawford (2003) and Rollings & Adams (2003) argue, the goal of graphics is not aesthetic excellence or stunning realism, though these may be desirable; the goal of graphics is, first and foremost, to communicate. This applies to all other elements of the representation as well. Thus, the rules and their representation must be reflexively congruent.

The structural definition of *self-consistent setting* accounts for important components of games and demonstrates their interrelationship as a functional composite. The definition of *self-consistent setting* does not eliminate other subcomponents or properties, but rather, provides a framework for their inclusion and discussion. Therefore, I submit that *self-consistent setting* is a core component of computer games.

Core Performance

For the game to work, players must be able to interact with it. As Crawford (2003) puts it, players must be able "to creatively influence the outcome of the game" (p. 87). However, Crawford (1984) and Salen and Zimmerman (2004) assert that designing an interface is not the starting point. Crawford (1984) argues,

The game designer must identify some key element from the topic environment and build the game around that key element. This key element must be central to the topic, representative or symbolic

of the issues addressed in the game, manipulable, and understandable. (Chapter 5 online)

The key element is initially conceptual, but must be translated into interface elements and controls (Crawford, 1984). Salen and Zimmerman (2004) propose a similar idea they term *core mechanic*. Salen and Zimmerman (2004) define the core mechanic as "the essential play activity players perform again and again in a game" (p. 316). They further indicate, "The core mechanic is the essential nugget of game activity" (p. 316). Interface elements and controls should then be designed around the core mechanic (Salen & Zimmerman, 2004). (A similar idea is also referred to by Avedon (1971) as *procedure*.)

To reduce the confusion of terms, the term *core performance* will be used to indicate a well-defined action or narrow set of integrated actions central to achieving the goal that the player must perform effectively to succeed. It is through the core performance that the player is imaginatively present in the game world and is metaphorically allowed to act, to speak, to create meaning (Costikyan, 1994; Crawford, 2003; Salen & Zimmerman, 2004). Interactivity and interface design are the means; the expression of agency is the end. It is this qualitative goal that should govern the design of the mechanical and computational systems (see also Laurel, 1991).

Consistent with the recommendations of Crawford (1984) and Salen and Zimmerman (2004), the core performance must be further translated into *elegant controls*. Further, the core performance is made manifest in the game world through *authentic consequences*. These two comprise subcomponents of the core performance.

Elegant Controls

Crawford's (2003) term of *elegant controls* is appropriate. Crawford counsels that a game's controls should be both simple and yet expressive.

It is not that the controls cannot be complex, but that the complexity is warranted for the fantasy of the game (Crawford, 1984). There is an inverse relationship between complexity of controls and the pace of the game; where the demands of the game on the player come faster, the controls (and the *core performance*), in general, should be simpler (Crawford, 1984). In slower paced games, the controls can be (but need not be) more complex. In all cases elegant controls are the ideal.

A qualitative criteria for elegant controls is that using the controls should recede into the background of the player's consciousness, while player action in the game moves into the foreground (Rollings & Adams, 2003). Initially, learning the controls often takes conscious effort. Ideally, using the controls should become like walking, or riding a bike; they can be done without consciously thinking about them, freeing up the conscious mind to deal with other matters—like winning the game.

Authentic Consequences

One of the touted strengths of computer games is that they provide immediate feedback (Dickey, 2005; Kirriemuir & McFarlane, 2004; Prensky, 2001; Salen & Zimmerman, 2004). However, the notion of feedback has become so common that it may have become a cultural blind spot (a blind spot shared by the author until this study; see Bogart, 1980; Rosen, 1985). Bogart (1980), citing Bertalanffy (1968), expresses a concern that feedback has become equated inaccurately with systems theory noting that the concept of feedback has become entrenched in everyday vocabulary. Indeed, the term feedback is sometimes loosely used in the game literature and seems to refer to almost any information presented as the player interacts with the game. Consequently, this study asserts that a more appropriate characterization is that games provide authentic consequences.

The type of relationship that is most often described when referring to immediate feedback is not a feedback loop (output fed back as input), but rather a cause-effect, or more appropriately an action-consequence relationship. If a child throws a baseball through a window, it is not generally referred to as feedback, yet it certainly is an action with a consequence. In a shooting game, for example, if a player "shoots" an alien monster, the death of the monster is more appropriately considered a consequence of the player's action not an output of the player's action.

Certainly, players need to know that their inputs have registered in the game world. Thus, in a shooting game, if the player "pulls the trigger" the player should immediately be informed that a shot was fired by a visual flash from the muzzle, for example, the sound of a gunshot, or both. But these again, are more accurately described (from the qualitative perspective of the game) in terms of action/consequence rather than input/output (notwithstanding this may be true from a technical computer programming standpoint).

Of course, the chain of action/consequence should continue through the entire effect of the action; representing the initial effect through the terminal effect of the action which brings us to another point—actions have multiple consequences that play out over different scales of time. Even in the simple example above, pulling the trigger has the consequence of firing the bullet which has a consequence at the end of its trajectory; and the consequence of hitting or missing the target may trigger other consequences which may affect unknown interactions in the future.

Thus, while there is an immediate consequence of an action, it may not be the immediate consequence that is the consequence of interest. Take, for example, games or simulations such as the *Sim* series, the *Tycoon* series, or the education game/ simulation of *VirtualU*—consequences of interest play out over much longer time scales than twitch-speed games, and are not always immediately detectable. Further, the consequence of interest may not be the result of a single action, but rather the interaction of multiple actions, consequences and reactions over time. This does not fit well with the notion of immediate feedback. Indeed, it may be precisely because players experience consequences and are not always given feedback that the game preserves some uncertainty and remains challenging and engaging.

In many cases, the computer game does not tell the player that what they did was right or wrong; it simply plays out the natural consequence of the action within the game. The evaluative function is most often left to the player. The player may use the same consequence to "turn on" or "turn off" a behavior (a feedback function), but may also use it to modify the strategy, the behavior, or both to improve future performance; or may use the event to signal a new goal or behavior. These uses are better described as serving a *feedforward* function which will be discussed in more detail later.

Nonetheless, there is an immediate need for information in a computer game. In computer games, the player acts indirectly through input devices. The often unconscious question to be answered is: "Did the game receive my input?" Thus, it is necessary to communicate that the player's expression through the joystick movement, the mouse click, or the keystroke has registered in the system and initiated the desired action through an immediate consequence. Players then expect the natural consequences of the action to play out over the natural timescale of the game.

Of course, consequences must be authentic; the monster should die *after* the gun is fired. At the same time, authenticity is determined in terms of the rules of the challenge and the setting (Swan, 2005). For example, waving a magic wand in a fantasy setting might reasonably result in turning someone into a frog. At the end of the interaction, however, the player ought to be able to unconsciously say to him or herself, "That makes sense."

Therefore, I submit that *authentic consequences* is a more descriptive term than immediate feedback (see also Crawford's (1984) discussion regarding natural flow of information). In sum-

mary, *elegant controls* and *authentic consequences* provide the means for players substantiate their agency within the game. They are the means by which the player executes and evaluates the *core performance* of the game. Thus, the core performance can be represented hierarchically as:

- Core performance (instantiated through)
- Elegant controls
- Authentic consequences

The player makes their presence felt in the game through the core performance. I would assert that the notion of agency—the *imaginative perception of being present* (Swan, 2008) and the ability, according to Crawford (2003), to "creatively influence the outcome of the game" (p. 85)—is at the heart of engagement and immersion.

Embedded Helps

Embedded helps are elements built into the game that assist or guide the player toward the goal. The core component of embedded helps is not obvious; it is not specified by any of the authors, although I would assert that it is implied. I believe it is not explicit in part because the forms of embedded helps are quite varied; thus this categorization would not be readily apparent. Further, it seems that the best of these embedded helps seem so "natural" to the game that they are not recognized for what they are. Also, they are often included in other categories such as interface or feedback, for example. Finally, it seems more fitting to consider embedded helps as a higher-level operational principle that encompasses other operational principles. Two categories of embedded helps identified from this study are *organic guides*, and *recoverability mechanisms*.

Organic Guides

Organic guides provide additional information beyond what is expected from the action-consequence flow of information from player-game interaction.

They can be visual, aural, or tactile (such as the rumble feature in some game controllers). For example, information can be transmitted aurally through sound effects, or through communications from friendly characters in the game. Visual displays can include status bars, or instrument panels; these often have narrative justification but are present to help guide the player. The best organic guides are incorporated into the theme and the flow of the game. For example, a number of games use non-player characters to provide direction effectively disguised as dialog that supports the narrative of the game. Reflecting on some of the better games I have played, I have been surprised at how much guidance was present and yet went largely unnoticed.

Recoverability Mechanisms

According to Crawford (2003),

Good games permit the player to undo his last move, or play it over, instantly. The quicker and more easily the player can correct a mistake, the safer he will feel and the more exploratory and playful his play will be. (p. 32)

The mechanisms mentioned above (undo, play over), allow the player to recover from a poor choice and try again. An interesting paradox of games is that players *expect to fail* (Crawford, 2003; Rouse, 2001), but ultimately, Crawford (2003) argues, play "must be safe" (p. 31). If recovery is difficult, players are more likely to disengage (Crawford, 2003; Rouse, 2001).

Thus, an appropriate term for this component from a design perspective would be *recoverability mechanisms*. Recoverability mechanisms also include the ability to save the game, or restart. On a smaller scale they can also include things such as healing potions, extra lives, etc. Note that these can be used as rewards, but they are also often placed strategically within the game and available whenever the player reaches that point—often at a point when the need is high. Recoverability provides that

balance that encourages risk-taking while providing the necessary safety. Indeed, *recoverability* is one of the key features that distinguishes computer games from real life.

Embedded helps, in general, should be non-intrusive and non-didactic; they should appear as if they arise naturally out of the interaction wherever possible. The quality of appearing to be natural parts of the environment preserves participants' sense of accomplishment. Certainly from the perspective of players, they prefer to "figure it out on their own;" they tend to seek didactic help as a last resort (Dempsey, Haynes, Lucassen, & Casey, 2002; Heeter, Winn, & Greene, 2005; Waelder, 2006). In short, *embedded helps* is an appropriate high-level descriptor for these elements and constitutes a core component of computer games.

SUMMARY OF CORE COMPONENTS OF COMPUTER GAMES

The first step of this analysis was to identify the core components of computer games. The above analysis addresses all of the potential components from the different authors although it frames all but two, termed here as self-consistent setting and meaningful challenge, as subcomponents or properties of larger core components (see Table 2). This analysis reduces the ambiguities between authors and better organizes and illustrates the interrelationships between the proposed essential components of computer games. It is to be expected that there are undoubtedly many important subcomponents and properties that could not be discussed here for reasons of space. At the same time, this analysis and the concept of operational principle provide a framework to define and relate additional subcomponents and their associated operational principles. Consequently, I conclude that the core components of an operational principle for the design of engaging experiences are as follows:

Table 2. Final core components compared to potential components by author

Crawford	Costikyan	Rollings & Adams	Salen & Zimmerman	Huizinga	Avedon & Sutton-Smith	Juul
Meaningful Challenge						
	Goals				Goals	
	Endogenous Meaning					Valorization of Outcome
Inter-player Conflict	Struggle	Challenge	Conflict	Test of Prowess	Opposition	Player Effort
Rules	Rules	Rules	Operational rules	Rules	Rules	Rules
	Resources				Equipment	
Implicit in Meaningful challenge						
			Quantifiable Outcome		Disequilibrial Outcome	Variable, Quantifiable Outcome
		Dramatic Tension	Uncertainty	Tension		
			Rewards and Punishments		Pay-off	
Self-consistent setting						
Focused Fantasy	Representation	Game World	Artificial Reality	Temporary World	Setting	
(Inherent Rules)			Constituative rules			
		Storytelling	Narrative descriptors			
Core performance						
Key element		Player's Role	Core Mechanic		Procedure	
					Role	
Elegant controls	Interactivity	User Interface	Narrow Input			
Organic Response		Presentation	Immediate Feedback			
Embedded helps						
Safety						

1. Meaningful challenge: An achievable goal of endogenous value that entails conflict constrained by operational rules and limited resources;
2. Self-consistent setting: A coconstructed alternate reality defined by constituative rules represented thematically;
3. Core performance: The action or narrow set of integrated actions central to achieve the goal transmitted through elegant controls and made manifest through authentic consequences;
4. Embedded helps: Resources or mechanisms within the setting that assist, encourage, or guide players to toward the goal.

ACTIVE PRINCIPLE OF ENGAGEMENT IN COMPUTER GAMES

As noted above, to complete the definition of an operational principle it is necessary to describe the active principle that animates the system. In my review, none of the designers or theorists directly addressed the idea of an active principle of engagement. Certainly, players invested their time, energy, and even a sense of self into the game (Costikyan, 1994; Crawford, 2003; Huizinga, 1944/1970; Juul, 2003; Rollings & Adams, 2003; Rouse, 2001; Salen & Zimmerman, 2004). But what forces or motivation underlie this investment? The realization that many features of computer games work to engender and sustain anticipatory behaviors emerged from the analysis described above. At the same time, a serendipitous encounter introduced a concept that encapsulates the anticipatory nature of computer games—the concept of *feedforward systems*.

Bogart (1980) and Rosen (1985) argue that the paradigm of feedback systems is so ubiquitous that it has, until recently, obscured anticipatory or *feedforward* systems. Indeed Rosen argues effectively that

The failure to recognize and understand the nature of anticipatory behavior has not simply been an oversight, but is the necessary consequence of the entire thrust of theoretical science since the earliest of times. ...the imperative to avoid even the remotest appearance of telic explanation in science is so strong that all modes of system analysis conventionally exclude the possibility of anticipatory behavior from the very outset." (p. 9)

Rosen (1985) recounts that once becoming acquainted with the idea of anticipatory systems, "To my astonishment, I found them everywhere, at all levels of biological organization" (p. 7). Similarly, the concept of feedforward applied to computer games resulted in many insights and provided a basis for an active principle of engagement in computer games—that the core components of computer games work together to engender and sustain a *feedforward effect*. Given that the concept of feedforward systems may be new to many readers, a brief discussion is warranted.

OVERVIEW OF SYSTEM TYPES AND FEEDFORWARD NATURE OF GAMES

To introduce feedforward systems, it is first helpful to provide an overview of feedback systems, as they are in many ways defined in opposition.

Feedback Systems

The concept of feedback comes out of cybernetics and systems theory (Ashby, 1956; Bogart, 1980; Heylighen & Joslyn, 2001; Joensuu, 2006). A feedback system is called so because the output of the system is "fed back" as input to the controller as shown in Figure 1 (Heylighen & Joslyn, 2001; Hubka & Eder, 1988; Macmillan, 1955; Shearer, Kulakowski, & Gardner, 1997). The most common type of feedback system works to counteract disturbances in order to maintain a desired state (Heylighen & Joslyn, 2001; Hubka & Eder, 1988; Joensuu, 2006; Shearer, et al., 1997). In other words, after an "error" has occurred, the system then reacts to correct the error (Macmillan, 1955; Rosen, 1985; Shearer, et al., 1997).

A simple example of a feedback system is a thermostat and furnace. The thermostat (controller) monitors the heat (input) in the room. When the heat dips behold a threshold value (the error condition) the process is invoked (the furnace turns on). The output of the process (heat) is fed back into the controller until the error condition is corrected, and the process (the furnace) is turned off.

Feedforward Systems

Although the idea of feedforward existed in the early development of systems theory (Bogart, 1980; Heylighen & Joslyn, 2001), practical successes in feedback systems overshadowed the research and development of feedforward systems (Bogart, 1980; Chalam, 1987; Shearer, et al., 1997). Thus, feedback is now a common

Figure 1. Diagram of a feedback system

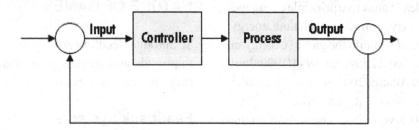

term in many fields while feedforward is not so well known (Bogart, 1980). However, with recent advances in microprocessors, feedforward systems have become more practical; consequently, interest in and development of these types of systems has been increasing (Chalam, 1987; Principe, Euliano, & Lefebvre, 2000; Sandberg, et al., 2001). As noted above, Rosen (1985) also expresses philosophical reasons why feedforward systems have been overlooked.

Simple Feedforward, or Open-loop Systems

Simple feedforward systems, sometimes referred to as open-loop systems (see Figure 2), are set up to anticipate future conditions and act, but do not monitor the outcome (Heylighen & Joslyn, 2001; Joensuu, 2006). An automatic sprinkler system is one example of an open-loop feedforward system (Skyttner, 2005); the user sets the system's program in anticipation of the need for watering the lawn at regular intervals. The system operates on the basis of the prediction, but the prediction may

not be accurate. The classic example, of course, is when the automatic sprinkler system turns on in the middle of a rainstorm.

Complex Adaptive Systems

There is another class of feedforward systems that have been given a variety of names—anticipatory systems, learning systems, feedforward neural networks, artificial neural networks, complex adaptive systems and more (Chalam, 1987; Holland, 1996; Principe, et al., 2000; Rosen, 1985). The critical distinction of this class of feedforward systems is that they learn; they can change their behavior based on past and present experience to make better predictions in order to achieve a desired future state or goal (Holland, 1996; Joensuu, 2006; Principe, et al., 2000; Rosen, 1985; Sandberg, et al., 2001). Adaptive systems can be artificial or organic; they can rely on feedforward mechanisms only, such as feedforward neural networks in computing, or they can also have both feedforward and feedback components (Principe, et al., 2000; Sandberg, et al., 2001). Feedforward

Figure 2. Diagram of a simple feedforward (open loop) system

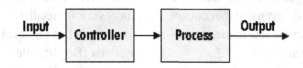

neural networks (such as the simple version displayed in Figure 3) do not use feedback to learn. There are a variety of methods, one of which is called back-propagation.[5]

To summarize, feedback systems have a reactive model. They can detect an error condition and correct it, but feedback systems do not of themselves change their model—they do not learn. Open-loop feedforward systems are anticipatory; they act in the present based on anticipations about the future. However, their anticipatory model is also fixed; they also do not learn. Complex adaptive systems, or agents, can change their own model to better anticipate future events. In other words, *they can learn*. Thus, agents act in the present based on predictions about the future, but can also correct or adapt their behavior relative to the goal by evaluating present and past results to refine the predictive model and its associated behaviors. In other words, feedback systems do not change their behavior; they act according to a fixed model. Feedforward learning systems, on the other hand, do change their behavior; they adapt their model to better approximate the desired outcome. It is important to emphasize that learning occurs for the purpose of improving the anticipatory, or *feedforward* component of the system. This notion more closely approximates the example of

the player trying to shoot an alien monster; the player uses the information to modify their own behavior to achieve the desired outcome.

According to Holland (1996), all living organisms are complex adaptive systems (see also Rosen, 1985, 2000). Holland (1996) also refers to complex adaptive systems as *agents*. Holland's term *agent* is very appropriate for this discussion and shall be used, especially to refer to human beings.

Feedforward Characteristics of Computer Games

Most computer games have elements of simple feedforward systems. The game systems have been built to anticipate the players' actions and to hinder or oppose players' progress to provide conflict. In many first-person shooter games, enemies have been placed in the probable path the player will take to reach the objective. Following this path tends to result in the greatest number of confrontations. However, if the player takes a path that avoids confrontation, these enemies do not detect the change in the player's strategy, but will remain in place in anticipation of an encounter that may never occur. In short, the game system is designed to anticipate players' probable actions, but may

Figure 3. Diagram of a simple feedforward neural network

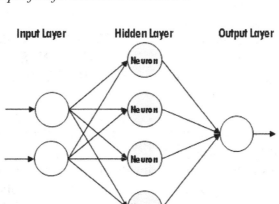

not necessarily adapt its own behaviors. (It should be noted that adaptivity is an area of research and development for computer games.)

However, the technical qualification of the game as a complex adaptive system may not be necessary. It may be enough that the game system requires the human player to adapt. Adaptation occurs in the face of competition (Holland, 1996; Rosen, 1985, 2000), but both systems do not have to be anticipatory to be in conflict. Heylighen and Joslyn (2001) assert that for any two interacting systems, "If the two goals are incompatible, this is a model of conflict or competition" (p. 17). Thus, if the game system hinders the player's ability to achieve the goal, the game is in conflict with the player.

In the board game *Monopoly*, for example, the use of two dice makes it impossible to acquire a monopoly of properties without circling the board at least once. With only one die, it would be possible to acquire a monopoly in two or three turns. Thus, the game's rules make it less likely that the player will achieve the goal quickly, which heightens the conflict. This example illustrates that adaptivity can be simulated by randomization methods, such as rolling dice or shuffling cards. Thus the game is never the same twice and the player must adapt to the novel circumstances, but the game itself is not adaptive.

Therefore, the essential requirement may simply be that the game challenges players' own anticipatory, adaptive capacity. According to Crawford (2003), it is sufficient that the players perceive (or pretend) that they are competing against another agent. (Of course, in many games adaptivity is provided by competing against other players.)

This formulation of challenging players' adaptive abilities also resolves the debate about puzzles and so-called "goalless" games such as Sim-City (Costikyan, 1994, 2002; Crawford, 2003; Salen & Zimmerman, 2004). These also provide suitable, albeit different, situations to safely test agentive abilities. Nonetheless, it would stand to reason that

the closer a game approximated an active adaptive agent, the more intense the gameplay experience would be. Further, it also explains why games that were once engaging become boring: no further adaptation is required of the player. Viewing games in this way gives us a mechanism to understand differences in games and the different forms and levels of engagement they elicit.

There is a convergence here with the game design theories particularly of Costikyan, Crawford, and Salen and Zimmerman and the ideas of feedforward systems, adaptivity and agency. The game requires players to invest something of themselves in the game; one's own anticipatory, adaptive abilities are on the line. This imaginative investment of self is the essential quality of entering the *magic circle* referred to by Salen and Zimmerman (2004)—that when one enters the magic circle, the game token is no longer a piece of plastic, the game token becomes "you" (see also Costikyan, 1994). It is this emotional investment of oneself—*to see if I am up to the challenge*—that supplies the motivational energy that underlies the significant expenditure of time and effort (see also Crawford, 2003; Rouse, 2001) which the game then channels and shapes through its structures and responses. Therefore, the well-designed game creates a feedforward effect on players' imaginative investment of themselves in the game.

INTERACTION OF CORE COMPONENTS AND ACTIVE PRINCIPLE

This section discusses ways in which the core components of computer games interact with the active principle of player agency. This section will discuss characteristics of agency based primarily on the writing of Holland (1996), Rosen (1985) and Kelly (1955/1963) and will then describe how the core components of games interact with these characteristics.

Agents take action based upon a predictive model of a given situation (Holland, 1996; Kelly, 1955/1963; Reigler, 2003; Rosen, 1985). An agent does not comprehend the entirety of a situation, but rather has an internal representation, or model that approximates the situation to a greater or lesser extent. The model is predictive and generates present actions based on anticipated goals with respect to the situation. Holland and Rosen primarily employ the term model. However, Kelly uses the term *construct* which he derives from construing, or the person's process of making meaning. Thus, the term *construct* also better implies the role of the human agent in creating the mental model. Consequently, this chapter will prefer the term construct as essentially synonymous with the term model.

According to Kelly, constructs are shaped by the experiential memories, emotions, and values through which an individual construes meaning. Thus, some aspects of a given construct will be learned and shared socially, while other aspects will be personal (Kelly, 1955/1963). For example, parts of the construct of *family* will be relatively common, but certainly, each individual, even within the same family, will have different experiences and therefore a similar yet different construct of *family*.

Constructs do not exist in isolation; they are interrelated by means of similarity and contrast with other constructs (Kelly, 1955/1963). For example, any given *planet* shares essential similarities with all other *planets*. Yet the construct *planet* stands in contrast to the construct *star* for example. Further, *Earth* is part of the classification *planet* yet stands in contrast by its individual differences to all other bodies of the same classification. Thus, a construct inherently comprises what is included, what is excluded, and what is irrelevant (Kelly, 1955/1963).

An agent uses their system of constructs to frame their current situation; to predict the likely course of events, and thus to guide their strategies and behaviors as they act in the world. Computer games are designed to work within and yet challenge players' constructs and agency.

Generating Anticipations through Thematic Signaling

According to Kelly (1955/1963), a construct is called to mind when we encounter a similar pattern or situation. Further, agents anticipate that the present situation will be substantially similar to previous situations that shaped the construct. They will, therefore, base their actions on those anticipations (Kelly, 1955/1963).[6]

Narrative descriptors in computer games function as thematic signals to evoke a familiar construct. To reiterate, narrative descriptors represent aspects of the game world; they are not a story, but communicate a sense of story (Salen & Zimmerman, 2004). The initial anticipations generated by *thematic signaling* must be appealing enough to overcome the threshold condition of suspension of disbelief. Once inside the game world, *thematic signaling* continues to reinforce or confirm these anticipations, often in the background of the participant's consciousness (Rollings & Adams, 2003). To violate the consistency of the theme is to call into question the current construct, and perhaps, to evoke a contradictory construct. The player may have to cognitively regroup, which pulls the player out of the illusion and the sense of immersion. In short, *thematic signaling* continuously evokes anticipations about the game world, how it operates, and how the player is expected to act within the game.

Testing Player Agency through Variable Challenge

To the extent that the construct allows the agent to adequately anticipate and/or control events, the construct is confirmed, and no substantial learning appears necessary (Kelly, 1955/1963).

Of course, validation—confirming that the construct still works—is also valuable. Nonetheless, when the construct is inadequate or fails, there is a natural desire to reevaluate the construct or to improve performance arises (see also "expectation failure" Schank, 2004). Thus, refining the construct, increasing adaptive ability, or in other words, *learning*, is an intrinsic drive of agents (Holland, 1996; Kelly, 1955/1963).

Games tap into this innate desire to learn (Crawford, 2003; Gee, 2003; Papert, 1998; Prensky, 2001; Rieber, 1996). In essence, the game challenges the player's constructs and adaptive abilities. Thus, challenge is central to learning in games. The challenge reveals the strengths or weaknesses of the agent's construct and the agent's execution of associated behaviors. Thus, the *meaningful challenge* affirms existing ability or exposes the need for new learning.

Games often require players to overcome multiple intermediate challenges in pursuit of the long-term goal. The long-term goal serves as a persistent object of anticipation, thereby creating a sustained feedforward effect. The long-term goal also provides justification and value to the intermediate challenges, while the intermediate challenges provide regular, near-term opportunities to test and affirm successful learning.

Intermediate challenges are similar to the device of dramatic tension or "plot hooks" in literature (Dickey, 2006; Huizinga, 1944/1970; Rollings & Adams, 2003); as one challenge ends another challenge arises enticing the player forward episodically. Intermediate challenges comprise iterations or cycles of *variable challenge* that lead up to the final "confrontation." Thus, games offer a stream of varying opportunities to develop and test adaptive abilities through *cycles of provocation and resolution*.

Provocation signals a challenge and an invitation to engage (Swan, 2005). The challenge calls into question players' ability or knowledge, and thus, stirs a natural desire to respond (Swan, 2005). But the challenge does not compel; always,

the player has the choice to engage or disengage. Once the player engages, the cycles of *variable challenge* continue to pull the player forward by presenting opportunities for continued adaptation. Adaptation may occur when the strategies and tactics of the opponent change even though the nature of the challenge is fundamentally unchanged. In basketball, for example, the challenge of scoring points remains basically the same. But each team is regularly changing players, changing offensive plays, and defensive strategies in response to strategies and tactics of the opposing team, and also in anticipation of disrupting the same opposing strategies and tactics. These ongoing responses to changing conditions create cycles of adaptation in terms of strategy and performance selection.

Each cycle of challenge has an outcome or resolution. This study will prefer the term *resolution* as it connotes both the outcome of the activity and the feeling of accomplishment and satisfaction in the player (The possibility of failure will be addressed in the following section on *recoverability*). The positive resolution of a challenge is innately satisfying because it affirms a successful adaptive strategy (Crawford, 2003; Kelly, 1955/1963). Further, current success engenders expectations of future success (Bandura & Locke, 2003; Hoffman, 2003). Crawford (2003) uses this analogy to refer to iterative success: "It's like eating popcorn; each piece is small but tastes so good that you readily move on to the next piece, until you suddenly realize that you have consumed a gallon of popcorn" (p. 47).

In summary, players desire to test and extend their adaptive abilities—or to put it more romantically—to "test their prowess" (Huizinga, 1944/1970). As Crawford (2003) asserts, "We measure ourselves by the challenges we face. ... We therefore go through life seeking new challenges that permit us to expand our identities" (p. 37). Thus, it is possible to conclude that the challenges of games tap in to the feedforward propensities of human agents.

Encouraging Engagement Through Recoverability

The test of adaptive abilities is a risk. Trying a new strategy or performance may fail. A new construct or behavior may be adaptive or maladaptive (Holland, 1996; Kelly, 1955/1963; Rosen, 1985, 2000). In other words, learning entails risk for the agent. Since survival of the agent is a superordinate goal (Holland, 1996; Rosen, 1985, 2000), safety is always a primary concern. Kelly (1955/1963) asserts that agents tend to make the choice they *think* will be the most advantageous. Of course, the agent's choice may or may not actually be the most advantageous.

At the most basic level then, an agent's expression of agency is to act based on the construct that appears to hold the promise of growth (Kelly, 1955/1963). Internal conflict can arise, however, because a riskier alternative may accrue advantages not available from the safest choice. As Zeelenberg (1999) indicates, "If you opt for the sure thing you normally do not learn whether the gamble would have been better" (p. 97). Testing the boundaries of a current construct or a trying a different construct—taking a risk—may yield more advantageous results. It would therefore be of considerable adaptive value to develop and test these strategies and abilities within a safe environment. This, of course, is one of the salient features of play and games—that they are safe (Crawford, 2003; Huizinga, 1944/1970; Papert, 1998; Rieber, 1996; Salen & Zimmerman, 2004). Thus, the ability to try out riskier strategies and behaviors in relative safety would be adaptively appealing.

Embedded helps in computer games promote a sense of safety in a variety of ways. In particular, *recoverability mechanisms* allow the player to take a risk and to try again if it fails. In the game context, punishments or failure simply pinpoint a weak construct or behavior. *Recoverability* provides an opportunity to develop and test changes to the construct and performances until one can

be found that succeeds. Knowing that they can quickly recover encourages players to practice and experiment (Crawford, 2003). *Recoverability* lessens the impact of failure and heightens the prospect of learning. Thus, *risk with recoverability* has a feedforward effect. Otherwise, as Crawford (2003) indicates, "players will resort to conservative, careful, plodding strategies—which aren't much fun" (p. 32).

Requiring Anticipatory Actions through the Core Performance

Execution of the core performance of a game also exhibits feedforward characteristics. Eventually, agents have to carry out their adaptive strategies and behaviors in the physical world. For human agents, this occurs through the use of their body. Therefore, to discuss this element of agency, the discussion must turn to the field of physiology and motor control.

Anticipatory mechanisms play an important role in motor control (Hatches, 2005; Schmidt & Lee, 2005; Seidler, Noll, & Thiers, 2004). In essence, physiological processes could not keep up with the computation and control of movement if it required moment-to-moment feedback control (Hatches, 2005; Miyamoto, Morimoto, Doya, & Kawato, 2004; Reigler, 2003; Seidler, et al., 2004; Williams, 1999). Athletes, in particular, must anticipate the needed action mentally and physically; then in-the-moment feedback can be used to refine the actual execution of the motion (Hoffmann, Stoecker, & Kunde, 2004; Miyamoto, et al., 2004; Schack, 2004). For example, Schack (2004) notes that quick-spikers in volleyball have to anticipate the opposing block and where to aim the hit prior to the execution of the spike.

One developing theory argues that motor control is composed of *movement primitives*: or modular units of learned anticipatory movements (Mussa-Ivaldi & Solla, 2004; Schaal, 2003, 2006; Sosnik, Hauptmann, Karni, & Flash, 2004). Small movement primitives can be combined into large movement primitives such as "grasping a cup," or a "tennis serve" (Schaal, 1999, 2003; Sosnik, et al., 2004). This seems to have its corollary cognitively in Kelly's (1955/1963) concept of a construct. In other words, the essential idea behind these cognitive and motor control units is that they can be aggregated as a single anticipatory entity rather than as a collection of discrete memory bits, signals and/or actions.

This relates to the *core performance* in that it appears that the performance required of players, both cognitive and physical, often needs to be learned and executed as an aggregate anticipatory unit. Further that performance of these strategy-action units needs to become relatively automatic. This automaticity is particularly necessary in twitch-speed games. Yet, even with slower strategy games, the psychological distance between thought and action should remain small for engagement to remain high.

When players have reached a reasonable level of mastery of the *core performance*, they can then perceive themselves as simply "acting in the world" and not consciously manipulating controls (Crawford, 2003; Rollings & Adams, 2003). Incidentally, in this one can also see the need for elegant controls (Crawford, 1984). Further, automaticity allows conscious activity to be geared toward the necessary in-the-moment adaptations of strategy and performance. The perception of relatively "effortless" action is necessary for immersion (see Csikszentmihalyi, 1990).

Thus to facilitate immersive engagement, the *core performance* should remain a single performance or a set of performances that can become an integrated unit (Crawford, 1984; Salen & Zimmerman, 2004). Keeping the *core performance* as a small integrated set of modular behaviors allows players to learn them as anticipatory units, to explore possible variations of the skills, and again, frees up cognitive resources for other purposes In conclusion, learning and executing the core performance interacts with and challenges the player's physiological feedforward mechanisms.

Defining an Operational Principle for the Design Engaging Experiences

In conclusion, the chapter proposes four core components for the design of engaging experiences: meaningful challenge, self-consistent setting, core performance, and embedded helps. The chapter also proposes that these components interact with players' anticipatory, adaptive nature, or agency. The successful result of this interaction is the player's imaginative investment of self which constitutes the active principle of our operational principle. The imaginative investment of self is defined here as the input of emotional, mental, and physiological energy in the social reality of the game. This allows us to formulate an operational principle for the design of engaging experiences as follows: the core components of games (meaningful challenge, self-consistent setting, core performance, and embedded helps) engage with player agency to engender and sustain a *feedforward* effect in players' imaginative investment of self in the designed experience.

FUTURE RESEARCH DIRECTIONS & IMPLICATIONS

The significant implications of this discussion for serious games are these:

1.   Serious games, as the name implies, may not have to stretch for "fun" to be engaging. As Kirriemuir and McFarlane (2004) suggest, trying to achieve "fun" may miss the mark. Although games may be very conducive to the achievement of *flow*, or optimal engagement according Csikszentmihalyi's (1990, 1996) theory, Csikszentmihalyi indicates that flow occurs in other venues as well including work. This chapter indicates that the critical feature may be the challenge to learner agency; a feature which should fit well with the intentions of serious games.

The learner's expansion of agency may not be perceived as a game, but nonetheless may be engaging and intrinsically satisfying.

2. Serious games have the added requirement of connecting to exogenous value. One of the oversights of most traditional education and most educational games—the connection to endogenous value is too often tenuous (see Fortugno & Zimmerman, 2005; Kirriemuir & McFarlane, 2004) and the connection to exogenous value, if present, is invisible. Serious games may face a greater challenge in design because they cannot sacrifice exogenous value for the sole purpose of engaging learners and still achieve the desired success. At the same time they cannot ignore endogenous value. This may require careful balancing.

Future avenues for research include:

1. Deriving and relating additional operational principles of the design of games and engagement. This chapter proposes a high-level operational principle for the design of games and engagement. Consistent with Vincenti's (1990) theory, it would be expected that there are additional components, subcomponents and operational principles within this domain that could be identified and placed in relationship to other operational principles and components.

2. Exploring the anticipatory nature of player/learner engagement. The conclusions of this chapter can serve as a starting hypothesis for continued research into the gameplay experience. The cross-disciplinary nature provides many possible avenues both qualitative and quantitative. There are also additional areas such as emotional self-regulation where the concept of feedforward is being explored and may have relevance to game design and engagement.

CONCLUSION

By formulating an operational principle for the design of engaging experiences, the chapter illustrates the utility of the concept of operational principle as a means to explore design problems. Further, the identification of core components of game design provides a cohesive and elegant framework to understand and relate the various ideas from game designers and game theorists and also provides a foundation for continued derivation and discussion of components and subcomponents.

The chapter also highlights the role of player/learner agency in engagement and makes explicit the notion of *feedforward* interactions as a key characteristic of engagement. This characteristic reveals more clearly the desired goal of game design and the design of engaging experiences—to create and sustain a feedforward effect in players' imaginative investment of self. Finally, the concept of feedforward and an expanded concept of agency open up new avenues of theoretical and experimental development for game design and instructional design.

REFERENCES

Aldrich, C. (2004). *Simulations and the future of learning: an innovative (and perhaps revolutionary) approach to e-learning*. San Francisco: Pfeiffer.

Ashby, W. R. (1956). *An introduction to cybernetics*. Retrieved from http://pespmc1.vub.ac.be/ASHBBOOK.html

Avedon, E. M. (1971). The structural elements of games. In Avedon, E. M., & Sutton-Smith, B. (Eds.), *The study of games* (1st ed., p. 530). New York: John Wiley & Sons, Inc.

Bandura, A., & Locke, E. A. (2003). Negative self-efficacy and goal effects revisited. *The Journal of Applied Psychology, 88*(1), 87–99. doi:10.1037/0021-9010.88.1.87

Bannan-Ritland, B. (2003). The role of design in research: The integrative learning design framework. *Educational Researcher, 32*(1), 21–24. doi:10.3102/0013189X032001021

Bannan-Ritland, B. (2008). *Design research and SCORM: From learning object reusability to the reuse of knowledge*. Paper presented at the ID+SCORM. Retrieved February 2008, from http://arclite.byu.edu/id+scorm/2008/Presentations/Bannan-Ritland/Bannan-Ritland.html

Barab, S., Thomas, M., Dodge, T., Carteaux, R., & Tuzun, H. (2005). Making learning fun: *Quest Atlantis*, a game without guns. *Educational Technology Research and Development, 53*(1), 86. doi:10.1007/BF02504859

Bayazit, N. (2004). Investigating design: A review of forty years of design research. *Design Issues, 20*(1), 16–29. doi:10.1162/074793604772933739

Bertalanffy, L. V. (1968). *General systems theory*. New York: George Brazeller.

Blumenfeld, P. C., Kempler, T. M., & Krajcik, J. S. (2006). Motivation and cognitive engagement in learning environments. In Sawyer, R. K. (Ed.), *Cambridge handbook of the learning sciences* (1st ed., pp. 475–488). New York: Cambridge University Press.

Bogart, D. H. (1980). Feedback, feedforward, and feedwithin: Strategic information in systems. *Behavioral Science, 25*(4), 237. doi:10.1002/bs.3830250402

Buchanan, K. (2006). *Beyond attention-getters: Designing for deep engagement*. Unpublished dissertation, Michigan State University, Michigan, USA.

Canfora, G., & Di Penta, M. (2007). *New frontiers of reverse engineering*. Paper presented at the Future of Software Engineering (FOSE '07), Minneapolis, MN.

Chalam, V. V. (1987). *Adaptive control systems: Techniques and applications*. New York: Marcel Dekker, Inc.

Chu, W. C., Lu, C. W., Chang, C. H., & Chung, Y. C. (2001). Pattern-based software re-engineering. In Chang, S. K. (Ed.), *Handbook of software engineering and knowledge engineering* (Vol. 1, pp. 767–786). Singapore: World Scientific Publishing Co.

Chu, W. C., Lu, C. W., Chang, C. H., Chung, Y. C., Liu, X., & Yang, H. (2002). Reverse engineering. In Chang, S. K. (Ed.), *Handbook of software engineering and knowledge engineering* (Vol. 2, pp. 447–466). Singapore: World Scientific Publishing Co.

Collins, A., Joseph, D., & Bielaczyc, K. (2004). Design research: Theoretical and methodological issues. *Journal of the Learning Sciences, 13*(1), 15–42. doi:10.1207/s15327809jls1301_2

Costikyan, G. (1994). I have no words & I must design. *Interactive Fantasy, 2*. Retrieved from http://www.costik.com/nowords.html

Costikyan, G. (2002). *I have no words & I must design: Toward a critical vocabulary for games*. Paper presented at the Computer Games and Digital Cultures. Retrieved from http://www.digra.org/dl/db/05164.51146.pdf

Crawford, C. (1984). *The art of computer game design*. Retrieved from http://www.vancouver.wsu.edu/fac/peabody/game-book/Coverpage.html

Crawford, C. (2003). *Chris Crawford on game design*. Thousand Oaks, CA: New Riders Publishing.

Csikszentmihalyi, M. (1990). *Flow: The psychology of optimal experience*. New York: Harper & Row.

Csikszentmihalyi, M. (1996). *Creativity: Flow and the psychology of discovery and invention* (1st ed.). New York: Harper Collins Publishers.

Csikszentmihalyi, M. (Producer). (2002, December). Mihalyi Csikszentmihalyi on motivating people to learn. *Video Gallery*. Podcast retrieved from http://www.glef.org.

Dempsey, J. V., Haynes, L. L., Lucassen, B. A., & Casey, M. S. (2002). Forty simple computer games and what they could mean to educators. *Simulation & Gaming, 33*(2), 157. doi:10.1177/1046878102332003

Dickey, M. D. (2005). Engaging by design: How engagement strategies in popular computer and video games can inform instructional design. *Educational Technology Research and Development, 53*(2), 67–83. doi:10.1007/BF02504866

Dickey, M. D. (2006). Game design narrative for learning: Appropriating adventure game design narrative devices and techniques for the design of interactive learning environments. *Educational Technology Research and Development, 54*(3), 245–263. doi:10.1007/s11423-006-8806-y

Eastman, C. M., McCracken, W. M., & Newstetter, W. C. (Eds.). (2001). *Design knowing and learning: Cognition in design education*. Amsterdam: Elsevier.

Edstrom, K. (2002). Design for Motivation. In Hazemi, R., & Hailes, S. (Eds.), *The Digital University: Building a Learning Community* (pp. 193–202). London: Springer.

Fortugno, N., & Zimmerman, E. (2005). Learning to play to learn: Lessons in educational game design. *Gamasutra*. Retrieved from http://www.gamasutra.com/features/20050405/zimmerman_01.shtml

Gardner, H. (Producer). (2002 November). *Howard Gardner on multiple intelligences and new forms of assessment*. Podcast retrieved from http://www.glef.org.

Gee, J. P. (2003). *What video games have to teach us about learning and literacy*. New York: Palgrave Macmillan.

Gibbons, A. S. (2000). *The practice of instructional technology*. Paper presented at the Annual International Conference of the Association for Educational Communications and Technology.

Hatches, P. L. (2005). *The effects of wrist proprioception on joint stability for forward falls*. Unpublished thesis, West Virginia University, Morgantown, WV.

Heeter, C., Winn, B. M., & Greene, D. D. (2005). *Theories meet realities: Designing a learning game for girls*. Paper presented at the Proceedings of the 2005 conference on Designing for User eXperience.

Heylighen, F., & Joslyn, C. (2001). Cybernetics and second-order cybernetics. In Meyers, R. A. (Ed.), *Encyclopedia of physical science & technology* (3rd ed., p. 24). New York: Academic Press.

Hoffman, J. (2003). Anticipatory behavior control. In Butz, M. V., Sigaud, O., & Gerard, P. (Eds.), *Anticipatory behavior in adaptive learning systems*. Berlin: Springer.

Hoffmann, J., Stoecker, C., & Kunde, W. (2004). Anticipatory control of actions. *International Journal of Sport and Exercise Psychology, 2*(4), 346–361.

Holland, J. H. (1996). *Hidden order: How adaptation builds complexity*. Reading, MA: Addison–Wesley.

Hubka, V., & Eder, W. E. (1988). *Theory of technical systems*. Berlin: Springer–Verlag.

Huizinga, J. (1944/1970). *Homo Ludens: A study of the play-element in culture*. New York: Harper & Row.

Inouye, D., Merrill, P., & Swan, R. H. (2005). Help: Toward a new ethics-centered paradigm for instructional design and technology. *IDT Record*. Retrieved from http://www.indiana.edu/~idt/

Joensuu, H. (2006). *Adaptive control inspired by the cerebellar system*. Unpublished thesis, Helsinki University of Technology, Finland, Helsinki.

Jonassen, D. H. (2000). Toward a design theory of problem solving. *Educational Technology Research and Development, 48*(4), 63. doi:10.1007/BF02300500

Juul, J. (2003). *The game, the player, the world: Looking for a heart of gameness*. Paper presented at the Digital Games Research Conference, Utrecht: Utrecht University.

Katzeff, C. (2000). *The design of interactive media for learners in an organisational setting–the state of the art*. Paper presented at the Nordic Interactive Conference, Copenhagen, Denmark.

Kelly, G. A. (1955/1963). *Theory of personality: The psychology of personal constructs*. New York: WW Norton & Company.

Kickmeier-Rust, M. D., Schwarz, D., Albert, D., Verpoorten, D., Castaigne, J. L., & Bopp, M. (2006). The ELEKTRA project: Towards a new learning experience. In Pohl, M., Holzinger, A., Motschnig, R., & Swertz, C. (Eds.), *M3 – Interdisciplinary aspects on digital media & education* (*Vol. 3*, pp. 19–48). Vienna: Österreichische Computer Gesellschaft.

Kirriemuir, J., & McFarlane, A. (2004). Literature review in games and learning. *Futurelab Series, Report 8*, 35. Retrieved from http://www.futurelab.org.uk/research/lit_reviews.htm

Laurel, B. (1991). *Computers as theatre*. Reading, MA: Addison–Wesley Pub.

Macmillan, R. H. (1955). *An introduction to the theory of control in mechanical engineering*. Cambridge, UK: Cambridge University Press.

Miyamoto, H., Morimoto, J., Doya, K., & Kawato, M. (2004). Reinforcement learning with via-point representation. *Neural Networks, 17*(3), 299–305. doi:10.1016/j.neunet.2003.11.004

Murmann, J. P., & Frenken, K. (2006). Toward a systematic framework for research on dominant designs, technological innovations, and industrial change. *Research Policy, 35*(7), 925–952. doi:10.1016/j.respol.2006.04.011

Mussa-Ivaldi, F. A., & Solla, S. A. (2004). Neural primitives for motion control. *IEEE Journal of Oceanic Engineering, 29*(3), 640–650. doi:10.1109/JOE.2004.833102

Papert, S. (1998). Does easy do it? Children, games, and learning. *Game Developer, 88*.

Polanyi, M. (1962). *Personal knowledge: Towards a post-critical philosophy*. London: Routledge.

Prensky, M. (2001). *Digital game-based learning*. New York: McGraw–Hill.

Principe, J. C., Euliano, N. R., & Lefebvre, W. C. (2000). *Neural and adaptive systems: Fundamentals through simulations*. New York: John Wiley & Sons, Inc.

Reigeluth, C. M., & Frick, T. W. (1999). Formative research: A methodology for creating and improving design theories. In Reigeluth, C. M. (Ed.), *Instructional-design theories and models: A new paradigm of instructional theory* (*Vol. 2*, pp. 633–651). Mahwah, NJ: Lawrence Erlbaum Associates.

Reigler, A. (2003). Whose anticipations? In Butz, M. V., Sigaud, O., & Gerard, P. (Eds.), *Anticipatory behavior in adaptive learning systems*. Berlin: Springer.

Rieber, L. P. (1996). Seriously considering play: Designing interactive learning environments based on the blending of microworlds, simulations, and games. *Educational Technology Research and Development*, *44*(2), 43–58. doi:10.1007/BF02300540

Rogers, P. C., Hsueh, S. L., & Gibbons, A. S. (2005). *The generative aspect of design theory.* Paper presented at the Fifth IEEE International Conference on Advanced Learning Technologies (ICALT'05).

Rollings, A., & Adams, E. (2003). *Andrew Rollings and Ernest Adams on game design.* Thousand Oaks, CA: New Riders Publishing.

Rosen, R. (1985). *Anticipatory systems: Philosophical, Mathematical and methodological foundations.* New York: Pergamon Press.

Rosen, R. (2000). *Essays on life itself.* New York: Columbia University Press.

Rouse, R. (2001). *Game design theory and practice.* Plano, TX: Wordware Publishing Inc.

Salen, K., & Zimmerman, E. (2004). *Rules of play: Game design fundamentals.* Cambridge, MA: MIT Press.

Sandberg, I. W., Lo, J. T., Fancourt, C. L., Principe, J. C., Katagiri, S., & Haykin, S. (2001). *Nonlinear dynamical systems: Feedforward neural network perspectives.* New York: John Wiley & Sons, Inc.

Schaal, S. (1999). Is imitation learning the route to humanoid robots? *Trends in Cognitive Sciences*, *3*(6), 233–242. doi:10.1016/S1364-6613(99)01327-3

Schaal, S. (2003). Computational approaches to motor learning by imitation. *Philosophical Transactions of the Royal Society of London. Series B, Biological Sciences*, *358*(1431), 537–547. doi:10.1098/rstb.2002.1258

Schaal, S. (2006). Dynamic movement primitives: A framework for motor control in humans and humanoid robotics. In Kimura, H., Tsuchiya, K., Ishiguro, A., & Witte, H. (Eds.), *Adaptive Motion of Animals and Machines* (pp. 261–280). Tokyo: Springer. doi:10.1007/4-431-31381-8_23

Schack, T. (2004). The cognitive architecture of complex movement. *International Journal of Sport and Exercise Psychology*, *2*, 403–438.

Schank, R. C. (1998). *Inside multi-media case based instruction.* Mahwah, NJ: Lawrence Erlbaum Associates.

Schank, R. C. (1999). *Dynamic Memory Revisited.* New York: Cambridge University Press. doi:10.1017/CBO9780511527920

Schank, R. C. (2004). *Making minds less well educated than our own.* Mahwah, NJ: Lawrence Erlbaum Associates, Inc.

Schmidt, R. A., & Lee, T. D. (2005). *Motor control and learning: A behavioral emphasis* (4th ed.). Champaign, IL: Human Kinetics.

Seidler, R. D., Noll, D. C., & Thiers, G. (2004). Feedforward and feedback processes in motor control. *NeuroImage*, *22*, 1775–1783. doi:10.1016/j.neuroimage.2004.05.003

Shearer, J. L., Kulakowski, B. T., & Gardner, J. F. (1997). *Dynamic modeling and control of engineering systems.* Upper Saddle River, NJ: Prentice Hall.

Silber, K. H. (2007). A principle-based model of instructional design: A new way of thinking about and teaching ID. *Educational Technology*, (September-October): 5–19.

Simon, H. A. (1996). *The sciences of the artificial.* Cambridge, MA: MIT Press.

Skyttner, L. (2005). *General systems theory: Problems, perspectives, practice* (2nd ed.). Singapore: World Scientific Publishing Co Inc.

Sloane, F. (2006). Normal and design sciences in education: Why both are necessary. In Van den Akker, J., Gravemeijer, K., McKenney, S., & Nieveen, N. (Eds.), *Educational design research: the design, development and evaluation of programs, processes, and products* (p. 163). London: Routledge.

Sosnik, R., Hauptmann, B., Karni, A., & Flash, T. (2004). When practice leads to co-articulation: The evolution of geometrically defined movement primitives. *Experimental Brain Research, 156*(4), 422–438. doi:10.1007/s00221-003-1799-4

Squire, K. (2005). *Game-based learning: Present and future state of the field.* Research paper presented at the e-learning CONSORTIUM.

Swan, R. H. (2005, October 2005). *Design structures for intrinsic motivation.* Paper presented at the The Interservice/Industry Training, Simulation & Education Conference (I/ITSEC) Orlando, FL.

Swan, R. H. (2008). *Deriving operational principles for the design of engaging learning experiences.* Unpublished dissertation, Brigham Young University, Provo, UT.

Van Aken, J. E. (2004). Management research based on the paradigm of the design sciences: The quest for field-tested and grounded technological rules. *Journal of Management Studies, 41*(2), 219–246. doi:10.1111/j.1467-6486.2004.00430.x

Van Eck, R. (2006). Digital game-based learning: It's not just the digital natives who are restless. *EDUCAUSE Review, 41*, 16–30.

Van Eck, R. (2007). Six ideas in search of a discipline. In Spector, M., Seel, N., & Morgan, K. (Eds.), *Educational design and use of computer simulation games.* The Netherlands: Sense Publishing.

Vincenti, W. G. (1990). *What engineers know and how they know it: analytical studies from aeronautical history.* Baltimore: Johns Hopkins University Press.

Waelder, P. (2006). *Bruised and happy: The addicted painstation players.* Paper presented at the medi@terra, September 27–October 1, 2006, Athens Greece.

Williams, A. M. (1999). *Visual perception and action in sport.* London: Spon Press.

Zeelenberg, M. (1999). Anticipated regret, expected feedback and behavioral decision making. *Journal of Behavioral Decision Making, 12*(2). doi: Document ID: 349484671

ENDNOTES

[1] (It is necessary to note that the most accessible examples of design are physical objects; however, Simon (1996) asserts that design principles apply to professions such as law, medicine, and education where the objects of design are more ephemeral (see also Gibbons, 2000).)

[2] (This brings to mind a rich literature from psychology regarding self-efficacy and a smaller literature on academic risk-taking to recommend as additional avenues of cross-disciplinary integration, but for which, there is too little space to discuss here.)

[3] (Interestingly, the definition of meaningful challenge to this point is very similar to Jonassen's (2000) definition of a problem as an unknown entity in a situation—a goal—the solution to which has some value. The challenge of a game, however, seems to go beyond the definition of a problem.)

[4] (For a discussion of rewards and punishments in games see Salen & Zimmerman (2004).)

5   (A reasonably accessible explanation of back-propagation can be found at http://www.ibm.com/developerworks/open-source/library/l-neural/)

6   (This is similar to Schank's (1998, 1999) concept of a script. He argues, for example, that the waitress and the patron know how to behave toward each other because they share the "restaurant script" developed by previous experiences in restaurants.)

APPENDIX: ADDITIONAL READING

"Must-Reads" for This Topic

Crawford, C. (1984). *The art of computer game design.* Retrieved from http://www.vancouver.wsu.edu/fac/peabody/game-book/Coverpage.html

Crawford, C. (2003). *Chris Crawford on game design.* Thousand Oaks, CA: New Riders Publishing.

Csikszentmihalyi, M. (1990). *Flow: The Psychology of Optimal Experience.* New York: Harper & Row.

Csikszentmihalyi, M. (1996). *Creativity: Flow and the psychology of discovery and invention* (1st ed.). New York: HarperCollinsPublishers.

Gee, J. P. (2003). *What Video Games Have to Teach Us About Learning and Literacy.* New York: Palgrave Macmillan. Holland, J. H. (1996). *Hidden order: How adaptation builds complexity.* Reading, MA: Addison–Wesley.

Kelly, G. A. (1955/1963). *Theory of personality: The psychology of personal constructs.* New York: WW Norton & Company.

Laurel, B. (1991). *Computers as theatre.* Reading, MA: Addison–Wesley Pub.

Rosen, R. (1985). *Anticipatory Systems: Philosophical, Mathematical and Methodological Foundations.* New York: Pergamon Press.

Salen, K., & Zimmerman, E. (2004). *Rules of play: Game design fundamentals.* Cambridge, MA: MIT Press.

Simon, H. A. (1996). *The sciences of the artificial.* Cambridge, MA: MIT Press.

Vincenti, W. G. (1990). *What engineers know and how they know it: Analytical studies from aeronautical history.* Baltimore: Johns Hopkins University Press.

Top Texts for Interdisciplinary Studies of Serious Games

DeFreitas, S. (2007). *Learning in immersive worlds: A review of game based learning* (Literature Review). London: Joint Information Systems Committee.

Entertainment & Leisure Software Publishers Association (ELSPA) (2006). *Unlimited learning: Computer and video games in the learning landscape.* Retrieved from http://www.elspa.com/assets/files/u/unlimitedlearningtheroleofcomputerandvideogamesint_344.pdf

Joint Information Systems Committee (JISC), UK. (2007). *Game-based learning.* Retrieved from http://www.jisc.ac.uk/media/documents/publications/gamingreportbp.pdf

Kirriemuir, J., & McFarlane, A. (2004). Literature review in games and learning. *Futurelab Series, Report 8,* 35. Retrieved from http://www.futurelab.org.uk/research/lit_reviews.htm

Chapter 6

Cognitive Load and Empathy in Serious Games:
A Conceptual Framework

Wen-Hao David Huang
University of Illinois, Urbana–Champaign, USA

Sharon Tettegah
University of Illinois, Urbana–Champaign, USA

ABSTRACT

The design of serious games does not always address players' empathy in relation to their cognitive capacity within a demanding game environment. Consequently players with inherent limitations, such as limited working memory, might feel emotionally drained when the level of empathy required by a game hinders their ability to cognitively attain the desired learning outcome. Because of the increasing attention being given to serious games that aim to develop players' empathy along with their cognitive competencies, such as Darfur is Dying (Ruiz et al., 2006), there is a need to investigate the empirical relationship between players' cognitive load and empathy development capacity during serious game play. Therefore this chapter examines cognitive load theory and empirical work on empathy development to propose a conceptual framework to inform the research and design of serious games that have empathy as part of the learning outcomes. Future research should focus on implementation and empirical validation of the proposed framework.

INTRODUCTION

The concept of serious games and their processes was first noted by Abt in 1970. In this seminal work, Abt argued that serious games should require players to make consecutive decisions in order to achieve predetermined game objectives. Players' actions, in turn, are bound by rules and constraints while

competing with others on various challenges (Abt, 1970). To these characteristics, Gredler (1994) and Suits (1978) add the aspects of voluntary participation of players and entertainment. Prensky (2001) expanded the notion of where and how serious games could be played, arguing for their use in education and training by designing games for computer-based environments. Many of today's serious games are digital games delivered via computers or video game consoles for instructional purposes. Both

DOI: 10.4018/978-1-61520-717-6.ch006

types of games have gained a substantial level of attention in recent years (Huang & Johnson, 2008). Hence, their broad educational applications across organizations and disciplines have been widely recognized by scholars and industries (Federation of American Scientists, 2006; Serious Games Initiative, 2010). These games are also capable of emulating and rendering scenarios with high fidelity, which gradually diminishes the boundary between serious games and simulations (Raybourn, 2007).

Despite serious games' emphasis on education and training in digital formats, their core game components remain unchanged from other games. Crawford (1982) identified four independent but interconnected game components: representation, interaction, conflict, and safety. The representation of the game system consists of all participating agents (e.g., players, system interface, game rules, game objectives), which enables intended interactions. Conflict is the means and/or the end of interactions that requires players to resolve complicated situations. The safety component encourages players to experience the outcome of their game-playing actions without any real harm. Amory (2007) further suggested that in order to understand the effect of serious games on learning, we should also include *Game Space* (play, exploration, authenticity, tacit knowledge, etc.), *Visualization Space* (critical thinking, storylines, relevance, goals, etc.), *Elements Space* (fun, emotive, graphics, sounds, technology, etc.), *Problem Space* (communication, literacy level, memory, etc.), and *Social Space* (communication tools and social network analysis). In addition to their multi-component architecture, serious games also encompass numerous characteristics that enable them to develop players' holistic and complex skills. It is suggested that challenges, fantasy, competition, multimedia representation, role-playing, and goal-oriented actions, to name a few, may enhance the learning experience in serious games (Huang & Johnson, 2008).

In addition to providing players with information about current issues and topics such as health, environment, and human rights, serious games have also become a major medium to train and teach skills such as social etiquette and prosocial behavior. The focus of this chapter is serious games for change, with a specific emphasis on games for cultural change. In games that are developed for cultural change, one common design strategy is getting the player to feel sympathy and/or empathy for the characters in the game. Most games for change simulate real physical casualties so that the player develops an awareness of a situation where war and genocide may be central to everyday life. While other educational serious games may focus on teaching a specific concept or subject (e.g., algebra), games for cultural change center on a different concept, one that concentrates on behavioral or attitudinal changes where the purpose is to raise awareness and evoke empathic concern. Empathy becomes one of the primary outcomes of the game.

Given serious games' complexity, it is commonly understood that players will engage in intense cognitive and emotional processing (Gray, Braver, & Raichle, 2002; Gunter, Kenny, & Vick, 2008). Such game-playing experiences would very likely overload players' limited cognitive processing capacity if gameplay and its resulting cognitive load were not carefully managed (Ang, Zaphiris, & Mahmood, 2007). Therefore, players' cognitive load levels should be considered when designing serious games (Huang & Johnson, 2008; Low, Jin, & Sweller, this volume). However, while serious game designers are beginning to consider issues of cognitive load, little attention has been paid to affective/emotional interactions with cognitive load. This may be particularly relevant for games for change that focus on cultural awareness. Since serious game tasks often require players to make multiple attempts before accomplishing the objectives, players' full participation and control in the game may solicit emotional fluctuation in response to the "ups and downs" (i.e., frustration, anxiety) of the game-playing process. In games for change, a primary objective is to get players to develop compassion and put themselves in the position of the person (i.e., characters) or persons at risk. Players might feel encouraged and joyful after accomplishing the game task or winning the competition, which could leave them with more cognitive resources, or having more cognitive resources might allow them to be more successful in the challenges, which in turn makes them feel encouraged and joyful. On the other hand, the feeling of frustration and annoyance might be induced by multiple failures in pursuing particular game objectives, and fewer cognitive resources may result in more failures. Consequently players' emotional responses and cognitive gain and loss might influence each other (Grodal, 2000, p. 208). Therefore, the level of empathy a player has for a character in the game may influence the player's cognitive load, and vice versa.

We further argue that cognitive and affective empathy play critical roles associated with engagement within games such as *Darfur is Dying*. We raise questions in this chapter about the relationship between cognitive load and empathy in serious games designed to induce and promote empathy. Some questions we ask are these: If empathy is a critical component in the learning outcome of serious games, can it be managed with a purposeful design? Are there cognitive load implications for empathy (or other affective constructs, for that matter)? In other words, given learners' limited cognitive information-processing capacity, could the existence of empathy improve or impede a learner's mental model development in serious games? Since current literature has not investigated the relationship between cognitive load and empathic aspects of learning with serious games, this chapter proposes a conceptual framework for empirical investigation of the relationship between cognitive load and empathy development. The following questions will guide the conceptual framework development in this chapter: What

might be the relationship between cognitive load and empathy, and how can we manage both cognitive load and empathic concern in serious games? To answer these questions, we will first provide a brief conceptual overview of empathy, including a discussion of empathic dispositions associated with factors that influence the social perspective-taking that is necessary for empathic learning. Next, we will discuss cognitive load as a theoretical framework in a complex learning environment such as serious games. We will then briefly describe the potential interaction of empathy and cognitive load, including some examples taken from the game *Darfur is Dying* (Ruitz et al., 2006). Finally, we will propose a conceptual framework for future investigations of cognitive load and empathy in serious games.

BACKGROUND

Empathy

There have been several definitions of empathy associated with perspective-taking experiences. The following have been most prominent in the literature: cognitive empathy, affective empathy, and multidimensional empathy. The primary means of designing for empathic outcomes lie in asking the player/users to infer the mental states and experiences of the characters in the game. The mental states of the player are provoked by the virtual experiences of the characters in the game, which hopefully promote cognitive and affective empathy on the part of the player.

Cognitive empathy refers to the ability of the player to infer something about the mental state of others, whereas affective empathy refers to the ability of the player to infer the emotional state of another person. (Davis 1994; Hoffman, 2000). The third kind of empathy, multidimensional, is conceptualized as encompassing both cognitive and affective aspects and includes personal distress, empathic concern, fantasy, and perspective-taking. Each of the aforementioned dimensions is presumed in the storyline of *Darfur is Dying*, and therefore, we focus our discussion of empathy in this and other persuasive games as multidimensional empathy.

Cognitive empathy is more than role taking. "Role taking refers to the process in which one individual attempts to imagine the world of another" (Davis, 1994, p. 17). Cognitive empathy refers only to the act of constructing for oneself another person's mental state (Davis, 1994). Hogan (1969) defined cognitive empathy as "the intellectual or imaginative apprehension of another's condition without actually experiencing that person's feelings" (p. 308). In cognitive empathy, an individual must have a cognitive sense of others; otherwise, empathy cannot occur through direct association. Direct association involves the cognitive process of developing new mental models in order to better relate to others' thinking patterns. Insufficient cognitive information processing capacity might impede such a mental modeling process, thus leading to a lack of cognitive empathy. In the context of serious games, this is very likely to occur since players are constantly situated in a cognitively demanding environment. Managing cognitive load in the serious game-playing process, therefore, becomes crucial so that players acquire the desired empathic concerns for the characters in the game.

Empathy is distinguished from sympathy. Sympathy involves "a heightened awareness of the suffering of another person as something to be alleviated" (Wispé, 1987, p. 318). Empathy involves a set of attributes that children develop and acquire through experiences with others who exhibit behaviors such as perspective-taking, an ability to put themselves in another place, and a feeling of believing that what is happening to another is also happening to the individual (Tettegah & Neville, 2007). Empathy is considered a moral emotion, which is defined as the capacity one person has to feel and relate her/himself into the consciousness of another person (Wispé, 1987).

It is the ability to step into someone else's shoes. Empathy involves a cognitive awareness of other's internal states, emotions, thoughts, feelings, and ways of perceiving and behaving in the world. As such, it involves perspective-taking, is multidimensional, and includes affective and cognitive aspects (Davis, 1994; Hoffman, 2000; Tettegah, 2007; Tettegah & Anderson 2007).

Cognitive Load

The gap between information structures presented in the instructional material and human cognitive architecture must be bridged so that learners can use their working memory more efficiently. In other words, learners should invest less mental effort to accomplish the learning task if the instructional material closely aligns with how learners cognitively process information. The level of mental effort investment during the learning process is defined as "cognitive load" (Paas, Tuovinen, Tabbers, & van Gerven, 2003). The purpose of cognitive load theory (CLT) (Chandler & Sweller, 1991), which has established a sound theoretical foundation to connect cognitive research on human learning with instructional design and development (van Merriënboer, Clark, & de Croock, 2002), is to be that bridge.

In the context of CLT, "learning" involves acquisition – the process of how learners construct schema and store them in long-term memory – and automation – how learners perform certain tasks *without* accessing working memory – of schema. Information required for the performance of a task is retrieved directly from the long-term memory (Paas et al., 2003). Since both attributes require little working memory capacity yet are still critical to meaningful learning, successful acquisition and automation of schema will lead to more efficient use of working memory for a desired performance (Mayer, 2001).

As suggested by CLT, there are three types of cognitive load which, combined, compose the total cognitive load: intrinsic, extraneous, and germane.

For learning to occur, the total cognitive load can never exceed a learner's working memory capacity. The total extraneous and germane cognitive load, combined, is assumed to be equal to the total cognitive load minus the intrinsic cognitive load. Since the intrinsic cognitive load is fixed (i.e., the load cannot be manipulated by instructional design), instructional design's main purpose is to *reduce* the extraneous while *increasing* the germane cognitive load (van Gerven, Paas, van Merriënboer, & Schmidt, 2006).

Intrinsic cognitive load is associated with the element interactivity – the degree to which information can be understood alone without the involvement of other elements – inherent to the instructional material itself. Information with high element interactivity is difficult to understand because it usually depends on the involvement of other information units in order to see the full interaction. Therefore, instructional material with high element interactivity is assumed to induce a higher intrinsic cognitive load, since the instruction requires more working memory for information processing (Paas et al., 2003). Intrinsic cognitive load is considered to be independent of instructional manipulations because the manipulation only involves the amount of information a learner needs to hold in working memory without decreasing the inherent element interactivity (Pollock, Chandler, & Sweller, 2002). The extraneous cognitive load and germane cognitive load, in contrast, *can* be manipulated by instructional design (Brüken, Plass, & Leutner, 2003).

Extraneous cognitive load, also known as *ineffective cognitive load,* as it only involves the process of searching for information within working memory as opposed to the process of constructing schemas in long-term memory, can be influenced by the way information is presented and the amount of working memory required for given learning tasks (Paas et al., 2003). Considered a necessary cost of processing information, yet not related to the understanding of that information, extraneous, or ineffective, cognitive load

must be reduced by instructional design. (Brüken et al., 2003). One method found to be successful in reducing extraneous cognitive load is the use of well-designed instructional multimedia components (Khalil, Paas, Johnson, & Payer, 2005; Mayer & Moreno, 2003). For the design of instructional materials, Cobb (1997) suggested the use of multimedia components (nonverbal and nontextual) as cognitive capacity external to learners' working memory, to facilitate cognitive efficiency and information processing. In theory, learners should spend less cognitive effort to understand the given information.

In contrast to the desired low degree of the extraneous cognitive load, instructional materials should be designed to *increase* the germane cognitive load. Also known as effective *cognitive load,* the germane cognitive load is described as the effort learners invest in order to facilitate the process of constructing schema and automation (Paas et al., 2003). The higher the germane cognitive load, the deeper the learning, since, by the design of the instructional material, learners are compelled to reexamine every new piece of information (de Crook, van Merriënboer, & Paas, 1998). Although the overall goal of manipulating cognitive load with instructional design is to *decrease* the level of ineffective cognitive load and to *increase* the effective cognitive load that promotes deeper learning, CLT suggests that the combination of extraneous and germane cognitive load should remain relatively constant after removing the fixed intrinsic cognitive load (Paas et al., 2003). The decrease of extraneous cognitive load should lead to the increase of germane cognitive load, or vice versa (Paas et al., 2003; van Gerven et al., 2006).

COGNITIVE LOAD AND EMPATHY IN SERIOUS GAMES

Cognition and emotion are regarded as two interrelated aspects of human functioning (Immordino-

Yang, & Damasio, 2008, p. 192). Immordino-Yang & Damasio, (2008) present a discussion of the neurological relationship between cognition and emotion. They argue that emotional thought encompasses processes of learning, memory, and decision making, in both social and nonsocial contexts (p. 193). Prior research on emotions and cognitive load in particular also indicates that there is an effect of emotions on learning and mental effort investment (Um, Song, & Plass, 2007). Emotions entail the perception of an emotionally competent trigger, a situation either real or imagined that has the power to induce an emotion, as well as a chain of physiological events that will enable changes in the body & mind (Immordino-Yang & Damasio, 2008, p. 192). Clearly, cognitive load is apt to be affected by the presence or absence of empathy. Emotions such as empathy help to direct our ability to reason in learning.

Learning with serious games is a complex process. Learners might engage in in-depth cognitive information processing while also experiencing intense emotional fluctuations. For instance, *Darfur is Dying* (http://www.darfurisdying.com/) (Ruitz, et al., 2006), an online game based on the genocide in Sudan, aims to evoke empathy in the player. Although players only interact with the game using a computer keyboard, the game designers hope its effect on learners' empathy level towards Darfur will be long-lasting. The game developers for *Darfur is Dying* state,

Darfur Is Dying is a narrative-based simulation where the user, from the perspective of the displaced Darfurian, negotiates forces that threaten the survival of his or her refugee camp. It offers a faint glimpse of what it's like for the more than 2.5 millions who have been internally displaced by the crisis in Sudan (http://www.darfurisdying. com/aboutgame.html).

The goals of the developers and instructional designers of *Darfur is Dying* include raising awareness so that the player/user shares fear, empathy, and other emotions associated with victims of war. *Darfur is Dying* was developed with goals to educate, provide support and inspire. The influence of the characters on the player can cause emotional responses that are positive, negative, or both. In addition to the basic cognitive information processing required in order to understand the rules of the gameplay, the interactions might play a significant role in affording high or low empathic experiences.

In gameplay of *Darfur is Dying* or other social games, learning outcomes are often associated with specific characters in the game and the things that happen to them. For example, in *Darfur is Dying*, the characters need to risk their lives to protect their village. An ideal outcome is for players to feel empathic about the character's experiences portrayed in the games. In serious games that focus on behavioral and attitudinal changes, it is necessary for the player to connect and take the perspective of the character. The developers are hoping that the connection is at such a deep level empathy the player may experience will transfer to empathy for the actual Darfurian's real-life experiences. Hence, a goal is for the player to seek further cognitive processing of the situation with hopes that those further actions will lead to more effort to save the characters (victims) in future actions in the game. We argue that if the player does not have empathy for the characters in the game, then it is quite likely the game designers have failed to attain their primary goal of getting the player to work hard to save the characters and their village.

Empathy is particularly important in gameplay that involves characters. *Darfur is Dying* is designed to make players feel empathy for, or take on the role of, the characters who are living in a dangerous environment. In this sense, the game designers intend to engage users in social perspective-taking. The designers expect for the player to "infer the mental state of others (their thoughts, motives, intentions)" (Davis, 1994, p.49). Characters in *Darfur is Dying* face snipers, thieves, and insurgents on a daily basis while carrying out simple tasks such as foraging for water. One expects players might be motivated to learn more about Darfur and/or develop empathy through social perspective-taking with the characters, and possibly with the genocide of the people in Darfur. Social perspective-taking in games such as *Darfur is Dying* is primary, and the game designers assume that the player will be able to associate with and take on the role of the characters in the game. Role or perspective-taking occurs when one imagines how the victim or character feels or how one would feel in the victim's situation (Hoffman, 2000). In this sense, the designers are attempting to induce empathy with the hope that the emotional response to the character's situation will encourage the user to play the game.

In light of the aforementioned observations on cognitive load and empathy development in serious games like *Darfur is Dying*, it is clear that the play–learn process not only provides ample cognitive stimulation but also fosters the complex development of empathy. Both outcomes require a substantial and concurrent amount of cognitive processing capacity from the player. As a result, if we design games without acknowledging the drain that empathy formulation may place on cognitive resources in addition to other cognitive drains associated with interface, message design, etc., we may unwittingly exhaust the cognitive capacity of our learners in games in general. This has particular relevance, obviously, to games with empathy as the intended outcome. We must investigate whether or not the management of effective cognitive load and empathy will lead us to better understand a character's role in gameplay and its effects on the cognitive load of individuals who are engaged in gameplay.

MANAGING COGNITIVE LOAD AND EMPATHY

You have real feelings for imaginary events, which—even as you laugh or weep—you know to be fictitious. ... cognitive evaluations that engender emotions are sufficiently crude that they contain no reality check. (Johnson-Laird & Oatley, 2000, p. 465)

This proposed framework focuses on how researchers can manipulate different types of cognitive load during the play–learn process in order to investigate the relation of cognitive load and empathy in serious games. Because a serious game is a closed system, researchers should be able to control variables in a systematic manner via purposeful design. That is, the investigative variables can be integrated at the beginning of the design process with corresponding independent and dependent variables. Because the serious game environment contains multiple layers and dimensions that influence players' cognitive and empathy development, initial empirical investigations should be conducted in well-controlled laboratory settings. For example, competitiveness as one prominent characteristic of a serious game (Huang & Johnson, 2008) could be one independent variable, while players' cognitive level and empathy could be the dependent variable. Or, using models that focus on the measurement of empathy associated with the visual representation of specific characters may affect cognitive load and empathy.

This framework recommends three interrelated research perspectives for systematically designing investigative treatments in serious games: environments, characters, and activities. Each perspective can have a significant impact on players' final learning outcomes, and also affords possibilities for researchers to isolate variables or factors to efficiently investigate the play–learn process. Because all perspectives are required simultaneously to provide a comprehensive play–learn experience, the interactions among all three perspectives must also be observed.

Because the ultimate goal is to enhance learning, all investigative treatments should focus on how they might help players reduce the ineffective cognitive load (extraneous cognitive load) while increasing the effective cognitive load (germane cognitive load) through empathy evoked by the characters in the game. By minimizing the ineffective cognitive load, players not only will have more cognitive capacity to develop desired mental models for the cognitive tasks (e.g., knowledge gain, skill development), but this minimization also allows cognitive space for the necessary development of empathy.

Environments in Serious Games

This perspective encompasses the information accessibility, scenario representation, and game event delivery in serious games. If managed improperly, any component alone would induce players' cognitive overload and leave insufficient cognitive capacity to enable the presence or absence of empathy for the characters in the game. Accessibility of information in serious games mainly concerns the design of how players interact with the information. The actions and information should facilitate the process for players to identify and retrieve relevant information in order to move forward in the game and not be stifled by high levels of cognitive load induced by a complex interface. Player control, for instance, often requires players to use game console controllers or personal computer input devices (keyboard and mouse) without consideration of how players might need time to get acquainted with the interface. Representation of scenarios in serious games usually requires heavy utilization of multimedia (e.g., audio, video, and animation) to create intense and immersive scenarios. But overly incorporated multimedia would overload players' limited cognitive capacity. In terms of

the delivery of game events, instead of pouring everything at the player at once, the delivery should focus on how often and in which manner game events should be made available to players to enable cognitively efficient information processing. Research in this perspective bears rich opportunities since all three components can be examined individually while monitoring their interaction effect on each other, which would also connect practical design issues of serious games with empirical research grounded in CLT.

Characters in Serious Games

This perspective emphasizes how players might empathize with, identify with, and relate themselves to the characters in the serious game. This perspective is particularly crucial for empathy development because players will dispense less mental effort in taking others' perspectives if they can easily identify with the character in the game. *Full Spectrum Warrior* (Institute for Creative Technologies, 2009), for example, is a serious game designed for training urban combat tactics. Characters in this game are designed based on real human experiences in refugee camps and combat positions in light infantry combat units in order to enable players (i.e., in-service armed forces personnel) to identify with the characters. Another approach to this research perspective is shifting the game character design to the game players. Once players have full control over the appearance of their characters, they might be expected to identify more with their characters and, therefore, be more likely to develop empathy.

Activities in Serious Games

This perspective aims to investigate the interaction between the player and the serious game environment and characters. Activities in serious games should require that players constantly retrieve relevant mental models from their long-term memory and repurpose them in various problem-solving tasks. In games that include empathy as an outcome, social interactions between players also need to be included in serious game activities since most tasks, in reality, demand collaborative efforts, and they may also facilitate the development of empathy between the player, his or her character, and individuals in the physical world. Activities irrelevant to cognitive as well as empathic gain, however, should be avoided. Most information-searching activities in serious games might fall into this less desired category.

FUTURE RESEARCH DIRECTIONS

Current research in serious games has not investigated the relationship between cognitive load and empathy. In games such as *Darfur is Dying*, characters depict actual situations that occur in real life. The objectives are to induce empathy for the characters in the game that will lead to cultural awareness and for a cultural group's true experiences in the Sudan. In other words, empathy becomes the main learning outcome as compared to learning about a specific content. Game designers in this case might have assumed that players already have a disposition for empathy for the characters in the game or, for that matter, have the ability to be empathic. The players might have some understanding about Darfur before participating in the game and therefore demand less cognitive capacity to process their empathic responses. It is also possible, however, that the game was designed without the aforementioned assumption. One intended outcome involves the development of the player's empathy for the character(s) in the game; however, the assumption here is that the individual has a similar experience that can help the player to connect through direct association with the victim characters in *Darfur is Dying*. With this approach, the characters within the game itself become the main source to provide critical information to evoke empathy in the player. Players must acquire an understanding of

the situation while developing empathy simultaneously in the game. Cognitive overload is likely to occur due to the dual-tasking if the design of game environment, characters, and activities lacks empirical ground.

In order to resolve issues associated with design, research must investigate the relationship between the management of cognitive load via grounded design and players' presence or absence of empathy as a learning outcome. Other research has begun to document the relationship between learning, emotions, and empathy (Bransford, Brown, & Cocking, 2000; Diamond & Hopson, 1998; Sousa, 2005), but cognitive load and empathy in serious games has not been systematically investigated. The research should begin with correlational design to explore preliminary relationships between design variables (e.g., ease of interaction/intuitiveness of the interface, the degree of multimedia utilization in scenario representation, players' control in creating their own game characters) and the intended learning outcome (i.e., empathy level). Cognitive load then could be used to gauge players' cognitive capacity efficiency during the game-playing process. With that exploratory finding in place, we can employ experimental design to investigate relationships between specific variables. For example, researchers grounded in CLT can manipulate the representation of game character information (audio versus textual) and investigate its impact on the player's empathy development.

Designers and researchers should examine the presence and absence of empathy in players to determine whether or not players have the ability to empathize with characters in general. The working memory of the player can be examined using empathy as a dependent variable. Player attitudes and perceptions about the characters can be examined through the following methods: Players could design their own personal avatars for the game to measure the level of ownership related to perspective-taking if a character shares similar physical attributes as the player. If game designers and developers seek social perspective-taking and the presence of empathy in serious games, they must consider the gender and appearance of the avatar. The consideration may be obtained through user/player control over the development of the avatar and connections with universal facial expressions, which can promote players empathic identification with the characters in the game (Hoffman, 2000). Furthermore, more flexibility can be given to the player so that the player can develop his or her own survival scenario after playing *Darfur is Dying* or similar games. A better understanding of players' moral internalization and motivations will also assist developers in ensuring the transference of empathy to physical world individuals instead of remaining isolated to the game.

Game developers, psychologists, neuroscientists, and designers should investigate possibilities to ensure players are not making negative causal attributions to characters in the game and transferring those negative causal attributions to Darfurians who experience everyday survival and victimization in the Sudan (Hoffman, 2000). Hoffman (2000) stated, "Training in multiple empathizing, which is not a natural thing to do, may capitalize on rather than be defeated by the natural human proclivity to empathize more with kin than strangers" (p. 298).

The relationship between cognitive load and empathy was laid out earlier in this chapter with a specific focus on games for change. As we continue to develop games with a focus on perspective-taking and empathy we have to consider the association between cognitive load and the absence or presence of empathy. We cannot assume that empathy is a given but must begin with investigating whether or not the player has the ability to empathize and to manage the interaction between cognitive load and empathy. Empathy is a very complex moral emotion that requires the ability to step into another's place cognitively. Game designers must realize that there must be a connection to prior experiences, or the long-

term memory, for the player to feel connected to the character's plight. Otherwise, the experience becomes a game, not a serious game.

CONCLUSION

Players enjoy the entertaining, playful aspects of interactive games, which could include an enthralling story; appealing characters; lush production values; a sense of social presence; making choices that affect the direction of the game; assuming the role of a character and playing with a new personality or identity; the extreme emotions that come with failure and success; and the pleasure of interacting with other characters and players. These experiences can heighten players' emotional responses to an interactive game and motive their effort to learn. (Lieberman, 2006, p. 381)

This chapter proposes several factors that inform how serious game designers can incorporate and manage elements to support the development of empathy while considering players' limited cognitive capacity. The first is cognitive load induced by the game environment, characters, and activities; the second is empathy and social perspective-taking resulting from the gameplay; and the last is the potential relationship between cognitive load and empathy and the impact of that relationship on learning in serious games. We argue that the ability to be empathic in serious games should affect the performance and learning of the player. In the meantime, players must have sufficient cognitive capacity allowance to develop their empathy. Thus the design of serious social games must consider the equilibrium between cognitive loads that engage players in the learning process and the cognitive allowance that supports empathy development.

REFERENCES

Abt, C. (1970). *Serious games*. New York: Viking Press.

Amory, A. (2007). Game object model version II: A theoretical framework for educational game development. *Educational Technology Research and Development*, *55*, 55–77. doi:10.1007/s11423-006-9001-x

Ang, C. S., Zaphiris, P., & Mahmood, S. (2007). A model of cognitive loads in massively multiplayer online role playing games. *Interacting with Computers*, *19*, 167–179. doi:10.1016/j.intcom.2006.08.006

Bransford, J., Brown, A., & Cocking, R. (2000). *How people learn: Brain, mind, and experience & school*. Washington, DC: National Academy Press.

Brünken, R., Plass, J., & Leutner, D. (2003). Direct measurement of cognitive load in multimedia learning. *Educational Psychologist*, *38*, 53–61. doi:10.1207/S15326985EP3801_7

Chandler, P., & Sweller, J. (1991). Cognitive load theory and the format of instruction. *Cognition and Instruction*, *8*, 293–332. doi:10.1207/s1532690xci0804_2

Cobb, T. (1997). Cognitive efficiency: Toward a revised theory of media. *Educational Technology Research and Development*, *45*, 1042–1062. doi:10.1007/BF02299681

Crawford, C. (1982). *The art of computer game design*. Retrieved from http://www.vancouver.wsu.edu/fac/peabody/game-book/Coverpage.html

Davis, M. H. (1994). *Empathy: A social psychological approach*. Dubuque, IA: Brown and Benchmark Publishers.

de Crook, M. B. M., van Merriënboer, J. J. G., & Paas, F. G. W. C. (1998). High versus low contextual interference in simulation-based training of troubleshooting skills: Effects on transfer performance and invested mental effort. *Computers in Human Behavior*, *14*, 249–267. doi:10.1016/S0747-5632(98)00005-3

Diamond, M., & Hopson, J. (1998). *Magic trees of the mind*. New York: Penguin.

Federation of American Scientists. (2006). Harnessing the power of video games for learning [report]. *Summit on Educational Games*. Federation of American Scientists, Washington, DC. Retrieved from http://fas.org/gamesummit/Resources/Summit%20on%20Educational%20Games.pdf

Gagné, R. M., & Driscoll, D. (1988). *Essentials of learning for instruction*. Englewood Cliffs, NJ: Prentice-Hall.

Gray, J. R., Braver, T. S., & Raichle, M. E. (2002, March 19). Integration of emotion and cognition in the lateral prefrontal cortex. *Proceedings of the National Academy of Sciences of the United States of America*, *99*(6), 4115–4020. doi:10.1073/pnas.062381899

Gredler, M. (1994). *Designing and evaluating games and simulations: A process approach*. Houston, TX: Gulf Publishing Company.

Grodal, T. (2000). Video games and the pleasures of control. In Zillmann, D., & Vorderer, P. (Eds.), *Media entertainment: The psychology of its appeal*. Mahwah, NJ: Lawrence Erlbaum Associates.

Gunter, G. A., Kenny, R. F., & Vick, E. H. (2008). Taking educational games seriously: Using the RETAIN model to design endogenous fantasy into standalone educational games. *Educational Technology Research and Development*, *56*, 511–537. doi:10.1007/s11423-007-9073-2

Hoffman, M. (2000). *Empathy & moral development: Implications for caring and justice*. New York: Cambridge University Press.

Hogan, R. (1969). Development of an empathy scale. *Journal of Consulting and Clinical Psychology, 33*, 307–316. doi:10.1037/h0027580

Huang, W. D., & Johnson, J. (2009). Let's get serious about E-games: A design research approach towards emergence perspective. In Cope, B., & Kalantzis, M. (Eds.), *Ubiquitous learning*. Champaign, IL: University of Illinois Press.

Huang, W. D., & Johnson, T. (2008). Instructional game design using Cognitive Load Theory. In Ferdig, R. (Ed.), *Handbook of research on effective electronic gaming in education*. Hershey, PA: Information Science Reference.

Immordino-Yang, M. H., & Damasio, A. (2008). *We feel, therefore we learn: The relevance of affective and social neuroscience to education. In the brain and learning. The Jossey-Bass reader*. San Francisco: Jossey-Bass.

Institute for Creative Technologies. (2009). *Full spectrum warrior*. Retrieved from http://ict.usc.edu/projects/full_spectrum_warrior

Johnson-Laird, P. N., & Oatley, K. (2000). Cognitive & social construction in emotions. In Lewis, M., & Haviland-Jones, J. M. (Eds.), *Handbook of emotions* (2nd ed.). New York: The Guildford Press.

Khalil, M., Paas, F., Johnson, T. E., & Payer, A. (2005). Design of interactive and dynamic anatomical visualizations: The implication of cognitive load theory. *Anatomical Record. Part B, New Anatomist, 286B*, 15–20. doi:10.1002/ar.b.20078

Lieberman, D. A. (2006). Can we learn from playing interactive games? In Vorderer, P., & Bryant, J. (Eds.), *Playing video games: Motives, responses, & consequences*. Mahwah, NJ: Lawrence Erlbaum Associates.

Low, R., Jin, P., & Sweller, J. (2010). Learner's cognitive load when using education technology. In Van Eck, R. (Ed.), *Interdisciplinary models and tools for serious games: Emerging concepts and future directions*. Hershey, PA: IGI.

Mayer, R. E. (2001). *Multimedia learning*. New York: Cambridge University Press.

Mayer, R. E., & Moreno, R. (2003). Nine ways to reduce cognitive load in multimedia learning. *Educational Psychologist, 38*, 43–52. doi:10.1207/S15326985EP3801_6

Paas, F., Tuovinen, J. E., Tabbers, H., & van Gerven, P. W. M. (2003). Cognitive load measurement as a means to advance cognitive load theory. *Educational Psychologist, 38*, 63–71. doi:10.1207/S15326985EP3801_8

Pollock, E., Chandler, P., & Sweller, J. (2002). Assimilating complex information. *Learning and Instruction, 12*, 61–86. doi:10.1016/S0959-4752(01)00016-0

Prensky, M. (2001). *Digital game-based learning*. New York: McGraw-Hill Publishing Company.

Raybourn, E. M. (2007). Applying simulation experience design methods to creating serious game-based adaptive training systems. *Interacting with Computers, 19*, 206–214. doi:10.1016/j.intcom.2006.08.001

Ruiz, S., York, A., Truong, H., Tarr, A., Keating, N., Stein, M., et al. (2006). *Darfur is Dying*. Thesis Project. Retrieved from http://interactive.usc.edu/projects/games/20070125-darfur_is_.php

Serious Games Initiative. (2010). Retrieved on January 14, 2010, from http://www.seriousgames.org/about2.html

Sousa, D. (2005). *How the brain learns*. Thousand Oaks, CA: Corwin Press.

Suits, B. (1978). *The grasshopper: Games, life, and utopia.* Ontario, CA: University of Toronto Press.

Tettegah, S. (2007). Pre-service teachers, victim empathy, and problem solving using animated narrative vignettes. *Technology, Instruction. Cognition and Learning, 5,* 41–68.

Tettegah, S., & Anderson, C. (2007). Pre-service teachers' empathy and cognitions: Statistical analysis of text data by graphical models. *Contemporary Educational Psychology, 32,* 48–82. doi:10.1016/j.cedpsych.2006.10.010

Tettegah, S., & Neville, H. (2007). Empathy among Black youth: Simulating race-related aggression in the classroom. *Scientia Paedagogica Experimentalis, XLIV, 1,* 33–48.

Um, E., Song, H., & Plass, J. L. (2007). *The effect of positive emotions on multimedia learning.* Paper presented at the World Conference on Educational Multimedia, Hypermedia & Telecommunications (ED-MEDIA 2007) in Vancouver, Canada, June 25–29, 2007.

van Gerven, P. W. M., Paas, F., van Merriënboer, J. J. G., & Schmidt, H. G. (2006). Modality and variability as factors in training the elderly. *Applied Cognitive Psychology, 20,* 311–320. doi:10.1002/acp.1247

van Merriënboer, J. J. G., Clark, R. E., & de Croock, M. B. M. (2002). Blueprints for complex learning: The 4C/ID-model. *Educational Technology Research and Development, 50,* 39–64. doi:10.1007/BF02504993

Wispé, L. (1987). History of the concept of empathy. In Eisenberg, N., & Strayer, J. (Eds.), *Empathy and its development.* Cambridge, UK: Cambridge University Press.

APPENDIX: ADDITIONAL READING

"Must-Reads" for This Topic

Aldrich, C. (2004). *Simulations and the future of learning*. San Francisco: Pfeiffer.

Blakemore, S.-J., & Frith, U. (2005). *The learning brain: Lessons for education*. Oxford, UK: Blackwell.

Clark, R., Nguyen, F., & Sweller, J. (2006). *Efficiency in learning: Evidence-based guidelines to manage cognitive load*. San Francisco, CA: Pfeiffer.

Restak, R. (2006). *The naked brain: How the emerging neuro-society is changing how we live, work, and love*. New York: Harmony Books.

Salen, K., & Zimmerman, E. (2004). *Rules of play: Game design fundamentals*. Cambridge, MA: The MIT Press.

Schroeder, R. & Axelsson, A.-S. (Eds.). (2006). *Avatars at work and play*. The Netherlands: Springer.

Vorderer, P., & Bryant, J. (Eds.). (2006). *Playing video games: Motives, responses, & consequences*. Hillsdale, NJ: Lawrence Erlbaum Associates.

Top Texts for Interdisciplinary Studies of Serious Games

Michael, D., & Chen, S. (2005). *Serious games: Games that educate, train & inform*. Washington, DC: Thomson Course Technology PTR.

Clark, R., Nguyen, F., & Sweller, J. (2006). *Efficiency in learning: Evidence-based guidelines to manage cognitive load*. San Francisco, CA: Pfeiffer.

Section 3
Theory Into Practice

Chapter 7
Effective Knowledge Development in Game-Based Learning Environments:
Considering Research in Cognitive Processes and Simulation Design

Amy B. Adcock
Old Dominion University, USA

Ginger S. Watson
Old Dominion University, USA

Gary R. Morrison
Old Dominion University, USA

Lee A. Belfore
Old Dominion University, USA

ABSTRACT

Serious games are, at their core, exploratory learning environments designed around the pedagogy and constraints associated with specific knowledge domains. This focus on instructional content is what separates games designed for entertainment from games designed to educate. As instructional designers and educators, the authors want serious game play to provide learners with a deep understanding of the domain, allowing them to use their knowledge in practice to think through multifaceted problems quickly and efficiently. Attention to the design of serious game affordances is essential to facilitating the development of domain knowledge during game play. As such, the authors contend that serious game designers should take advantage of existing prescriptions found in research on knowledge development in exploratory learning environments and tests of adaptive instructional designs in these environments. It is with this intention that the authors use evidence from research in cognitive processes and simulation design to propose design heuristics for serious game affordances to optimize knowledge development in games.

DOI: 10.4018/978-1-61520-717-6.ch007

INTRODUCTION

Zyda (2005) defines serious games as "a mental contest, played with a computer in accordance with specific rules, that uses entertainment to further government or corporate training, education, health, public policy and strategic communication objectives" (p. 26). Serious games present players with a contextualized problem, rules (guided by constraints associated with the content), multiple interacting elements, and cognitive tools that allow users to freely discover solution paths in the tradition of exploratory, problem-based learning. In a way, serious games can be thought of as a sense-making activity; players are constrained by the rules associated with their domains (situated context) but otherwise use the affordances in the game to make sense of domain-related concepts needed to complete game objectives. For example, to represent the fact that mixing acids and bases will cause an explosion, it is necessary to generate a rule to restrict actions in a chemistry game.

Unlike training simulations, which are held to realistic representations and high levels of detail at all levels, serious games are able to place players in fantastic situations where they are asked to take on specific roles and where representations might be simplified to focus on target knowledge (Crawford, 1984). While in the game world, players observe the consequences of their decisions and are constantly challenged to fill knowledge gaps through problem solutions that require retrieval of prior knowledge (Van Eck, 2007). As they work to fill these knowledge gaps, players integrate domain knowledge into their cognitive systems, thus gaining knowledge of the domain (Foster & Mishra, 2009).

Serious game environments are inherently complex, as there are many elements working in harmony to create the game experience. Potential for collaboration, cross disciplinary activities and situated learning are all possible in a well-designed serious game. Gee (2004) suggests designers focus on designing games to keep learners hooked (even when dealing with complex information). He suggests approaches like well-defined problem statements and practice in context to sustain the players' interest throughout the life of the game. Certain properties such as motivation (Low, this volume), flow (Reese, this volume), and adaptability (Magerko, Heeter & Medler, this volume) are also essential to creating an environment where learners want to play and are motivated to come back and replay.

Designers of serious games can take advantage of the freedom to simplify representations, insert features such as custom avatars, transition scenes, inventories, maps, and non-player characters and focus on necessary domain knowledge by carefully crafting problems, rules and cognitive tools: what we refer to as serious game affordances. To design a serious game that is not only entertaining but also educational, these affordances should be designed with careful attention to the cognitive development of the players; we feel these considerations are critical to the serious game design process. The purpose of this chapter is to provide heuristics for the design of serious game affordances to support the learner as they develop their domain understanding.

To construct these heuristics, we will examine research in cognitive processes related to knowledge development from within the framework of the development of expertise. We begin with a review of the literature on development of expertise to provide evidence of the most efficient means of supporting a learner as they move from domain novice to expert thinker and beyond. We use these findings to address a critical issue in serious game design: the development of a player-driven exploratory learning environment that supports the development of domain-related schema through verified supports and affordances. To facilitate optimal serious game design, we propose a set of design heuristics specifically aimed at supporting knowledge development for meaningful learning outcomes.

SUPPORTING THE KNOWLEDGE CONTINUUM

The Process of Knowledge Development

Human memory systems consist of a sensory, short-term (working) and long-term memory stores (Atkinson & Shiffrin, 1968; Baddeley, 1992). Theories of knowledge development account for the strengths and limitation of each memory type and the processing that occurs when information moves from short- to long-term memory (encoding) and back for later use (retrieval). Optimal learning environments are designed to facilitate the encoding of information through the design of affordances to support every knowledge level of the learner, allowing for either rehearsal or practice with increasingly complex problems. Ideally, it is this process that helps novice learners develop into seasoned domain experts who can transfer knowledge from instructional environments to practice, solve divergent problems, and present creative solutions. It is the organization and storage of information chunks into long-term memory schemas that truly allows for a flexible approach to situated problems even over long periods of time (Mayer, 2009).

Stages of Knowledge Acquisition: The Knowledge Continuum

Domain expertise can be quantified in several different ways (e.g. ability to solve complex problems, level of automaticity when recalling prior knowledge). Anderson (2000) presents three stages of skill acquisition leading to the development of a domain expert. In the cognitive (novice) stage, learners begin to understand the processes or concepts related to the domain through the acquisition of declarative or foundational knowledge. Learners at this stage require a high level of detailed information about the domain area and any necessary supports for understanding or

visualizing. In the associative (experienced) stage, connections are made linking individual knowledge units together into procedural knowledge. At this point, the level of detail is reduced, as the learner is able to create larger chunks of information. Learners can begin working autonomously as long as proper scaffolding is provided. In the final level of knowledge development, the autonomous (expert) stage, connections among essential domain knowledge are internalized and learners can make automatic associations. Supports can be gradually faded as learners are able to perform tasks without the support an expert model. It is in this stage that learners are able to think conditionally, divergently and transfer knowledge from one problem set to an isomorphic problem.

This sequence of knowledge development can be visualized as the progressive strengthening of associations between small pieces of foundational knowledge creating a deep understanding of the domain (i.e. McClelland, 2000). This understanding gives learners the ability to make connections internally so they can figure out novel approaches to problems. They are also able to deal with ill-structured problem spaces more efficiently (Bransford, Brown & Cocking, 1999; Jonassen, 1997). Learners at the automatic level are able to quickly retrieve the most efficient and effective solutions rather than having to go through a trial-and-error process, which in turn gives them the ability to tackle complex problems.

To foster learning across these various levels of domain knowledge, instructional systems must facilitate recognition and recall of learned content, illustrate the associations of learned and new content, and extend associations to new or novel situations. In serious game environments, which we argue are primarily player-directed, open-ended exploratory or discovery spaces, examining what is known about the needs of learners at every stage of development is critical to determine what is needed to support meaningful learning (Kirschner, Sweller & Clark, 2006).

THE IMPORTANCE OF PRIOR KNOWLEDGE IN DESIGN

As with any instructional environment, the goal of a well-designed serious game is the development and support of the learner's (in this case, player's) knowledge base. To support this development, serious game designers must be aware of research precedents associated with message design and prior knowledge of learners. Cognitive load theory (CLT; Chandler & Sweller, 1991; Sweller, 1999) provides a theoretical framework for designing instruction that uses different forms of media representations (i.e., text and pictures, text and narration) or multimedia to support the learner. CLT accounts for the load on working memory resources during each stage of knowledge development and can guide designers as they create environments to support not only novices but also learners with a higher level of prior knowledge. CLT provides empirical evidence that instructional messages are most effective when they are designed to account for the learner's cognitive system.

Using what is known about human cognitive architecture, CLT defines three types of cognitive load evidenced when instructional messages are presented to learners (Chandler & Sweller, 1991). Intrinsic cognitive load is associated with the complexity of the elements of the instructional domain and is much higher in domain novices than in experts. Germane cognitive load refers to the mental resources necessary to develop relevant schema for learning independent of the learner's expertise in the particular domain. Extraneous cognitive load is found in poorly designed instructional messages that present unnecessary details in the message, thereby distracting the learner from the instruction. These three types are additive and too much load on the learner's cognitive system is found to hinder learning at any level of prior knowledge.

In an effort to inform the field of instructional design working within a CLT framework, van Gog, Ericsson, Rikers and Paas (2005) discuss how different cognitive systems (novice vs. expert) are affected by the design of the instructional environment. They argue that in order for instructional designers to create sound learning environments for each stage of knowledge, we must attend to both the initial development of schema (novice stage) and the continuing reinforcement of domain knowledge for experienced learners (automatic stage). Leveraging findings on the effects of deliberate practice and expert characteristics, van Gog et al. suggest that as learners develop, their instructional environments should adapt to their knowledge base. They call on instructional design research to verify their assertions by creating adaptive systems. It is this ability to create an adaptive system that holds promise for the design of self-directed but meaningful exploratory learning environments like serious games (van Merrienboer & Ayres, 2005). In serious game design, this can be realized by providing concrete examples and more restricted learner controls in the early stages of learning, and gradually providing less structure and more learner control as the learner gains expertise.

Supporting Knowledge Development in Player-Driven Exploratory Learning Environments

As Mayer (2009) points out, tests of multimedia environments have shown marked differences in the way high- and low-domain knowledge users interact with instruction. Empirical research indicates that differences in levels of expertise call for differences in the design of instructional messages (Kalyuga, Ayres, Chandler & Sweller, 2003; van Gog et al. 2005). Understanding human cognitive architecture, the basis of CLT, allows us to see that as knowledge is developed, learners are able to use cognitive resources in different ways (e.g., taking on new and divergent problems). Given what we know about the stages of knowledge acquisition and the importance of adapting instruction to learners' knowledge development, serious game designers should think about evoking the behavior of experts during game play as a means to facilitate encoding of domain specific knowledge for later transfer into practice.

In the context of serious game design, we define the effective development of knowledge as a progression towards deep understanding of the domain and support once this level is achieved and the learner has become a more expert thinker. Given both the overall nature of serious games in providing a space for discovery learning and the lack of confidence many have in completely unguided discovery based learning (i.e. Kirschner et al., 2006) this is a difficult thing to achieve. Nonetheless, with the proper attention to guidelines it might be possible to create expert thinkers from serious game play.

To guide serious game designers in the behaviors we strive to evoke through continuing explorations in the serious game space, we first examined Bransford, Brown and Cocking's (1999) characteristics of domain experts. These characteristics are based on research which observed the differences between novice and expert behavior in certain disciplines (e.g. de Groot, 1965, Chi, Glaser & Rees, 1982), and are listed in Table 1. The list contains the behaviors we want to see after learners interact with open-ended exploratory

learning environments (including both instructional simulations and games). Table 1 summarizes these characteristics and provides general design considerations and possible adaptations meant to support learners during their development from novice to expert. These adaptations are especially critical in serious game design where supports should be self-contained as affordances within the game environment, and they form the basic structure for the heuristics proposed in the next section.

SUPPORTING KNOWLEDGE DEVELOPMENT IN SERIOUS GAMES

Serious games are more than simple multimedia instructional environments. Many complex elements go into a well-designed game. Elements of narrative, fantasy, pedagogical structure and competition are critical for game effectiveness (Amory, 2007; Killi, 2005). Affordances such as custom avatars, inventories, non-player character interactions, tool sets, reflection journals and collaborative spaces present multiple opportunities for instructional designers to create pedagogically meaningful learning environments. As instructional designers, we think it is important to pay special attention to what past research tells us in

Table 1. Characteristics of expertise (adapted from Bransford et al. 1999) and their related supports and design considerations

Expert Characteristics	Design Considerations	Serious Game Adaptations to Support Knowledge Development
Notice patterns in problem spaces	Vary levels of problem detail and complexity to further build and extend expertise	Reduce level of overt help and increase complexity of problems as knowledge is developed
Understand domain conditionally	Domain-Related Information can be presented that take advantage of this conditional knowledge.	Gradually present problems that require less procedural and more conditional knowledge
Easily retrieve domain knowledge without expending a large amount of mental resources	Added layers of capability and tool sets can be provided to experts as it is not necessary to use mental resources to figure out problem solution paths	Gradually release more complex affordances as knowledge progresses
Approach new situations flexibly	Ill-structured problems can be solved with reduced mental resource expenditure	Increase the use of multifaceted problems that require the chunking of domain knowledge

terms of a careful balance of instructional message and supports to facilitate effective knowledge development. By designing for the support of knowledge development, we increase the chances of skills transfer from the serious game into the real world of practice.

To quickly review what we have discussed regarding research in cognitive processes and support of knowledge development, domain novices (i.e. learners in the cognitive stage) do best when presented with a high level of informational detail and guidance in a simplified but very contextual environment in order to build a mental model of necessary knowledge and/or procedures (Mayer, 2009). This sequencing and structure allows novice learners to encounter and solve each necessary procedural step in a task so that associations are facilitated and connections are strengthened (Anderson, 2000; McClelland, 2000). On the other side of the equation, learners with a higher level of domain knowledge can work in a richer representation of the problem space but with a lower level of scaffolds and supports (primarily available upon request) as long as practice opportunities are structured to support domain-relevant schema (Kalyuga, Ayres, Chandler & Sweller, 2003; Mayer, 2009; van Gog, Ericsson, Rikers & Paas, 2005). One promise of complex exploratory learning environments like serious games is that adaptations for facilitating and supporting knowledge development can be built into several different game features.

Adapting Features From Simulation Design for Serious Game Design Heuristics

The heuristics presented in this next section of the chapter deal with four critical features of exploratory learning environment design; models, interface, learning activities and learner control. These features are derived from precedents in simulation design research (Alessi, 1988; Alessi & Trollip, 2001; de Jong, de Hoog, & De Vries,

1993) and are easily adapted through the use of design heuristics.

Consider as an example, a serious game designed to train investigators in crime scene analysis. The game starts with the learner navigating a vehicle to a house where a crime has occurred. At the cognitive stage, a player might navigate the vehicle into the driveway and immediately enter the house. In contrast, a player with more expertise would begin earlier in the scenario to observe the street, the driveway and yard for tire marks, footprints, and other evidence related to the crime *before* entering the house. Varying the starting point of the game, the overt aspects of the evidence, and the amount of coaching can provide a very different amount of complexity and support to learners at different stages of expertise within the game. Without this support for knowledge development, a stand-alone serious game environment can overwhelm the novice, thus leading to incorrect and/or inefficient actions and possible misconceptions. On the other side of the continuum, serious game environments with minimal guidance will provide the right amount of challenge along for the expert investigator (Kirschner et al. 2006).

Model Feature

Models represent the underlying structure of the knowledge domain. The model may or may not be available to the learner; however, some propose allowing learners at more advanced stages to see the model in order to facilitate knowledge development (Alessi, 1988; de Jong, et al., 1993). The type, design, and fidelity of the underlying simulation model are driven by the level of realism needed to support the underlying scenario, instructional interface and learner activities. As previously stated, serious games are not constrained by reality, so this feature can be adapted as needed to support the learners.

As a player interacts with the game, their actions are reflected in reactions within the game world. When domain-related, these interactions/ reactions serve as declarative knowledge items, the building blocks of understanding the connections that comprise a deep understanding of the domain. As domain knowledge develops, learners are more able to see the connections between the smaller domain-related challenges (Bransford, Brown & Cocking, 1999). By presenting these tasks gradually and with increasing elaboration and detail, we support the learner by slowly facilitating the associations in their cognitive structures (de Jong & van Joolingen, 1998).

General design heuristics related to the presentation of the model in serious game environments are:

1. Early in knowledge development, activities are very simple and straightforward to avoid complexity (high intrinsic cognitive load; Chandler & Sweller, 1991). This allows the learner to use mental resources to understand the basic structure of the domain.

2. Layers of model complexity are added gradually as knowledge develops. As the learner gains domain-related knowledge, information on how the pieces of knowledge are related (i.e. connections or associations) can gradually be revealed. This supports the strengthening of these connections that occur in the associative stage (Anderson, 2000) of developing domain knowledge.

Serious game affordances that can be designed to reflect these heuristics include:

*   Inventory
*   Transition narratives
*   Level completion tasks

Let's take the example of the crime scene investigation training game for novice investigators as an example of how these heuristics might be implemented for the expertise continuum.

Cognitive: In the beginning stages of knowledge development, players will begin their investigation but their focus is not distracted by the presentation of how these pieces fit together. Instead, their attention is guided by narrative (e.g., via non-player characters—NPCs—or text) and the player is directed to the necessary procedures and tools (revealed in inventory) for collecting evidence. Level goals are small scale problems (e.g., "note potential evidence for further inquiry" or "pick up the magnifying glass to examine this fingerprint").

Associative: As players proceed through the game, the pieces of evidence are collected in the inventory making the underlying model of how much and what evidence to collect to facilitate the investigative process viewable. Narrative is still frequent to refocus attention and connect pieces of evidence to the deduction process. Level goals become more complex and require more than one action to complete. Guidance for actions is reduced.

Automatic: Players have full access to both evidence collection tools in inventory and the model of the deductive process showing the relationship of each piece of evidence and how they are related to the investigative process. Level goals are more complex, investigations must be resolved to level up.

Interface Feature

The most commonly recognized aspect of an exploratory learning environment (e.g. simulations and serious games) is the instructional interface that provides a text or graphical representation of the phenomenon, process, or situation being simulated. A graphical interface provides a visual image of the phenomenon, equipment, or scenario environment. In the context of a serious game, the interface refers to explanatory scaffolds and supports for task accomplishment including help from text-based cues and/or non-player characters serving as guides.

General design heuristics related to the presentation serious game interface:

1. Game instructional interface adjusts levels of help and scaffolding to account for learners knowledge level
2. Learners with a low level of prior knowledge are presented with simple tasks and explanatory scaffolds such as worked examples.
3. As learner knowledge develops, explanatory scaffolds become available on request.

Serious game affordances that can be designed to reflect these heuristics include:

*   Help access
*   Feedback to player

Let's go back to our example of a investigation training game to illustrate how this might work:

Cognitive: The interface appears as a simple frame of the immediate area where the player will be collecting evidence. Explanations of *each* element on the screen are provided via rollovers providing text-based or verbal explanations of necessary tools and to give the player a situational awareness of the environment (i.e. "You are standing in front of the house where a crime has occurred, the first piece of evidence is in front of you.").

Associative: As players proceed through the game, the interface view is expanded to include more of the surrounding environment, which might be distracting for players at the cognitive stage. Help and feedback via scaffolding from text or verbal messages is still available but only when critical errors occur.

Automatic: As the learner develops knowledge, the interface is fully available to the player, while scaffolds from text or verbal messages are eventually are made available only upon request.

Learning Activities Feature

The learning activities comprise the actual tasks given to the player to promote the development of

their knowledge. Learner activities in a simulation may include dissecting a frog, mixing a chemical compound, docking a spacecraft, or breeding mice. Strategies for learning activities include specifying the experimental setting with initial values and parameters (de Jong, et al., 1993), explaining or demonstrating the phenomenon or procedure (Alessi, 2000), allowing the learner to choose the next step in the process or the format of data presentation and providing realistic interface and immediate feedback after learner inputs (de Jong, et al.), and giving summary feedback or debriefing at program completion (Alessi and Trollip, 2001).

In order to facilitate the development of knowledge without interfering with necessary mental resources, careful attention should be paid to the tasks given at each stage of knowledge development. At a lower level of knowledge, learners need to interact with small elements (or units of knowledge). As associations or connections develop, activities can become more complex leading to the presentation of ill-structured problems.

Design considerations related to the learning activities in the serious game environment are:

1. Learners with low prior knowledge are given simple tasks. Detailed explanations accompany tasks
2. As knowledge develops, tasks become more complex.
3. Explanations begin with high levels of detail and are given at each step of the process. As the game progresses, explanations are available on request or automatically occur if several errors are made.

Serious game affordances that can be designed to reflect these heuristics include:

*   Problem statements
*   Level completion tasks
*   Feedback to player

Let's go back to our example of a investigation training game to illustrate how this might work:

Cognitive: Players are not simply allowed to take a course of action. Instead they are told stepwise (via text-based or verbal presentation of problem statements from a non-player character) each procedure involved in the arrival of a crime scene (i.e. look around to see if there is evidence outside the area). They are then directed to collect single pieces of evidence and these pieces are stored in an inventory. Players complete levels after they complete each small step.

Associative: As they progress through the game, units of evidence collected are combined and players are shown the collection to form a "big picture" of how single units of evidence add up to conclusions about what occurred during the crime. Players are allowed to level up after they complete larger tasks but do not have to complete the entire investigation.

Automatic: At this stage, a new complex crime scene with many interacting elements is presented. Players are not allowed to level up until they complete the entire investigation and report their findings.

Learner Control Feature

Features for learner control include affordances meant to control the flow of information in the game. These controls support knowledge development by providing necessary domain information. Because learners at lower knowledge levels need mental resources to process foundational knowledge, it is advisable to focus their attention to the domain-related knowledge. There must also be consideration for the granularity of knowledge (chunks) at this stage. At this stage, navigation should be as tightly controlled as possible. As learners gain knowledge, their mental resources are somewhat freed up and they can be gradually given access to the controls of amount and kind of information.

Design heuristics related to the learning activities in the serious environment include:

- Options for controlling the flow of domain-related information are not available for learners at the cognitive stage
- As knowledge develops, options are gradually unlocked allowing learners to control the flow of domain-related information.

Serious game affordances that can be designed to reflect these heuristics are:

- Control panels
- Navigation
- Transition narratives

Let's go back to our example of a investigation training game to illustrate how this might work:

Cognitive: Players are brought into the game and given direct instructions on how they will proceed through evidence collection. Navigational options are hidden and players are not allowed to travel around the crime scene at will. Transition narratives are very detailed indicating the next step of the procedure and any necessary situational information (i.e. you now need to look around outside the crime scene for footprints; your next stop is outside). Any evidence collection tools needed are provided directly for the learner, they are not allowed to choose. When they successfully complete small tasks, the game navigates them to the next step. In the beginning of knowledge development, players are presented with direct domain-related information in a controlled manner through the hiding or disabling of certain options (i.e. navigation to access the underlying model of the information). Navigational guidance is provided through textual or verbal feedback. Transition narratives give detailed indications of the next step in the game.

Associative: As players progress, the navigational functions such as moving back and forth from outside to inside the crime scene area are made available. Transition narratives are less detailed but are still used to provide some information to orient the player to the next task needed to complete evidence collection. Tools are available on a limited basis and feedback is provided to facilitate correct tool selection.

Automatic: Players are given full control of tools and navigation needed to complete evidence collection. Transition narratives provide very little explanation as to the next step of the task. Feedback as to the correct evidence collection procedures and necessary tools is minimal. Navigation is open and players can move around the crime scene at will.

This section presented design heuristics intended to support the development of knowledge in a serious game environment. Using features derived from design research in simulation, we were able to extract four features that are easily adaptable within a game. With these heuristics, we have striven for generality so that they can apply to a wide range of serious game taxonomies. Table 2 presents the primary serious game affordances and the adaptations needed based on these heuristics.

FUTURE RESEARCH DIRECTIONS

A still relevant criticism of the field of serious game design research is the lack of sound empirical studies documenting the advantages of learning from games. As such, it makes sense to begin a discussion of future research directions by prescribing these types of studies. In relation to the focus of this chapter, we propose the implementation of design research examining the effectiveness of the heuristics and empirical measures to determine the correlation between knowledge development and affordance adaptations recommended in the heuristics. Two separate research tracks are discussed below. One will test the effectiveness of each heuristics through controlled design research experiments. The second will test the heuristics as a whole through a process of formative and summative assessments.

Some general research questions we would like to address using the proposed research protocols are:

- Do affordance adjustments suggested by research in simulation design apply to the design of serious games?
- What is the general effectiveness of the heuristics in the design of effective serious games?
- Which affordance adjustments are most critical to effective support of knowledge development
- Is this affected by the domain?
- What other game affordances can be adjusted to support knowledge development?

Assessment of Design Heuristics

In order to verify the effectiveness of each heuristic in terms of supporting and sustaining knowledge development, we propose that each heuristic be tested in a series of controlled design experiments. The procedure for these experiments will be the same but will test each heuristic separately. Experimental conditions include variations of content knowledge and adaptation algorithms to determine the optimal progression of affordances to support the progression to expertise.

Measures

One of the greatest challenges of game research is the need for meaningful measures of learning outcomes. Research needs to move beyond measures of time in game, fun, and perception to assess gains in content knowledge, problem solving and causal reasoning which are critical for high-order activities (Jonassen & Ionas, 2008). Research should also focus on the near and far transfer of problem solving and causal reasoning to other content areas and performance in related environments.

More advanced technologies today allow researchers to collect physiological data from learners interacting with computer-based and virtual learning environments to measure individual learners' response to sensory, motor, and cognitive stimuli in the simulation or serious

Table 2. Design heuristics for serious game affordances

Game Affordance	Knowledge Level	Heuristics
Inventory	Cognitive	Access to inventory items is restricted by the program. Only tools relevant to the needed task are released.
	Associative	Players allowed to select from limited items
	Automatic	Players have full access to all tool sets
Transition Narratives	Cognitive	Narratives contain detailed domain-related information Narratives provide a high level of domain related scaffolding
	Associative	Narratives contain less detailed domain-related information Narratives provide minimal domain related scaffolding
	Automatic	Narratives are minimal and only used when changing context Domain related scaffolding is available upon request
Level Completion Tasks	Cognitive	Level completion tasks represent simple procedures
	Associative	Level completion tasks are more involved requiring integration of prior knowledge
	Automatic	Level completion tasks are more complex and require the use of conditional knowledge
Help Access	Cognitive	Help is integrated into the narrative and contains a high level of domain related detail
	Associative	Help is still integrated into game narrative but level of detail is reduced
	Automatic	Help is available upon request
Problem Statements	Cognitive	Problems are reduced to small procedural steps
	Associative	Problems are more complex but are still presented in steps
	Automatic	Problem statement is complex and presented as a whole
Feedback to Player	Cognitive	Feedback is immediate, elaborative and corrective. Detailed explanations are provided
	Associative	Feedback is immediate, not as detailed. Players are encouraged to try again
	Automatic	Feedback is delayed, either available at final debriefing or on request
Control Panels	Cognitive	Access to controls is limited.
	Associative	Some access to controls released to player
	Automatic	Player given full access to controls
Navigation	Cognitive	Navigation through game space is controlled by the program
	Associative	Players are allowed to navigate restricted areas of the game space
	Automatic	Players are allowed full control of navigation

game. Technologies such as eye tracking and electroencephalogragh (EEG) facilitate measuring visual attention and cognitive response continuously throughout game play. These physiological measures allow the researcher or developer to link the stimuli in a simulation or game to continuous attention and processing on the part of the learner, offering promise for adapting the program to individual learners. For example, in the investigation game discussed previously, if a learner is having difficulty identifying clues at a crime scene the game could highlight a set of items or fade out unnecessary details in the scene. With eye tracking, the program can detect if the learner now "looks" at the individual clues, and with EEG it can discriminate if the learner is cognitively processing that clue. Such technologies can be used to assess individual learner cognition, the effectiveness of instructional approaches, and the efficacy of supports provided to learners at various stages of knowledge development.

It is worth noting that the equipment used to collect these data continues to evolve and is still in early stages for such applications. Similarly, current research in neuroscience continues to localize neurological processing. Techniques such as event-related potential facilitate measurement of P300, which has been linked to cognitive processing (Hillyard, 2008). As these technologies advance, it is conceivable that physiological measures such as eye tracking and EEG could become commonplace even using a web camera available on most computers and a headband that can be put on by the player. In the meantime, they are research tools that allow us to literally look into the minds of learners during instruction.

Formative and Summative Evaluation of Serious Games Employing Heuristics

The traditional formative evaluation design approach iteratively evaluates the system, which results in increasingly more robust prototypes.

Data from the evaluation of each prototype is used to modify both the instruction and the interface. Furthermore, evidence-based instructional intervention design isolates various attributes of the instructional environment to determine the most effective approach. So while the serious game environment is being developed and formative evaluations are conducted, the evaluation should focus on interface design and the development of simulations and representative scenarios designed to teach foundational skills and knowledge.

Evaluations should also be made of the contexts to determine if they are appealing and motivational, and whether they help develop and support the appropriate knowledge and skills. The user interface should be evaluated to determine the most effective design. The formative evaluation should begin with a review from an expert in either interview or written form, and proceed from there to a one-to-one evaluation that involves an early storyboard or prototype version of the game. Next, a small group evaluation should take place to verify that the recommendations for changes made by the expert and one-to-one evaluations have been successfully completed. The last stage of field test should then take a more complete version of the prototype that has been modified through the expert review, the one-to-one, and the small group stages of the formative evaluation. The field test will measure the efficacy of the game in the actual environment with a sample of the actual learners that will be using the game. Feedback from this last stage of field testing is conducted on a mostly completed game and may provide feedback for both the current and future iterations of the game (Tessmer, 1993).

After a final version of the game is constructed, summative evaluations can occur through checks of knowledge development using different versions of the game. Four levels of evaluation may be used to determine the efficacy of the design including (a) level 1 learner affective reactions such as like or dislike of the game, (b) learning evaluation with pre and post test assessments,

(c) transfer to see if behavior has changed in the learners' environment and (d) results or the "bottom line" of measurable results such as reduction of waste or increase in production, (Kirkpatrick, 1994). Researchers must move beyond a level 1 evaluation to provide designers and decision-makers with valid research-based, data-driven reasons for allocating resources to game design and development.

CONCLUSION

As evidenced by the publication of new texts, journals and conferences specifically focused on game-based learning research, the concept of learning from playing games is beginning to cohere into a discipline of its own. In 2005, a report from the Federation of American Scientists called for a greater use of serious games for educational purposes (2005). The multifaceted exploratory learning environments afforded by serious games have the potential to transform learning. However, instructional designers are still at the beginning stages of realizing the potential for serious games. Our contribution to the growing field of serious games is to emphasize the need to look to established research on the development of knowledge (via message and interface design guidelines) and to apply these principles to some of the unique features found in serious game environments. These heuristics were carefully constructed to guide the design of what are usually self-directed, exploratory learning environments. By using existing simulation design research to construct the heuristics, we take advantage of existing research precedents.

Van Eck (2007) suggests one of the issues related to the widespread acceptance of serious game research and development is a lack of cohesion of ideas related to how game-based learning environments work as cognitive tools. He contends that as game-based researchers and designers, we must look to research from other fields to add important contributions to the pursuit of principles to make research in game-based learning a valid scientific enterprise. Research in the development of expertise not only tells us about the cognitive processes that occur while a learner gains expertise but also gives us a window into domain experts' thought processes. This information contains useful indications of what affordances are needed by learners at every stage of their knowledge development. By incorporating these findings into a typical serious game environment with all of the required affordances (story, competition, problem sets) we strengthen the legitimacy of claims for serious games as a means to deliver meaningful learning.

Our design heuristics provide instructional supports within serious game environments for the underlying model, interface, learner activities, and learner controls of the game. These heuristics are intended to create a serious environment that adapts to provide varying levels of support for learners with varying levels of knowledge. Research is needed to fully test the model and heurisics and to determine the most effective ways to implement and adapt them relative to traditional game elements such as story, narrative, fantasy, and competition.

REFERENCES

Alessi, S. M. (1988). Fidelity in the design of instructional simulations. *Journal of Computer-Based Instruction, 15*(2), 40–47.

Alessi, S. M. (2000). Simulation design for training and assessment. In O'Neill, H. F. Jr, & Andrews, D. H. (Eds.), *Aircrew training and assessment* (pp. 197–222). Mahwah, NJ: Lawrence Erlbaum Associates.

Alessi, S. M., & Trollip, S. R. (2001). *Multimedia for learning: Methods and development*. Boston, MA: Allyn & Bacon.

Amory, A. (2007). Game object model version II: A theoretical framework for educational game development. *Educational Technology Research and Development, 55*(1), 51–77. doi:10.1007/s11423-006-9001-x

Anderson, J. R. (2000). *Cognitive psychology and its implications* (5th ed.). New York: Worth Publishing.

Atkinson, R. C., & Shiffrin, R. M. (1968). Human memory: A proposed system and its control processes. In Spence, K. W., & Spence, J. T. (Eds.), *The psychology of learning and motivation* (*Vol. 2*, pp. 89–195). New York: Academic Press.

Baddeley, A. (1992). Working memory. *Science, 255*, 556–559. doi:10.1126/science.1736359

Bransford, J., Brown, A., & Cocking, R. (Eds.). (1999). *How people learn: Brain, mind, experience, and school*. Washington, DC: National Academy Press.

Chandler, P., & Sweller, J. (1991). Cognitive load theory and the format of instruction. *Cognition and Instruction, 8*(4), 293–332. doi:10.1207/s1532690xci0804_2

Chi, M. T. H., Glaser, R., & Rees, E. (1982). Expertise in problem solving. In Sternberg, R. J. (Ed.), *Advances in the psychology of human intelligence* (*Vol. 1*, pp. 7–76). Hillsdale, NJ: Erlbaum.

Crawford, C. (1984). *The art of computer game design*. Berkeley, CA: Osborne/McGraw-Hill.

de Jong, T., de Hoog, R., & de Vries, F. (1993). Coping with complex environments: The effects of providing overviews and a transparent interface on learning with a computer simulation. *International Journal of Man-Machine Studies, 39*(4), 621–639. doi:10.1006/imms.1993.1076

de Jong, T., & Van Joolingen, W. R. (1998). Scientific discovery learning with computer simulations of conceptual domains. *Review of Educational Research, 68*(2), 179–201.

deGroot, A. D. (1965). *Thought and choice in chess*. The Hague, Netherlands: Mouton.

Federation of American Scientists. (2005). *Harnessing the power of educational games*. Retrieved from http://fas.org/gamesummit/Resources/Summit%20on%20Educational%20Games.pdf

Foster, A., & Mishra, P. (2009). Disciplinary knowledge construction while playing a simulation strategy game. In I. Gibson, R. Weber, K. McFerrin, R. Carlsen & D. Willis (Eds.), *Proceedings of Society for Information Technology and Teacher Education International Conference 2009* (pp. 1439-1444). Chesapeake, VA: AACE.

Gee, J. P. (2004). Learning by design: Games as learning machines. *Interactive Educational Multimedia, 8*, 15–23.

Hillyard, S. A. (2008). Event-related potentials (ERPs) and cognitive processing. In Squire, L. R. (Ed.), *Encyclopedia of neuroscience* (3rd ed., pp. 13–18). San Diego, CA: Academic Press.

Jonassen, D. H. (1997). Instructional design models for well-structured and ill-structured problem-solving learning outcomes. *Educational Technology Research and Development, 45*(1), 65–94. doi:10.1007/BF02299613

Jonassen, D. H., & Ionas, I. G. (2008). Designing effective supports for causal reasoning. *Educational Technology Research and Development, 56*(3), 287–308. doi:10.1007/s11423-006-9021-6

Kalyuga, S., Ayres, P., Chandler, P., & Sweller, J. (2003). The expertise reversal effect. *Educational Psychologist, 38*(1), 23–31. doi:10.1207/S15326985EP3801_4

Killi, K. (2005). Digital game-based learning: Towards an experiential gaming model. *The Internet and Higher Education, 8*(1), 13–24. doi:10.1016/j.iheduc.2004.12.001

Kirkpatrick, D. L. (1994). *Evaluating training programs: The four levels*. San Francisco, CA: Berrett-Koehler.

Kirschner, P. A., Sweller, J., & Clark, R. E. (2006). Why minimal guidance during instruction does not work: An analysis of the failure of constructivist, discovery, problem-based, experiential and inquiry-based teaching. *Educational Psychologist, 41*(2), 75–86. doi:10.1207/s15326985ep4102_1

Low, R. (in press). Examining motivational factors in serious educational games. In Van Eck, R. (Ed.), *Gaming & cognition: Theories and practice from the learning sciences*. Hershey, PA: IGI Global.

Magerko, B., Heeter, C., & Medler, B. (in press). Individual differences in students: How to adapt games for better learning experiences. In Van Eck, R. (Ed.), *Gaming & cognition: Theories and practice from the learning sciences*. Hershey, PA: IGI Global.

Mayer, R. E. (2009). *Multimedia learning* (2nd ed.). Cambridge, UK: Cambridge University Press.

McClelland, J. L. (2000). Connectionist models of memory. In Tulving, E., & Craik, F. I. M. (Eds.), *The Oxford handbook of memory* (pp. 583–596). New York: Oxford University Press.

Reese, D. D. (in press). Games to evoke and assess readiness to learn conceptual knowledge. In Van Eck, R. (Ed.), *Gaming & cognition: Theories and prctice from the learning sciences*. Hershey, PA: IGI Global.

Sweller, J. (1999). *Instructional design in technical areas*. Camberwell, Victoria, Australia: Australian Council for Educational Research.

Tessmer, M. (1993). *Planning and conducting formative evaluation*. London: Kogan Page Limited.

Van Eck, R. (2007). Six ideas in search of a discipline. In Shelton, B., & Wiley, D. (Eds.), *The design and use of simulation computer games in education*. Rotterdam, The Netherlands: Sense Publishing.

van Gog, T., Ericsson, K., Rikers, R., & Paas, F. (2005). Instructional design for advanced learners: Establishing connections between the theoretical frameworks of cognitive load and deliberate practice. *Educational Technology Research and Development, 53*(3), 73–81. doi:10.1007/BF02504799

van Merriënboer, J., & Ayres, P. (2005). Research on cognitive load theory and its design implications for e-learning. *Educational Technology Research and Development, 53*(3), 5–13. doi:10.1007/BF02504793

Zyda, M. (2005). From visual simulation to virtual reality to games. *IEEE Computer, 38*(9), 25–32.

APPENDIX: ADDITIONAL READING

"Must-Reads" for This Topic

Alessi, S. M. (1988). Fidelity in the design of instructional simulations. *Journal of Computer-Based Instruction, 15*(2), 40-47.

Alessi, S. M. (2000). Simulation design for training and assessment. In H. F. O'Neill, Jr., & D. H. Andrews (Eds.), *Aircrew training and assessment* (pp.197-222). Mahwah, NJ: Lawrence Erlbaum Associates.

Alessi, S. M., & Trollip, S. R. (2001). *Multimedia for learning: Methods and development*. Boston, MA: Allyn & Bacon.

Anderson, J. R. (2000). *Cognitive Psychology and its implications* (5th ed.) New York: Worth Publishing.

Bransford, J., Brown, A., & Cocking, R. (Eds.). (1999). *How people learn: Brain, mind, experience, and school*. Washington, DC: National Academy Press.

Chandler, P., & Sweller, J. (1991). Cognitive load theory and the format of instruction. *Cognition and Instruction, 8*(4), 293-332.

Chi, M. T. H., Glaser, R., & Rees, E. (1982). Expertise in problem solving. In R. J. Sternberg (Ed.), *Advances in the psychology of human intelligence* (Vol. 1, pp. 7-76). Hillsdale, NJ: Erlbaum.

de Jong, T., de Hoog, R., & de Vries, F. (1993). Coping with complex environments: The effects of providing overviews and a transparent interface on learning with a computer simulation. *International Journal of Man-Machine Studies, 39*(4), 621-639.

Jonassen, D. H. (1997). Instructional design models for well-structured and ill-structured problem-solving learning outcomes. *Educational Technology, Research and Development, 45*(1), 65-94.

Jonassen, D. H., & Ionas, I. G. (2008). Designing effective supports for causal reasoning. *Educational Technology Research and Development, 56*(3), 287-308.

Mayer, R. E. (2009). *Multimedia learning* (2nd ed.). Cambridge, UK: Cambridge University Press.

Sweller, J. (1999). *Instructional design in technical areas*. Camberwell, Victoria, Australia: Australian Council for Educational Research.

van Joolingen, W. R., & de Jong, T. (1991). Characteristics of simulations for instructional settings. *Education & Computing, 6*, 241-262.

Top Texts for InterDisciplinary Studies of Serious Games

Alessi, S. M., & Trollip, S. R. (2001). *Multimedia for learning: Methods and development*. Boston, MA: Allyn & Bacon.

Beck, J. C., & Wade, M. (2006). *The kids are alright: How the gamer generation is changing the workplace*. Boston: Harvard Business School.

Gee, J. (2007). *What video games have to teach us about learning and literacy* (2nd ed.). New York: Palgrave Macmillan.

Gibson, D., Aldrich, C., & Prensky, M. (2007). *Games and simulations in online learning: Research and development frameworks*. Hershey, PA: Information Science Publishing.

Harrigan, P. (2004). *First person: New media as story, performance, and game*. Cambridge, MA: MIT Press.

Kafi, Y. (1995). *Minds in play: Computer game design as a context for children's learning.* Hillsdale, NJ: Lawrence Erlbaum.

Koster, R. (2004). *A theory of fun for game design.* Scottsdale, AZ: Paraglyph Press.

Mayer, R. E. (2001). *Multimedia learning.* Cambridge, UK: Cambridge University Press.

Shaffer, D. (2006). *How computer games help children learn.* New York: Palgrave Macmillan.

Shelton, B., & Wiley, D. (2007). *The design and use of computer simulation games in education.* Rotterdam, Netherlands: Sense Publishers.

Chapter 8
Learners' Cognitive Load When Using Educational Technology

Renae Low
University of New South Wales, Australia

Putai Jin
University of New South Wales, Australia

John Sweller
University of New South Wales, Australia

ABSTRACT

Taking advantage of the rapid evolution of educational technology, simulations and games have been embodied in a variety of teaching and learning procedures. To a large extent, their effectiveness, in common with the effectiveness of all instructional design relies on how material and activities are optimally organized. That organization should be determined by the nature of human cognitive architecture when dealing with complex, biologically secondary information. Cognitive load theory has been devised to deal with such knowledge. Therefore, embodied simulations and serious games should take evidence-based cognitive load principles into account in both design and implementation.

INTRODUCTION

Games, with features such as voluntariness, fantasy, specific rules/goals, artificial gains/payoffs, competition or cooperation, sensory and motor involvement, challenge, control, low costs of trial and error, and associated amusement (Garris, Ahlers, & Driskell, 2002), might have existed as a type of leisure activity as early as the dawn of civilization, when adults had sufficient food and children were not habitually starving (Dempsey, Haynes, Lucassen,

& Casey, 2002). Games not only can be used for recreation but also for educational/training purposes. For instance, in ancient China, individuals learned to play games like Weiqi, or "Go" as it is known in Western countries, to practice various moves in order to become commanders or military strategists. In the modern world, serious, game-based computer systems are widely used for military training as well as for classroom learning (Raybourn, 2007). Currently, learners have an exponentially increasing quantity and variety of educational games available to them (Dipietro, Ferdig, Boyer, & Black, 2007).

DOI: 10.4018/978-1-61520-717-6.ch008

During the last two decades, software developers and instructors have introduced a variety of educational games to learners at all levels. According to a recent review of 55 popular educational games and relevant publications/information, 22 games were claimed by their designers to be constructed and developed on the basis of established learning theories or instructional strategies (Kebritchi & Hirumi, 2008). Educational game developers have shown increasing interest in understanding and implementing various pedagogical principles. The pedagogical foundations for some educational games include (a) behaviorist learning theory (e.g., the educational game *Destination Math* uses a stimulus–response model that reinforces desirable learning outcomes during problem solving); (b) experiential learning theory (e.g., students in medical science assume the role of authentic medical practitioners and refer to their authentic experience when playing the *BioHazard* game to deal with simulated medical emergencies); (c) discovery learning theory (e.g., college students are guided to discover a number of basic concepts and underlying processes of market economy by playing *Gamenomics*, which allowed players to explore demands, change purchasing or selling prices, and manipulate supplies and other marketing parameters); (d) situated cognition (e.g., cognitive apprenticeship is employed for teacher education in a classroom management game *simSchool*, which includes a database of realistic student profiles and provides trainees with step-by-step scaffolding, hints, and feedback to acquire essential classroom management skills); and (e) constructivist learning theory (e.g., students learnt electromagnetism by playing *SuperCharged!*, in which they have the discretion to construct their own game level and build up their new knowledge "blocks" toward an optimized level). These examples indicate a growing trend of using extant learning theories and instructional principles in the design and delivery of educational games.

Dempsey and colleagues (2002) attempted to evaluate the features and components of forty computer games that could be used in educational settings. It was found that the most common strategy employed by game players was trial-and-error, even when players were aware of knowledge-based strategies. A trial-and-error strategy, although perhaps being the only option when no knowledge-based strategy is available, can be time-consuming and inefficient. Why do learners not choose a more efficient strategy? Is it because the alternative strategies are not explicitly presented to players/learners during instruction? Or have computer game players become used to the characteristic trial-and-error behavior that has been reinforced by numerous games not equipped with sound instructional principles? In fact, Dempsey and colleagues found game participants complained about poor or no instruction and insufficient feedback. Nevertheless, they did tend to use an "adviser" (i.e., help, hint, and other game tools) and to adopt effective strategies such as mind imagery techniques, memorization, and pattern matching. The study indicated that games designed for educational purposes should not be overly complex, otherwise cognitive overload may occur. Dempsey and associates (2002) further recommend that worked examples (winning prototypes) should be provided to facilitate engagement and learning. The use of worked examples is one of the most effective instructional strategies and is supported by a series of empirical studies in the field of cognitive load theory (Sweller, 2003).

The aims of this chapter are threefold: a) to introduce cognitive load theory in the context of human cognitive architecture; b) to explore aspects of feasible applications of cognitive load theory to the design and delivery of learning programs, in particular, gaming using educational technology; and c) to identify the cognitive mechanisms at work in gaming. In the following sections, we elaborate a framework of human cognitive architecture and indicate the use of cognitive load theory for effective instructional design followed by a discussion of opportunities that serious educational games can provide for facilitating cognitive processes. We conclude by suggesting some important aspects to link cognitive load theory and educational technology for future research and professional activities.

HUMAN COGNITIVE ARCHITECTURE FROM AN EVOLUTIONARY PERSPECTIVE

Knowledge can be categorized in many different ways. Two categories of knowledge have clear instructional implications: biologically primary knowledge and biologically secondary knowledge (Geary, 2002, 2005, 2007, 2008; Sweller, 2008). Biologically primary knowledge is associated with the long process of human evolution for survival. It is knowledge we have evolved to acquire easily, rapidly, and unconsciously just by immersion in a society (family and wider community). Examples of such knowledge are oral language, the "reading" of facial expressions as well as body language, simple tool usage, counting by using one's own fingers, and folk theory of mind. However, biologically secondary knowledge, which has been accumulated more recently in human history, such as written language and mathematics, requires a conscious effort and often additional assistance to learn. Therefore, effective instruction specifically designed for the acquisition of certain biologically secondary knowledge is often needed in education (Geary, 2002; Kirschner, Sweller, & Clark, 2006). Because the target of most serious educational games is to deliver biologically secondary knowledge (e.g., algebra), one cannot assume that a child, by just using easily acquired biologically primary knowledge (e.g., clicking a mouse — manipulating a relatively simple tool), will learn efficiently if the instruction embedded in the game is not in accord with evidenced-based cognitive principles.

How is biologically secondary knowledge acquired? The cognitive architecture required to allow the acquisition of biologically secondary knowledge is remarkably similar to the information structures required by evolution by natural selection. In a summary by Sweller and Sweller (2006), five general principles are proposed to identify the analogy between human cognitive architecture and biological evolution in terms of natural selection and inheritable changes. The principles of natural information-processing systems and their implications for learning and instruction are briefly explained below.

The Information Store Principle

During biological evolution, massive amounts of information are stored in the genomes of all organisms. If a genome remains the same, then no changes (i.e., evolution) will occur within the organism (or a species). Similarly, an enormous amount of knowledge that is critical for human cognitive activity is stored in long-term memory. The central role of long-term memory in cognitive functioning has been demonstrated in classical studies using the game of chess (Chase & Simon, 1973; De Groot, 1965). These studies demonstrated that chess masters have a much better memory than novices for board configurations taken from real games, while both masters and novices have a poor memory for random configurations. Chess masters are good at chess because they have memorized tens of thousands of board configurations along with the best moves for the various configurations (Simon & Gilmartin, 1973). For an educational game, one of the ultimate indicators of its effectiveness is to examine whether, compared with alternative instructional procedures, there are favorable changes in long-term memory.

The Borrowing and Reorganizing Principle

In biological systems, this mechanism permits rapid transmission of biological information between generations. For instance, in sexual reproduction the new generation takes and re-shuffles parental genetic material to create a novel, individual genome. In human cognition, a person can borrow information from other individuals by imitating what they do, listening to what they say and reading what they write. The new information can be reorganized and combined with information already held in long-term memory to form particular schemas. This kind of learning takes advantages of others' existing knowledge, and such information should be transferred and built into educational games.

The Randomness as Genesis Principle

All variations between all organisms can ultimately be sourced back to random mutations. Every mutation is tested for effectiveness, with adaptive mutations surviving and maladaptive mutations reducing reproductive rates. Since most random mutations will not be adaptive, subsequent real-life tests of their effectiveness (i.e., natural selection) is essential for long-term survival. Likewise, during human problem solving when only limited solution information is available in long-term memory, a person may use randomly generated ideas or moves and then check their feasibility in order to find a solution. This process is often related to creativity and novelty (Sweller, 2009). It is not uncommon for computer game players and other users to employ the strategy of randomness to deal with uncertainty, particularly under circumstances where no obvious solutions are available. There are two categories of gaming from the systems perspective: a) the closed system that constrains possible moves and b) the semiopen system, such as alternate reality games (ARGs) and massively multiplayer online games (MMOGs). Currently, the majority of serious games are in the former category because of their operational mode and specific purposes. Game designers need to assess the affordance of their products in terms of support as well as constraints of the random generation of

users' ideas and moves. In particular, educational game designers need to be aware that the "random generate" strategy will be used by learners when faced with game-generated problems for which information in long-term memory is either not available, or its relation to the problem at hand is unrecognized. Explicit instruction may be preferable to having learners engage in random generate-and-test strategies.

The Narrow Limits of Change Principle

Biological evolution has two different but complementary systems, the genetic and epigenetic systems. The genetic system enables mutations to occur, as addressed in the randomness as genesis principle. The epigenetic system handles environmental impacts. By influencing phenotypes, the epigenetic system can determine which mutations are relevant and which are irrelevant. Changes that result from mutations must occur at a relatively slow pace and be of a small magnitude to ensure the system is not destroyed.. Slow changes are necessary for survival because dramatic, uncontrolled changes are likely to be harmful to organisms.

Human cognition has an analogue to the epigenetic system—working memory, which plays a similar role to the epigenetic system in biological evolution. Both the epigenetic system and working memory can be used to handle novel, external information. Working memory controls the amount and flow of information from the external world via the sensory system to the central information store (i.e., long-term memory). Working memory is limited in capacity (Miller, 1956) and duration (Peterson & Peterson, 1959). This "bottleneck" is not "unfortunate" but indeed necessary for the effectiveness and efficiency of human information processing. In line with evolution theory, massively generated random ideas, if simultaneously or sequentially presented for judgment, would compromise effective information processing. Constraints of working memory functionally protect long-term memory from dramatic random changes, most of which are likely to be inconsistent and dysfunctional. The limited capacity of working memory is one of the major aspects to be considered when designing instruction. It is crucial to consider this principle of narrow limits of change in the formation and operation of educational programs, such as serious learning games. Because of working memory limitations, the working memory resources distributed to any game components should not be at the expense of working memory that is needed for the acquisition of the knowledge and skills for which the game has been created. Therefore, serious games should maintain a reasonable balance between the effective utility of working memory and the "freedom" of random changes.

The Environmental Organizing and Linking Principle

From the perspective of evolutionary biology, the epigenetic system's interaction with the genetic system has a dual function: (a) the epigenetic system deals with external input and moderates its impact on the genome (as shown in the narrow limits of change principle) and (b) the epigenetic system uploads and interprets information from the genetic code so that an organism can function appropriately in a particular environment. In other words, the epigenetic system provides a link between the genetic code and the environment. This environmental organizing and linking principle can also be shown in the functioning of working memory, which acts as a transmission system that retrieves large amounts of organized information from long-term memory in order to swiftly respond to environmental demands. For instance, if a question such as $1-\cos^2\theta=0$ appears on the map of an electronic learning game, a learner with particular mathematical knowledge may retrieve relevant information about trigonometry and algebra from long-term memory, such as $\sin^2\theta+\cos^2\theta=1$ or $a^2-b^2=(a+b)(a-b)$, bring the organized information

to working memory, and then determine suitable, often personalized actions (choosing either $\sin^2\theta=1$ or $(1+\cos\theta)(1-\cos\theta)=0$ as the next move) that meet environmental demands (in this case, trigonometric equation solving). This case illustrates that if relevant knowledge has previously been stored in long-term memory, such information can often be organized in a vast and complex format and uploaded to working memory for cognitive operations. To differentiate this structure from the short-duration, limited-capacity work memory mentioned in the previous section on the narrow limits of change principle, the structure has been termed long-term working memory, indicating the linkage between long-term storage and working memory (Ericsson & Kintsch, 1995; Sweller & Sweller, 2006). In instructional design, including the design of serious games, it is important to incorporate the learner's prior knowledge (expertise), which can be used as schema-based information to increase the capacity of working memory (Simon, 1990; Sweller & Sweller, 2006). By the same token, a serious game as a form of intelligent tutoring system should be based on a dynamically generated and modified "model" of student learning that incorporates what the learner knows and uses the acquired schemata to inform users of other aspects of the game. The environmental organizing and linking principle provides the ultimate justification for instruction. Broadly, learning is the acquisition of a variety of features such as new knowledge, skills, beliefs, attitudes, values, and behaviour. However, all of these changes can only occur with changes in long-term memory. Once information is stored in long-term memory, the characteristics of working memory are dramatically altered, with capacity and duration limits essentially eliminated. As a consequence, cognitive tasks that would otherwise be difficult or impossible can become simple after learning. Educational games have the same instructional requirements. The ultimate justification of an educational game should be to increase knowledge in long-term memory that alters the characteristics of working memory when dealing with the relevant information. Educational games are justified to the extent that they can accomplish this aim more effectively than other instructional procedures.

THE NEED TO CONSIDER COGNITIVE LOAD THEORY WHEN INTRODUCING A NEW LEARNING TECHNOLOGY

Although there have been different perspectives supported by research in laboratory or educational settings to depict the features of human cognitive architecture (see Reed, 2006; Sweller, 2004), the basic principles summarized above can be regarded as the foundations of various models, in which the interacting effects between long-term memory and working memory in response to the specific information input from the environment via sensory memory have been emphasized and studied. In instructional contexts, cognitive load theory uses the above human cognitive architecture as a framework to generate and test a series of propositions for teaching and learning (Sweller, 1994, 1999, 2004). Specifically, cognitive load theory proposes that (a) effective instruction should facilitate knowledge building in long-term memory, and this should be the fundamental goal of instruction; (b) working memory has a limited capacity to integrate and process information, especially in a learning environment where novel information is introduced, and thus appropriate guidance/instruction is needed; (c) prior knowledge stored in long-term memory can be organized as relevant information and sent back to working memory to enhance its functioning, and therefore. instruction should take learner's expertise into account; (d) in educational settings, instruction usually imposes an intrinsic cognitive load determined by the complexity of the learning material as well as an extraneous cognitive load caused by instructional design factors; (e) if instruction

is able to reduce cognitive load, more working memory will be released for information processing and thus optimum learning outcomes can be achieved; (f) instructional tasks and activities, if optimally structured and properly implemented, can provide an efficient central executive function to minimize learners' uncertainty and thus to some extent reduce their need for time-consuming random generation and subsequent effectiveness checking; and (g) instructional procedures and instruments that are designed to ameliorate cognitive overloads and their effects can be examined by randomized, controlled experiments. In sum, cognitive load theory provides a conceptual framework of effective instruction and permits a number of working hypotheses to be generated for empirical research. It should be noted that any instructional task, be it an exercise, quiz, simulation or game, should be challenging enough to elicit and maintain learners' high motivation (see Low, this volume). The following sections will present instructional procedures that have been tested in experiments and discuss some implications for the design of serious educational games.

Worked Example Effect

According to cognitive load theory, learners, especially beginners, can achieve more in less time by using instructions that conform to the borrowing and reorganizing principle. In other words, such instructions can enable learners to take advantage of another person's acquired knowledge instead of wandering in a trial-and-error, problem-solving maze. A typical case of this type of application is to provide less experienced learners with worked examples, which take the role of an instructionally central executive, act as a substitute for random generation and test, reduce extraneous cognitive load, and thus save working memory resources for the acquisition of knowledge and its subsequent transmission to long-term storage. The positive worked example effect, in particular, at a learner's early stages of skill development, has been reported and analyzed frequently (e.g., Moreno & Durán, 2004; Quilici & Mayer, 1996; Sweller & Cooper, 1985; Zhang & Lin, 2005), and some studies and reviews further indicated that worked examples are effective when combined with additional procedures, such as self-explanation prompts (Crippen & Earl, 2007), fading (Renkl, 2005), and mixed modality presentations (Moreno & Mayer, 2002; Mousavi, Low, & Sweller, 1995).

Developers of educational games need to consider issues such as whether or not to use worked examples and, if the decision is yes, how to present worked examples in an effective way. Initial research has demonstrated that the worked example technique is useful for novices in domains like science and mathematics using well-defined problems. More recently, the effect has been demonstrated in ill-defined areas such as learning to recognize designers' styles (Rourke & Sweller, 2009). In general, research has shown that the worked example technique is one of the most effective methods for knowledge acquisition and problem solving. Worked examples should be useful if they are contextualized within game strategies.

Modality Effect

It has been suggested that working memory can be subdivided into partially independent information processors consisting of a visual subsystem to handle images and an auditory subsystem to deal with sounds (Baddeley, 1992, 2003; Low & Sweller, 2005; Mayer, 2005). Under certain clearly defined conditions, presenting some information in visual mode and other information in auditory mode may to some extent increase the capacity of working memory and thus facilitate information processing. The conditions are that (a) the two different sources of information must be unintelligible if each is assessed separately and (b) the two different sources of information have to be mentally integrated to be meaningful and

understandable. For instance, a geometry problem and its solution may contain a diagram and textual information. These two sources of information are difficult to comprehend in isolation and must be mentally integrated before a solution can be processed. While the diagram must be in the visual mode, the textual information can be in either the visual or auditory mode. It has been found that, in comparison with the single mode instruction (i.e., a visually presented diagram together with visual text), dual-mode instruction (i.e., a visually presented diagram together with auditory text) resulted in more effective capacity of working memory and thus more positive learning outcomes (Mousavi et al., 1995). Consistently, learners given an "animation + narration" presentation had higher retention scores than those given an "animation + text" presentation (Mayer & Moreno, 1998). This modality effect has been confirmed by a number of subsequent studies (e.g., Brünken, Plass, & Leutner, 2004; Brünken, Steinbacher, Plass, & Leutner, 2002; Jeung, Chandler, & Sweller, 1997; Moreno & Mayer, 1999, Tindall-Ford, Chandler, & Sweller, 1997).

Most educational games, especially on-screen games, are in the form of multimedia presentations. It is very common for players to receive mixed mode information. The "enjoyment" component built into serious games may impose additional cognitive load. Effective use of both the visual and auditory capacities appears to be a sound strategy to accommodate such additional enjoyment-related demands. It is beneficial for designers to check some essential aspects of the sources of information to be presented: Are the sources of information unintelligible in isolation? If so, must the sources of information be mentally integrated to ensure the theme is understandable? Such steps are necessary not only because constructing multimedia material is costly but also to avoid replicating the same information via different channels (the redundancy effect discussed below). It is also important to distinguish in the game between episodes designed for learning and those used solely for enjoyment, transitions, or ancillary but not critical information.

Split-Attention Effect

When learners are exposed to multiple sources of information that are not arranged in a spatially or temporally integrated manner by the instructor, they need to use additional working memory resources to mentally integrate those spatially or temporally separated sources of information for further processing. Such instructional procedures split learners' attention between multiple sources of information resulting in an elevated extraneous cognitive load, reduced working memory resources available to deal with intrinsic cognitive load, with consequent poor learning outcomes. The negative consequences of such split-attention instructions were initially identified by Tarmizi & Sweller (1988) in their study of the effectiveness of geometry worked examples comparing spatially split and integrated materials. Mayer and Anderson's (1991) work demonstrated that students who received words and pictures simultaneously performed better then those receiving words before pictures, indicating a temporal version of the split-attention effect. Subsequent research has confirmed this split-attention effect in various domains, such as physics (Ward & Sweller, 1990), industrial skill training (Chandler & Sweller, 1991), computer skill training (Chandler & Sweller, 1996), e-learning (Mayer & Moreno, 1998), and second language learning (Yeung, Jin, & Sweller, 1998).

The design of educational games needs to take the well-documented split-attention effect into consideration. The educational effectiveness of games that require learners to unnecessarily split their attention between multiple sources of information is likely to be compromised. Eliminating the split-attention effect is frequently a simple process. For instance, in an educational game for vocabulary learning, features of an adventurous journey to find treasures (i.e., gems that represent new words to be learned), the new words and their definitions should be physically close enough to avoid the split-attention effect and to elicit appropriate responses. By analyzing material for split attention and eliminating it where possible, the instructional effectiveness of games should be substantially enhanced.

Redundancy Effect

Redundant information can interfere with learning. There are two conditions under which the redundancy effect can be triggered. First, a learner may receive identical information in multiple forms. For example, a student may view information on a screen and at the same time hear the same message being read. Because both of the two forms are fully understandable in isolation, one form is unnecessary and technically redundant. A second category of conditions under which information may be redundant occurs when presented information is sufficient for learners to achieve their learning goals but the instructional procedures unnecessarily provide additional elaborating information. Under those two conditions, learners are required to unproductively coordinate and cross-check replicated information in multiple forms or process unnecessary explanatory information, leading to an increased extraneous cognitive load. This seemingly counterintuitive phenomenon, although discovered decades ago (e.g., Miller, 1937; Reder & Anderson, 1980, 1982), was later interpreted in terms of cognitive load theory by Chandler and Sweller (1991). Subsequent studies showed that the elimination of redundant material improved learning (e.g., Diao & Sweller, 2007; Kalyuga, Chandler, & Sweller, 1999; Mayer, Heiser, & Lonn, 2001; Sweller & Chandler, 1994; Yeung et al., 1998).

In educational game design, there is always a temptation for the designer to insert more features into the game and learning material. Although adding more features may be technically feasible, it is psychologically counterproductive. Redundant information is rarely neutral and usually harmful to learning because sources of redundant information compete for limited cognitive resources.

Element Interactivity Effect

Cognitive load theory has been used to examine the relations between characteristics of learning material and corresponding delivery procedures. One of the issues that educators often encounter is the interactivity of elements contained in the learning material. Some material is very high in element interactivity because in order to understand and learn the material, students must simultaneously consider a large number of interacting elements resulting in a high working memory load. Dealing with equations provides an example since, in order to understand an equation, all elements of the equation must be considered simultaneously. In contrast, low element interactivity material allows learners to consider each element individually, resulting in a low working memory load. Learning the meaning of the symbols of chemical elements provides an example. When element interactivity is high, learning material is characterized by a high level of complexity that requires a learner to hold and process content elements collectively and simultaneously in working memory in order to understand the information contained in the material. Such material is assumed to have a high intrinsic cognitive load. If the number of interacting elements exceeds the capacity of working memory, resulting in a high intrinsic cognitive load, learning will be hindered. Cognitive load effects only are obtainable using high element interactivity material (Sweller & Chandler, 1994; Tindall-Ford et al., 1997) with a high intrinsic cognitive load.

If element interactivity is too high to allow understanding and learning, a solution is to artificially reduce intrinsic cognitive load. Pollock, Chandler and Sweller (2002) initially presented high element interactivity information to learners in an isolated form without indicating the interactions between elements. For material with very high

element interactivity, the presentation of isolated elements followed by information indicating the interactions between elements appears to be a beneficial instructional procedure.

Cognitive load theory particularly applies when developing educational games that are complex in terms of element interactivity. Under high element interactivity conditions it is particularly important to reduce extraneous cognitive load. Under very high element interactivity conditions, it may be necessary to reduce intrinsic cognitive load as well. For instance, a game designed to train electricians on very complex, high element interactivity material such as electrical safety tests can use a two-stage strategy as highlighted by Pollock and colleagues (2002). First, an introductory version of isolated elements (how to set the voltmeter to a given value, make sure the switch is "on," etc.) can be used to master basic elements one by one; second, once the relevant schemata have been established in the learner's long-term memory, a new version of instruction that requires learners to consider all necessary elements simultaneously and interactively, such as a comprehensive insulation resistance test, should be adopted.

Learners' Prior Knowledge and the Expertise Reversal Effect

A learner's expertise or prior knowledge is another variable that needs to be included when designing effective instruction. It should not be taken for granted that an instruction design that is effective for novices will remain effective for more expert learners. Some information presented to novices, though initially useful, may be redundant for more advanced learners who possess sufficient prior knowledge (e.g., Kalyuga, Ayres, Chandler, & Sweller, 2003; Tuovinen & Sweller, 1999; Yeung et al., 1998). Continuing to use instructional procedures that are effective for novices even when those novices have become more knowledgeable imposes an extraneous cognitive load. Techniques that are effective for novices may be quite counterproductive as expertise increases.

Educational games suitable for beginners in a domain may need to be substantially modified as knowledge increases. One of the characteristics of computer-based games is that they frequently can be adjusted for levels of experience. Such adjustments are necessary and could provide one of the major advantages of using computer games in an educational environment. For instance, consider an educational game designer who constructs a reading comprehension game for players who are at a relatively advanced level. In comparison to players using "gathered gems" as rewards that are suitable for vocabulary building, the advanced learners may find gem-gathering episodes for less frequently used words unnecessary, distracting, and annoying. In this case, the game can be designed to include a vocabulary screen test initially to gauge learners' language proficiency and then adjust game procedures to accommodate advanced learners' learning needs. In fact, many games are already appropriately formatted by allowing players to choose their own initial level of competence.

Guidance Fading Effect

This effect is based on and closely related to the expertise reversal effect. At a certain point, the accumulation of a learner's knowledge in a particular domain may be sufficient to provide a knowledge-based central executive, which can gradually replace the intensive instruction provided initially. For instance, in a study on transition from studying examples to solving problems, it was found to be beneficial to have some multimedia elaborations for the learning of probability principles faded out step by step (Atkinson, Renkl, & Merrill, 2003). At this stage, the learner's specific schema-based knowledge, after the initial period of scaffolding, can be immediately retrieved from long-term memory and effectively uploaded to working memory for information processing. Under such circumstances, if the experienced learner is still given high-structure

instruction with redundant details, the learner will find it hard to ignore the redundant information and the ensuing cross-referencing process may result in an excessive extraneous cognitive load. Therefore, as a learner's schema-based knowledge develops, high-structure instruction can be replaced by low-structure instruction to facilitate more advanced levels of learning. Research has in general shown that this promising strategy can be combined with worked example approaches under various circumstances to improve learning (Atkinson et al., 2003; Renkl & Atkinson, 2003; Renkl, Atkinson, Maier, & Staley, 2002; Van Merriënboer & de Croock, 1992).

This guidance fading strategy may be well suited for educational computer games. For instance, if worked examples are included in the content of an educational computer game, when the learner's knowledge increases, some now redundant, fully worked out examples can be replaced firstly by partial worked examples followed by full problems. Today, many games adopt this strategy by providing detailed guidance at the beginning which fades out as players move up in the level of difficulty or select higher levels of difficulty at the start of a gaming session.

SOME COGNITIVE FACTORS IN SERIOUS EDUCATIONAL GAMES

There are basically two types of educational games: a) games that attempt to have learning content incorporated into the playing procedures, b) games that are inserted into different learning phases as an extrinsic reward (bonus) after the fulfillment of a certain learning task. We will consider games that attempt to incorporate learning. It should be noted that some previous reviews (e.g., Vogel et al., 2006) cover both computer gaming and interactive simulation in assessing the effectiveness of using educational technology. Although computer games and interactive simulations have some similarities, such as the low costs of error for participants, games do not intend to simulate external reality, whereas simulations represent an operational model of a real system. According to a meta-analysis conducted by Vogel and associates (2006), participants using interactive games or simulations overall had significantly higher cognitive gains and more positive attitudes toward learning than those receiving traditional teaching methods for instruction. A number of researchers (e.g., Dipietro et al., 2007; Reese, 2007) have pointed out this question of interest: What are the underlying mechanisms for increased cognitive gains?

Apart from the possibility of elevated motivation (due to novelty, for example) that is conducive to increased effort and enhanced attention (see Low, this volume, for a further discussion of this aspect), the cognitive processes discussed above and associated with such interactive activities should be scrutinized. There are some indications of deeper cognitive processes revealed in well-controlled experiments in this field. For instance, in a study using a computer-based simulation game to assist middle school students to learn Grades 7 and 8 mathematics (number sense, measurement, geometry, spatial sense, etc.), participants were requested to help "Auntie Ann and Uncle Bob" to repair their house under various conditions (Van Eck & Dempsey, 2002). In the noncompetitive context, the students using a contextualized video "adviser" that could provide learners with assistance had significantly higher transfer scores than those without access to the contextualized video adviser. In another experiment, Dempsey and Van Eck (2003) examined the function of the adviser by conducting a 2 (the placement of the adviser: on-screen access vs. pull-down access) X 2 (the modality of the adviser: digitized video of a human adviser providing spoken text vs. a written-text-based adviser) experiment, in which adult participants were requested to learn basic statistics concepts. It was found that (a) participants in the on-screen video-based adviser group used the adviser more frequently than those in

both the text-based and video-based pull-down adviser groups, and (b) the usage of the adviser was significantly correlated with performance during the instruction period. Whereas it is understandable that using the adviser when needed can somehow facilitate learners' comprehension of abstract concepts, why did the on-screen condition result in more frequent use of advice than the pull-down condition? According to Dempsey and Van Eck (2003), about 80% of the participants in the pull-down adviser groups never attempted to access the advice. It has long been noticed that the existence of online help, often in a pull-down format, can be a distraction from the task that is being undertaken (e.g., Schuerman & Peck, 1991). A pull-down format is likely to impose an extraneous cognitive load.

De Jong (2006) described an educational cognitive tool (a computer-aided system with specially designed software), *SimQuest*, which was introduced to learners in their studying of the physics of moments. Using *SimQuest*, students can manipulate relevant parameters such as the magnitude of forces and the distances to the center of a seesaw to obtain balance. They can also use an on-screen hypothesis scratchpad to develop testable hypotheses and explore the relations among variables. The same report warns educational cognitive tool developers and educators not to make and adopt an overly complex technological system, which could require too much working memory capacity and thus obstruct the learning process. In particular, the instructional design and course delivery must minimize extraneous cognitive load and take individual learners' characteristics and expertise into account (Sweller, 2003). Most educational games are multimedia in nature, hence the principles derived from multimedia learning research can be used as guidelines for effective instruction (Mayer, 2005).

Since an educational game typically consists of certain learning material and a particular game and both require cognitive involvement, an emerging issue is to examine the cognitive activities in gaming itself. Ang, Zaphiris and Mahmood (2006) investigated the cognitive loads in massively multiplayer online role playing games (MMOR-PGs). In this exploratory study, they employed qualitative methods to analyze 20 hours of data obtained from three players (one expert and two novices) in *Maple Story*, a typical MMORPG. The game players reported a variety of cognitive overload categories during MMORPG, including multiple game interaction overloads (interacting with a large number of game objects), user interface overloads (keeping track of the information in the game user interface), identity construction overloads (constructing and identifying different roles), parallel game and social interaction overloads (interacting with both game objects and other participants simultaneously), and multiple social interaction overloads (interacting with other game players or instructors). In such situations, players tended to miss important information, failed to seize opportunities for quick actions that could create a more advantageous situation, and made frequent mistakes that could lead to "game over" and frustration. The study recommended that further research should be carried out on the issue of how to balance cognitive overload effects with the challenging features of a game. The bottom line is that a game should be easy to learn or play but not too easy so that it becomes a "boring" game. Meanwhile, we have to bear in mind that an educational game is not "pure" entertainment. It has to include serious academic content. Devising such tasks can be challenging.

FUTURE RESEARCH DIRECTIONS

Development of Educational Games from a Cognitive Load Perspective

The following provides some suggestions for future directions from a cognitive load perspective.

1. Communication between educational technologists and cognitive scientists should be enhanced. Analogously, the current situation in this field is somewhat akin to the situation faced by educational psychologists and educators in the 1970s when, as highlighted by Mayer (1999), a two-way street between psychology and education was required to develop joint studies and evidence-based applications. A community project of learning initiatives can be an appropriate catalyst that involves computer experts as educational game designers, users as game testers, parents as game monitors, school teachers and administrators as educational game organizers, and researchers as consultants.

2. The computer-aided environment has unique features. For instance, animations and prompts can be used in educational games at a moderate cost (e.g., Atkinson et al., 2003; Clark, 2005; Moreno, 2005), and PowerPoint presentations can be immersed in a virtual computer game engine world (Price, 2008). Many multimedia functions can be included in educational games on the basis of human cognitive architecture. Future research examining the effectiveness of various computer-generated multimedia presentations using cognitive load approaches appears promising.

3. Whereas the guidance fading and other strategies need to be further tested under various conditions (Moreno, 2005), a similar approach deserves specific attention—adaptive learning. Since it is relatively easy to monitor computer users' performance by using log data and gauge their levels of progress by using online tests, learner-adapted instruction can be employed in educational games to maximize learning outcomes (Kalyuga & Sweller, 2004, 2005; Moreno-Ger, Burgos, Martínez-Orti, Sierra, & Fernández-Manjón, 2008; Raybourn, 2007).

4. The cognitive principles discussed above have been mainly tested among schoolchildren and young adults. It is not uncommon for adults to use simulations and educational games to learn new skills or to release work stress. A specifically designed educational game, as a tool for mental exercise, can be used for educational entertainment of the aged as well. A general trend in cognition for the elderly is the decline of cognitive efficiency, which is characterized by decreased working memory capacity, reduced cognitive speed, weakened inhibition, and downgraded integration (Paas, Van Gerven, & Tabbers, 2005). Efforts (e.g, the project of ElderGames in the European Union) have been made to enhance the usability of information and communication technologies (ICTs) for the elderly to use games for their learning, mental "jogging," socialization, and enjoyment (Gamberini et al., 2006). Research in the area of cognitive aging is much needed in order to establish age-related design principles and to produce educational games for the aging population (Van Gerven, Paas, Van Merriënboer & Schmidt, 2000).

5. Many studies in cognitive psychology are intended to assist in understanding the capacity/limits of the human cognitive processing system and to explore procedures for optimizing instructional procedures. We need to consider also the impact of instructional procedures on cognitive abilities. In a recent study to examine the efforts of playing violent and nonviolent computer games on cognitive performance, it was found that (a) the participants who did not play any video games had no change in their cognitive performance and (b) the participants who played video games, regardless of the degree of violence, had a noticeable increase in their cognitive performance (Barlett, Vowels, Shanteau, Crow, & Miller, 2009). Although the compounding effect of self-selection needs to be ruled out in such investigations, future research should ascertain the long-term impact of game playing on cognitive abilities. Will action gaming as part of daily computer usage enhance the player's psychomotor skills? Likewise, will strategic gaming during childhood increase the player's decision-making and logistic ability? Furthermore, will learners' long-term intensive engagement in educational games that incorporate established cognitive principles speed up the learning process (e.g., completing Stage 4 mathematics in a shorter period), increase the retention rate of intended knowledge/skills (i.e., building up long-term memory in relevant domains), and enhance learners' commitment (e.g., choosing to study engineering after engaging in a submarine simulation game)?

CONCLUSION

The ultimate utility of an educational game is, to a large extent, indicated by whether playing the game can effectively transfer the particular knowledge contained in the game to the users' long-term memory. This information processing can be analyzed within a cognitive load framework, which specifies the relations between human cognitive architecture and instruction. Research in cognition and instruction has demonstrated that a reduced extraneous cognitive load is conducive to efficient learning. It is suggested that many applications of cognitive load theory can be used in educational game design. It would be beneficial for educational game designers to carefully take into consideration the worked example effect, modality effect, split-attention effect, redundancy effect, element interactivity of learning materials, learners' prior knowledge and the expertise reversal effect, and the guidance fading effect. Enhancing communication and collaboration between educational technologists and cognitive scientists should be given priority.

REFERENCES

Ang, C. S., Zaphiris, P., & Mahmood, S. (2006). A model of cognitive loads in massively multiplayer online role playing games. *Interacting with Computers, 19*, 167–179. doi:10.1016/j.intcom.2006.08.006

Atkinson, R. K., Renkl, A., & Merrill, M. M. (2003). Transitioning from studying examples to solving problems: Effects of self-explanation prompts and fading worked-out steps. *Journal of Educational Psychology, 95*, 774–783. doi:10.1037/0022-0663.95.4.774

Baddeley, A. D. (1992). Working memory. *Science, 255*, 556–559. doi:10.1126/science.1736359

Baddeley, A. D. (2003). Working memory: Looking back and looking forward. *Nature Reviews. Neuroscience, 4*, 829–839. doi:10.1038/nrn1201

Barlett, C. P., Vowels, C. L., Shanteau, J., Crow, J., & Miller, T. (2009). The effect of violent and non-violent computer games on cognitive performance. *Computers in Human Behavior, 25*, 96–102. doi:10.1016/j.chb.2008.07.008

Brünken, R., Plass, J. L., & Leutner, D. (2004). Assessment of cognitive load in multimedia learning with dual task methodology: Auditory load and modality effects. *Instructional Science, 32*, 115–132. doi:10.1023/B:TRUC.0000021812.96911.c5

Brünken, R., Steinbacher, S., Plass, J. L., & Leutner, D. (2002). Assessment of cognitive load in multimedia learning using dual-task methodology. *Experimental Psychology, 49*, 109–119. doi:10.1027//1618-3169.49.2.109

Chandler, P., & Sweller, J. (1991). Cognitive load theory and the format of instruction. *Cognition and Instruction, 8*, 293–332. doi:10.1207/s1532690xci0804_2

Chandler, P., & Sweller, J. (1996). Cognitive load while learning to use a computer program. *Applied Cognitive Psychology, 10*, 151–170. doi:10.1002/(SICI)1099-0720(199604)10:2<151::AID-ACP380>3.0.CO;2-U

Chase, W. G., & Simon, H. A. (1973). Perception in chess. *Cognitive Psychology, 4*, 55–81. doi:10.1016/0010-0285(73)90004-2

Clark, R. E. (2005). Multimedia learning in e-course. In Mayer, R. E. (Ed.), *The Cambridge handbook of multimedia learning* (pp. 589–616). New York: Cambridge University Press.

Crippen, K. J., & Earl, B. L. (2007). The impact of Web-based worked examples and self-explanation on performance, problem solving, and self-efficacy. *Computers & Education, 49*, 809–821. doi:10.1016/j.compedu.2005.11.018

De Groot, A. (1965). *Thought and choice in chess*. The Hague, Netherlands: Mouton. (Original work published 1946)

de Jong, T. (2006). Computer simulations: Technological advances in inquiry learning. *Science, 312*, 532–533. doi:10.1126/science.1127750

Dempsey, J. V., Haynes, L. L., Lucassen, B. A., & Casey, M. (2002). Forty simple computer games and what they could mean to educators. *Simulation & Gaming, 33*, 157–168. doi:10.1177/1046878102332003

Dempsey, J. V., & Van Eck, R. (2003). Modality and placement of a pedagogical adviser in individual interactive learning. *British Journal of Educational Technology, 34*, 585–600. doi:10.1046/j.0007-1013.2003.00352.x

Diao, Y., & Sweller, J. (2007). Redundancy in foreign language reading comprehension instruction: Concurrent written and spoken presentations. *Learning and Instruction, 17*, 78–88. doi:10.1016/j.learninstruc.2006.11.007

Dipietro, M., Ferdig, R. E., Boyer, J., & Black, E. W. (2007). Toward a framework for understanding electronic educational gaming. *Journal of Educational Multimedia and Hypermedia, 16*, 225–248.

Ericsson, K. A., & Kintsch, W. (1995). Long-term working memory. *Psychological Review, 102*, 211–245. doi:10.1037/0033-295X.102.2.211

Gamberini, L., Alcaniz, M., Barresi, G., Fabregat, M., Ibanez, F., & Prontu, L. (2006). Cognition, technology and games for the elderly: An introduction to ELDERGAMES Project. *PsychNology Journal, 4*, 285–308.

Garris, R., Ahlers, R., & Driskell, J. E. (2002). Games, motivation, and learning: A research and practice model. *Simulation & Gaming, 33*, 441–467. doi:10.1177/1046878102238607

Geary, D. (2002). Principles of evolutionary educational psychology. *Learning and Individual Differences, 12*, 317–345. doi:10.1016/S1041-6080(02)00046-8

Geary, D. (2005). *The origin of mind: Evolution of brain, cognition, and general intelligence.* Washington, DC: American Psychological Association. doi:10.1037/10871-000

Geary, D. (2007). Educating the evolved mind: Conceptual foundations for an evolutionary educational psychology. In Carlson, J. S., & Levin, J. R. (Eds.), *Psychological perspectives on contemporary educational issues* (pp. 1–99). Greenwich, CT: Information Age Publishing.

Geary, D. (2008). An evolutionarily informed education science. *Educational Psychologist, 43*, 179–195. doi:10.1080/00461520802392133

Jeung, H., Chandler, P., & Sweller, J. (1997). The role of visual indicators in dual sensory mode instruction. *Educational Psychology, 17*, 329–343. doi:10.1080/0144341970170307

Kalyuga, S., Ayres, P., Chandler, P., & Sweller, J. (2003). Expertise reversal effect. *Educational Psychologist, 38*, 23–31. doi:10.1207/S15326985EP3801_4

Kalyuga, S., Chandler, P., & Sweller, J. (1999). Managing split attention and redundancy in multimedia instruction. *Applied Cognitive Psychology, 13*, 351–371. doi:10.1002/(SICI)1099-0720(199908)13:4<351::AID-ACP589>3.0.CO;2-6

Kalyuga, S., & Sweller, J. (2004). Measuring knowledge to optimize cognitive load factors during instruction. *Journal of Educational Psychology, 96*, 558–568. doi:10.1037/0022-0663.96.3.558

Kalyuga, S., & Sweller, J. (2005). Rapid dynamic assessment of expertise to improve the efficiency of adaptive e-learning. *Educational Technology Research and Development, 53*, 83–93. doi:10.1007/BF02504800

Kebritchi, M., & Hirumi, A. (2008). Examining the pedagogical foundations of modern educational computer games. *Computers & Education, 51*, 1729–1743. doi:10.1016/j.compedu.2008.05.004

Kirschner, P. A., Sweller, J., & Clark, R. E. (2006). Why minimal guidance during instruction does not work: An analysis of the failure of constructivist, discovery, problem-based, experiential, and inquiry-based teaching. *Educational Psychologist, 41*, 75–86. doi:10.1207/s15326985ep4102_1

Low, R. (in press). Examining motivational factors in serious educational games. In Van Eck, R. (Ed.), *Gaming & cognition: Theories and practice from the learning sciences.* Hershey, PA: IGI Global.

Low, R., & Sweller, J. (2005). The modality principle in multimedia learning. In Mayer, R. E. (Ed.), *The Cambridge handbook of multimedia learning* (pp. 147–158). New York: Cambridge University Press.

Mayer, R. E. (1999). *The promise of educational psychology.* Upper Saddle River, NJ: Prentice–Hall.

Mayer, R. E. (2005). Introduction to multimedia learning. In Mayer, R. E. (Ed.), *The Cambridge handbook of multimedia learning* (pp. 1–16). New York: Cambridge University Press.

Mayer, R. E., & Anderson, R. (1991). Animations need narrations: An experimental test of a dual-coding hypothesis. *Journal of Educational Psychology, 83,* 484–490. doi:10.1037/0022-0663.83.4.484

Mayer, R. E., Heiser, J., & Lonn, S. (2001). Cognitive constraints on multimedia learning: When presenting more material results in less understanding. *Journal of Educational Psychology, 93,* 187–198. doi:10.1037/0022-0663.93.1.187

Mayer, R. E., & Moreno, R. (1998). A split-attention effect in multi-media learning: Evidence for dual processing systems in working memory. *Journal of Educational Psychology, 90,* 312–320. doi:10.1037/0022-0663.90.2.312

Miller, G. A. (1956). The magical number seven, plus or minus two: Some limits on our capacity for processing information. *Psychological Review, 63,* 81–97. doi:10.1037/h0043158

Miller, W. (1937). The picture crutch in reading. *Elementary English Review, 14,* 263–264.

Moreno, R. (2005). Multimedia learning with animated pedagogical agents. In Mayer, R. E. (Ed.), *The Cambridge handbook of multimedia learning* (pp. 507–523). New York: Cambridge University Press.

Moreno, R., & Durán, R. (2004). Do multiple representations need explanations? The role of verbal guidance and individual differences in multimedia mathematics learning. *Journal of Educational Psychology, 96,* 492–503. doi:10.1037/0022-0663.96.3.492

Moreno, R., & Mayer, R. E. (1999). Cognitive principles of multimedia learning: The role of modality and contiguity. *Journal of Educational Psychology, 91,* 358–368. doi:10.1037/0022-0663.91.2.358

Moreno, R., & Mayer, R. E. (2002). Learning science in virtual reality multimedia environments. Role of methods and media. *Journal of Educational Psychology, 94,* 598–610. doi:10.1037/0022-0663.94.3.598

Moreno-Ger, P., Burgos, D., Martínez-Orti, I., Sierra, J. L., & Fernández-Manjón, I. (2008). Educational game design for online education. *Computers in Human Behavior, 24,* 2530–2540. doi:10.1016/j.chb.2008.03.012

Mousavi, S., Low, R., & Sweller, J. (1995). Reducing cognitive load by mixing auditory and visual presentation modes. Journal of Educational Psychology, 87, 319–334. Paas, F., Van Gerven, P., Tabbers, H. K. (2005). The cognitive aging principle in multimedia learning. In R. E. Mayer (Ed.), The Cambridge handbook of multimedia learning (pp. 339–351). New York: Cambridge University Press.

Peterson, L., & Peterson, M. J. (1959). Short-term retention of individual verbal items. *Journal of Experimental Psychology, 58,* 193–198. doi:10.1037/h0049234

Pollock, E., Chandler, P., & Sweller, J. (2002). Assimilating complex information. *Learning and Instruction, 12,* 61–86. doi:10.1016/S0959-4752(01)00016-0

Price, C. B. (2008). Unreal PowerPoint: Immersing PowerPoint presentations in a virtual computer game engine world. *Computers in Human Behavior, 24,* 2486–2495. doi:10.1016/j.chb.2008.03.009

Quilici, J. L., & Mayer, R. E. (1996). Role of examples in how students learn to categorize statistics word problems. *Journal of Educational Psychology, 88*, 144–161. doi:10.1037/0022-0663.88.1.144

Raybourn, E. M. (2007). Applying simulation experience design methods to creating serious game-based adaptive training systems. *Interacting with Computers, 19*, 206–214. doi:10.1016/j.intcom.2006.08.001

Reder, L., & Anderson, J. R. (1980). A comparison of texts and their summaries: Memorial consequences. *Journal of Verbal Learning and Verbal Behavior, 19*, 121–134. doi:10.1016/S0022-5371(80)90122-X

Reder, L., & Anderson, J. R. (1982). Effects of spacing and embellishment on memory for main points of a text. *Memory & Cognition, 10*, 97–102.

Reed, S. K. (2006). Cognitive architectures for multimedia learning. *Educational Psychologist, 41*, 87–98. doi:10.1207/s15326985ep4102_2

Reese, D. D. (2007). First steps and beyond: Serious games as preparation for future learning. *Journal of Educational Multimedia and Hypermedia, 16*, 283–300.

Renkl, A. (2005). The worked-out examples principle in multimedia learning. In Mayer, R. E. (Ed.), *The Cambridge handbook of multimedia learning* (pp. 229–246). New York: Cambridge University Press.

Renkl, A., & Atkinson, R. K. (2003). Structuring the transition from example study to problem solving in cognitive skills acquisition: A cognitive load perspective. *Educational Psychologist, 38*, 15–22. doi:10.1207/S15326985EP3801_3

Renkl, A., Atkinson, R. K., Maier, U. H., & Staley, R. (2002). From example study to problem solving: Smooth transitions help learning. *Journal of Experimental Education, 70*, 293–315. doi:10.1080/00220970209599510

Rourke, A., & Sweller, J. (2009). The worked-example effect using ill-defined problems: Learning to recognise designers' styles. *Learning and Instruction, 19*, 185–199. doi:10.1016/j.learninstruc.2008.03.006

Schuerman, R. L., & Peck, K. L. (1991). Pull-down menus, menu design, and usage patterns in computer-assisted instruction. *Journal of Computer-Based Instruction, 18*, 93–98.

Simon, H., & Gilmartin, K. (1973). A simulation of memory for chess positions. *Cognitive Psychology, 5*, 29–46. doi:10.1016/0010-0285(73)90024-8

Simon, M. A. (1990). Invariants of human behavior. *Annual Review of Psychology, 41*, 1–19. doi:10.1146/annurev.ps.41.020190.000245

Sweller, J. (1994). Cognitive load theory, learning difficulty, and instructional design. *Learning and Instruction, 4*, 295–312. doi:10.1016/0959-4752(94)90003-5

Sweller, J. (1999). *Instructional design in technical areas*. Melbourne: ACER Press.

Sweller, J. (2003). Evolution of human cognitive architecture. In Ross, B. (Ed.), *The psychology of learning and motivation* (*Vol. 43*, pp. 215–266). San Diego: Academic Press.

Sweller, J. (2004). Instructional design consequences of an analogy between evolution by natural selection and human cognitive architecture. *Instructional Science, 32*, 9–31. doi:10.1023/B:TRUC.0000021808.72598.4d

Sweller, J. (2008). Instructional implications of David Geary's evolutionary educational psychology. *Educational Psychologist, 43*, 214–216. doi:10.1080/00461520802392208

Sweller, J. (2009). Cognitive bases of human creativity. *Educational Psychology Review, 21*, 11–19. doi:10.1007/s10648-008-9091-6

Sweller, J., & Chandler, P. (1994). Why some material is difficult to learn. *Cognition and Instruction, 12*, 185–233. doi:10.1207/s1532690xci1203_1

Sweller, J., & Cooper, G. (1985). The use of worked examples as a substitute for problem solving in learning algebra. *Cognition and Instruction, 2,* 59–89. doi:10.1207/s1532690xci0201_3

Sweller, J., & Sweller, S. (2006). Natural information processing systems. *Evolutionary Psychology, 4,* 434–458.

Tarmizi, R., & Sweller, J. (1988). Guidance during mathematical problem solving. *Journal of Educational Psychology, 80,* 424–436. doi:10.1037/0022-0663.80.4.424

Tindall-Ford, S., Chandler, P., & Sweller, J. (1997). When two sensory modes are better than one. *Journal of Experimental Psychology. Applied, 3,* 257–287. doi:10.1037/1076-898X.3.4.257

Tuovinen, J., & Sweller, J. (1999). A comparison of cognitive load associated with discovery learning and worked examples. *Journal of Educational Psychology, 91,* 334–341. doi:10.1037/0022-0663.91.2.334

Van Eck, R., & Dempsey, J. (2002). The effect of competition and contextualized advisement on the transfer of mathematics skills in a computer-based instructional simulation game. *Educational Technology Research and Development, 50,* 23–41. doi:10.1007/BF02505023

Van Gerven, P. W. M., Paas, F. G. W. C., Van Merriënboer, J. J. G., & Schmidt, H. G. (2000). Cognitive Load Theory and the acquisition of complex cognitive skills in the elderly: Towards an integrative framework. *Educational Gerontology, 26,* 503–521. doi:10.1080/03601270050133874

Van Merriënboer, J. J. G., & de Croock, M. B. M. (1992). Strategies for computer-based programming instruction: Program completion vs. program generation. *Journal of Educational Computing Research, 8,* 365–394.

Vogel, J. J., Vogel, D. S., Cannon-Bowers, J., Bowers, C. A., Muse, K., & Wright, M. (2006). Computer games and interactive simulations for learning: A meta-analysis. *Journal of Educational Computing Research, 34,* 229–243. doi:10.2190/FLHV-K4WA-WPVQ-H0YM

Ward, M., & Sweller, J. (1990). Structuring effective worked examples. *Cognition and Instruction, 7,* 1–39. doi:10.1207/s1532690xci0701_1

Yeung, A. S., Jin, P., & Sweller, J. (1998). Cognitive load and learner expertise: Split-attention and redundancy effects in reading with explanatory notes. *Contemporary Educational Psychology, 23,* 1–21. doi:10.1006/ceps.1997.0951

Zhang, Q., & Lin, H. (2005). Worked example learning about the rules of the four fundamental Admixture operations of arithmetic. *Acta Psychologica Sinica, 37,* 784–790.

APPENDIX: ADDITIONAL READING

"Must-Reads" for This Topic

Ericsson, K. A., & Kintsch, W. (1995). Long-term working memory. *Psychological Review, 102*, 211–245.

Geary, D. (2002). Principles of evolutionary educational psychology. *Learning and Individual Differences, 12*, 317–345.

Kirschner, P. A., Sweller, J., & Clark, R. E. (2006). Why minimal guidance during instruction does not work: An analysis of the failure of constructivist, discovery, problem-based, experiential, and inquiry-based teaching. *Educational Psychologist, 41*, 75–86.

Low, R., & Sweller, J. (2005). The modality principle in multimedia learning. In R. E. Mayer (Ed.), *The Cambridge handbook of multimedia learning* (pp. 147–158). New York: Cambridge University Press.

Mayer, R. E., & Moreno, R. (1998). A split-attention effect in multi-media learning: Evidence for dual processing systems in working memory. *Journal of Educational Psychology, 90*, 312–320.

Mousavi, S., Low, R., & Sweller, J. (1995). Reducing cognitive load by mixing auditory and visual presentation modes. *Journal of Educational Psychology, 87*, 319–334.

Raybourn, E. M. (2007). Applying simulation experience design methods to creating serious game-based adaptive training systems. *Interacting with Computers, 19*, 206–214.

Reed, S. K. (2006). Cognitive architectures for multimedia learning. *Educational Psychologist, 41*, 87–98.

Reese, D. D. (2007). First steps and beyond: Serious games as preparation for future learning. *Journal of Educational Multimedia and Hypermedia, 16*, 283–300.

Renkl, A. (2005). The worked-out examples principle in multimedia learning. In R. E. Mayer (Ed.), *The Cambridge handbook of multimedia lLearning* (pp. 229–246). New York: Cambridge University Press.

Rieber, L. P. (2005). Multimedia learning in games, simulations, and microworlds. In R. E. Mayer (Ed.), *The Cambridge handbook of multimedia learning* (pp. 549–567). New York: Cambridge University Press.

Sweller, J. (2009). Cognitive bases of human creativity. *Educational Psychology Review, 21*, 11–19.

Tarmizi, R., & Sweller, J. (1988). Guidance during mathematical problem solving. *Journal of Educational Psychology, 80*, 424–436.

Tindall-Ford, S., Chandler, P., & Sweller, J. (1997). When two sensory modes are better than one. *Journal of Experimental Psychology: Applied, 3*, 257–287.

Van Eck, R., & Dempsey, J. (2002). The effect of competition and contextualized advisement on the transfer of mathematics skills in a computer-based instructional simulation game. *Educational Technology, Research and Development, 50*, 23–41.

Van Gerven, P. W. M., Paas, F. G. W. C., Van Merriënboer, J. J. G., & Schmidt, H. G. (2000). Cognitive Load Theory and the acquisition of complex cognitive skills in the elderly: Towards an integrative framework. *Educational Gerontology, 26*, 503–521.

Vogel, J. J., Vogel, D. S., Cannon-Bowers, J., Bowers, C. A., Muse, K., & Wright, M. (2006). Computer games and interactive simulations for learning: A meta-analysis. *Journal of Educational Computing Research, 34*, 229–243.

Yeung, A. S., Jin, P., & Sweller, J. (1998). Cognitive load and learner expertise: Split-attention and redundancy effects in reading with explanatory notes. *Contemporary Educational Psychology, 23*, 1–21.

Top Texts for Interdisciplinary Studies of Serious Games

Baddeley, A.D. (2003). Working memory: Looking back and looking forward. *Nature Reviews Neuroscience, 4,* 829–839.

Clark, R. E. (2005). Multimedia learning in e-course. In R. E. Mayer (Ed.), *The Cambridge handbook of multimedia learning* (pp. 589–616). New York: Cambridge University Press.

de Jong, T. (2006). Computer simulations: Technological advances in inquiry learning. *Science, 312,* 532–533.

Dempsey, J. V., Haynes, L. L., Lucassen, B. A., & Casey, M. (2002). Forty simple computer games and what they could mean to educators. *Simulation and Gaming, 33,* 157–168.

Kebritchi, M., & Hirumi, A. (2008). Examining the pedagogical foundations of modern educational computer games. *Computers and Education, 51,* 1729–1743.

Mayer, R. E. (2005). Introduction to multimedia learning. In R. E. Mayer (Ed.), *The Cambridge handbook of multimedia learning* (pp. 1–16). New York: Cambridge University Press.

Geary, D. (2008). An evolutionarily informed education science. *Educational Psychologist, 43,* 179–195.

Sweller, J. (2008). Instructional implications of David Geary's evolutionary educational psychology. *Educational Psychologist, 43,* 214–216.

Van Eck, R., & Dempsey, J. (2002). The effect of competition and contextualized advisement on the transfer of mathematics skills in a computer-based instructional simulation game. *Educational Technology, Research and Development, 50,* 23–41.

Vogel, J. J., Vogel, D. S., Cannon-Bowers, J., Bowers, C. A., Muse, K., & Wright, M. (2006). Computer games and interactive simulations for learning: A meta-analysis. *Journal of Educational Computing Research, 34,* 229–243.

Chapter 9
Making a Connection:
Game Genres, Game Characteristics, and Teaching Structures

Dennis Charsky
Ithaca College, USA

ABSTRACT

This chapter will make a connection between game genres, game characteristics, and constructivist teaching structures. Constructivist teaching structures, like open learning environments and anchored instruction, have the same aims as serious games – to facilitate higher order learning skills and knowledge. However, constructivist teaching structures are not games and serious games are grappling with how to design games and keep the fun and learning in perfect balance. Making connections between game genres and characteristics (where much of the fun resides) and teaching structures (where much of the learning resides) will highlight commonalities that can be taken advantage of in the design of good serious games – where learning and fun are in perfect balance.

INTRODUCTION

In the past decade, there has been significant support for creating serious games (Aldrich, 2004, 2005; Gee, 2003, 2007; Prensky, 2001; Squire, 2002). Serious games are focused on non-entertainment purposes, (i.e. training and instruction) in a variety of fields (i.e., public policy, education, corporate management, healthcare, military; Abt, 1965; B. Sawyer, 2006). The reemergence of interest in games for learning transpired from advances in technol-

ogy, media, and game design has reinvigorated the movement to look to games as sound venues for instruction and training.

While the reemergence of the interest in games for learning/training has spurred the development of serious games, there is a lack of research and analysis supporting how learning is facilitated. There is support for the contention that game activities provide the engagement needed to motivate learners to persist in serious games (Aldrich, 2004; Annetta & Cheng, 2008; Malone & Lepper, 1987; Prensky, 2001; Shaffer, 2006; Squire, 2002). Exploring the motivational aspects and their impact on learning is

DOI: 10.4018/978-1-61520-717-6.ch009

a viable and worthy goal for serious games. Also of value to this emerging field is linking games to learning theory and practice. Doing so may help develop design heuristics and strategies that facilitate learning and retain the playful joy of games. Making these connections between games and learning theory and practices will help move the field to new heights and away from the mistake of combining games with drill and practice activities (Becker, this volume; Van Eck, 2007a).

BACKGROUND

Game designers strive to create games that are fun and games that will engage players (Crawford, 2003; Koster, 2005; Rollings & Adams, 2003; Rouse, 2005). Game design strategies that are believed to lead to engagement can include story, shooting, racing, fighting, collaboration, role playing, constructing, managing, and many, many more (Rollings & Adams, 2003). It is because of these exciting and entertaining strategies that the commercial video game industry is so popular and profitable. Dickey (2005) has argued that many of the engagement strategies used in entertainment-based video games can inform instructional design practice because they mirror sound instructional practices. The sound instructional practices that Dickey refers to can be found in many teaching structures grounded in the constructivist philosophy.

Constructivism encompasses a wide array of perspectives; yet while each perspective is different they share some common values and assumptions (Duffy & Cunningham, 1996; Land & Hannafin, 2000). A common assumption among the many perspectives is that individuals create their own knowledge from their unique experiences, background, and value system (Duffy & Cunningham, 1996; Duffy, Lowyck, Jonassen, & Welch, 1993; Jonassen, 1991; Jonassen, Cernusca, & Ionas, 2007). Further, constructivists believe that learning is not simply the result of transferring knowledge from one to another, but that

knowledge is created by the individual's unique interpretation. Learners actively seek to construct their understanding by negotiating different perspectives. The learner's negotiation of different perspectives results in learning; which is always open to change as the learner continues to learn and gain experience (Duffy & Cunningham, 1996; Land & Hannafin, 2000)

Further, most constructivist perspectives advocate that learners are active processors of information and learning is an active process as well. To facilitate this active process, learners are typically situated in a learning environment that can be structured in a variety of ways. Some constructivist perspectives emphasize providing more social avenues for learners to negotiate and construct understanding (Land & Hannafin, 2000). The social avenues provide opportunities for learners to share their understanding, debate the relevance of others' contentions, and collaborate on ideas that further and deepen their understanding (Duffy & Cunningham, 1996; Jonassen, 1999). Others advocate emphasizing technology tools (simulation, databases, websites) as means for assisting learners in negotiating and constructing meaning (Hannafin, 1992).

Serious games seek to facilitate the type of learning advocated by many perspectives of constructivistism. Since the learning aims of serious games and constructivism are the same, this chapter will attempt to make connections between teaching structures, grounded in constructivist philosophies, and game genres and characteristics.

Various teaching structures have been developed in order to fulfill constructivist principles, including problem-based learning, goal-based scenarios, and open learning environments. Some constructivist teaching structures will be compared to a few game genres in order to highlight the aspects that may work well in serious games. The impetus for this analysis is that highlighting the commonalities between the genres and the teaching structures may lead to the identification of design heuristics for particular genres that will help fulfill the mandate of serious games – good games for learning that are still fun.

Comparing game genres to teaching structures will further provide a valuable perspective, but we must also consider what aspects of the teaching structures are best suited for serious games. Becker (this volume) has stated that games are so different today that a "fresh approach" is needed. To do this, the teaching structures discussed here will also be compared to common characteristics of games in order to determine if the new gameplay embodied in current commercial video games can be transparently integrated into teaching structures. The analysis will focus on self-contained serious games and whether the role of a live instructor can be fulfilled by the features of a particular genre.

TEACHING STRUCTURES

The values and assumptions of constructivism that have facilitated the development of learning environments have been fulfilled in a variety of different forms. Open learning environments (Hannafin, Land, & Oliver, 1999), goal based scenarios (Schank, Berman, & Macpherson, 1999; Schank, Fano, Bell, & Jona, 1994), problem-based learning (Savery & Duffy, 1995), cognitive apprenticeship (Collins, Brown, & Holum, 1991), and anchored instruction (Cognition & Technology Group at Vanderbilt, 1992) are just some of the different teaching structures that embody the values and assumptions of constructivism. No one teaching structure is superior to another; in fact, all approaches are ideal for facilitating a deep level of understanding that is unique yet socially negotiated (Duffy et al., 1993; Perkins & Unger, 1999).

The aforementioned teaching structures have been selected from a plethora of teaching structures, and from here forward will be referred to as "the teaching structures." In this analysis each teaching structure will be described and related

to games. This analysis differ from others (e.g., Becker, 2007) in that it involves teaching structures not previously considered and further narrows the analysis to a comparison of game genres and game characteristics in regards to the teaching structures.

Open Learning Environments

According to Hannafin, et al. (1999), open learning environments (OLEs) have values that are central to developing instruction that assists learners in knowledge construction. They have identified four core values for creating OLE: enabling contexts, resources, tools, and scaffolds (1999), each of which will be discussed below.

Enabling Contexts

Enabling contexts themselves take three different forms: externally imposed, externally induced, and individually generated. In the first enabling context, **externally imposed**, the learner is presented with a particular problem or project that needs to be solved or completed. However, the learner is not given any specific means to solve the problem or complete the project (Hannafin et al., 1999).

The second type of enabling context, **externally induced**, requires the learner to identify the problem *and* create a competent solution. In this context, the learner is only presented a scenario(s) or case(s) which s/he must analyze in order to identify the problem and design the means to solve it (Hannafin et al., 1999).

The third context is **individually generated**. In this context the learner pursues his/her own interests, concerns, questions and devises the means to solve or answer them. In this context, the "instruction" cannot be anticipated or planned for; essentially the learner needs to create the context, the problem, and the means to solve it (Hannafin et al., 1999).

Resources

Hannafin, Land, and Oliver's (1999) second core value of OLEs is providing learners with resources to support their learning. Resources provide learners with a plethora of information key for answering or solving the driving problem(s). Resources can be other people inside and outside the OLE, print materials, media, databases, and web-based materials.

In OLEs, tools provide learners with the means to interact with the resources and the context. Tools enable learners to get support, coaching, feedback, and scaffold their efforts in solving the problem. Tools also support learners' information seeking, organizing their thoughts and ideas, exploring explanations and hypotheses, monitoring and reflecting upon their learning, and communicating with the teacher, outside experts, and their peers (Hannafin et al., 1999).

Scaffolds

The last core value of OLEs is scaffolds. Scaffolds, similar to tools, help support the learners' efforts in solving the problem. Yet, unlike tools, scaffolds are strategies that the teacher can use to effectively integrate the tools and guide their instruction. Conceptual scaffolds assist learners in identifying, contemplating, and organizing key concepts, and theories. Integrating advanced organizers, graphic organizers, concept maps, diagrams, expert/teacher advice, and related cases can help learners understand the OLE's content (Hannafin et al., 1999). Jonassen (1999) recommends using related cases in order to teach learners the complexity of the domain under study. Providing learners with a wealth of related cases or experiences helps scaffold the learner's memory through case-based reasoning and better represents complexity via multiple perspectives. Metacognitive scaffolding can be done through informal conversations with a learner(s) or through formal class presentations, class discussions, and assessments (Hannafin et

al., 1999). Teachers and instructors can support their learners' metacognitive skills by helping students link their prior knowledge to new learning, through using appropriate questioning tactics and allowing learners to demonstrate their knowledge. Procedural scaffolds assist the learner in finding and/or using the OLE tools and resources. The teacher/instructor can tutor the learner(s) as needed to use or locate items that will help the learner(s) perform better (Hannafin et al., 1999).

The Connection to Games

The enabling contexts of OLEs are similar to the levels in many games as well as to the different problems that drive the gameplay in many games. The different enabling contexts could be used to create levels of varying difficulty. The first enabling context, externally imposed, is very scripted, the second, externally induced, is driven by a mission, but allows for many solutions, while the last enabling context, individually generated, requires greater autonomy by the learner. The contexts seems to increase in difficulty, much as games do, by increasing the level of autonomy given to the learner while reducing the reliance on the instructor, this could lead to a means for structuring game play and designing levels in serious games. The resources and tools in OLEs are already a part of many games, whether by the various objects and artifacts in games, the ability to converse with others (NPC or real persons), or the searchable indexes inside many games, current game design and technology can support this aspect of OLEs. However, the scaffolding required for OLEs are not entirely possible with current game technology. NPCs could serve as pedagogical agents (PAs) and assist learners by via procedural scaffolding. Many games already do this with the training stage where an NPC teaches the player how to use the interface, perform basic movements, etc. Providing the conceptual and metacognitive scaffolds, however, would require the NPC to become much more involved in instructional aspects while still remaining true to the fun aspects of the game. Van Eck (2007) has stated that making NPCs part of the game's overall theme alone does not make them adept at delivering scaffolding, nor would using NPCs as PAs that merely lecture to learners or constantly questions them be any less disruptive to game flow. Van Eck recommends the use of intelligent tutoring systems to drive NPC/PAs, but Iuppa and Borst (2007) contend that NPCs can be valuable instructional tools if the right multi-dimensional characters are developed to help fulfill the learning goals and keep game play flowing.

Goal-Based Scenarios

Goal-Based Scenarios (GBS) are referred to as 'learning by doing' (Schank, Berman, & Macpherson, 1999; Schank, Fano, Bell, & Jona, 1994). Created by Schank et al. (1999; 1994), these scenarios are designed to develop expertise by placing learners in complex situations. The seven components of GBS are: learning objectives, mission, cover story, scenarios, role, resources, and feedback. The components facilitate the creation of a narrative that also creates the context. The mission and cover story provides an engaging and motivating opening event that delivers the goal to the learners. The mission and cover story need to be somewhat realistic and crafted in a manner that will facilitate knowledge development. Here is an example: Tom is the chief athletic trainer at a high school in Louisiana. Tom's job is to assist the school's injured athletes, find out how they were injured, diagnose their injuries, and depending on the severity of said injuries, send them to the nurse, call their parents, or send them to a physician or a hospital. Over the weekend, Tom was in a car crash and he can no longer continue his duties at the high school. On Monday morning, you [as student] get called in by the athletic director to serve as a substitute athletic trainer. You must take care of the athletic team's injuries or their championship season is doomed! You must interview the injured athletes, diagnose their injuries, and either continue or change their care.

The role defines whom the learner will play in the narrative. The role must be one that allows them to both learn and apply content. The role needs to be interesting to the learner and it does not matter that the role may not be one the learner would assume, i.e. president of the United States (Schank et al., 1999).

The scenario defines the learner's instructional tasks and activities. The tasks should be explicitly linked to the goals and mesh with the cover story and mission. The tasks should have positive outcomes for correctly completing them and consequences for not completing them or completing them poorly (Schank et al., 1999). The remaining components—goals, resources, feedback—provide activities that must be carried out by the instructor in order to support learners.

The instructor will typically write the goals, but that does not exclude the learners from creating the goal(s) or any sub-goals. Resources include the information needed to achieve the mission's goal(s). The information should be readily accessible and formulated as additional anecdotes that contribute to the cover story and mission. The additional stories can come from experts, clients, mentors, and any other character that can be integrated into the cover story and mission. For example, in our hypothetical GBS on athletic training we could bring in additional stories from athletes, coaches, parents, other trainers, a past professor, etc., that can deliver information as well as contribute to the authenticity of the GBS (Schank et al., 1999). Schank, Berman, and McPherson (1999) claim that feedback can be delivered in three manners: critically, positively, and anecdotally. Critical feedback lets learners know that they have made a mistake and that their proposed solution is inadequate. Positive feedback is usually delivered from coaches or instructors that reinforce the learners' efforts and offer advice and/or just in time guidance. Anecdotal feedback usually comes from experts that offer additional information in the form of stories and/or similar cases.

The Connection to Games

The obvious connection between games and GBS are the strong narrative components. The mission, cover story, role development, and embedded tasks within those components are nearly identical to many narrative components in role-playing and adventure games. More importantly, GBS provide ideas for the use of PAs that flows with the gameplay and narrative. Games have a variety of narratives and stories, so it is feasible that an appropriate narrative could be crafted that would be able to integrate the type of agents that could deliver the three types of feedback required of GBS; critical, positive, anecdotal. Iuppa and Borst (2007) recommend having different types of NPCs in serious games. The various NPCs might be argumentative, constantly offering alternative perspectives, characters that offer a different cultural perspective, and others. GBS seem to offer a heuristic for the design of NPCs that minimize disruptions in the flow of the game while still supporting learning.

Problem-Based Learning

Problem-Based Learning (PBL) has been used successfully for over thirty years in a variety of disciplines and different levels of education (Savery, 2006). In typical (non-PBL) instructional environments, learners are taught the foundations or lower level skills first and then are given problems that allow them to apply their understanding. In PBL, learners are given the problem at the outset and need to figure out how to solve the problem. Hence, the problem drives the instruction, making learning the foundational knowledge necessary (Savery, 2006).

The problem itself needs to be developed so that it pulls from a wide range of disciplines and

in return requires learners to explore and pull from those same disciplines in developing their answer. The problem also needs to be ill-structured, meaning that there is not a single correct answer, but, rather a plethora of possible answers. The ill-structured problem must also be situated in an authentic context; this context assists learners in developing relevant skills and knowledge (Savery, 2006; Savery & Duffy, 1995).

The problem can be presented in a rich context which provides all possible information or it can be presented in a series of short, but connected problems, or it can be a single question that requires learners to seek the information needed to solve the problem (Hoffman & Ritchie, 1997; Savery & Duffy, 1995). Once the problem has been presented, learners must analyze the problem, create solutions to the problem, and agree on a schedule of how to complete the tasks required to craft the solutions. This process will be repeated as the learners refine and discover more about both the problem and the appropriate solution. Most PBL environments require learners to work in small teams so that they can negotiate and share their developing understanding of the problem, collectively brainstorm solutions, and support one another through the problem solving process (Savery, 2006). Collaboration within small teams is key because it affords learners the opportunity to share what they have learned. Collaborating with others helps each individual hone their own understanding and make a significant contribution to the solution (Savery, 2006).

The instructor's role in PBL is to be a facilitator of learning and manager of the problem-solving process. It is a significant level of work to properly scaffold, guide, and coach learners who may be both new to the content areas and new to PBL. Further, the instructor must be adept at helping learners consider and explore the other perspectives and disciplines essential for crafting a tenable solution. The instructor must question the validity and impact the solution(s) will have on the problem because challenging the learners' thinking develops sound solutions and metacognitive skills (Savery & Duffy, 1995).

The PBL typically ends with a debrief that details what was learned, topics encountered, how the answer(s) was developed, and facilitates learner reflection on what they learned and the learning process. Debriefing is an important aspect of PBL because it consolidates the various efforts of individuals and teams so that each learner better understands the complexity of the problem, the complexity of the solutions, and how the problem-solving process facilitated their understanding (Savery, 2006).

The Connection to Games

Gee (2003, 2007), Van Eck (2007b) and Kiili (2007) have made convincing cases for games as fun problem-solving activities. Hung & Van Eck (in press) discuss the relationships between problems and serious games by analyzing how different game genres may better support particular types of problems. PBL and serious games are similar in that both present problems in an authentic context, can have a mission, scenario, or narrative, are goal oriented, support complexity, and provide a space, virtual or face-to-face, for working on the problem. The critical role the instructor must play in PBL is clear, as with the other teaching structures. Again, redesigning NPCs with or without intelligent tutoring systems may help fill the role typically played by the instructor.

PBL is the only teaching structure that explicitly states that learners must be grouped, although this is supported by many. PBL is clear that the negotiation, debate, and collaboration that happens among teammates is an essential part of their learning. Many games are online, and massively multiplayer online games (MMOG) in particular require gamers to team up, organize, discuss, and collaborate if they are to be successful. Anderson (this volume) discusses how MMORPG (role playing games) support developing problem-solving

skills through collaboration and socialization. The ability for learners to collaborate within MMOG makes them a unique venue appropriate for the collaboration required in PBL.

Cognitive Apprenticeship

Cognitive Apprenticeship (CA) stems from traditional apprenticeships. In traditional apprenticeships, learners watched as the master demonstrated the task. When it was the apprentice's turn, the master guided and provided help as the apprentice tried to replicate the task that was modeled by the master. The modeling, guiding, and coaching happened within the context of the work environment made learning the task more relevant (Collins, Brown, & Holum, 1991).

CA uses the traditional apprenticeship model and integrates it with cognitive skills and knowledge development strategies. The task(s) conducted in traditional apprenticeships were visible and concrete, i.e. tailoring a suit (Collins et al., 1991). The cognitive skills and knowledge that CA facilitates are abstract or invisible. Reading comprehension, writing skills, problem solving, negotiation, etc. are just a few of the cognitive skills/knowledge that learners must master, but cannot see. The four components, identified by Collins et al. (1991), that comprise CA are: content, method, sequence, and sociology.

Content involves learning the domain knowledge, heuristic strategies, metacognitive strategies, and learning strategies. These different strategies facilitate learning the foundational knowledge, as well as the complex knowledge that leads to expertise. All four of these processes are interdependent and required for true mastery (Collins et al., 1991).

Method involves the teaching strategies that need to be employed in order to facilitate learning. Collins et al. (1991) identified six strategies that needed to facilitate learning: modeling, scaffolding, coaching, articulation, reflection, and exploration. In modeling, the instructor shows the learner how to perform tasks. Scaffolding is the aid that an instructor gives to a learner to help finish a task. Coaching occurs through the instructor offering feedback, challenging the learner's understanding, and providing words of encouragement. Articulation includes methods that have learners verbalize their understanding. Reflection occurs when the learner evaluates their performance or understanding against an expert's. Exploration is intended to let learners try on their own as supports are faded (Collins et al., 1991).

Sequence refers to the manner in which the content is organized and presented. The content should focus on a broad perspective and the overarching purpose of the activity or content. Collins et al. (1991) refer to this as global skills before local skills. Further, the content should increase in complexity or difficulty and this increase should be gradual; meaning that once a learner has successfully completed a task they can then move onto a more difficult task. Not only should these tasks increase in difficulty; they should also be diverse. Tasks should vary in the way that they are solved requiring the learner to utilize other strategies.

Sociology means that the learning is situated in a relevant and authentic context. Learners need to apply their knowledge in various contexts to help promote transfer. Further, learners should be part of a community that allows for the sharing of their understanding as well as opportunities for collaborating with others. All of these aspects are designed to facilitate learner's intrinsic motivation (Collins et al., 1991).

The Connection to Games

The sequence and content components of CA offers guidance for designing challenges in serious games. Sequencing the content from easy to difficulty and global to local is achieved in many games by level design. Unfortunately, while level design does have some similarities to basic in-

structional theory, it is not sufficient to facilitate learning because it fails to address mastery and transfer (Gunter, Kenny, & Vick, 2007).

CA content component recommends that learners develop the basic foundational knowledge, heuristics, meta-cognitive skills, and learning strategies. These aspects could be used to create challenges within a given level or to structure four sequential levels. Using these components in serious game may address issues of level design not leading to mastery and transfer identified by Gunter et al., (2007). Further, transfer could also be improved by adding levels that vary from previous levels but which rely on the same skills. Anchored instruction, PBL, and OLE advocate for the use of multiple cases or perspectives so that learners can attain a flexible understanding that they can transfer to diverse and novel situations. The use of diverse, novel situations within level design could retain the engaging aspects while supporting the transfer of learning.

The modeling and exploration methods of CA are similar to the training phase and expansive virtual environments of many games. Role-playing games (RPGs) could allow learners to follow the master (modeling), who in turn could also help players learn tasks by guiding and/or coaching them through activities. Games also help learners explore alternative strategies because most games allow nearly endless opportunities to try a variety of strategies; even those that fail to bring success. Even if gamers are killed in the game, they are typically "reborn" in the exact location and are free to try again. CA calls for articulation and reflection, which could also be designed into NPCs so that they occur seamlessly. However, the scaffolding, coaching, articulation, and reflection methods, typically carried out by the instructor in CA, are difficult to integrate in serious games. As mentioned previously, these methods could be carried out by NPCs designed as PA or ITS.

Game worlds can easily replicate the sociology component of CA by creating contexts using three or two-dimensional interfaces. Further, online games like MMOGs can facilitate this component because of their inherent social nature in virtual worlds. Of course, this type of socialization may have to be appropriately structured in order to attain the type of interactions needed for collaboration and sharing.

Anchored Instruction

Anchored instruction is a term first used to describe the work of the Cognition and Technology Group at Vanderbilt University (CTGV; 1990) that used videodiscs as a means of presenting problems to learners. The problems in anchored instruction are situated, meaning that they naturally spring from the context. CTGV (1990) refers to these problem spaces as macrocontexts that allow learners to explore the macrocontext in order to find the relevant information needed to solve the problem. For example, in the CTVG (1990) project *Jasper Woodbury*, Jasper finds himself in a predicament when after sailing down the river in his motorboat; he becomes worried about whether he has enough gas to make the return journey. Once the problem has been proposed (does he have enough gas to get home) learners need to develop an answer and get Jasper back home. To do this the learners must explore the previous scenes where they were provided clues and bits of information that they must identify and use to create an answer.

Obviously, the presentation of the macrocontext and the accompanying narrative are vital aspects to anchored instruction. The macrocontext allows learners to experience an authentic story and situation out of which the problem arises (CTVG, 1990). The macrocontext puts learners in an authentic situation that subsequently spawns their problem-solving process. As in the previous teaching structures, the instructor plays a key role in scaffolding, guiding, and coaching learners in exploring the macrocontext and embarking on the problem solving process.

The Connection to Games

Once again we see that narrative and the instructor are essential parts. The anchored instruction macrocontext is very similar to the game world in many games. Game worlds can provide all the necessary narrative dialogue, evidence, and information for creating a macrocontext. Game worlds also allow for exploration in either a three-dimensional world or two-dimensional interface capable of supporting all the information and narrative of the macrocontext. Yet instead of watching previous scenes on a videodisc, game worlds allow learners to walk around, enter buildings, use vehicles, consult characters, maps, etc. and watch video scenes. Explorations of game worlds are essential activities in many games where gamers move to and from a variety of scenes, places, encounters, objects, etc. and apply the information found towards their understanding of how to solve the problem presented by the game.

THOUGHTS ON THE TEACHING STRUCTURES AND GAMES

The aim of serous games and constructivist teaching methods are identical— to facilitate the development of higher order thinking, knowledge, and skills. Games and the teaching structures use authentic contexts in which to situate relevant problems, activities, and tasks. Narrative and scenarios are aspects used in games and the teaching structures to motivate the players/learners and to provide a mechanism for revealing content and information that is relevant to both the game world and context. A wealth of resources and appropriate tools need to be available in both games and the teaching structures. PBL specifically states that teams are a key component, while many of the other teaching structures recommend learners be in contact with experts and peers. The instructor plays a critical role in all the teaching structures by coaching, scaffolding, guiding, and assisting learners. NPCs, if designed to support the learning goals and not disrupt the gameplay, may be a viable option for fulfilling the role of the instructor in serious games.

Connecting the Teaching Structures to Game Genres

RPGs & Adventure Games

There are some unique commonalities between RPGs, adventure games, and the teaching structures. The most obvious commonality is the use of narratives and scenarios that are embedded in a game world or context. OLE enabling contexts, the macrocontexts in AI, and GBS all use some form of narrative to set the stage for learning. RPG and adventure games do so as well, but the narratives are immensely longer and have more plot twist and turns. The structure provided by OLE enabling context, GBS' narrative components, and exploration of the macrocontext for relevant information in anchored instruction provide basic means for structuring narratives in serious games. Quests could be designed into learning quests that are seamlessly a part of the narrative but also serve a learning purpose. All disciplines have foundational knowledge and information that can become the focus of quests, (e.g., find the *Declaration of Independence*, Euler's equation). These items then need to serve a purpose that fulfills higher order learning goals, (e.g., interpret the first line of the *Declaration of Independence*, apply Euler's formula). While quests are more akin to edutainment tasks, they could help deliver the foundational knowledge within the game structure. They should not, however, be the only challenges.

Anchored instruction requires learners to explore previous scenes in order to find relevant information to solve the problem. The exploration of the macrocontext for information could be driven by quests. Initially the exploration could be very structured, but as the learner levels up to more difficult macrocontexts, the quests could be faded to help facilitate higher order learning skills and metacognition. Further, many RPG/adventure games allow for repeated attempts at solving the problem, an aspect called for in CA exploration method.

The modeling method of CA could be easily designed into RPG/adventure serious games because there is an authentic game world and context, the player assumes a role, and there are NPCs that the player has to interact with. NPCs could easily be designed to act as the master in the game and conduct various modeling tasks, turn the task over to the learner and subsequently assume a coaching, scaffolding, critical role, or ask learners to articulate or reflect upon their learning. Although current game technology would restrict the articulation and reflection to basic text conversations with canned responses, it could still be effective. Inclusion of more advanced artificial intelligence in NPC or inclusion of intelligent tutoring systems would make these interactions more valuable.

Construction and Management Simulations

Construction and management simulations (CMSs) typically involve building up some entity, country, business, space station, etc., by managing the in-game economy of resources that are needed to construct the entity. CMSs are very similar to strategy games and for purposes of this chapter we will consider the two as one. The *SimCity* series and the *Civilization* series are two very popular CMS games. Typically in a CMS, gamers must secure resources and then use some or all of those resources in order to construct the entity. To make the game compelling, CMSs often have drains within the game economy that take away from the resources. Plus, some games have random disasters that disrupt the economy and make the game more challenging. Some CMSs have a war component that can impact the game and add in another engaging aspect (Rollings & Adams, 2003).

The core gameplay of CMS (e.g., managing the resources, drains, and pitfalls) can be linked to the tools inside many teaching structures. OLEs specifically call for tools that allow learners to experiment with different hypotheses and a CMS would allow for this. CMS gameplay is also similar to the goal setting requirements of GBS and OLE enabling context II (identify the problem *and* create a competent solution) and III (learner pursues his/her own interests, concerns, questions and devises the means to solve or answer them). The goal setting in CMSs is like the exploration aspect of CA that requires that learners try solutions on their own. Overall, the CMS gameplay is like many of the teaching structures because it allows learners to ask different questions, propose and try out possible solutions, and reflect on whether those solutions were appropriate. However, this thought process needs to be articulated and shared with others (instructor, experts, peers) in order to fulfill the requirements of PBL.

The constant decision-feedback loop is made more difficult as the CMS game progresses. The game gets more difficult because there are more and more decisions as disruptions occur and throw the game and the gamer's strategy into disarray. This increasingly difficult and complex gameplay is very similar to the sequencing of content suggested by CA where the content gradually becomes more complex and more diverse. Yet, as the game gets more difficult, the gamer will seek out access to help from advisors and/or other information screens, and this mirrors the role of the instructor in many of the teaching structures. The teaching structures call for the instructor to scaffold the learners as their knowledge develops; many of the advisor/information screens in CMSs provide the scaffolding because they often provide tips, hints, or specific instructions on how to do better in the game. However, these advisor/information screens do not help learners reflect on their decisions or articulate their reasoning behind their strategy.

The overarching perspective of CMSs is also similar to PBL and OLE enabling contexts, because the perspective is shaped by the perspective of the driving problem. The CMS overarching perspective may be best suited for facilitating learning about overall systems, processes, and theories. For example, creating a serious game RPG about storming the beaches of Normandy on D-Day provides the learner with a soldier's perspective on that endeavor: seeing lives lost, the terrifying aspects of war, etc., But does this RPG provide the same type of learning as a serious game CMS from Gen. Eisenhower's or President Roosevelt's perspective? Would students develop a different understanding of D-Day because of the different perspective? RPGs may be ideal for teaching a culture's history because students can be put into specific contexts and roles. CMSs may be ideal for teaching historical theory, such as Jarod Diamond's (1997) theory of civilization development, articulated in his book *Guns, Germs, and Steel,* because learners could get to play with whole systems, processes, and entities (see Crawford, in press, for more on this).

Massively Multiplayer Online Games

While MMOGs have many of the same gameplay features of other game genres, especially RPGs, the unique aspects of online play have specific connection to aspects of the teaching structures, especially those that emphasize socialization and collaboration. PBL specifically states that learners should be placed in small teams in order to propel negotiation of meaning and debate of the developing solution. The other teaching structures also stress that fostering opportunities for learners to share their understanding, converse with experts, and freely express their ideas is a valuable aspect to facilitating higher order learning. MMOGs seem to provide a means to fulfill those requirements. MMOGs already have social interactions designed into the gameplay. In many MMOGs, gamers must work together in groups to complete certain tasks, and typically MMOGs have an informal social structure where new players are mentored by veteran players (Steinkuehler, 2004). Given the MMOG gameplay and social structure, it seems possible that the role of the instructor could be fulfilled by others in the game world and/or the instructor could be embedded in the game world.

Yet, to keep the immersive experience believable, the instructor would have to enter the game in disguise. Many MMOGs have in-game moderators with administrative powers to regulate the game space. This same tactic could be used to plant instructors in the game so that they can manipulate the game space to provide more instruction or create learning opportunities. The instructor could be allowed to enter the game in various roles to scaffold, guide, and coach in a manner that would be consistent with the fantasy, context, and narrative of the game world. For example, consider a civilization/history building game where the learners are constantly taking over other countries and dominating the game by warfare. Pretend now that the teacher can go in and change some aspect or impose some calamity that cripples the learners' civilization. The teacher chooses to change the game by inserting financial disaster into the game because they are moving into studying the US stock market crash of 1929. Within an instant, the virtual world that they dominated is now quickly dominating them and the instructor has created a teachable moment! The potential for having the instructor in game and with a suite of abilities, powers, information, etc., to shape the game as well as coach, scaffold, guide and model for learners offers an intriguing set of possibilities.

MMOGs are by nature very team-oriented; you must interact with other people in order to accomplish most of the activities in the virtual world (Anderson, this volume). With thousands of players playing nearly around the clock from all over the world, all looking to collaborate, it is easy to "friend" someone. Hence, it makes perfect sense to build teaming into serious MMOGs.

Having MMO serious games built for classes, grade levels, departments, and employee levels, rather than opening up a MMO serious game to every 6-12 student in the world or even the United States could facilitate their integration into the existing school network. Further, limiting the MMO serious game to entities that resemble our current class designations retains our current student-teacher ratios and allows instructors to retain the amount of feedback, coaching, scaffolding, and facilitating that many are already doing, albeit it in a virtual world. Yet, with the rise of eLearning and virtual schools, there is a new educational landscape that might be ready for truly *massive* multiple-player online serious games.

Game Genres & the Teaching Structures: Closing Thoughts

While it would seem logical to combine game genres and their inherent activities with constructivist teaching structures in order to create serious games, doing so over-simplifies two complex design processes: game design and instructional design, to a level that seemingly trivializes the work of both fields. Simply mixing together the 'best' of game design with the 'best' of instructional design is easier said than done.

Serious games should strive for transparency: where the game design blends seamlessly with instructional design in order to create serious game where it is hard, hopefully impossible, to discern the learning from the fun (Dickey, 2005; Gee, 2005, 2006, 2007; Gunter et al., 2007; Habgood, Ainsworth, & Benford, 2005). The game genres have been detailed because they have many characteristics that are similar to the characteristics found in the teaching structures. Subsequently, the characteristics of games themselves, regardless of genre, also need to be considered because they are what makes different games genres unique and appealing to different audiences. There are many titles in each of the game genres, but each title is different because of how the designers manipulated the game characteristics to create engaging game play (Rouse, 2005).

GAME CHARACTERISTICS

While game genres are useful for categorizing the different types of gameplay, game characteristics are useful for discussing specific aspects of games. There are, of course, far too many game characteristics to address in a single chapter, but a few are worth mentioning here for their relation to the teaching structures. Game characteristics can include game rules (Alessi & Trollip, 2001); challenging activities (Malone & Lepper, 1987); and choices, and fantasy elements (Lepper & Cordova, 1992). Figure 1 charts the connections between game characteristics and the teaching structures.

The game characteristics are inherently interdependent—discussing one characteristic inevitably leads to discussing others. Discussing them independently is like trying to separate the different colors from a multicolor ball of *Play-doh*. However, for the sake of clarity, and

in order to connect the teaching structures to the characteristics, each characteristic will be discussed separately.

Rules

Rules are constraints that limit the actions a gamer can and cannot take. In some games, the rules can be fixed: impossible to break or alter. Such is the case with many edutainment titles that use rules to rigidly structure content; breaking the rules means the gamer did not select the correct answer. For example, in the game *Number Munchers* (Minnesota Educational Computer Consortium, 1988), the gamer is asked to munch the correct answer to the posed math problem, (i.e. "munch all even numbers"). When the gamer 'breaks' the rules by munching an incorrect answer, they lose points. The rules are very fixed in order to teach the content.

Rules are also important because they can be set to represent reality or a real phenomenon (Alessi & Trollip, 2001). The rules in CMS games determine the outcome of the gamer's decisions. Complex CMSs like *RollerCoaster Tycoon III* (Frontier, 2004), *SimCity IV* (Maxis, 2003), and

Figure 1. Game characteristics and teaching structures

	Game Characteristics						
Teaching Structures	Rules	Choice			Challenges	Fantasy	
		Expressive	Strategic	Tactical		Fidelity	Context
Cognitive Apprenticeship	~	-	-	-	~	~	~
Anchored Instruction	~	-	-	-	+	~	~
Open Learning Environments	~	-	-	-	~	~	`
Goal Based Scenarios	~	-	-	-	+	~	+
Problem Based Learning	~	-	-	-	~	~	~
Key: + = fulfilled ~ = partially - = not fulfilled							

Civilization IV (Firaxis, 2005) have their own ruleset that best represents the real-world forces depicted in the game, physics, economics, and urban planning (*RollerCoaster Tycoon III*; *SimCity IV*), theory of civilization development (*Civilization IV*). The rules in these CMS games create a world that is representative of the real world in some important ways, and gamers must first learn the simulated environment and then exploit it to their advantage in order to achieve their goal(s). In RPGs and adventure games, rules restrict the gamer's access to game spaces, NPCs, and/or the ability to take on challenges until their avatar has reached a certain level. In MMOGs, the rules are nearly absent and made up by the gamers as they collectively shape the game world culture.

Connection to the Teaching Structures

The rules can be connected to the limitations inherent in, or imposed by, the teaching structures. The contexts in OLE and anchored instruction, the mission in GBS, and the degree of ill-structuredness of the problem in PBL impose parameters on the scope and depth of the content. Further, access to resources, tools, information, experts, communication tools, etc., can also be restricted.

Rules can also be used to craft structured levels in games that can facilitate the learning of prerequisite skills. Very strict rules in levels may work best for teaching foundational knowledge before moving onto higher order knowledge. Rules can be used to increase the difficulty of the level by restricting the available choices, decisions, or actions a learner can take. Adcock, Watson, Morrison, & Belfore, (this volume) discuss structuring levels based on available items in the interface. They use the example of a detective training serious game that employs different scenarios for solving crimes. In each scenario, some items are grayed out and cannot be selected by the learner, thus restricting their choices (and subsequently their learning) to only the items that are active. This

is a perfect example of using the rule structure that creates a prerequisite stream that is tied to the fantasy and gameplay. This structure may be most suitable for novice learners, while experts with much prior knowledge and experience (in this case a seasoned detective) might find the game to be too easy or restrictive. Low, Sweller, Jin (this volume) state that prior knowledge and experience should be purposefully designed into serious games. They note that many games allow learners to selected the level of difficulty and also suggest that adjusting the game by analyzing pre-testing might be another accommodation for prior knowledge and experience.

Choice

Choice refers to the number of options and decisions a gamer has prior to and during gameplay (Hannafin & Peck, 1988; Malone & Lepper, 1987). Three different types of choice have been outlined by Charsky (in press): Expressive, Strategic, and Tactical. When a gamer decides she wants to be a sorceress, she has made a strategic choice; if she did so because she likes the wardrobe options, she has made an expressive choice.) How she develops her avatar (good, evil, warrior, healer) is a tactical choice. All are different kinds of choices, and are independent of each other.

Expressive choices are choices that the gamer makes which may have little impact on gameplay, but can improve engagement (e.g., by allowing them to customize their avatar or entity). Allowing the gamer to make these expressive choices can help develop their "projective identity" (Gee, 2003). Gee refers to projective identity as the development of empathy and pride in a game entity (2003). The projective identity develops because the gamer is infusing some of his/her personality into the entity. This may be the reason Hallford and Hallford (2001) categorize some gamers as naval gazers because their overarching goal and motivation to play is to improve their entity.

When the learner makes choices that affect the manner in which a game is played, those decisions can be categorized as strategic choices. Strategic choice refers to the gamer's ability to change some game attributes, such as level of difficulty, allotted time, number of players (Hannafin & Peck, 1988) and to make selections like country to develop a civilization with or type of avatar to develop (ranger, wizard, fairy).

Tactical choice refers to the gamer's ability to make decisions about how they play the game. How the gamer decides to do "x" instead of all the other possible options in a situation is a tactical choice (Charsky, in press). Further, another tactical choice is whether or not the gamer chooses to access help from the in-game resources (Hannafin & Peck, 1988).

Connection to the Teaching Structures.

The open, self-directed nature of both the teaching structures and games inherently provides a great deal of choice. Some genres offer more choices than others; CMSs typically are designed to constantly provide gamers with a plethora of choices presented as decisions that escalate in both number and difficulty as the game progresses. RPG/adventure games provide a structured set of choices for each level that ultimately propels the narrative. The choices that games provide allow for structured exploration—the ability to act freely within a closed system. The structured exploration consists of the types of choices as well as the number of possible choices in a game. Each of the teaching structures crafts an environment that allows for structured exploration, yet some of the choices in games are absent in the teaching structures.

Expressive choice (Charsky, in press) is one type of choice that is present in many commercial games and which has no equivalent in the teaching structures. The challenge is to cater to the navel gazers and character chasers by building expressive choices into serious games beyond

simply including a reward scheme appropriately tied to the context and fantasy. For example, in a hypothetical serious game on project management, rewarding a learner with money so that they can go shopping for new clothes before their first day as project manager is a way of catering to the navel gazers. Yet this tactic comes eerily close to the mistakes made with edutainment by including a game design tactic within a traditional instruction simulation. Serious games need to take the next step and design reward structures that are tied to the learning goals.

For example, using our same hypothetical project management serious game, the reward structure might allow the learners to use their points to emphasize the traits that they want their avatar to have, charisma, intellect, empathy, organization. The traits they emphasize, by distributing points among those traits, would affect the strategies available to them in the game. If the learner distributed most of his/her points towards charisma, that would focus gameplay on solving managerial problems using strategies akin to charismatic leaders because the other strategies would not be available due to the gamer's point distribution. The opposite would be true if the gamer stressed power, empathy, or took a balanced approach to distributing their points across all traits—how they develop their avatar (point distribution) determines the strategies available. The gameplay would lead to situations where the gamer would need to handle a particular situation using the available strategies. With these choices in place it sets up the use of diverse situations: some where the strategies will have great success, and somewhere they will not. The gamer will have to further develop their avatar or develop the avatar in a different way in order to handle situations where they do not succeed. The point is that the expressive choices can be connected to the learning and be seamlessly tied to the content, context, world, and game play. Whether or not this connection has an effect on learning is an area in need of research.

Challenges

Challenges are the game's events, tasks, and activities faced during gameplay (Malone, 1981; Malone & Lepper, 1987; Rollings & Adams, 2003). Challenges are influenced by the genre of the game. If the game is an action-adventure-shooter, then most of the challenges involve shooting and other fast-paced activities. RPG/adventure games usually involve completing many quests and conversing with NPCs. CMSs typically involve negotiating the resources and drains of the simulated world. Context also plays a significant role in the design of challenges. A WWII based game would obviously have many challenges involving military weapons, vehicles, and enemies (Rollings & Adams, 2003). The genre and the context contribute to the design of challenges be they quests, shooting, managing, constructing, etc. This combination of context, narrative, content, and game world can create a feeling of immersion and escapism with an intensity not found in other media (Gee, 2007; Rouse, 2005).

Connection to the Teaching Structures

Games are difficult and gamers pay to be entertained by difficult challenges. Easy games do not do well in the marketplace because gamers want tough challenges (Rollings & Adams, 2003; Rouse, 2005). Yet, this increased challenge does not necessarily mean increased competition where victory or success occurs at the expense or defeat of another. Rather, challenge can come in managing a team, developing a character, fixing a problem, collaborating with others, etc. In these instances, gamers analyze the challenge, decipher possible options for overcoming that challenge, and implement their ideas until they achieve success and meet their goal.

The challenges presented in many of the teaching structures require learners to structure their own learning using the content provided, with the help of others, and under the guidance of the instructor. The means of how the learner achieves the overarching goal is not set in stone; learners must develop their own processes using the resources and tools provided.

Tools have been defined as representing complex, real-world systems (Jonassen & Reeves, 1996). Some games genres fit this definition. CMS games, for instance, fulfill this definition because they have an underlying model that represents some complex, possibly real world, phenomenon. *SimCity IV* (Maxis, 2003) has an underlying model reflecting urban planning and development. *Civilization IV* (Firaxis, 2007) and *Age of Empires III* (Ensemble Studios, 2005) both have underlying models of how civilizations developed, and *RollerCoaster Tycoon III* (Frontier, 2004) has an underlying model of how amusement parks function.

If tools are defined as things that support cognitive processes (LaJoie, 2000), then these types of tools must be designed into serious games. Types of tools that support cognitive processes can include concept maps, graphic organizers, searchable databases, simulations, ability to communicate with experts, etc. These tools might offer strategic choices that provide challenges that seamlessly integrate with gameplay and help meet the learning goals.

For example, a serious game could redesign the typical inventory of many games to be an inventory of knowledge and skills, arranged like a concept map. The arrangement of that concept map could have an impact on the player's access to his/her knowledge and abilities. Arranging the map to emphasize one skillset over others would impact game play because when the gamer returned to the game world their avatar would first try the primary skills and then secondary, etc. based on the arrangement of the concept map. This idea could be employed in our hypothetical project management game instead of distributing points to traits.

Many games also provide resources via built-in glossaries, help menus, and guides. For example, the game *Civilization IV* (Firaxis, 2007) has its own encyclopedia ("Civlopedia") about the game that includes entries for actual historical concepts, events, and people. Again, the challenge is not *if* resources can be made available, but rather how to connect them to the game and the learning. A possibility for integrating in-game resources might be to structure the information that the learner obtains from the game into a database, spreadsheet, table, or graphic organizer where learners can search, filter and sort the information collected. The configuration of the database, spreadsheet, table, etc. would impact game play just as the arrangement of the concept map would impact game play. Creating a knowledge system that the learner constructs as part of the serious game, and how the corresponding arrangement of the knowledge system impacts gameplay is based on the use of computers as mindtools. Jonassen and Carr (2000) and Jonassen, Carr, and Yeuh (1998) advocate using various computer applications (e.g., databases or spreadsheets) as cognitive tools for facilitating critical thinking and multiple knowledge representations, but their research has not been integrated with virtual worlds or serious games.

While these notions (e.g., concept maps, knowledge systems, and mindtools) offer possible solutions to endogenously integrating challenges, tools, and resources, these ideas have not been evaluated and more research is needed to evaluate their integration into serious games.

Fantasy

Nearly every game contains fantasy elements (Rollings & Adams, 2003; Rouse, 2005). Fantasy allows gamers to immerse themselves in a totally different world. Games provide the same types of fantasy as movies, television, and books, but games allow the gamer to control the experience rather than passively watch the fantasy unfold. Two aspects that contribute to fantasy and help suspend reality for the gamer are fidelity and context.

Fidelity is the virtual backdrop for the game world that facilitates the game's challenges. Fidelity is the result of using graphics, audio, video, three-dimensional virtual worlds, and artificial intelligence to authentically represent reality and/or the game world. Providing true-to-life processes, images, landscapes, sound, video, and dialogue can create an exciting and immersive game context that makes the fantasy more believable. (Alessi & Trollip, 2001; Rollings & Adams, 2003; Rouse, 2005).

Context is the setting, narrative, scenario, characters, backstory, mission, etc. of the game. Context, like fidelity, can enhance the believability of the fantasy. Developing rich, heroic protagonists, vile antagonists, and loveable supporting characters within a tantalizing storyline can greatly contribute to the escapist feelings just as fidelity can by the use of excellent graphics, audio, video, three-dimensional virtual worlds, and artificial intelligence (Dickey, 2005, 2006; Gee, 2005; Rollings & Adams, 2003).

Many games make use of both fidelity and context, but to different degrees. RPG/adventure games emphasize the context more than the fidelity; conversely CMS games typically emphasize fidelity over context.

Connection to the Teaching Structures

Fantasy elements can be blended with content and instruction in two ways: exogenously and endogenously (Gunter et al., 2007). Exogenous means that the learning elements are inserted into the fantasy elements. Essentially, there is an obvious disconnect between the learning and the fantasy because, typically, the learning interrupts the fantasy (Malone & Lepper, 1987). For example, the learner is chasing the villain who has just crossed a river. In order for the learner to continue chasing the villain he/she must correctly answer the following: ___ + 2 = 2.

Endogenous means that there is no disconnect between the game and the learning (Malone

& Lepper, 1987). The game is, as Gunter et al., 2007 state "tightly coupled to the instructional challenges" (p. 514). This is the key to serious games: delivering a highly engaging gameplay while facilitating learning without disrupting the escapism the fantasy provides (Gee, 2007; Gunter et al., 2007; Habgood et al., 2005; Lepper & Cordova, 1992; Malone & Lepper, 1987; Shaffer, 2006).

While most entertainment games use fantastic narratives and contexts (*Star Wars*, hobbits, aliens, monsters) many serious games use narratives that are more relevant to the everyday lives of learners, and this relevance can help with transfer of learning. The narrative components in the teaching structures can help serious game designers craft the narrative in a manner that contextualizes the content within a relevant yet fantastic situation that, when other instructional components are built in, provides a rich learning environment. The teaching structures focus on using narratives as anchors, the cover story, the role, the context, and even the problem in PBL.

GBS' narrative components provide a solid guide for developing the initial narrative, cover story, and role. However, in a serious game these components would need to be extended into a full narrative that would provide a full assortment of plot twists, characters, situations, etc. CA offers no specific guidelines for writing a narrative, but the context of following a master and the context in which those skills need to be applied offer enough components that could drive a narrative. Anchored instruction makes use of a narrative that leads up to the problem along the way dropping hints or clues that may help solve the problem or achieve the goal.

Shaffer's (2005; 2006) epistemic games make a significant contribution to the field and the desire to seamlessly blend fantasy with learning. Epistemic games situate learners in professional roles. Within these professional roles they are given a significant number of challenges. For example, if the learner assumes the role of an en-

vironmental scientist, they conduct experiments; if they are an urban planner, they design city spaces; if they are a president of a country, they make decisions regarding national matters. The fantasy is playing a role in an authentic context that provides relevant challenges.

FUTURE RESEARCH DIRECTIONS

Based on the connections outlined between the teaching structures, game genres, and game characteristics, there are design implications for serious games. GBS feedback types may constitute a potential design heuristic for structuring the use of NPCs as pedagogical agents, but more research is needed in the role of pedagogical agents and intelligent tutoring systems in serious games.

Another possible area for research lies in designing serious games that integrate the instructor by disguising him/her within the context and narrative. Disguising the instructor would help remove any disruption of the immersive experience and provide opportunities to deliver the necessary coaching, scaffolding, and guiding.

One other area that suggests the need for research is on the differences in facilitating learning by using a RPG/adventure game versus a CMS. While RPG/adventure games appear to be well suited for serious games, CMSs (as discussed earlier) offer unique gameplay perspectives that might be best suited for certain types of instructional goals, namely understanding theories and models. Creating a serious game that takes advantage of both genres is an intriguing option worthy of research and development.

CONCLUSION

Problems are the essence of games, and solving problems is the essence of the challenges that games present. Serious games and the teaching structures have the same aim, and both strive to create authentic, relevant learning environments. Yet, the teaching structures make no mention of housing their components in a three-dimensional world, and the virtual worlds and context of games are enticing aspects for creating instructional environments. This begs the question; is that all we are using games for—to better present learning problems? To provide a better anchor for the instruction? To provide a more believable cover story? The answer is no, but without going beyond good stories, authentic contexts, and a sweet looking virtual world, serious games are only presenting a more believable anchor/problem/mission. This would not be a bad thing, as there is a long history of using technology to improve upon instruction (Cuban, 1986, 2001; Hannafin, Hannafin, Hooper, Rieber, & Kini, 1996), but in the end, if all this serious game movement amounts to is using the game technology to improve the teaching structures then we would have failed to live up to the potential of serious games.

If we use games to better present the problem, anchor, mission, etc., the next step is to make sure that the challenges, choices, and goals that spring from the presentation are structured to facilitate learning. This chapter made some connections between game genres, game characteristics, and constructivist teaching structures. Through elaborating on these connections, some design heuristics and ideas have emerged that may help serious games keep the fun and learning in perfect balance.

REFERENCES

Abt, C. (1970). *Serious games*. New York: Viking Press.

Adcock, A. B., Watson, G. S., Morrison, G. R., & Belfore, L. A. (in press). Effective knowledge development in game-based learning environments: Considering research in cognitive processes and simulation design. In Van Eck, R. (Ed.), *Gaming & cognition: Theories and practice from the learning sciences*. Hershey, PA: IGI Global.

Aldrich, C. (2004). *Simulations and the future of learning*. San Francisco, CA: Pfeiffer.

Aldrich, C. (2005). *Learning by doing*. San Francisco: Pfeiffer.

Alessi, M. S., & Trollip, S. R. (2001). *Multimedia for learning: Methods and development* (3rd ed.). Boston: Allyn and Bacon.

Anderson, B. (in press). The use of massive multiplayer online games in support of learning: An overview of current trends and future use. In Van Eck, R. (Ed.), *Gaming & cognition: Theories and practice from the learning sciences*. Hershey, PA: IGI Global.

Annetta, L. A., & Cheng, M. (2008). Why educational video games? In Annetta, L. A. (Ed.), *Serious educational games* (pp. 1–12). Rotterdam: Sense Publishers.

Becker, K. (2007). Pedagogy in commercial video games. In Gibson, D., Aldrich, C., & Prensky, M. (Eds.), *Games and simulations in online learning: Research and development frameworks* (p. 20). Hershey, PA: IGI.

Becker, K. (in press). Distinctions between games and learning? A review of the literature on games in education. In Van Eck, R. (Ed.), *Gaming & cognition: Theories and practice from the learning sciences*. Hershey, PA: IGI Global.

Charsky, D. (in press). From edutainment to serious games: A change in the use of game characteristics. *Games and Culture*.

Cognition & Technology Group at Vanderbilt. (1990). Anchored instruction and its relation to situated cognition. *Educational Researcher*, *19*(6), 2–10.

Cognition & Technology Group at Vanderbilt. (1992). Technology and the design of generative learning environments. In Jonassen, D. H., & Duffy, T. M. (Eds.), *Constructivism and the technology of instruction: A conversation*. Mahwah, NJ: Lawrence Erlbaum.

Collins, A., Brown, J. S., & Holum, A. (1991). Cognitive apprenticeship: Making thinking visible. *American Federation of Teachers, Winter*, 1-18.

Crawford, C. (2003). *Chris Crawford on game design*. Berkeley, CA: New Riders.

Crawford, C. (in press). Interactivity, process, and algorithm. In Van Eck, R. (Ed.), *Interdisciplinary models and tools for serious games: Emerging concepts and future directions*. Hershey, PA: IGI Global.

Cuban, L. (1986). *Teachers and machines: The classroom use of technology since 1920*. New York: Teacher's College Columbia University.

Cuban, L. (2001). *Oversold and underused: Computers in the classroom*. Cambridge, MA: Harvard University Press.

Dickey, M. D. (2005). Engaging by design: How engagement strategies in popular computer and video games can inform instructional design. *Educational Technology Research and Development, 53*(2), 67–83. doi:10.1007/BF02504866

Dickey, M. D. (2006). Game design narrative for learning: Appropriating adventure game design narrative devices and techniques for the design of interactive learning environments. *Educational Technology Research and Development, 54*(3), 245–264. doi:10.1007/s11423-006-8806-y

Duffy, T. M., & Cunningham, D. J. (1996). Constructivism: Implications for the design and delivery of instruction. In Jonassen, D. H. (Ed.), *Handbook of research for educational communications and technology* (pp. 170–198). New York: Simon & Schuster Macmillan.

Duffy, T. M., Lowyck, J., Jonassen, D. H., & Welch, T. M. (1993). *Designing environments for constructive learning*. New York: Springer-Verlag.

Ensemble Studios. (2005). *Age of Empires III* [Computer game]. USA: Microsoft Game Studios.

Firaxis. (2007). *Civilization IV* [Computer game]. USA: 2K Games.

Frontier. (2004). *RollerCoaster Tycoon III* [Computer game]. USA: Atari.

Gee, J. P. (2003). *What video games have to teach us about learning and literacy*. New York: Palgrave MacMillan.

Gee, J. P. (2005). What would a state of the art instructional video game look like? *Innovate, 1*(6). Retrieved from http://www.innovateonline.info/index.php?viewarticle&id=80

Gee, J. P. (2006). Learning and games [Electronic Version]. In K. Salen (Ed.), *The ecology of games: connecting youth, games, and learning* (pp. 21-40). Retrieved from http://www.mitpressjournals.org/doi/abs/10.1162/dmal.9780262693646.021

Gee, J. P. (2007). *Good video games + good learning*. New York: Peter Lang Publishing Inc.

Gunter, G. A., Kenny, R. F., & Vick, E. H. (2007). Taking educational games seriously: Using the RETAIN model to design endogenous fantasy into stand alone educational games. *Educational Technology Research and Development, 56*(5/6), 511–537.

Habgood, M. P. J., Ainsworth, S. E., & Benford, S. (2005). Endogenous fantasy and learning in digital games. *Simulation & Gaming, 36*(4), 483–498. doi:10.1177/1046878105282276

Hallford, N., & Hallford, J. (2001). *Swords & circuitry: A designers guide to computer role playing games*. Roseville, CA: Prima Publishing.

Hannafin, M. J. (1992). Emerging technologies, ISD, and learning environments: Critical perspectives. In Ely, D., & Plomp, T. (Eds.), *Classic writings on instructional technology* (Vol. 2, pp. 95–112). Englewood, CO: Libraries Unlimited, Inc.

Hannafin, M. J., Hannafin, K. M., Hooper, S. R., Rieber, L. P., & Kini, A. S. (1996). Research on and research with emerging technologies. In Jonassen, D. H. (Ed.), *Handbook of research for educational communications and technology* (pp. 378–402). New York: Simon & Schuster.

Hannafin, M. J., Land, S., & Oliver, K. (1999). Open learning environments: Foundations, methods, and models. In Reigeluth, C. M. (Ed.), *Instructional-design theories and models* (pp. 115–140). Mahwah, NJ: Lawrence Erlbaum.

Hannafin, M. J., & Peck, K. (1988). *The design, development and evaluation of instructional software*. New York: MacMillan Publishing Company.

Hoffman, B., & Ritchie, D. (1997). Using multimedia to overcome the problems with problem based learning. *Instructional Science*, *27*(25), 97–115. doi:10.1023/A:1002967414942

Hung, W., & Van Eck, R. (in press). Aligning problem solving and gameplay: A model for future research and design. In Van Eck, R. (Ed.), *Interdisciplinary models and tools for serious games: Emerging concepts and future directions*. Hershey, PA: IGI Global.

Iuppa, N., & Borst, T. (2007). *Story and simulations for serious games: Tales from the trenches*. Oxford, UK: Elsevier.

Jonassen, D. H. (1991). Objectivism versus constructivism: Do we need a new philosophical paradigm? In Ely, D. P., & Plomp, T. (Eds.), *Classic writings on instructional technology* (*Vol. 2*, pp. 53–65). Englewood, CO: Libraries Unlimited, Inc.

Jonassen, D. H. (1999). Designing constructivist learning environments. In Reigeluth, C. M. (Ed.), *Instructional-design theories and models* (*Vol. 2*). Mahwah, NJ: Lawrence Erlbaum Associates.

Jonassen, D. H., & Carr, C. S. (2000). Mindtools: Affording multiple knowledge representations for learning. In S. P. LaJoie (Ed.), Computers as cognitive tools, Volume II: No more walls. Mahwah, NJ: Lawrence Erlbaum Associates.

Jonassen, D. H., Carr, C. S., & Yeuh, H. (1998). Computers as mindtools for engaging learners in critical thinking. *TechTrends*, *43*(2), 24–32. doi:10.1007/BF02818172

Jonassen, D. H., Cernusca, D., & Ionas, G. (2007). Constructivism and instructional design: The emergence of the learning sciences and design research. In Reiser, R. A., & Dempsey, J. V. (Eds.), *Trends and issues in instructional design and technology* (2nd ed.). Upper Saddle River, NJ: Pearson.

Jonassen, D. H., & Reeves, T. C. (1996). Learning with technology: Using computers as cognitive tools. In Jonassen, D. H. (Ed.), *Handbook of research for educational communications and technology* (pp. 693–719). New York: Simon & Schuster Macmillan.

Kiili, K. (2007). Foundation for problem-based gaming. *British Journal of Educational Technology*, *38*(3), 394–404. doi:10.1111/j.1467-8535.2007.00704.x

Koster, R. (2005). *A theory of fun for game design*. Scottsdale, AZ: Paraglyph Press.

(2000). In LaJoie, S. P. (Ed.). Computers as cognitive tools: *Vol. II. No more walls*. Mahwah, NJ: Lawrence Erlbaum Associates.

Land, S., & Hannafin, M. (2000). Student-centered learning environments. In Jonassen, D. H., & Land, S. (Eds.), *Theoretical foundations of learning environments*. Mahwah, NJ: Lawrence Erlbaum Associates.

Lepper, M. R., & Cordova, D. L. (1992). A desire to be taught: Instructional consequences of intrinsic motivation. *Motivation and Emotion*, *16*(3), 187–208. doi:10.1007/BF00991651

Low, R., Sweller, J., & Jin, P. (in press). Learner's cognitive load when using educational technology. In Van Eck, R. (Ed.), *Gaming & cognition: Theories and practice from the learning sciences*. Hershey, PA: IGI Global.

Malone, T. W. (1981). Towards a theory of intrinsic motivation. *Cognitive Science, 4*, 333–369.

Malone, T. W., & Lepper, M. R. (1987). Making learning fun: A taxonomy of intrinsic motivations for learning. In Snow, R., & Farr, M. (Eds.), *Aptitude, learning and instruction: III. Cognitive and affective process analysis* (pp. 223–253). Hillsdale, NJ: Erlbaum.

Maxis. (2003) *SimCity IV* [Computer game]. USA: Electronic Arts.

Minnesota Educational Computer Consortium. (1988). *Number Munchers* [Computer game]. USA: Minnesota Educational Computer Consortium.

Perkins, D. N., & Unger, C. (1999). Teaching and learning for understanding. In Reigeluth, C. M. (Ed.), *Instructional-design theories and models*. Mahwah, NJ: Lawrence Erlbaum.

Prensky, M. (2001). *Digital game-based learning*. New York: McGraw-Hill.

Rollings, A., & Adams, E. (2003). *Andrew Rollings and Ernest Adams on game design*. Berkeley, CA: New Riders Publishing.

Rouse, R. (2005). *Game design: Theory & practice*. Plano, TX: Wordware Publishing, Inc.

Savery, J. R. (2006). Overview of problem based learning: Definitions and distinctions. *Interdisciplinary Journal of Problem Based Learning, 1*(1), 9–20.

Savery, J. R., & Duffy, T. M. (1995). Problem based learning: An instructional model and its constructivist framework. *Educational Technology, 35*, 31–38.

Sawyer, B. (2006). *Serious games*. Retrieved from http://www.seriousgames.org./index.html

Schank, R. C., Berman, T. R., & Macpherson, K. A. (1999). Learning by doing. In Reigeluth, C. M. (Ed.), *Instructional-design theories and models*. Mahwah, NJ: Lawrence Erlbaum.

Schank, R. C., Fano, A., Bell, B., & Jona, M. (1994). The design of goal based scenarios. *Journal of the Learning Sciences, 3*(4), 305–345. doi:10.1207/s15327809jls0304_2

Shaffer, D. (2005). *Epistemic games*. Retrieved from http://www.innovateonline.info/index.php?view=article&id=79

Shaffer, D. W. (2006). *How computer games help children learn*. New York: Palgrave MacMillan. doi:10.1057/9780230601994

Squire, K. (2002). Cultural framing of computer games. *The international journal of computer game research*. Retrieved February 2003, from http://www.gamestudies.org/0102/squire/

Steinkuehler, C. A. (2004). *Learning in massively multiplayer online games*. Paper presented at the International Conference on Learning Sciences, Santa Monica, CA.

Van Eck, R. (2007a). Building intelligent learning games. In Gibson, D., Aldrich, C., & Prensky, M. (Eds.), *Games and simulations in online learning research & development frameworks*. Hershey, PA: Idea Group.

Van Eck, R. (2007b). Six ideas in search of a discipline. In Shelton, B. E., & Wiley, D. A. (Eds.), *The design and use of simulation computer games in education*. Rotterdam, The Netherlands: Sense Publishing.

APPENDIX: ADDITIONAL READING

"Must-Reads" for This Topic

Becker K. (2007). Pedagogy in commercial video games. In D. Gibson, C. Aldrich and M. Prensky (Eds.), *Games and simulations in online learning: research and development frameworks*, Hershey, PA: Idea Group. (pp. XX)

Cognition & Technology Group at Vanderbilt. (1992). Technology and the design of generative learning environments. In D. H. Jonassen, and Duffy, T. M. (Ed.), *Constructivism and the technology of instruction: A conversation*. Mahwah, NJ: Lawrence Erlbaum.

Collins, A., Brown, J. S., & Holum, A. (1991). Cognitive apprenticeship: Making thinking visible. *American Federation of Teachers, Winter*, 1-18.

Dickey, M. D. (2005). Engaging by design: How engagement strategies in popular computer and video games can inform instructional design. *Educational Technology, Research, & Development, 53*(2), 67-83.

Hannafin, M. J., Land, S., & Oliver, K. (1999). Open learning environments: Foundations, methods, and models. In C. M. Reigeluth (Ed.), *Instructional-design theories and models* (pp. 115-140). Mahwah, NJ: Lawrence Erlbaum.

Rollings, A., & Adams, E. (2003). *Andrew Rollings and Ernest Adams on game design*. Berkeley, CA: New Riders Publishing.

Rouse, R. (2005). *Game design: Theory & practice*. Plano, TX: Wordware Publishing, Inc.

Savery, J. R. (2006). Overview of problem based learning: Definitions and distinctions. *Interdisciplinary Journal of Problem Based Learning, 1*(1), 9-20.

Schank, R. C., Berman, T. R., & Macpherson, K. A. (1999). Learning by doing. In C. M. Reigeluth (Ed.), *Instructional-design theories and models*. Mahwah, NJ: Lawrence Erlbaum.

Van Eck, R. (2007). Building intelligent learning games. In D. Gibson, C. Aldrich, & M. Prensky (Eds.) *Games and simulations in online learning research & development frameworks*. Hershey, PA: Idea Group.

Top Texts for Interdisciplinary Studies of Serious Games

Aldrich, C. (2005). *Learning by doing*. San Francisco: Pfeiffer.

Alessi, M. S., & Trollip, S. R. (2001). *Multimedia for learning: Methods and development* (3rd ed.). Boston: Allyn and Bacon.

Bogost, I. (2007). *Persuasive games: The expressive power of videogames*. Cambridge, MA: The MIT Press.

Garris, R., Ahlers, R., & Driskell, J. E. (2002). Games, motivation, and learning: A research and practice model. *Simulation & Gaming, 33*(4), 441 - 467.

Gee, J. P. (2003). *What video games have to teach us about learning and literacy*. New York: Palgrave MacMillan.

Iuppa, N., & Borst, T. (2007). *Story and simulations for serious games: tales from the trenches*. New York: Focal Press.

Laveault, P., & Corbeil, P. (1990). Assessing the impact of simulation games on learning: A step-by-step approach. *Simulation/games for learning, 20*(1), 42-54.

Rieber, L. P., Smith, L., & Noah, D. (1998). The value of serious play. *Educational Technology, 38*(6), 29-37.

Van Eck, R. (2007). Building intelligent learning games. In D. Gibson, C. Aldrich, & M. Prensky (Eds.) *Games and simulations in online learning research & development frameworks*. Hershey, PA: Idea Group.

Van Deventer, S., & White, J. (2002). Expert behavior in children's videogame play. *Simulation & Gaming, 33*(1).

Chapter 10
Activity–Based Scenario Design, Development, and Assessment in Serious Games

Tim Marsh
National University of Singapore, Singapore

ABSTRACT

Serious gaming environments provide the potential to create player activities and opportunities to design for experience. A flexible, powerful and rich way to create, represent and characterize player activities in serious games is through scenarios. Scenarios are stories: they are realized through text descriptions and supporting artwork such as storyboards and sketches. In this way, they illustrate a game's scenes, settings, circumstances and situations, as well as the possible future sequence or choice of events that make-up a game's narrative flow. While the flexibility of scenarios makes them useful for describing player activities, the lack of tools and methodologies to guide their design may lead to the use of ad hoc non-standardized language. Borrowing from film, HCI, and activity theory, this chapter describes a hierarchical activity-based framework that on the one hand is sufficiently flexible to support the design and development of scenarios at any level of complexity, while on the other hand provides a standard template and language with which to frame scenarios in serious game design. The proposed framework provides a way to bridge the gaps between design, development, and implementation of serious games. In addition, it incorporates a multi-level structure providing multiple units of analysis (a variable lens) for analyzing learning from objectives to goals and subgoals.

INTRODUCTION

Although users have been interacting with computer and video games for decades, published work on gaming in the literature of human-computer interac-

tion (HCI) has been limited until recently. Despite this lack of research, the computer games industry has become one of the most lucrative technological and media industries, raising questions about whether the HCI community really has anything to offer the industry in terms of the advancement of games development. What HCI can provide, how-

DOI: 10.4018/978-1-61520-717-6.ch010

ever, is a research base to inform design theories and methodologies to guide design and evaluation of games and player experience. Over time, methods become validated through extensive trial and testing, leading to wider use and standardization. Another sector that would arguably gain from this is simulation and game-based learning. This is because the development of validated and standardized evaluation and design methodologies opens opportunities to create digital games for learning based on sound design principles and pedagogical theories, integrate learning objectives, help design for anticipated outcomes, and incorporate or develop valid techniques for the assessment of learning. In addition, standardized and validated evaluation and design methodologies can inform researchers and educators as they develop their own games and strive to assess the learning that results.

It has been widely touted that the engaging and motivational aspects of video games can be incorporated with educational components to transform the way people learn and make learning more enjoyable. It is because of this that many sectors and organizations from business, health, military, and education the world over are considering the potential of serious games to support learning and to complement existing teaching materials and resources. Despite the fact that advocates of serious games and game-based learning now have the world's attention, there remains little in the way of standardized tools and approaches for assessment of learning in serious games (Chen & Michael, 2005) and little in the way of design guidelines that embrace "well-established and practical instructional theories" and "good game design principles" (Gunter, Kenny, & Vick, 2006). To overcome this, several researchers have argued for taking game-based learning more 'seriously.' For example, Zyda (2007) suggests a need for "creating a science of games," Van Eck (2007) argues for a more rigorous research approach with game-based learning, and Marsh (2007) calls for "serious approaches and methodologies

for serious games." While some propose "design dimensions" (Hendriksen, 2006) and "formal design principles," incorporating learning theories (Gunter et al., 2006) for serious games, is largely theoretical work rather than operationalized, applied, and tested research.

Recently we have witnessed an increase in published serious games literature outside of HCI. However, rather than pursuing a complementary research and development approach, much of this work focuses on development alone. Generally this involves building ad-hoc games for a specific purpose or situation, paying little attention to research that can go towards the creation of tried and tested design guidelines or tools supporting underlying theories of learning to demonstrate a game's learning or educational value or how it can generalize to a wide range of serious games learning environments.

Serious games provide designers and developers with opportunities to create activities for players and the potential to design for experience. Activities in serious games are for purposes other than, but also including, entertainment. An increasing array of categories are used to encapsulate emerging purposes for serious games (e.g., learning, training, education, health, well-being, for change, persuasion, experiential). Specifically, purpose in a serious game is achieved by undertaking a number of actions in order to reach or fulfill the serious game's objective. A flexible, powerful and rich way to represent actions in serious games is through story, narrative or scenario. While such approaches imply a narratological approach to tell a story (Crawford, 2004) and engage the player (Murray, 1997), it is also argued that they can incorporate rules (i.e., ludology, where mastery of rules leads to player engagement, Juul, 2005) or that at least narrative and rules can coexist side-by-side in a game.

This chapter describes a framework that addresses important challenges facing serious games development; namely, the creation of scenarios in such a way as to also allow assessment of learning outcomes. I start by describing earlier work in scenario and scenario-based design from the HCI literature to support interaction design. This is, in many respects, analogous to storytelling, narrative, and scenario in film and theatre. Next, I describe a framework based on extended research in activity theory and scenario design research in HCI that generalizes to many serious games purposes. The framework will then be applied to the development of a serious game. Finally, directions for future work are described.

SCENARIO CREATION IN HCI AND FILM

Scenarios and scenario-based design methods have a long history in HCI. Scenario-based design methods in HCI are narrative descriptions or a "sketch of use" of people using technologies (Rosson & Carroll, 2002a, p. 1032). They have been found to be particularly appropriate for interaction design, both in analyzing how future technologies shape people's activities and in guiding the design and development of technologies that enable use experiences (Rosson & Carroll, 2002b). Crampton Smith & Tabor (2006) refer to scenarios as "the imagining of a fictional situation and its representation as a written narrative... storyboard, performance, or video, within which possible interactive behaviors between users and systems emerge."

Nardi (1995, p. 393) describes scenarios succinctly as deriving from two things:

i.   the inclusion of context
ii. a narrative format, as in a text narrative or storyboard

She suggests that if these characteristics are missing, then the term scenario can seem very similar to other areas of design and analysis in HCI such as, "user requirement," or "feature," or "test pattern," or "system configuration," etc.

The key advantage of scenarios as used in HCI is that they can be adapted to different styles of human practice (Karat, 1995; Nardi, 1995). While work with scenarios in HCI is usually restricted to human practice involving work and work-related activities, a key advantage arising from the flexibility of scenarios is their potential to describe a plethora of genres (e.g., learning, training, education, entertainment). Furthermore, scenarios provide a means of "embodying and communicating user experience" (Nardi, 1995, p. 396), offer "a rich view of ...experiences of users," (Rosson & Carroll, 1995, p. 268) and as suggested by (Nardi, 1995, p. 398), "will undoubtedly remain a part of our design repertoire as we push forward toward more theoretical means of predicting and explaining user experience."

In spite of their flexibility, Kuutti (1995) argues that there is no generally accepted definition and their use and scope in different contexts varies drastically. He divides these varying definitions into two main approaches. The first is scenario as an external description of what a system does, for example, "to specify use scenarios that cover all possible pathways through the system functions" (Rubin, 1994). The second approach sets scenarios in a wider context. For example, this is "the 'big picture' of how some particular kind of work gets done" in social settings, with resources, and goals of users (Kuutti, 1995, p. 21, citing Nardi, 1992). In addition, Crampton Smith & Tabor (2006) draw our attention to a third approach elucidated in the work of Brenda Laurel, to account for the improvisational ("improv") or unpredictable way that things occur or are played out.

It is no stretch to see how these different approaches to defining scenarios might just as easily apply to simulation, games and serious games environments. The combination of all three approaches makes scenarios potentially powerful for use in simulation, games and serious games environments. This is because of their flexibility to either cover all possible pathways or the improvisational or unpredictable nature of interaction (e.g., to travel between two points, in the use of an artifact, or communication between characters) or the "big picture" approach focusing on context, setting, situation, resources and player goals.

Other areas where a more creative approach to scenario development is central and which games and serious game scenario development can draw upon is film and theatre. As scenarios imply temporal components or episodes, they begin to resemble the unfolding events of a film or theatrical performance.

In Carroll's (2000) description of scenarios in HCI, we can see the close resemblance to scenarios in film and games. They "presuppose setting," "include agents or actors" and "have a plot; they include sequences of actions and events, things that actors do, things that happen to them, changes in the circumstances of the setting, and so forth" (pp. 46-47).

The similarity between scenarios, scripts/ screenplays of films or theatrical plays, and scenarios with virtual, gaming and serious games environments is further illustrated by looking at dictionary definitions of scenarios in film and theatre.

1a. A sketch or outline of the plot of a play, ballet, novel, opera, story, etc., giving particulars of the scenes, situations etc; 1b. ...A film script with all the details of scenes, appearances of characters, stage-directions, etc., necessary for shooting the film; 2. A sketch, outline, or description of an imagined situation or sequence of events; esp. (a) ...outline of any possible sequence of future events; (b) an outline of an intended course of action; (c) ...circumstances, situation, scene, sequence of events, etc. (Oxford English Dictionary 1989)

Indeed, story or script writers of early film were referred to as scenario writers. For example, D. W. Griffith, who is considered one of the leading pioneers of filmmaking, began his career by writing scenarios whose emergence marks the beginning of narrative film (Loughney, 1990). It is no surprise then, that scenarios have long been

proposed as a means of representing participant actions in virtual and gaming environments by virtue of their connection to theatre (Laurel, 1993) and film (Laurel, Strickland & Tow, 1994; Pausch, Snoddy, Taylor, Watson & Haseltine, 1996).

Thus, by drawing parallels between scenarios in games and scenarios in film, theatre and HCI, a natural next step is to look to the more mature scenario processes used in HCI as well as to the creative scenario processes of film and theatre to inform scenario creation in games.

While the flexibility of scenarios makes them useful for describing human actions in wider contexts, as argued herein, this flexibility can also be a limitation in their application to gaming and serious game environments. Kuutti (1995, p. 33) suggests that one problem with scenarios lies in their ad hoc language (i.e., non-formalized and left up to the developer) and that a challenge for the future is to find "a more standard language" in which to talk about and structure scenarios. One approach to solving this challenge is to provide a standard "template" in which to describe scenarios. For example, in HCI Beyer & Holtzblatt (1998) provide five complementary models for describing work (e.g., flow, cultural, sequence, artifact and physical). However, the focus of this approach is centered primarily on work-related activities.

Another example appropriate to non-work as well as work-related activities is Kenneth Burke's "Pentad," (e.g., Wertsch, Del Rio & Alvarez, 1995). This approach includes agent, act, agency, scene and purpose to study human motivation through analysis of drama. While this is an interesting direction for future research, my interest in this chapter is in the extension of the hierarchical framework and concepts provided by activity theory. Indeed, Kuutti (1995, p. 33) provides support to this direction by suggesting that activity theory is a potential approach for structuring scenarios. The next section extends concepts from activity theory to provide a standard template and language in which to structure scenarios in serious games.

ACTIVITY-BASED SCENARIOS IN SERIOUS GAMES

Originating from Soviet psychology, activity theory has been usefully applied to interaction design and analysis in HCI because it is "a powerful and clarifying descriptive tool" (Nardi, 1996, p. 7). However, it can be argued that the adoption of activity theory is not as widespread as it could be because it is relatively difficult and time consuming to understand in comparison to other analysis and design methodologies in HCI. Compounding this difficulty, two activity theory approaches currently co-exist: the original approach of activity theory proposed in Leontiev's (1978; 1981) hierarchical framework of activity and Engeström's (1987; 1999 expanded activity triangle to incorporate social/collective activity.

While essentially developing from similar roots found in the work of Vygotsky, the two approaches are different and even have "different views" for the same concept (e.g., object; Kaptelinin & Nardi 2006, p. 141). However, I argue that a clear distinction between these two approaches isn't always made and at worse concepts from both approaches have been mixed together, and subsequently this has led to misunderstandings and confusion. A detailed account of the historical developments and the similarities, differences, and tensions between Leontiev's (1978; 1981) and Engeström's (1987; 1999 activity theory approaches is beyond the scope of this chapter. For an informed discussion, the interested reader is referred to Kaptelinin & Nardi (2006).

The focus in HCI has been primarily on Engeström's (1987; 1990) approach, largely because of its expansion to analysis of social/collective activities. However, this chapter focuses on Leontiev's activity theory approach in general, and in particular the work contained in Leontiev (1981). This is because it is arguably the most practical and operationalized theory in terms of the support for design and development of scenarios in serious games, and because it incorporates a multilevel structure providing multiple units of analysis (variable lens) that can be extended to analysis of learning. To aid the reader, each concept and feature of the activity theory-based framework will be clearly described and annotated.

As illustrated in Figure 1, central to activity theory is Leontiev's (1981) hierarchical framework of activity composed of *activity, actions* and *operations* and characterized respectively by *objective, goals and conditions*, as discussed below. The hierarchical structure is not static, but dynamic, with shifts between activity, actions and operations determined by situations and circumstances of the scenario.

Activity is directed towards achieving an *objective* as denoted by "a." The objective is a process characterizing the activity as a whole. For example, consider a hypothetical game in which the objective is to overthrow an unscrupulous ruler. When the objective is fulfilled the activity ends. The objective is closely related to motive, and the motive is the intention that stimulates and drives a player in a game / to play a game. In our hypothetical example, the motive is to return the kingdom to its rightful heir and restore peace. In activity theory, the objective's outcome and motive have to be considered in the analysis of "activity proper" (Leontiev, 1981, pp. 399-400). This provides the basis for framing activity for assessment. With serious games this provides the basis to reason about learning.

Activity is made up of a combination of *actions* as denoted by "b" in Figure 1. "Activity is what gives meaning [intention] to our actions" (Bannon & Bødker, 1991, p. 242). The action level contains the heart of the scenario, using text, graphics, storyboards, etc. to describe the game environment (e.g., settings, surroundings, circumstances), the game mechanics, and what players do. Actions are performed with conscious thought and effort, and are planned and directed towards achieving a *goal*. Nardi (1996) states that actions can be considered similar to what the HCI literature refers to as tasks. Objectives

Figure 1. Hierarchical Framework of Activity applied to games: (a) activity; (b) action; (c) operation; (d) shift in focus of attention from actions to operations; (e) shift in focus of attention from operations to actions; (f) transformation from action to activity; (g) shift in focus of attention from gaming to real world; (h) boundary for gaming context of use

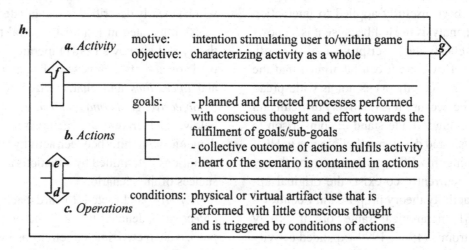

and goals provide units for analysis through the fulfillment of activities and actions respectively, and this informs design.

Actions may themselves be made up of subactions directed towards subgoals, and subactions can be made up of sub-subactions directed to sub-subgoals, and so on. This depends on the level of complexity that is required by the scenario. Each subaction/subgoal has to be fulfilled in order to fulfill the higher-level action. For example, consider an action/goal in the aforementioned hypothetical game to enter a castle. In order to enter the castle, the player first has to fulfill the subaction/subgoal of lowering and then crossing a drawbridge. Before lowering the drawbridge, the player has to fulfill the sub-subaction/sub-subgoal to find gold coins to pay the gatekeeper. The fulfillment of actions/goals, subactions/subgoals and so on, not only provides an indication of task-level completion, but in serious games can also serve as an indication of learning.

Actions are performed by a combination of *operations.* Operations are processes performed with little conscious thought or effort in the use of physical interactive and virtual in-game artifacts

triggered by conditions of actions as denoted by "c" in Figure 1. Players' shifts in focus between action and operation levels provide an indication of learning. For example, the early phases of learning to use an artifact will have been performed with deliberate and conscious attention. At this point they are actions. When they become well practiced and experienced, actions become routine. That is, they do not need to be planned and at such a point are performed with little conscious thought or effort. In this way, actions become operations as represented by the downward pointing vertical arrow "d" in Figure 1. This provides a way to reason about the *mastery of artifacts/tools.* Conversely, operations become actions when something goes wrong, impedes interaction, or is associated with user-player learning. Unfamiliarity with interaction or an interface, or reflecting on the learning content of a serious game are examples of operations becoming actions. Players' shifts in focus of attention are represented by the upward pointing lower vertical arrow "e" in Figure 1. Following the work of Bødker (1996) and Winograd & Flores (1986), this provides a way to reason about and design for "focus shifts" and "breakdown," respectively.

Breakdown and learning may also be the cause of shifting players' focus of attention from the virtual or gaming environment context (depicted by rectangle "h") to the real world (denoted by the horizontal arrow "g"). The cause of this shift in focus of attention can be design problems, interruption or disruption, shifting from in-game to off-game learning actions/activities, or momentarily taking time out from interacting with the serious game to reflect/contemplate on the subject matter.

Activity Proper: Objective Outcome Coincides with Motive as a Measure of Learning

As previously discussed, an objective is a process characterizing the activity as a whole and is closely related to *motive*. According to Leontiev (1981), an activity without motive cannot exist. Whether intrinsically or extrinsically driven (Malone, 1981), motive stimulates a player to begin an encounter or to continue an encounter in a serious game. A player's motive for playing a serious game may be, for example, "some special need," interest, "to understand," "to comprehend," for fun, enjoyment, or pleasure (Leontiev, 1981, p. 36). Both the outcome from an objective and the motive have to be considered in the analysis of activity (Leontiev, 1981).

If the objective outcome of performing actions of an activity with a serious game is the inducement of appropriate and/or stimulating learning experience, the objective outcome will coincide with the motive that stimulated the player to begin or to continue an encounter. Then, in the words of Leontiev, (1981: 399-400) it is "activity proper." Hence, the encounter is successful. When the objective is fulfilled the activity ends. On the other hand, if the objective outcome does not provide appropriate and/or stimulating learning experience then it does not coincide with motive (Leontiev, 1981). So for example, returning to our hypothetical game, if the outcome of the objective is to overthrow the unscrupulous ruler then it has been fulfilled and coincides with the motive to return the kingdom to its rightful heir and restore peace.

Stimulating Experience: Doing it Because we Want to Do It

One of the interesting implications of activity theory, especially as applied to games, is that it is possible for an action to be so stimulating that it actually becomes its own activity. According to Leontiev (1981), this transformation is the result of "an action's result [outcome] being more significant…than the motive that actually induces it" (p. 403). Hence, it can be postulated that if actions performed within serious games are stimulating enough, then players continue to engage with the game because they want to, which transforms the action itself into "activity proper" as illustrated by the upper arrow "f" in Figure 1.

This provides a way for evaluators to reason about extrinsic drives (e.g., having to learn) transforming into intrinsic motives (playing/learning because we want to) through innovative design that is stimulating. Hence, this can provide an operational definition for engagement in serious games learning environments. The implication for designers is then to design serious games that promote stimulating actions that transform into their own activities.

Summary: Hierarchical Activity-Based Scenario

To summarize, the hierarchical activity-based scenario approach provides a flexible and dynamic conceptual framework that supports serious game design, development and analysis in the following ways:

1.   Hierarchical structure aids design, creation and modeling of scenarios and narratives (from high-level activities/objectives,

through actions/goals to low-level operations of physical/virtual artifacts) to any level of complexity from conception to finished game.

2. Action level contains the heart or guts of the scenario, describing and representing (e.g., through text, graphic, and storyboards, etc.) what players do, as well as settings, surroundings, circumstances.

3. Concepts and framework to dynamically trace and model player behavior/acting in the scenario during gameplay.

4. Shifts in focus of attention between levels from operations to actions as represented on the bottom vertical arrow in Figure 1 help identify when something goes wrong and/or where there is problematic design (e.g., glitch or design bug), or is associated with player learning (e.g., contemplating the serious games' subject matter).

5. Incorporates a method to frame and reason about: (i) the degree to which a game's scenario or backstory has been successful through the fulfillment of actions/goals and objectives; (ii) the degree to which learning experience from gameplay has been successful (through the objective outcome of activity coinciding with the motive that stimulates a player to or within the game).

6. The framework incorporates a way to reason about the situation in which an action becomes so stimulating that it drives itself and transforms into an activity. This transformation is the result of "an action's result [outcome] being more significant...than the motive that actually induces it" (Leontiev, 1981). Hence, it can be postulated that if any outcome from game-based learning is stimulating enough then, players/users do it because they want to do it.

Putting it all Together: Activity-Based Scenario Support for Serious Game Development

The hierarchical activity-based scenario approach can be used throughout the development cycle from conception to finished game. In the very early stages of design, it can be used as a guide to identify and partition processes/elements that will make up the activity (e.g., learning objective, scenario of what the player will do, actions/goals in order to fulfill the objective, etc.).

The hierarchical activity-based scenario approach can be used to support game writers, designers, and/or development teams to generate a high-level set of ideas and concepts for gameplay during or after the creation of a scenario. Fullerton (2008) provides an informative practical guide to game brainstorming, idea and concept generation. In addition, the hierarchical activity-based scenario approach can be used to guide and support students in the constructionist approach of making games to learn as opposed to the instructionist approach of playing games to learn (e.g., Kafai, 2006; Papert, 1993).

To illustrate how the hierarchical activity-based scenario approach supports the development of serious games, I describe the development of a serious game learning environment for University of Southern California undergraduate students whose major is engineering and minor is Biology. The development of the game was part of an NSF funded research project. The purpose of the game was to allow players to learn about topics from the curriculum relating to physical and biological processes of human organs.

In reference to Figure 2, the gaming scenario or backstory provided an overall motive for students to interact within the game (i.e., help to save humankind) by attempting to fulfill the activity's objective (i.e., to revive a world renowned medical research scientist from a coma so he can continue his research) that characterizes the activity as a whole. We recall from activity theory that a successful activity is one in which the motive and objective outcome are aligned. Accordingly, for our game, the scenario would be successful to the extent that reviving the scientist from his coma (objective outcome) would allow him to continue his research to help save humankind (motive).

It is important to recognize that when designing a serious game, the learning objectives of a course may or may not correspond with a game activity's objective, depending for example on the complexity of the topics for learning and the crafting of the games' scenarios. In our example, learning objectives for topics of the undergraduate course were carefully integrated into the game's scenarios. Hence, the learning objectives were integrated into the high-level actions. In keeping with the scenario or backstory of the educational serious game, the high-level actions, containing the heart of the scenario as outlined in (2) above, were referred to as missions and are shown below:

- provide energy source and reactivate digestion and adsorption processes
- regulate available blood sugar and restore systems that maintain blood glucose

The fulfillment of these main goals then provides an indication of the degree to which the outcome from the objective (i.e., to revive world-renowned scientist) was successful as outlined in (5) above. Figure 2 illustrates the representation of one action-goal in the hierarchical activity-based framework. The goal to *regulate available blood sugar and restore systems that maintain blood glucose* involves the subgoal of *unlocking the wormhole* to enter the scientist's organs and is fulfilled by carrying out the sub-subgoal to identify the *pancreas, liver and muscle*; and the subgoal to *increase blood glucose level* is fulfilled by *collecting glucagons,* and so on. So the lowest level goal must be fulfilled first, followed by the fulfillment of the next higher-level goal, and so on, in order to fulfill the highest-level goal.

As mentioned previously, actions are performed by a combination of *operations*. Operations are processes performed with little thought or attention in the use of artifacts both physical (e.g., keyboard, mouse, novel devices) and virtual (e.g., artifacts, objects, environment) triggered by conditions of actions (physical and virtual). Hence, using the activity-based scenario approach, evaluators and developers can dynamically observe and model player's behavior and interactions with the

Figure 2. Example showing one goal of the hierarchical activity-based scenario for a serious game

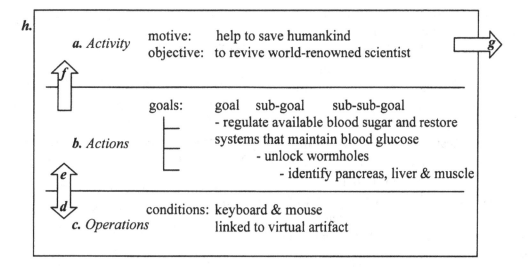

scenario as outlined in (3) above. Observing and coding shifts in levels of the activity provides a way to identify disruptions, problematic design and learning. This information can in turn be used to inform design to make improvements or as an indication of learning as outlined in (4) above. Finally, as observed through observation, and confirmed in debriefing sessions, playing this educational serious game and attempting to fulfill its actions-goals was enjoyable for students. As outlined in (6) above, this provides some evidence to show that having to play this game for most students may have transformed into playing because it was enjoyable for them. Hence, in turn, it is not difficult to see that students may be learning because they want to learn through innovative serious games design that is stimulating.

FUTURE RESEARCH DIRECTIONS

There are many possible extensions and potential future research directions building on the work presented herein. One important future direction for research is the extension of the activity-based scenario approach to support design and analysis of in-game as well as off-game learning. For example, the use of serious games in the classroom in which the learning activity encompasses both the actions in the game and in the classroom. Another future research direction is the extension of the activity-based scenario approach presented herein with Engeström's (1987; 1990) expanded activity triangle, for example, to incorporate collective play. Steps in this direction are already underway. While I have presented an activity-based scenario approach that builds on scenario development in HCI, film and theater, the integration of these approaches can be further tightened. While the activity-based scenario approach provides a way to structure text descriptions and supporting artwork (e.g., storyboards and sketches) of scenarios, future work should draw more upon the creative process of scenario development in

film and theater to further support the creative development of scenarios in serious games. At the same time, more consideration should be given to the player as coauthor in the unfolding scenario of a game.

CONCLUSION

Borrowing from film, HCI and activity theory, this chapter has described a framework, tool and approach to support scenario design and development through stages of a serious game's life cycle. On the one hand, the framework is sufficiently flexible to support the design and development of scenarios at any level of complexity, while on the other hand it provides a standard template (i.e., activity-objective, action-goal, operation-condition, etc.) and language with which to frame scenarios in serious games. This provides a way to bridge the gap between the processes of design, development, and implementation of serious games. In addition, the framework also incorporates a variable lens for analyzing learning objectives, goals, subgoals, and so on. The focus of this chapter is on how the activity-based scenario approach incorporates concepts to support learning, is informed by scenario-based design in HCI and film and theater, and how it can be used to support the development of serious games.

REFERENCES

Bannon, L., & Bødker, S. (1991). Beyond the interface: Encountering artifacts in use. In Carroll, J. M. (Ed.), *Designing Interaction: Psychology at the Human-Computer Interface* (pp. 227–253). New York: Cambridge University Press.

Beyer, H., & Holtzblatt, K. (1998). *Contextual design: Defining customer-centered systems*. London: Academic Press.

Bødker, S. (1996). Applying activity theory to video analysis: How to make sense of video data in human-computer interaction. In Nardi, B. (Ed.), *Context and consciousness: Activity theory and human-computer interaction* (pp. 147–174). Cambridge, MA: MIT Press.

Carroll, J. M. (2000). *Making use: Scenarios and scenario-based design*. London: MIT Press.

Chen, S., & Michael, D. (2005 October). Proof of learning: Assessment in serious games. *Gamasutra*.

Crampton Smith, G., & Tabor, P. (2006). More Than One Way of Knowing. In Bagnara, S., & Crampton Smith, G. (Eds.), *Theories and Practice in Interaction Design* (pp. 117–124). Mahwah, NJ: Lawrence Erlbaum Associates, Inc.

Crawford, C. (2004). *Chris Crawford on Interactive Storytelling*. Indianapolis, IN: New Riders.

Engeström, Y. (1987). *Learning by Expanding: An activity-theoretical approach to developmental research*. Helsinki, Finland: Orienta–Konsultit.

Engeström, Y. (1999). Activity theory and individual and social transformation. In Engeström, Y., Miettinen, R., & Punamäki, P. (Eds.), *Perspectives on activity theory-learning in doing social, cognitive and computational perspectives, part 1: Theoretical issues* (pp. 19–38). Cambridge, UK: Cambridge University Press.

Fullerton, T. (2008). *Game design workshop: A playcentric approach to creating innovative games* (2nd ed.). Burlington, MA: Morgan Kaufman.

Gunter, G., Kenny, R., & Vick, E. (2006). A case for a formal design paradigm for serious games. *The Journal of the International Digital Media and Arts Association, 3*(1), 93–105.

Hendriksen, T. D. (2006). *Educational role-play: Moving beyond entertainment. Seeking to please or aiming for the stars*. Conference paper presented at "On Playing Roles" Seminar, Tampere, FL.

Juul, J. (2005). *Half-real. Video games between real rules and fictional worlds*. Cambridge, MA: MIT Press.

Kafai, Y. (2006, January). Playing and making games for learning: Instructionist and constructionist perspectives for game studies. *Games and Culture, 1*(1), 36–40. doi:10.1177/1555412005281767

Kaptelinin, V., & Nardi, B. (2006). *Acting with technology: Activity theory and interaction design*. Boston, MA: MIT Press.

Karat, J. (1995). Scenario use in the design of a speech recognition system. In Carroll, J. (Ed.), *Scenarios as design representations* (pp. 109–133). London: Academic Press.

Kuutti, K. (1995). Work processes: Scenarios as a preliminary vocabulary. In Carroll, J. M. (Ed.), *Scenario-based design: Envisioning work and technology in system development* (pp. 19–36). New York: John Wiley and Sons.

Laurel, B. (1993). *Computers as theatre* (2nd ed.). Reading, MA: Addison–Wesley.

Laurel, B., Strickland, R., & Tow, R. (1994). Placeholder: Landscape and Narrative in virtual environments. *ACM SIGGRAPH Computer Graphics, 28*(2), 118–126. doi:10.1145/178951.178967

Leontiev, A. N. (1978). *Activity, consciousness, and personality*. Englewood Cliffs, NJ: Prentice–Hall.

Leontiev, A. N. (1981). *Problems of the development of the mind*. Moscow: Progress.

Loughney, P. G. (1990). In the beginning was the word: Six pre-griffith motion picture scenarios. In Elsaesser, T. (Ed.), *Early cinema: space, frame, narrative* (pp. 211–219). London: BFI Publishing.

Malone, T. W. (1981). Toward a theory of intrinsically motivating instruction. *Cognitive Science, 4*, 333–369.

Marsh, T. (2007). *Informing design and evaluation methodologies for serious games for learning. Presented at Learning with Games 2007.* France: Sofia Antipolis.

Murray, J. H. (1997). *Hamlet on the holodeck – The future of narrative in cyberspace.* Cambridge, MA: MIT Press.

Nardi, B. (1992). The Use of Scenarios in Design. *ACM SIGCHI Bulletin. International Perspectives: Some Dialogue on Scenarios, 24*(4), 13–14.

Nardi, B. (1995). Some reflections on scenarios. In Carroll, J. (Ed.), *Scenarios as design representations* (pp. 387–399). London: Academic Press.

Nardi, B. (1996). Activity theory and human-computer interaction. In Nardi, B. (Ed.), *Context and consciousness: Activity theory and human-computer interaction* (pp. 7–16). Cambridge, MA: MIT Press.

Papert, S. (1993). *The children's machine: Rethinking school in the age of the computer.* New York: Basic Books.

Pausch, R., Snoddy, J., Taylor, R., Watson, S., & Haseltine, E. (1996). Disney's *Aladdin*: First steps toward storytelling in virtual reality. In Dodsworth, C. Jr., (Ed.), *Digital illusion: Entertaining the future with high technology* (pp. 357–372). London: Addison–Wesley.

Rosson, M. B., & Carroll, J. M. (1995). Narrowing the specification-implementation gap in scenario-based design. In Carroll, J. M. (Ed.), *Designing interaction: Psychology at the human-computer interface* (pp. 247–278). New York: Cambridge University Press.

Rosson, M. B., & Carroll, J. M. (2002a). Scenario-based design. In Jacko, J., & Sears, A. (Eds.), *The human-computer interaction handbook: Fundamentals, evolving technologies and emerging applications* (pp. 1032–1050). Mahwah, NJ: Lawrence Erlbaum Associates.

Rosson, M. B., & Carroll, J. M. (2002b). *Usability engineering: Scenario-based development of human-computer interaction.* San Francisco: Morgan Kaufmann.

Rubin, J. (1994). *Handbook of usability testing: How to plan, design, and conduct effective tests.* Chichester, UK: John Wiley and Sons.

Simpson, J. A., & Weiner, E. S. C. (Eds.). (1989). *Oxford English Dictionary* (2nd ed.). Oxford, UK: Clarendon Press.

Van Eck, R. (2007). Six ideas in search of a discipline. In Shelton, B., & Wiley, D. (Eds.), *The educational design and use of computer simulation games* (pp. 31–60). Rotterdam, The Netherlands: Sense Publishers.

Wertsch, J. V., Del Río, P., & Alvarez, A. (1995). Sociocultural studies: History, action, and mediation. In Wertsch, J. V., Del Río, P., & Alvarez, A. (Eds.), *Sociocultural studies of mind* (pp. 1–34). Cambridge, UK: Cambridge University Press.

Winograd, T., & Flores, F. (1986). *Understanding computers and cognition: A new foundation for design.* Norwood, NJ: Ablex Publishing Corporation.

Zyda, M. (2007). Creating a science of games. *Communications of the ACM, 50*(7), 27–29.

APPENDIX: ADDITIONAL READING

"Must-Reads" for This Topic

Bogost, I. (2007). *Persuasive games.* Cambridge MA: MIT Press.

Gunter, G., Kenny, R., & Vick, E. (2006). A case for a formal design paradigm for serious games. *The Journal of the International Digital Media and Arts Association, 3*(1), 93–105.

Gee, J. P. (2004). *What video games have to teach us about learning and literacy.* New York: Palgrave Macmillan.

Hendriksen, T. D. (2006). *Educational role-play: Moving beyond entertainment. Seeking to please or aiming for the stars.* Conference paper presented at "On Playing Roles" Seminar, Tampere, FL.

Kafai, Y. (2006 January). Playing and making games for learning: instructionist and constructionist perspectives for game studies. *Games and Culture, 1*(1), 36–40.

Koster, R. (2005). *A theory of fun for game design.* Phoenix, AZ: Paraglyph Press.

Malone, T. W. (1981). Toward a theory of intrinsically motivating instruction. *Cognitive Science, 4,* 333–369.

Prensky, M. (2001). *Fun, play and games: What makes games engaging. Digital game-based learning.* Columbus, OH: McGraw–Hill,

Squire, K., & Jenkins, H. (2003). Harnessing the power of games in education, insight. *Vision, 3,* 1–33.

Van Eck, R. (2007). Six ideas in search of a discipline. In B. Shelton & D. Wiley (Eds.), *The educational design and use of computer simulation games* (pp. 31–60). Rotterdam, The Netherlands: Sense Publishers.

Top Texts for Interdisciplinary Studies of Serious Games

Chen, S., & Michael, D. (2005 October). Proof of learning: Assessment in serious games. *Gamasutra.*

Csikszentmihalyi, M. (1975). *Beyond boredom and anxiety – experiencing flow in work and play.* San Francisco, CA: Jossey–Bass.

Khoo, E. T., Merritt, T., Lim Fei, V., Liu, W., Rahaman, H., Prasad, J., & Marsh, T. (2008). *Body music: Physical exploration of music theory.* Presented at ACM SIGGRAPH Video Games Symposium, Los Angeles, USA, ACM Press.

Gunter, G., Kenny, R., & Vick, E. (2006). A case for a formal design paradigm for serious games. *The Journal of the International Digital Media and Arts Association, 3*(1), 93–105.

Hendriksen, T.D. (2006). *Educational role-play: Moving beyond entertainment. Seeking to please or aiming for the stars.* Conference paper presented at: "On Playing Roles" Seminar, Tampere, FL.

Marsh, T. (2007). *Informing design and evaluation methodologies for serious games for learning.* Presented at Learning with games 2007, Sofia Antipolis, France.

Papert, S. (1993). *The children's machine: Rethinking school in the age of the computer.* New York: Basic Books.

Shaffer, D.W., Squire, K.A., Halverson, R. & Gee, J.P. (2005). Video games and the future of learning. *Phi Delta Kappan, 87,* 104–111.

Zyda, M. (2005). From visual stimulation to virtual reality to games. *IEEE Computer, 38*(9), 25–32.

Section 4
Research and Design

Chapter 11
Introducing Flowometer:
A CyGaMEs Assessment Suite Tool

Debbie Denise Reese
Wheeling Jesuit University, USA

ABSTRACT

A CyGaME is an online instructional game designed to make concept learning more intuitive while assessing changes in players' targeted knowledge and self-perceptions of flow. CyGaMEs stands for Cyberlearning through Game-based, Metaphor Enhanced Learning Objects, a research program supporting federal education road maps targeting cyberlearning and assessment as key to 21st-century learner-centered education. The author situates the CyGaMEs approach to instructional game design and assessment within structure mapping, flow, and game design theories. She introduces the CyGaMEs toolset for assessing game-based learning as realized in Selene: A Lunar Construction GaME. Identifying similarities between CyGaMEs and production-oriented approaches, she suggests CyGaMEs' design and assessment generalize across both methods. She presents the CyGaMEs adaptation of the double transfer paradigm as a research design for studying game-based learning. Then she derives the flowometer tool, illustrates a flowometer research implementation, and suggests scholars use the CyGaMEs Selene environment to investigate the relationship between game-based learning and flow.

INTRODUCTION

Successful video games are powerful technologies. The Cyberlearning Through Game-based, Metaphor Enhanced Learning Objects (CyGaMEs) project seeks to harness that power and put it to work for teaching and learning. CyGaMEs derives from the belief that effective game-based technologies are powerful learning tools with the potential to facili-

tate acquisition of targeted *conceptual* knowledge if and only if they are well designed. Sound research, measurement, and design require strong methods. CyGaMEs methods derived from established instructional, cognitive, and game design theories.

CyGaMEs is a cyberlearning project. The 2008 National Science Foundation (NSF) Task Force on Cyberlearning recognizes that "cyberlearning offers new learning and educational approaches and the possibility of redistributing learning experiences over time and space, beyond the classroom and

DOI: 10.4018/978-1-61520-717-6.ch011

throughout a lifetime" (Borgman et al., p. 5). The task force recommends:

interoperable resources that support developers so that they can concentrate on their innovation and contribute to the community. Rather than expecting individual projects to take responsibility for all aspects of learning, developers should be able to test their ideas with available tools for such activities as recording student data, designing assessments, acquiring sensor data, or storing data that would be applicable to a wide variety of cyberlearning activities. (Borgman et al., p. 23)

In other words, the task force calls for suites of tools for design, assessment, data collection, data management, data storage, and data reporting. The NSF panel believes "cyberlearning has reached a turning point where learning payoffs can be accelerated" (Borgman et al., p. 5). However, the panel also warns "that this moment could be fleeting because, without deliberate efforts to coordinate cyberlearning approaches, we will miss the opportunity to provide effective support for the convergence of learning and technology" (p. 5). For these reasons NSF funds research programs such as CyGaMEs to design, develop, and evaluate assessment toolsets for use as shared resources within cyberlearning research and implementation.

Many assessment instruments measure change in conceptual or procedural knowledge. Assessments may also measure change in aspects of affect, such as perceived experience. Flow theory defines flow as a state of personally perceived optimal experience (e.g., Csikszentmihalyi & Csikszentmihalyi, 1988). Flow theory provides measures of flow and other states of experience, such as arousal, anxiety, worry, apathy, boredom, and relaxation. Flow is intrinsically rewarding. This means people will attempt to revisit and repeat flow experience. To remain in flow, an individual must meet progressively greater challenge with corresponding greater skill. Flow can derive

from positive life choices, but it can also derive from negative choices, such as violent crime. It is imperative to enable humans, especially young people, to experience flow in connection with positive life choices. Academic endeavor is one such positive life choice that could promote flow. Flow and the other states of experience are identified as key aspects of both computer-mediated learner experience (e.g., Craig, Graesser, Sullins, & Gholson, 2004; D'Mello, Taylor, & Graesser, 2007; Kort, Reilly, & Picard, 2001; McQuiggan, Robison, & Lester, 2008; Pearce, Ainley, & Howard, 2005) and videogame experience (e.g., Fullerton, Swain, & Hoffman, 2004; Salen & Zimmerman, 2004; Schell, 2008). Thus it is important to investigate flow with respect to instructional videogames. The CyGaMEs research program has produced a game-based instructional environment and assessment toolset to investigate learner state during optimal learning, identify characteristics and causes of learning-flow trajectories, and refine the learning environments to optimize player state. The long-term goal is enhanced achievement through learner experience involving flow and the states of experience that accompany successful patterns of learning.

This chapter introduces the CyGaMEs suite of assessment tools with a focus on the flowometer. The flowometer measures flow and the other states of experience. Within the background section, I contextualize the suite by summarizing the CyGaMEs approach to instructional video game design, research, and assessment as derived from cognitive science analogical reasoning theory, video game design theory, flow theory, and the preparation for future learning paradigm. Next, I define the CyGaMEs assessment toolset, describe the CyGaMEs research environment, and illustrate flowometer application and potential. I conclude by proposing the research community use the CyGaMEs game, methods, tools, and research environment to investigate the relationship between CyGaMEs learning and CyGaMEs flow.

BACKGROUND

Luminary video game designers within the entertainment industry characterize their field as young and just developing the principles of its practice[1] (Langhoff et al., 2009; Schell, 2008). Although the entertainment industry invests heavily in video game research and development efforts, it documents a 90% failure rate[2]. Because instructional video games are even younger than their entertainment siblings, it is essential that educational scholars and game developers coordinate their own research and development effort to produce instructional video games that work.

An Instructional Game R & D Agenda

Readers find it helpful when I define CyGaMEs and clarify my usage patterns for pronouns and the word CyGaMEs. The terms in the CyGaMEs name mean:

- Cyberlearning: "Learning that is mediated by networked computing and communications technologies," as coined and defined by the NSF Task Force on Cyberlearning (Borgman et al., 2008, p. 10).
- Game-based: A virtual world in which a user's behavior is procedural gameplay directed by that world's embedded goal structures. The world is virtual in that it allows the learner to conduct embodied transactions with virtual objects. The world does not have to be persistent, multiplayer, or 3-D—although any specific CyGaME may be.
- Metaphor enhanced: The relational system that is and runs the game world is the analog of a targeted conceptual domain's relational structure. The mapping between game world and targeted learning domain is directed by the principles of structure mapping analogical reasoning theory (Gentner, 1983).

- Learning object(s): A self-contained, computer-mediated learning environment about one topic, in this case a particular conceptual domain, which can be inserted into any variety of related educational units that employ any variety of instructional approaches and/or delivery systems. CyGaMEs are designed specifically for introductory conceptual domains and serve as virtually embodied experience that readies the player for learning a targeted concept.

Now to clarify my usage conventions. I refer to my own CyGaMEs work and thoughts using the pronoun *I*. I refer to efforts or thoughts held by the CyGaMEs team using the pronoun *we*. And I refer to the CyGaMEs program as *it*. Second, I refer to a CyGaMEs *team* working with a CyGaMEs *approach* to develop, implement, and analyze learning and perceived experience (flow) within a CyGaMEs *research environment* using a CyGaME *instructional video game* and a suite of CyGaMEs assessment tools. I will often use CyGaMEs to represent the CyGaMEs team, approach, or instructional video games.

Theoretical Framework

Prior Knowledge

"People interpret new information with the help of prior knowledge and experience" (Anderson, Reder, & Simon, 1998, p. 232). Therefore, instructional designers produce instructional events to activate learners' prior knowledge (Gagné, Briggs, & Wager, 1992). Schwartz, Martin, and their colleagues (e.g., Schwartz, Bransford, & Sears, 2005) argued that the process through which students use prior knowledge to make sense of what is told to them during direct instruction is "essentially... a transfer process, but one where learners are transferring in rather than out of the observed situation" (Schwartz & Martin, 2004, p. 132). When prior knowledge is not available, instruction should provide experience to serve as apt prior knowledge (Merrill, 2002); that is, instruction should "help students develop useful forms of prior knowledge that are likely to help them interpret the meaning of subsequent lessons" (Schwartz & Martin, 2004, p. 132). Schwartz and his colleagues conceptualize prior knowledge as a type of anchor for new knowledge.

The role of prior knowledge in new learning has been known for a long time. For example, back in 1968, David Ausubel advised: "If I were to reduce all of educational psychology to just one principle, I would say this: The most important single factor influencing learning is what the learner already knows. Ascertain this and teach him accordingly" (epitaph). The importance of prior knowledge is now so well established it drives the scope and sequence techniques applied to development of national standards (e.g., American Association for the Advancement of Science, 2001; National Research Council, 1995) and curricula of all levels. Prior knowledge is the rationale behind pretest and placement tests: The goal is to support learner success by aligning learner placement with learner readiness. Instructional designers specify skills and knowledge as learner prerequisites for instruction (e.g., Smith & Ragan, 2005). Even so, educational scientists have documented that many introductory concepts are so counterintuitive or unfamiliar that they continue to handicap learners in all areas, including physics (e.g., Hestenes, Wells, & Swackhamer, 1992) and statistics,(e.g., Schwartz & Martin, 2004). Learners need effective ways to develop apt prior knowledge as readiness for learning challenging introductory concepts. Schwartz and Martin have argued that "preparing [students] for future learning requires the development of new instructional methods and the development of assessments that can evaluate whether students have been prepared to learn" (2004, p. 130).

Prior Knowledge (transfer in) and Future Learning (transfer out)

Schwartz, Bransford, and their colleagues bring a new perspective to learner readiness by incorporating the concept of transfer. Spiro, Collins, Thota, and Feltovich define transfer as "reconfiguring use of old knowledge in new situations that differ from the initial conditions and contexts of learning" (2003, p. 6). Schwartz et al. explicitly design with and for transfer (see Figure 1). They suggest an expanded perspective of transfer that considers the roles of prior knowledge, mental model building, and assessment (Bransford & Schwartz, 1999; Schwartz, et al., 2005; Schwartz & Martin, 2004). They conceptualize old knowledge (prior knowledge) as something students transfer "in" to direct instruction, and new knowledge as something students transfer "out" when they encounter subsequent novel scenarios or learning (e.g., Schwartz, et al., 2005). Within this paradigm, initial instruction includes procedural activities to encourage mental model building. These activities lead the student to infer relational characteristics of the to-be-learned concept. The first stage, while the learner is building a model, is preconceptual. The next stage is direct instruction. The learner's preconceptual inferences, though incomplete, anchor new learning as the learner continues to build a mental model for the targeted concept. The effectiveness of that initial instruction can be assessed by requiring the learner to transfer new knowledge out to address or solve a novel scenario. In research terms that initial instruction may be operationalized as the treatment or intervention.

CyGaMEs has applied this double transfer paradigm to the design of game-based learning objects and research environments. Game Level 1 is designed to scaffold mental model building. The student transfers this preconceptual knowledge into direct instruction as inferences about the to-be-learned content. Game Level 2 is designed as a novel scenario. The student transfers out new

Figure 1. Prior knowledge (transfer in) and future learning (transfer out). CyGaMEs applies the double transfer paradigm (e.g., Bransford & Schwartz, 1999; Schwartz et al., 2005; Schwartz & Martin, 2004) within the CyGaMEs instructional videogame research program. Copyright 2009 Debbie Denise Reese. Used with permission

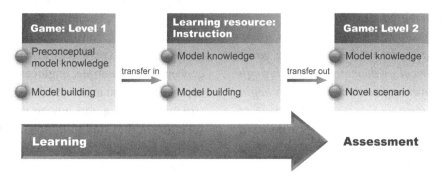

knowledge constructed during direct instruction to accomplish game goals set within the new game level.

Bransford, Schwartz, and their colleagues have already developed several methods to support the development of learners' early knowledge, such as anchored instruction (Bransford, Sherwood, Hasselbring, Kinzer, & Williams, 1990), comparison of contrasting cases (Schwartz & Bransford, 1998), and invention (or "inventive production," see Schwartz & Martin, 2004). These interventions support learner readiness by scaffolding the development of apt prior knowledge, preconceptual knowledge that learners can transfer "in" to anchor their experience of direct instruction. Schwartz, Martin, Bransford and their colleagues use the transfer out stage, i.e., a novel scenario, as an assessment to evaluate the effectiveness of the preconceptual model building.

Procedural Interventions

Although these methods are a good start, preparation for future learning (transfer in) requires additional design and assessment methods. These methods should support procedural interventions that ready learners by making new learning more intuitive. A procedural intervention is instruction that translates content into a series of rules that the learner enacts. CyGaMEs is a procedural intervention because the method translates abstract concepts from inside the minds of experts into procedural gameplay executed by the learner.

Concept learning is currently conceptualized as an active process of meaning-making through discovery via theory formulation, testing, and revision (Jonassen, 2006). If this is true, procedural interventions targeting readiness for concept formation[3] should engage the learner in an active process of meaning-making through discovery via theory formulation, testing, and revision.

Game Worlds to Enhance Learner Readiness

Today's cyberlearning technologies hold promise for the design, development, and investigation of innovative procedural activities that enhance learner preparation while supporting the assessment required for research, iterative development, and evaluation. One strong contender is the video game. This is because game worlds can be conceptualized and designed for meaning-making. Game-based technologies lead players to construct mental models by meeting challenges—the game goals and subgoals (Wright, 2004). Video games are "possibility spaces" (Wright, 2004) on which players act as agents while constructing a mental model of how the systems works and how to act to obtain the game goal (Fullerton et al., 2004; Wright, 2006). According to Wright (2006):

This isn't a random process; it's the essence of the scientific method. Through trial and error, players build a model of the underlying game based on empirical evidence collected through play. As the players refine this model, they begin to master the game world. It's a rapid cycle of hypothesis, experiment, and analysis. And it's a fundamentally different take on problem solving than the linear, read-the-manual-first approach of their parents. (2)

So:

- Each individual's conceptual domains are personal mental models formed through iterative cycles of theory formation, testing, and revision.
- Videogames are goal-driven virtual world systems that lead players to discover and construct viable mental models of the game world through procedurally enacted, goal-oriented gameplay.
- Sound instruction provides experience that enables learners to construct relevant prior knowledge when apt prior knowledge is inadequate or missing.
- Transfer can be conceptualized as two stages of knowledge application (a) transfer in—use prior knowledge to infer and construct new mental model and (b) transfer out—apply new mental model as a result of learning.

Putting this all together, we should find it possible to construct game worlds that enable students to build preconceptual mental models of targeted conceptual domains. That is, game worlds would provide [virtually] embodied experience that leads learners to make viable inferences about targeted conceptual domains. This

requires a design methodology for developing [virtually] concrete game worlds that lead students to make viable inferences about the abstract concepts required for academic success. Sound methodology requires an empirically supported theoretical foundation that describes how the mind uses concrete experiences to construct abstract concepts. For example, engineers apply the concepts of force and motion to design machines and structures that support human work and play. If scientists of the mind could specify the principles for how people infer abstract concepts from their concrete experiences, then game designers could apply them to design instructional game worlds that support human learning. Structure mapping theory is one approach from cognitive science that explains how people infer abstract concepts from their concrete and familiar experiences (Gentner, 1983). CyGaMEs applies structure mapping to instructional game design.

Comparison to Other Approaches

The CyGaMEs player conducts transactions within a *completed* CyGaME environment. Today there is a passion to design educational video games that require the player to design part of the game world during game play. Player as codesigner may be instantiated as scripted objects and social interactions such as occur in *Second Life*, as mods such as with *Neverwinter Nights*™, or as evolution and colonization of the universe as in *Spore*™. These designers characterize their players as *producers* of knowledge (http://www. gameslearningsociety.org/macarthur.php, para. 9). Theorists and designers like Kurt Squire, David Shaffer, Eric Zimmerman, and Katie Salen also develop games to immerse players in simulations of authentic professional activities. In their games, players explore the habits of mind and values of professionals like engineers, urban planners, journalists, lawyers, and game designers. Matthew Gaydos and Kurt Squire (in press) designed their role-playing game *Citizen Science* to develop scientific civic literacy by engaging players in authentic practices of ecological investigations and scientific argumentation. Shaffer's *Digital Zoo* players participate in the authentic practice by working with a client and engineers as they use *Sodaconstructor* software (http://sodaplay. com/creators/soda/items/constructor) to design character prototypes for an animated film (http:// www.epistemicgames.org/eg/?cat=5). Salen and Zimmerman's *Gamestar Mechanic* players engage in systems thinking as they progress within the game to design playable prototypes for original games (Salen, 2007). According to Salen, games like *Gamestar Mechanic* emphasize young people as "producers" rather than "consumers of knowledge and media" (http://www.gameslearning society.org/macarthur.php, para. 9).

CyGaMEs takes an overtly instructional design approach to instructional video game design: The prime motive is the instructional goal. Design begins with the content:

- What do you want the student to learn?
- Specify the learning goal/s.
- Conduct a task analysis!

A CyGaMEs instructional video game derives from a task analysis using a process that applies structure mapping. Unlike real-world parameters that often exist a priori or outside personal control, a game world derives from mechanics that are coded by programmers. If a concept's relational system is not scripted into the CyGaMEs world model, the player cannot learn it. The CyGaMEs approach assumes that progression toward the game goal in any well-designed game requires that the player discover the game world's predesigned, underlying relational structure. Salen termed this "reading" the game system (2007, p. 308). Will Wright (2006) explained that this process:

is the essence of the scientific method. Through trial and error, players build a model of the underlying game based on empirical evidence collected

through play. As the players refine this model, they begin to master the game world. It's a rapid cycle of hypothesis, experiment, and analysis. And it's a fundamentally different take on problem-solving than the linear, read-the-manual-first approach of their parents. (2)

Salen (2007) characterized *Gamestar Mechanic* as "an imprint" of the designers' expert knowledge of game design. In other words, the game system scaffolds the player through a *game world that is an analog of her design team's mental model of game design.* Squires and Gaydos (in press) worked with subject matter experts to identify "enduring" understandings and develop "an understanding of how to instantiate [their] content as a [game] world." Thus, both games designed for the learner-as-producer and those designed as situated instruction align with the CyGaMEs approach to the degree that their game worlds are analogs of the targeted learning domain.

Whether design is accomplished intuitively or through a formalism like the CyGaMEs approach, it appears essential that designers, even designers of production-oriented instructional games, should conduct a task analysis to specify the components of targeted expert practice. And, whether intuitively or through a formalism like the CyGAMEs approach, even production-oriented instructional games must map the targeted expert practice onto the game world analog.

Utility of a Formalism for Instructional Game Design and Assessment

In 1998, Anderson, Reder, and Simon wrote, "What is needed more than a philosophy of education is a science of education" (p. 237). Today, we also need a science of instructional video game design. The CyGaMEs method is a formal instructional approach to video game design that specifies the target domain and designs a game world that maps to it. Elsewhere, Anderson et al. wrote that a cognitive approach based upon task analysis has had "large, positive educational payoffs" and that "what is critical" in computer-mediated learning is "not the computer but the careful cognitive task analysis of the units that need to be learned" (1997, p. 21). I suggest that any instructional video game requires an approach that specifies the to-be-learned domain and applies structure mapping as well or better than CyGaMEs to design and map the aligned game world. Furthermore, to the degree that Salen's and other production-oriented processes informally or formally align a game world with a targeted domain, the tenets of CyGaMEs, structure mapping, and the aligned toolset of assessment instruments should apply to their design and assessment practice. The CyGaMEs assessment instruments are conceptualized and specified as interoperable tools for use in data collection and analysis within the gamut of game-based, computer-mediated learning environments. As instantiated within the *Selene* environment, they are a prototype that can guide subsequent development and implementation practice.

CyGaMEs TO EVOKE AND ASSESS LEARNING

CyGaMEs is an innovative instructional design method developed to help prepare students for direct instruction. CyGaMEs focuses on game-based technologies and a particular type of instructional game: a game that comes at the start of a unit of study and prepares the learner with viable intuitions about a targeted conceptual domain. In other words, the game is designed to "help students generate the types of early knowledge that are likely to help them learn" (Schwartz & Martin, 2004, p. 132).

Structure Mapping Applied to Instructional Game Design

The CyGaMEs approach to the design of instructional game worlds is applied cognitive science structure mapping theory. Structure mapping theory (Gentner, 1983) explains that people learn through analogy by mapping relational structure from a concrete or relatively familiar domain to an abstract or relatively unfamiliar domain. The left-hand rectangle in Figure 2 can represent either the concrete real world or the concrete game world. The right-hand rectangle displays a conceptual domain represented via concept mapping (see Novak & Gowin, 1984, for concept-mapping procedures). In the left-hand rectangle, ovals stand for objects or familiar concepts. In the right-hand rectangle, ovals represent subconcepts within a conceptual domain. The labeled arrows (arcs) represent relations between objects (left) or subconcepts (right). People form analogies by mapping relational structure from the left (base domain) to the right (the target domain). The CyGaMEs approach specializes in (a) base domains that are concrete source domains, like the real world and game worlds, and (b) targets that are conceptual domains. A CyGaMEs designer actually uses a target domain as a base and specifies the game world as its analog. The game world (left) is designed so that it is relationally isomorphic to the target. The assumption is that playing the game will produce a viable preconceptual mental model that readies the learner for subsequent direct instruction. Thus the game world acts as a source domain, inspiring candidate inferences that facilitate acquisition of targeted domain knowledge.

Although children and novices often map from a familiar (source) domain to an unfamiliar to-be-learned domain (target) according to superficial similarities (Gentner & Markman, 1997), human cognitive preference is for mapping due to shared *relational* structure that is deep and large (Gentner,

Figure 2. Structure mapping theory as applied within the CyGaMEs approach to instructional game design. This mapping is an excerpt from the specification used to design Selene: A Lunar Construction GaME. Copyright 2009 Debbie Denise Reese and Charles A. Wood. Used with permission

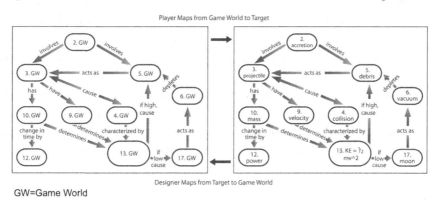

1989). Analogical reasoning is a natural (Lakoff & Johnson, 1980) and typically ubiquitous process in human cognition (Holyoak & Thagard, 1995); however, it is often enacted by the mind without conscious awareness (Lakoff & Johnson, 1999).

Superficial analogies can be helpful mnemonic devices suitable for low-end tasks like memorizing lists or labels or facts, but higher order learning such as concept formation or problem solving requires relational mapping between source and target domains. The best analogical match is the mapping with "the maximally systematic and consistent match of relational structure" (Gentner, 1989, p. 221). This is the structure mapping principle of systematicity (Gentner, 1983). As Smith and Ragan noted, "the more this mapping is related by 'deep structure' (i.e., with meaningful and conceptual links) rather than by similarities on 'surface features' (e.g., similarities in actual working, or similarities in contexts in which learning occurred) the more the knowledge will support facile problem solving" (Smith & Ragan, 2005, p. 220).

The CyGaMEs approach allows a design team to develop an instructional context that obviates access problems while leading the analogizer to map apt relational restructure. Detailed description of the CyGaMEs approach to instructional game

design is outside the scope of the present chapter, but components of the approach are described elsewhere (Reese, 2003a, 2003b, 2007a, 2008, 2009b; Reese & Coffield, 2005).

Spiro and his colleagues conceptualized their instructional interventions as "experience acceleration systems" (Spiro et al., 2003). An experience acceleration system is designed to prepare learners to respond more expertly to real-world cases than preparation by traditional instruction or years of real-world experience. CyGaMEs applies structure mapping theory to design game-based instructional environments in an effort to produce instructional games that act as experience acceleration systems by making introductory, domain-specific learning more intuitive while supporting the requirements of advanced study.

A Virtual Lab for Game-Based Research

I used the CyGaMEs approach to create the online, single-player game *Selene: A Lunar Construction GaME* and the CyGaMEs suite of embedded and external assessment tools. *Selene* is set within an encapsulating online environment with the same name. The *Selene* environment contains the game, embedded assessments, video instruction, and external assessments. The environment transitions players seamlessly through assessment, instruction, and gameplay components (see Figure 3). The CyGaMEs team designed the *Selene* environment as an online laboratory for studying learning and assessment within an instructional game while piloting prototypes for embedded assessment. Embedded assessments occur within the game world, often as a component of gameplay. The *Selene* environment is modularized to allow researchers to manipulate game, assessment, and instructional parameters.

The Double Transfer Paradigm

At the highest level, the *Selene* research environment is modeled after the double transfer paradigm introduced by learning scientists Daniel Schwartz and Taylor Martin (2004). The paradigm allows the CyGaMEs team to organize the *Selene* environment modules as conditions for testing interventions (e.g., the effect of scaffolds and feedback on learning and experience). For example, one *Selene* study investigated the effect of passive participation (watching gameplay and/or video

instruction) versus active participation (playing game) on gameplay and self-reported flow experience. There were four conditions, and each followed its own path through the environment (see Figure 3). For instance, the Play-Instruction-Play (PIP) condition routed through the environment as (a) Play Round 1, (b) Watch Round 1 instruction, and (c) Play Round 2. PIP condition players constructed preconceptual knowledge during Round 1 game play. This preconceptual knowledge was available for players to *transfer in* as scaffolding for learning during Round 1 instruction. Players could *transfer out* new knowledge and apply it to meet Round 2 game play and goals.

Assessing Learning in Game-Based Instructional Environments

How might researchers, developers, and educators approach assessment of experience and learning within computer-mediated, game-based instructional environments? What types of relevant information could cyberlearning environments collect? Might assessment be designed so that a game system collects evidence of learning

Figure 3. The CyGaMEs research environment experimental paradigm. At the highest level, the structure was adapted from the double transfer paradigm and experimental design developed by Schwartz and Martin (2004, pp. 148–149). The four Selene experimental conditions illustrated in this figure are WPI = Watch–Play–Instruction; WIP = Watch–Instruction–Play; PIP = Play–Instruction–Play; PPI = Play–Play–Instruction. Copyright 2009 by Debbie Denise Reese. Used with permission of the author

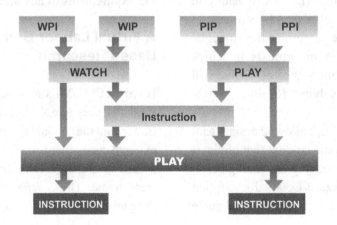

during game play? If so, this assessment would be *embedded* within the game. It would collect procedural evidence of cognitive growth. How might designers operationalize constructs as embedded measures of experience and learning? I address these questions from the perspective of the CyGaMEs approach.

CyGaMEs explicitly designs a game world aligned with the targeted learning domain. CyGaMEs designs the game goal so that it is the analog of the targeted learning. Alignment supports direct mapping from the game goal to the targeted learning goal. When the game goal and subgoals align with targeted learning and the game world aligns with the target domain's relational structure, player progress demonstrates the player's application of the targeted knowledge. An embedded instrument that could continually report player progress toward the game goal would provide both a measure of learning and a trace of the learning trajectory.

When a research program is in its infancy or the instructional game environment is young, it may be important to design external assessments to validate embedded measures of learning. External assessments should also align with content. CyGaMEs was able to derive an assessment instrument from the structure mapping theoretical framework and research program. Gentner and her colleagues had used structure mapping theory to develop mutual alignment tasks as facilitators of learning through analogical reasoning (Kurtz, Miao, & Gentner, 2001). Mutual alignment tasks serve as a CyGaMEs external assessment of learning. Correlations between embedded and external measures of learning can be calculated to investigate, improve, and validate the efficacy of the embedded measures.

Please note that the type of instructional game I am describing contains procedural gameplay that requires the player to conduct transactions within a virtual world while discovering and applying conceptual knowledge in order to progress toward the game goal. Not all instructional games meet

these requirements. A quiz game that follows a question-and-answer format contains insufficient relational alignment between the targeted domain and the interface (gameplay and game world) to qualify for CyGaMEs assessment techniques. Even a 3-D quiz game with avatars that talk and run and jump and fly and collaborate to answer questions would not meet CyGaMEs requirements for aligned gameplay and game world transactions based upon the content of the quiz. This is because quiz game content is projected onto the quiz game world. The content domain is irrelevant to the quiz game goal and the core game mechanics. A quiz game interface is therefore domain-general, while a CyGaMEs interface is domain-specific. In the CyGaMEs approach, each conceptual domain requires its own game world and its own idiosyncratic gameplay.

Assessing Perceived Experience in Game-Based Instructional Environments

Claims of relationships between player perceptions of gameplay experience and learning require measures of both gameplay *experience* and game-based *learning*. I discussed embedded and external assessment of learning above. Where might researchers look for the measures of gameplay experience? One coveted gameplay experience is flow (Fullerton et al., 2004; Salen & Zimmerman, 2004; Schell, 2008). Game designers strive to place players in a state of flow. Flow is a state of intense concentration, focus, and productivity in which an individual's self-perceptions of skill and challenge are high (for that individual) and balanced (e.g., Csikszentmihalyi & Csikszentmihalyi, 1988). Being in flow, or in the zone, is said to keep gamers playing and coming back for more. Game players were among the populations Csikszentmihalyi (1990) studied when he discovered flow, its characteristics, and its parameters. It is by design, not coincidence, that measures of flow and flow states can provide evidence about gameplay experience.

To understand flow, we must go back to Mihaly Csikszentmihalyi's (1988) doctoral research in the 1960s. As he tells the story, while studying creativity in artists, he observed that "the activity of painting produced its own autonomous positive rewards" (p. 4). Although the peak experiences Abraham Maslow identified seemed similar, Csikszentmihalyi needed to define the experience as a construct that could support an empirical research program. Csikszentmihalyi was primarily interested in "the quality of subjective experience that made a behavior intrinsically rewarding" (p. 7). At that time, the intrinsic motivation construct had not yet been identified. It developed in the 1970s as psychologists investigated intrinsically motivated behavior. Csikszentmihalyi, his students, and his colleagues originally used interview techniques to collect their data. Analyses identified that participants commonly described an autotelic experience that they often characterized as flow-like. Later, flow scholars developed open-ended protocols to explore flow. For example,

- Participants might read three quotations describing the flow experience "that were taken from original flow interviews" (Massimini, Csikszentmihalyi, & Delle Fave, 1988, p. 67) "and asked if they had ever had a similar experience, and if yes, what activities were they engaged in when they had such an experience" (Han, 1988, p. 139). Three examples of the flow quotations are:
  1. My mind isn't wandering. I am not thinking of something else. I am totally involved in what I am doing. My body feels good. I don't seem to hear anything. The world seems to be cut off from me. I am less aware of myself and my problems.
  2. My concentration is like breathing. I never think of it. I am really quite oblivious to my surroundings after I really get going. I think that the phone could ring, and the doorbell could ring or the house burn down or something like that. When I start I really do shut out the whole world. Once I stop, I can let it back in again.
  3. I am so involved in what I am doing. I don't see myself as separate from what I am doing. (pp. 139–140)
- Participants might be asked to describe the quality, quantity, and degree of personal experiences. For example:

When I stop to think about it, I realize that an important part of this state of mind is enjoyment. I get so involved in what I'm doing, I almost forget about time. When I experience this state of mind, I feel really free from boredom and worry. I feel like I am being challenged or that I am very much in control of my actions and my world. I feel like I am growing and using my best talents and skills; I am master of my situation. (Allison & Duncan, 1988)

Qualitative research led Csikszentmihalyi and his colleagues to operationalize flow and the related states of apathy, boredom, relaxation, control, anxiety, and worry as degrees of self-reported skill and challenge. In an eight-channel model of flow, relative degrees of skill and challenge are (see Figure 4):

- Flow: High skill–high challenge.
- Apathy: Low skill–low challenge.
- Boredom: Medium skill–low challenge.
- Relaxation: High skill–low challenge.
- Control: High skill–medium challenge.
- Arousal: Medium skill–high challenge.
- Anxiety: Low skill–high challenge.
- Worry: Low skill–medium challenge.

This eight-channel model of flow can be used to report assessment measures of flow, which will be described in more detail later in this chapter.

Figure 4. The eight-channel model of states of perceived experience. The labeled eight-channel flow models illustrate the skill and challenge combinations corresponding to each state. The eight-channel flow trace on the left illustrates the mean self-reported skill and challenge ratings for the Play–Instruction–Play condition within the Selene Phase 1 study targeting players age 13–18. The eight-channel flow trace on the right plots all the self-reported skill and challenge ratings for one Play–Instruction–Play condition Selene player (ID No. 1714). The eight-channel flow concept and graph implemented within CyGaMEs analyses are adapted from work by Csikszentmihalyi and his colleagues (e.g., Csikszentmihalyi, 1997, p. 31). Copyright 2009 Debbie Denise Reese. Used with permission

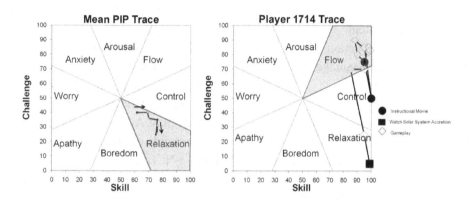

In order to interpret player experience effectively, however, we need a means of coding and collecting player interactions with the game, so I turn next to a discussion of how this can be done before moving into a discussion of the CyGaMEs assessment suite of tools in general, and the flowometer in more detail.

Game Play Gestures

Player interactions are fine-grained units that reveal how players negotiate the game world, when they learn, and how they behave. When measuring gameplay experience, it is helpful to have a record of these "gestures" as documentation of each player's interaction with the game world. Gestures can be correlated with learning and perceived experience. Videotape is one approach to recording such gestures, but videotape transcriptions and analyses are expensive and time-consuming, and they delay data analysis. Current video analysis techniques also make video records impractical for large-scale cyber-learning formative assessment and quantitative

research. Another way to code player gestures is to automate a parsimonious, digital gesture collection and reporting system and embed it within the game world. The game would record each gameplay gesture by identifying the gesture, its occurrences, and its parameters. The game would report to a database. A well-designed gesture data system would enable review and mental replay of a player's entire set of game gestures through a simple visual scan of the data report. A trained report recipient could quickly identify and summarize a participant's gameplay as key aspects and critical incidents. CyGaMEs analyzes gameplay gesture parameters in such a manner in order to indicate learning. For example, a trace of a *Selene* player's velocity parameter indicates when a player has learned the concept that collisions with too much kinetic energy prevent accretion.

CyGaMEs Suite: Embedded and External Assessments

CyGaMEs designed three embedded assessment instruments and two external instruments. I will briefly introduce the five tools before focusing in more depth on the flowometer tool.

Embedded Assessment: Gesture

CyGaMEs defines a gesture as a passive or active action:

- Active: A player action that causes some change to the game system.
- Passive: A game system action in response to the state of the game that makes a change to the state of the game.

Each gesture has multiple parameters. Some are standard across all gestures. Standard gesture parameters identify the player (player identification number), the time of the gesture (time stamp), the gesture identification number, and the location within the environment at which the gesture was triggered (trigger point). Gestures also report gesture-specific parameters that contain information specific to their own properties. The *Selene* slingshot gesture is a good example of both standard and gesture-specific parameters. Procedurally, the slingshot gesture works like this:

Clicking on a particular chunk of debris will momentarily "freeze" the game's system of asteroids and bring up a "slingshot" interface. The player will aim the piece of debris at the proto-Moon and pull back to "sling" the object at the proto-Moon. (Hankinson, 2007, p. 185)

The slingshot gesture is an assessment item. Within a slingshot gesture report *Selene* posts standard information about the game time, location and context. Gesture-specific parameters are density of the particle, radius of the particle, the player's accuracy in choosing the correct particle, radioactive state of the particle, the velocity of the shot, and the accuracy of the shot. I have coded video footage identifying procedural evidence of players' learning accretion concepts (Reese &

Tabachnick, 2010). Then I have matched that exact time with gameplay data. Graphed, the data indicate to the millisecond where learning occurred, what it was, and that it persisted over time.

The *Selene Classic* game may take 90 minutes or more to play, but it posts only 11 types of player gestures.

Embedded Assessment: Timed Report

The CyGaMEs timed report measures player progress toward game goal or subgoal at the gesture level. In *Selene,* the system calculates a timed report at the conclusion of each 10 seconds of game play. An algorithm idiosyncratic to each game module calculates and reports player progress as a "1" (progress toward the game goal), "-1" (moved away from the game goal), or "0" (no change in progress). As with the gesture report, timed reports post standard parameters that identify the player (player identification number), the time of the report (time stamp), and the location within the environment at which the gesture was triggered (trigger point). I have matched the timed report output by millisecond with those gesture parameters that quantify the learning captured in video segments. Graphed, the data indicated to the millisecond where learning occurred and how long it persisted (Reese & Tabachnick, 2010).

External Assessment: Mutual Alignment

According to structure mapping theory, when people engage in analogical reasoning, they place the source and target domains into structural alignment (Markman & Gentner, 1993). When that alignment is due to relational structure, the mapping between target and source domain can be represented as illustrated in Figure 2. Kurtz et al. (2001) found that learning improved when participants engaged in a mutual alignment task; that is, participants explicitly matched source and target domain subconcept dyads and provided rationales for the matches. I derived the CyGaMEs mutual alignment assessment from structure mapping theory and research. The CyGaMEs mutual alignment assessment prompts the learner that a "[subconcept label] is like" and displays movies (screen captures of gameplay) excerpted from that module of the game (Reese, Diehl, & Lurquin, 2009). For *Selene* there are four prompts: one for each of the four game modules.

External Assessment: Procedural

The procedural assessment translates gameplay into procedural task challenges. Effectively solving a challenge demonstrates the player's ability to correctly apply and interpret content. For example, the *Selene* surface features module requires the player to discover and replicate when and how the processes of impact cratering and volcanism occurred on the Moon. The procedural assessment for this module presents five paintings of the same lunar region as it evolved over time and asks the player to (a) place the five images in order on a time line and (b) provide the rationale for the placement of each painting.

Embedded Assessment: The Flowometer

Flow is typically measured through a randomly prompted self-report of the two dimensions, skill and challenge, each on a Likert scale (Hektner, Schmidt, & Csikszentmihalyi, 2007). Based on the video game design theory literature (Schell, 2008), it may be that game designers are unaware that researchers can measure the degree of game-induced flow during gameplay.

CyGaMEs developed the flowometer to measure flow during cyberlearning and embedded the tool within the *Selene* game and interstitial environment. The flowometer prompts each participant at a random but preselected time every 5 minutes. Players are prompted to report their current (i.e., at the moment of prompting) levels of skill and challenge within every segment of

the *Selene* environment *except* during the external assessments.

FLOWOMETER

The remainder of the chapter will describe the theory and design of the flowometer tool and analyses in more detail, illustrated by findings from two phases of *Selene* data collection.

ESM and ESF

Quantitatively, flow is typically measured via self-report of skill and challenge, typically using a 9-point Likert scale. Many flow studies measure flow experience across the gamut of everyday, real-life activity in a process referred to as the Experience Sampling Method, or ESM. Measurement requires a signaling device and a self-report questionnaire (Csikszentmihalyi & Larson, 1987). The questionnaires are typically referred to as the Experience Sampling Form, or ESF.

In the ESM, participants typically wear a pager that pings at random but preset times of the day over the course of a week, typically "seven to ten signals" over "seven consecutive days" (Csikszentmihalyi & Larson, 1987, p. 528). The "awake" day is broken into blocks of time; signals are scheduled at random times such that no two signals occur within 15 minutes of each other. Studies may also concentrate signals during crucial points of the day or in different situations. At each signal the participant completes a paper and pencil report (the ESF) describing the qualities of the experience and the context, including the level of skill and challenge. The ESF is designed to be completed in two minutes or less. A typical ESF contains the two flow prompts (skill and challenge), Likert-like items to measure quality of experience (I've seen as many as 26 items), fill-in/open-ended items, and any additional items targeted by the study (Csikszentmihalyi & Schneider, 2000).

Each ESF becomes a record in a response-level data set. These records may be aggregated by person at the level of analysis to form person-level data sets. Data sets can be recompiled at many levels, and:

One can think of the database as a permanent laboratory in which an almost unlimited number of relationships may be tested. To the extent that new records are continuously being added and the number of observations in each cell increases, ever more refined questions can be asked of the data. (Csikszentmihalyi & Larson, 1987, p. 529)

Validity and Reliability of the ESF

The interested reader should consult Csikszentmihalyi and Larson (1987) and the more recent Hektner, et al. volume (2007) for detailed guidance about ESM and ESF logistics and methods. In summary, flow scholars have documented strong validity and reliability (Csikszentmihalyi & Larson, 1987). For example:

- Comparison with diary records: $r = .93$.
- Correlation between first half of week with the second at the individual response level for the mean of eight variables: $r_{adolescent} = .60$; $r_{adult} = .74$.
- Five self-esteem items from 2,287 observations collected from 49 mothers of small children: $\alpha = .94$, first half of week to second $r = .86$, $p = .0001$.

In general, the data suggest (a) that ESM reports of psychological states covary in expected ways with the values for physical conditions and with situational factors such as activity, location, and social context; (b) that measures of individual differences based on the ESM correlate with independent measures of similar constructs; and (c) that the ESM differentiates between groups

expected to be different, e.g., patient and nonpatient groups or gifted and average mathematics students. (Csikszentmihalyi & Larson, 1987, p. 531)

Csikszentmihalyi and Larson summarized that their 1987 paper offered "ample evidence that [ESM provides] a plausible representation of reality" (p. 533). Most importantly for the CyGaMEs research program, "adding up patterns within a person, it becomes possible to use ESM to *evaluate the common experience of situations*" (emphasis in the original, Csikszentmihalyi & Larson, 1987, p. 531). Our two initial phases of *Selene* data collection indicate that the experience sampling method can also be used to evaluate the common experience of instructional gameplay situations.

The ESF Scantron Form

The flowometer is my second adaptation of the ESF. The first occurred 3 years ago when I led a large flow study called Inspiration in 50 classrooms in states from Vermont to Hawaii, conducted in science classrooms daily over the course of 4 weeks (Reese, 2006b, 2007b; Reese, Kim, Palak, Smith, & Howard, 2005; Reese & McFarland, 2006). We collected one or two ESM reports from every participating student every science class period at a random but preselected time—totaling about 44,000 reports. To ease the processing of so much data, we had translated the ESF into a Scantron sheet (see Figure 5). We reduced the number of Likert-like items to 23 and retained seven contextual items. Based upon teachers' reports (Reese, 2006b), middle school students took about 90 seconds to complete the forms.

Anecdotally, we found evidence that ESF could be a quick way for teachers to monitor their students. For example, a participating teacher picked up her class's ESM sheets and noticed that one student had marked the scale proud (1)

Figure 5. Scantron version of the experience sampling method (ESM) form. Copyright 2006, Center for Educational Technologies. Used with permission

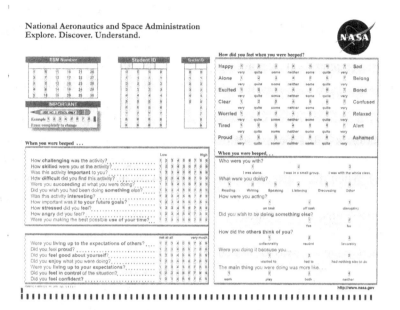

to ashamed (7) as a 7. The teacher felt the class had been positive and nonthreatening and was concerned that the student felt so ashamed. The teacher contacted a counselor who visited with the student. The student reported his family had been evicted from their home the previous evening. The counselor was able to provide support to assist the student.

During the Inspiration study, students completed a 4-week unit of study about volcanoes and hurricanes and then participated in a computer-mediated, live leader-moderated simulation in which they took on roles as disaster unit specialists planning and conducting emergency analyses and procedures to protect the population of the island of Montserrat against a simultaneous hurricane and volcano. ESF collections were divided into instructional waves: baseline (before the unit of study), three successive pre-simulation waves, and the final simulation. We don't argue the possibility, presence, or absence of a novelty effect. The relevance to the present discussion

is that we would expect flow or anxiety to rise during the 2-hour simulation and expect apathy and boredom/relaxation to decrease. And this is what we found. Calculating at the response level, students reported a 24% rise in flow ($\mu_{simulation}$ = 43%, $\mu_{presimulation}$ = 24%), a 12% decrease in apathy ($\mu_{simulation}$ = 10%, $\mu_{presimulation}$ = 22%), a 13% increase in anxiety ($\mu_{simulation}$ = 33%, $\mu_{presimulation}$ = 20, and a 25% drop in relaxation/boredom ($\mu_{simulation}$ = 10%, $\mu_{presimulation}$ = 35).

Developing the Flowometer

As we designed our game assessment instruments, we planned to minimize the intrusiveness of the ESM instrument. We wanted an even quicker version of the ESF, one that could take 1 to 5 seconds rather than 90. So we retained only the skill and challenge flow items. We did not include the quality of experience items that are typically used to correlate with flow and measure the quality of experience. We translated the two key prompts (level of skill and level of challenge) into an interactive tool and called it flowometer (see Figure 6).

Scholars in the medical field had found that patients' self-reports of pain were much more accurate if patients indicated pain level by pointing on a scale that ran from left to right than if they verbally indicated pain level (e.g., Sriwatanakul, et al., 1983; Wewers & Lowe, 1990). Scholars studying Albert Bandura's self-efficacy scales (Pajares, Hartley, & Valiante, 2001) had found greater discrimination when the scales ran from 0–100 than when they ran over a smaller interval (e.g, 1–10). For these reasons, we formatted our flowometer as a click-and-drag tool ranging from 0–100. The original flowometer was designed using Flash for measures during video of game play or instruction and translated into Java for reports during the Java-based *Selene* game. The two implementations shared look and feel, and the flowometer transitions from *Flash* and *Java* are not discernable to study participants.

Selene study participants complete a flow report within every 5-minute segment of participation in the online study at a random but preselected time. Coding constrains the flowometer such that

(a) no two flowometer prompts should ever be closer than 1 minute or farther apart than 5 minutes and (b) the flowometer prompt is postponed until the player completes a current gesture. That is, a flow prompt never interrupts a gesture but waits until the current gesture is complete. Furthermore, prompts were designated for each 5-minute time block within each of the four game stages (Round 1 accretion, Round 1 surface features, Round 2 accretion, and Round 2 surface features). Each player could progress idiosyncratically through the game, but every player who played in the same 5-minute segment of any stage would be prompted by the flowometer at the same number of milliseconds into that 5-minute block. Our first *Selene* study contained two conditions that watched screen captures (Camtasia) of Round 1 game play (WIP and WPI) and two that played (PIP and PPI, see Figure 3). Flowometer prompts for the game play videos were set according to the same 5-minute blocks as they were for game play.

Selene Exploratory Flow Analyses

We knew we would be collecting a lot of game play and self-report data from *Selene* players. But

Figure 6. The CyGaMEs Selene flowometer. Copyright 2008 Debbie Denise Reese and James Coffield. Used with permission

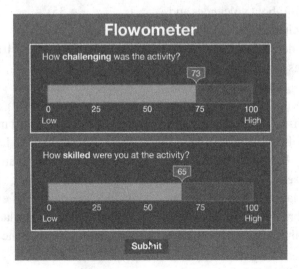

would that data carry information? In other words, would flowometer data allow us to evaluate the common experience of situations encountered within the *Selene* environment? We found the *Selene* flowometer data do:

- Differentiate situations expected to be different. In general, over time, player skill increases and player challenge decreases (Reese, 2009a).
- Covary in expected ways with other measures. Case studies indicate flowometer data correlate with other measures indicating learning and gameplay experience (Reese & Tabachnick, 2010).
- Support screening. Flowometer data enable comparison of Selene experience between individual cases and group averages.

The CyGaMEs team is working toward prototype design of a data reporting system that can analyze and present player data as immediate feedback to the player and as assessment and evaluation data for researchers, teachers, parents, administrators, and other stakeholders. One application of aggregate and individual data is the possibility for efficient screening for aptitude and interest. For example, the eight-channel flow trace on the left-hand side of Figure 4 displays an aggregate graph for the Phase 1 condition PIP players across the seven segments of the environment. The eight-channel flow trace on the right-hand side of Figure 4 displays all the flow reports for one player. The PIP players reported ever-increasing relaxation as they progressed through the environment. This means that, on the average, skill increased and challenge decreased over time spent interacting with Selene. Please note that as used within flow research, relaxation is similar to the concept of routine expertise. A rock climber ascending a familiar formation the climber has often traversed experiences routine expertise. The climber must be alert and proficient, but the cliff no longer presents the challenge it

once held. In contrast, Player 1714 reported high relaxation only while watching solar system accretion and during the first 5 minutes of game play. Subsequent reports were all in flow, except for one segment of video instruction, which was a state of control. These data and analyses easily identify Player 1714 as a candidate to be considered for science enrichment, extracurricular activities, or National Aeronautics and Space Administration (NASA) student pipeline.

FUTURE RESEARCH DIRECTIONS

CyGaMEs flowometer research to date suggests three research questions:

- Which eight-channel flow states are most conducive to what types of learning?
- How do cognitive, affective, and physiological data (e.g., EEG, facial expressions) correlate with flowometer self-reports?
- How can gameplay mechanics be calibrated to accurately measure flow states?

Play Interruptus

Scholars warn that no matter how quickly a player completes a measure of flow like the flowometer, *play interruptus* will dispel the focus and concentration that define and engage the flow state. However, recent CyGaMEs video footage demonstrates that, in the lab at least, CyGaMEs players respond to the flowometer with as much intensity as they play the game.

If a solution to play interruptus is desirable, and I'm not certain it is, CyGaMEs has identified two routes to solutions (Reese, 2006a). First, social science flow research began by identifying and qualifying flow through open-ended survey questionnaires and interviews. Through analyses, Csikszentmihalyi has identified the elements that cause a flow experience, such as degree of challenge, perceived level of control, awareness of goal structure, and feedback. As the flow construct was refined, the research technique progressed to more quantifiable self-reports. Alignment between the flow construct and its role as a game design element suggests that game mechanics and game-play choices could be operationalized to track and measure flow. Then, tracked flow-related software activity and player response could be analyzed as a performance measure of flow. A second solution is the "The Flow Design Challenge":

- Build the flow prompt as an integral component of gameplay.
- Motivate the player to want to provide the information.

A third solution? Use the flowometer. Flow prompts may increase learner mindfulness and metacognition. Flow prompts and analyses might help learners become more aware of flow, how the states of experience interact with their idiosyncratic learning process, and how to make productive life choices.

Learning and Eight-Channel Flow

We currently lack definitive information about which of the eight-channel flow states is optimal for learning, however. Is it flow or one of the other states? Does an optimal state for learning depend upon characteristics of the learner and task? Csikszentmihalyi (2008) said, "Arousal is the area where most people learn from because that's where they are pushed beyond their comfort zone and that to [re]enter. .. flow. .. they develop higher skills" (16m 46s). Does arousal correspond with learning? Is there a stage in learning where the individual transitions from anxiety or arousal and into flow? CyGaMEs designed *Selene* and the flowometer to help answer these questions. CyGaMEs exploratory analyses suggest that together the *Selene* assessment suite (flowometer, timed reports, gestures, and external assessments) will support exploration of the relationship between

learning and flow—for this game, for this domain, and for future games that aid learner construction of introductory mental models for complex concepts.

CONCLUSION

Charles M. Reigeluth, codirector of the Association for Educational Communications and Technology initiative, "FutureMinds: Transforming American School Systems®" (http://futureminds. us/index.html), is concerned that people don't understand the concept of paradigm change and how it should be employed to transform floundering education practice and systems "from time-based to attainment-based, from standardized to customized, from sorting-focused to learning-focused, from teacher-centered to learner-centered, from grade levels to continuous progress, and so forth" (C. M. Reigeluth, personal communication, March 29, 2009). Reigeluth warns that equality does not mean equity. To this effect, he wrote:

Two things educators know for certain are that different children learn at different rates, and different children have different learning needs, even from their first day of school. And yet our Industrial Age system presents a fixed amount of content to a group of students in a fixed amount of time, so it is like a race in which we see who receives the A's and who flunks out. Our current system is not designed for learning; it is designed for selection. (Reigeluth, 1994, p. 7)

I cannot specify the exact methods by which we guarantee productive paradigm change, but I do know instructional, game-based environments could be used to assist and assess learning of complex concepts within an attainment-based, customized, learning-focused, learner-centered, and continuous progress education paradigm. This chapter summarized the CyGaMEs approach to instructional game design and assessment, an approach derived from the convergence of well-substantiated cognitive, learning science, and game design theories. It introduced the CyGaMEs toolset for assessment within game-based instructional environments. Then it focused on the flowometer: a tool to assess learner perception of eight flow theory states: flow, arousal, anxiety, worry, apathy, boredom, relaxation, and control. The CyGaMEs *Selene* data support the viability of the flowometer as a tool to measure and study player perception of gameplay experience within cyberlearning environments.

It would be valuable in the learner-centered education system of the future to have simple, reliable, efficient, and accurate methods to *guide* our students to experience intrinsic satisfaction through academic study and to *assess* the degree to which our learners prosper and our learning environments succeed. It will be helpful to produce a mindfulness within our learners connected with flow experience so they can self-reliantly lead themselves to find fulfillment in making productive life choices. To this end, an overt flowometer might be a very effective tool. Over time, gameplay and flowometer calibration can support system monitoring of player response to target for abnormalities that signal sub- and supernormal atypical behavior in reporting (e.g,. effort or honesty) or flow response. A culture educated to expect and experience flow through life choices beneficial to themselves and others would be a great advance for humankind.

Video game technologies are powerful. When they are used for instructional goals, they must be carefully designed to ensure they evoke viable mental models. Entertainment games do not have to meet this parameter. For example, some evolutionary biologists have been quoted as enjoying *Spore* but concerned that "the step-by-step process by which *Spore's* creatures change does not have much to do with real evolution. The mechanism is severely messed up" (Prum, as cited in Zimmer, 2008, ¶11–12). An entertainment or persuasive game may bend the facts for effect. What if, just

what if, the goal of *Spore* were to teach evolution? How would game design practice have to change to support an instructional goal? This is the CyGaMEs research mission and CyGaMEs is its approach.

AUTHOR NOTE

Debbie Denise Reese, Center for Educational Technologies®, Wheeling Jesuit University, Wheeling, West Virginia.

This material is based upon work supported by the National Science Foundation under Grant DRL-0814512 awarded to the author and Charles A. Wood, Ben Hitt, and Beverly Carter and work supported by the National Aeronautics and Space Administration under awards NCC5-451, NNX06AB09G-Basic, NNX06AB09G-Sup-1, NNX06AB09G-Sup-2, NAG-13782, and NNX08AJ71A-Basic to the NASA-sponsored Classroom of the Future. *Selene* derived from Charles A. Wood's mental model of lunar and planetary geology, and he is the project's subject matter expert. The *Selene* database was designed and is maintained by Andrew Harrison. *Selene* player recruitment is managed by Lisa McFarland. Ben Hitt, director of the Schenk Center for Informatic Sciences at Wheeling Jesuit University, oversees planning of data cleaning algorithms and knowledge discovery work, aided by Ralph J. Seward. Ian Bogost led his Georgia Tech graduate students, William Hankinson and Matt Gilbert, in design and development of the original *Selene* game concept. Any opinions, findings, and conclusions or recommendations expressed in this material are those of the authors and do not necessarily reflect the views of the National Science Foundation or the National Aeronautics and Space Administration.

REFERENCES

Allison, M. T., & Duncan, M. C. (1988). Women, work, and flow. In Csikszentmihalyi, M., & Csikszentmihalyi, I. S. (Eds.), *Optimal experience: Psychological studies of flow in consciousness* (pp. 118–137). New York: Cambridge University Press.

American Association for the Advancement of Science. (2001). *Atlas of science literacy*. Washington, DC: American Association for the Advancement of Science and National Science Teachers Association.

Anderson, J. R., Reder, L. M., & Simon, H. A. (1997). Situative versus cognitive perspectives: Form versus substance. *Educational Researcher*, *26*(1), 18–21.

Anderson, J. R., Reder, L. M., & Simon, H. A. (1998). Radical constructivism and cognitive psychology. In Ravitch, D. (Ed.), *Brookings papers on educational policy: 1998* (p. 384). Washington, DC: The Brookings Institution Press.

Ausubel, D. P. (1968). *Educational psychology: A cognitive view*. New York: Holt, Rinehart, and Winston, Inc.

Borgman, C. L., Abelson, H., Johnson, R., Koedinger, K. R., Linn, M. C., Lynch, C. A., et al. (2008). *Fostering learning in the networked world: The cyberlearning opportunity and challenge: A 21st century agenda for the National Science Foundation*. Retrieved August 13, 2008, from http://www.nsf.gov/pubs/2008/nsf08204/nsf08204.pdf?govDel=USNSF_124

Bransford, J. D., & Schwartz, D. L. (1999). Rethinking transfer: A simple proposal with multiple implications. *Review of Research in Education*, *24*, 61–100.

Bransford, J. D., Sherwood, R. D., Hasselbring, T. S., Kinzer, C. K., & Williams, S. M. (1990). Anchored instruction: Why we need it and how technology can help. In Nix, D., & Spiro, R. (Eds.), *Cognition, education, and multimedia: Exploring ideas in high technology* (pp. 115–141). Hillsdale, NJ: Lawrence Erlbaum Associates.

Craig, S. D., Graesser, A. C., Sullins, J., & Gholson, B. (2004). Affect and learning: An exploratory look into the role of affect in learning. *Journal of Educational Media*, *29*(3), 241–250.

Crandall, R. W., & Sidak, J. G. (2006). *Video games, Serious business for America's economy*. Entertainment Software Association.

Csikszentmihalyi, M. (1988). Introduction. In Csikszentmihalyi, M., & Csikszentmihalyi, I. S. (Eds.), *Optimal experience: Psychological studies of flow in consciousness* (pp. 3–14). New York: Cambridge University Press.

Csikszentmihalyi, M. (1990). Flow: The psychology of optimal experience (HarperPerennial ed.). New York: Harper & Row.

Csikszentmihalyi, M. (1997). *Finding flow: The psychology of engagement with everyday life*. New York: HarperCollins Publishers.

Csikszentmihalyi, M. (2008, October 24). Creativity, fulfillment, and flow. *TED: Ideas worth spreading*. Retrieved March 23, 2009, from http://www.youtube.com/watch?v=fXIeFJCqsPs

Csikszentmihalyi, M., & Csikszentmihalyi, I. S. (Eds.). (1988). *Optimal experience: Psychological studies of flow in consciousness*. New York: Cambridge University Press.

Csikszentmihalyi, M., & Larson, R. (1987). Validity and reliability of the experience sampling method. *The Journal of Nervous and Mental Disease*, *175*(9), 526–536. doi:10.1097/00005053-198709000-00004

Csikszentmihalyi, M., & Schneider, B. (2000). *Becoming adult: How teenagers prepare for the world of work.* New York: Basic Books.

D'Mello, S., Taylor, R. S., & Graesser, A. C. (2007). Monitoring affective trajectories during complex learning. In *Proceedings of the 29th Annual Meeting of the Cognitive Science Society*, 203–208.

Fullerton, T. (2008). *Game design workshop: A Playcentric approach to creating innovative games* (2nd ed.). Burlington, MA: Elsevier.

Fullerton, T., Swain, C., & Hoffman, S. (2004). *Game design workshop: Designing, prototyping, and playtesting games.* San Francisco: CMP Books.

Gagné, R. M., Briggs, L. J., & Wager, W. W. (1992). *Principles of instructional design* (4th ed.). Belmont, CA: Wadsworth/Thomson Learning.

Gaydos, M., & Squire, K. (in press). Citizen science: Designing a game for the 21st century. In Van Eck, R. (Ed.), *Interdisciplinary models and tools for serious games: Emerging concepts and future directions.* Hershey, PA: IGI Global.

Gentner, D. (1983). Structure mapping: A theoretical framework for analogy. *Cognitive Science, 7,* 155–170.

Gentner, D. (1989). The mechanisms of analogical learning. In Vosniadou, S., & Ortony, A. (Eds.), *Similarity and analogical reasoning* (pp. 199–241). New York: Cambridge University Press. doi:10.1017/CBO9780511529863.011

Gentner, D., & Markman, A. B. (1997). Structure mapping in analogy and similarity. *The American Psychologist, 52*(1), 45–56. doi:10.1037/0003-066X.52.1.45

Han, S. (1988). The relationship beween life satisfaction and flow in elderly Korean immigrants. In Csikszentmihalyi, M., & Csikszentmihalyi, I. S. (Eds.), *Optimal experience: Psychological studies of flow in consciousness* (pp. 138–149). New York: Cambridge University Press.

Hankinson, W. (2007). Stage Two: Early Moon Formation. In Reese, D. D. (Ed.), *The Collected Selene (Classic) Game and Research Environment Design Documentation* (pp. 184–186). Wheeling, WV: Wheeling Jesuit University.

Hektner, J. M., Schmidt, J. A., & Csikszentmihalyi, M. (2007). *Experience sampling method: Measuring the quality of everyday life.* Thousand Oaks, CA: Sage.

Hestenes, D., Wells, M., & Swackhamer, G. (1992). Force concept inventory. *The Physics Teacher, 30,* 141–158. doi:10.1119/1.2343497

Holyoak, K. J., & Thagard, P. (1995). Mental leaps analogy in creative thought

Jonassen, D. H. (2006). On the role of concepts in learning and instructional design. *Educational Technology Research and Development, 54*(2), 177–196. doi:10.1007/s11423-006-8253-9

Kort, B., Reilly, R., & Picard, R. W. (2001). An affective model of interplay between emotions and learning: Reengineering educational pedagogy—building a learning companion. In *Proceedings of the International Conference on Advanced Learning Technologies (ICALT 2001).*

Kurtz, K. J., Miao, C.-II., & Gentner, D. (2001). Learning by analogical bootstrapping. *Journal of the Learning Sciences, 10*(4), 417–446. doi:10.1207/S15327809JLS1004new_2

Lakoff, G., & Johnson, M. (1980). *Metaphors we live by.* Chicago: The University of Chicago Press.

Lakoff, G., & Johnson, M. (1999). *Philosophy in the flesh: The embodied mind and its challenge to Western thought.* New York: Basic Books.

Langhoff, S., Cowan-Sharp, J., Dodson, E., Damer, B., Ketner, B., & Reese, D. D. (2009). *Workshop report: Virtual worlds and immersive environments (No. NASA/CP–2009-214598).* Moffett Field, CA: NASA Ames Research Center.

Markman, A. B., & Gentner, D. (1993). Splitting the difference: A structural alignment view of similarity. *Journal of Memory and Language, 32,* 517–535. doi:10.1006/jmla.1993.1027

Massimini, F., Csikszentmihalyi, M., & Delle Fave, A. (1988). Flow and biocultural evolution. In Csikszentmihalyi, M., & Csikszentmihalyi, I. S. (Eds.), *Optimal experience: Psychological studies of flow in consciousness* (pp. 60–81). New York: Cambridge University Press.

McQuiggan, S. W., Robison, J. L., & Lester, J. C. (2008). Affective transitions in narrative-centered learning environments. *Proceedings of the Ninth International Conference on Intelligent Tutoring Systems,* 490–499.

Merrill, M. D. (2002). First principles of instruction. *Educational Technology Research and Development, 50*(3), 43–59. doi:10.1007/BF02505024

National Research Council. (1995). *National Science Education Standards.* Washington, DC: National Academy Press.

Novak, J. D., & Gowin, D. B. (1984). *Learning how to learn.* New York: Cambridge University Press.

Pajares, F., Hartley, J., & Valiante, G. (2001). Response format in writing self-efficacy assesment: Greater discrimination increases prediction. *Measurement & Evaluation in Counseling & Development, 33,* 214–221.

Pearce, J., Ainley, M., & Howard, S. (2005). The ebb and flow of online learning. *Computers in Human Behavior, 21,* 745–771. doi:10.1016/S0747-5632(04)00036-6

Reese, D. D. (2003a). *Metaphor and content: An embodied paradigm for learning.* Unpublished dissertation, Virginia Polytechnic Institute and State University, Blacksburg, VA.

Reese, D. D. (2003b). Trees of knowledge: Changing mental models through metaphorical episodes and concept maps. In Griffin, R. E., Williams, V. S., & Lee, J. (Eds.), *Turning trees: Selected readings* (pp. 205–214). Loretto, PA: International Visual Literacy Association.

Reese, D. D. (2006a). *Foundations of serious games design and assessment (No. COTF/LVP/Sep-2006).* Wheeling, WV: Center for Educational Technologies, Wheeling Jesuit University.

Reese, D. D. (2007a). First steps and beyond: Serious games as preparation for future learning. *Journal of Educational Media and Hypermedia, 16*(3), 283–300.

Reese, D. D. (2007b, April). *Increasing flow during middle school science with the e-Mission live simulation and the DiSC argumentation tool.* Roundtable presented at the American Educational Research Association, Chicago.

Reese, D. D. (2008). Engineering instructional metaphors within virtual environments to enhance visualization. In Gilbert, J. K., Nakhleh, M., & Reiner, M. (Eds.), *Visualization: Theory and practice in science education* (pp. 133–153). New York: Springer. doi:10.1007/978-1-4020-5267-5_7

Reese, D. D. (2009a, October 27-31). *Replication supports flowometer: Advancing cyberlearning through game-based assessment technologies.* Paper presented at the 2009 International Conference of the Association for Educational Communications and Technology, Louisville, KY.

Reese, D. D. (2009b). Structure mapping theory as a formalism for instructional game design and assessment. In D. Gentner, K. Holyoak, & B. Kokinov (Eds.), *Proceedings of the 2nd International Analogy Conference* (pp. 394–403). Sofia, Bulgaria: New Bulgarian University Press.

Reese, D. D., & Coffield, J. (2005). Just-in-time conceptual scaffolding: Engineering sound instructional metaphors. *International Journal of Technology, Knowledge, and Society*, *1*(4), 183–198.

Reese, D. D., Diehl, V. A., & Lurquin, J. L. (2009, May). *Metaphor enhanced instructional video game causes conceptual gains in lunar science knowledge*. Poster presented at the Association for Psychological Science 21st Annual Convention, San Francisco.

Reese, D. D., Kim, B., Palak, D., Smith, J., & Howard, B. (2005). *Inspiration brief 1: Defining inspiration, the Inspiration Challenge, and the informal event (concept paper) (No. COTF/IB1/6-2005)*. Wheeling, WV: Wheeling Jesuit University.

Reese, D. D., & McFarland, L. (2006). *Inspiration brief 2: The DiSC and RoboKids tools and labs (design and testing) (No. COTF/B2/Jan-2006)*. Wheeling, WV: Center for Educational Technologies, Wheeling Jesuit University.

Reese, D. D., & Tabachnick, B. G. (2010). *The moment of learning: Quantitative analysis of exemplar gameplay supports CyGaMEs approach to embedded assessment [structured abstract]*. Paper to be presented at the Society for Research on Educational Effectiveness 2010 Annual Research Conference, Washington, DC. Retrieved from http://www.sree.org/conferences/2010/program/abstracts/191.pdf

Reese, D. D. (2006b). *Inspiration Brief 3: Enhancing perceived challenge/skill and achievement (DiSC 2005)* (No. COTF/B3/Mar-2006). Wheeling, WV: Center for Educational Technologies, Wheeling Jesuit University.

Reigeluth, C. M. (1994). *The imperative for systemic change. Systemic change in education* (pp. 3–11). Englewood Cliffs, NJ: Educational Technology Publications.

Salen, K. (2007). Gaming literacy studies: A game design study in action. *Journal of Educational Media and Hypermedia*, *16*(3), 301–322.

Salen, K., & Zimmerman, E. (2004). *Rules of play: Game design fundamentals*. Cambridge, MA: MIT Press.

Schell, J. (2008). *The art of game design: A book of lenses*. New York: Elsevier.

Schwartz, D. L., & Bransford, J. D. (1998). A time for telling. *Cognition and Instruction*, *16*(4), 475–522. doi:10.1207/s1532690xci1604_4

Schwartz, D. L., Bransford, J. D., & Sears, D. (2005). Efficiency and innovation in transfer. In Mestre, J. P. (Ed.), *Transfer of learning from a modern multidisciplinary perspective* (pp. 1–51). Greenwich, CT: Information Age.

Schwartz, D. L., & Martin, T. (2004). Inventing to prepare for future learning: The hidden efficiency of encouraging original student production in statistics instruction. *Cognition and Instruction*, *22*(2), 129–184. doi:10.1207/s1532690xci2202_1

Smith, P. L., & Ragan, T. J. (2005). *Instructional design* (3rd ed.). Hoboken, NJ: John Wiley & Sons.

Spiro, R. J., Collins, B. P., Thota, J. J., & Feltovich, P. J. (2003). Cognitive flexibility theory: Hypermedia for complex learning, adaptive knowledge application, and experience acceleration. *Educational Technology*, *43*(5), 5–10.

Sriwatanakul, K., Kelvie, W., Lasagna, L., Calimlim, J. F., Weis, O. F., & Mehta, G. (1983). Visual analogue scales: Measurement of subjective phenomena. *Clinical Pharmacology and Therapeutics*, *34*(2), 234–239.

Wewers, M. E., & Lowe, N. K. (1990). A critical review of visual analogue scales in the measurement of clinical phenomena. *Research in Nursing & Health, 13*(4), 227–236. doi:10.1002/nur.4770130405

Wright, W. (2004). *Sculpting possibility space*. Paper presented at the Accelerating Change 2004: Physical Space, Virtual Space, and Interface conference (keynote address). Retrieved June 16, 2006, from http://cdn.itconversations.com/ITC. AC2004-WillWright-2004.11.07.mp3

Wright, W. (2006). Dream machines. *Wired, 14*(4). Retrieved from http://www.wired.com/wired/archive/14.04/wright.html

Zimmer, C. (2008, September 2). Gaming evolves. *The New York Times*. Retrieved from http://www.nytimes.com/2008/09/02/science/02spor.html?_r=1&8dpc&oref=slogin

ENDNOTES

[1] Jesse Schell (2008) explains there "is no 'unified theory of game design,' no simple formula that shows us how to make good games," and video game designers "are in a position something like the ancient alchemists. .. [i]n the time before Mendeleev discovered the periodic table.. . ." Today's designers work with a "patchwork of principles and rules" (p. xxv). Furthermore, according to Will Wright, what is known has not widely disseminated within university game design programs (Langhoff et al., 2009).

[2] Although the entertainment video game industry annually invests about $1.6 billion in research and development (Crandall & Sidak), successful entertainment game design is a challenge. For example, since 2002, Electronic Arts (EA) has annually invested between 16% and 20% of its sales revenue back into research and development (p. 20). EA's 2004 sales totaled almost $3 billion dollars (p. 17), so that's between $473 million and $592 million in R&D. Despite R&D investment the majority of entertainment video games "fail to find commercial or critical success" (Fullerton, 2008, p. 266), and "only 10 percent of games earn a profit" (Crandall & Sidak, p. 14).

[3] The method would be generic, but each instantiation of the intervention would be specific for one or more targeted concepts. That is, the method is domain-general, but each learning object developed through the method is domain- specific.

APPENDIX: ADDITIONAL READING

"Must-Reads" for This Topic

Fullerton, T., Swain, C., & Hoffman, S. (2004). *Game design workshop: Designing, prototyping, and playtesting games.* San Francisco: CMP Books.

Gentner, D. (1983). Structure mapping: A theoretical framework for analogy. *Cognitive Science, 7,* 155–170.

Hatano, G., & Inagaki, K. (1986). Two courses of expertise. In H. Stevenson, H. Azuma, & K. Hakuta (Eds.), *Child development and education in Japan* (pp. 262–272). New York: W. H. Freeman and Company.

Hestenes, D., Wells, M., & Swackhamer, G. (1992). Force concept inventory. *The Physics Teacher, 30,* 141–158.

Huizinga, J. (1950). *Homo ludens: A study of play–element in culture* (paperback ed.). Boston: Beacon Press.

Jonassen, D. H. (2006). On the role of concepts in learning and instructional design. *Educational Technology, Research, & Development, 54*(2), 177–196.

Norman, D. (1995). *Things that make us smart: Defending human attributes in the age of the machine.* Reading, MA: Addison Wesley.

Reese, D. D. (2007). First steps and beyond: Serious games as preparation for future learning. *Journal of Educational Media and Hypermedia, 16*(3), 283–300.

Reese, D. D. (2008). GaME design for intuitive concept knowledge. In R. E. Ferdig (Ed.), *Handbook of research on effective electronic gaming in education* (Vol. 3, pp. 1104–1126). Hershey, PA: Idea Group.

Reese, D. D. (2009). Structure mapping theory as a formalism for instructional game design and assessment. In D. Gentner, K. Holyoak, & B. Kokinov (Eds.), *Proceedings of the 2nd International Analogy Conference* (pp. 394–403). Sofia, Bulgaria: New Bulgarian University Press.

Schell, J. (2008). *The art of game design: A book of lenses.* NY: Elsevier.

Schwartz, D. L., & Martin, T. (2004). Inventing to prepare for future learning: The hidden efficiency of encouraging original student production in statistics instruction. *Cognition and Instruction, 22*(2), 129–184.

Smith, P. L., & Ragan, T. J. (2005). *Instructional design* (3rd ed.). Hoboken, NJ: John Wiley & Sons.

Wright, W. (2004). *Sculpting possibility space.* Keynote presented at the Accelerating Change 2004: Physical Space, Virtual Space, and Interface conference. Retrieved June 16, 2006, from http://cdn.itconversations.com/ITC.AC2004-WillWright-2004.11.07.mp3

Top Texts for Interdisciplinary Studies of Serious Games

CyGaMEs methods and theory are interdisciplinary, and important references are listed in the preceding section. Jesse Schell posed the question, "What Skills Does a Game Designer Need?" and then listed and discussed a set of skills (Schell, 2008, pp. 2–5):

- Animation
- Anthropology

- Architecture
- Brainstorming
- Business
- Cinematography
- Communication
- Creative writing
- Economics
- Engineering
- History
- Management
- Mathematics
- Music
- Psychology
- Public speaking
- Sound design
- Technical writing
- Visual arts
- Listening

At this time, the best advice I can give an inquiring game scholar is to combine Jesse Schell's list of options with instructional design, cognitive science, and learning science.

Chapter 12

Different Strokes for Different Folks:
Tapping Into the Hidden Potential of Serious Games

Brian Magerko
Georgia Institute of Technology, USA

Carrie Heeter
Michigan State University, USA

Ben Medler
Georgia Institute of Technology, USA

ABSTRACT

Digital game-based learning experiences are typically presented to a captive audience that has to play, as opposed to entertainment games that players can select themselves and choose to play. The captive nature of learning games introduces an interesting issue: Not everyone may be familiar with the genre of the game they have to play or be motivated to play it. Students have individual differences that may make a learning game particularly ineffective, uninteresting, or inappropriate for some learners. The authors present work that frames important differences between students in terms of their game literacy, motivation, goal orientation, and mind-set. This understanding leads us to envision game design variations to serve specific combinations of particular individual differences at the intersection of learning and gaming. The authors present their initial work on identifying and automatically accommodating these differences within a single digital game-based learning experience.

INTRODUCTION

Computer games for entertainment are purchased from stores, played online at certain Web sites, or borrowed from friends as part of a selective, free

market culture of choice. Game players decide what games they want to play, when and where they will play them, etc. In other words, playing games for fun is a voluntary and highly selective experience. Games for learning, on the other hand, can be quite the opposite. There are informal learning games, mainly distributed on the Web, that players can

DOI: 10.4018/978-1-61520-717-6.ch012

voluntarily choose to play, however there are many other learning games that are presented within the context of a school or training curriculum. Serious games played within a military training context, as part of a high school curriculum, or used in corporate training are relatively involuntary mandatory learning experiences that are equivalent to assigned lab experiments, interactive training videos, simulation exercises, etc.

Games for learning face a much more diverse player audience than players of entertainment games, because the audience is not self-selected. A learning game's audience may include those who rarely play any kind of game (i.e., "non-gamers") and those who dislike and normally avoid playing the genre used by that particular learning game. The ramifications of this are obvious, although surprisingly overlooked in the digital game-based learning community at present: while certain games may be fun for many people (e.g., the best-selling *Civilization* series of games which are widely used for education; Squire, 2005), they may not be "fun," "engaging," and "motivating" for an entire class. Even the most wonderful learning games will undoubtedly fail to reach all members of the target audience.

If the only consequence of using a learning game with non-gamers were a lack of fun, there would be little cause for concern. However, unfamiliarity with gaming in general or with a particular learning game genre can present barriers to achieving learning goals. A player must effectively master how to play a learning game in order to experience the desired learning content. From the perspective of cognitive load, we might infer that mental attention devoted to trying to figure out how to play is attention not devoted to the intended learning (Low, Jin, & Sweller, this volume; Mayer, 2005a; Mayer, 2005b). Non-gamers need to exert much more effort figuring out how to play most games than do experienced gamers. Furthermore, feeling lost and incompetent trying to play a learning game introduces negative thoughts that can create performance deficits by diverting

cognitive load (Cadinu, Maass, Rosabianca & Kiesner, 2005; Croizet et al., 2004), with negative consequences for learning (Covington, Omelich, & Schwarzer, 1986; Thomas et al., 2006). Other students may have extensive gaming experience but may find playing a particular learning game uninteresting or even unpleasant, regardless of their interest in the subject matter the game is designed to teach. In other words, using games for learning as a one-size-fits-all educational approach leaves some students unmotivated and presents others with a distinctly unfamiliar and potentially inscrutable experience.

Individual Differences

This inherent disparity in the effectiveness of even well-designed serious games is a problem that needs to be addressed by recognizing important individual differences amongst students and by changing our game design and development practices to accommodate those differences. The authors contend that four key obstacles to digital game-based learning should be considered in this respect: gaming literacy, gaming motivation, gaming mindset, and the congruence of student's goal orientation with the game design. This is in contrast to Low (in press), who states that goals, intrinsic vs. extrinsic motivation, interest, and self-schema are the main motivational principles.

Gaming Literacy

K-6 education teaches reading, writing, and oral language, carefully preparing students to learn from books and other forms of writing (ACEI, 2007). K-12 education does not teach gaming. Gaming literacy is acquired (or not) outside of school, through voluntary leisure activities. In order to learn from a game, players must learn how to play and they must experience the intended learning content by playing. Salen (2007, p. 10) points out that "learning about games and learning with games take place simultaneously." Players must figure out how to "read" the game. They must understand how systems operate within a game, what actions are and are not possible. Simple learning games tend to be designed with a goal of providing the same learning experience to all players. Researchers have noticed that in the case of complex games like the *RollerCoaster Tycoon* series, different student players are motivated to develop specific areas of expertise (Foster & Mishra, 2009). Myriad obvious and not so obvious factors about the game and the learner contribute to successful learning from a game. Gaming literacy plays an obvious role.

Like other media, games are often categorized by genre. The classification helps audiences locate preferred content and provides designers with a core framework to work with. Each individual game has its own unique learning curve, but games in the same genre typically share similar mechanics and gaming conventions. A player who has a lot of experience playing games in a particular genre has developed genre-specific literacy. He or she will almost certainly have an easier pathway to learning how to play another game in that same genre than those unfamiliar with the genre. Learners who are less experienced with the genre used by a particular learning game will have to work harder to learn how to play the game than players experienced with that genre, before they can focus on learning the content the game is intended to teach.

Serious games that emulate a known genre inherit player expectations and player expertise. Serious games where the designers do not follow any common genre present all players with a new learning curve. Although unique game designs sound like they would equalize the gaming literacy disparity, because designers start from scratch, inventing how play happens, they fail to capitalize on decades of game design progress (which may help explain why educational games have historically been considered not very fun). Gaming literacy, including game genre literacy, has deep implications for learning game design.

The needs of novices and experts both need to be accommodated.

Motivation

Motivation refers to needs, goals, interests, concerns, and other kinds of pleasures or pains a learner experiences or anticipates experiencing as a result of trying to learn something; it is a central correlate to learning. Students who are more motivated either because of intrinsic fascination with the subject matter or extrinsic desire to earn good grades are more likely to learn (Lepper & Henderlong, 2000). Successful commercial games attract players because they are fun and engaging, using both intrinsic and extrinsic motivation to entice players. Consequently, a key reason that teachers consider using learning games in their classes is the hopes of motivating their students. The motivational benefit teachers anticipate from using a game can range from a modest hope that students find it "more fun than a boring lecture" (Winn & Heeter, 2007) to an idealized expectation that great games engender great pedagogy to such an extent that they "recruit learning as a form of fun and mastery" (Gee, 2007b). Different students may be intrinsically or extrinsically motivated (or unmotivated) to learn the subject matter. Gaming adds another level of motivation. Players may be motivated by intrinsic and/or extrinsic rewards within the game, separate from their interest in the subject matter.

Mindset

Achievement or goal orientation refers to how individuals perceive and respond to achievement situations (Dweck & Leggett, 1988). Theories about mindset and motivation suggest that some individuals welcome hard challenges and others avoid failure. According to Dweck (2006), mindsets can "change the meaning of effort" (p. 39). She explains that people with a *Mastery* mindset relish challenge (Dweck, 2000, 2006). They find easy challenges boring and are resilient in the face of failure because they believe in their capacity to learn and improve. The converse is a *Fixed*, or *Helpless* mindset (Dweck, 2000). People who have a Fixed mindset worry about how they are performing instead of whether they are learning. They seek easy challenges to avoid failure and validate their self-worth. Dweck describes American popular culture as reinforcing the idea that people have to either be smart or hardworking, but not both, to succeed. Our culture expects and reveres effortless perfection. Mindset theories have deep implications for game design because players who play with a fixed mindset will be overly worried about failure in the game, whereas players with a Mastery mindset will relish learning through trial and error.

Congruence of Goal Orientation

Matching teaching methods to learning styles has not been shown to impact learning (Coffield, Moseley, Hall, & Ecclestone, 2004). However, a related psychological theory, the theory of regulatory fit (Aaker & Lee, 2006), does support the idea of matching goal orientation with process to increase motivation and learning. Higgins proposes "people experience regulatory fit when the manner of their engagement in an activity sustains their goal orientation or interests regarding that activity" (Higgins, 2005, p. 209). The theory distinguishes *eager* and *vigilant* goal orientations. Someone with an eager goal orientation is trying to satisfy a need for accomplishment; he or she seeks positive rewards from an activity. Someone with a vigilant goal orientation is trying to satisfy a need for security or to fulfill a sense of duty; he or she wants to avoid negative consequences.

Individuals have a predilection toward either vigilance or eagerness, but researchers have also found they can manipulate goal orientation based on how instructions for a task are described. These variations seem subtle but have profound consequences. Regulatory fit between goal orientation

and task behavior strengthens engagement. It has a magnifying effect—it makes you feel worse about a bad thing or better about a good thing. The idea of regulatory fit has interesting implications for learning game design. Learning games could either cater to individual differences by providing two distinctly different modes of play, each designed to maximize either eager or vigilant play or they could frame game play to help induce the goal orientation that best suits the game mechanics.

Proposed Solution

These four critical ways individual learners may differ when they are exposed to a new digital game-based learning experience (Fixed or Mastery mindset, and eager or vigilant goal orientation) are likely to impact engagement with and learning from a game. Unfortunately, games for learning are not typically designed with these individual differences in mind. The game industry has begun to consider how games might appeal to diverse player preferences in the entertainment realm such as gender- and age-related predilections (for example, see Kafai et al., 2008), but the kind of fine-grained analysis of student needs and interests (and resulting design accommodations) the authors introduce in this chapter has simply not been done to date. Once we reach a sophisticated understanding of the variations in gaming literacy, motivation, and mindset that students can have, what can be done with that knowledge to design better, more effective games for learning?

The initial step to improving the efficacy of learning games is to map the most important individual differences among students noted above to possible game design features. For instance, we need to understand how a game should be different for those with extrinsic versus intrinsic motivation or what features of games such players enjoy (and dislike) the most. We need to arrive at a set of design principles that can help designers better target a varied student population (a similar approach is described in Low, in press).

Once we have a firm understanding of how individual student differences can map to potential variations in game designs, we have to answer the question of how these different design principles can be incorporated into the design of games for learning. The obvious, brute force approach is to simply publish multiple versions of a game that reflect the different combinations of learner motivations and gaming literacy (e.g., one for intrinsically motivated gamers, one for intrinsically motivated non-gamers, extrinsically motivated gamers, one for extrinsically motivated non-gamers, etc.). Developers could then ship these multiple versions as distinct games. This would be expensive, of course, and given the reluctance of commercial developers to develop even single-title games, perhaps prohibitively so.

Alternatively, the variations could be shipped as a single game with different "modes," giving the player the power to choose the learning mode they prefer. This approach would essentially allow players to self-diagnose their individual differences and decide what kind of game would be best for them. This approach does have possible drawbacks, however. For instance, player self-perception of differences may not be terribly accurate, thus failing to optimally match game style with a player's true motivational and literacy needs.

An alternate approach to self-selection of game variation would be to automatically identify or detect each student's individual differences (i.e., game literacy, motivation, goal orientation, and mindset) and assign game mechanics based on that assessment. Automatic assessment could be done in one of two ways: asking the player to answer a questionnaire before playing the game that would help map the player to a certain player type or to have the player play a diagnostic game that provides enough feedback through game play for the system to recognize the player type from observation. The former is a much more straightforward, although obvious and obtrusive, approach while the latter is much less direct but

more difficult to execute. The end result with either approach will be a seamless game experience where students begin with an assessment period and then are provided with a game experience that is accurately mapped to their player type.

This chapter will explore in more detail the individual differences in motivation, mindset, and goal orientation the authors have highlighted here and how those can potentially relate to game design. The authors will explore the mappings from player types to design principles. Finally, the authors present a prototype game, called S.C.R.U.B., which employs their theories on player types and game design, and discuss future work.

BACKGROUND

Motivation to learn varies from student to student and it can be different for each individual depending on the topic. Students' motivation to achieve at school can be based on extrinsic goals external to the learning content, such as earning good grades or teacher approval. Intrinsic goals can also motivate learning, such as the pleasure felt when mastering a new topic or some new content, general curiosity about the subject matter, or a general sense of expertise over time as knowledge grows. Intrinsic and extrinsic motivation can coexist, but as the authors will discuss later, offering learners extrinsic rewards can have a detrimental impact on intrinsic motivation (Lepper & Henderlong, 2000). Studies show that students generally have higher intrinsic than extrinsic motivation but that intrinsic motivation declines significantly between third and eighth grades (Henderlong & Lepper, 2002).

Adding motivation possibilities to a game for learning adds complexity to an already complex milieu. In general, games are motivating for students who love games. However, games are likely to interfere with learning for students who dislike games. Games also vary in the extent to which they offer intrinsic and extrinsic rewards

(Heeter, Magerko, Medler, & Fitzgerald, 2009). Researchers have hypothesized that some game genres appeal more to extrinsically motivated player types (called *Achievers*) who enjoy earning high scores and winning, while other game genres attract intrinsically motivated players who enjoy discovery, collecting, and role play (called *Explorers*) (Bartle, 1996; Yee, 2006). As the authors will discuss in this section, research shows that the individual student differences of motivation, mindset, and goals affect a student's learning experience.

Intrinsic Motivation and Learning

Intrinsic rewards arise from the process of learning or play and extrinsic rewards from the results (grades, points, winning, or approval). Fostering intrinsic goals can create self-directed learners and expand a student's productivity into other areas (Low, in press). Experimental schools such as Montessori schools, which nurture intrinsic motivation to drive learning, are rare exceptions. Rather than structuring a learning progression through standardized curriculum and standardized grades, Montessori tries to instill an internal sense of purpose. It avoids setting learners up to compete for the highest grade in the class. According to Montessori President Tim Seldin, "Students learn not to be afraid of making mistakes; they come to see them as natural steps in the learning process" (Seldin, 2008, p. 2). Maintaining this level of intrinsic motivation is important, as removing it may hinder the student's learning experience (Low, in press).

Beswick (1971, 1974) found that intrinsically motivated individuals need time to explore. He explains that intrinsically motivated individuals "tend [to] be more aware of a wide range of phenomena, while giving careful attention to complexities, inconsistencies, novel events, and unexpected possibilities. They need time and freedom to make choices, to gather and process information. . . ." (Beswick, 2007, p.1). Therefore,

intrinsic motivation and extrinsic motivations cannot always be equally well served. For example, meeting the need of time to explore can directly compete with competition based on a time limit.

Extrinsic Motivation and Learning

Formal education tends to be structured to use the threat of poor grades to motivate homework and learning. At the beginning of a semester or school year, teachers describe how standardized grades will be fairly assigned. Students are expected to do what is necessary to "pass" or, better yet, to excel on the exams and other kinds of performances. Report cards document standardized achievement, informing students and parents about the learner's performance. In the context of this kind of achievement-focused education, learning scientists have looked at the impact of *achievement orientation* on learning, which refers to how individuals perceive and respond to achievement situations (Dweck & Leggett, 1988). People who have a high achievement motivation enjoy challenges much more than those with a low achievement motivation (Lee, Sheldon, & Turban, 2003).

Additionally, Elliot and Church (1997) considered two quite different reasons individuals might have for pursuing extrinsic performance goals such as grades. *Performance-approach goals* are linked to displaying competence and earning a favorable judgment. *Performance-avoidance goals* focus on trying to avoid failure. Elliot and Church found positive outcomes for performance-approach goals including positive emotions and absorption in the given task. Performance-avoidance prompted efforts to escape the potential consequences of failure and was associated with anxiety. Performance-avoidance interfered with mental focus, blocking the individual's ability to concentrate and become absorbed in an activity, while the performance-approach goals approach enhanced mental focus.

Mindset

Dweck (2006) made similar observations to those of Elliot and Church. She studied how people approach or avoid challenge in a school context. She found that about 42% of students have what she calls a growth, or Mastery, mindset. These people believe that intelligence is malleable; that they are capable of improving it if they try. Another 42% have a Fixed, or helpless, mindset. They believe that intelligence is fixed at birth and cannot improve. They avoid situations that they cannot easily do well at. Failure undermines their confidence, and if they fail, they become depressed and ineffective. (The remaining 16% could not be classified as either Fixed or Mastery mindset). Having a Fixed mindset can undo a natural love of learning. In contrast, effort and learning make mastery-motivated students feel good about their intelligence; easy tasks waste their time rather than raise their self-esteem. Dweck describes the conundrum of the Fixed mindset. "If you're in a Fixed mindset, both positive and negative labels can mess with your mind. When you're given a positive label, you're afraid of losing it. When you're given a negative label, you're afraid of deserving it" (Dweck, 2006, pp 75–76).

Mangels worked with Dweck and other colleagues to measure brain activation among individuals with a Fixed and Mastery mindset (Mangels et al., 2006). Participants completed a pretest that allowed researchers to classify them as one or the other mindset. They answered a series of knowledge questions and were given feedback about whether their answers were right or wrong and what the right answer was. Brain scans revealed people with a Mastery mindset paid close attention to what the right answer was. Those with a Fixed mindset showed activation of the limbic, or emotional system, but paid much less attention to learning the right answer. In other words, Fixed mindset people focused on their own emotional response to being told they were right or wrong, whereas Mastery mindset people paid most attention to learning new information.

Having a Fixed mindset is considered dysfunctional for learning because it focuses learners on performance instead of mastery. Educators who are aware of the research look for ways to ease learners out of a Fixed mindset and into a Mastery mindset. They also craft feedback to focus on ways the learner can improve, rather than on labeling the person a success or failure (Dweck, 2006, Lepper and Henderlong, 2000).

Combining the research discussed, Fixed mindset, performance-avoidance individuals are likely to experience anxiety when faced with achievement situations. Impression management is a similar psychological construct that refers to ways individuals consciously and unconsciously try to influence or control other people's perceptions of them (Goffman, 1959). Those with a Fixed mindset might be considered *Validators* because, when called upon to perform on a test at school or in a game, they worry about their impression in front of others if they fail; not failing is a way for them to validate their existence with the group. This concern may motivate studying, but this preoccupation with appearing to be successful can also interfere with performance.

Regulatory Fit and Goal Orientation

In a series of studies between 1995 and the present, Higgins and colleagues have developed and tested the theory of regulatory fit (Higgins, 2000, Higgins, 2005). When people pursue a goal, such as earning a good grade in a class, they begin with a motivational orientation. That motivational focus may be prevention-oriented (the need to not get a bad grade because doing so is important to get into medical school) or the focus may be promotion-oriented (getting an "A" would provide a personal sense of accomplishment). Those with a prevention orientation will experience regulatory fit when they pursue a vigilant strategy, carefully completing all course requirements. Those with a promotion orientation will experience regulatory fit when they pursue an eager strategy (such as reading extra materials).

Regulatory fit has been shown to improve motivational strength, task performance, and changes in attitude and behavior (Forster, Higgins, & Idson, 1998; Higgins 2000, 2005). When regulatory fit occurs, people also feel better about what they are doing. These results have been found when study participants' natural motivational predilections are designed for and when a prevention or promotion orientation was experimentally induced.

Higgins' work strongly supports the idea of matching player motivation with learning game features to enhance learning. Higgins' work echoes Dweck's Fixed versus Mastery mindset and Elliot and Church's performance-approach versus performance-avoidance extrinsic motivations. However, rather than considering promotion-focused need for achievement as superior to prevention-focused need for vigilance and caution, Higgins has shown that matching an individual's goal orientation (either prevention or promotion) with the task can enhance task performance (Higgins, 2006).

Motivation Dichotomies

Let's review the motivation, mindset, and goal orientation dichotomies that have been discussed so far.

Extrinsic motivation vs. intrinsic motivation – These represent whether a student is motivated to learn material because of an external reward (extrinsic) or for the pleasure of learning (intrinsic). Intrinsic and extrinsic motivations can coexist, and, unfortunately, students may also be not motivated at all. Self-determination theory also explores the relationship between extrinsic and intrinsic motivation (Low, in press).

Achievement goal orientation vs. Performance goal orientation – Students who strive for achievement goals may either work for extrinsic achievements (an "A" grade) or intrinsic ones ("I have learned something new"). Performance goals are strictly pursued for extrinsic motivations and can be split into two types (stated next).

Performance-approach goals vs. Performance-avoidance goals – These extrinsic goals are related to how students manage their image in front of other students. Students pursue performance-approach goals when they wish to show competency in the learning content (showing they understand the material to other students), while performance-avoidance goals are pursued when students do not wish to fail in front of their peers (for instance, not raising their hand if they are unsure about an answer).

Mastery mindset vs. fixed mindset – Students who have Mastery mindsets relish challenges and can accept failure as a learning experience. Fixed mindset individuals experience failure and success as evidence of low intelligence rather than as a learning experience. They enjoy the validation of success but would choose safe challenges.

Prevention-oriented goals vs. promotion-oriented goals – A person's reasons for pursuing a goal influences whether a person's goal is prevention-oriented or promotion-oriented. A prevention-oriented goal focuses on the extrinsic rewards for accomplishing a goal, while a promotion-oriented goal focuses on the intrinsic rewards for accomplishing a goal.

The motivations, mindsets, and goals of a student can vary wildly, given these various dichotomies and their combinations. Extrinsic and intrinsic motivations are one of the major factors in determining the student's best learning experience, but a student's mindset and chosen goals have just as much effect on the type of learning experience that will help that student the most. However, our discussion so far is missing the last student difference, game literacy, which may affect the design of the learning game the most. After all, understanding how to play a game itself is the main barrier of entry for any learning game.

This means that instead of focusing solely on the type of learning experience a student should have in order to learn we must also focus on the type of game experience they should have. Combining learning and game experiences means we must leave the research that revolves around understanding motivation's effects on learning and explore how motivation (as well as mindsets and goals) affects how individuals play games.

MOTIVATION, PLAY STYLE, AND GAMES

Most of the research on motivation and mindset reviewed in the previous sections looked at motivation in relation to learning, particularly learning in the context of formal education. Turning to the realm of games, is there such a thing as gaming motivations, gaming mindset, and gaming goal orientation? Games and learning scholar James Gee writes, "Good computer and video games are complex, challenging, and long; they can take 50 or more hours to finish" (Gee, 2007a, p. 45). Gee goes on to point out that failing is part of playing a video game: "[failure in video games] allow[s] players to take risks and try out hypotheses" (Gee, 2007a, p. 153). In other words, playing entertainment games is fraught with the same kinds of performance and achievement issues and intrinsic and extrinsic motivations that have been studied in relation to classroom learning. In this respect, game players are subject to the same motivation and learning dichotomies that the authors discussed above. The authors find that gaming motivations have indeed been a focus of some academic and game industry research, studied primarily in the context of player types and games for entertainment.

Player Types

Player types, a term that is sometimes used interchangeably with player style, categorize players based on their motivations for playing. The authors differentiate player type from play style, which can be defined as a particular "style of play" available within a particular game or the style of play a player enacts while playing a particular game.

Hence, player type is conceived of as a trait or underlying characteristic of the player, whereas a player's play style is actual play behavior enacted while playing a specific game. Play style is constrained by the mechanics available in a game. Particular game genres only offer players certain game mechanics and tactics. Thus, players may not be free to engage in the play style that fits their player type, a play style the authors assume they would most prefer if it were available. The tug of intrinsic and extrinsic motivations for an individual may depend on the circumstance of play and the nature of the game. In her research on motivation and learning, Dweck points out that people tend to have a Mastery mindset in some realms and a Helpless mindset in other domains (Dweck, 2006). Furthermore, players may sometimes choose a play style that is inconsistent with their player type, whether for variety, for mood management purposes, or other reasons.

Previous studies on player types have categorized the different motivations that players experience while playing games. Richard Bartle researched player behavior in "multi-user dungeon" (MUD) games in 1996 and classified players into four general categories of motivation (1996). Two player types focus on the player's relationship with the game's environment. The first, Achievers, enjoy acting in the game, scoring points and winning the game. The second, Explorers, are motivated by interaction and wish to learn about how a game functions. Bartle's other player types focus on the social aspects of MUDs and include Socializers, who interact with other players, and Killers, who impede other players in a game (for example, killing another player or helping another player without being asked).

Nearly a decade after Bartle's research, Nick Yee's *Daedalus Project* (2008) focused its attention on the new wave of social games, which have become known as massively multiplayer online games or MMOs. Yee's project surveyed thousands of MMO players and found three main motivating factors for play: achievement, socializing, and immersion. While socializing proved to be similar to Bartle's social player type, these new motivation categories found were in some ways similar to Bartle's four player types, but in other ways they were different.

The two motivation areas that Yee declares as achievement and immersion include multiple subcategories. These subcategories contain a mix of both Achiever and Explorer player types laid out by Bartle. Players that were motivated by achievements included the motivations for Advancement (progress, power accumulation, and status), Mechanics (numbers optimization, templating, and analysis), and Competition (challenging others, provocation, and domination).

Players motivated by immersion included motivations for discovery (exploration, lore, finding hidden things), role-playing (storyline, character history, roles, fantasy), customization (appearances, accessories, style, color scheme), and escapism (relax, escape from real life, avoiding real-life problems). Motivations such as mechanics, discovery, and customization have similar traits but can be found in different motivation categories. Players thus do not always adhere to a strict player type or set of motivations. For our purposes the authors use *Achiever* and *Explorer* as loose player type titles that focus on whether the player is extrinsically motivated or intrinsically motivated, respectively.

Along with Achiever and Explorer player type, the authors have proposed a third type, *Validators*, not found in any previous player type studies (Heeter et al., 2009). In proposing this new type, the authors integrate Dweck's mindset theories; Validators are players who approach gaming with a Fixed mindset. Validators enjoy the validation of positive feedback but experience failure as a commentary on their worthiness. They seek easy challenges where positive validation is likely and avoid hard challenges so as not to risk failure. Validators face a vicious cycle when it comes to digital games for learning. Validators who try playing an unfamiliar entertainment game genre

and fail in their early attempts would probably avoid the genre. Overall, Validators probably play easier games for entertainment or choose easier levels within a game, so that playing and winning becomes rewarding validation of self-worth. This results in Validators having lower gaming literacy in game genres based on hard challenges. When forced to play a learning game in a genre they already avoid, Validators will be less literate in the genre and would likely be more devastated by negative feedback. Even if a Validator has simply never tried a game genre, his or her unfamiliarity makes failure more likely, while aversion to failure makes failure more painful. Validators are the player type most at risk of not learning from a learning game.

Gaming literacy and mindset also intersect with gender. Boys spend more time gaming than girls do—an average of at least 100 more hours per year from middle school through college (Winn & Heeter, 2009), and they play more different genres than girls (Lenhart et al., 2008). The result is that boys develop more diverse and extensive gaming literacy. Dweck notes that boys encounter more criticism and girls more praise at school, setting girls up to equate other people's feedback with their sense of self-worth and encouraging a helpless mindset (Dweck, 2006, p. 78). Girls are probably more likely to be Validators and, for that reason as well as girls' limited gaming literacy, are more at risk of not learning from a learning game. The authors feel that designing games that address the needs of Validators, along with Achiever and Explorer player types, is key to developing universally accessible learning games.

The figure below (Figure 1) maps hypothetical "flow" trajectories for our two extrinsically motivated player types: Achievers and Validators. The chart reflects the interests of pure types. The Y axis represents challenge and the X axis represents player ability. There is an assumption that players' skill will improve as they play; therefore, the challenge should also increase to maintain optimal engagement.

Keeping different player types motivated requires different trajectories. Achievers thrive on difficult challenge, and the challenge needs to increase in relation to their growing skill as they learn while playing. Validators follow a much gentler trajectory. Challenge can increase slightly as their skill increases, but success should always be within reach. The idea of "easy fun" would appeal to Validators, but these players would likely prefer that the fun not be labeled "easy." It might be better to use a less humiliating label for players concerned about saving face. Explorers may experience a mix of extrinsic and intrinsic motivation or they may be purely intrinsic. Pure Explorers may prefer not to be distracted from their exploration by irrelevant challenges. Explorers interested in extrinsic rewards could be either Explorer–Achievers or Explorer–Validators.

Each player motivation implies a different trajectory for optimal amount of challenge relative to growing player skill. Figure 1 shows hypothetical trajectories over time for each player type. Compared to Achievers, Validators prefer a much gentler increasing of challenge, ensuring easy victories. For explorers challenge is irrelevant. Their primary interest is the intrinsic curiosity of discovery, whether it is easy or difficult. Of course, players may be part Explorer and part Achiever or Validator. Most players probably do not fit a single pure type.

Our discussion extends player type research to characterize player types that are grounded in theories and research on motivation, mindset, and goal orientation, as discussed in the introduction. Achievers, Explorers and Validators are the three player types the authors arrived at when they combined the motivation and player type research. Moving forward, we must now attempt to combine our player types with the idea of automatically assessing and adapting to these player types in a serious game.

MAPPING INDIVIDUAL DIFFERENCES TO GAME DIFFERENCES

Given that players may be motivated by extrinsic or intrinsic rewards and have fixed or mastery mindsets, how do these translate into game content? Can game designers support Achievers, Explorers and Validators at the same time or must they focus their attention on a smaller subset of them? Understanding the differences between the player types helps answer these questions and discover design principles for building games to match each player's motivation and mindset.

Figure 1. Trajectories of optimal challenge and skill by player type

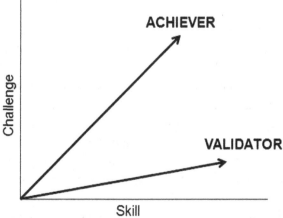

The main difference between motivating players with extrinsic and intrinsic rewards is how the reward itself relates to the game's content. Extrinsic rewards are represented by concepts like points, health, mana, or any other arbitrary numbers given to the player. Acquiring more points or keeping a character's health high offers challenges for the extrinsic player or Achievers. Having quantitative number systems like "points" or "damage dealt" allow game designers to alter difficulty level much easier. Achievers are then motivated by these difficult challenges and by giving Achievers specific goals a designer helps these players understand what they need to do. Scoreboards and ranking systems are an easy way to set goals for Achievers and are used to support the competition between players. Competition with an entire game community offers the greatest, and most dynamic, challenge for a player who is extrinsically motivated.

Intrinsically motivated players, or Explorers, focus on the specifics of a game's content. They do not need specific challenges that are offered to Achievers (in fact, such challenges may interfere with free exploration) but they do need a rich enough environment to explore. Allowing Explorers to customize their avatars or game world, incorporating discovery and collection, or providing authoring tools would appeal to these players. Extended storylines or diverse sets of game mechanics could also give Explorers other dimensions to explore. These features can engage Explorers much like a scoreboard challenges an Achiever, except Explorers may prefer to invent their own challenges and rewards.

Achievers follow a mastery mindset; they seek new challenges in the environment and as a result, if the game is well designed, grow and learn with their new experiences. Rewards are just as desirable for the Validator as they are for the Achiever but they must be more prevalent and easier to win. Achievers want rewards that they have earned for mastering difficult tasks while Validators want to be told that they are wonder-ful and to avoid failure. Validators may also want control over the exposure of these rewards. Hiding bad performances could be a welcomed feature for these players, as they just want to prove to themselves that they can play a game. They do not want to receive negative feedback for performing tasks slower or differently than other more experienced players.

Genre Preferences and Player Types

The authors' research has determined that commercial games tend to specialize in pleasing a single player type (Heeter et al., 2009). For example, role-play games (RPGs) and first-person shooters (FPS) strongly support extrinsic motivations. Life simulation games support intrinsic motivations. In a prior content analysis study, the authors classified eight entertainment games by genre and by whether they primarily offered extrinsic or intrinsic player rewards. (See Table 1.)

Four of the games, *Bioshock* (2K Boston/2K Australia, 2007), *Guitar Hero* (RedOctane, 2005), *Keep It in Mind* (Brain Powered Games, 2009) *and Puzzle Quest* (D3 Publisher, 2007), offer extrinsic rewards to the player and thus may support the Achiever and Validator player types. The other four games, *Animal Crossing* (Nintendo, 2001), *Budget Hero* (American Public Media, 2008), *FlOw* (Sony, 2006), and *Play the News* (Impact Games, LLC, 2008) mainly offer intrinsic rewards and thus may support Explorer player types. The genres examined include first-person shooters, or FPS, play along, brain games, puzzle/role-play games, or RPG, virtual life, sensory experience, current events, and budget simulation.

Research on player types has so far only looked within a particular game or game genre. We do not know the extent to which players may have a different player type when they play different game genres, or if people tend to only choose game genres that accommodate a single underlying player type. We do know that people don't simply play games; they tend to specialize in one or a few

Table 1. A list of the eight games that were analyzed, including their genre and whether the game caters to intrinsically or extrinsically motivated players (Heeter et al., 2009)

Game	Genre	Player motivation
Bioshock (2K Boston/2K Australia, 2007)	FPS	EXTRINSIC
Guitar Hero (RedOctane, 2005)	Play along	EXTRINSIC
Keep It in Mind (Brain Powered Games, 2009)	Brain game	EXTRINSIC
Puzzle Quest (D3 Publisher, 2007)	Puzzle/RPG	EXTRINSIC
Animal Crossing (Nintendo, 2001)	Virtual life	INTRINSIC
Budget Hero (American Public Media, 2008)	Budget simulation	INTRINSIC
FlOw (Sony, 2006)	Sensory experience	INTRINSIC
Play the News (Impact Games, LLC, 2008)	Current events	INTRINSIC

genres of game. One consequence is that they are likely to be unfamiliar with how to play the genres they avoid, which they probably rejected because they were unappealing to them.

There are also gender differences in genre preferences, which have implications for creating universally accessible learning games. According to a recent Pew Foundation study of teens and gaming (Lenhart, Kahne, Middaugh, Evans, & Vitek, 2008), 97% of American teens play games (Table 2 reports the results). Boys play for more time and they play more different genres of games than girls do (an average of eight different genres compared to an average of six genres). Boys play more action, strategy, sports, adventure, first-person shooter, fighting, role-play, survival-horror, and multiplayer games. Girls play more puzzle games. There is no difference in amount of play of racing, rhythm, simulation or virtual worlds games. Girls who are frequent gamers tend to play the same games as do boys who are frequent gamers. Gender differences in genres played are found primarily among girls who game less frequently. Table 2 also characterizes each genre as tending to favor extrinsic or intrinsic player motivations, extrapolating from our earlier research.

Most entertainment genres orient towards extrinsic rewards. The exceptions are puzzle games (played more by girls), simulation games, and virtual worlds. Two of the three more intrinsic oriented genres are played significantly more by girls than boys.

While it may be efficient for game developers to focus on one player type, which allows them to focus on the core game features, it also means part of their potential game playing audience will likely not want to play their game. Commercial games can get away with this so long as their game reaches enough players to be profitable. Learning games have less leverage; students are required to play these games and if a game is not engaging students may be discouraged from learning the game's material. One option for learning games would be to offer a series of games on the same topic and students can pick which game version to play. However, because of time and cost factors there may be better ways to achieve the same breadth of player type coverage for learning games.

ADAPTIVE GAMES

Building games to reach a wider audience is not a new idea. Challenge in games is moderated in at least in two ways: selectable difficulty, and levels. Games for entertainment often offer players a selection of difficulty levels (such as easy,

Table 2. Player percentages by gender per genre (Lenhart et al., 2008) and tendency to favor extrinsic or intrinsic rewards (A "*" in the table indicates that males play significantly more than females. A "+" indicates that females play significantly more than males. Grey rows reflect genres not significantly different by gender.)

	% Boy gamers	% Girl gamers	Favors
*Action games	84%	48%	EXTRINSIC
*Strategy games	83%	55%	EXTRINSIC
*Sports games	80%	55%	EXTRINSIC
Racing games	77%	71%	EXTRINSIC
*Adventure games	75%	57%	EXTRINSIC
*First-person shooter	74%	17%	EXTRINSIC
*Fighting games	67%	29%	EXTRINSIC
Rhythm games	58%	64%	EXTRINSIC
+Puzzle games	58%	87%	INTRINSIC
Simulation games	46%	52%	INTRINSIC
*Role playing games	45%	26%	EXTRINSIC
*Survival–horror games	45%	18%	EXTRINSIC
*MMOs	30%	11%	EXTRINSIC
Virtual worlds	11%	10%	INTRINSIC

medium, or hard). Within a difficulty level, the challenge of the game may ramp up as the player succeeds. Sometimes ramping up is overt—the player completes one level to advance to the next. Exactly how quickly and how much to ratchet up the challenge within and between levels would presumably be different for Validators and for Achievers, but games today do not make that distinction. These changes in difficulty are usually quantifiable, meaning that Achievers gain the most out of these systems because they can crank up the difficulty for more extrinsic rewards (Validators also benefit by being allowed to choose their difficulty). Serious games are less likely to incorporate selectable difficulty in part due to their typically smaller scale and lower budgets. In fact, the authors argue that accommodating Achiever and Validator player types is even more important in a serious game than in a game for entertainment, because play is required rather than voluntary.

Incorporating game mechanics to appeal to Explorers could also enhance the palatability and

effectiveness of serious games. Subject material that is considered advanced may in fact be easy for some students. Offering extra content in a game (side quests, extra levels, more material, user generated content) can make up for such problems with classification of material. This would help Explorers in commercial games by offering more content to search through and alter. Learning games that can provide extra content would similarly benefit from having lots of material for a student to explore. This could enhance experience with the game for self-directed learners and learners with a mastery mindset. On the other hand, too much information may intimidate fixed mindset learners. Players cannot always be expected to know what they need from a game, and learners should not have to guess as to which material they should cover next.

There have been approaches created in educational digital media that attempt to alter the learning experience to better suit the individual in a more dynamic fashion that what the authors have described above. Intelligent tutoring systems (ITSs), which are built for helping with a student's aptitude in various subject domains (Gomez-Martin, Gomez-Martin, & Gonzalez-Calero 2004; Johnson, Vilhjálmsson, & Marsella, 2005), are a good example. The defining feature of an ITS is that it carefully oversees a learner's work on problems to provide needed guidance and content selection. ITSs identify the need for instructional interventions by comparing a model of expert performance with a model of the learner's performance (Koedinger, Anderson, Hadley, & Mark, 1997). ITSs traditionally employ a model trace, which is a cognitive model designed to help identify what strategies a student is employing to solve a problem. When the student is having trouble arriving at the correct answer, the systems can use the model trace to identify what strategy is being employed and then decide what kind of guidance or feedback would best fit that specific situation. A traditional ITS will also measure student aptitude in the concepts being taught (called a knowledge trace) and will select content to address student deficiencies.

Games have already employed intelligent tutoring systems to teach such topics as language (Johnson et al., 2005), computer programming (Gomez-Martin et al., 2004), and interpersonal and intercultural skills (Lane, Core, Gomboc, Karnavat, & Rosenberg, 2007). However, these systems employ model and knowledge in the same way as ITS systems have been used in non-game-based media. This approach does not try to alter the features of a game experience that are most closely tied to player motivation (e.g., game mechanics, game goals, story, etc.), however. Instead, we need to move the state-of-the-art in learning games beyond the "games plus intelligent tutoring" approach that has existed thus far in games research. Doing so will fundamentally change how learning games are developed and their efficacy in classrooms around the world. This approach, which the authors call "adaptive games," is discussed below.

Identifying Player Type

When building an adaptive game, a crucial element of the system is the ability to recognize the relevant individual differences of the players who play the game. Once this recognition occurs, the game can configure itself to accommodate those differences. Three possible approaches could be used to determine player type: giving players a survey, allowing players to customize the game on their own, or identifying player type by observing play behavior.

Surveys

Participants could complete a short survey prior to playing an adaptive game in order to quickly assess their gaming motivation, mindset, and immediate goal. If games for learning are going to be used frequently, perhaps learners could complete a gaming motivations profile once and then simply select ACHIEVER, VALIDATOR, or EXPLORER mode when they start a game, or the game could select the mode based on learners' previous survey answers.

Customization

An interface could be created to allow participants a large amount of control over how the game functions. Some entertainment games already permit considerable customization before play. Customization features related to motivations, mindset, and goal orientation could include control over how the game functions (e.g., how points are awarded, how much time is allotted to perform certain actions, etc.), how the user interface appears to the participant, whether intriguing extra content is included (for explorers), and/or how learning information is presented to the participant.

Research on customization could also provide insight into whether the selections players make result in the same game adaptations as would have happened if the game adapted to them based on a motivation survey. Which approach leads to the more optimal learning experience? It is unclear whether students are aware of their motivation and mindset (when completing a survey) and whether the game configuration choices they make do in fact result in their most preferred game. Furthermore, allowing players to choose their style of play prevents the gaming system from making configuration choices based on what is best for learning rather than what is most enjoyable.

Automatic Adaption

Instead of asking the players survey questions or allowing them to change the game personally, this method opts for intelligently tracking game play. There could be a short "initial calibration game" players play as a warm-up activity or introduction to the adaptive learning game, which is then used by the system to define that player's type. Tracking players in this way is similar to tracking a user in a recommendation system where preferences are continually recorded and updated (Medler, 2009). This would allow the system to form an initial hypothesis and update it as the player continued to play, possibly observing changes in motivation or play style. The authors hypothesize that this will be the least obtrusive and potentially most

accurate method for identifying player type, since the measures will be based on the observation of behavior rather than relying on self-report.

S.C.R.U.B.

The authors created an adaptive game prototype called S.C.R.U.B. (Super Covert Removal of Unwanted Bacteria) (Magerko et al., 2008). This mingame focuses on the topic of microbial pathogens and is intended to teach players about the effects of hand washing (see Figure 2). S.C.R.U.B. is envisioned to be a simple arcade game, incorporating typical arcade values like ammunition, kills, time limits, and points. Players play through three rounds using soap and three rounds using antibacterial gel, permitting players to experience and compare the effects of each hand-washing approach for getting rid of microbes.

Within this basic game design, the authors identified game mechanics that could be added to or subtracted from the game mechanics to meet the needs of Explorers, Achievers, and Validators. Table 3 presents five potential adaptive game mechanics that could be changed for different player types. Explorers, who are intrinsically motivated, would benefit from an explore mode which turns off the game clock and opens extra exploration

Figure 2. Screenshot of the S.C.R.U.B. mini-game

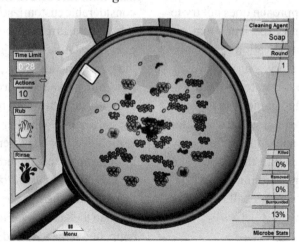

tools such as a microscope view (because a timer would interfere with explorers' game play). Extra content, which in the case of S.C.R.U.B. takes the form of trivia questions, might appeal to explorers. Explorers might also enjoy a "show me" option to see deeper explanations, while Achievers and Validators simply want to win quickly without extraneous distracting information. Leader boards, bonus points and the tutorial are irrelevant but not harmful to Explorers. Achievers and Validators have common interests, but there are important differences in optimizing their game mechanics. Both enjoy speed bonus points, but the more delicate Validators may do better if they do not face failure for not finishing in time.

If player monitoring were built into S.C.R.U.B., we could use that information to adaptively display these different features and mechanics to offer somewhat different gaming experiences. Players who are found to score a lot of points and beat each level's time limit could be given harder challenges (we would guess that they are Achievers). Players who take their time during each round and spend time on the trivia questions would be classified as Explorers. These players could be offered extra information about S.C.R.U.B.'s subject matter and time constraints could be removed.

Players who choose to watch the tutorial might be classified as Validators since they are choosing to learn to play in this way instead of by trial and error. Their error messages might be gentler, and their time limits a bit longer. Validators must be dealt with carefully because these are players who may find games difficult to play, dislike the way the game is presented or have a fixed mindset. The game could offer hints or choices that

Table 3. Inclusion or exclusion of game mechanics for player types

	Intrinsic	Extrinsic	
	Explorer	Achiever	Validator
Mindset	Can be either	Mastery	Fixed/helpless
Goal orientation	Can be either	Eager	Vigilant
Explore mode	Yes	No	No
Timer			
Speed bonus	No	Yes	Yes
Fail if too slow	No	Yes	No
Leader board			
Always		Yes	No
If I'm doing well			Yes
Trivia Qs			
Bonus points		Yes	Yes
Extra content	Yes	No	No
Show me option	Yes	No	Yes
Tutorial			Yes

point the player in new directions. For instance, if a Validator continues to play each round very slowly, a choice to try and play the game with a time constraint could be offered to see if the player could be interested in more extrinsic rewards. Alternatively, when Validators finish a round, they could be given a new hint or technique to use the next time they play (e.g., rinse your hands before applying soap to remove more microbes). Hinting at how the player can move forward will help those players gain more confidence in their game play.

Finally, while each player may show a predilection for one player type over another, we should not lump players into one static type. Players who both beat the rounds under the given constraints and spend a lot of time in between levels looking at extra content might be classified as both Achievers and Explorers. In this case, features and mechanics suitable to both player types could be offered, so long as those features are not incompatible. If at any time players begin to exhibit signs that they are only interested in one type or the other (say they stop playing the game competitively), then that player type's features could be scaled back, leaving the features that the player is still interested in. Each feature would be modular and scalable, being turned off and on as it is needed in the game.

DESIGNING FOR ADAPTIVE GAMES

One of the products of our preliminary work on S.C.R.U.B. is the unique process that has arisen from building a game that represents a space of possible game features and mechanics as opposed to what is conventionally considered a typical game design. This process involved several additional steps to the typical iterative process we normally take: analysis, identification, and mapping.

When building the S.C.R.U.B. prototype game, the authors first analyzed the game experience to identify the different features that make up the

game play, the interface, and the knowledge presented to the player (e.g., having a high score, the visualization of facts about methicillin-resistant Staphylococcus aureus infection, or MRSA, and having a time limit). Once these different features were identified (which of course can change during iterative design), the authors then identified which alternate approaches they could take within each of these features (e.g., having a high score vs. not having one) and finally how each of those differences mapped onto possible player preferences (e.g., having a high score fits an achiever profile).

The authors ended up with six initial adaptive features of particular importance to Explorers, Achievers, or Validators. The authors found that it is important that Explorers have enough time provided to them to explore. Therefore, a countdown clock and bonus speed points are omitted for them. The countdown is also left out for Validators, on the expectation that added pressure only further interferes with their mental focus. Explorers also have a means of entering an "explore mode," in which game play ceases, and they can more closely examine aspects of interest in the interface (while learning more about MRSA). Achievers get bonus speed points and a prominent Leader Board. The authors avoid distracting Validators with superfluous options or pressures, guide them into the game with a built-in tutorial, and offer a "show me" alternative to answering trivia quiz questions.

FUTURE RESEARCH DIRECTIONS

Player Motivation Survey

Our theoretical approach integrates player types, mindset, and the theory of intelligence. Extensive research on player types supports the validity of Achiever and Explorer player types. Our own preliminary survey research on play behavior and related educational research provides strong evidence of and rationale for considering the additional Validator player type. Essentially, extrinsically motivated players are divided Achievers (Mastery mindset and an eager goal orientation) and Validators (Fixed mindset and a vigilant goal orientation).

Further research is needed to develop survey instruments to measure gaming motivations and gaming mindsets and to determine the distribution of Explorers, Achievers, and Validators in different populations and in relation to different game genres. Games for learning perversely conjure up both an individual's entertainment gaming motivations as well as that person's formal education learning motivations and mindset. These two worlds are often in opposition. What is the relationship between learning and gaming motivations? How do players reconcile potential conflicts? Which predilection wins out when playing a game for learning?

Identifying Player Motivation

Work on player motivation is needed to design and apply adaptations in a finer-grained manner, such as weighting features with "how much" they relate to a particular style or assigning features proportionately based on the model of the player (e.g., assigning 60% of the features for Achiever and 40% for Explorer, or better yet, deciding which features can coexist and which must remain true to the player's primary type). We need to understand how individual differences in players change over time and if any of the aforementioned techniques need to accommodate these changes over time. One way to determine individual differences may be to use a motivation framework (e.g., Keller's ARCS framework, as discussed by Low, in press).

Design Process for Adaptation

Our initial work focused on an arcade-style game. It has been fairly straightforward to conceptualize

adaptive features of S.C.R.U.B. since it is a simple minigame. This process needs to be generalized for other game genres or larger games. How such a design process applies to other kinds of games appears straightforward for some (e.g., first-person shooter-style games) but less obvious for others (e.g., turn-based strategy games). Ultimately, a pan-genre design process could be developed that addresses the individual differences in gaming and learning motivations and how those differences could be mapped to design decisions for adaptive games in general and for serious games in particular.

CONCLUSION

The ramifications of serious games that adapt to player motivations, mindset, and goal orientation are potentially large. Computer games for learning are increasing in use every year, whether they are off-the-shelf games co-opted for an unintended purpose (Van Eck, 2006) or multiuser virtual environments created for communities of elementary and middle school students (e.g., Barab, Thomas, Dodge, Carteaux, & Tuzun, 2005). These and other digital media approaches to education have the same opportunity that intelligent tutoring researchers saw in computer-based education: computers have the ability to model and adapt educational content to fit the user's needs.

Adaptive serious games can potentially help serious games, including digital game-based learning, more effectively motivate and teach a much broader player audience. Intrinsically motivated players would be able to exercise their curiosity and go beyond the minimum-content mastery necessary to complete and win the game without being rushed by timers and without being limited by the competitive interests of achievement-oriented players. Validators, a group that likely includes non-gamers as well as more experienced gamers, will find a gentler game. Achievers will be able to immerse themselves in hard challenges and well-deserved success, indulging their mastery mindset.

If different students respond differently to different game situations, genres, etc., then progress in the games for learning community will surely be slowed until we can experimentally identify these differences and accommodate them in our games. The future is bright for digital game-based learning. However, the authors contend that the future can be even brighter when games are designed to identify and accommodate the differences in students who wind up playing them. We have the potential to engage more players in a more effective manner by creating learning games that adapt to the individual differences that each player brings with them to the gaming experience.

REFERENCES

2K2007). *Bioshock*. [Video game]. Boston, MA: 2K Games.

D3 Publisher. (2007). Puzzle Quest. Los Angeles: D3

Aaker, J., & Lee, A. (2006). Understanding regulatory fit. *JMR, Journal of Marketing Research, 43*, 15–19. doi:10.1509/jmkr.43.1.15

American Public Media. (2008). *Budget Hero* [Video game]. St. Paul, MN: American Public Media.

Association for Childhood Education International. (2007). *ACEI: Elementary Standards and Supporting Explanation*. Retrieved from http://www.ncate.org/ProgramStandards/ACEI/ACEIscoringGuide_07.doc

Barab, S., Thomas, M. K., Dodge, T., Carteaux, B., & Tuzun, H. (2005). Making learning fun: *Quest Atlantis*, a game without guns. *Educational Technology Research and Development, 5*(1), 86–108. doi:10.1007/BF02504859

Bartle, R. A. (1996). Hearts, clubs, diamonds, spades: Players who suit muds. *Journal of MUD Research, 1*, 1.

Beswick, D. G. (1971). Cognitive process theory of individual differences in curiosity. In Day, H. I., Berlyne, D. E., & Hunt, D. E. (Eds.), *Intrinsic motivation: A new direction in education* (pp. 156–170). Toronto, ON: Holt, Rinehart and Winston.

Beswick, D. G. (1974). Intrinsic motivation in senior secondary school students. *Education Research and Perspectives, 1*, 1525.

Beswick, D. G. (2007). Management implications of the interaction between intrinsic motivation and extrinsic rewards. *Beswick recent psychological research*. Retrieved from http://www.beswick.info/psychres/management

Brain Powered Games. (2009). Keep It. In *Mind* [computer game]. Lansing, MI: Brain Powered Games.

Cadinu, M., Maass, A., Rosabianca, A., & Kiesner, J. (2005). Why do women underperform under stereotype threat? Evidence for the role of negative thinking. *Psychological Science, 16*(7), 572–578. doi:10.1111/j.0956-7976.2005.01577.x

Coffield, F., Moseley, D., Hall, E., & Ecclestone, K. (2004). *Learning styles and pedagogy in post-16 learning: A systematic and critical review.* Retrieved from http://www.lsrc.ac.uk/publications/index.asp

Covington, M., Omelich, C., & Schwarzer, R. (1986). Anxiety, aspirations, and self-concept in the achievement process: A longitudinal model with latent variables. *Motivation and Emotion, 10*, 71–88. doi:10.1007/BF00992151

Croizet, J. C., Després, G., Gauzins, M. E., Huguet, P., Leyens, J. P., & Méot, A. (2004). Stereotype threat undermines intellectual performance by triggering a disruptive mental load. *Personality and Social Psychology Bulletin, 30*(6), 721–731. doi:10.1177/0146167204263961

Dweck, C. (2000). *Self-theories: Their role in motivation, personality, and development.* New York: Psychology Press.

Dweck, C. (2006). *Mindset: The new psychology of success.* New York: Random House.

Dweck, C. S., & Leggett, E. L. (1988). A social-cognitive approach to motivation and personality. *Psychological Review, 95,* 256–273. doi:10.1037/0033-295X.95.2.256

Elliot, E. S., & Church, M. A. (1997). A hierarchal model of approach and avoidance achievement motivation. *Journal of Personality and Social Psychology, 72,* 218–232. doi:10.1037/0022-3514.72.1.218

Förster, J., Higgins, E. T., & Idson, L. C. (1998). Approach and avoidance strength during goal attainment: Regulatory focus and the "goal looms larger" effect. *Journal of Personality and Social Psychology, 75,* 1115–1131. doi:10.1037/0022-3514.75.5.1115

Foster, A., & Mishra, P. (2009). *Disciplinary knowledge construction while playing a simulation strategy game.* Society for Information Technology & Teacher Education International Conference, March 2–6, Charleston, SC.

Gee, J. P. (2007a). Games and learning: Issues, perils and potentials. In Gee, J. P. (Ed.), *Good video games and good learning: Collected essays on video games, learning and literacy (New Literacies and Digital Epistemologies)* (pp. 129–174). New York: Palgrave/Macmillan.

Gee, J. P. (2007b). Learning and Games. In Salen, K. (Ed.), *The ecology of games: Connecting youth, games, and learning* (pp. 21–40). Cambridge, MA: MIT Press.

Goffman, E. (1959). *The presentation of self in everyday life.* New York: Doubleday.

Gómez-Martín, M., Gómez-Martín, P., & González-Calero, P. (2004). *Game-driven intelligent tutoring systems.* Third International Conference on Entertainment Computing (ICEC). September 1–3, Eindhoven, The Netherlands.

Heeter, C., Magerko, B., Medler, B., & Fitzgerald, J. (2009). Game design and the challenge-avoiding "validator" player type. *International Journal of Gaming and Computer-Mediated Simulations, 1*(3), 53–67.

Heeter, C., Winn, B., Winn, J., & Bozoki, A. (2008). *The challenge of challenge: Avoiding and embracing difficulty in a memory game.* Meaningful Play Conference, October 9–11, East Lansing, MI.

Henderlong, J., & Lepper, M. (2002). The effects of praise on children's intrinsic motivation: A review and synthesis. *Psychological Bulletin, 128,* 774–795. doi:10.1037/0033-2909.128.5.774

Higgins, E. T. (2000). Making a good decision: Value from fit. *The American Psychologist, 55,* 1217–1230. doi:10.1037/0003-066X.55.11.1217

Higgins, E. T. (2005). Value from regulatory fit. *Current Directions in Psychological Science, 14,* 209–213. doi:10.1111/j.0963-7214.2005.00366.x

Higgins, E. T. (2006). Value from hedonic experience and engagement. *Psychological Review, 113*(3), 439–460. doi:10.1037/0033-295X.113.3.439

Impact Games, L. L. C. (2008). *Play the News* [Video game]. Pittsburgh, PA: Impact Games.

Johnson, W. L., Vilhjálmsson, H., & Marsella, S. (2005). *Serious games for language learning: How much game, how much AI?* 12th International Conference on Artificial Intelligence in Education. July 18–22, Amsterdam, The Netherlands.

Kafai, Y., Heeter, C., Denner, J., & Sun, J. (Eds.). (2008). *Beyond Barbie and Mortal Kombat: New perspectives on gender and gaming.* Cambridge, MA: MIT Press.

Koedinger, K. R., Anderson, J. R., Hadley, W. H., & Mark, M. A. (1997). Intelligent tutoring goes to school in the big city. *Journal of Artificial Intelligence in Education, 8,* 30–43.

Lane, H. C., Core, M. G., Gomboc, D., Karnavat, A., & Rosenberg, M. (2007). *Intelligent tutoring for interpersonal and intercultural skills.* Interservice/Industry Training, Simulation, and Education Conference (I/ITSEC). November 26–29, Orlando, FL.

Lee, F. K., Sheldon, K. M., & Turban, D. B. (2003). Personality and the goal striving process: The influence of achievement goal patterns, goal level, and mental focus on performance and enjoyment. *The Journal of Applied Psychology, 88,* 256–265. doi:10.1037/0021-9010.88.2.256

Lenhart, A., Kahne, J., Middaugh, E., Evans, C., & Vitek, J. (2008). Teens' gaming experiences are diverse and include significant social interaction and civic engagement. *Pew Internet and American Life Project.* Retrieved April 2, 2009, from http://www.pewinternet.org/~/media//Files/Reports/2008/PIP_Teens_Games_and_Civics_Report_FINAL.pdf

Lepper, M. R., & Henderlong, J. (2000). Turning "play" into "work" and "work" into "play": 25 years of research on intrinsic versus extrinsic motivation. In Sansone, C., & Harackiewicz, J. M. (Eds.), *Intrinsic and extrinsic motivation: The search for optimal motivation and performance* (pp. 257–307). San Diego, CA: Academic Press. doi:10.1016/B978-012619070-0/50032-5

Low, R. (in press). Examining motivational factors in serious educational games. In Van Eck, R. (Ed.), *Gaming and cognition: Theories and practice from the learning sciences.* Hershey, PA: IGI Global.

Low, R., Jin, P., & Sweller, J. (in press). Learner's cognitive load when using educational technology. In Van Eck, R. (Ed.), *Gaming and cognition: Theories and practice from the learning sciences.* Hershey, PA: IGI Global.

Magerko, B., Heeter, C., Medler, B., & Fitzgerald, J. (2008). *Intelligent adaptation of digital game-based learning.* Conference on Future Play: Research, Play, Share. Toronto, ON.

Mangels, J. A., Butterfield, B., Lamb, J., Good, C. D., & Dweck, C. S. (2006). Why do beliefs about intelligence influence learning success? A social cognitive neuroscience model. [SCAN]. *Social Cognitive and Affective Neuroscience, 1*(2), 75–86. doi:10.1093/scan/nsl013

Mayer, R. E. (2005a). Principles for managing essential processing in multimedia learning: Segmenting, pretraining, and modality principles. In Mayer, R. E. (Ed.), *The Cambridge handbook of multimedia learning* (pp. 169–182). New York: Cambridge University Press.

Mayer, R. E. (2005b). Principles for reducing extraneous processing in multimedia learning: Coherence, signaling, redundancy, spatial contiguity, and temporal contiguity principles. In Mayer, R. E. (Ed.), *The Cambridge handbook of multimedia learning* (pp. 183–200). New York: Cambridge University Press.

Medler, B. (2009.). Using recommendation systems to adapt gameplay. *International Journal of Gaming and Computer-Mediated Simulations.*

Nintendo. (2001). *Animal Crossing.* [Video game]. Kyoto, Japan: Nintendo.

RedOctane. (2005). *Guitar Hero* [Video game]. Mountain View, CA: RedOctane.

Salen, K. (2007). Toward an ecology of gaming. In Salen, K. (Ed.), *The ecology of games: Connecting youth, games, and learning* (pp. 1–20). Cambridge, MA: MIT Press.

Seldin, T. (2008). *Montessori 101: Some basic information that every Montessori parent should know*. Retrieved June 11, 2008, from http://www.montessori.org/sitefiles/Montessori_101_non-printable.pdf

Sony. (2006). *FlOw*. [Computer software]. Japan: Sony.

Squire, K. D. (2005). Changing the game: What happens when videogames enter the classroom? *Innovate*, *1*, 6.

Thomas, J., Bol, L., Warkentin, R., Wilson, M., Strage, A., & Rohwer, W. (2006). Interrelationships among students' study activities, self-concept of academic ability, and achievement as a function of characteristics of high-school biology courses. *Applied Cognitive Psychology*, *7*(6), 499–532. doi:10.1002/acp.2350070605

Van Eck, R. (2006). Digital game-based learning: It's not just the digital natives who are restless. *EDUCAUSE Review*, *41*(2), 16–30.

Winn, B., & Heeter, C. (2007). Resolving conflicts in educational game design through playtesting. *Innovate*, *3*(2).

Winn, J., & Heeter, C. (2009). Gaming, gender, and time: Who makes time to play? *Journal of Sex Roles*, *61*(1–2), 1–13. doi:10.1007/s11199-009-9595-7

Yee, N. (2006). Motivations of play in online games. *Cyberpsychology & Behavior*, *9*(6), 772–775. doi:10.1089/cpb.2006.9.772

Yee, N. (2008). Maps of digital desires: Exploring the topography of gender and play in online games. In Kafai, Y., Heeter, C., Denner, J., & Sun, J. (Eds.), *Beyond Barbie and Mortal Kombat: New perspectives in gender and gaming*. Cambridge, MA: MIT Press.

APPENDIX: ADDITIONAL READING

"Must-Reads" for This Topic

Aaker, J., & Lee, A. (2006). Understanding regulatory fit. *Journal of Marketing Research, 43*, 15–19.

Barab, S., Thomas, M., Dodge, T., Carteaux, R., & Tuzun, H. (2005). Making learning fun: Quest Atlantis, a game without guns. *Educational Technology Research and Development, 1*, 86–107.

Bartle, R. A. (1996). Hearts, clubs, diamonds, spades: Players who suit MUDs. *Journal of MUD Research, 1*, 1. Available at http://www.mud.co.uk/richard/hcds.htm

Beswick, D. G. (1974). Intrinsic motivation in senior secondary school students. *Education Research and Perspectives, 1*, 15–25.

Beswick, D. G. (2007). Management implications of the interaction between intrinsic motivation and extrinsic rewards. *Beswick recent psychological research.* Retrieved from http://www.beswick. info/psychres/management

Brain Powered Games. (2009). *Keep it in mind.* [Video game]. USA: Brain Powered Games.

Coffield, F. Moseley, D. Hall, E. & Ecclestone, K. (2004). *Learning styles and pedagogy in post-16 learning: A systematic and critical review.* Retrieved from http://www.lsrc.ac.uk/publications/ index.asp

Dweck, C. (2000). Self-theories: Their role in motivation, personality, and development. *Essays in social psychology.* Philadelphia, PA: Taylor & Francis.

Dweck, C. (2006). *Mindset: The new psychology of success.* New York: Random House.

Dweck, C. S., & Leggett, E. L. (1988). A social-cognitive approach to motivation and personality. *Psychological Review, 95*, 256–273.

Elliot, E. S., & Church, M. A. (1997). A hierarchal model of approach and avoidance achievement motivation. *Journal of Personality and Social Psychology, 72*, 218–232.

Gómez-Martín, M., Gómez-Martín, P., & González-Calero, P. (2004). Game-driven intelligent tutoring systems. In *Third International Conference on Entertainment Computing* (ICEC), Eindhoven, The Netherlands.

Heeter, C., Magerko, B, Medler, B., & Fitzgerald, J. (2009). Game design and the challenge-avoiding "validator" player type. *International Journal of Gaming and Computer-Mediated Simulations, 1*(3), 53–67.

Heeter, C., Winn, B., Winn, J., & Bozoki, A. (2008). *The challenge of challenge: Avoiding and embracing difficulty in a memory game.* Presented at Meaningful Play Conference, Oct. 9–11, East Lansing, MI.

Henderlong, J., & Lepper, M. (2002). The effects of praise on children's intrinsic motivation: A review and synthesis. *Psychological Bulletin, 128*, 774–795.

Higgins, E. T. (2005). Value from regulatory fit. *Current Directions in Psychological Science, 14*, 209–213.

Koedinger, K. R., Anderson, J. R., Hadley, W. H., & Mark, M. A. (1997). Intelligent tutoring goes to school in the big city. *Journal of Artificial Intelligence and Education, 8*, 30–43.

Lane, H. C., Core, M. G., Gomboc, D., Karnavat, A., & Rosenberg, M. (2007). *Intelligent tutoring for interpersonal and intercultural skills.* Interservice/Industry Training, Simulation, and Education Conference (I/ITSEC). Orlando, FL.

Lepper, M. R., & Henderlong, J. (2000). Turning "play" into "work" and "work" into "play": 25 years of research on intrinsic versus extrinsic motivation. In C. Sansone & J. M. Harackiewicz (Eds.), *Intrinsic and extrinsic motivation: The search for optimal motivation and performance* (pp. 257–307). San Diego, CA: Academic Press.

Mangels, J. A., Butterfield, B., Lamb, J., Good, C. D., & Dweck, C. S. (2006). Why do beliefs about intelligence influence learning success? A social cognitive neuroscience model. *Social Cognitive and Affective Neuroscience (SCAN), 1*(2), 75–86.

Yee, N. (2006). Motivations of play in online games. *CyberPsychology and Behavior, 9*(6), 772–775.

Top Texts for Interdisciplinary Studies of Serious Games

Csikszentmihalyi, M. (1991). *Flow: The psychology of optimal experience.* New York: Harper Perennial.

Ferdig, R., (Ed.). (2008). *Handbook of research on effective electronic gaming in education.* Hershey, PA: IGI Global.

Gee, J. (2007). *What video games have to teach us about learning and literacy.* New York: Palgrave Macmillan.

Gee, J. P. (2007). *Good video games and good learning: Collected essays on video games, learning and literacy.* New York: Palgrave–Macmillan.

Jenkins, H. (2006). *Convergence culture: Where old and new media collide.* New York: NYU Press.

Jenkins, H., Clinton K., Purushotma, R., Robinson, A. J., & Weigel, M. (2006). *Confronting the challenges of participatory culture: Media education for the 21st century.* Chicago, IL: The MacArthur Foundation. Retrieved from http://www.google.com/url?sa=t&source=web&ct=res&cd=1&url=http%3A%2F%2Fwww.digitallearning.macfound.org%2Fatf%2Fcf%2F%257B7E45C7E0-A3E0-4B89-AC9C-E807E1B0AE4E%257D%2FJENKINS_WHITE_PAPER.PDF&ei=RBzWSez7BYzNlQej0qnCDA&usg=AFQjCNFIkObOp5TawNj0J4ZmqsQFouXcPw&sig2=L8tSQ8jYOYYZQ35Ukrdt1w

Ritterfeld, U., Cody, M., & Vorderer, P. (2009). *Serious games: Mechanisms and effects.* New York: Routledge Press.

Salen, K. (2007). *The ecology of games: Connecting youth, games, and learning.* Cambridge, MA: MIT Press.

Vorderer, P., & Bryant, J. (Eds.). (2006). *Playing video games—Motives, responses, and consequences.* Mahwah, NJ: Lawrence Erlbaum Associates.

Wardrip-Fruin, N., & Monfort, N. (2003). *The new media reader.* Cambridge, MA: The MIT Press.

Vygotsky, L. S. (1978). *Mind in society: Development of higher psychological processes.* Cambridge, MA: Harvard University Press.

Section 5
Practitioner Perspectives

Chapter 13
Developing Serious Games for Learning Language-in-Culture

K. A. Barrett
University of New Mexico, USA

W. Lewis Johnson
Alelo, Inc., USA

ABSTRACT

This chapter will focus on the instructional design process used to create Alelo's language and culture training programs. The objective of the design process is not just a serious game, but an integrated learning environment which combines serious games with other supporting learning activities. Learners apply their newfound communication skills and cultural knowledge to complete tasks in a simulated environment. The chapter will specifically focus on the design and development phases of the process, which uses interdisciplinary teams combined with an iterative approach to meet customer needs. The authors employ innovative learning technologies such as artificial intelligence and speech recognition; these add greatly to the learning experience but also introduce unique challenges for instructional design. Central to the instructional design process is situated instructional design and rapid prototyping. Authoring techniques that facilitate the creation of lessons and games that scaffold the learner from beginning- to intermediate-level proficiency are also be described. In addition, the chapter will explain how Alelo's technology instantiates current theories, models, and research findings in the fields of language learning, serious games, and artificial intelligence.

INTRODUCTION

This chapter will describe how Alelo designs and develops serious games that teach foreign languages and intercultural communication skills. Immersive, interactive 3-D video games simulate real-life communication, allowing users to role-play with animated "socially intelligent virtual humans" that recognize the user's speech, intent, gestures and behavior. These game experiences are combined with interactive multimedia learning materials to provide learners with comprehensive learning environments that enable them to progress from no knowledge of the language and culture to significant levels of job-related communicative proficiency.

DOI: 10.4018/978-1-61520-717-6.ch013

Although there many educational computer games available in the market today, there are relatively few that, like Alelo games, are complete learning environments designed with learning theory in mind. Alelo's games are in widespread use, particularly by military personnel deploying overseas. At least 50,000 people have trained so far with these games for self-paced learning, supervised learning programs, and blended learning programs. Developing these games and getting feedback from the users has provided valuable knowledge and insights into how to use game-based learning effectively to teach foreign languages and cultures.

The pedagogy used is based upon constructivist learning theory, situated cognition theory, sociocultural learning theory and, more specifically, on task-based second-language learning theory. Task-based language learning emphasizes learning in the context of tasks that require learners to communicate meaning, as in real life (Ellis, 2003). Alelo's game-based learning approach immerses learners in a variety of simulations of real-world settings in which they must communicate with nonplayer characters (NPCs) using spoken language to accomplish tasks. The artificially intelligent NPCs are designed to engage in dialogue with learners on topics related to the current task. The learner experience is thus qualitatively different from typical computer-based language learning software in which speech recognition is either not used at all or focuses on learner pronunciation rather than the learner's ability to convey meaning.

We strive to align the tasks in the learning environment with the real-life tasks that learners can expect to engage in when they use the language in the foreign country. This approach is aligned with sociocultural learning theory, which seeks to study the mediated mind in the environments in which people engage in normal living activities and thus seeks to maintain the richness and complexity of living reality instead of deconstructing it (Lantolf & Thorne, 2006). In 3-D worlds, learners interact with virtual avatars

in nonthreatening environments. This has been shown to be important to adult learners who are often intimidated by the live language classroom experience (Johnson, Wang, & Wu, 2007). Learners who practice communicative skills in the context of these realistic communicative tasks find it relatively easy to transfer their communication skills to comparable real-life situations even though they have experienced them only in a computer simulation.

Moreover, by placing learners in an immersive game context, we can employ a variety of game design methods to promote learner motivation. Motivation is often a significant barrier to language learning. Language learners frequently find foreign language curricula to be boring and/or frustrating (Franc, Lawton, & Morton, 2008). This tends to lower learners' motivation to engage in foreign language study. Many learners have low self-efficacy for foreign language learning, particularly for more difficult languages such as Arabic or Chinese. When these factors are combined, the result can be high rates of learner attrition (Doughty, Nielsen, & Freynik, 2008). Alelo's game-based learning approach strives to counteract these common motivational impediments. For example, the immersive games provide extensive levels of engagement, motivation, and practice through "free-form" storylines with very wide ranges of gameplay paths, interactive dialogues, and action options. The storyline's drama, exploration, and elements of surprise include many different opportunities to learn.

The learning environments combine immersive games with interactive instructional materials and utilize advanced speech recognition and conversational artificial intelligence (AI) capabilities to give learners opportunities to develop and practice their communication skills. Figures 1 and 2 illustrate how this is done in a pilot *Encounters Chinese* language course, developed in collaboration with Yale University and Chinese International Publishing Group. Figure 1 shows an exercise from one of the interactive Web-based lessons (known as "skill builders") in the Encounters course. Here, learners are prompted to introduce themselves to the lady in the top left in Chinese. Wearing a headset microphone, they must speak in Chinese to perform the exercise. The automated speech-processing system evaluates what the learner says so that the virtual coach (shown at bottom) can provide specific constructive feedback. In this case the coach critiques the learner's word choice, using "xìng" (family name) instead of "jiào" (name). Through such exercises, learners acquire basic conversational skills. They then apply these communication skills in the immersive 3-D game, as shown in Figure 2. Here the learner is able to walk up to NPCs and engage in extended conversations with them to locate a named individual.

Designing such complex learning environments, which combine multiple learning activities and which use advanced technologies to simulate real-life situations and interactions, is potentially very challenging. To meet this challenge, we have established a design and methodology that draws on principles of situated instructional design. Situated instructional design, as described by Wilson (1995), is adaptive and community-oriented, involving multiple stakeholders and multidisciplinary design teams. Rather than taking a prescriptive, rigid approach to instructional design as some approaches do, customers are closely involved in the process, providing iterative feedback to the course development team, which consists of applied linguists and anthropologists, animators, artists, sound engineers, speech recognition experts, and programmers. This approach has resulted in engaging and effective language-in-culture instruction for such challenging languages as Dari, Iraqi Arabic, and Chinese.

THEORETICAL FOUNDATIONS IN COGNITION AND LEARNING

There are a number of issues to take into consideration when designing serious games. Among these are an understanding of learning, cognition, motivation, emotion, and play. There are several theories that, woven together, provide a foundation for the instructional design approach to game development used by Alelo. We will start

Figure 1. Example mini-dialogue exercise

Figure 2. Example episode of encounters Chinese: "Find Your Friend in a Hutong" Game

by reviewing the relevant research in cognition and learning.

Situated Cognition and Language Learning

The notion of situated cognition is fundamental to the creation of 3D worlds that are effective learning environments for language and culture. Lave (1988) put forward the idea that learning is situated within activity and occurs through legitimate peripheral participation. Miller and Gildea (1987) showed that when young people learn vocabulary words within the context of every day cognition the gains are rapid and successful. Yet when vocabulary is learned in an abstract way, in other words, taken out of context, learning is slow and many errors are made. People learn languages and their associated ways of thinking best when they can tie the words and structures of those languages to experiences they have had (Gee, 2004). Activity and situations are integral to cognition and learning (Brown, Collins, & Duguid, 1989). In terms of learning a language and appropriate discourse, Lave and Wenger (1991)

write that issues regarding language may well have more to do with legitimacy of participation and access to peripherality than they do with actual knowledge transmission. Roth (2001) notes that there are different ways in which cognition is situated, for example, across settings, in group interactions, and embodied in practices.

Constructivism

The theoretical framework underlying the model used to develop our instructional approach is constructivism. Constructivist learning theory is used to describe portions of the collective works of Piaget, Vygotsky, Bruner, and others. Constructivism acknowledges that learners themselves are active agents who engage in their own knowledge construction by integrating new information into their existing schema and by associating and representing it in possibly unique ways that are meaningful to them (Miller & Fallad, 2005). Constructivist learning takes place when learners actively create their own knowledge by trying to make sense out of material that is presented to them (Mayer, 1999). Knowledge is constructed and socially constructed by learners based upon their interpretations of experiences in the world (Reigeluth, 1999) and, by extension, their interpretations of experiences in virtual worlds.

Phillips (1995) described constructivism along a spectrum of differing forms. The three axes are (1) individual psychology versus public discipline; (2) humans the creators versus nature the instructor; and (3) the construction of knowledge as an active process, whether individual or in terms of social and political processes. Constructivism theory underlies the foundation of serious games that teach language and culture with the assumption that meaning exists within the learner rather than in external forms.

Social constructivists see knowledge as:

constructed when individuals engage in talk and activity about shared problems or tasks. Making meaning is thus a dialogic process involving person-in-conversation, and learning is seen as the process by which individuals are introduced to a culture by more skilled members. (Driver et al., 1994, p. 7)

Task-Based Language Learning

Alelo's learning approach is heavily influenced by research in task-based learning, an approach that has a high degree of currency in the field of second language learning (Ellis, 2003). The fundamental assumption underlying task-based language learning is that language is not an isolated skill but rather a skill that people employ to accomplish tasks in the world. Therefore, learners should develop and practice their language skills in the context of authentic tasks (e.g., making an airline reservation, ordering a meal) that are similar to the tasks that one might encounter in everyday life. Tasks typically involve communication of meaning with other foreign language speakers and require learners to both construct meaning from the language that they hear and

construct utterances to convey their own meaning. Task-based learning exercises contrast with exercises such as grammar drills that focus on language forms but not on their meaning or use in particular situations.

One shortcoming of task-based learning in classroom contexts is that such tasks tend to be divorced from reality; they may involve make-believe situations or may be focused on the context of the classroom. Virtual worlds and artificially intelligent NPCs can help to overcome these limitations. They make it possible to put learners in realistic simulations of real-world situations and to have them perform tasks that are very similar to real-life communication tasks. The resulting learning experiences combine the benefits of situated learning and task-based learning.

Task-based language learning theorists draw a distinction between *task-supported* language teaching in which tasks are one element of the curriculum, and *task-based* language teaching, in which tasks provide the basis for the entire curriculum. Alelo curricula use a task-supported approach. They are organized around tasks, such as inquiries and introductions as in Figures 1 and 2. These task-oriented exercises are coupled with language lessons and exercises that introduce learners to the vocabulary and language forms that they need in order carry out the tasks.

Cognitive Flexibility Theory

Another supporting theory underlying Alelo's immersive games is Spiro's cognitive flexibility theory (CFT), which focuses on the nature of learning in complex and ill-structured domains:

By cognitive flexibility, we mean the ability to spontaneously restructure one's knowledge, in many ways, in adaptive response to radically changing situational demands. ... This is a function of both the way knowledge is represented (e.g., along multiple rather single (sic) conceptual dimensions) and the processes that operate on those mental representations (e.g., processes of schema assembly rather than intact schema retrieval). (Spiro & Jehng, 1990, p. 165)

CFT is premised on the notion that most knowledge domains are complex and ill-structured, as are the situations faced by many learners in today's world. An ill-structured knowledge domain is one in which individual cases of knowledge application are multidimensional with considerable variability of structure in cases of the same type. The foundational principle of CFT is that by offering students opportunities to apply multiple representations of new learning tailored to a particular context, they will then be able to master increasingly complex content. Concomitantly, students acquire the ability to spontaneously structure and restructure this knowledge in ways that anticipate and meet the demands of variable situations. CFT is being used to train police in the United States and abroad, and in other work environments where rapid adaptation to changing conditions is necessary, such as medicine and meteorology (Jonassen, 1992).

Thus, knowledge restructuring is a critical component of a learners' training vector as s/he engages with the content. CFT is inherently constructivist, stressing the importance of constructed knowledge in that learners must be given an opportunity to develop their own representations of information in order to properly learn. A key principle of CFT is that instructional materials should avoid oversimplifying the content domain and should support context-dependent knowledge.

CFT is especially appropriate for interactive technology (Park & Hannafin, 1993). It is consistent with and provides a useful complement to situated and task-based learning. Many of the cultural norms that we try to teach are not easily reduced to hard-and-fast rules of dos and don'ts and are best introduced in the context of a variety situations in which they may apply. By giving learners practice performing tasks in a variety of situations, and practice using language forms in the context of a variety of tasks, learners gain flexibility in their language skills and acquire the ability to apply those skills in real-world situations that are similar to, but distinct from, the experiences that they encountered in the virtual world.

Sociocultural Theory and Language Learning

The research tradition of sociocultural theory informs the instructional design approach used to design and develop the skillbuilders and immersive games for language and culture learning because it guides the observation and interpretation of people engaged in the activity of teaching, learning, and using foreign languages. Sociocultural theories of learning posit that individuals learn by socially interacting and conversing with others. Moreover, sociocultural theory seeks to study the mediated mind in the environments in which people engage in normal living activities (Lantolf & Thorne, 2006). Therefore, game-based environments for educational purposes that employ pedagogical agents, in particular those that teach language, are fertile ground for learning socially appropriate ways of interacting across languages and cultures.

Vygotsky (1978) began what would become the sociocultural movement in education by stating that in order to understand individual psychological development it is necessary to understand the system of social relations in which the individual lives and grows. For Vygotsky, culture and community play a significant role in the early development of a child. He felt that this development is applied primarily to mental development, such as thought, language, reasoning functions, and mental processes (1986). Vygotsky observed that these abilities develop through social interactions with significant people in a child's life, including parents and other adults. Through these interactions, children come to learn the habits of mind of their culture: speech patterns, written language, and other symbolic knowledge that effects construction of knowledge. Moreover, the specific knowledge gained from these interactions represents the shared knowledge of a culture.

The challenge for language educators is to create learning environments for gaining fluency in another language that take advantage of the new technologies available while also building on theories of second language acquisition (SLA) that foster language learning within the context of culture. Sociocultural theory posits that social interaction facilitates the construction of knowledge. This theory of learning and development suggests that learning is also a form of language socialization between individuals. A fundamental principle in sociocultural theory as it relates to language learning is the notion that learners' communicative resources are formed and reformed in the very activity in which they are used. In other words, in linguistically mediated social and intellectual activity (Lantolf & Thorne, 2006).

Beginning with the end of the 1960s, the paradigm of language development shifted from static to dynamic and began to address social and psychological factors. Into this new paradigm stepped Wong-Fillmore (1991), who firmly placed language development within a social context. She proposed three components of SLA: (a) learners, (b) speakers of the target language, and (c) the social setting. Wong-Fillmore added that there are three processes inherent in SLA: (a) social, (b) linguistic, and (c) cognitive. Thus, learning a foreign language is a multidimensional process.

ISSUES IN DESIGNING LANGUAGE AND CULTURE TRAINING USING SERIOUS GAMES

Computer simulation gaming offers the opportunity for instructional designers of language and culture training to design learning environments that are at once engaging and content-rich. Through placing learners at the locus of control (first person), they are able to become full participants in

the simulation, experiencing the results of their decision making (affect) in a safe environment. Simulation and gaming theory is based upon learning theories where behavioral, attitudinal, and cognitive changes due to experience are foremost (Garcâia-Carbonell, Rising, Montero, & Watts, 2001). In turn, these experiential learning theories are rooted in the theories of early educational theorists who include Dewey, Piaget and Ausebel (Garcâia-Carbonell et al., 2001). More contemporary researchers, such as Klabbers (2000), differentiate between learning as acquisition and learning as interaction, suggesting that system dynamics play a role in the design of computer-based interactive learning environments for a wide variety of audiences. Activity theory and situated learning, with their emphasis on providing an environment and tools that are transferable (Reigeluth, 1999), also support and underlie the design of serious games. Design factors that play major roles in serious game design, and which are particularly relevant to the games described in this chapter, are learner control, feedback, and motivation.

Learner Control

Learner control in technology-mediated environments has been shown to be instrumental in creating effective learning for participants (Chou & Liu, 2005). Alelo's courses are designed with learner control as a principal element in order to help learners quickly acquire basic communication skills in foreign languages and cultures. Learners are able to repeat lessons as necessary and are given continuous, targeted feedback in the mission games to guide them to successful completion. Learners can move from instruction pages to game scenarios as their skill sets and confidence improve. The immersive games implicitly present learners with a variety of choices as to who to talk to, what to say, and what to do. In addition, learners are free to make choices as to how they divide their time between the focused lessons and the game scenarios. They can even make choices as to their learning objectives, resulting in automatically tailored curricula that address those objectives. According to Plass and Jones (2005), there are indications that providing learners with a choice of the order in which they proceed through a multimedia environment may allow them to manage the cognitive load they experience. Plass and Jones state that this finding may be specific to second language acquisition, where the materials are not necessarily presented in an order that needs to be followed to ensure comprehension. Plass and Jones suggest that instructional designers consider the task requirements of the learning environment and learner characteristics such as language proficiency when deciding how much learner control to provide.

Tennyson (1980) demonstrated that learner control conditions can be valuable instructional management systems, in particular for computer-based instruction, if learners receive enough information about their development. The amount of choice provided to learners should depend upon the characteristics of learners and the nature of the topic (Okey & Jones, 1990). Okey and Jones suggest that when the complexity and importance of the topic (e.g., safety) provide no margin of error in learning, less choice in what is learned is required. They add that if it is essential that certain knowledge and skills be acquired, then choices need to be proscribed for learners. Adaptive advisement has been shown to result in higher posttest performance than evaluative advisement when used in computer-based instruction with learner control conditions (Santiago & Okey, 1990). The appeal to learners was the ability to make decisions on their own after receiving the information. Santiago and Okey suggest that instructional designers apply adaptive advisement as an improvement to computer-based training. Alelo courses employ a similar approach: they offer recommendations as to what tasks and activities to perform next but give learners the option to choose different activities if they prefer.

Learner Feedback

Studies show that the manner in which systems provide tutorial feedback has an effect on learning outcomes (Dempsey & Van Eck, 2003; Johnson et al., 2007). Feedback that is encouraging and sensitive to the learner's sense of self-esteem leads to better learning than simply telling learners when their responses are right or wrong. Corrective feedback is most effective when it is embedded in the game, instead of being in tutorial critiques. For example, if the learner inadvertently is rude to a virtual Iraqi in the Tactical Iraqi course, the Iraqi may call the learner a "son of a dog." This very effectively gets the learner's attention without either damaging the learner's self-esteem or interrupting the flow of the game.

Our feedback approach distinguishes *inner-loop feedback* (immediate feedback to learner actions during gameplay) and *outer-loop feedback* (feedback between gaming episodes and other activities). Outer-loop feedback encourages learners to reflect on mistakes they made in the previous activity and choose what activity they should undertake next. We increasingly provide such feedback via virtual coaches (i.e., animated pedagogical agents), as shown in Figure 1. Inner-loop feedback is designed so as not to distract the learner from the game or disrupt the gameplay. As a result, we currently avoid using virtual coaches for inner-loop feedback and instead rely on the game interaction (i.e., the consequences of the learner's actions in the virtual world) to provide the feedback, supplemented with a review of the learner's performance at the end of the gaming episode, i.e., in the outer loop. Thus, although we agree with intelligent tutoring theorists such as VanLehn (2006) that feedback can be conceptualized in a two-loop model, we see a contrast with typical intelligent tutoring systems where the tutor provides feedback in both loops. In fact, the type of feedback in the inner loop is often very different from the feedback in the outer loop, because it should be designed in such a way as not to interrupt the flow of the game (Czikszentimihalyi, 1990; Van Eck, 2006). While we design our virtual coaches to be polite, encouraging, and supportive by following the principles of politeness theory in tutorial discourse (Wang & Johnson, 2008) and motivational tutoring (Lepper, 1988), we consider it very appropriate for in-game characters to be very direct in their responses (e.g., calling the learner "a son of a dog"), so that learners understand clearly the consequences of their actions and can learn from their mistakes.

Motivation

Motivation, particularly intrinsic, is an integral part of adult education (Knowles, 1984) and is an important aspect of language and culture learning. Data from a series of studies on motivation which were designed to test whether making learning more fun would produce corresponding increases in learning, retention, and interest in the subject matter showed that there are cognitive and motivational benefits of appropriately designed motivational additions to educational activities (Lepper, 1988).

Studies of second-language learning have repeatedly shown a strong correlation between motivation and learning outcomes (e.g., Johnson & Wu, 2008). Although motivation depends upon the goals of each learner, motivation can be influenced by the learner's experience with the learning environment and can vary over time (Johnson & Beal, 2005). A common complaint about foreign language courses is that they are boring or tedious, which surely has a negative effect on motivation.

Optimizing learner motivation is a common concern in game-based learning design, and the topic has been explored extensively by other serious game researchers (Gee, 2005; Low, in press). Our design approach is informed by Lepper's model of the 4 Cs in learner motivation: curiosity, challenge, control, and confidence. Learning experiences are designed to provide an optimal level of challenge. For example, beginning-level spoken dialogues are highly tolerant of learner mistakes, while more advanced dialogues demand more accurate speech. Learners are also given a high degree of control over which learning activities to perform and in which order. Curiosity plays a further role in the selection of tasks that are clearly relevant to learner needs and job responsibilities, as well as aspects of the culture that are unique or unexpected. And most importantly, the beginning learning experiences are designed to build up learners' self-confidence in speaking the foreign language by having them practice their conversational skills in a nonthreatening simulated game world.

AGENT-BASED LEARNING ENVIRONMENTS

Although game-based learning and social-learning approaches have promise for language learning, they also pose design challenges, particularly for beginning language learners. Most language learning games in use today (e.g., word puzzles and word-matching exercises) may be engaging but bear little relation to the use of language in face-to-face conversation and so may be of limited value in promoting spoken language proficiency. Educational game designs can have a tendency to incorporate what Mayer and Moreno (2002) have referred to as seductive details—engaging multimedia elements that distract the learner's attention away from the concepts being learned and thus interfere with learning. Social learning environments can provide advanced learners with opportunities to practice their language skills, but beginning learners can find them difficult and intimidating. These problems are illustrated in Foti & Hannafin's (2008) multiplayer Chinese game study, where it was found that learners tended to engage in game activities that were unrelated to language learning and conversed with each other mainly in English instead of in the target language.

Intelligent agent technology, and conversational agent technology in particular, offer exciting possibilities for computer and online learning environments and for overcoming the design challenges mentioned above. Agents can be used to create games that simulate actual human conversation and social interaction so that the skills acquired in the game transfer more easily to real-life language use. They can actively engage learners in language use, making the learners less likely to engage in distracting game activities unrelated to language learning. For example, agents that communicate only in the target language, and not in the learner's native language, can encourage learners to use the target language and discourage them from switching back to their native language. Finally, we can carefully control the level of difficulty of conversational interactions with agents to provide learners with an optimal level of challenge. For beginning learners, we can create conversational agents that are very tolerant of learner mistakes and hesitations to reduce the intimidation factor in foreign language dialogue. For advanced learners, we can create agents that demand a much higher standard of language fluency and so help learners to overcome the well-known plateau effect in second language learning, where learners progress only to the point where they are understandable by native speakers, and no farther.

Negroponte (1970) was the first to conceive of a computerized intelligent agent with his notion of a personal butler or assistant. Agents are increasingly being shown to be valuable for learning (Atkinson, 2002; Johnson, Rickel, & Lester, 2000; Moreno, Mayer, Spires, & Lester, 2001). Although computer agents can never simulate an actual human instructor, agents can better operationalize human aspects of instruction than other methods of computer-based tutoring (Baylor, 2002). Pedagogical agents can respond to learners in a social manner through human-like interactions (Kim & Baylor, 2006). Pedagogical agents have also been found to be viable and effective with educationally appropriate personas (Baylor, 2000).

In their phenomenological study of human–agent interactions, Veletsianos and Miller (2008) described one aspect of the experience of conversing with a pedagogical agent as humanizing the agent somewhere between fantasy and reality.

According to Sengers (2004), one of the challenges of building complex artificial agents is that their design often results in fragmented depersonalized behavior, which mimics the fragmentation and depersonalization of schizophrenia in psychiatry. Sengers offers that the "juice" that is missing is narrative. She adds that narrative psychology suggests that "narrative comprehension is context-sensitive, focuses on agent motivation, and seeks connections between events over time" (p. 106). To address the schizophrenic nature of agents, Sengers proposes a move away from agent-as-autonomous to the socially situated AI notion of agent-as-communication, a concept embraced in our immersive games.

Although agent technology offers promise for game-based learning and language learning in particular, it offers significant challenges from an instructional design perspective. It is a very new technology and so calls for new design methods that can apply it effectively. Because it is a new technology, it is hard to predict with certainty how learners will interact with agent-based learning solutions. This makes rapid prototyping and iterative design extremely important. Finally, authoring tools and methods are needed that are suitable for use by instructional designers, not just specialists in AI. These are key factors underlying our instructional design approach.

INSTRUCTIONAL DESIGN STRATEGIES

The instructional design approach used to create Alelo's skill builders and immersive games is fundamentally an ADDIE process, a heuristic shared by many instructional design models. More specifically, aspects of Wilson's (1995) situated instructional design model and Tripp & Bichelmeyer's (1990) rapid prototyping model are used to design and develop the overall content for the game-based courses. Our approach also has similarities with the Dick and Carey systems approach model for designing instruction (Dick & Carey, 1996), which consists of a process of design, development, implementation and evaluation, placing lesser emphasis on the analysis phase. Instruction is carefully targeted on the skills and knowledge to be taught, given certain conditions of learning.

Tripp and Bichelmeyer argue that rapid prototyping applies to instructional design for computer-based instruction, just as it does to software engineering. They state that rapid prototyping methods allow greater flexibility when dealing with the complexity of a human factors intensive field such as the process of instruction. Central to designing and developing a serious game is the reality that various processes do not occur in a linear fashion. Instead, the analysis of needs and content depends partially upon the knowledge gained by building and using a game-based system. This issue comes up frequently in the design of interactive dialogues for our game environments. Each dialogue is designed to practice and reinforce particular communicative skills and vocabulary, but in the course of authoring the dialogue, we may discover that it requires the learner to have knowledge of additional vocabulary and skills that have not yet been covered in the curriculum; these must then be worked into the curriculum. Play testing of the completed game episode with learners may uncover other problems either with the episode design (e.g., learners attempt to communicate with the game characters in ways that the designers did not anticipate) or with the supporting learning materials (learners are unable to play through the episode because they have failed to master critical communication skills). These may necessitate further adjustments to the design.

Tripp and Bichelmeyer point out that the design environment in rapid prototyping makes it practi-

cal to quickly synthesize and modify instructional artifacts, offering a high degree of plasticity for instructional design. Plans can easily be changed throughout the design and development process because the model takes advantage of the medium's flexibility, using it to create the instructional sequence and strategy. A major disadvantage of rapid prototyping is that feature creep is almost inevitable, leading to cost overruns and longer time lines (Whitten, Bentley, & Dittman, 1989). In the media-rich environment of serious games, feature creep is a constant battle. In our case, we permit prototyping and revisions up to a certain point but then must freeze the design before the game goes into final production, and sometimes we remove game elements that are not yet ready for inclusion in the final design.

Wilson's (1995) situated instructional design model is also relevant to our approach. It incorporates a constructivist, situated view of learning and expertise, while concomitantly viewing the instructional design process itself in situated terms. Additionally, situated instructional design has as its foundation a situated cognition view of human learning and performance, adapting itself to the constraints of situations in ways that traditional instructional design models do not (Wilson, 1995). Similar to rapid prototyping, in situated instructional design, implementation and design are ultimately inseparable. A focal point of this method is that instruction should support learners as they become efficient in procedural performance and deliberate in their self-reflection and understanding. In addition, Wilson suggests that successful programs must attempt to make complex performance possible while avoiding simplistic proceduralization. For serious games that teach complex notions of language-in-culture, this approach suggests the need for rich contextualized game episodes in which learners can practice and integrate the communication skills that they have been acquiring in the course.

A key challenge is properly integrating presentation, practice, and assessment into the game-based curriculum. Gagné (Gagné, Briggs, and Wager, 1992) identified nine events shared by all instruction, involving preparing and orienting learners, presenting material, providing practice opportunities, assessing performance, and review and reflection. However as Van Eck (2006) has noted, if this approach is applied in a simplistic, linear fashion, it can result in rigid, didactic learning materials incompatible with game-based learning. Nevertheless, Gagne's nine events are very relevant, and neglecting them can often result in game environments that focus just on the practice opportunities and neglect both presentation and assessment. We address this issue through a close coupling of interactive learning materials in what we call skillbuilders and game episodes that offer opportunities to practice the skills that are covered in the skillbuilders. Assessment is incorporated both in the skillbuilders and in the game episodes; in the latter case, learners are scored based on their ability to apply their communication skills in the context of the game. Following Quinn's (2005) convergent model of instructional design, we also provide dramatic introductions that introduce the communication skills being taught, present examples of the communication skills in use, and give multiple opportunities for scaffolded practice and feedback. These culminate in free-play game episodes in which learners apply and integrate the skills that they have learned to that point.

THE ALELO APPROACH TO DESIGNING SERIOUS GAMES

We will now describe in detail how these concepts and strategies are applied in Alelo's instructional design approach. Underlying the instructional design approach is Alelo's situated culture model, which informs the teaching of task-based cultural knowledge to learners so that they can successfully interact and communicate with people from other linguistic and cultural backgrounds. The process of designing the skillbuilders and immersive games

is iterative in nature and highly dependent upon communication between subject matter experts (SMEs) and the production and technical staff in order to realize a course of instruction that is at once effective and engaging.

Situated Culture Model: A Foundation for Teaching Culture

Underlying the instructional design of Alelo's products is a dynamic methodology for identifying and teaching situated culture (i.e., the cultural knowledge needed to successfully perform tasks or higher-level projects in a foreign country). Students and learners learn the cultural knowledge they need in order to successfully interact and communicate with people who have grown up in a different linguistic and cultural context. One of the major goals of Alelo products is the acquisition of cultural competence. In addition, learners are trained to be more aware of cultural differences and cultural relativity, also known as metacultural awareness. This improved metacultural awareness is meant to be a tool kit that learners take with them to the foreign context: once they are living and immersed in a foreign country, this metacultural awareness helps them continue to learn culturally appropriate and effective ways of speaking and behaving.

The Situated Culture Methodology (SCM) is used to develop all of our courses (See Figure 3). The methodology is broken down into three major groupings: context, cultural factors, and curriculum. All of the groupings are integrated to support learners in reaching performance objectives and in becoming more culturally aware and adaptable. The goal here is to help learners acquire both the skills they need to handle common tasks and situations that they are likely to face and the cognitive flexibility to apply their skills in a variety of situations.

Working With Subject Matter Experts (SMEs) – Analysis Phase

SMEs are an integral part of the course development effort. SMEs are interviewed early in the course design phase using a modified job/task analysis approach where applicable. We also encourage participation of customer SMEs as a way to promote cooperative design involving all stakeholders.

Nevertheless, one of the challenges faced by the content design and development team is the lack of SME availability to answer substantive questions when they arise. Indeed, decision making without adequate information is typical of design (Tripp & Bichelmeyer, 1990). Optimally, SMEs from target cultures and the customer would have a hand in every step of content development, including initially assisting in identifying tasks that would be interesting and relevant to learners. Once the tasks have been outlined, SMEs would continue to be involved in the curriculum development process by identifying cultural and language interest points and helping to author exercises by suggesting common errors and possible false responses. In reality, while SMEs are involved at many stages of development, the decision-making process in the design phase often must proceed without complete information. Schön (1988) suggested that uncertainty, uniqueness, and conflict are the defining characteristics of design activities. In the rapid prototyping model, the complexity and uncertainty of situations is acknowledged rather than minimized as in traditional Instructional Systems Design (Tripp & Bichelmeyer, 1990). Once adequate information is gathered, content development proceeds in an iterative process as current content is validated and additional information becomes available from SMEs.

Cultural protocols involve cultural knowledge, sensitivity and awareness—including nonverbal gestures, etiquette, and norms of politeness—that are critical for successful communication. During the design phase, SMEs familiar with the target culture provide and validate cultural content, working closely with course authors to design interactive learning experiences for participants.

Task-Based Module Design: Task Identification

As a first step in curriculum design, we identify the tasks that anchor each of the learning modules, consistent with the task-based approach to

Figure 3. Situated culture model

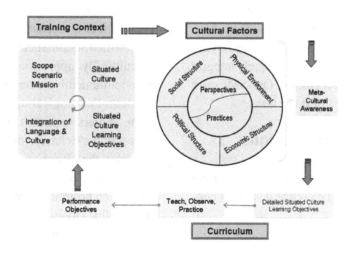

second language instruction (Ellis, 2003). The task-selection process is based on a number of factors summarized below.

Interest to the Learner

Foremost, the selection of tasks has to reflect situations that a learner may encounter in his or her daily life and that the learner has a particular interest in mastering. This helps to tap into learner motivation to learn.

Skill Transferability

Some tasks are chosen because the skills learned in mastering that task are readily transferable to other practical situations, adding to cognitive flexibility. These sorts of tasks provide the opportunity for learners to pick up on language for expressing opinions and reflecting on choices made. Learners can also pick up on patterns for turning opinions into questions and posing them to their conversation partners. This enables learners to feel more confident engaging others in conversation and to feel a sense of ownership of their opinions.

Richness of Cultural Content

Another factor in determining tasks to include hinges on identifying aspects of the target language and culture that fascinate and capture the imaginations of our learners and provoke their curiosity. We identify topics that will be both relevant and interesting precisely because they are so foreign to our learners and so uniquely integral to members of the target culture. Our SMEs are key to the identification of these tasks.

Key Facets of Course Design

Once the tasks have been identified, there are a number of facets of the course design to consider:

Dialogue Models

Alelo applies (AI technologies to create game characters that are capable of engaging in rich, natural dialogue with learners, giving them opportunity to practice their communication skills.

Speech Recognition

People often badly mispronounce language and blame the software when it misrecognizes their speech. Our speech recognition technology combines grammar-based and "garbage" speech models to determine the probability of when learners' speech is correct and when it isn't, and provide them with meaningful, immediate feedback. The speech recognition capability is tightly integrated with the AI dialogue models and the game scenarios, so that it is tailored to recognize utterances that learners are likely to say in the context of the scenario, using the language skills that they have acquired to that point in the curriculum.

Believable Virtual Humans

The AI methods generate virtual humans who can choose believable courses of action such as complaining, cooperating, making requests, and answering questions; exhibit believable physical behavior adapted to dynamically changing social contexts; and express rich communicative acts that combine appropriate speech and gestures. This utilizes a mechanism called Cultural Puppets, which automatically generates sequences of culturally appropriate behaviors matching the communicative intent of the NPC at a given moment. Pedagogical agents play a central role in the immersive games. The politeness effect is built into the behavior of the agents. This effect indicates that learning systems that adhere to social norms of politeness in human–computer interaction promote better learning than learning systems that violate those norms. These principles guide the behavior of the virtual coaches and socially intelligent virtual humans in our intelligent learning environments.

Learner Models

Each correct or incorrect use of relevant linguistic, cultural, and task skills provides probabilistic evidence of mastery of that skill. Although it is not possible to tell whether each individual usage is an instance of guessing an answer, making an unconscious mistake, or the speech recognizer's misinterpretation of the learner's response, after a series of such usages, our learner models can quickly identify the learner's mastery level.

Content Authoring

Authoring tools allow authors to create the rich content representations required by our AI-based products and perform AI-based processing themselves. For example, one tool proposes phonetic transcriptions for utterances written in the foreign language's standard orthography.

Designing and Developing Courses Using the Situated Culture Model

Once the tasks and context have been determined, Alelo anthropologists and content developers can begin work on determining and documenting the cultural factors that will be relevant for learners. These cultural factors come from all levels of social organization: macrosocial, microsocial, and individual; together, they form the "cultural lens" through which learners and the local citizens with whom they will be interacting view and interpret the world (Valente et al., 2009).

The more a learner is able to accurately interpret the behavior, speech, and implicit ways of communicating of the people with whom they're interacting, the more effectively they will be in building trust, managing perceptions, and making progress towards task completion. This means that the learner needs to have a basic working knowledge of local cultural norms, sociolinguistic etiquette, the ways that expectations for conversations vary from culture to culture, and cultural taboos. Teaching situated culture through task-based and relevant exposure to the culture in question helps guide learners toward both cultural competence and metacultural awareness.

Knowledge is not presented solely for knowledge's sake; the cultural notes that are integrated into training modules are not random lists of interesting historical facts and what might be seen as cultural exoticisms. Instead, all information presented to learners about the context is designed to be relevant to learning how to communicate appropriately with a range of potential interlocutors in the target country.

Other relevant cultural factors are extracted from the context of the projected interactions that learners are learning to participate in appropriately. For example, in order to conduct a meeting with a bureaucrat or official of some kind, a learner will need to know, at minimum, information about the following cultural norms:

- Understandings of time. For example, does 10 o'clock really mean 10 o'clock? Or does it mean 11:00 or 11:30? Cultures vary in their views about time and punctuality, and in norms and expectations concerning meetings and appointments.
- Greetings, especially differences between formal and informal greetings.
- Types of appropriate small talk for meetings between strangers, and just how much small talk needs to take place before getting down to business. In more relationship-oriented cultures, initial meetings are often concerned entirely with relationship building, not with the actual conduct of business.

Table 1 presents a sample curriculum for a game-based program to teach cultural awareness.

Table 1. Sample curriculum

Unit 3: Relationships and Communication	Detailed Situated Culture Learning Objectives	Suggested Content
The purpose of this lesson is to introduce you to the multiple aspects of communication and relationship development with people in Sahel Africa. These units focus on the importance of communication, the different elements of communication, and some types of interactions between aid workers and people in Sahel Africa.		
Meet Strangers	. Terminal Performance Objective: Initiate preliminary greetings with people in both formal (e.g., meeting military counterpart) and informal (e.g., interacting with new people in the marketplace) situations in a culturally appropriate manner. . Enabling Objectives: 1) Ask someone's name. 2) Apply culturally appropriate levels of intonation, pitch, and, loudness given the context you are in. 3) State your name. 4) Say please and thank you. 5) Appropriately express that you don't understand. 6) Name where you are from. 7) Say goodbye at different times of the day. 8) Address people of the opposite sex with respect for culturally specific gender roles. Introduce dialects of French and Arabic spoken in Sahel Africa. 9) Identify appropriate titles and forms of address for men, women, and children in Sahel Africa.	. The aid worker approaches a person in a village. He must ask for directions. The aid worker wants to introduce himself, and he asks the man's name before getting directions.

Skillbuilders – Development

Curricula begin with a larger task and then break it down into smaller components. For example, a content developer may need to write a curriculum to help train people with the language and cultural knowledge they will need to set up a medical mission. This overarching task, with the help of SMEs, is then broken down into smaller lessons that cover different necessary components, such as explaining your mission, locating your mission site, managing requests, inspecting potential mission sites, and coordinating security. These lessons are then broken down further into smaller component parts, with information on how to set up meetings and speak appropriately with local bureaucrats and officials, how to deal with implicit and explicit requests for bribes, and how to manage local employees, for example. Curriculum development goes hand in hand with definition and analysis of cultural factors and is an iterative process with repeated feedback loops.

Immersive Games – Development

Curricula incorporate a number of immersive games in which the learner is given objectives that they must complete by interacting with virtual characters in a virtual world. These objectives normally reflect realistic tasks learners are likely to need to complete in a foreign country like finding a taxi, purchasing something at a market, or completing military missions such as house searches and partner military training. Each task is covered by at least one "scenario" which connects the immersive game episodes into an overarching storyline.

Believability, as opposed to photorealism, has been shown to be a more appropriate instructional strategy for our serious games (Vilhjalmsson, Merchant, & Samtani, 2007). The virtual world should be similar enough to the real foreign country so that when people are immersed in the foreign country, it will feel familiar to them. However, the virtual world need not be a faithful rendering of any specific locale in the foreign country. NPCs should react to players in a manner that is appropriate for the target culture from the perspective of the player. However, there are limits to the amount of behavioral realism that is practical and necessary. For one thing, learners tend to overlook certain behavioral details when they are actively and cognitively engaged in the game. We often do not bother to synchronize lips with speech in our game characters, because we find that learners playing the games tend to focus more on body posture and gesture when they are engaged in conversation with the characters on the screen. Sometimes we deliberately depart from reality by adding scaffolds to the gameplay so that learners can more readily understand the behavior that they are seeing. For example, if the learner has offended a NPC, a red minus sign often appears above the head of the NPC. This is useful both because beginning learners often have trouble interpreting the facial expressions of people from other cultures, and it is difficult to depict subtle facial cues using current game animation technologies.

Alelo's games are designed from the perspective of a player character to help learners gain first-hand experience interacting with people from another culture. We do not, however, employ a first-person view as in shooter games, but rather adopt a third-person perspective that enables the learner to see his or her character interacting with other characters. This makes it easier for learners to see the nonverbal behavior of their own characters, as well as the NPC responses.

Task-based curricula provide learners with contexts that are highly relevant to their missions and daily lives. Virtual world simulations let learners transfer their acquired skills to the real world by practicing realistic, extensive interpersonal communication (as opposed to merely repeating uninteresting phrases) at their own pace and as often as they need to without embarrassment.

Conversational agents have been used effectively in task-based approaches such as the Tactical Language and Culture Training System, where learners converse with Iraqi NPCs to complete tasks such as a civil reconstruction mission (Johnson, 2007). Other tasks modeled in these military training courses include basic survival skills (passing through customs, obtaining transportation, lodging, food, etc.), arranging and conducting meetings (with officials, military officers, police, tribal leaders, village elders, etc.), gathering information, conducting house searches, maintaining base and embassy security, and mastering foreign military advisor skills.

In the mission games, learners are given a specific task to complete, such as in Tactical Dari where they must talk with locals on the street in order to gain an introduction to the village elders. "Performance before competence" is one of the 16 principles of "good learning" using video games outlined by Gee (2005). While this is the opposite of most traditional instruction, Gee cites in particular the example of language acquisition, in which students can gain competence through reading before actual performance. In Tactical Iraqi, learners acquire appropriate language and cultural points in the skillbuilder lessons, then enter the Mission Game, where they then "man" a checkpoint in one scene. If learners do not have all of the requisite skills, they are provided hints to enable them to successfully complete the mission—although their game score is less than if they had completed it without hints. Designers work closely with military SMEs and language and culture experts to create appropriate dialogues and believable environments. In the Chinese *Virtual Encounters* game, for instance, students must find their friend in a hutong using survival language. The *Virtual Encounters* game was carefully designed to include only those words and phrases which were taught in the first unit of instruction.

Integration of Scenarios With Skillbuilder Lessons

Immersive games provide a practice area for the skills taught in the skillbuilder lessons. The learner is expected to first learn the skills needed to complete a task, and then practice completing the task in an immersive game. To learn the skills they need, the learner will complete approximately one unit (usually about three to five lessons) of language and culture instruction before entering the first scenario. In some systems, tutor advice specifies which skills are prerequisites for a scenario and whether or not the learners have mastered these skills. The scenarios are also dependent on the lessons in a key way: the learner can only use the language that is explicitly taught in the lessons. No prior knowledge of a foreign language is assumed. Figure 4 shows the Main Menu, in which the learner chooses whether to enter the Mission Game or the Skillbuilder lessons:

Developing a Scenario Specification Using Skillbuilder Lesson Content

Scenarios must be designed to incorporate language and culture skills learned in the preceding skillbuilder lessons. This instructional design step is complex since scenario and skillbuilder lesson outlining must be done in parallel. The first step in scenario creation is to obtain an outline for a unit of skillbuilder lesson material (see Table 2). After determining the key learning objectives for the unit, authors can begin constructing an overall storyline, including scenario specifications, for the system. Below is an example outline of a unit of skillbuilder lesson for Tactical Indonesian.

From this information, a scenario specification is created that includes the following:

1. A summary of the overall story and objectives
2. Names of primary characters involved
3. A simple description of the setting
4. Possible ways to fail
5. Possible ways to pass
6. A small sample of dialogue in the scenario

Since the language in the unit outlined in the curriculum revolves around greetings and introductions, the scenario needs to test these communicative functions. As an example, the learner will try to meet with her driver, who is picking her up at the airport. This type of scenario should cover all of the following communicative functions: saying hello, introducing oneself, saying where one is going, and introducing anyone else who is

Figure 4. Main menu of Tactical French showing both skillbuilder and mission game components

Table 2. Sample outline of a skillbuilder lesson for Tactical Indonesian

Lesson	Learning Objectives	Vocabulary:	Grammar:	Culture:
Greet someone	Saying hello formally	Pak / Bu – sir / ma'am Selamat pagi/sore/siang/malam. Good morning/ afternoon/day/evening. Mau ke mana? Where are you going? Jalan-jalan. Traveling around. Halo. Hi. Hai. Hey.		Use proper greeting gestures
	Saying hello to someone Muslim	Asalamu aleykum. Peace be upon you. Wa aleykum salam. (reply)		Introduction to Islam in Indonesia
Introduce yourself	Tell someone to sit	Silakan duduk. Please sit. Terima kasih. Thank you.		
	Say your name	(Nama) saya… My name is…	Form possessives Form sentences without "be"	
	Ask someone else's name	Siapa (nama) anda? What is your name? Siapa (nama) bapak? What is sir's name?		Use proper form of "you"
	Locate someone	Permisi, (apa) anda…? Excuse me, are you..? Ya. Yes Tidak. No. Saya bukan… I'm not… …kan? …right?	Form Yes–No questions	
Introduce your team	Ask the name of a third person	Siapa ini/itu/dia? Who is this/that/he? Siapa namanya? What is his name?/your name?	Possessive suffixes	Use proper pointing gestures
	Introduce a third person using proper ranks	Ini…/itu… This is/That is… Mayor – major Kapten – captain Letnan – lieutenant Sersan – sergeant Kopral – corporal Prajurit – private		
	Say which force you're from	Kami dari Korps Marinir. We're from the Marine (Corps).		

present. Based on this simple description, the first part of the scenario specification is written:

1. Your goal is to meet with your driver at the airport, and get transportation to Jakarta.
2. Main characters: Ramelan, your driver
3. Setting: Jakarta airport

The scenario could be made more difficult by having other drivers in the area try to tempt the learner to use their services. This gives the learner more people to interact with and makes the scenario richer. It also gives learners practice applying their skills in a variety of situations to increase the flexibility of their skills. Moreover, if the learner is extremely polite, as a bonus outcome,

she could obtain additional valuable information that will help her on her mission.

Once the language skills are incorporated into the scenario, cultural skills learned in this unit are added. The unit outline includes learning about the use of Muslim greetings, proper greeting/ pointing gestures, and appropriate ways to address strangers. The final step is to add sample dialogue to the outline using the language in the unit outline. The following is an example of a completed scenario outline.

1. Your goal is to meet with your driver at the airport and get transportation to Jakarta.
2. Main characters: Ramelan, your driver; Budi, an angkot driver, Dian, another taxi driver.

3. Setting: Jakarta airport, crowded and some other drivers in the background.
4. Possible ways to fail:
   a. Choose to go with the wrong driver. This means that you snub the driver who was sent to pick you up, and it's also a waste of money, since his services have already been paid for.
   b. Use informal "you," which is disrespectful for a stranger.
   c. Use American pointing gestures, which are considered vulgar.
   d. Fail to use a greeting gesture, which would possibly cause you to lose points, although not too many, since it is not always obvious in the game that you have the option of choosing a gesture.
5. Possible ways to pass:
   a. Build rapport with Ramelan. Since he is well connected in Jakarta, he has access to a lot of valuable information about your mission. This can be accomplished by:
   i. Using very polite forms of "you" ("sir")
   ii. Responding appropriately to Muslim greetings and gestures
   iii. Using polite phrases like "nice to meet you" and "thank you"
       1. T: Selamat pagi, Pak. Good morning, sir.
       2. R: Selamat pagi. Good morning.
       3. T: Siapa nama bapak? What's your name?
       4. R: Nama saya Ramelan. Apa bapak John? My name's Ramelan. Are you John?
       5. T: Ya, nama saya Sersan John. Yes, my name is Sergeant John.
       6. R: Selamat datang! Siapa ini? Welcome! Who is this?
       7. T: Itu Kopral Tom. That's Corporal Tom.
       8. R: Mau ke Jakarta, kan? You want to go to Jakarta, right?
       9. T: Ya, betul. Yes, that's correct.
       10. R: Oke! Silakan duduk. Okay! Please take a seat!

Examples of Scenarios in the Immersive Game

Figure 5 shows the Mission Game menu for Tactical French, with five possible scenarios available to learners. Under the "Scene Description" box, learners receive instructions about what objectives they must complete in a given scenario. In "Leave the Airport," for example, the learner's goals are to find the driver, load the bags, and leave for the hotel.

Some tasks are comprehensive enough that they require multiple scenarios. For example, in Tactical French, Weapons Training is divided into four subscenarios: Safety Rules Lecture, Shooting Position, Courses of Fire, and After Action Review. In this case, the parent is referred to as a "scenario," and the daughters as "episodes" of that scenario, as can be seen in Figure 6.

The Production Team creates believable worlds to match the given curriculum design and specifications. 3-D artists build the worlds, and 3-D animators build the characters and gestures that are placed in those worlds. Audio specialists record voice actor lines for the dialogues. The end result is the development of believable worlds, which are made to look authentic with collaborating support from SMEs, who verify the content at every step.

Once in a scenario, the learner normally can choose to approach and interact with different people. Figure 7 shows the scenario "Leave the Airport," where the learner has the option to speak to any of five characters. A few of these characters can help him satisfy his objectives, and the rest are not central to the plotline, but are capable of carrying on a basic conversation and sometimes giving hints as to how to satisfy the objectives.

Figure 5. "Mission Game" Main Menu for Tactical French showing five possible scenarios

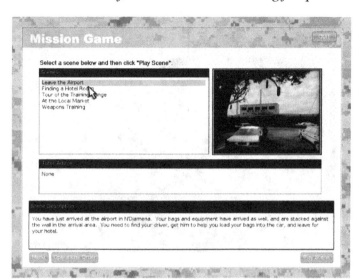

Figure 6. Hierarchical relations of parent (scenario) and daughter (episode) for complex scenarios

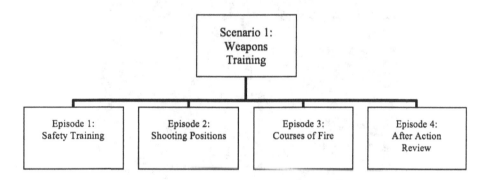

The learner can select people to talk to by clicking on them and then selecting "Talk" from the pop-up box.

Once a learner approaches someone, he must carry on a conversation with that person. At any time, learners can choose to view what they are allowed to say or do by clicking on "Courses of Action." In most systems, users interact with characters by speaking to them via a microphone. The system uses speech recognition technology to understand what the learner said (e.g., "What's your name?") and AI technology to assign an appropriate response (e.g., "My name's Laila"). Systems that teach primarily culture do not require the learner to speak in order to complete

the scenario. Instead, learners can click on one of their Courses of Action; their character will then speak for them.

If they select the right person and complete their objectives in a culturally sensitive way, learners win the game and can move on to the next scenario. If the learner says or does something culturally inappropriate, they will fail and the debrief will explain what was done wrong.

Active Dialogues: A Mini-Game

Active dialogues are essentially scaled-down scenarios. The fundamental purpose of an active dialogue is to provide opportunities to practice

Figure 7. Leaving the airport scenario

Figure 8. The learner has initiated a conversation with the agent "Laila"

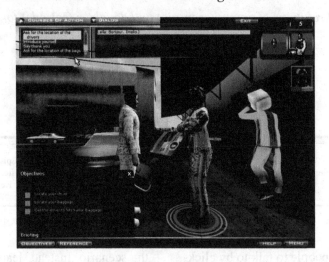

the specific communicative functions taught in the lesson where they are introduced. While a Mission Game episode normally corresponds to three or four lessons and can exercise material from all of those lessons, an active dialogue corresponds to one skillbuilder lesson and sometimes only part of a lesson.

As a result of this conceptual distinction, active dialogues are placed directly in the skillbuilder lesson that they are relevant to, while scenarios are separated into the Mission Game segment of the system. In addition, the learner's control

is much more limited, the logic is less complex, less advanced language is required, and fewer possible courses of action are available in active dialogues. While active dialogues can have good and bad outcomes, they are not a fundamental requirement.

Scenarios are intended to function as "transfer tasks," while active dialogues are not. In order to prepare learners to perform communicative functions in real life, learners must successfully complete active dialogues, where they can practice what they learned in a familiar context similar to the way learners typically practice speaking inside of a classroom. When they reach a more advanced level, users can progress to the scenarios. Since the scenarios typically follow a separate storyline and involve different characters and places, the learner is required to practice the same skills but in an unfamiliar context. The assumption given cognitive flexibility theory, or CFT, is that in transferring their skills to different virtual situations, learners will become more prepared to transfer their knowledge to different real-world situations.

To complete each active dialogue, the learner must speak its character's lines. There are many different things that the learner can say, and the virtual humans in the scenario may respond differently to the learner, depending upon whether or not the learner interacts with the Iraqi characters in culturally appropriate ways. The learner can say a range of things to this character and express each utterance in a variety of different ways. Furthermore, the learner can speak to multiple virtual humans within the scene.

EXAMPLES OF IMMERSIVE GAMES AND INTEGRATED SKILLBUILDERS

The following are some further examples of serious games that we have developed using this framework. These give an example of the range of learning experiences that have been developed using the methods described above.

Encounters: Chinese Language and Culture

Encounters Chinese includes a suite of multimedia language materials anchored by a new textbook being written. Alelo developed a pilot Web site portal named "Virtual Encounters" and Web-based instructional materials for the program. "Virtual Encounters" is media-rich, incorporating audio, text, and multimedia features. The pilot unit

contains 13 interactive skillbuilders, including introductions, greetings, tones, radicals, and writing simple Chinese characters. "Getting Started with Encounters Chinese" gives learners an initial overview of the main components of the skillbuilder section and how to employ the material presented most effectively in learning. This section includes an animated virtual guide accompanied by voiceovers which explain the main features of the course. "Review Your Progress" shows a view of what modules and games learners have completed and what scores they have achieved. This progress page is viewable at various places throughout the program. "The Hutong Game" challenges learners to find their friend in a hutong by using language learned in the first few lessons of the skillbuilders.

Virtual Cultural Awareness Trainer (VCAT): Teaching Cultural Awareness for the Horn of Africa

The overall objective of the Virtual Cultural Awareness Trainer (VCAT) is to provide cultural awareness training over the Web using a fully embedded social simulation model. Only survival language skills are taught, as the focus is on teaching culture. Learners are guided through the program using "metacultural checkpoints" that teach fundamental cultural knowledge and skills that would be needed to become culturally aware in the Horn of Africa, regardless of the country being visited. Learners follow a loose storyline in the game, which consists of task-based lessons appropriate to their rank and mission (e.g., humanitarian assistance), as well as casual games. As learners move through the game, they gain points depending upon successful completion of culturally challenging situations where they must decide upon various courses of action that determine whether or not they are able to achieve a mission objective. Integrated into the gameplay is a full spectrum of media such as cultural notes with voiceovers, video interviews with cultural experts, and interactive maps which show the fluidity of tribal migration across national borders, a concept foreign to many American learners. VCAT is designed to be delivered using SCORM-compliant learning management systems. The system automatically generates a customized module sequence for each learner, depending upon the learner's country of focus, mission, and level of responsibility. Figure 9 below shows an interactive scenario; the index on the left shows the lessons and sublessons.

RezWorld: Teaching Cherokee Language and Culture

Tribal language revitalization is more important now than ever. More than 90% of American tribal languages will be gone within 20 years if effective measures are not taken. In collaboration with Thornton Media, we have developed *RezWorld*, a pilot immersive game for teaching the Cherokee language. The immersive Cherokee game teaches spoken language and cultural knowledge. The game has lesson plans that teach basic pronunciations, grammar, sentence structure, and much more (see Figure 10).

EVALUATION AND PILOT STUDY RESULTS

An evaluation of the Tactical Iraqi course by the U.S. Special Operations Command found that learners learn Arabic to an Interagency Language Roundtable (ILR) proficiency level of 0+ (ACTFL proficiency level of novice high) after as little as a week of study. A study by the Marine Corps Center for Lessons Learned (MCCLL) documented strong evidence of Tactical Iraqi's effectiveness. It examined the experience of the 2nd Battalion and 3rd Battalion, 7th Marine Regiment (2/7 and 3/7 Marines), who trained with Tactical Iraqi prior to their most recent tour of duty in Iraq. The 3/7 attracted the attention of MCCLL because it did not suffer a single combat casualty during its entire tour of duty. The 3/7 was deployed in Anbar province, and had been involved in heavy fighting in Ramadi during its previous tour of duty. Interviews of the commanding officers of the 3/7 reveal several interesting and important findings. In the opinion of the officers, the training greatly increased the battalion's operational capability as it enabled it to operate more efficiently, with an increased understanding of the situation and better relationships with the local people. They felt that the Marines who trained with Tactical Iraqi

Figure 9. Interactive scenario in VCAT

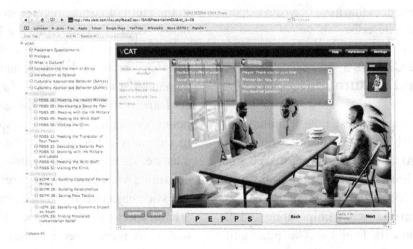

Figure 10. RezWorld scene

achieved a substantial level of language proficiency; so much so that they deserved to receive college credit for the language proficiency they gained. While this evidence is anecdotal, it points to the effectiveness of serious games to transfer knowledge and skills to the field.

Pilot studies for the *Encounters Chinese* and *Voice of America GoEnglish* online language and culture programs provided positive feedback on the instructional strategy and approach. Young learners at a summer camp for learning Chinese reported that the *Encounters* course was a fun way to learn a difficult language. Students especially liked the ability to speak and listen, and to have their speech recognized by the software. Results of a focus group study on *Encounters* provided similar feedback, offering that this interactive way to learn a language and culture was engaging and effective. A formative evaluation of *GoEnglish* with Farsi and Chinese learners of varying skill levels produced positive results regarding the content and delivery. Learners enjoyed the story-based approach to learning American idiomatic English, saying that this was practical language that they could use in everyday situations. One tester reported later using the language on what

to say when in a car accident when she was side-swiped on a Los Angeles freeway.

FUTURE RESEARCH DIRECTIONS

The costs of designing and developing serious games are continuing to decrease, and new authoring tools are becoming more widely available. Thus, the opportunity to use this instructional strategy becomes increasingly affordable and attractive to a larger audience. Future research should delve into how using rapid prototyping combined with Wilson's situated instructional design model facilitates the creation of pedagogically sound games for fields beyond language and culture training. Future research should also include evaluative studies that determine the effectiveness of serious games that were designed with accelerated learning and performance outcomes in mind.

CONCLUSION

Instructional designers are increasingly challenged to design serious games that take advantage

305

of emerging technologies with an eye toward addictive learning, much like the engagement present in entertainment games such as *World of Warcraft*. Immersive games offer learners an opportunity to practice their linguistic skills and cultural knowledge in a safe environment while receiving constructive feedback. This chapter has described an approach to teaching second language and cultural skills that integrates game-based learning with other interactive instruction methods. It describes a methodology for developing such learning environments that is well grounded in research on learning. Initial results on the impact of serious games in achieving language and cultural competency are positive. With rapid advancements in technology and in the field of AI combined with widely available broadband accessibility, serious games are poised to play an important role in bridging language and culture barriers.

ACKNOWLEDGMENT

The authors wish to acknowledge the contributions of various members of the Alelo team to the work presented here, particular Ellen O'Connor and Michelle Flowers. This work was funded in part by DARPA, USSOCOM, PM TRASYS, and other US government agencies. It reflects the opinions of the authors and not of the U.S. Government.

REFERENCES

Atkinson, R. K. (2002). Optimizing Learning from Examples Using Animated Pedagogical Agents. *Journal of Educational Psychology, 94*(2), 416–427. doi:10.1037/0022-0663.94.2.416

Baylor, A. L. (2000). Beyond butlers: Intelligent agents as mentors. *Journal of Educational Computing Research, 22*(4), 373–382. doi:10.2190/1EBD-G126-TFCY-A3K6

Baylor, A. L. (2002). Agent-based learning environments as a research tool for investigating teaching and learning. *Journal of Educational Computing Research, 26*(3), 227–248. doi:10.2190/PH2K-6P09-K8EC-KRDK

Brown, J. S., Collins, A., & Duguid, P. (1989). Situated cognition and the culture of learning. *Educational Researcher, 18*(1), 32–42.

Chou, S.-W., & Liu, C.-H. (2005). Learning effectiveness in a web-based virtual learning environment: A learner control perspective. *Journal of Computer Assisted Learning, 21*(1), 65–76. doi:10.1111/j.1365-2729.2005.00114.x

Dempsey, J. V., & Van Eck, R. (2003). Modality and placement of a pedagogical adviser in individual interactive learning. *British Journal of Educational Technology, 34*(5), 585–600. doi:10.1046/j.0007-1013.2003.00352.x

Dick, W. C., & Carey, L. (1996). *The systematic design of instruction* (4th ed.). New York: Longman.

Doughty, C., Nielsen, K., & Freynik, S. (2008). *Final report E.3.2: Rosetta Stone findings*. Center for Advanced Study of Language, Univ. of Maryland.

Driver, R., Asoko, H., Leach, J., Mortimer, E., & Scott, P. (1994). Constructing scientific knowledge in the classroom. *Educational Researcher, 23*(7), 5–12.

Ellis, R. (2003). Task-based language learning and teaching. New York: Oxford University Press, USA.

Flowers, M. (2009). *Virtual Cultural Awareness Trainer preliminary design document. Alelo TLT.* LLC.

Foti, L. T., & Hannafin, R. D. (2008). Games and multimedia in foreign language learning-using back-story in multimedia and avatar-based games to engage foreign language learners: A pilot study. *International Journal of Emerging Technologies in Learning*, *3*(3), 40–44.

Franc, C., Lawton, J., & Morton, A. (2008). *EBL for EBL: Enquiry-based learning for an end to boring language learning*. Centre for Excellence in Enquiry-Based Learning, University of Manchester. Retrieved from http://www.campus.manchester.ac.uk/ceebl/projects/casestudies/17.pdf

Gagné, R. M., Briggs, L. J., & Wager, W. W. (1992). *Principles of Instructional Design* (4th ed., *Vol. 365*). Fort Worth, TX: Harcourt Brace Jovanovich College Publishers.

Garcâia-Carbonell, A., Rising, B., Montero, B., & Watts, F. (2001). Simulation/gaming and the acquisition of communicative competence in another language. *Simulation & Gaming*, *32*(4), 481–491. doi:10.1177/104687810103200405

Gee, J. P. (2004). *Situated language and learning: A critique of traditional schooling*. New York: Routledge.

Gee, J. P. (2005). *Why are video games good for learning?* [Electronic Version]. Retrieved from http://www.academiccolab.org/resources/documents/Good_Learning.pdf

Johnson, W. L. (2007). Serious use of a serious game for language learning. *Artificial Intelligence in Education: Building Technology Rich Learning Contexts that. Work (Reading, Mass.)*, 67.

Johnson, W. L., & Beal, C. (2005). Iterative evaluation of a large-scale, intelligent game for language learning. In C.-K. Looi et al. (Eds.), *Proceedings of the International Conference on Artificial Intelligence in Education* (pp. 290-297). Amsterdam: IOS Press.

Johnson, W. L., Rickel, J. W., & Lester, J. C. (2000). Animated pedagogical agents: Face-to-face interaction in interactive learning environments. *International Journal of Artificial Intelligence in Education*, *11*(1), 47–78.

Johnson, W. L., Wang, N., & Wu, S. (2007). *Experience with serious games for learning foreign languages and cultures*. Paper presented at the SimTecT 2007, Brisbane, Queensland, Australia.

Johnson, W. L., & Wu, S. (2008). Assessing aptitude for learning with a serious game for foreign language and culture. In *Intelligent Tutoring Systems* (pp. 520–529). Berlin: Springer-Verlag. doi:10.1007/978-3-540-69132-7_55

Jonassen, D. H. (1992). Cognitive flexibility theory and its implications for designing CBI. In Dijkstra, S., Krammer, H., & van Merriënboer, J. (Eds.), *Instructional models in computer-based learning environments* (pp. 385–403). Berlin: Springer.

Kim, Y., & Baylor, A. L. (2006). A social-cognitive framework for pedagogical agents as learning companions. *Educational Technology Research and Development*, *54*(6), 569–596. doi:10.1007/s11423-006-0637-3

Klabbers, J. H. G. (2000). Learning as acquisition and learning as interaction. *Simulation & Gaming*, *31*(3), 380–406. doi:10.1177/104687810003100304

Knowles, M. S. (1984). *Andragogy in action*. San Francisco: Jossey-Bass.

Lantolf, J. P., & Thorne, S. L. (2006). *Sociocultural theory and the genesis of second language development*. Oxford, UK: Oxford University Press.

Lave, J. (1988). *Cognition in practice*. New York: Cambridge University Press. doi:10.1017/CBO9780511609268

Lave, J., & Wenger, E. (1991). *Situated learning: Legitimate peripheral participation*. New York: Cambridge University Press.

Lepper, M. R. (1988). Motivational considerations in the study of instruction. *Cognition and Instruction, 5*(4), 289–309. doi:10.1207/s1532690xci0504_3

Low, R. (in press). Examining motivational factors in serious educational games. In Van Eck, R. (Ed.), *Interdisciplinary models and tools for serious games: Emerging concepts and future directions*. Hershey, PA: IGI Global.

Mayer, R. E., & Moreno, R. (2002). Aids to computer-based multimedia learning. *Learning and Instruction, 12*(1), 107–119. doi:10.1016/S0959-4752(01)00018-4

Mayer, R. W. (1999). Designing instruction for constructivist learning. In Reigeluth, C. M. (Ed.), *Instructional design theories and models* (*Vol. 141-159*). Mahwah, NJ: Lawrence Erlbaum Associates.

Miller, G. A., & Gildea, P. M. (1987). How children learn words. *Scientific American, 257*(3), 94–99.

Miller, R., & Fallad, J. (2005). *Constructivist Theory & Social Constructivism. Unpublished class paper*. University of New Mexico.

Moreno, R., Mayer, R. E., Spires, H. A., & Lester, J. C. (2001). The case for social agency in computer-based teaching: Do students learn more deeply when they interact with animated pedagogical agents? *Cognition and Instruction, 19*(2), 177–213. doi:10.1207/S1532690XCI1902_02

Negroponte, N. (1970). *The architecture machine*. Cambridge, MA: MIT Press.

O'Connor, E. (2009). *Alelo Immersive game process document. Alelo TLT*. LLC.

Okey, J. R., & Jones, M. G. (1990). *Learner decisions and information requirements in computer-based instruction*. Paper presented at the International Conference of the Association for the Development of Computer-Based Instructional Systems

Park, I., & Hannafin, M. J. (1993). Empirically-based guidelines for the design of interactive multimedia. *Educational Technology Research and Development, 41*(3), 63–85. doi:10.1007/BF02297358

Phillips, D. C. (1995). The good, the bad, and the ugly: The many faces of constructivism. *Educational Researcher, 24*(7), 5–12.

Plass, J. L., & Jones, L. C. (2005). Multimedia learning in second language acquisition. In Mayer, R. (Ed.), *The Cambridge handbook of multimedia learning* (p. 467). New York: Cambridge University Press.

Quinn, C. N. (2005). *Engaging learning: Designing e-learning simulation games*. Hoboken, NJ: Pfeiffer.

Reigeluth, C. M. (Ed.). (1999). *Instructional-design theories and models* (*Vol. II*). Mahwah, NJ: Lawrence Erlbaum Associates.

Roth, W. M. (2001). Situating cognition. *Journal of the Learning Sciences, 10*(1/2), 27–61. doi:10.1207/S15327809JLS10-1-2_4

Santiago, R. S., & Okey, J. R. (1990). *The effects of advisement and locus of control on achievement in learner-controlled instruction*. Paper presented at the 32nd international conference of the Association for the Development of Computer-based Instructional Systems, San Diego, California, October 29-November 1, 1990.

Schön, D. A. (1988). Designing: Rules, types and worlds. *Design Studies, 9*(3), 181–190. doi:10.1016/0142-694X(88)90047-6

Sengers, P. (2004). Schizophrenia and narrative in artificial agents. In Wardrip-Fruin, N., & Harrigan, P. (Eds.), *First person: New media as story, performance, and game* (pp. 95–116). Cambridge, MA: MIT Press.

Spiro, R. J., & Jehng, J. C. (1990). Cognitive flexibility and hypertext: Theory and technology for the nonlinear and multidimensional traversal of complex subject matter. In Nix, D., & Spiro, R. J. (Eds.), *Cognition, education, and multimedia: Exploring ideas in high technology* (pp. 163–205). Hillsdale, NJ: Lawrence Erlbaum.

Tennyson, R. D. (1980). Instructional Control Strategies and Content Structure as Design Variables in Concept Acquisition Using Computer-Based Instruction. *Journal of Educational Psychology*, *72*(4), 525–532. doi:10.1037/0022-0663.72.4.525

Tripp, S. D., & Bichelmeyer, B. (1990). Rapid prototyping: An alternative instructional design strategy. *Educational Technology Research and Development*, *38*(1), 31–44. doi:10.1007/BF02298246

Valente, A., Johnson, W. L., Wertheim, S., Barrett, K., Flowers, M., & LaBore, K. (2009). *A dynamic methodology for developing situated culture training content. Alelo TLT*. LLC.

Van Eck, R. (2006). Building artificially intelligent learning games. In Gibson, D., Aldrich, C., & Prensky, M. (Eds.), *Games and simulations in online learning research & development frameworks*. Hershey, PA: Idea Group.

VanLehn, K. (2006). The behavior of tutoring systems. *International Journal of Artificial Intelligence in Education*, *16*(3), 227–265.

Veletsianos, G., & Miller, C. (2008). Conversing with pedagogical agents: A phenomenological exploration of interacting with digital entities. *British Journal of Educational Technology*, *39*(6), 969–986. doi:10.1111/j.1467-8535.2007.00797.x

Vilhjalmsson, H., Merchant, C., & Samtani, P. (2007). Social puppets: Towards modular social animation for agents and avatars. *Lecture Notes in Computer Science*, *4564*, 192. doi:10.1007/978-3-540-73257-0_22

Vygotsky, L. S. (1978). *Mind in society*. Cambridge, MA: Harvard University Press.

Vygotsky, L. S. (1986). *Thought and language*. Cambridge, MA: MIT Press.

Wang, N., & Johnson, W. L. (2008). The politeness effect in an intelligent foreign language tutoring system. *Lecture Notes in Computer Science*, *5091*, 270–280. doi:10.1007/978-3-540-69132-7_31

Whitten, J. L., Bentley, L. D., & Dittman, K. (1989). *Systems analysis and design methods* (2nd ed.). Homewood, IL: Irwin.

Wilson, B. G. (1995). *Situated instructional design: Blurring the distinctions between theory and practice, design and implementation, curriculum and instruction*. Paper presented at the Association for Educational Communications and Technology, Anaheim, CA.

Wong Fillmore, L. (1991). Second-language learning in children: A model of language learning in social context. In Bialystok, E. (Ed.), *Language processing in bilingual children* (pp. 49–69). Cambridge, UK: Cambridge University Press. doi:10.1017/CBO9780511620652.005

APPENDIX: ADDITIONAL READING

"Must-Reads" for This Topic

Bateman, C. M., & Boon, R. (2006). *21st century game design.* Florence, KY: Charles River Media.

Garcâia-Carbonell, A., Rising, B., Montero, B., & Watts, F. (2001). Simulation/gaming and the acquisition of communicative competence in another language. *Simulation & Gaming, 32*(4), 481-491.

Johnson, W. L., Rizzo, P., Bosma, W., Kole, S., Ghijsen, M., & Van Welbergen, H. (2004). Generating socially appropriate tutorial dialog. *Lecture Notes in Computer Science, 3068*, 254-264.

Johnson, W. L. (2007). Serious use of a serious game for language learning. *Artificial Intelligence in Education: Building Technology Rich Learning Contexts that Work*, 67.

Johnson, W. L., Wang, N., & Wu, S. (2007). *Experience with serious games for learning foreign languages and cultures.* Paper presented at the SimTecT 2007, Brisbane, Queensland, Australia.

Jonassen, D. H. (1992). Cognitive flexibility theory and its implications for designing CBI. In S. Dijkstra, H. Krammer & J. van Merriënboer (Eds.), *Instructional models in computer-based learning environments* (pp. 385-403). Berlin: Springer.

Lee, S., Kim, J. W., & Lee, J. (2005). *The Effectiveness of online situated environments for language Learning.* Paper presented at the 21st Annual Conference on Distance Teaching and Learning, Madison, WI.

Quinn, C. N. (2005). *Engaging learning: Designing e-learning simulation games.* Hoboken, NJ: Pfeiffer.

Reigeluth, C. M., & Goldman, S. R. (2001). Instructional-design theories and models: A new paradigm of instructional theory. *Contemporary psychology, 46*(3), 3.

Tripp, S. D., & Bichelmeyer, B. (1990). Rapid prototyping: An alternative instructional design strategy. *Educational Technology Research and Development, 38*(1), 31-44.

Wilson, B. G. (1995). *Situated instructional design: Blurring the distinctions between theory and practice, design and implementation, curriculum and instruction.* Paper presented at the Association for Educational Communications and Technology, Washington, DC.

Top Texts for Interdisciplinary Studies of Serious Games

Constantine, L. L. (2004). Beyond user-centered design and user experience. *Cutter IT Journal, 17*(2), 2-11.

Ellis, R. (2003). *Task-based language learning and teaching.* New York: Oxford University Press.

Gee, J. P. (2003). What video games have to teach us about learning and literacy. *Computers in Entertainment (CIE), 1*(1), 20.

Klemmer, S. R., Hartmann, B., & Takayama, L. (2006). *How bodies matter: Five themes for interaction design.*

Mulligan, K., & Smith, B. (1986). A Husserlian theory of indexicality. *Grazer Philosophische Studien, 28*, 133-163.

Prensky, M. (2001). *Digital game-based learning.* Colombus, OH: McGraw-Hill.

Raybourn, E. M. (2005). Adaptive thinking & leadership training for cultural awareness and communication competence. *Interactive Technology & Smart Education, 2*, 127-130.

Stubblefield, W. A. (2007). *Hacking sense: Understanding design and use as situated sensemaking.* Technical report, Sandia National Laboratories.

Suchman, L. A. (1987). *Plans and situated actions.* New York: Oxford University Press.

Tomasello, M., & Whiten, A. (1999). *The cultural origins of human cognition.* Cambridge, MA: Harvard University Press.

Chapter 14
Principles and Signatures in Serious Games for Science Education

Otto Borchert
North Dakota State University, USA

Lisa Brandt
North Dakota State University, USA

Guy Hokanson
North Dakota State University, USA

Brian M. Slator
North Dakota State University, USA

Bradley Vender
North Dakota State University, USA

Eric J. Gutierrez
Northern Arizona University, USA

ABSTRACT

The World Wide Web Instructional Committee at North Dakota State University has developed a number of serious games aimed at science education. Their games are all multiuser, with a role-based orientation, promoting a task-and-goal cultural awareness. Constructed in collaboration with content experts, these games were developed under a proven set of design guidelines (design principles and signature elements) that serve to preserve consistency among the applications. As a consequence of this high-concept design constraint, their systems share important cognitive and pedagogical features that assist players in learning the serious game content while also allowing for consistent evaluation of learning outcomes across games. The authors have formatively evaluated these games and found them to be effective. It is now their hope that by sharing their design guidelines, others may be able to use and evaluate them to their advantage. The authors continue to develop and refine these design principles and signature elements through basic and evaluative research.

DOI: 10.4018/978-1-61520-717-6.ch014

INTRODUCTION

The World Wide Web Instructional Committee (WWWIC) has developed a number of serious learning games, all sharing the same strategic principles and signature elements. The games provide an immersive, spatially oriented, game-like, highly interactive, exploratory, goal oriented, learn by doing, role-based, and multiplayer experience. The underlying argument is that experiences and rehearsal lead to expertise, and so WWWIC games provide serious experiences to maximize learner achievement (Slator & Associates, 2006).

BACKGROUND

The WWWIC at North Dakota State University (NDSU) is an ad hoc group of faculty, staff, and students dedicated to the development of immersive virtual environments, or IVEs, for education. These serious games focus on physical and social science topics such as geology, cell biology, anthropology, and economics.

WWWIC games share a common "signature" on both the pedagogical design and implementation level. At a pedagogical design level are the qualities listed above: immersive, spatially oriented, game-like, highly interactive, exploratory, goal-oriented, learn by doing, role-based, and so forth. These principles are echoed by others working in this field such as Gaydos & Squire's chapter on "designed experience" (in press).

At the interface and implementation level, NDSU WWWIC games combine the specificity of science-based educational games with techniques developed both academically and commercially to increase productivity and decrease development costs. We have developed a model for the creation of serious games based on this signature that we describe here for review, use, and evaluation by others working in this field.

This chapter will begin with a description of the design principles and signature elements of the WWWIC IVE model, followed by descriptions of a number of serious games and how they fit into the model. We end with a discussion for further research.

DESIGN PRINCIPLES

IVE Cultural Context

Contextual learning is the catalyst for new frontiers of learning research between anthropology and immersive virtual role-based learning computer sciences. The IVE "world" is both cultural artifact and sociocultural experience. This virtual world can be described as a semi-isolated cultural system.

The anthropological contribution to a science of learning involves understanding how student engagement of problems in a cultural context affects learning and affects individual and group knowledge. Following examples of ethnographic studies in education (Wolcott, 1985, 1991), immersive virtual role-based environments can be described as cognitive artifacts for education, that is, as tools for learning. Cognitive artifacts are fundamental to most of humanity's learning processes (Bidney, 1947; D'Andrade, 1989; Norman, 1993). As cognitive artifacts, the virtual role-based worlds for education are constructed purposefully for student immersion in scientific and humanities problems.

Immersion in IVEs

Immersion in IVEs means the student is plunged into a virtual environment in the role of a particular persona. Scientists and scholars working with IVEs refer to these immersive contexts for learning as authentic scenarios. Anthropology defines these authentic scenario worlds as cultural in the sense that the world is made up by a selection of traits from a universe of possibilities (Batteau, 2000). Specifically, the world is designed to offer a limited set of facts in a rich context of scientific practice (Edelson, Pea, & Gomez, 1996). The resulting context has an effect on students that can be described, in part, in terms of the linguistic relativity principle as developed by Sapir and Whorf. That is, the virtual world is limited, and hence, it constrains through language and symbolic communicative experience and behavior how the student understands the virtual reality. Because the virtual reality is an archetype of real-world reality (what Dempsey, this volume, refers to as elemental learning outcomes), the student's understanding of the virtual problem can be transferred to real-world problems, using the same class of psychological and social processes that are associated with individual learning through problem exposure (Spindler, 1955) and innovation diffusion found within a cultural system (Rogers, 1962). By taking the role of scientist, scholar, or artist (depending on the discipline), the student advances in the problem scenario by learning to think scientifically, as shown through the use of methods, tools, nomenclature, and analytical approaches learned in the virtual world and demonstrated in both the virtual world and the real world.

Role-Based

Elsewhere, we have described in detail the anthropological theory behind role-based learning in IVEs (please see Slator & Associates, 2006). Briefly, the virtual role-based worlds are specially constructed to engage the student at theory and method levels for the content-specific IVE. Role-based means that the student appears in the virtual world, to self and others, as an individual and unique persona (an avatar in the visual virtual worlds) capable of engaging objects and others through language and virtual physical movement. The role may be as a scientist, businessperson, or student, depending on the discipline involved and the goals of the problem scenarios. No matter the environment, the pattern of engagement in the virtual world is driven by individual experi-

ences and "other-dependent learning" in both the virtual and real worlds. Other-dependent learning involves "conditions of informally guided discovery" (D'Andrade, 1981, p. 186). We learn best not on our own but through engagement with others. Student engagement in the world is both formal and informal, made possible through interaction with things and other people online in the virtual world. These other people include instructors (software agents and real people online) whose virtual behavior is that of "powerful hints and occasional correction," which are so important to other-dependent learning. The interaction of the instructors with the students in the virtual world is deliberately patterned and is part of the selection of the traits (elements) of the world.

Levels of Cognizance

The patterns of theory and method constructed into the virtual world are recognized at various levels of cognizance by the student as the student proceeds to work with the problems presented in the scenarios (similar to processes of cognizance and learning as reported by D'Andrade, 1984). A student's recognition of patterns in the world is indicative of learning stages: Increasing comprehension requires many rearrangements of understanding. Hence, as the student learns, so the understanding of the virtual world changes for the student. Learning is both accumulative and transformational, whether the learning environment is constructed for science or the workplace (e.g., Clancey, 1995).

To interact, and therefore to learn, in the virtual world, the student must engage virtual objects, virtual agents, and real-time personas of real people also in the virtual world. Formal teaching of this type of engagement learning can only reach a rudimentary level. Basically, the student is told the problem scenarios and reasons for being in the virtual world. The student is told how to use the interface technology that is the mechanism of physical engagement in the virtual world. The student is given a vocabulary and interaction etiquette guidelines. Students are encouraged to work together. But the students have no real experiential understanding of the virtual world until they are in it. Students who have previously experienced virtual worlds and virtual role-based interaction may explore the world with confidence, often acting as informal mentoring agents to newer students. The more experienced virtual student teaches others how to get along in the virtual world, usually through various informal behaviors and discourse.

Virtual Enculturation

The catalyst that transforms the virtual world into a cultural learning experience is enculturation affected within the virtual conditions. Enculturation traditionally refers to the processes by which cultural ideas and behaviors are passed from one generation to the next (Dix, 2000; Harris, 1968, p. 11, 78–79, 132; Spindler, 1955). Enculturation in contemporary anthropological usage refers to cultural learning in general through social observation and interaction (Ortuno, 1991). Enculturation is an intrinsically social process relying on material and symbolic context and content of experience to bridge the gap between cognizance of new ideas and practice relying on those ideas (Rogers & Shoemaker, 1971).

From the interactions among player students, we find there is an ordering of interaction through a complex set of rules, formal and informal, of a class described by Sapir. Specifically, the virtual worlds represent a diversity of learning levels. Hence, the culture of the virtual world is unequally shared among the members of the group, much like what occurs in the real world (Bailey, 1983; D'Andrade, 1992). Yet, through a significant reliance on informal other-dependent learning, the culture perpetuates the advancement of knowledge in new generations of learners. This can be explained as enculturative context (Harris, 1968) affected by diffusion process (Rogers & Shoe-

maker, 1971) made salient through *performative interaction*. This understanding of the processes by which virtual enculturation works informs, whether explicitly or implicitly, the design of many IVE serious games today (e.g., Barrett & Johnson, this volume).

Communicative Competence

In the virtual world, there are performative social interactions that directly affect learning processes (Guimarães, 2001). Performative interactions are social interplay that produces effects either on the performers and/or on the other social actors. Specifically, there is reflexive behavior as categorized by Turner (1987, p. 81), where the student learns by observing or engaging in social interactions generated by other people. The student's sense of self and knowledge is altered through these reflexive cognitive performative encounters. At the textual discourse level, performative behavior occurs when the students are aware of their language interaction and use and perceive their role as one "to display for others" a certain grasp of other or specialized concepts and language. This is proactive shifting of the language-style presentation of self to others (Schilling-Estes, 1998, p. 53).

For the virtual learner, performative social interaction develops and changes as the student progresses through levels of understanding and learning. These various developments are salient where the student displays increasing levels of communicative competence (similar to that described by Bonvillain, 1997, p. 247). That is, as the student expands knowledge and confidence in the information and interactions encountered in the virtual environment, the student's learning is reflected and made measurable, in part, in the ability to deal with a stylized speech and presentation form specific to the virtual scenario discipline. Today, an anthropology of performance focused on virtual environments is concerned with "the way by which the multimedia resources. ..

platform are appropriated and resignified by the users through the analysis of the interactions that take place inside it" (Guimarães 2001, p. 1). Performance for learning is associated with studies on "the cultural meanings associated to the physical behavior of the avatars" (Ibid).

Culture as Process and Commitment to Interaction

The performance approach is related to a conception of culture as a process, a flux of facts embedded on a web of meanings that flow through time. The IVE culture is not considered as homogeneous or fixed but as being in continuous movement and change. Indeed, all the student's virtual social interactions are innovations derived from the fundamental set of instructions given to the student prior to the student's entrance into the virtual world. However, the virtual world reflects archetypes of communication processes extant in the real world, hence, activity in the virtual world, no matter how open-ended, will find itself reflecting hegemonic rules of interaction from the real world. As in the real world, learning through social interaction in the virtual world is encased in rules of interaction built into the IVE (similar to those described by Moerman, 1969, p. 459). This pushes research to ask, "How does the individual's commitment to social interaction support or undermine the individual's learning?"

Anthropologists are aware that individual learning is affected by the degree of commitment of an individual to interaction with others and the environment (Morris, 1994), especially interaction with change agents (Rogers, 1962). Thus, in the role-based scenario of the virtual world, the amount of social role-based interaction directly bears on the effectiveness of the learning environment for the student. In other words, the more the student interacts with objects and persons, the more possible is engagement of other-dependent learning and through that, diffusion of knowledge.

In the authentic scenarios of the virtual world, study of learning processes expands to open new ideas on the degree of commitment students have to virtual interaction with others. Pushing the limits of interaction study, we find that students interact in more professional and serious ways with one another within the IVE than we find in the conventional classroom. This is attributed, in part, to the freedom of expression under the guise of a role, and the lack of immediate physical presence may be releasing inhibitions that affect learning processes.

Pedagogy

The unifying research questions binding our multidisciplinary approach are these: (1) how do students learn in virtual educational worlds and (2) what can be done to enhance these processes of learning to higher levels of performance? These questions involve the relationship between humans and machines, cognition and behavior, symbolic performance and enculturation, social organization and learning, play and learning, stress and learning, among others. The fields involved span the biophysical sciences, social sciences, and humanities. Virtual learning context projects are reported from such diverse areas as medical and health sciences, political science, geology, chemistry, English, archaeology, business, microbiology, psychology, language, and others. In K-12, virtual learning contexts are being hand-created and launched by teachers anxious to explore a learning environment already familiar to their students. In the private sector and in government, projects are reported for training, marketing, and familiarization of duties. The future of a science of learning in immersive virtual role-based contexts requires organizing and advancing all of these appropriate partnerships among academia, industry, all levels of education, and other public and private entities.

Assessment, Data Collection, Maintenance

In brief, there are two areas for which data must be collected: (1) assessment of student performance and (2) evaluation of the IVE for maintenance issues and future developments.

Results have repeatedly shown that students in the virtual environments perform significantly higher on assessments than their counterparts in traditional settings. For instance, in controlled experiments (n = 281) where assessment measures of an IVE group using the *Geology Explorer* environment were compared to both a WEB group (alternative Web-based instruction) and a control group (traditional instruction without computers), a two-way main effects MANOVA model indicated a significant group effect (p = 0.0143). The Bonferroni intervals indicated that the IVE group outperformed both the WEB group and the control group. That is, there were no significant differences in mean net improvement between these two groups. Hence, because of large sample sizes and sound statistical analyses, we can conclude that our virtual world is benefiting student learning ability (McClean, Saini-Eidukat, Schwert, Slator, & White, 2001).

Similar positive effects are noted in controlled studies with the biology software. In one such study (n = 332), students in an introductory biology course were divided into three groups: (1) students who address specific questions based on additional textbook readings; (2) students who complete a WWW activity consisting of content similar to that found in the *Virtual Cell*, or *VCell*, modules; and (3) students who completed two *VCell* modules. A significant difference was observed between the scores among the three experimental groups. Those students using the *VCell* scored significantly higher (p < 0.05) on post-treatment assessments than the other two groups. In our most recent study, we measured both students' achievement and their confidence levels (how certain were they that their responses

on the assessment were correct). Not only did the technology group significantly outperform the others but their posttest confidence scores were twice as high.

In Slator et al. (2005), a study was conducted with the *Geology Explorer* and the *VCell* to determine the impact of specific player traits on the effectiveness of learning in IVEs. From this study, one of the factors being tested was gender. This study has shown that these games are not biased towards gender, meaning that the t-test results from this experiment show no significant differences in performance between male and female students in the *Geology Explorer* and the *VCell* experiments.

These studies, taken together with other published results (e.g., McClean et al., 2005), lead to the conclusion that IVEs such as the *Geology Explorer* and the *VCell* are not only valuable tools for the delivery of course content, but also support higher order thinking skills.

SIGNATURE ELEMENTS

WWWIC IVE signature elements were developed over time to address the needs and requirements of the design principles. The WWWIC IVEs share nine general elements that create a consistent approach across all of our serious games:

- *Multiple players.* Enculturation requires social interaction. The use of a multiplayer environment forces the student to begin immediate interaction with other players, promotes teamwork and leadership (factors often required in real world problems), and engages quickly the enculturative conditions present in the IVE. The IVEs are specifically designed to be multiuser and are played on a client-server architecture that supports multiple simultaneous users. Multiple players can change the IVE simulation in many ways, reflecting the changes that can happen in real-world situations where multiple experts work together to address problems and achieve goals.

- *Game-like*. The value of play in learning can hardly be overemphasized. Games are common to children across all cultures, and learning by playing is a well-recognized attribute of human learning through enculturation. Many of today's students grew up playing video games, and therefore the idea of learning through a game will seem normal to them, effectively reducing some of the resistance to learning something new. Furthermore, games can be fun, thereby encouraging the player to continue despite setbacks and frustrations. The WWWIC game *Geology Explorer* can be set up to be competitive if desired by the teacher.

- *Navigation*. The need to explore the virtual environment causes the students to interact with the environment in the game while at the same time allowing the students to control their own experiences while pursuing their own interests. This approach also takes into account the user-centered metaphor, where virtual physicality can be transposed to problems in the real world, thereby encouraging the curiosity necessary to successful scientific endeavors.

- *Library*. Professionals have many tools at their fingertips to help them succeed in their work. The library is a virtual place visually represented where students can find documents, materials, and other items necessary to fulfill their roles. These documents are similar to those in the real world, and thus student use of the library is transferable to real-world situations. Furthermore, the library is a place where those overseeing the use of the game can insert help, advice, and other resources for students as the game progresses. Additionally, items created by students, such as a logbook, can be stored

in the library. Typically, WWWIC games have, at a minimum, a dictionary of terms immediately available to the student. In addition, the library contains a manual that helps the player successfully engage with the IVE interface.

- *Tool kit*. All professionals have tool kits. Tools are not just for manipulation but also for reference. A tool can be an object with which to manipulate another object, an analytical approach, a mathematical formula, and other ideas as well as items. Tool kits are specific to the IVE content and are intentionally not all encompassing, instead reflecting the general range of fundamental tools necessary to complete tasks. Scientific inquiry requires the use of instruments for a multitude of purposes: to make measurements, to modify the environment, and to more accurately observe the natural world. To be immersed in the role of a scientist, students need access to these instruments, the tools of scientific study. Serious games provide these tools to varying degrees. Some are extremely realistic, while others abstract away some of the details to focus on other scientific pursuits. All WWWIC IVE tool kits contain the objects and processes necessary to complete the tasks required of the students.

- *Goals/tasks*. Goals are the overall focus of the teaching environment, and tasks are the strategically ordered components students must realize and undertake to reach their goals. Using the constructivist proposition of scaffolded learning, students are given goals and must undertake a set of tasks to reach those goals. Task models are specific to the discipline under study. Some training models adapt well to linear, sequential goal structures, while others require branching trees, and still others have a more dynamic task structure where masters guide apprentices based on experience levels.

Tasks force the students into learning by doing and can be understood as rehearsals for real-world problems. Furthermore, the tasks are the principal place in which the software tutoring agents in the IVE can monitor and assess students' performances for correction and assessment. Software agents monitor the students as the students go about performing tasks. They are not intrusive as a rule, interacting on their own with students (visiting) only when the need arises, as determined by the content experts. Tutoring falls into three general categories: diagnostic tutoring, case-based tutoring, and rule-based tutoring. (For a more in-depth explanation of these tutoring realms, please see Slator & Associates, 2006.) Tutoring harnesses the informal "other-dependent learning" conditions that help guide students to discovery and practice found in the real world.

- *Social interaction.* Learning through enculturation is intrinsically a social process. That is, it takes two or more actors. One actor is the student. The other actor can be another student, a tutor, or other software agent. Social interaction, especially through language, is a key element for evaluating the learning processes engaged in by students (see the previous section on *communicative competence*). Without social interaction, students are compelled to learn through rote memorization, binary searches, or other nonsocial interactions, all of which can slow down, frustrate, or even skew knowledge. Furthermore, social interaction is fundamental to the real world, at least in the physical and social sciences, and as such bears directly on the student's ability to begin approaching problems in the ways found in real-world disciplines.

- *Data collection for a) assessment of student performance and b) future IVE testing and development.* It is imperative that data be collected during the playing of the game to measure the performance of the students during and at the end of the game. The main assessment within the game is tracking students in terms of their goals and success or failure in achieving them. This is primarily accomplished through software agents and materials submitted within the game by the student. Additionally, for purposes of evaluating the IVE and future IVE developments, certain data about student behavior and performance can be sampled for rigorous scientific assessment. The type of data collected and the way data are collected varies from game to game. These data are also used with data collection strategies external to the game (such as pregame/postgame surveys and scenarios) that enable instructors as well as developers to assess the impact of the game on student knowledge and practice.

- *Help and Detail Editors.* It is important that those overseeing the use of the game by their students have the opportunity to assist their students indirectly. For example, they can insert new terms into the dictionary, add hyperlinks to references, and generally assist students who go to the library looking for help. The software editors require no programming knowledge and instructions for their use and are provided during implementation of the game.

These elements and the design principles they support are summarized in Table 1.

WWWIC GAMES

In this section, we provide overviews of five of the serious games WWWIC has developed (and continues to develop). Our examples begin with reviews of *Geology Explorer* and *On-A-Slant* village. Each successive game we discuss more

Table 1. WWWIC IVE design guidelines

Design Principles	Traits	Signature Elements	Examples
IVE Cultures: IVEs are cultural artifacts; semi-isolated cultural systems	Internet hosted Infrastructural constraints; limited set of traits	Multiple players	Varying levels of players' confidence and exposure to IVE-style serious games
		Game-like	"Backstories" and premise, modules, or levels; endgame scenarios
Immersion: enculturative conditions; authentic scenarios	Problem exposure; levels of cognizance	Navigation	Spatially oriented; exploratory; visual
		Library	Reference materials (e.g., glossaries, manuals) and student-created works (e.g., logbooks)
Role-based, goal-oriented: rehearsal in authentic contexts leading to expertise	Performance; Commitment to social interaction; Communicative competence	Tool kit	Specific to content, involves use of methods, tools, language, analytical approach. Also includes items such as a toolbox, logbooks, and other items created by the player
		Goals/tasks	Scaffolding of goals (both required goals and optional goals). Linear as well as branching, depending on content.
		Social interaction	In-game "conversations," in-game and outside-game messaging, virtual physicality. In-game interaction and feedback with other student players, tutors, guides, other agents
Assessment and evaluation; data collection; maintenance	Pregame, during game, postgame	Data collection and feedback for assessment of student in-game performance	Embedded assessments based on performance of tasks and data collected by software agents or other devices
		Data collection for future IVE development	Chronological sampling of in-game "conversations" between students and associated performance activities logged for postgame analysis.
		Help and Detail Editors	Available to those overseeing the use of the game.

briefly, highlighting the similarities and differences among the games (for more in-depth discussion of our games, please see Slator & Associates, 2006, as well as Brandt et al., 2006; Daniels et al., 2009; McClean et al., 2001; Slator et al., 2003, 2006). Taken altogether, in this section we work to indicate the breadth and depth of the games designed and implemented by WWWIC and the direction of our work. It is our intent that readers will see how we apply our principles and signature elements in these games and take away

from this discussion insights and opportunities for exploring and evaluating their own creations and/or use of games.

Geology Explorer

The *Geology Explorer* (Saini-Eidukat, Schwert, & Slator, 2001) is a goal-oriented computer game in which students learn about geology by acting like scientists exploring a new world. Within this virtual world, students "travel" to an imaginary

Planet Oit in order to gather geologic data about this newly discovered planet. Students act as geologists by performing various tests in order to identify unknown rocks and minerals and create a geologic map, which serves as an interpretation of the underlying geology of the area.

In the game, students are transported to the planet's surface and acquire a standard set of field instruments. Students are issued an "electronic logbook" with which to record their findings and are assigned a sequence of exploratory goals. These goals are structured using the scaffolding learning strategy and are intended to motivate the students to view their surroundings with a critical eye, as a geologist would. The students make field observations, conduct small experiments, take note of the environment, and generally act like geologists as they work toward their goals. A scoring system has been developed, so students can compete with each other and with themselves.

Tasks

The virtual environment of the *Geology Explorer* allows students to identify, investigate, and analyze scientific questions, to apply multiple process skills (manipulation, cognitive, and procedural) in context, to use evidence and strategies for developing or revising explanations, to manage ideas and information obtained on the planet, and to apply results of experiments to scientific arguments and explanations. The strategies employed direct the student explorer toward making logical conclusions based on the rules of evidence and following the methods and procedures practiced within the discipline of geology. Current learning objectives align with the following National Science Education Standards (National Research Council, 1995):

- Standard A: Science as Inquiry
- Standard D: Earth and Space Science
- Standard E: Science and Technology
- Standard G: History and Nature of

Science

The initial set of tasks in the *Geology Explorer* game is a series of five embedded pretreatment assessment tasks. These assessments measure content knowledge, confidence, attitude, and critical thinking. The information gathered allows for comparative statistics to discern any learning gains and attitudinal changes that occurred in students using the *Geology Explorer* immersive virtual environment. Each of the assessments is administered by a software avatar that is able to answer questions and provide hints that guide the students through completion of the tasks. The first assessment measures students' existing knowledge of geology instrumentation. The second measures their understanding of the scientific method. The third assessment is an interview with the leader of the mission. During the interview, students are asked a series of multiple-choice interview questions that are meant to discern their attitudes toward computers and geosciences. The fourth task is a problem-solving scenario that presents a problem in the domain of interest. Students are encouraged to "think like a geologist," record any questions they might have about the scenario, and pose possible solutions. The final assessment task is a series of content questions related to their existing knowledge on the subject of geology.

After students complete the assessments, they land on the newly discovered planet and receive their next set of tasks. These tasks contain simple step-by-step instructions and form a short tutorial that introduces students to some of the basic functions of the game. These include how to move, where to find geology instruments, and how to use the instruments to perform tests on rock samples.

The rest of the game is divided up into two main modules. The first is an identification module where students are asked to explore the planet and locate and identify a series of rocks and minerals. To begin with, rocks and minerals are relatively easy to find and identify. Players are given several hints to aid in the location and identification of this goal. Upon correctly identifying each rock or mineral, the student is given progressively more difficult rocks and minerals to find and the information in the hints is reduced. During this module, software tutors help students by pointing out what equipment players are lacking to successfully identify their goal, showing players what tests should be performed to come up with the correct conclusion, and explaining why their hypothesis is incorrect by pointing out contradictory experiments that would disprove its identity.

The second module is an interpretive module where students are asked to create a geologic map of a region of the planet. Here, students build on the outcrop identification skills by painting a map of the underlying geology of a region featuring an intrusive basalt dike. This is a fairly advanced procedure that enables the students to interpret a geologic setting as a geologist would. The student's job is to identify all the outcrops in the region, perform strike-and-dip measurements on specific outcrops, create the map, and use it to answer some questions about the underlying geology. Tutors in this module provide the same rock and mineral help as in the interpretive module. They also inform students if they have missed outcrops, provide help on creating a valid geologic map, and provide information necessary to answer questions about the region's underlying geologic structure.

After students have completed both modules of the *Geology Explorer*, they return to the landing area, where a posttreatment summative assessment is performed using a variation of the five tasks given in the pretreatment assessment.

User Interface Tools

The *Geology Explorer* game interface has five main tools: a Detail Window that allows close-up views of samples and thin sections, a Map of Planet Oit, a Sample Bag that contains items the student has collected, a Tool Kit that contains a collection of geology testing equipment, and a Bookcase. The Bookcase has six sections: a Dictionary panel that contains the many terms and concepts a player will encounter in the game, a Goal panel that contains the instructions for the student's current goal, a Tests panel that lists all of the experiments that a student has performed on various samples and outcrops, a Tutors Panel that contains a record of all contacts a student has had with the various tutors, a Notes panel where students can record their own notes, and a Who panel that shows the location of the other players in the game.

Maintenance Tools

The *Geology Explorer* environment contains several online maintenance and editing tools that anyone on the development team can use to make changes to the environment without having any prior programming experience.

The environment may contain terms and concepts that a player may not be familiar with, so an embedded dictionary database is provided to allow players easy access to definitions and explanations. The Help Editor was created so that updates or additional dictionary entries could be added using a simple Web-based HTML interface. The Detail Editor allows creating or editing of object descriptions and appearance using a simple form-based Web interface.

The simulation encourages students to complete the game collaboratively, so the Group Editor was created for teachers to form their students into groups of two.

Supplementary Material

The game is supplemented by a teachers' manual and a comic book as a graphical resource, both available in print and digital format on the Web. The plot of the comic is a "how to play" manual and the history of the game. The comic creatively depicts the scenario that a *Geology Explorer* player encounters—a new planet is discovered, and seven student geologists volunteer to explore it and identify its rocks and minerals. The comic book world has many parallels to the game, introducing players to the appearance of the game interface, the tools they can use, the landscapes they visit, and the tutors they may encounter.

On-A-Slant Virtual Village

On-A-Slant (Hokanson et al., 2008; Slator et al., 2001), is a virtual reconstruction of a sedentary Native American village that was located along the Missouri River near Mandan, North Dakota, USA. The *On-A-Slant* village was established in the second half of the sixteenth century and was abandoned around 1781, more than two decades before the Lewis and Clark expedition would explore that region for the United States. The environment is a "learn by doing" simulation based on a 3-D reconstruction of the archeologically important *On-A-Slant* Mandan village where students will explore the site, discover artifacts, and develop an interpretation of the relationship

between the archeology and society by interacting with the visualized context.

In the game, students are sent back in time to explore the village, learn about the food, family, lifestyle, education, and other cultural elements of the Mandan people before the full impact of Euro-American expansion was felt. At the same time, students are taught the methods and logic of anthropology and archaeology at an introductory level (see Figure 1).

Tasks

The tasks in the *On-A-Slant* learning environment are structured using the scaffolding learning strategy. The strategy originates from Lev Vygotsky's (1986) concept of the zone of proximal development (ZPD). This ZPD is the distance between what students can achieve by themselves and the learning they can acquire with competent assistance. Scaffolding provides individualized support based on the student's ZPD. Typically, a more knowledgeable other provides support (scaffolds) to facilitate a student's development.

Figure 1. The on-a-slant client

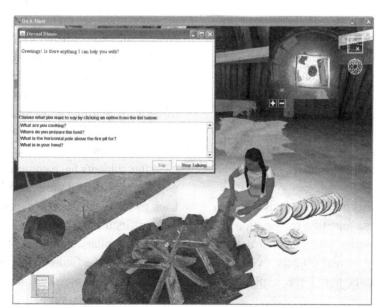

In the case of *On-A-Slant*, these more knowledgeable "others" are software agents that take the form of excavation team members and Mandan villagers who provide enough information and assistance to allow students to complete their current task(s). This scaffolding helps students build on prior knowledge and assimilate new information by providing instructional activities that are just beyond what they can accomplish alone.

Interactive and inquiry-based activities are currently under development. Students are given certain tasks to investigate in the environment (i.e., determine what foods the village population ate). As students move through and explore the environment, they can click on the various village inhabitants (avatars) and items to receive additional information and prompts. Activities are designed to align with the following national science standards (National Research Council, 1995).

Science as Inquiry

- Identify questions that can be answered through scientific investigation.
- Use appropriate tools and techniques to gather, analyze, and interpret data.
- Develop descriptions, explanations, predictions, and models using evidence.
- Think critically and logically to make the relationships between evidence and explanations.
- Recognize and analyze alternative explanations and predictions.

Unifying Concepts and Processes

- Evidence consists of observations and data on which to base scientific explanations.
- Models are tentative schemes or structures that correspond to real objects, events, or classes of events that have explanatory power.
- Scientific explanations incorporate existing scientific knowledge and new evidence from observations, experiments, or models into internally consistent, logical statements.

The first tasks in the *On-A-Slant* game contain simple step-by-step instructions and collectively form an immersive tutorial that introduces students to the game and familiarizes them with the various aspects of the interface. At the beginning, students find themselves on a virtual field trip to a present-day archaeological dig site. At the site, several avatars help the students through the tutorial by showing them how to communicate with other avatars, interact with in-game objects, move around the environment, and use the various tools provided by the game interface.

Once the students have completed the tutorial tasks, they are assigned two pretreatment assessment tasks. The first task is an interview with the leader of the excavation. During the interview, the student is asked a series of multiple-choice interview questions that are meant to discern their attitude toward computers and social science. After the interview, the students are sent on their second assessment task. They are asked to find a laptop at the excavation site and use it to answer a series of content questions related to their existing knowledge of the Mandan people. The embedded assessments measure content knowledge, confidence, and attitude and allow for comparative statistics to discern any learning gains and attitudinal changes that occurred while using the *On-A-Slant* immersive virtual environment.

After students have completed the tutorial and assessment tasks, they are "accidently" transported back to 1776, where they experience the Mandan village firsthand. In order to guide the students through the village environment, periodic messages are sent from the future to the students' electronic logbooks. These messages are in the form of requests for information and contain tasks for the students to perform.

These knowledge acquisition tasks are divided into five categories: food, shelter, games and leisure, community and family, and religion. The tasks are also designed around tools that anthropologists and archaeologists use to learn about a past culture. Archaeologists examine artifacts, evaluate primary source documents, and make ethnographic analogies. Anthropologists examine present cultures by observing, participating when possible, and asking questions of native peoples. We employ all of these tools to teach students about the Mandan culture.

The first category of tasks involves learning about the harvesting and processing of food. These tasks are divided into two sets. The first set of tasks are "examine artifact" tasks where students receive a series of messages from the archaeologists in the future, asking them to identify some artifacts discovered at the archaeological dig site. To accomplish the tasks, students need to explore the village and visit with Mandan villager avatars that tell them about each artifact's use and construction. Once the students believe they have identified an artifact, they report their findings back to the archaeologists by answering a series of multiple-choice questions about each of the artifacts. If a student answers incorrectly, hints are given to point the student toward the right answers. The second set of tasks involves examining primary source documents. Students are given excerpts from stories told by an old Hidatsa woman and are asked to verify the authenticity of their content. These tasks also require students to report their findings back to the archaeologists by answering a series of multiple-choice questions. Since the Hidatsa were culturally very similar to the Mandan, these excerpts also let students learn about ethnographic analogy.

The second category of knowledge acquisition tasks involves learning about the typical Mandan earth lodge dwelling. These tasks are similar to the earlier examine artifact tasks, but the students are provided with less initial information and are expected to accomplish more during each task.

In these tasks, students are asked to explore the lodges in the village and create a floor plan for a typical earth lodge dwelling including fire pits, beds, food preparation and preserving areas, horse corrals, and storage pits. Students are also tasked with determining how an earth lodge is built by visiting several lodges that are under various stages of construction. Again, avatars explain the process, and students complete formative evaluations showing they understand the content.

The final category of tasks involves observing three elements of the Mandan culture: games and leisure, community and family, and religion. Students are divided into groups of three, and each student in a group is assigned to learn about one of the above three cultural elements. This divided activity is based on the "jigsaw" method (Aronson, Stephan, Sikes, Blaney, & Snapp, 1978) and provides individual accountability for cooperative learning. Using this method, each student in a group learns about one part of a larger topic. After individual study, the students combine their knowledge by teaching each other about their respective areas of expertise. In the *On-A-Slant* game, students are each assigned a specific earth lodge to visit where they can talk to avatars and observe events in progress. After the assigned lodge is explored, students are each asked to use a paint program to draw a concept pictorial about their topic. The concept pictorial is a strategy that helps students to determine the main ideas of a learning activity. When all students have completed their drawings, they meet in a chat room and explain their pictorials to each other. Students take turns explaining their diagrams and answering questions other group members may have about their portion of the Mandan culture. In order to ensure that each group member is exposed to the same material, a "teacher check" avatar provides each student with a summary of what the other students experienced. Formative assessment of the cultural tasks is assessed using a matching exercise.

After the students have completed all of the goals in the Mandan village, they return to the future where a posttreatment summative assessment is performed using two tasks that are essentially the same as the two pretreatment assessment tasks.

An extension to the *On-A-Slant* environment is under development. A contemporary Lakota village is being created where students will complete tasks similar to those in the Mandan village that will help them understand the differences between sedentary and nomadic Native Americans.

User Interface Tools

The *On-A-Slant* game interface has five tools: a compass for indicating direction, a map that provides an aerial view of the player's surroundings, a teleportation tool that allows players to jump ahead as far as they can see, and an "archaeologist's logbook." The logbook also has five sections: a dictionary that contains the many of terms and concepts a player will encounter in the game, a task section that contains all of the information a player has gathered while working on current task(s), a task history log where players can access the information gathered on previously completed tasks, a chat log of all conversations a player has had with any of the game's avatars, and a diagrams section that contains several interactive diagrams where students are asked to record the placement of various objects found in the game.

Maintenance Tools

The *On-A-Slant* environment contains several online maintenance and editing tools that anyone on the development team can use to make changes to the environment without having any prior programming experience.

The Task Editor allows for the creating or editing of task descriptions and associated assessment questions, using a simple form-based Web interface. Tasks are built using a simple form layout that provides options for inserting, deleting, editing, and ordering of assessment questions and responses in hierarchal order.

The simulation contains a number of software agents with which players can interact. The Bot Conversation Editor allows creating or editing of agent conversations. Conversations are built using a simple form layout that provides options for inserting, deleting, editing, and ordering of conversational statements and responses in hierarchal order.

The environment may contain terms and concepts that a player may not be familiar with, so an embedded dictionary database is provided to allow players easy access to definitions and explanations. The Dictionary Editor was created so that updates or additional dictionary entries could be added using a simple Web-based HTML interface.

Dollar Bay

The focus of the *Dollar Bay* project is microeconomics—economics at the scale of a retail business owner (Slator et al., 2006). The setting for *Dollar Bay* is a fictitious seaside town, and the goal of the project is to teach the principles and practices of retailing. Each player assumes control of a newly created character and acts as a store owner. Given a retail space and a starting budget, players have the simple goal of making money (see Figure 2).

In *Dollar Bay*, each player is given control of a small business and given complete control over hiring an employee, advertising, and ordering and pricing goods. An economic simulation and a set of consumer agents respond to the player's actions, and as time progresses, customers will come to the store, examine the goods available to them and either purchase or not purchase goods as dictated by the economic simulation. The economic simulation is sensitive to a number of factors, including advertising efforts, store locations, and pricing. Success or failure is as simple as whether the player still has an operational business at the end of play.

While simple success or failure of the store can be used to determine whether the player has successfully played the game, there are a myriad of

Figure 2. A player in Dollar Bay buying goods from a specialty supplier

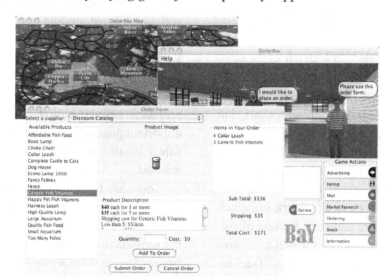

possible stumbling blocks that a player could encounter. For example, a player may be succeeding one week and losing money the next because new players have entered the game, and their pricing is no longer competitive. To guide the player past these obstacles, the system employs a combination of simple static tutoring and case-based tutoring. The simple static tutoring covers simple errors such as not having any employees, not having anything to sell, or attempting to sell toasters for $1,000,000. The case-based tutoring attempts to guide the player around the more subtle obstacles by comparing the player's actions to those of previous players and guiding the player away from paths that have led to failure for others. Figure 3 shows an example message as it was delivered via the game's internal mail system.

The language of retailing is presented immersively in *Dollar Bay*. While some terms such as "manufacturer's suggested retail" are displayed in the interface and defined in the help documents, the expectation is that the importance of those

Figure 3. Message from the case-based tutor concerning product choice

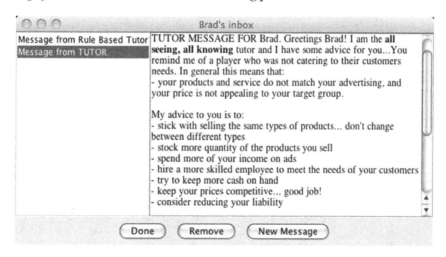

terms will be discovered through a combination of interactions with the tutoring agents and first-hand experience.

As shown in Figure 3, in addition to the automatic feedback of the tutoring system, players can get additional feedback from other sources in the game. Among these sources are the score chart, Hall of Fame, and the store ledger. These tables provide a way for the players to compare their accumulated wealth with the totals of both current players and players from previous sessions.

The game also provides a set of market research tools as a second, more authentic method of collecting feedback. The market research tools give the player estimates of the current values of various economic values, along with a sample of previous values and simple projections of those values. In addition, the market research functions also provide information concerning other stores that may be competing to sell the same products. Using these tools, a player could observe that competition for

a product has increased and adjust prices and advertising for that product to compensate.

Virtual Cell

The subject matter for the *Virtual Cell*, or *VCell*, project is cellular biology, but one of the more important goals of the game is to improve scientific reasoning and understanding of the scientific method.

There are three modules in the *Virtual Cell*: Organelle Identification, Electron Transport Chain (ETC), and Photosynthesis. Sample images from the introduction and other modules are shown in figures 5 and 6. The Organelle Identification module is used as an introduction to the game play and the acts of performing tests and comparing results. The Electron Transport Chain module focuses on one part of the respiration process and traces the movement of hydrogen and electrons during the conversion of ADP to ATP in the mitochondria.

Figure 4. Other sources of feedback in Dollar Bay

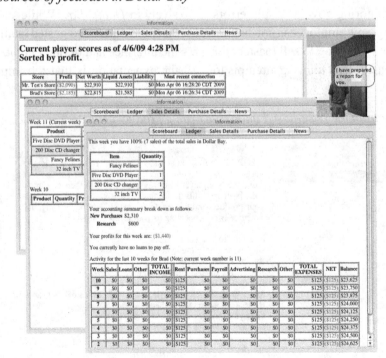

The Photosynthesis module similarly focuses on the movement of hydrogen and electrons in one segment of the photosynthesis reaction in the chloroplast.

In the first two modules, the culminating tasks are diagnostic in nature, with introductory steps explaining the process being studied and understanding being tested through comparing malfunctioning systems to the canonical ideal. For example, late in the Organelle Identification module, the player is asked to confirm the cause of an illness linked to a protein deficiency, and in order to do so, the player must confirm the presence of an irregularity in one of the organelles. The diagnostic approach is more explicitly employed in the last activity for the ETC module when the player is asked to observe various systems containing partially functional versions of the normal system and "repair" the systems by locating the partially functional complexes with fully functional versions.

The Photosynthesis module for the *Virtual Cell* in its current form differs from the ETC module by having a final task to induce an inactive section of the chloroplast to produce ATP. That is, the player is asked to add the necessary photons and substrates to the system and induce a temporary imbalance in the hydrogen equilibrium, and as a side effect of the hydrogen imbalance being removed, the system will produce ATP from ADP.

As the player works through each module, a help and information system is available. In that system, the player can find descriptions of the system being studied and information about the structures and chemicals involved. For ETC, diagrams and animated representations of the system are presented, but the players also work through activities that examine the behavior of parts of the system before being asked to perform diagnoses.

Feedback for the diagnostic activities is divided into four categories using the orthogonal characterizations of correctness and sufficiency of evidence. In other words, one response is given if the player's diagnosis is correct but not enough evidence has been collected, as might happen if the player guessed. A different response is used if the diagnosis is incorrect despite having enough evidence, indicating that the player misunderstood the evidence collected or miscalculated.

In each case, situations posed in the current *Virtual Cell* Organelle Identification and ETC

Figure 5. Interacting with the virtual lab assistant as a new player

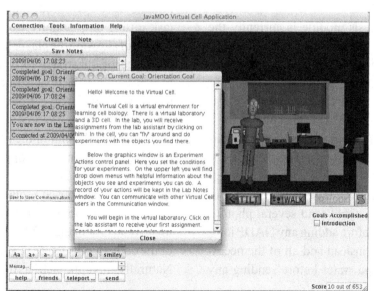

Figure 6. A sample of the activities from the various modules

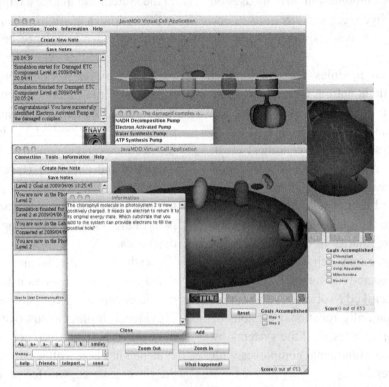

modules have answers that are distinct so as to avoid uncertainty as to the final answer. In every case, scenarios are arranged to try to prevent confusion about whether the answer should be, for example, 2.3 mg or 2.35 mg, answers such as "Cell line A is defective" or "Cell line B is defective" are used instead.

The Photosynthesis module is currently the weakest module for assessment and feedback. As mentioned earlier, the final task of the Photosynthesis module is causing an inactive chloroplast to produce ATP. In order for the player to cause the simulation to create ATP, the player must add water and NADP and send several photons to each of the photo systems. The difficulty is that there are many possible correct orderings of activities that produce the desired result. For example, the player could send several photons to Photo system II before adding any NADP ions, or the player could instead add all of the necessary NADP ions and water before sending any

photons into the system. As a result, a majority of the feedback possible for that task involves informing the player that there is already enough of the selected substrate present in the simulation and that a different shortage exists.

Two alternate tasks for the Photosynthesis module have been proposed. The first proposed task differs only slightly from the current task. Instead of allowing the player to use an open-ended sequence of substrates to drive the simulation forward, an artificial substrate budget would be used to prevent the player from getting sidetracked. In addition, running out of substrates would be used to signal the end of the player's answer and provide the system a clear opportunity to provide diagnostic feedback.

The other proposed replacement task for the Photosynthesis module is a diagnostic task similar to the final task in the ETC module, identification of the defective structure in a sample chloroplast. Naturally, this approach has the appeal of leveraging the pattern used in the ETC module but may be considered repetitious.

Blackwood

The *Blackwood* project is an attempt to construct a setting like *Dollar Bay* for history. The two primary goals are to explore a slightly different economic perspective and to study how effective immersion in the details of a time period can be for improving the experiences of students studying historical periods.

The significant difference in *Blackwood*'s game play compared to *Dollar Bay*'s model is that *Blackwood* places the various players in different roles in the economy. Instead of all players having the role of retailers, one player may be a blacksmith, another player may be a farmer, and another player a cartwright. The agents for each player, and various non-player-controlled agents as needed to fill vacancies, will form a mixed economy and trade goods, services, and money to accomplish their goals.

Blackwood remains a work in progress, with only initial work completed on the employee agents and time line. Under the current design, employee agents will perform actions on a schedule calculated to try to accomplish player requests. For example, a blacksmith employee may fill its schedule with work shifts in order to fulfill a large order of horseshoes; and a farm hand may instead fill its schedule with tending the fields during summer and general chores during the winter.

Blackwood is expected to use *Dollar Bay*'s combination of simple, rule-based feedback and more situational, case-based feedback.

WWWIC Games Section Summary

WWWIC environments are focused on teaching students about a particular scientific discipline. Each discipline has its own set of tools used in experiments. These tools are emergent to the enculturative situation, taught in context, and rely on student performance for learning. For example, geologists use a scratch plate to determine hardness, while biologists use reagents to discover cellular defects. Tools are implemented as objects on the LambdaMOO server, which send results to the client via the message-passing schema. In turn, the client displays test results to students. Students thus learn how to be scientists in their discipline by performing experiments that would be conducted by experts in the field. The design principles and signature elements that make up the consistent frame of reference for WWWIC IVEs (for review, see Table 1) have been found to increase student learning (for example, Brandt et al., 2006; Daniels et al., 2009; McClean et al., 2001; Slator & Associates, 2006; Slator et al., 2003, 2006).

FUTURE RESEARCH DIRECTIONS

Virtual role-based learning research during the past decade has transformed our understanding of human–machine and cognition–culture impacts on college-level learning. Powerful new technologies for visual worlds and multiuser interaction combined with sciences of cognition and performance, learning, and education, have resulted in a new subfield of scientific knowledge: a science of learning in immersive virtual role-based environments. Although the research outcomes and products from these new multidisciplinary research teams have increased our understanding of many aspects of human and machine learning, the scattered and uncoordinated research results in large gaps of knowledge and little public–private sector coordination to meet the challenges of educating students for current and future challenges in science and the workforce. Especially complex but fundamental questions, such as the difference between learning in single-user worlds and multiuser worlds, the differences in visual- and non-visual-world learning, and the relationship between real-world learning simultaneously with virtual-world learning, remain largely unexplored by virtual learning scientists. Not only do we know very little about the long-term impact of virtual learning, we know even less about how sociocultural experience within and outside the virtual world sculpts the learning process.

WWWWIC has worked, and continues to work, on addressing these shortcomings in the science of learning in immersive virtual environments, or IVEs. Our group of scientists and scholars address the various problems through basic and applied research and testing. Role-based IVEs for education and the assessment of role-based learning continue to be core activities. These role-based, multiuser, content-laden, systems are computerized educational games of a specific and particular design that emphasize immersion, exploration, and learning-by-doing. Based on the core competencies already established at NDSU, the future mission will be to expand its efforts in three directions: horizontally, vertically, and laterally. We discuss these in order.

Horizontal expansion is simply the mission to add content to existing systems. For example, the *Geology Explorer* (Saini-Eidukat et al., 2001) has modules for mineral and rock identification and for geologic mapping. These modules represent several hours of activities but still only begin to provide experience with the many activities offered in the geology curriculum. Each of the projects currently under way has a list of horizontal expansion ideas to pursue.

Vertical expansion is the mission to seek opportunities to extend IVE content both upward to the graduate level and, more importantly, downward to the public schools, the technical and community college arena, and the "informal education" opportunities of museums and other public education. The pedagogical goals of the NDSU systems have been mainly centered on undergraduate education. This is where the core principles are located. However, even now the WWWIC approach shows little regard for traditional curriculum in favor of a more "organic"

approach. For example, the *Geology Explorer* begins with a freshman-level activity (mineral and rock identification) and then builds on that experience by moving directly to a geologic mapping exercise (sometimes not covered until junior year in the "normal" course sequence). In these cases, it is often an accident of tradition and custom that dictates the order of concepts as presented to students. WWWIC IVE systems build from one idea to another in an organic progression illuminated by the practice of working geologists in the field. Vertical expansion requires further partnership between academia, the government, industry, and other public and private sectors.

Lateral expansion refers to moving into other disciplines and specialties. Perhaps the most important activity will be to identify the disciplines and subdisciplines that lend themselves to our theory of enculturation through role-based learning by doing—and those that do not. For example, we have determined that geology and biology are natural fits with our pedagogical strategies. Practitioners in these sciences tend to practice their science "in the field" (where that field might be a hillside or a wet lab). Archaeology, botany, and paleontology might seem to be obvious extensions. However, what about psychology? Or political science? Perhaps these can be visualized within the framework. But then what about more fundamental pursuits like arithmetic and reading? These are not so obvious. These are the confounding questions embedded in lateral expansion.

CONCLUSION

When Marshall McLuhan (1964) said, "People want roles, not goals," he put his finger on a principle that is both ancient and prescient. Cultures have always preserved themselves by providing models of behavior for society members to integrate and assimilate as they learn to function in their worlds. This can be observed in common-sense terms as children are seen to copy the influences that surround them (parental, educational, and societal), and it has been examined in countless studies of sociological and anthropological change in cultures both "western" and "primitive."

One illustrative example is Like-A-Fishhook Village (Smith, 1972) in what is now northwestern North Dakota. This is a case where three "sedentary" (earth lodge) tribes banded together in the 1840s in the aftermath of a smallpox epidemic (after centuries of internecine feuding), on a strategically defensible bluff in the shadow of an army fort as a means of defending themselves against the predations of ancient enemies. This was the last great earth lodge village and the scene of a fascinating cultural movement as the three tribes learned to coexist for mutual protection. Meanwhile, they attempted to preserve their own identities, while both absorbing and resisting the modern influences of the soldiers and traders in the fort. There are stories of heartbreaking struggle and uplifting accommodation, tales of children crossing tribal lines for the sake of marriage and adoption, movements to preserve cultural integrity along with defections to jobs as traders and scouts, and a remarkable account of "early adoption" as a new rifle was bartered and swapped from hand to hand, passing from North Dakota to New Mexico in a week's time. It was an era of change, marked by fluidity, absorption, adaptation, accommodation, and ultimately transition to a new synthesized culture.

While this might remind the reader of the current American educational landscape, that is not the point to the example. The point is learning through enculturation. The children of the tribes did not, as one example, take classes on hunting and trading. They went out and experienced hunting and trading. They watched, they asked questions, they tried it for themselves, they failed in various ways, they received additional advice, and because they had seen it done all their lives, they learned how to do it. Meanwhile, they accumulated new skills and new technologies, and learned new ways

of surviving in their world. Then, with varying levels of success, they passed these customs and practices on to their own children.

This is a story of learning as enculturation, where learners are informed by their context and social interactions, and develop the skills and conceptual understanding that comes with practicing a discipline under the watchful eye of more experienced practitioners, eventually learning concepts and techniques that are both new and old. The immersive experiences and cognitive apprenticeship this describes extends from the study of carpentry and retailing to the sciences, medicine and law. Teaching by "field trip" in geology, and by laboratory in biology, and by residency in medicine, and by cases in business and law are all examples of "role-based learning"—that margin where concept is put into practice and learning passes from memorizing and reciting facts to developing what the mathematicians call "intuition."

Working from the critical intersection of computer science educational technology and the anthropologies of learning, cognition, and performance, we are breaking new ground in learning research on immersive virtual environments. It is our intent that the NDSU WWWIC IVE design principles and signature elements we have presented in this chapter will assist others in their development and evaluation of effective virtual learning environments. We welcome your feedback and constructive criticism, and we look forward to developing more informal and formal partnerships with others as we continue on this exhilarating path.

REFERENCES

Aronson, E., Stephan, C., Sikes, J., Blaney, N., & Snapp, M. (1978). *The jigsaw classroom*. Beverly Hills, CA: Sage.

Bailey, F. G. (1983). *The tactical uses of passion: An essay on power, reason, and reality*. Ithaca, NY: Cornell University Press.

Barrett, K., & Johnson, L. (in press). Designing and developing serious games for teaching language-in-culture: Creating engaging learning experiences that accelerate performance outcomes. In Van Eck, R. (Ed.), *Gaming & cognition: Theories and practice from the learning sciences*. Hershey, PA: IGI Global.

Batteau, A. W. (2000). Negations and ambiguities in the cultures of organizations. *American Anthropologist, 102*(4), 726–740. doi:10.1525/aa.2000.102.4.726

Bidney, D. (1947). Human nature and the cultural process. *American Anthropologist, 49*(3), 375–399. doi:10.1525/aa.1947.49.3.02a00010

Bonvillain, N. (1997). *Language, culture, and communication* (2nd ed.). Upper Saddle River, NJ: Prentice Hall.

Brandt, L., Borchert, O., Addicott, K., Cosmano, B., Hawley, J., & Hokanson, G. (2006). *Roles, culture, and computer supported collaborative work on* Planet Oit. *Journal of Advanced Technology for Learning, 3*(2), 89–98.

Clancey, W. J. (1995). Practice cannot be reduced to theory: Knowledge, representations, and change in the workplace. In Bagnara, S., Zuccermaglio, C., & Stucky, S. (Eds.), *Organizational learning and technological change* (pp. 16–46). Berlin: Springer.

D'Andrade, R. G. (1981). The cultural part of cognition. *Cognitive Science, 5*, 179–195. doi:10.1207/s15516709cog0503_1

D'Andrade, R. G. (1984). Cultural meaning systems. In Shweder, R. A., & Levine, R. A. (Eds.), *Culture theory: Essays on mind, self and emotion* (pp. 88–119). Cambridge, UK: Cambridge University Press.

D'Andrade, R. G. (1989). Culturally based reasoning. In Gellatly, A. D., & Slobada, J. A. (Eds.), *Cognition and social worlds* (pp. 132–143). Oxford: Clarendon Press.

D'Andrade, R. G. (1992). Schemas and motivation. In D'Andrade, R. G., & Strauss, C. (Eds.), *Human motives and cultural models* (pp. 23–44). Cambridge, UK: Cambridge University Press.

Daniels, L., Borchert, O., Hokanson, G., Clark, J., Saini-Eidukat, B., Schwert, D., et al. *(2009). Effects of immersive virtual environments on student achievement and confidence. In* Proceedings of the American Educational Research Association Annual Meeting *(AERA-09), April 13-17, San Diego.*

Dempsey, J. (in press). Elemental learning and the pyramid of fidelity. In Van Eck, R. (Ed.), *Gaming & cognition: Theories and practice from the learning sciences*. Hershey, PA: IGI Global.

Dix, C. *(2000)*. Education, culture, and the transmission of identity: A case study in a central Illinois school. *Unpublished thesis, Dept. Sociology-Anthropology, Illinois State University, Normal, IL. Retrieved from* http://www.soa.ilstu.edu/anthrothesis/dix/

Edelson, D., Pea, R., & Gomez, L. (1996). Constructivism in the collaboratory. In Wilson, B. G. (Ed.), *Constructivist learning environments: Case studies in instructional design* (pp. 151–164). Englewood Cliffs, NJ: Educational Technology Publications.

Guimarães, M. J. L., Jr. *(2001)*. Investigating physical performance in cyberspace: Some notes about methods. *Middlesex, UK: Centre for Research into Innovation, Culture and Technology, Brunel University, Uxbridge. Retrieved at* http://www.brunel.ac.uk/depts/crict/vmpapers/mario.html

Harris, M. (1968). *The rise of anthropological theory*. New York: Crowell.

Hokanson, G., Borchert, O., Slator, B. M., Terpstra, J., Clark, J. T., Daniels, L. M., et al. *(2008). Studying Native American culture in an immersive virtual environment. In* Proceedings of the IEEE International Conference on Advanced Learning Technologies *(ICALT-2008) (pp. 788-792). Washington, DC: IEEE Computer Society Press.*

McClean, P., Johnson, C., Rogers, R., Daniels, L., Reber, J., & Slator, B. (2005). Molecular and cellular biology animations: Development and impact on student learning. *Cell Biology Education, 4*(2), 169–179. doi:10.1187/cbe.04-07-0047

McClean, P., Saini-Eidukat, B., Schwert, D., Slator, B., & White, A. *(2001). Virtual worlds in large enrollment biology and geology classes significantly improve authentic learning. In J. A. Chambers (Ed.),* Selected Papers from the 12th International Conference on College Teaching and Learning *(ICCTL-01) (pp. 111-118). Jacksonville, FL: Center for the Advancement of Teaching and Learning.*

McCluhan, M. H. (1964). *Understanding media: The extensions of man.* Cambridge, MA: MIT Press.

Moerman, M. (1969). A little knowledge. In Tyler, S. A. (Ed.), *Cognitive Anthropology* (pp. 449–469). New York, NY: Holt, Rinehart, and Winston, Inc.

Morris, B. (1994). *Anthropology of the self: The individual in cultural perspective.* Boulder, CO: Pluto Press.

National Research Council. (1995). *National science education standards.* National Academy Press.

Norman, D. A. (1993). *Things that make us smart: Defending human attributes in the age of the machine.* Reading, MA: Addison-Wesley Pub.

Ortuno, M. M. (1991). Cross-cultural awareness in the foreign language class: The Kluckhohn model. *Modern Language Journal, 75*(4), 449–460. doi:10.2307/329494

Rogers, E. M. (1962). *The diffusion of innovations.* Glencoe, IL: The Free Press of Glencoe.

Rogers, E. M., & Shoemaker, F. F. (1971). *Communication of innovations: A cross-cultural approach.* New York: The Free Press.

Saini-Eidukat, B., Schwert, D. P., & Slator, B. M. (2001). Geology explorer: Virtual geologic mapping and interpretation. *Journal of Computers and Geosciences, 27*(4).

Schilling-Estes. (1998). Investigating 'self-conscious' speech: The performance register in Ocracoke English. *Language in Society, 27,* 53–83.

Slator, B., Dong, A., Erickson, K., Flaskerud, D., Halvorson, J., Myronovych, O., et al. (2005). Comparing two immersive virtual environments for education. In Proceedings of E-Learn 2005, Vancouver, Canada, October 24-28.

Slator, B. M., Beckwith, R., Brandt, L., Chaput, H., Clark, J. T., & Daniels, L. M. (2006). *Electric worlds in the classroom: Teaching and learning with role-based computer games.* New York: Teachers College Press.

Slator, B. M., Chaput, H., Cosmano, R., Dischinger, B., Imdieke, C., & Vender, B. (2006). A multi-user desktop virtual environment for teaching shopkeeping to children. *Virtual Reality Journal, 9,* 49–56. doi:10.1007/s10055-005-0003-5

Slator, B. M., Clark, J. T., Landrum, J., III, Bergstrom, A., Hawley, J., Johnston, E., & Fisher, S. *(2001). Teaching with immersive virtual archaeology. In* Proceedings of the 7th International Conference on Virtual Systems and Multimedia *(VSMM-2001), Berkeley, CA, Oct. 25-27.*

Slator, B. M., Daniels, L. M., Saini-Eidukat, B., Schwert, D. P., Borchert, O., Hokanson, G., & Beckwith, R. T. *(2003). Software tutors for scaffolding on Planet Oit. In* Proceedings of the 3rd IEEE International Conference on Advanced Learning Technologies *(ICALT) (pp. 398-399). Athens, Greece, July 9-11.*

Smith, G. H. (1972). Like-A-Fishhook Village and Fort Berthold, Garrison Reservoir North Dakota. Anthropological Papers 2. Washington, DC: National Park Service, US Department of the Interior.

Spindler, G. (1955). *Sociocultural and psychological processes in Menomini acculturation. Culture and Society #5.* Berkeley, CA: University of California Press.

Squire, K., & Gaydos, M. (in press). Citizen science: Designing a game for the 21st century. In Van Eck, R. (Ed.), *Interdisciplinary models and tools for serious games: Emerging concepts and future directions.* Hershey, PA: IGI Global.

Turner, V. (1987). *The anthropology of performance.* New York: PAJ Publications.

Vygotsky, L. (1986). *Thought and language.* Cambridge, MA: MIT Press.

Wolcott, H. F. (1985). On ethnographic intent. *Educational Administration Quarterly, 21*(3), 187–203. doi:10.1177/0013161X85021003004

Wolcott, H. F. (1991). Propriospect and the acquisition of culture. *Anthropology & Education Quarterly, 22*(3), 251–273. doi:10.1525/aeq.1991.22.3.05x1052l

APPENDIX: ADDITIONAL READING

"Must-Reads" for This Topic

Brandt, L., Borchert, O., Addicott, K., Cosmano, B., Hawley, J., Hokanson, G., Reetz, D., Saini-Eidukat, B., Schwert, D. P., Slator, B. M. & Tomac, S. (2006). Roles, culture, and computer supported collaborative work on Planet Oit. *Journal of Advanced Technology for Learning. 3*(2), 89–98.

Daniels, L., Borchert, O., Hokanson, G., Clark, J., Saini-Eidukat, B., Schwert, D.,. .. Terpstra, J. (2009). Effects of immersive virtual environments on student achievement and confidence. *Proceedings of the American Educational Research Association Annual Meeting (AERA-09)*. April 13–17. San Diego.

McClean, P., Saini-Eidukat, B., Schwert, D., Slator, B., & White, A. (2001). Virtual worlds in large enrollment science classes significantly improve authentic learning. In J. A. Chambers (Ed.), *Selected Papers from the 12th International Conference on College Teaching and Learning* (pp. 111–118). Jacksonville, FL: Center for the Advancement of Teaching and Learning.

Kaptelinin, V., & Cole, M. (2002). Individual and collective activities in educational computer game playing. In T. Koschmann, R. Hall, and N. Miyake (Eds.), *CSCL2: Carrying Forward the Conversation* (pp. 303–316). Mahwah, NJ: Lawrence Erlbaum Associates, Inc.

Kolodner, J. L. (Ed.). *Journal of the Learning Sciences.* Routledge.

Rieber, L. P. (1996). Seriously considering play: Designing interactive learning environments based on the blending of microworlds, simulations, and games. *Educational Technology Research and Development, 44*(2), 43–58.

Slator, B. M., Beckwith, R., Brandt, L., Chaput, H., Clark, J. T., Daniels, L. M.,. .. White, A. R. (2006). *Electric worlds in the classroom: Teaching and learning with role-based computer games.* New York, NY: Teachers College Press.

Slator, B. M., Clark, J. T., Daniels, L. M., Hill, C., McClean, P., Saini-Eidukat, B.,. .. White, A. R. (2002). Use of virtual worlds to teach the sciences. In Jain, L. C., Howlett, R. J., Ichalkaranje, N. S., Tonfoni, G. (Eds.), *Virtual environments for teaching and learning,* (1–40). Singapore: World Scientific Publishing Co. Pte. Ltd.

Tennyson, R. D. (Ed.). *Computers in Human Behavior*. San Diego, CA: Elsevier.

Crookall, D. (Ed.). *Simulation & Gaming*. Beverly Hills, CA: Sage.

Top Texts for Interdisciplinary Studies of Serious Games

Brown, J. S., Collins, A., & Duguid, P. (1989). Situated cognition and the culture of learning. *Educational Researcher, 18*(1), 32–42.

Bruce, B., Peyton, J., & Batson, T. (1993). Introduction. In P. Bruce and T. Batson (Eds.), *Network-based classrooms: Promises and realities* (pp. 1-6). Cambridge, UK: Cambridge University Press.

Gee, J.P. (2003). What video games have to teach us about learning and literacy. *New York: Palgrave Macmillan.*

Johnson, D. W., & Johnson, R. T. (1991). Learning together and alone: Cooperative, competitive, and individualistic learning. *Englewood Cliffs, NJ: Prentice Hall.*

Koschmann, T. (Ed.). (1996). CSCL: *Theory and practice: An emerging paradigm.* Mahwah, NJ: Lawrence Erlbaum Associates, Inc.

Lave, J., & Wenger, E. (1991). *Situated learning: Legitimate peripheral participation*. Cambridge, UK: Cambridge University Press.

Piaget, J. (1977). Science of education and the psychology of the child. In H. E. Gruber, J. J. Vonèche, and J. Jacques (Eds.), *The essential Piaget* (pp. 695-725). New York: Basic Books.

Scardamalia, M., Bereiter, C., & Lamon, M. (1994). The CSILE project: Trying to bring the classroom into world 3. In K. McGilly (Ed.), *Classroom lessons: Integrating cognitive theory and classroom practice* (pp. 201-228). Cambridge, MA: MIT Press.

Shaffer, D. W. (2006). *How computer games help children learn*. New York: Palgrave Macmillian.

Vygotsky, L. S. (1978). *Mind in society: The development of higher psychological processes*. (M. Cole, Trans.), Cambridge, MA: Harvard University Press.

Top Texts for Interdisciplinary Studies of Serious Games

The authors of each chapter were asked to list the top texts that all researchers and practitioners interested in interdisciplinary perspectives on serious games should be aware of. Each chapter listed these individually, but I present them here as a compiled list. Texts are listed first in descending order by the number of citations, and then alphabetically by first author.

Title of Text	Times Cited
Gee, J. (2003 & 2007). *What video games have to teach us about learning and literacy.* New York: Palgrave Macmillan.	11
Shaffer, D. (2006). *How computer games help children learn.* New York, NY: Palgrave Macmillan.	5
Bogost, I. (2007). *Persuasive games: The expressive power of videogames.* Cambridge, MA: MIT Press.	4
Alessi, M. S., & Trollip, S. R. (2001). *Multimedia for learning: Methods and development* (3rd ed.). Boston: Allyn and Bacon.	3
Csikszentmihalyi, M. (1990). *Flow: The psychology of optimal experience.* New York: Harper and Row.	3
Huizinga, J. (1950). *Homo ludens: A study of play-element in culture* (paperback ed.). Boston: Beacon Press.	3
Kirriemuir, J., & McFarlane, A. (2004). Literature review in games and learning. *Futurelab Series, Report 8*, 35. http://www.futurelab.org.uk/research/lit_reviews.htm	3
Koster, R. (2004). *A theory of fun for game design.* Scottsdale, AZ: Paraglyph Press.	3
Prensky, M. (2001 & 2007). *Digital game-based learning.* New York: McGraw-Hill.	3

Wardrip-Fruin, N., & Harrigan, P. (Eds.). (2004). *First person: New media as story, performance, and game*. Cambridge, MA: MIT Press. 3

Wolf, M. J. P., & Perron, B. (2003). *Video game theory reader*. New York: Routledge 3

Campbell, J. (1993). *The hero with a thousand faces*. London: Fontana Press. 2

de Jong, T. (2006). Computer simulations: Technological advances in inquiry learning. *Science, 312*(5773), 532-533. 2

Dempsey, J. V., Haynes, L. L., Lucassen, B. A., & Casey, M. (2002). Forty simple computer games and what they could mean to educators. *Simulation and Gaming, 33*, 157–168. 2

Geary, D. (2008). An evolutionarily informed education science. *Educational Psychologist, 43*, 179-195. 2

Gee, J. P. (2007). *Good video games and good learning: Collected essays on video games, learning and literacy*. New York: Palgrave/Macmillan. 2

Lave, J., & Wenger, E. (1991). *Situated learning: Legitimate peripheral participation*. Cambridge, UK: Cambridge University Press. 2

Michael, D., & Chen, S. (2005) *Serious Games: Games that educate, train & inform*. Washington, DC: Thomson Course Technology PTR. 2

Raessens (2005). *Handbook of computer game studies*. Cambridge, MA: MIT Press. 2

Salen, K. (2007). *The ecology of games: Connecting youth, games, and learning*. Cambridge, MA: MIT Press. 2

Salen, K., & Zimmerman, E. (2004). *Rules of play: Game design fundamentals*. Cambridge, MA: MIT Press. 2

Squire, K. (2006). From content to context: Video games as designed experiences. *Educational Researcher, 35*(8), 19-29. 2

Van Eck, R. (2007). Six ideas in search of a discipline. In B. E. Shelton & D. A. Wiley (Eds.), *The design and use of simulation computer games in education* (pp. 31–60). Rotterdam, Netherlands: Sense Publishing. 2

Vorderer, P., & Bryant, J. (Eds.) .(2006). *Playing video games: Motives, responses, and consequences*. New York: Routledge. 2

Vygotsky, L. S. (1978). *Mind in society: The development of higher psychological processes*. (M. Cole, Trans.), Cambridge, MA: Harvard University Press. 2

Aldrich, C. (2005). *Learning by doing*. San Francisco: Pfeiffer. 1

Aldrich, C. (2009). *The complete guide to simulations and serious games: How the most valuable content will be created in the age beyond Gutenberg to Google*. San Francisco: Pfeiffer. 1

Baddeley, A.D. (2003). Working memory: Looking back and looking forward. *Nature Reviews Neuroscience, 4*, 829–839. 1

Barab, S., Ingram-Goble, A., Warren, S. (2008). Conceptual play spaces. In R. Ferdig (Ed.), *Handbook of research on effective electronic gaming in education* (pp. 1-20). Hershey, PA: IGI Global publications. 1

Beck, J. C., & Wade, M. (2006). *The Kids are alright: How the gamer generation is changing the workplace* (Paperback). Boston: Harvard Business School. 1

Bettelheim, B. (1991). *The uses of enchantment: The meaning and importance of fairy tales.* 1
London: Penguin Books.

Blumberg, F. C. (2000). The effects of children's goals for learning on video game performance. 1
Journal of Applied Developmental Psychology, 21(6), 641-653.

Bransford, J., Vye, N., Stevens, R., Kuhl, P., Schwartz, D., Bell, P., Meltzoff, A., 1
Barron, B., Pea, R., Reeves, J., Roschelle, J., & Sabelli, N. (2006). Learning
theories and education: Toward a decade of synergy. In P. Alexander & P.
Winne (Eds.), *Handbook of educational psychology* (2nd ed., pp. 209-244).
Mahwah, NJ: Lawrence Erlbaum Associates.

Brown, J. S., Collins, A., & Duguid, P. (1989). Situated cognition and the culture of learning. 1
Educational Researcher, 18(1), 32-42.

Bruce, B., Peyton, J., & Batson, T. (1993). Introduction. In P. Bruce and T. Batson (Eds.), 1
Network-based classrooms: Promises and realities (pp. 1-6). Cambridge, UK:
Cambridge University Press.

Bruner, J. (1990). *Acts of meaning.* Cambridge, MA: Harvard University Press. 1

Calleja, G. (2007). Digital game involvement: A conceptual model. *Games and Culture, 2*(3), 1
236-260.

Carroll, J. M. (2003). *HCI models, theories and frameworks: Toward a multidisciplinary* 1
science. San Francisco: Morgan Kaufmann Publishers.

Cassell, J., & Jenkins, H. (Eds.). (2000). *From Barbie to Mortal Kombat: Gender and* 1
computer games. Cambridge, MA: MIT Press.

Chen, S., & Michael, D. (October, 2005). Proof of learning: Assessment in Serious Games. 1
Gamasutra.com.

Clark, R. E. (2005). Multimedia learning in e-course. In R. E. Mayer (Ed.), *The Cambridge* 1
handbook of multimedia learning (pp. 589–616). New York: Cambridge University
Press.

Clark, R., Nguyen, F., & Sweller, J. (2006). Efficiency in learning: Evidence-based guidelines 1
to manage cognitive load. San Francisco: Pfeiffer.

Cobley, P. (2001). *Narrative.* New York: Routledge. 1

Constantine, L. L. (2004). Beyond user-centered design and user experience. *Cutter IT* 1
Journal, 17(2), 2-11.

Cooper. R. (2007). *Alter ego: Avatars and their creators.* London: Chris Boot. 1

Craig, R. T. (1999). Communication theory as a field. *Communication Theory, 9*(2), 119- 1
161.

Crawford, C. (2002). *The art of interactive design,* San Francisco: No Starch. 1

Crawford, C. (2003). *Chris Crawford on game design.* Indianapolis: New Riders. 1

Csikszentmihalyi, M. (1975). *Beyond boredom and anxiety – experiencing flow in work and* 1
play. San Francisco: Jossey-Bass.

De Aguilera, M., & Méndiz, A. (2003). Video games and education: Education in the face of 1
a parallel school. *ACM Computers in Entertainment, 1*(1).

de Freitas, S., & Jarvis, S. (2007). Serious games – engaging training solutions: A research and 1
development project for supporting training needs. *British Journal of Educational*
Technology, 38(3), 523-525.

DeFreitas, S. (2007). *Learning in immersive worlds: A review of game based learning* (Literature Review). London: Joint Information Systems Committee.   1

Dempsey, J. V., & Johnson, R. B. (1998). The development of an ARCS gaming scale. *Journal of Instructional Psychology, 25*(4), 215-221.   1

Dodge, T., Barab, S., & Stuckey, B. (2008). Children's sense of self: Learning and meaning in the digital age. *Journal of Interactive Learning Research, 19*(2), 225-249.   1

Educational games research. http://edugamesblog.wordpress.com/   1

Egenfeldt-Nielsen, S. (2005). *Beyond edutainment: Exploring the educational potential of computer games.* Copenhagen, Denmark: IT-University.   1

Egenfeldt-Nielsen, S., Smith, J. H., & Tosca, S. P. (2008). *Understanding video games: The essential introduction.* New York: Routledge.   1

Ellis, R. (2003). *Task-based language learning and teaching*: New York: Oxford University Press.   1

Entertainment & Leisure Software Publishers Association (ELSPA), (2006). *Unlimited learning: Computer and video games in the learning landscape.* 1-66. Retrieved from http://www.elspa.com/assets/files/u/unlimitedlearningtheroleofcomputerandvideogamesint_344.pdf.   1

Federation of American Scientists. (2006). *Harnessing the power of video games for learning.* Retrieved December 6, 2006, from http://fas.org/gamesummit/   1

Ferdig, Rick, Ed. (2008). *Handbook of research on effective electronic gaming in education.* Hershey, PA: IGI Global.   1

Field, J. (2006). *Lifelong learning and the new educational order.* London: Routledge.   1

Frasca, G. (2001) Ephemeral games: Is it barbaric to design videogames after Auschwitz? In M. Eskelinen & R. Koskimaa (Eds.), *Cybertext yearbook 2000* (pp. 172–182). Jyväskylä, Finland: University of Jyväskylä. Retrieved August 20, 2009, from http://cybertext.hum.jyu.fi   1

Frasca, G. (2004). Video games of the oppressed: Critical thinking, education, tolerance and other trivial issues. In P. Harrington & N. Wardrip-Fruin (Eds.), *First person: New media as story, performance, and game.* Cambridge, MA: The MIT Press.   1

Fullerton, T., Swain, C., & Hoffman, S. (2004). *Game design workshop: Designing, prototyping, and playtesting games.* San Francisco: CMP Books.   1

Funk, J. B., & Buchman, D. D. (1996). Playing violent video and computer games and adolescent self-concept. *Journal of Communication, 46*(2), 19.   1

Galloway, A. R. (2006). *Gaming: Essays on algorithmic culture.* Minneapolis: University of Minnesota Press.   1

Gardner, J. E., Wissick, C. A., Schweder, W., & Canter, L. S. (2003). Enhancing interdisciplinary instruction in general and special education: Thematic units and technology. *Remedial and Special Education, 24*, 161-172.   1

Garris, R., Ahlers, R., & Driskell, J. E. (2002). Games, motivation, and learning: A research and practice model. *Simulation & Gaming, 33*(4), 441 - 467.   1

Gee, J. P. (2008). Video games and embodiment. *Games and Culture, 3*(3–4), 253–263.   1

Gee, J.P. (2001). Learning by design: Good video games as learning machines. *E-Learning, 2*(1).   1

Genette, G. (1997). *Paratexts: Thresholds of interpretation.* New York: Cambridge University 1 Press.

Gentner, D. (1983). Structure mapping: A theoretical framework for analogy. *Cognitive* 1 *Science, 7*, 155-170.

Gibson, D., Aldrich, C. & Prensky, M. (2007). *Games and simulations in online learning:* 1 *Research and development frameworks.* Hershey, PA: Information Science Publishing.

Gibson, J. J. (1977). The theory of affordances. In R. Shaw & J. Bransford (Eds.), *Perceiving,* 1 *acting, and knowing: Toward an ecological psychology* (pp. 67–82). Hillsdale, NJ: Lawrence Erlbaum.

Giddens, A. (1984). *The constitution of society: Outline of the theory of structuration.* Berkley, 1 CA: University of California Press.

Gray, C. H. (Ed.). (1995). *The cyborg handbook.* New York: Routledge Press. 1

Gredler, M. E. (2004). Games and simulations and their relationships to learning. In D. 1 H. Jonassen (Ed.), *Handbook of research on educational communications and technology* (2nd ed.). Mahwah, N.J.: Association for Educational Communications and Technology, Lawrence Erlbaum.

Green, C. S., & Bavelier, D. (2003). Action video game modifies visual selective attention. 1 *Nature, 423*, 534- 537.

Green, S. & Bavelier D. (2006) The cognitive neuroscience of video games. In *Digital media:* 1 *Transformations in human communication*, Messaris & Humphreys, Eds. New York: Peter Lang.

Gunter, G., Kenny, R., & Vick, E. (2006). A case for a formal design paradigm for serious 1 games. *The Journal of the International Digital Media and Arts Association, 3*(1), 93–105.

Hatano, G., & Inagaki, K. (1986). Two courses of expertise. In H. Stevenson, H. Azuma, & K. 1 Hakuta (Eds.), *Child development and education in Japan* (pp. 262-272). New York: W. H. Freeman and Company.

Hays, R. T. (2005). *The effectiveness of Instructional games: A literature review and* 1 *discussion.* Naval Air Warfare Center Training Systems Division (No 2005-004). http://stnet.dtie.mil/oai/

Hendriksen, T.D. (2006). *Educational role-play: Moving beyond entertainment. Seeking to* 1 *please or aiming for the stars.* Conference paper presented at: "On Playing Roles" Seminar, Tampere, FI.

Hestenes, D., Wells, M., & Swackhamer, G. (1992). Force concept inventory. *The Physics* 1 *Teacher, 30*, 141-158.

Iuppa, N., & Borst, T. (2007). *Story and simulations for serious games: Tales from the* 1 *trenches.* New York: Focal Press.

Jenkins, H. (2006). *Convergence culture: Where old and new media collide.* New York: NYU 1 Press.

Jenkins, H., Clinton K., Purushotma, R., Robinson, A.J., & Weigel, M. (2006). *Confronting the* 1 *challenges of participatory culture: Media education for the 21st century.* Chicago, IL: The MacArthur Foundation. Retrieved April 24, 2007, from http://digitallearning. macfound.org/atf/cf/{7E45C7E0-A3E0-4B89-AC9C-E807E1B0AE4E}/ JENKINS_WHITE_PAPER.PDF

Johnson, D. W., & Johnson, R. T. (1991). *Learning together and alone: Cooperative, competitive, and individualistic learning.* Englewood Cliffs, NJ: Prentice Hall.

Joint Information Systems Committee (JISC), U. K. (2007). *Game-based learning.* Retrieved from http://www.jisc.ac.uk/media/documents/publications/gamingreportbp.pdf.

Jonassen, D. H. (2006). On the role of concepts in learning and instructional design. *Educational Technology, Research, & Development, 54*(2), 177-196.

Juul, J. (2004). *Half-real: Video games between real rules and fictional worlds.* Unpublished doctoral dissertation, IT University of Copenhagen, Copenhagen, Denmark.

Kafi, Y. (1995). *Minds in play: Computer game design as a context for children's learning.* Hillsdale, NJ: Lawrence Erlbaum Associates.

Kankaanranta, M., & Neittaanmäki, P. (Eds.). *Design and use of serious games.* Dordrecht: Springer.

Kebritchi, M., & Hirumi, A. (2008). Examining the pedagogical foundations of modern educational computer games. *Computers and Education, 51*, 1729–1743.

Keller, J. M. (1987). Motivational design and multimedia: Beyond the novelty effect. *Strategic Human Resource Development Review, 1(1)*, 188-203.

Khoo, E.T., Merritt, T., Lim Fei, V., Liu, W., Rahaman, H., Prasad, J., & Marsh, T. 2008. *Body music: Physical exploration of music theory.* ACM SIGGRAPH Video Games Symposium, Los Angeles, USA, ACM Press.

King, M. (2008). Remapping Rhetorical Peaks: A video game for first-year writing. *Computers and Composition Online*, Fall 2008. Retrieved from http://www.bgsu.edu/cconline/gaming_issue_2008/King_Rhetorical_peaks/index.html

Kirsh, D. & Maglio, P. (1994). On distinguishing epistemic from pragmatic action. *Cognitive Science, 18*, 513-549.

Klemmer, S. R., Hartmann, B., and Takayama, L. (2006). How bodies matter: five themes for interaction design. In DIS '06: *Proceedings of the 6th ACM conference on Designing Interactive systems*, 140-149, New York: ACM Press.

Koschmann, T. (Ed.). (1996). *CSCL: Theory and practice: An emerging paradigm.* Mahwah, NJ: Lawrence Erlbaum Associates.

Lakoff, G., & Johnson, M. (1980). *Metaphors we live by.* University of Chicago Press.

Lanigan, R. L. (1988). *Phenomenology of communication: Merleau-Ponty's thematics in communicology and semiology.* Pittsburgh: Duquesne University Press.

Laveault, P., & Corbeil, P. (1990). Assessing the impact of simulation games on learning: A step-by-step approach. *Simulation/games for learning, 20*(1), 42-54.

Lee, D. & Larose, R. (2007) A socio-cognitive model of game usage. *Journal of Broadcasting and Electronic Media*, 632-647.

Lepper, M. R. & Cordova, D. (1992). A desire to be taught: Instructional consequences of intrinsic motivation. *Motivation and Emotion, 16*(3), 187-208.

Low, R., & Sweller, J. (2005). The modality principle in multimedia learning. In R. E. Mayer (Ed.), *The Cambridge Handbook of Multimedia Learning* (pp. 147-158). New York: Cambridge University Press.

Loyens, S. M. & Gijbels, D. (2008). Understanding the effects of constructivist learning environments: Introducing a multi-directional approach. *Instructional Science, 36*, 351-357.

Malone, T. W. (1981). Toward a theory of intrinsically motivating instruction. *Cognitive Science*, (4), 333-369.

Marsh, T. (2007). Informing design and evaluation methodologies for serious games for learning, *Learning with games 2007*, Sofia Antipolis, France.

Mayer, R. , Mautone, P., Prothero, W. (2002). Pictorial aids for learning by doing in a multimedia geology simulation game. *Journal of Educational Psychology, 94*(1), 171-185.

Mayer, R. E. (2001). *Multimedia learning*. Cambridge, UK: Cambridge University Press.

Mayer, R. E. (2005). Cognitive theory of multimedia learning. In R. E. Mayer (Ed.), *The Cambridge handbook of multimedia learning* (pp. 31-48). New York: Cambridge University Press.

Mayer, R. E. (2005). Introduction to multimedia learning. In R. E. Mayer (Ed.), *The Cambridge handbook of multimedia learning* (pp. 1-16). New York: Cambridge University Press.

Mayo, M. J. (2009). Video games: A route to large-scale stem education? *Science*, 323(5910) ,79-82.

McAllister, K. S. (2004). *Game work: Language, power, and computer game culture.* Tuscaloosa, AL: University of Alabama Press.

Mead, G. H. (1934). *Mind, self, and society*. Chicago University Press.

Mezirow, J. (1991). *Transformative dimensions of adult learning*. San Francisco: Jossey-Bass.

Mitchell, E. (1985). The dynamics of family interaction around home video games. Special Issue: Personal computers and the family. *Marriage and Family Review 8*(1-2), 121)-135.

Moeller, R. M., & White, K. (2008). Enter the game factor: Putting theory into practice in the design of Peer Factor. *Computers and Composition Online*, Fall 2008. Retrieved from http://www.bgsu.edu/cconline/gaming_issue_2008/Moeller_White_Enter_the_game/index.html

Mookerjee, A., & Kharma, M. (1977). *The tantric way*. London: Thames and Hudson.

Moulthrop, S. (2005). After the last generation: Rethinking scholarship in the days of serious play. *Proceedings of the 6th Digital Arts & Culture Conference*. Copenhagen, Denmark: IT University of Copenhagen.

Mulligan, K., & Smith, B. (1986). A Husserlian theory of indexicality. *Grazer Philosophische Studien, 28*, 133-163.

Murphy, P. K., & Alexander, P. A. (2000). A motivated exploration of motivation terminology. *Contemporary Educational Psychology, 25*, 3-53.

Myers, D. (2003). *The nature of computer games: Play as semiosis*. New York: Peter Lang.

Nardi, B., & Harris, J. (2006). Strangers and friends: collaborative play in *World of Warcraft*, 2006 20th Anniversary *Conference on Computer Supported Cooperative Work* (pp. 149-158). New York: ACM.

Newmann, F. M. (2007). Improving achievement for all students: The meaning of staff-shared understanding and commitment. In W. D. Hawley & D. L. Rollie (Eds.), *The keys to effective schools: Education reform as continuous improvement* (2nd ed., pp. 33-49). Thousand Oaks, CA: Corwin Press.

Norman, D. (1995). *Things that make us smart: Defending human attributes in the age of the machine*. Reading, MA: Addison Wesley.

Nousiainen, T. (2008). Children's involvement in the design of game-based learning environments. *Jyväskylä Studies in Computing*, No. 95. Jyväskylä, Finland: University of Jyväskylä.

Papert, S. (1993). *The children's machine: Rethinking school in the age of the computer*. New York: BasicBooks.

Pease, D. E. (1995). Author. In F. Lentricchia & T. McLaughlin (Eds.), *Critical terms for literary study*. University of Chicago Press.

Perron, B. (2009). *Video game theory reader 2*. New York: Routledge.

Piaget, J. (1977). Science of education and the psychology of the child. In H. E. Gruber, J. J. Vonèche, and J. Jacques (Eds.), *The essential Piaget* (pp. 695-725). New York: Basic Books, Inc.

Pintrich, P. R., Smith, D., Garcia, T., & McKeachie, W. (1993). Predictive validity and reliability of the Motivated Strategies for Learning Questionnaire (MSLQ). *Educational Psychological Measurement, 53*, 801-813.

Propp, V. (1st Ed. Transl. by Scott, L.; 2nd Ed. Revised & Edited by Wagner, L.A.). (1977). *Morphology of the folk tale*. Austin: University of Texas.

Randel, J., Morris, B., Wetzel, C., & Whitehill, B. (1992). The effectiveness of games for educational purposes: A review of recent research. *Simulation and Gaming, 23*(3), 261–276.

Raybourn, E. M. (2005). Adaptive thinking & leadership training for cultural awareness and communication competence. *Interactive Technology & Smart Education, 2*, 127-130.

Reese, D. D. (2007). First steps and beyond: Serious games as preparation for future learning. *Journal of Educational Media and Hypermedia, 16*(3), 283-300.

Reese, D. D. (2009). Structure mapping theory as a formalism for instructional game design and assessment. In D. Gentner, K. Holyoak, & B. Kokinov (Eds.), *Proceedings of the 2nd International Analogy Conference* (pp. 394-403). Sofia, Bulgaria: New Bulgarian University Press.

Rice, J. (2007). Assessing higher order thinking in video games. *Journal of Technology and Teacher Education, 15*(1) ,87-100.

Rieber, L. P. (1996). Seriously considering play: Designing interactive learning environments based on the blending of microworlds, simulations, and games. *Educational Technology Research and Development, 44*(2), 43-58.

Rieber, L. P., Smith, L., & Noah, D. (1998). The value of serious play. *Educational Technology, 38*(6), 29-37.

Ritterfeld, U., Cody, M., & Vordered, P. (in press). *Serious games: Mechanisms and effects*. New York: Routledge Press.

Robison, A. J. (2008). The design is the game: Writing games, teaching writing. *Computers and Composition, 25*(3), 359-370.

Rodriguez, H. (2006). The playful and the serious: An approximation to Huizinga's *Homo Ludens*. *Game Studies—The International Journal of Game Studies, 6* (1). Retrieved August 20, 2009, from http://gamestudies.org/0601/articles/rodriges

Rotman, A. (translator). (2008). *Divine stories, Divyavadana part 1*. Boston: Wisdom Publications.

Ruesch, J., & Bateson, G. (1951). *Communication: The social matrix of psychiatry*. New York: W. W. Norton & Co., Inc.

Ryan, M. L. (2001). *Narrative as virtual reality*. Baltimore: The Johns Hopkins University Press

Salen, K. (2007) *Game ecologies*. The John D. and Catherine T. MacArthur Foundation series on digital media and learning. (167-198) Cambridge, MA: MIT Press.

Satwicz, T., & Stevens, R. (2008). Playing with representations: How do kids make use of quantitative representations in video games? *International Journal of Computers for Mathematical Learning, 13*, 179–206.

Sawyer, B. (2002). Serious Games: Improving public policy through game-based learning and simulation. *Foresight and Governance Project, Woodrow Wilson International Center for Scholars*. Retrieved December 5, 2006, from http://wwics.si.edu/subsites/game/Serious2.pdf

Scardamalia, M., Bereiter, C., & Lamon, M. (1994). The CSILE project: Trying to bring the classroom into world 3. In K. McGilly (Ed.), *Classroom lessons: Integrating cognitive theory and classroom practice*, 201-228. Cambridge, MA: MIT Press.

Schell, J. (2008). *The art of game design: A book of lenses*. New York: Elsevier.

Scholes, R., Phelan, J., & Kellogg, R. (2006). *The nature of narrative*. New York: Oxford University Press.

Schwaber, K. (2004). *Agile project management with scrum*. Redmond, WA: Microsoft.

Schwartz, D. L., & Martin, T. (2004). Inventing to prepare for future learning: The hidden efficiency of encouraging original student production in statistics instruction. *Cognition and Instruction, 22*(2), 129-184.

Selfe, C. L., & Hawisher, G. E. (Eds.). (2007). *Gaming lives in the twenty-first century: Literate connections*. New York: Palgrave Macmillan.

Sell, R.D. (2000). *Literature as communication*. Amsterdam and Philadelphia: John Benjamins Publishing.

Shaffer, D. (2006). Epistemic frames for epistemic games. *Computers & Education, 46*(3), 223-234.

Shaffer, D.W., Squire, K.A., Halverson, R. & Gee, J.P. (2005). Video games and the future of learning. *Phi Delta Kappan, 87*: 104-111

Shelton, B. & Wiley, D. (2007). *The design and use of computer simulation games in education*. Rotterdam, Netherlands: Sense Publishers.

Sheridan, D. M., & Hart-Davidson, W. (2008). Just for fun: Writing and literacy learning as forms of play. *Computers and Composition, 25*(3), 323-340.

Smith, P. L., & Ragan, T. J. (2005). *Instructional design* (3rd ed.). Hoboken, NJ: John Wiley & Sons.

Squire, K. D, & Jan, M. (2007). Mad city mystery: Developing scientific argumentation skills with a place-based augmented reality game on handheld computers. *Journal of Science Education and Technology, 16*, 5-29.

Steinkuehler, C. (2006). Virtual worlds, learning, & the new pop cosmopolitanism. *Teachers College Record.* Retrieved July 12, 2009, from http://www.tcrecord.org ID Number: 12843.

Steinkuehler, C. A. (2004). Learning in massively multiplayer online games. In Y. B. Kafai, W. A. Sandoval, N. Enyedy, A. S. Nixon, & F. Herrera (Eds.), *Proceedings of the Sixth International Conference of the Learning Sciences* (pp. 521–528). Mahwah, NJ: Erlbaum.

Stephenson, N. (1995). *The diamond age: Or, a young lady's illustrated primer.* New York: Bantam Spectra.

Stubblefield, W. A. (2007). *Hacking sense: Understanding design and use as situated sensemaking.* Sandia National Laboratories.

Suchman, L. A. (1987). *Plans and situated actions* [Electronic Version]. Retrieved 3/2/2007.

Sutton-Smith, B. (1997). *The ambiguity of play.* Cambridge, MA: Harvard University Press.

Sweller, J. (2008). Instructional implications of David Geary's evolutionary educational psychology. *Educational Psychologist, 43*, 214–216.

Thomas, M., & Penz, F. (Eds.). (2003). *Architectures of illusion: From motion pictures to navigable interactive environments.* Bristol, UK: Intellect Books.

Tomasello, M., & Whiten, A. (1999). *The cultural origins of human cognition.* Cambridge, MA: Harvard University Press

Van Deventer, S., & White, J. (2002). Expert behavior in children's videogame play. *Simulation & Gaming, 33*(1).

Van Eck, R. (2006). The effect of contextual pedagogical advisement and competition on middle-school students' attitude toward mathematics and mathematics instruction using a computer-based simulation game. *Journal of Mathematics and Science Teaching, 25(2)*, 165-195.

Van Eck, R. (2007). Building intelligent learning games. In D. Gibson, C. Aldrich, & M. Prensky (Eds.) *Games and simulations in online learning research & development frameworks.* Hershey, PA: Idea Group.

Van Eck, R., & Dempsey, J. (2002). The effect of competition and contextualized advisement on the transfer of mathematics skills in a computer-based instructional simulation game. *Educational Technology, Research and Development, 50*, 23–41.

Vansteenkiste, M., Lens, W., & Deci, E. L. (2006). Intrinsic versus extrinsic goal contents in self-determination theory: Another look at the quality of academic motivation. *Educational Psychologist, 41(1)*, 19-31.

Vogel, J. J., Vogel, D. S., Cannon-Bowers, J., Bowers, C. A., Muse, K., & Wright, M. (2006). Computer games and interactive simulations for learning: A meta-analysis. *Journal of Educational Computing Research, 34*, 229–243.

Vogler, C. (1999). *The writer's journey: Mythic structure for storytellers and screenwriters.* London: Pan Books.

Wardrip-Fruin, N. and Monfort, N. (2003). *The new media reader.* The MIT Press.

Wark, M. (2007). *Gamer theory.* Cambridge, MA: Harvard University Press.

Wilden, A. (1987). *The rules are no game: The strategy of communication.* New York: Routledge.

Wood, D. (Ed.). (1991). *On Paul Ricœur, narrative and interpretation.* London: Routledge.

Woods, S. (2004). Loading the dice: The challenge of serious videogames. *Game Studies— The International Journal of Game Studies, 4*(1). Retrieved August 20, 2009, from http://www.gamestudies.org/0401/woods/   1

Wright, W. (2004). *Sculpting possibility space.* Keynote presented at the Accelerating Change 2004: Physical Space, Virtual Space, and Interface conference. Retrieved June 16, 2006, from http://cdn.itconversations.com/ITC.AC2004-WillWright-2004.11.07. mp3   1

Zimmerman, B. J. (2008). Investigating self-regulation and motivation: Historical background, methodological development, and future prospects. *American Educational Research Journal, 45*, 166-183.   1

Zyda, M. (2005). From Visual Stimulation to Virtual Reality to Games. *IEEE Computer, 38*(9), 25-32.   1

Compilation of References

2K. (2007). Bioshock. [Video game]. Boston, MA: 2K Games.

Aaker, J., & Lee, A. (2006). Understanding regulatory fit. *JMR, Journal of Marketing Research, 43*, 15–19. doi:10.1509/jmkr.43.1.15

Aarseth, E. (2003). *Playing research: Methodological approaches to game analysis.* Paper presented at the 5th International Digital arts and culture conference, Melbourne.

Abt, C. (1970). *Serious games.* New York: Viking Press.

Adcock, A. B., Watson, G. S., Morrison, G. R., & Belfore, L. A. (in press). Effective knowledge development in game-based learning environments: Considering research in cognitive processes and simulation design. In Van Eck, R. (Ed.), *Gaming & cognition: Theories and practice from the learning sciences.* Hershey, PA: IGI Global.

Albanese, M. A., & Mitchell, S. (1993). Problem-based learning: A review of literature on its outcomes and implementation issues. *Academic Medicine, 68*, 52–81.

Aldrich, C. (2004). *Simulations and the future of learning: an innovative (and perhaps revolutionary) approach to e-learning.* San Francisco: Pfeiffer.

Aldrich, C. (2005). *Learning by doing.* San Francisco: Pfeiffer.

Alessi, M. S., & Trollip, S. R. (2001). *Multimedia for learning: Methods and development* (3rd ed.). Boston: Allyn and Bacon.

Alessi, S. M. (1988). Fidelity in the design of instructional simulations. *Journal of Computer-Based Instruction, 15*(2), 40–47.

Alessi, S. M. (2000). Simulation design for training and assessment. In O'Neill, H. F. Jr, & Andrews, D. H. (Eds.), *Aircrew training and assessment* (pp. 197–222). Mahwah, NJ: Lawrence Erlbaum Associates.

Allison, M. T., & Duncan, M. C. (1988). Women, work, and flow. In Csikszentmihalyi, M., & Csikszentmihalyi, I. S. (Eds.), *Optimal experience: Psychological studies of flow in consciousness* (pp. 118–137). New York: Cambridge University Press.

American Association for the Advancement of Science. (2001). *Atlas of science literacy.* Washington, DC: American Association for the Advancement of Science and National Science Teachers Association.

American Public Media. (2008). *Budget Hero* [Video game]. St. Paul, MN: American Public Media.

Amory, A. (2007). Game object model version II: A theoretical framework for educational game development. *Educational Technology Research and Development, 55*(1), 51–77. doi:10.1007/s11423-006-9001-x

Amory, A., & Seagram, R. (2003). Educational game models: Conceptualization and evaluation. *South African Journal of Higher Education, 17*(2), 206–217.

Anderson, B. (2007). *The role of place deixis in massive multiplayer online games.* Retrieved from http://pine.ucc.nau.edu/boa/mmorpgdeixis/

Anderson, B. (2008). *Operationalizing online interaction in distance education: A register comparison of IRC and*

MMORPG corpora. Retrieved from http://pine.ucc.nau.edu/boa/mmoircinteraction/

Anderson, B. (in press). The use of massive multiplayer online games in support of learning: An overview of current trends and future use. In Van Eck, R. (Ed.), *Gaming & cognition: Theories and practice from the learning sciences.* Hershey, PA: IGI Global.

Anderson, C. A., & Bushman, B. J. (2001). Effects of violent games on aggressive behavior, aggressive cognition, aggressive affect, physiological arousal, and prosocial behavior: A meta-analytic review of the scientific literature. *Psychological Science, 12,* 353–359. doi:10.1111/1467-9280.00366

Anderson, D. (1982). *Informal features.*

Anderson, D. R. (1983, April). *Home television viewing by preschool children, and their families.* Paper presented at the Society for Research in Child Development.

Anderson, J. R. (2000). *Cognitive psychology and its implications* (5th ed.). New York: Worth Publishing.

Anderson, J. R., Reder, L. M., & Simon, H. A. (1997). Situative versus cognitive perspectives: Form versus substance. *Educational Researcher, 26*(1), 18–21.

Anderson, J. R., Reder, L. M., & Simon, H. A. (1998). Radical constructivism and cognitive psychology. In Ravitch, D. (Ed.), *Brookings papers on educational policy: 1998* (p. 384). Washington, DC: The Brookings Institution Press.

Anderson, L. W. E., Krathwohl, D. R. E., Airasian, P. W., Cruikshank, K. A., Mayer, R. E., Pintrich, P., et al. (Eds.). (2001). A taxonomy for learning, teaching, and assessing: A revision of Bloom's taxonomy of educational objectives (Complete Ed.). New York: Longman.

Ang, C. S., Zaphiris, P., & Mahmood, S. (2007). A model of cognitive loads in massively multiplayer online role playing games. *Interacting with Computers, 19,* 167–179. doi:10.1016/j.intcom.2006.08.006

Annetta, L. A., & Cheng, M. (2008). Why educational video games? In Annetta, L. A. (Ed.), *Serious educational games* (pp. 1–12). Rotterdam: Sense Publishers.

Arnfalk, P., & Kogg, B. (2003). Service transformation—Managing a shift from business travel to virtual meetings. *Journal of Cleaner Production, 11*(8), 859–872. doi:10.1016/S0959-6526(02)00158-0

Aronson, E., Stephan, C., Sikes, J., Blaney, N., & Snapp, M. (1978). *The jigsaw classroom.* Beverly Hills, CA: Sage.

Ashby, W. R. (1956). *An introduction to cybernetics.* Retrieved from http://pespmc1.vub.ac.be/ASHBBOOK.html

Association for Childhood Education International. (2007). *ACEI: Elementary Standards and Supporting Explanation.* Retrieved from http://www.ncate.org/ProgramStandards/ACEI/ACEIscoringGuide_07.doc

Atkinson, R. C., & Shiffrin, R. M. (1968). Human memory: A proposed system and its control processes. In Spence, K. W., & Spence, J. T. (Eds.), *The psychology of learning and motivation* (*Vol. 2*, pp. 89–195). New York: Academic Press.

Atkinson, R. K. (2002). Optimizing Learning from Examples Using Animated Pedagogical Agents. *Journal of Educational Psychology, 94*(2), 416–427. doi:10.1037/0022-0663.94.2.416

Atkinson, R. K., Renkl, A., & Merrill, M. M. (2003). Transitioning from studying examples to solving problems: Effects of self-explanation prompts and fading worked-out steps. *Journal of Educational Psychology, 95,* 774–783. doi:10.1037/0022-0663.95.4.774

Au, J. (2007). *Lord of the Rings online: MMORPG meets Web 2.0.* Retrieved from http://gigaom.com/2007/10/25/lord-of-the-rings-online-mmorpg-meets-web-20/

Ausubel, D. P. (1968). *Educational psychology: A cognitive view.* New York: Holt, Rinehart, and Winston, Inc.

Avedon, E. M. (1971). The structural elements of games. In Avedon, E. M., & Sutton-Smith, B. (Eds.), *The study of games* (1st ed., p. 530). New York: John Wiley & Sons, Inc.

Baddeley, A. (1992). Working memory. *Science, 255,* 556–559. doi:10.1126/science.1736359

Baddeley, A. (2000). The episodic buffer: A new component of working memory? *Trends in Cognitive Sciences*, *4*(11), 417–423. doi:10.1016/S1364-6613(00)01538-2

Baddeley, A. D. (2003). Working memory: Looking back and looking forward. *Nature Reviews. Neuroscience*, *4*, 829–839. doi:10.1038/nrn1201

Baek, Y. K. (2008). What hinders teachers in using computer and video games in the classroom? Exploring factors inhibiting the uptake of computer and video games. *Cyberpsychology & Behavior*, *11*(6), 665–671. doi:10.1089/cpb.2008.0127

Bailey, F. G. (1983). *The tactical uses of passion: An essay on power, reason, and reality*. Ithaca, NY: Cornell University Press.

Bandura, A., & Locke, E. A. (2003). Negative self-efficacy and goal effects revisited. *The Journal of Applied Psychology*, *88*(1), 87–99. doi:10.1037/0021-9010.88.1.87

Bannan-Ritland, B. (2003). The role of design in research: The integrative learning design framework. *Educational Researcher*, *32*(1), 21–24. doi:10.3102/0013189X032001021

Bannan-Ritland, B. (2008). *Design research and SCORM: From learning object reusability to the reuse of knowledge*. Paper presented at the ID+SCORM. Retrieved February 2008, from http://arclite.byu.edu/id+scorm/2008/Presentations/Bannan-Ritland/Bannan-Ritland.html

Bannon, L., & Bødker, S. (1991). Beyond the interface: Encountering artifacts in use. In Carroll, J. M. (Ed.), *Designing Interaction: Psychology at the Human-Computer Interface* (pp. 227–253). New York: Cambridge University Press.

Barab, S., Thomas, M. K., Dodge, T., Carteaux, B., & Tuzun, H. (2005). Making learning fun: *Quest Atlantis*, a game without guns. *Educational Technology Research and Development*, *5*(1), 86–108. doi:10.1007/BF02504859

Barlett, C. P., Vowels, C. L., Shanteau, J., Crow, J., & Miller, T. (2009). The effect of violent and non-violent computer games on cognitive performance. *Computers in Human Behavior*, *25*, 96–102. doi:10.1016/j.chb.2008.07.008

Barrett, K., & Johnson, L. (in press). Designing and developing serious games for teaching language-in-culture: Creating engaging learning experiences that accelerate performance outcomes. In Van Eck, R. (Ed.), *Gaming & cognition: Theories and practice from the learning sciences*. Hershey, PA: IGI Global.

Bartle, R. (1996). Hearts, clubs, diamonds, spades: Players who suit MUDs. *Journal of Virtual Environments* (Vol. 1). Retrieved from http://www.brandeis.edu/pubs/jove/index.html

Bartle, R. A. (1996). Hearts, clubs, diamonds, spades: Players who suit muds. *Journal of MUD Research*, *1*, 1.

Barton, M. (2007). *The history of computer role playing games: Parts I, II and III*. Retrieved from http://www.gamasutra.com/features/20070223b/barton_01.shtml

Batteau, A. W. (2000). Negations and ambiguities in the cultures of organizations. *American Anthropologist*, *102*(4), 726–740. doi:10.1525/aa.2000.102.4.726

Bayazit, N. (2004). Investigating design: A review of forty years of design research. *Design Issues*, *20*(1), 16–29. doi:10.1162/074793604772933739

Baylor, A. L. (2000). Beyond butlers: Intelligent agents as mentors. *Journal of Educational Computing Research*, *22*(4), 373–382. doi:10.2190/1EBD-G126-TFCY-A3K6

Baylor, A. L. (2002). Agent-based learning environments for investigating teaching and learning. *Journal of Educational Computing Research*, *26*(3), 249–270. doi:10.2190/PH2K-6P09-K8EC-KRDK

Baylor, A. L. (2003). *Evidence That Multiple Agents Facilitate Greater Learning*. Paper presented at the AI-ED. Sydney, Australia.

Baylor, A. L., & Kim, Y. (2006). A social-cognitive framework for pedagogical agents as learning companions. *Educational Technology Research and Development*, *54*(6), 569–596. doi:10.1007/s11423-006-0637-3

Beale, I. L., Kato, P. M., Marin-Bowling, V. M., Guthrie, N., & Cole, S. W. (2007). Improvement in cancer-related knowledge following use of a psychoeducational video game for adolescents and young adults with cancer. *Journal of Adolescent Health, 41*(3), 263–270. doi: DOI: 10.1016/j.jadohealth.2007.04.006

Becker, K. (2001). Teaching with games: The *Minesweeper* and *Asteroids* experience. *Journal of Computing in Small Colleges, 17*(2), 23–33.

Becker, K. (2005a, July 4–6). *Games and learning styles.* Paper presented at the Special Session on Computer Games for Learning and Teaching, at the The IASTED International Conference on Education and Technology, ICET 2005, Calgary, Alberta, Canada.

Becker, K. (2005b, June 16–20). *How are games educational? Learning theories embodied in games.* Paper presented at the DiGRA 2005 2nd International Conference, "Changing Views: Worlds in Play," Vancouver, B.C.

Becker, K. (2006b, Sept 21–24). *A psycho-cultural approach to video games.* Paper presented at the Canadian Games Studies Association Symposium, York, University, Toronto, Ontario.

Becker, K. (2007). Pedagogy in commercial video games. In Gibson, D., Aldrich, C., & Prensky, M. (Eds.), *Games and simulations in online learning: Research and development frameworks* (p. 20). Hershey, PA: IGI.

Becker, K. (2008a). *The invention of good games: Understanding learning design in commercial video games.* Unpublished dissertation, University of Calgary, Calgary, Canada.

Becker, K. (2008b). Video game pedagogy: Good games = good pedagogy. In Miller, C. T. (Ed.), *Games: Their purpose and potential in education.* New York: Springer Publishing.

Becker, K. (in press). Distinctions between games and learning? A review of the literature on games in education. In Van Eck, R. (Ed.), *Gaming & cognition: Theories and practice from the learning sciences.* Hershey, PA: IGI Global.

Becker, K., & Jacobsen, D. M. (June 16–20, 2005). *Games for learning: Are schools ready for what's to come?* Paper presented at the DiGRA 2005 2nd International Conference, "Changing Views: Worlds in Play," Vancouver, B.C.

Becker, K., & Parker, J. R. (October 13–15, 2005). *All I ever needed to know about programming, I learned from re-writing classic arcade games.* Paper presented at Future Play, The International Conference on the Future of Game Design and Technology, Michigan State University, East Lansing, Michigan.

Berkeley, E. (1853). The world's laconics, or, the best thoughts of the best authors in prose and poetry. New York: M.W.Dodd.

Bernard, R. M., Abrami, P. C., Lou, Y., Borokhovski, E., Wade, A., Wozney, L., & Wallet, P. (2004). How does distance education compare with classroom instruction? A meta-analysis of the empirical literature. *Review of Educational Research, 74*(3), 379–439. doi:10.3102/00346543074003379

Bertalanffy, L. V. (1968). *General systems theory.* New York: George Brazeller.

Bertozzi, E. (2008). You play like a girl!: Cross-gender competition and the uneven playing field. *Convergence, 14*(4), 473–487.

Beswick, D. G. (1971). Cognitive process theory of individual differences in curiosity. In Day, H. I., Berlyne, D. E., & Hunt, D. E. (Eds.), *Intrinsic motivation: A new direction in education* (pp. 156–170). Toronto, ON: Holt, Rinehart and Winston.

Beswick, D. G. (1974). Intrinsic motivation in senior secondary school students. *Education Research and Perspectives, 1*, 1525.

Beswick, D. G. (2007). Management implications of the interaction between intrinsic motivation and extrinsic rewards. *Beswick recent psychological research.* Retrieved from http://www.beswick.info/psychres/management

Beyer, H., & Holtzblatt, K. (1998). *Contextual design: Defining customer-centered systems.* London: Academic Press.

Biber, D., Conrad, S., & Leech, G. (1999). *The Longman grammar of spoken and written English*. Essex, UK: Longman.

Bidney, D. (1947). Human nature and the cultural process. *American Anthropologist*, *49*(3), 375–399. doi:10.1525/aa.1947.49.3.02a00010

Blizzard Entertainment Inc. (2009). *World of Warcraft*. [Online game].

Bloom, B. S. (1956). *Taxonomy of educational objectives: The classification of educational goals, Handbook 1: Cognitive domain*. New York: David McKay.

Bloom, B. S. (1984). The 2 sigma problem: The search for methods of group instruction as effective as one-to-one tutoring. *Educational Researcher*, *13*(6), 4–16.

Blumenfeld, P. C., Kempler, T. M., & Krajcik, J. S. (2006). Motivation and cognitive engagement in learning environments. In Sawyer, R. K. (Ed.), *Cambridge handbook of the learning sciences* (1st ed., pp. 475–488). New York: Cambridge University Press.

Bødker, S. (1996). Applying activity theory to video analysis: How to make sense of video data in human-computer interaction. In Nardi, B. (Ed.), *Context and consciousness: Activity theory and human-computer interaction* (pp. 147–174). Cambridge, MA: MIT Press.

Bogart, D. H. (1980). Feedback, feedforward, and feedwithin: Strategic information in systems. *Behavioral Science*, *25*(4), 237. doi:10.1002/bs.3830250402

Bonk, C., & Dennen, V. (2005). *Massive multiplayer online gaming: A research framework for military training and education* (Technical Report No. 2005-1). Washington, DC: U.S. Department of Defense (DUSD/R), Advanced Distributed Learning (ADL) Initiative. Retrieved from http://mypage.iu.edu/cjbonk/GameReport_Bonk_final.pdf

Bonvillain, N. (1997). *Language, culture, and communication* (2nd ed.). Upper Saddle River, NJ: Prentice Hall.

Borgman, C. L., Abelson, H., Johnson, R., Koedinger, K. R., Linn, M. C., Lynch, C. A., et al. (2008). *Fostering learning in the networked world: The cyberlearning opportunity and challenge: A 21st century agenda for the National Science Foundation*. Retrieved August 13, 2008, from http://www.nsf.gov/pubs/2008/nsf08204/nsf08204.pdf?govDel=USNSF_124

Brain Powered Games. (2009). Keep It. In *Mind* [computer game]. Lansing, MI: Brain Powered Games.

Brandt, L., Borchert, O., Addicott, K., Cosmano, B., Hawley, J., & Hokanson, G. (2006). *Roles, culture, and computer supported collaborative work on* Planet Oit. *Journal of Advanced Technology for Learning*, *3*(2), 89–98.

Bransford, J. D., & Schwartz, D. L. (1999). Rethinking transfer: A simple proposal with multiple implications. *Review of Research in Education*, *24*, 61–100.

Bransford, J. D., Sherwood, R. D., Hasselbring, T. S., Kinzer, C. K., & Williams, S. M. (1990). Anchored instruction: Why we need it and how technology can help. In Nix, D., & Spiro, R. (Eds.), *Cognition, education, and multimedia: Exploring ideas in high technology* (pp. 115–141). Hillsdale, NJ: Lawrence Erlbaum Associates.

Bransford, J., Brown, A., & Cocking, R. (2000). *How people learn: Brain, mind, and experience & school*. Washington, DC: National Academy Press.

Broderbund. (1985). *Where in the world is Carmen San Diego?* [Video game].

Brooks, J. D. (1983). *Video games and human development A research agenda for the '80s*. Cambridge, MA: Monroe C. Gutman Library, Harvard Graduate School of Education.

Brown, J. S., Collins, A., & Duguid, P. (1989). Situated cognition and the culture of learning. *Educational Researcher*, *18*(1), 32–42.

Bruckman, A., & Resnick, M. (1996). The MediaMOO project: Constructionism and professional community. In Y. B. Kafai & M. Resnick (Eds.), Constructionism in practice: designing, thinking, and learning in a digital world (pp. xii, 339). Mahwah, NJ: Lawrence Erlbaum Associates.

Bruner, J. (1960). *The process of education.* Cambridge, MA: Harvard University Press.

Bruner, J. (1961). The act of discovery. *Harvard Educational Review, 31*(1), 21–32.

Bruner, J. S. (1977). Structures in learning. In Hass, B. (Ed.), *Curriculum planning: A new approach* (pp. 192–194). London: Allyn & Bacon.

Brünken, R., Plass, J. L., & Leutner, D. (2004). Assessment of cognitive load in multimedia learning with dual task methodology: Auditory load and modality effects. *Instructional Science, 32,* 115–132. doi:10.1023/B:TRUC.0000021812.96911.c5

Brünken, R., Plass, J., & Leutner, D. (2003). Direct measurement of cognitive load in multimedia learning. *Educational Psychologist, 38,* 53–61. doi:10.1207/S15326985EP3801_7

Brünken, R., Steinbacher, S., Plass, J. L., & Leutner, D. (2002). Assessment of cognitive load in multimedia learning using dual-task methodology. *Experimental Psychology, 49,* 109–119. doi:10.1027//1618-3169.49.2.109

Bryant, T. (2008). Using *World of Warcraft* and other MMORPGs to foster a targeted, social, and cooperative approach toward language learning. *Academic Commons, 12*(4), 23–35.

Buchanan, K. (2006). *Beyond attention-getters: Designing for deep engagement.* Unpublished dissertation, Michigan State University, Michigan, USA.

Buckingham, D., & Scanlon, M. (2004). Connecting the family? 'Edutainment' web sites and learning in the home. *Education Communication and Information, 4.*

Cadinu, M., Maass, A., Rosabianca, A., & Kiesner, J. (2005). Why do women underperform under stereotype threat? Evidence for the role of negative thinking. *Psychological Science, 16*(7), 572–578. doi:10.1111/j.0956-7976.2005.01577.x

Caillois, R. (1961). *Man, play, and games.* Glencoe, IL: Free Press of Glencoe.

Calleja, G. (2007). Digital game involvement: A conceptual model. *Games and Culture, 2*(3), 236–260. doi:10.1177/1555412007306206

Cameron, B., & Dwyer, F. (2005). The effect of online gaming, cognition and feedback type in facilitating delayed achievement of different learning objectives. *Journal of Interactive Learning Research, 16*(3), 243–358.

Cancerland. (2009). Retrieved August 1, 2009 from http://slurl.com/secondlife/Kula%203/197/86/21

Canfora, G., & Di Penta, M. (2007). *New frontiers of reverse engineering.* Paper presented at the Future of Software Engineering (FOSE '07), Minneapolis, MN.

Carroll, J. M. (2000). *Making use: Scenarios and scenario-based design.* London: MIT Press.

Caspian Learning. (2008). *Serious Games in Defence Education.* White Paper Retrieved from http://www.caspianlearning.co.uk/MoD_Defence_Academy_Serious_games_Report_04.11.08.pdf

Castronova, E., Bell, M., Cornell, R., Cummings, J., Falk, M., & Ross, T. (2009). Synthetic worlds as experimental instruments. In Wolf, M., & Perron, B. (Eds.), *The video game theory reader 2.* New York: Routledge.

CCP. (2009). *EVE Online* [Online game]. Winch Gate Property Limited.

Ceer, D. (2006). Pervasive medical devices: less invasive, more productive. *Pervasive Computing IEEE, 5*(2), 85–87. doi:10.1109/MPRV.2006.37

Center for Social Organization of Schools. (1983, April). *School uses of microcomputers: Reports from a national survey.* Center for Social Organization of Schools, John Hopkins University.

Chaffin, J. D., Maxwell, B., & Thompson, B. (1982). ARC-ED curriculum: The application of video game formats to educational software. *Exceptional Children, 49,* 173–178.

Chalam, V. V. (1987). *Adaptive control systems: Techniques and applications.* New York: Marcel Dekker, Inc.

Chandler, P., & Sweller, J. (1991). Cognitive load theory and the format of instruction. *Cognition and Instruction, 8*, 293–332. doi:10.1207/s1532690xci0804_2

Chandler, P., & Sweller, J. (1996). Cognitive load while learning to use a computer program. *Applied Cognitive Psychology, 10*, 151–170. doi:10.1002/(SICI)1099-0720(199604)10:2<151::AID-ACP380>3.0.CO;2-U

Chapman, G. (2009, Mar 13, 2009). Second Life finding new life. *AFP*. Retrieved from http://www.google.com/hostednews/afp/article/ALeqM5hHXGgsClglmLWwN-2hCXGS-fqYwqQ

Charsky, D. (in press). From edutainment to serious games: A change in the use of game characteristics. *Games and Culture*.

Charsky, D., & Mims, C. (2008). Integrating commercial off-the-shelf video games into school curriculums. *TechTrends, 52*(5), 38–44. doi:10.1007/s11528-008-0195-0

Chase, W. G., & Simon, H. A. (1973). Perception in chess. *Cognitive Psychology, 4*, 55–81. doi:10.1016/0010-0285(73)90004-2

Chen, C., Sun, C., & Hsieh, J. (2008). Player guild dynamics and evolution in massively multiplayer online games. *Cyberpsychology & Behavior, 11*(3), 293–301. doi:10.1089/cpb.2007.0066

Chen, S., & Michael, D. (2005 October). Proof of learning: Assessment in serious games. *Gamasutra*.

Chi, M. T. H., Glaser, R., & Rees, E. (1982). Expertise in problem solving. In Sternberg, R. J. (Ed.), *Advances in the psychology of human intelligence* (Vol. 1, pp. 7–76). Hillsdale, NJ: Erlbaum.

Chi, M. T. H., Siler, S. A., Jeong, H., Yamauchi, T., & Hausmann, R. G. (2001). Learning from human tutoring. *Cognitive Science: A Multidisciplinary Journal, 25*(4), 471–533.

Childress, M., & Braswell, R. (2006). Using massively multiplayer online role-playing games for online learning. *Distance Education, 27*(2), 187–196. doi:10.1080/01587910600789522

Choi, D., & Kim, J. (2004). Why people continue to play online games: In search of critical design factors to increase customer loyalty to online contents. *Cyberpsychology & Behavior, 7*(1), 11–24. doi:10.1089/109493104322820066

Chou, S.-W., & Liu, C.-H. (2005). Learning effectiveness in a web-based virtual learning environment: A learner control perspective. *Journal of Computer Assisted Learning, 21*(1), 65–76. doi:10.1111/j.1365-2729.2005.00114.x

Christakis, D. A., Ebel, B. E., Rivara, F. P., & Zimmerman, F. J. (2004). Television, video, and computer game use in children under 11 years of age. *The Journal of Pediatrics, 145*, 652–656. doi:10.1016/j.jpeds.2004.06.078

Chu, W. C., Lu, C. W., Chang, C. H., & Chung, Y. C. (2001). Pattern-based software re-engineering. In Chang, S. K. (Ed.), *Handbook of software engineering and knowledge engineering* (Vol. 1, pp. 767–786). Singapore: World Scientific Publishing Co.

Chu, W. C., Lu, C. W., Chang, C. H., Chung, Y. C., Liu, X., & Yang, H. (2002). Reverse engineering. In Chang, S. K. (Ed.), *Handbook of software engineering and knowledge engineering* (Vol. 2, pp. 447–466). Singapore: World Scientific Publishing Co.

Clancey, W. J. (1995). Practice cannot be reduced to theory: Knowledge, representations, and change in the workplace. In Bagnara, S., Zuccermaglio, C., & Stucky, S. (Eds.), *Organizational learning and technological change* (pp. 16–46). Berlin: Springer.

Clariana, R. B. (1989). Computer simulations of laboratory experiences. *Journal of Computers in Mathematics and Science Teaching, 2*, 14–19.

Clark, R. E. (1983). Reconsidering research on learning from media. *Review of Educational Research, 53*(4), 445–459.

Clark, R. E. (2005). Multimedia learning in e-course. In Mayer, R. E. (Ed.), *The Cambridge handbook of multimedia learning* (pp. 589–616). New York: Cambridge University Press.

Clark, R. E. (2007). Learning from serious games? Arguments, evidence, and research suggestions. *Educational Technology*, (May–June): 56–59.

Cobb, T. (1997). Cognitive efficiency: Toward a revised theory of media. *Educational Technology Research and Development*, *45*, 1042–1062. doi:10.1007/BF02299681

Coffield, F., Moseley, D., Hall, E., & Ecclestone, K. (2004). *Learning styles and pedagogy in post-16 learning: A systematic and critical review.* Retrieved from http://www.lsrc.ac.uk/publications/index.asp

Cognition & Technology Group at Vanderbilt. (1990). Anchored instruction and its relation to situated cognition. *Educational Researcher*, *19*(6), 2–10.

Cognition & Technology Group at Vanderbilt. (1992). Technology and the design of generative learning environments. In Jonassen, D. H., & Duffy, T. M. (Eds.), *Constructivism and the technology of instruction: A conversation.* Mahwah, NJ: Lawrence Erlbaum.

Colella, V. S., Klopfer, E., & Resnick, M. (2001). *Adventures in modeling: exploring complex, dynamic systems with StarLogo.* New York: Teachers College Press.

Collins, A., Brown, J. S., & Holum, A. (1991). Cognitive apprenticeship: Making thinking visible. *American Federation of Teachers, Winter*, 1-18.

Collins, A., Joseph, D., & Bielaczyc, K. (2004). Design research: Theoretical and methodological issues. *Journal of the Learning Sciences*, *13*(1), 15–42. doi:10.1207/s15327809jls1301_2

Colliver, J. A. (2000). Effectiveness of problem-based learning curricula: Research and theory. *Academic Medicine*, *75*, 259–266. doi:10.1097/00001888-200003000-00017

Conole, G. (2008). New schemas for mapping pedagogies and technologies. *Ariadine*, *56*.

Costikyan, G. (1994). I have no words & I must design. *Interactive Fantasy*, *2*. Retrieved from http://www.costik.com/nowords.html

Costikyan, G. (2002). *I have no words & I must design: Toward a critical vocabulary for games.* Paper presented at the Computer Games and Digital Cultures. Retrieved from http://www.digra.org/dl/db/05164.51146.pdf

Covington, M., Omelich, C., & Schwarzer, R. (1986). Anxiety, aspirations, and self-concept in the achievement process: A longitudinal model with latent variables. *Motivation and Emotion*, *10*, 71–88. doi:10.1007/BF00992151

Craig, S. D., Graesser, A. C., Sullins, J., & Gholson, B. (2004). Affect and learning: An exploratory look into the role of affect in learning. *Journal of Educational Media*, *29*(3), 241–250.

Crampton Smith, G., & Tabor, P. (2006). More Than One Way of Knowing. In Bagnara, S., & Crampton Smith, G. (Eds.), *Theories and Practice in Interaction Design* (pp. 117–124). Mahwah, NJ: Lawrence Erlbaum Associates, Inc.

Crandall, R. W., & Sidak, J. G. (2006). *Video games, Serious business for America's economy.* Entertainment Software Association.

Crawford, C. (1984). *The art of computer game design.* Retrieved from http://www.vancouver.wsu.edu/fac/peabody/game-book/Coverpage.html

Crawford, C. (2003). *Chris Crawford on game design.* Indianapolis, IN: New Riders.

Crawford, C. (2004). *Chris Crawford on Interactive Storytelling.* Indianapolis, IN: New Riders.

Crawford, C. (in press). Interactivity, process, and algorithm. In Van Eck, R. (Ed.), *Interdisciplinary models and tools for serious games: Emerging concepts and future directions.* Hershey, PA: IGI Global.

Crippen, K. J., & Earl, B. L. (2007). The impact of Web-based worked examples and self-explanation on performance, problem solving, and self-efficacy. *Computers & Education*, *49*, 809–821. doi:10.1016/j.compedu.2005.11.018

Croizet, J. C., Després, G., Gauzins, M. E., Huguet, P., Leyens, J. P., & Méot, A. (2004). Stereotype threat undermines intellectual performance by triggering a disruptive mental load. *Personality and Social Psychology Bulletin, 30*(6), 721–731. doi:10.1177/0146167204263961

Csikszentmihalyi, M. (1988). Introduction. In Csikszentmihalyi, M., & Csikszentmihalyi, I. S. (Eds.), *Optimal experience: Psychological studies of flow in consciousness* (pp. 3–14). New York: Cambridge University Press.

Csikszentmihalyi, M. (1990). *Flow: The psychology of optimal experience*. New York: Harper & Row.

Csikszentmihalyi, M. (1996). *Creativity: Flow and the psychology of discovery and invention* (1st ed.). New York: Harper Collins Publishers.

Csikszentmihalyi, M. (1997). *Finding flow: The psychology of engagement with everyday life*. New York: HarperCollins Publishers.

Csikszentmihalyi, M. (2008, October 24). Creativity, fulfillment, and flow. *TED: Ideas worth spreading*. Retrieved March 23, 2009, from http://www.youtube.com/watch?v=fXIeFJCqsPs

Csikszentmihalyi, M. (Producer). (2002, December). Mihalyi Csikszentmihalyi on motivating people to learn. *Video Gallery*. Podcast retrieved from http://www.glef.org.

Csikszentmihalyi, M., & Csikszentmihalyi, I. S. (Eds.). (1988). *Optimal experience: Psychological studies of flow in consciousness*. New York: Cambridge University Press.

Csikszentmihalyi, M., & Larson, R. (1987). Validity and reliability of the experience sampling method. *The Journal of Nervous and Mental Disease, 175*(9), 526–536. doi:10.1097/00005053-198709000-00004

Csikszentmihalyi, M., & Schneider, B. (2000). *Becoming adult: How teenagers prepare for the world of work*. New York: Basic Books.

Cuban, L. (1986). *Teachers and machines: The classroom use of technology since 1920*. New York: Teacher's College Columbia University.

Cuban, L. (2001). *Oversold and underused: Computers in the classroom*. Cambridge, MA: Harvard University Press.

D'Andrade, R. G. (1981). The cultural part of cognition. *Cognitive Science, 5*, 179–195. doi:10.1207/s15516709cog0503_1

D'Andrade, R. G. (1984). Cultural meaning systems. In Shweder, R. A., & Levine, R. A. (Eds.), *Culture theory: Essays on mind, self and emotion* (pp. 88–119). Cambridge, UK: Cambridge University Press.

D'Andrade, R. G. (1989). Culturally based reasoning. In Gellatly, A. D., & Slobada, J. A. (Eds.), *Cognition and social worlds* (pp. 132–143). Oxford: Clarendon Press.

D'Andrade, R. G. (1992). Schemas and motivation. In D'Andrade, R. G., & Strauss, C. (Eds.), *Human motives and cultural models* (pp. 23–44). Cambridge, UK: Cambridge University Press.

D'Mello, S., Taylor, R. S., & Graesser, A. C. (2007). Monitoring affective trajectories during complex learning. In *Proceedings of the 29th Annual Meeting of the Cognitive Science Society*, 203–208.

D3 Publisher. (2007). Puzzle Quest. Los Angeles: D3

Daniels, L., Borchert, O., Hokanson, G., Clark, J., Saini-Eidukat, B., Schwert, D., et al. *(2009). Effects of immersive virtual environments on student achievement and confidence. In* Proceedings of the American Educational Research Association Annual Meeting *(AERA-09), April 13-17, San Diego.*

Davis, M. H. (1994). *Empathy: A social psychological approach*. Dubuque, IA: Brown and Benchmark Publishers.

De Corte, E. (1999). On the road to transfer: An introduction. *International Journal of Educational Research, 31*(7), 555–559. doi:10.1016/S0883-0355(99)00023-3

de Crook, M. B. M., van Merriënboer, J. J. G., & Paas, F. G. W. C. (1998). High versus low contextual interference in simulation-based training of troubleshooting skills: Effects on transfer performance and invested mental effort. *Computers in Human Behavior, 14*, 249–267. doi:10.1016/S0747-5632(98)00005-3 de Freitas, S., & Griffiths, M. (2007). Online gaming as an educational tool in learning and training. *British Journal of Educational Technology*, *38*(3), 535–537. doi:10.1111/j.1467-8535.2007.00720.x

De Groot, A. (1965). *Thought and choice in chess*. The Hague, Netherlands: Mouton. (Original work published 1946)

de Jong, T. (2006). Computer simulations: Technological advances in inquiry learning. *Science*, *312*, 532–533. doi:10.1126/science.1127750

de Jong, T., & Van Joolingen, W. R. (1998). Scientific discovery learning with computer simulations of conceptual domains. *Review of Educational Research*, *68*(2), 179–201.

de Jong, T., de Hoog, R., & de Vries, F. (1993). Coping with complex environments: The effects of providing overviews and a transparent interface on learning with a computer simulation. *International Journal of Man-Machine Studies*, *39*(4), 621–639. doi:10.1006/imms.1993.1076

De Lisi, R., & Cammarano, D. M. (1996). Computer experience and gender differences in undergraduate mental rotation performance. *Computers in Human Behavior*, *12*, 351–361. doi:10.1016/0747-5632(96)00013-1

De Lisi, R., & Wolford, J. L. (2002). Improving children's mental rotation accuracy with computer game playing. *The Journal of Genetic Psychology*, *163*, 272–282. doi:10.1080/00221320209598683

Dede, C. J. (1992). The future of multimedia: Bridging to virtual worlds. Educational Technology. *British Journal of Educational Technology*, *38*(3), 535–537.

deGroot, A. D. (1965). *Thought and choice in chess*. The Hague, Netherlands: Mouton.

Dempsey, J. (in press). Elemental learning and the pyramid of fidelity. In Van Eck, R. (Ed.), *Gaming & cognition: Theories and practice from the learning sciences*. Hershey, PA: IGI Global.

Dempsey, J. V. (1986). Using the rational set generator with computer-based instruction for creating concept

examples: A template for instructors. *Educational Technology*, *26*(4), 43–46.

Dempsey, J. V., & Driscoll, M. P. (1996). Error & feedback: The relation between content analysis and confidence of response. *Psychological Reports*, *78*, 1079–1089.

Dempsey, J. V., & Litchfield, B. C. (2001). HyperInquiry: Surfing below the surface of the Web. In Web-based training (pp. 229–234). Englewood Cliffs, NJ: Educational Technology Publications.

Dempsey, J. V., & Van Eck, R. (2003). Modality and placement of a pedagogical adviser in individual interactive learning. *British Journal of Educational Technology*, *34*, 585–600. doi:10.1046/j.0007-1013.2003.00352.x

Dempsey, J. V., Driscoll, M. P., & Litchfield, B. C. (1992). Feedback, retention, discrimination error, and feedback study time. *Journal of Research on Computing in Education*, *25*(2), 303–326.

Dempsey, J. V., Driscoll, M. P., & Swindell, L. (1993). Text-based feedback. In Dempsey, J. V., & Sales, G. C. (Eds.), *Interactive instruction and feedback* (pp. 21–53). Englewood Cliffs, NJ: Educational Technology Publications.

Dempsey, J. V., Haynes, L. L., Lucassen, B. L., & Casey, M. A. (2002). Forty simple computer games and what they could mean to educators. *Simulation & Gaming*, *33*(2), 157–168. doi:10.1177/1046878102332003

Dewey, J. (1910). *How we think*. Boston, D. C.: Heath. doi:10.1037/10903-000

Diamond, M., & Hopson, J. (1998). *Magic trees of the mind*. New York: Penguin.

Diao, Y., & Sweller, J. (2007). Redundancy in foreign language reading comprehension instruction: Concurrent written and spoken presentations. *Learning and Instruction*, *17*, 78–88. doi:10.1016/j.learninstruc.2006.11.007

Dick, W. C., & Carey, L. (1996). *The systematic design of instruction* (4th ed.). New York: Longman.

Dickey, M. D. (2005). Engaging by design: How engagement strategies in popular computer and video games can inform instructional design. *Educational Technology Research and Development*, *53*(2), 67–83. doi:10.1007/BF02504866

Dickey, M. D. (2006). Game design narrative for learning: Appropriating adventure game design narrative devices and techniques for the design of interactive learning environments. *Educational Technology Research and Development*, *54*(3), 245–264. doi:10.1007/s11423-006-8806-y

Din, F. S., & Calao, J. (2001). The effects of playing educational video games on kindergarten achievement. *Child Study Journal*, *31*(2), 95–102.

Dipietro, M., Ferdig, R. E., Boyer, J., & Black, E. W. (2007). Toward a framework for understanding electronic educational gaming. *Journal of Educational Multimedia and Hypermedia*, *16*, 225–248.

Dix, C. *(2000)*. Education, culture, and the transmission of identity: A case study in a central Illinois school. *Unpublished thesis, Dept. Sociology-Anthropology, Illinois State University, Normal, IL. Retrieved from* http://www.soa.ilstu.edu/anthrothesis/dix/

Dobson, M., Ha, D., Mulligan, D., & Ciavarro, C. (2005, June 16–20). *From real-world data to game world experience: Social analysis methods for developing plausible & engaging learning games*. Paper presented at the DiGRA 2005 2nd International Conference, "Changing Views: Worlds in Play," Vancouver, B.C.

Dormann, C., & Biddle, R. (2006). Humour in game-based learning. *Learning, Media & Technology. Special Issue: Digital Games and Learning*, *31*(4), 411–424.

Dorval, M., & Pepin, M. (1986). Effect of playing a video game on a measure of spatial visualization. *Perceptual and Motor Skills*, *62*, 159–162.

Doughty, C., Nielsen, K., & Freynik, S. (2008). *Final report E.3.2: Rosetta Stone findings*. Center for Advanced Study of Language, Univ. of Maryland.

Driver, R., Asoko, H., Leach, J., Mortimer, E., & Scott, P. (1994). Constructing scientific knowledge in the classroom. *Educational Researcher*, *23*(7), 5–12.

Ducheneaut, N., Yee, N., Nickell, E., & Moore, R. (2006). Building an MMO with mass appeal: A look at gameplay in *World of Warcraft. Games and Culture*, *1*, 281–317. doi:10.1177/1555412006292613

Duffy, T. M., & Cunningham, D. J. (1996). Constructivism: Implications for the design and delivery of instruction. In Jonassen, D. H. (Ed.), *Handbook of research for educational communications and technology* (pp. 170–198). New York: Simon & Schuster Macmillan.

Duffy, T. M., Lowyck, J., Jonassen, D. H., & Welch, T. M. (1993). *Designing environments for constructive learning*. New York: Springer-Verlag.

Dweck, C. (2000). *Self-theories: Their role in motivation, personality, and development*. New York: Psychology Press.

Dweck, C. (2006). *Mindset: The new psychology of success*. New York: Random House.

Dweck, C. S., & Leggett, E. L. (1988). A social-cognitive approach to motivation and personality. *Psychological Review*, *95*, 256–273. doi:10.1037/0033-295X.95.2.256

Eastman, C. M., McCracken, W. M., & Newstetter, W. C. (Eds.). (2001). *Design knowing and learning: Cognition in design education*. Amsterdam: Elsevier.

Eatough, V., Davies, M. N. O., Griffiths, M. D., & Chappell, D. (2006). *Everquest*—It's just a computer game right? An interpretative phenomenological analysis of online gaming addiction. *International Journal of Mental Health and Addiction*, 4205–4216.

Ebbinghaus, H. (1885/1962). *Memory: A contribution to experimental psychology*. New York: Dover. Retrieved from http://psychclassics.yorku.ca/Ebbinghaus/index.htm

Ebner, M., & Holzinger, A. (2007). Successful implementation of user-centered game based learning in higher education: An example from civil engineering. *Computers & Education*, *49*(3), 873–890. doi:10.1016/j.compedu.2005.11.026

Edelson, D., Pea, R., & Gomez, L. (1996). Constructivism in the collaboratory. In Wilson, B. G. (Ed.), *Constructiv-*

ist learning environments: Case studies in instructional design (pp. 151–164). Englewood Cliffs, NJ: Educational Technology Publications.

Edstrom, K. (2002). Design for Motivation. In Hazemi, R., & Hailes, S. (Eds.), *The Digital University: Building a Learning Community* (pp. 193–202). London: Springer.

Egenfeldt-Nielsen, S. (2005). *Beyond edutainment: Exploring the educational potential of computer games.* Unpublished dissertation, IT University Copenhagen, Copenhagen.

Egenfeldt-Nielsen, S. (2007). *Educational potential of computer games.* New York: Continuum.

Egenfeldt-Nielsen, S., Smith, J. H., & Tosca, S. P. (2008). *Understanding video games: The essential introduction.* New York: Routledge.

Elliot, E. S., & Church, M. A. (1997). A hierarchal model of approach and avoidance achievement motivation. *Journal of Personality and Social Psychology, 72,* 218–232. doi:10.1037/0022-3514.72.1.218

Ellis, H., Heppell, S., Kirriemuir, J., Krotoski, A., & McFarlane, A. (2006). *Unlimited learning: The role of computer and video games in the learning landscape.* Retrieved from http://www.elspa.com/assets/files/u/unlimitedlearningtheroleofcomputerandvideogames-int_344.pdf

Ellis, R. (2003). Task-based language learning and teaching. New York: Oxford University Press, USA.

Engeström, Y. (1987). *Learning by expanding: An activity-theoretical approach to developmental research.* Paper presented at the Orienta-Konsultit, Helsinki.

Engeström, Y. (1999). Activity theory and individual and social transformation. In Engeström, Y., Miettinen, R., & Punamäki, P. (Eds.), *Perspectives on activity theory- learning in doing social, cognitive and computational perspectives, part 1: Theoretical issues* (pp. 19–38). Cambridge, UK: Cambridge University Press.

Ensemble Studios. (2005). *Age of Empires III* [Computer game]. USA: Microsoft Game Studios.

Ericsson, K. A., & Kintsch, W. (1995). Long-term working memory. *Psychological Review, 102,* 211–245. doi:10.1037/0033-295X.102.2.211

Fabricatore, C. (2000). *Learning and videogames: An unexplored synergy.* Paper presented at the International Conference of the Association for Educational Communications and Technology, Denver, Colorado.

Federation of American Scientists. (2005). *Harnessing the power of educational games.* Retrieved from http://fas.org/gamesummit/Resources/Summit%20on%20Educational%20Games.pdf

Federation of American Scientists. (2006). Harnessing the power of video games for learning [report]. *Summit on Educational Games.* Federation of American Scientists, Washington, DC. Retrieved from http://fas.org/gamesummit/Resources/Summit%20on%20Educational%20Games.pdf

Firaxis. (2007). *Civilization IV* [Computer game]. USA: 2K Games.

Flowers, M. (2009). *Virtual Cultural Awareness Trainer preliminary design document. Alelo TLT.* LLC.

Förster, J., Higgins, E. T., & Idson, L. C. (1998). Approach and avoidance strength during goal attainment: Regulatory focus and the "goal looms larger" effect. *Journal of Personality and Social Psychology, 75,* 1115–1131. doi:10.1037/0022-3514.75.5.1115

Fortugno, N., & Zimmerman, E. (2005). Learning to play to learn: Lessons in educational game design. *Gamasutra.* Retrieved from http://www.gamasutra.com/features/20050405/zimmerman_01.shtml

Foster, A., & Mishra, P. (2009). Disciplinary knowledge construction while playing a simulation strategy game. In I. Gibson, R. Weber, K. McFerrin, R. Carlsen & D. Willis (Eds.), *Proceedings of Society for Information Technology and Teacher Education International Conference 2009* (pp. 1439-1444). Chesapeake, VA: AACE.

Foster, A., & Mishra, P. (2009). *Disciplinary knowledge construction while playing a simulation strategy game.*

Society for Information Technology & Teacher Education International Conference, March 2–6, Charleston, SC.

Foti, L. T., & Hannafin, R. D. (2008). Games and multimedia in foreign language learning-using back-story in multimedia and avatar-based games to engage foreign language learners: A pilot study. *International Journal of Emerging Technologies in Learning, 3*(3), 40–44.

Franc, C., Lawton, J., & Morton, A. (2008). *EBL for EBL: Enquiry-based learning for an end to boring language learning.* Centre for Excellence in Enquiry-Based Learning, University of Manchester. Retrieved from http://www.campus.manchester.ac.uk/ceebl/projects/casestudies/17.pdf

Freeman, D. (2003). *Creating emotion in games: The craft and art of emotioneering.* New Riders Games.

Freitas, S. d. (2007). Learning in immersive worlds: A review of game based learning. London: Joint Information Systems Committee (JISC).

Friedman, T. L. (2006). The world is flat: A brief history of the twenty-first century (1st Updated and Expanded ed.). New York: Farrar, Straus and Giroux.

Fröbel, F. (1912). *Froebel's chief writings on education* (Fletcher, S. S. F., & Welton, J., Trans.). London: Arnold.

Frontier. (2004). *RollerCoaster Tycoon III* [Computer game]. USA: Atari.

Fullerton, T. (2008). *Game design workshop: A Playcentric approach to creating innovative games* (2nd ed.). Burlington, MA: Elsevier.

Fullerton, T., Swain, C., & Hoffman, S. (2004). *Game design workshop: Designing, prototyping, and playtesting games.* San Francisco: CMP Books.

Gagné, R. M. (1962). *Psychological principles in system development.* New York: Holt, Rinehart & Winston.

Gagné, R. M. (1985). *The conditions of learning and theory of instruction.* Fort Worth, TX: Holt, Rinehart and Winston.

Gagné, R. M., & Driscoll, D. (1988). *Essentials of learning for instruction.* Englewood Cliffs, NJ: Prentice-Hall.

Gagné, R. M., Briggs, L. J., & Wager, W. W. (1992). *Principles of Instructional Design* (4th ed., *Vol. 365*). Fort Worth, TX: Harcourt Brace Jovanovich College Publishers.

Gagnon, D. (1985). Video games and spatial skills: An exploratory study. *Educational Technology and Communication Journal, 33*, 263–275.

Gamberini, L., Alcaniz, M., Barresi, G., Fabregat, M., Ibanez, F., & Prontu, L. (2006). Cognition, technology and games for the elderly: An introduction to ELDERGAMES Project. *PsychNology Journal, 4*, 285–308.

Garcâia-Carbonell, A., Rising, B., Montero, B., & Watts, F. (2001). Simulation/gaming and the acquisition of communicative competence in another language. *Simulation & Gaming, 32*(4), 481–491. doi:10.1177/104687810103200405

Gardner, H. (1983, March 27). When television marries computers [Review of *Pilgrim in the microworld* by Robert Sudnow]. *New York Times,* 12.

Gardner, H. (Producer). (2002 November). *Howard Gardner on multiple intelligences and new forms of assessment.* Podcast retrieved from http://www.glef.org.

Garris, R., Ahlers, R., & Driskell, J. E. (2002). Games, motivation, and learning: A research and practice model. *Simulation & Gaming, 33*(4), 441–467. doi:10.1177/1046878102238607

Gaydos, M., & Squire, K. (in press). Citizen science: Designing a game for the 21st century. In Van Eck, R. (Ed.), *Interdisciplinary models and tools for serious games: Emerging concepts and future directions.* Hershey, PA: IGI Global.

Geary, D. (2002). Principles of evolutionary educational psychology. *Learning and Individual Differences, 12*, 317–345. doi:10.1016/S1041-6080(02)00046-8

Geary, D. (2005). *The origin of mind: Evolution of brain, cognition, and general intelligence.* Washington, DC:

American Psychological Association. doi:10.1037/10871-000

Geary, D. (2007). Educating the evolved mind: Conceptual foundations for an evolutionary educational psychology. In Carlson, J. S., & Levin, J. R. (Eds.), *Psychological perspectives on contemporary educational issues* (pp. 1–99). Greenwich, CT: Information Age Publishing.

Geary, D. (2008). An evolutionarily informed education science. *Educational Psychologist*, *43*, 179–195. doi:10.1080/00461520802392133

Gee, J. P. (2003). *What video games have to teach us about learning and literacy* (1st ed.). New York: Palgrave Macmillan.

Gee, J. P. (2004). Learning by design: Games as learning machines. *Interactive Educational Multimedia*, *8*, 15–23.

Gee, J. P. (2004). *Situated language and learning: A critique of traditional schooling*. New York: Routledge.

Gee, J. P. (2005). What would a state of the art instructional video game look like? *Innovate*, *1*(6). Retrieved from http://www.innovateonline.info/index.php?viewarticle&id=80

Gee, J. P. (2005). *Why are video games good for learning?* [Electronic Version]. Retrieved from http://www.academiccolab.org/resources/documents/Good_Learning.pdf

Gee, J. P. (2006). Learning and games [Electronic Version]. In K. Salen (Ed.), *The ecology of games: connecting youth, games, and learning* (pp. 21-40. Retrieved from http://www.mitpressjournals.org/doi/abs/10.1162/dmal.9780262693646.021

Gee, J. P. (2007). *Good video games + good learning*. New York: Peter Lang Publishing Inc.

Gee, J. P. (2007). *What video games have to teach us about learning and literacy* (2nd ed.). New York: Palgrave/Macmillan.

Gee, J. P. (2007a). Games and learning: Issues, perils and potentials. In Gee, J. P. (Ed.), *Good video games and good learning: Collected essays on video games, learning and literacy (New Literacies and Digital Epistemologies)* (pp. 129–174). New York: Palgrave/Macmillan.

Gee, J. P. (2007b). Learning and Games. In Salen, K. (Ed.), *The ecology of games: Connecting youth, games, and learning* (pp. 21–40). Cambridge, MA: MIT Press.

Gee, J. P. (2008). Video games and embodiment. *Games and Culture*, *3*(3–4), 253–263. doi:10.1177/1555412008317309

Gentile, D. A., Anderson, C. A., Yukawa, S., Ihori, N., Saleem, M., & Ming, L. K. (2009)... *Personality and Social Psychology Bulletin*, *35*, 752–763. doi:10.1177/0146167209333045

Gentner, D. (1983). Structure mapping: A theoretical framework for analogy. *Cognitive Science*, *7*, 155–170.

Gentner, D. (1989). The mechanisms of analogical learning. In Vosniadou, S., & Ortony, A. (Eds.), *Similarity and analogical reasoning* (pp. 199–241). New York: Cambridge University Press. doi:10.1017/CBO9780511529863.011

Gentner, D., & Markman, A. B. (1997). Structure mapping in analogy and similarity. *The American Psychologist*, *52*(1), 45–56. doi:10.1037/0003-066X.52.1.45

Gibbons, A. S. (2000). *The practice of instructional technology*. Paper presented at the Annual International Conference of the Association for Educational Communications and Technology.

Gibson, J. J. (1977). The theory of affordances. In Shaw, R., & Bransford, J. (Eds.), *Perceiving, acting, and knowing: Toward an ecological psychology* (pp. 67–82). Hillsdale, NJ: Lawrence Erlbaum.

Goffman, E. (1959). *The presentation of self in everyday life*. New York: Doubleday.

Gómez-Martín, M., Gómez-Martín, P., & González-Calero, P. (2004). *Game-driven intelligent tutoring systems*. Third International Conference on Entertainment Computing (ICEC). September 1–3, Eindhoven, The Netherlands.

Gould, S. J. (1981). *The mismeasure of man.* New York: W. W. Norton & Company.

Gray, J. R., Braver, T. S., & Raichle, M. E. (2002, March 19). Integration of emotion and cognition in the lateral prefrontal cortex. *Proceedings of the National Academy of Sciences of the United States of America, 99*(6), 4115–4020. doi:10.1073/pnas.062381899

Gray, M. (2008). World of Warcraft hits 11 million subscribers worldwide. *WoW Insider.* Retrieved from http://www.wowinsider.com/2008/10/28/world-of-warcraft-hits-11-million-subscribers-worldwide/

Gredler, M. (1994). *Designing and evaluating games and simulations: A process approach.* Houston, TX: Gulf Publishing Company.

Gredler, M. E. (1996). Educational games and simulations: A technology in search of a research paradigm. In Jonassen, D. H. (Ed.), *Handbook of research on educational communications and technology* (pp. 521–540). New York: Simon & Schuster Macmillan.

Gredler, M. E. (2004). Games and simulations and their relationships to learning. In Jonassen, D. H. (Ed.), *Handbook of research on educational communications and technology* (2nd ed.). Mahwah, NJ: Association for Educational Communications and Technology, Lawrence Erlbaum.

Gredler, M. E. (2009). *Learning and instruction: Theory into practice* (6th ed.). Upper Saddle River, NJ: Pearson Education, Inc.

Green, S., & Bavelier, D. (2003). Action video game modifies visual selective attention. *Nature, 423,* 534–537. doi:10.1038/nature01647

Greenfield, P. M. (1972). Oral or written language: The consequences for cognitive development in Africa, the United States, and England. *Language and Speech, 15,* 169–178.

Greenfield, P. M. (1984). Video games. In *Mind and media: The effects of television, video games, and computers* (pp. 97–126). Cambridge, MA: Harvard University Press.

Greenfield, P. M. (2009). Technology and informal education: What is taught, what is learned. *Science, 323,* 69–71. doi:10.1126/science.1167190

Greenfield, P. M., Brannon, C., & Lohr, D. (1994). Two-dimensional representation of movement through three-dimensional space: The role of video game expertise. *Journal of Applied Developmental Psychology, 15,* 87–103. doi:10.1016/0193-3973(94)90007-8

Greenfield, P. M., Camaioni, L., Ercolani, P., Weiss, L., Lauber, B., & Perucchini, P. (1994). Cognitive socialization by computer games in two cultures: Inductive discovery or mastery of an iconic code? *Journal of Applied Developmental Psychology, 15,* 59–85. doi:10.1016/0193-3973(94)90006-X

Greenfield, P. M., deWinstanley, P., Kilpatrick, H., & Kaye, D. (1994). Action video games and informal education: Effects on strategies for dividing visual attention. *Journal of Applied Developmental Psychology, 15,* 105–123. doi:10.1016/0193-3973(94)90008-6

Greeno, J. G. (1997). On claims that answer the wrong questions. *Educational Researcher, 26*(1), 5–17.

Griffiths, M., Davies, N., & Chappell, D. (2004). Online computer gaming: A comparison of adolescent and adult gamers. *Journal of Adolescence, 27,* 87–96. doi:10.1016/j.adolescence.2003.10.007

Grodal, T. (2000). Video games and the pleasures of control. In Zillmann, D., & Vorderer, P. (Eds.), *Media entertainment: The psychology of its appeal.* Mahwah, NJ: Lawrence Erlbaum Associates.

Guimarães, M. J. L., Jr. (2001). Investigating physical performance in cyberspace: Some notes about methods. *Middlesex, UK: Centre for Research into Innovation, Culture and Technology, Brunel University, Uxbridge.* Retrieved at http://www.brunel.ac.uk/depts/crict/vmpapers/mario.html

Gunawardena, L., & McIsaac, M. (2003). Theory of distance education. In Jonassen, D. H. (Ed.), *Handbook of research for educational communications and technology.* New York: Simon and Schuster Macmillan.

Gunter, G. A., Kenny, R. F., & Vick, E. H. (2008). Taking educational games seriously: Using the RETAIN model to design endogenous fantasy into standalone educational games. *Educational Technology Research and Development*, *56*, 511–537. doi:10.1007/s11423-007-9073-2

Gunter, G., Kenny, R., & Vick, E. (2006). A case for a formal design paradigm for serious games. *The Journal of the International Digital Media and Arts Association*, *3*(1), 93–105.

Habgood, M. P. J., Ainsworth, S. E., & Benford, S. (2005). Endogenous fantasy and learning in digital games. *Simulation & Gaming*, *36*(4), 483–498. doi:10.1177/1046878105282276

Hadziomerovic, A., & Biddle, R. (2006, October 10–12). *Tracking engagement in a role play game.* Paper presented at the Future Play, The International Conference on the Future of Game Design and Technology, The University of Western Ontario, London, Ontario, Canada.

Hallford, N., & Hallford, J. (2001). *Swords & circuitry: A designers guide to computer role playing games.* Roseville, CA: Prima Publishing.

Han, S. (1988). The relationship beween life satisfaction and flow in elderly Korean immigrants. In Csikszentmihalyi, M., & Csikszentmihalyi, I. S. (Eds.), *Optimal experience: Psychological studies of flow in consciousness* (pp. 138–149). New York: Cambridge University Press.

Hankinson, W. (2007). Stage Two: Early Moon Formation. In Reese, D. D. (Ed.), *The Collected Selene (Classic) Game and Research Environment Design Documentation* (pp. 184–186). Wheeling, WV: Wheeling Jesuit University.

Hannafin, M. J. (1992). Emerging technologies, ISD, and learning environments: Critical perspectives. In Ely, D., & Plomp, T. (Eds.), *Classic writings on instructional technology* (*Vol. 2*, pp. 95–112). Englewood, CO: Libraries Unlimited, Inc.

Hannafin, M. J., & Peck, K. (1988). *The design, development and evaluation of instructional software.* New York: MacMillan Publishing Company.

Hannafin, M. J., Hannafin, K. M., Hooper, S. R., Rieber, L. P., & Kini, A. S. (1996). Research on and research

with emerging technologies. In Jonassen, D. H. (Ed.), *Handbook of research for educational communications and technology* (pp. 378–402). New York: Simon & Schuster.

Hannafin, M. J., Land, S., & Oliver, K. (1999). Open learning environments: Foundations, methods, and models. In Reigeluth, C. M. (Ed.), *Instructional-design theories and models* (pp. 115–140). Mahwah, NJ: Lawrence Erlbaum.

Harden, R. M., & Stamper, N. (1999). What is a spiral curriculum? *Medical Teacher*, *21*(2), 141–143. doi:10.1080/01421599979752

Harris, M. (1968). *The rise of anthropological theory.* New York: Crowell.

Hatches, P. L. (2005). *The effects of wrist proprioception on joint stability for forward falls.* Unpublished thesis, West Virginia University, Morgantown, WV.

Heeter, C., & Winn, B. (2008). Implications of fender, player type and learning strategies for the design of games for learning. In Kafai, Y., Heeter, C., Denner, J., & Sun, J. (Eds.), *Beyond Barbie to Mortal Combat: New perspectives on games, gender, and computing.* Cambridge, MA: MIT Press.

Heeter, C., Chu, C. K., Maniar, A., Winn, B., Punya, M., Egidio, R., & Portwood-Stacer, L. (2003, 4–6 November). *Comparing 14 plus 2 forms of fun (and learning and gender issues) in commercial versus educational space exploration digital games.* Paper presented at the International Digital Games Research Conference, University of Utrecht: Netherlands.

Heeter, C., Egidio, R., Mishra, P., Winn, B., & Winn, J. (2009). Alien games: Do girls prefer games designed by girls? *Games and Culture*, *4*(1), 74–100. doi:10.1177/1555412008325481

Heeter, C., Magerko, B., Medler, B., & Fitzgerald, J. (2009). Game design and the challenge-avoiding "validator" player type. *International Journal of Gaming and Computer-Mediated Simulations*, *1*(3), 53–67.

Heeter, C., Winn, B. M., & Greene, D. D. (2005). *Theories meet realities: Designing a learning game for girls.* Paper presented at the Proceedings of the 2005 conference on Designing for User eXperience.

Heeter, C., Winn, B., Winn, J., & Bozoki, A. (2008). *The challenge of challenge: Avoiding and embracing difficulty in a memory game.* Meaningful Play Conference, October 9–11, East Lansing, MI.

Hektner, J. M., Schmidt, J. A., & Csikszentmihalyi, M. (2007). *Experience sampling method: Measuring the quality of everyday life.* Thousand Oaks, CA: Sage.

Henderlong, J., & Lepper, M. (2002). The effects of praise on children's intrinsic motivation: A review and synthesis. *Psychological Bulletin, 128*, 774–795. doi:10.1037/0033-2909.128.5.774

Hendriksen, T. D. (2006). *Educational role-play: Moving beyond entertainment. Seeking to please or aiming for the stars.* Conference paper presented at "On Playing Roles" Seminar, Tampere, FL.

Hestenes, D., Wells, M., & Swackhamer, G. (1992). Force concept inventory. *The Physics Teacher, 30*, 141–158. doi:10.1119/1.2343497

Heylighen, F., & Joslyn, C. (2001). Cybernetics and second-order cybernetics. In Meyers, R. A. (Ed.), *Encyclopedia of physical science & technology* (3rd ed., p. 24). New York: Academic Press.

Higgins, E. T. (2000). Making a good decision: Value from fit. *The American Psychologist, 55*, 1217–1230. doi:10.1037/0003-066X.55.11.1217

Higgins, E. T. (2005). Value from regulatory fit. *Current Directions in Psychological Science, 14*, 209–213. doi:10.1111/j.0963-7214.2005.00366.x

Higgins, E. T. (2006). Value from hedonic experience and engagement. *Psychological Review, 113*(3), 439–460. doi:10.1037/0033-295X.113.3.439

Hill, M. (2005). *The RPG evolution.* Retrieved from http://iml.jou.ufl.edu/projects/Spring05/Hill/

Hillyard, S. A. (2008). Event-related potentials (ERPs) and cognitive processing. In Squire, L. R. (Ed.), *Encyclopedia of neuroscience* (3rd ed., pp. 13–18). San Diego, CA: Academic Press.

Hoffman, B., & Ritchie, D. (1997). Using multimedia to overcome the problems with problem based learning. *Instructional Science, 27*(25), 97–115. doi:10.1023/A:1002967414942

Hoffman, J. (2003). Anticipatory behavior control. In Butz, M. V., Sigaud, O., & Gerard, P. (Eds.), *Anticipatory behavior in adaptive learning systems.* Berlin: Springer.

Hoffman, M. (2000). *Empathy & moral development: Implications for caring and justice.* New York: Cambridge University Press.

Hoffmann, J., Stoecker, C., & Kunde, W. (2004). Anticipatory control of actions. *International Journal of Sport and Exercise Psychology, 2*(4), 346–361.

Hogan, R. (1969). Development of an empathy scale. *Journal of Consulting and Clinical Psychology, 33*, 307–316. doi:10.1037/h0027580

Hokanson, G., Borchert, O., Slator, B. M., Terpstra, J., Clark, J. T., Daniels, L. M., et al. (2008). *Studying Native American culture in an immersive virtual environment. In* Proceedings of the IEEE International Conference on Advanced Learning Technologies *(ICALT-2008) (pp. 788-792). Washington, DC: IEEE Computer Society Press.*

Holland, J. H. (1996). *Hidden order: How adaptation builds complexity.* Reading, MA: Addison–Wesley.

Holyoak, K. J., & Thagard, P. (1995). Mental leaps analogy in creative thought

Huang, W. D., & Johnson, J. (2009). Let's get serious about E-games: A design research approach towards emergence perspective. In Cope, B., & Kalantzis, M. (Eds.), *Ubiquitous learning.* Champaign, IL: University of Illinois Press.

Huang, W. D., & Johnson, T. (2008). Instructional game design using Cognitive Load Theory. In Ferdig, R. (Ed.), *Handbook of research on effective electronic gaming in education.* Hershey, PA: Information Science Reference.

Hubka, V., & Eder, W. E. (1988). *Theory of technical systems.* Berlin: Springer–Verlag.

Huizinga, J. (1950). *Homo Ludens: a study of the play element in culture.* New York: Roy Publishers.

Hung, W., & Van Eck, R. (in press). Aligning problem solving and gameplay: A model for future research and design. In Van Eck, R. (Ed.), *Interdisciplinary models and tools for serious games: Emerging concepts and future directions.* Hershey, PA: IGI Global.

Hunn, E. (1982). The utilitarian factor in folk biological classification. *American Anthropologist, 84*(4), 830–847. doi:10.1525/aa.1982.84.4.02a00070

Hussain, Z., & Griffiths, M. D. (2008). Gender swapping and socializing in cyberspace: An exploratory study. *Cyberpsychology & Behavior, 11*(1), 47–53. doi:10.1089/cpb.2007.0020

Huston, A. C., & Wright, J. C. (1983). Children's processing of television: The informative functions of formal features. In Bryant, J., & Anderson, D. R. (Eds.), *Watching TV, Understanding TV: Research on children's attention and comprehension.* New York: Academic Press.

Immordino-Yang, M. H., & Damasio, A. (2008). *We feel, therefore we learn: The relevance of affective and social neuroscience to education. In the brain and learning. The Jossey-Bass reader.* San Francisco: Jossey-Bass.

Impact Games, L. L. C. (2008). *Play the News* [Video game]. Pittsburgh, PA: Impact Games.

Inouye, D., Merrill, P., & Swan, R. H. (2005). Help: Toward a new ethics-centered paradigm for instructional design and technology. *IDT Record.* Retrieved from http://www.indiana.edu/~idt/

Institute for Creative Technologies. (2009). *Full spectrum warrior.* Retrieved from http://ict.usc.edu/projects/full_spectrum_warrior

Instructional Technology Council. (2008). *2007 Distance education survey results* [report]. Retrieved from http://4.79.18.250/file.php?file=/1/ITCAnnualSurvey-March2008.pdf

Iuppa, N., & Borst, T. (2007). *Story and simulations for serious games: Tales from the trenches.* Oxford, UK: Elsevier.

Jacobs, J. W., & Dempsey, J. V. (1993). Simulation and gaming: Fidelity, feedback, and motivation. In Dempsey, J. V., & Sales, G. C. (Eds.), *Interactive instruction and feedback* (pp. 197–228). Englewood Cliffs, NJ: Educational Technology Publications.

Jacobs, J. W., Dempsey, J. V., & Salisbury, D. F. (1990). An attention reduction training model: Educational and technological applications. *Journal of Artificial Intelligence in Education, 1*(4), 41–50.

Jakobsson, M., & Taylor, T. (2003). *The Sopranos meets EverQuest: Social networking in massively multiplayer online games.* Melbourne International Digital Arts and Culture Conference (MelbourneDAC). Retrieved from http://hypertext.rmit.edu.au/dac/papers/Jakobsson.pdf

Jeung, H., Chandler, P., & Sweller, J. (1997). The role of visual indicators in dual sensory mode instruction. *Educational Psychology, 17*, 329–343. doi:10.1080/0144341970170307

Joensuu, H. (2006). *Adaptive control inspired by the cerebellar system.* Unpublished thesis, Helsinki University of Technology, Finland, Helsinki.

Johnson, W. L. (2007). Serious use of a serious game for language learning. *Artificial Intelligence in Education: Building Technology Rich Learning Contexts that. Work (Reading, Mass.)*, 67.

Johnson, W. L., & Beal, C. (2005). Iterative evaluation of a large-scale, intelligent game for language learning. In C.-K. Looi et al. (Eds.), *Proceedings of the International Conference on Artificial Intelligence in Education* (pp. 290-297). Amsterdam: IOS Press.

Johnson, W. L., & Wu, S. (2008). Assessing aptitude for learning with a serious game for foreign language and culture. In *Intelligent Tutoring Systems* (pp. 520–529). Berlin: Springer-Verlag. doi:10.1007/978-3-540-69132-7_55

Johnson, W. L., Rickel, J. W., & Lester, J. C. (2000). Animated pedagogical agents: Face-to-face interaction in interactive learning environments. *International Journal of Artificial Intelligence in Education, 11*(1), 47–78.

Johnson, W. L., Vilhjálmsson, H., & Marsella, S. (2005). *Serious games for language learning: How much game, how much AI?* 12th International Conference on Artificial Intelligence in Education. July 18–22, Amsterdam, The Netherlands.

Johnson, W. L., Wang, N., & Wu, S. (2007). *Experience with serious games for learning foreign languages and cultures.* Paper presented at the SimTecT 2007, Brisbane, Queensland, Australia.

Johnson-Laird, P. N., & Oatley, K. (2000). Cognitive & social construction in emotions. In Lewis, M., & Haviland-Jones, J. M. (Eds.), *Handbook of emotions* (2nd ed.). New York: The Guildford Press.

Jonassen, D. H. (1991). Objectivism versus constructivism: Do we need a new philosophical paradigm? In Ely, D. P., & Plomp, T. (Eds.), *Classic writings on instructional technology* (*Vol. 2*, pp. 53–65). Englewood, CO: Libraries Unlimited, Inc.

Jonassen, D. H. (1992). Cognitive flexibility theory and its implications for designing CBI. In Dijkstra, S., Krammer, H., & van Merriënboer, J. (Eds.), *Instructional models in computer-based learning environments* (pp. 385–403). Berlin: Springer.

Jonassen, D. H. (1997). Instructional design models for well-structured and ill-structured problem-solving learning outcomes. *Educational Technology Research and Development, 45*(1), 65–94. doi:10.1007/BF02299613

Jonassen, D. H. (1999). Designing constructivist learning environments. In Reigeluth, C. M. (Ed.), *Instructional-design theories and models* (*Vol. 2*). Mahwah, NJ: Lawrence Erlbaum Associates.

Jonassen, D. H. (2000). Toward a design theory of problem solving. *Educational Technology Research and Development, 48*(4), 63. doi:10.1007/BF02300500

Jonassen, D. H. (2006). On the role of concepts in learning and instructional design. *Educational Technology Research and Development, 54*(2), 177–196. doi:10.1007/s11423-006-8253-9

Jonassen, D. H., & Carr, C. S. (2000). Mindtools: Affording multiple knowledge representations for learning. In S. P. LaJoie (Ed.), Computers as cognitive tools, Volume II: No more walls. Mahwah, NJ: Lawrence Erlbaum Associates.

Jonassen, D. H., & Ionas, I. G. (2008). Designing effective supports for causal reasoning. *Educational Technology Research and Development, 56*(3), 287–308. doi:10.1007/s11423-006-9021-6

Jonassen, D. H., & Reeves, T. C. (1996). Learning with technology: Using computers as cognitive tools. In Jonassen, D. H. (Ed.), *Handbook of research for educational communications and technology* (pp. 693–719). New York: Simon & Schuster Macmillan.

Jonassen, D. H., Carr, C. S., & Yeuh, H. (1998). Computers as mindtools for engaging learners in critical thinking. *TechTrends, 43*(2), 24–32. doi:10.1007/BF02818172

Jonassen, D. H., Cernusca, D., & Ionas, G. (2007). Constructivism and instructional design: The emergence of the learning sciences and design research. In Reiser, R. A., & Dempsey, J. V. (Eds.), *Trends and issues in instructional design and technology* (2nd ed.). Upper Saddle River, NJ: Pearson.

Jones, K. (1984). Simulations versus professional educators. In Jaques, D., & Tippen, E. (Eds.), *Learning for the future with games and simulations* (pp. 45–50). Loughborough, UK: SAGSET/Loughborough, University of Technology.

Jones, K. (1987). *Simulations: A handbook for teachers and trainers.* London: Kogan Page.

Juel, C. (1991). Cross-age tutoring between student athletes and at-risk children. *The Reading Teacher, 45*(3), 178–186.

Juul, J. (2003). *The game, the player, the world: Looking for a heart of gameness.* Paper presented at the Digital Games Research Conference, Utrecht: Utrecht University.

Juul, J. (2005). *Half-real. Video games between real rules and fictional worlds.* Cambridge, MA: MIT Press.

Juul, J. (2005). *Half-real: Video games between real rules and fictional worlds*. Cambridge, MA: MIT Press.

Kafai, Y. B. (2006). Playing and making games for learning: Instructionist and constructionist perspectives for game studies. *Games and Culture*, *1*(1), 36–40. doi:10.1177/1555412005281767

Kafai, Y., Heeter, C., Denner, J., & Sun, J. (Eds.). (2008). *Beyond Barbie and Mortal Kombat: New perspectives on gender and gaming*. Cambridge, MA: MIT Press.

Kahn, T. M. (1981). *An analysis of strategic thinking using a computer-based game*. Ph.D. dissertation, University of California, Berkeley.

Kalyuga, S., & Sweller, J. (2004). Measuring knowledge to optimize cognitive load factors during instruction. *Journal of Educational Psychology*, *96*, 558–568. doi:10.1037/0022-0663.96.3.558

Kalyuga, S., & Sweller, J. (2005). Rapid dynamic assessment of expertise to improve the efficiency of adaptive e-learning. *Educational Technology Research and Development*, *53*, 83–93. doi:10.1007/BF02504800

Kalyuga, S., Ayres, P., Chandler, P., & Sweller, J. (2003). The expertise reversal effect. *Educational Psychologist*, *38*(1), 23–31. doi:10.1207/S15326985EP3801_4

Kalyuga, S., Chandler, P., & Sweller, J. (1999). Managing split attention and redundancy in multimedia instruction. *Applied Cognitive Psychology*, *13*, 351–371. doi:10.1002/(SICI)1099-0720(199908)13:4<351::AID-ACP589>3.0.CO;2-6

Kaptelinin, V., & Nardi, B. (2006). *Acting with technology: Activity theory and interaction design*. Boston, MA: MIT Press.

Karat, J. (1995). Scenario use in the design of a speech recognition system. In Carroll, J. (Ed.), *Scenarios as design representations* (pp. 109–133). London: Academic Press.

Katona, G. (1940). *Organizing and memorizing*. New York: Columbia University Press.

Katzeff, C. (2000). *The design of interactive media for learners in an organisational setting–the state of the art*. Paper presented at the Nordic Interactive Conference, Copenhagen, Denmark.

Kay, A. (2007). The real computer revolution hasn't happened yet (VPRI Memo M-2007-007-a). (Viewpoints Research Institute, Ed.).

Kearney, P. R. (2005). Cognitive calisthenics: Do FPS computer games enhance the player's cognitive abilities? *Proceedings of the DIGRA World Conference*.

Kebritchi, M. (2008). *Effects of a computer game on mathematics achievement and class motivation: An experimental study*. Unpublished doctoral dissertation University of Central Florida, FL, USA.

Kebritchi, M., & Hirumi, A. (2008). Examining the pedagogical foundations of modern educational computer games. *Computers & Education*, *51*, 1729–1743. doi:10.1016/j.compedu.2008.05.004

Kelly, G. A. (1955/1963). *Theory of personality: The psychology of personal constructs*. New York: WW Norton & Company.

Khalil, M., Paas, F., Johnson, T. E., & Payer, A. (2005). Design of interactive and dynamic anatomical visualizations: The implication of cognitive load theory. *Anatomical Record. Part B, New Anatomist*, *286B*, 15–20. doi:10.1002/ar.b.20078

Kickmeier-Rust, M. D., Schwarz, D., Albert, D., Verpoorten, D., Castaigne, J. L., & Bopp, M. (2006). The ELEKTRA project: Towards a new learning experience. In Pohl, M., Holzinger, A., Motschnig, R., & Swertz, C. (Eds.), *M3 – Interdisciplinary aspects on digital media & education* (*Vol. 3*, pp. 19–48). Vienna: Österreichische Computer Gesellschaft.

Kiili, K. (2007). Foundation for problem-based gaming. *British Journal of Educational Technology*, *38*(3), 394–404. doi:10.1111/j.1467-8535.2007.00704.x

Killi, K. (2005). Digital game-based learning: Towards an experiential gaming model. *The Internet and Higher Education*, *8*(1), 13–24. doi:10.1016/j.iheduc.2004.12.001

Kim, J. (2008). *Narrative or tabletop RPGs*. Retrieved from http://www.darkshire.net/~jhkim/rpg/whatis/tabletop.html

Kim, Y., & Baylor, A. L. (2006). A social-cognitive framework for pedagogical agents as learning companions. *Educational Technology Research and Development, 54*(6), 569–596. doi:10.1007/s11423-006-0637-3

Kirkpatrick, D. L. (1994). *Evaluating training programs: The four levels*. San Francisco, CA: Berrett-Koehler.

Kirriemuir, J., & McFarlane, A. (2004). *Literature review in games and learning*. Retrieved from http://www.nestafuturelab.org/research/reviews/08_01.htm

Kirriemuir, J., & McFarlane, A. (2004). Literature review in games and learning. *Futurelab Series, Report 8*, 35. Retrieved from http://www.futurelab.org.uk/research/lit_reviews.htm

Kirschner, P. A., Sweller, J., & Clark, R. E. (2006). Why minimal guidance during instruction does not work: An analysis of the failure of constructivist, discovery, problem-based, experiential, and inquiry-based teaching. *Educational Psychologist, 41*, 75–86. doi:10.1207/s15326985ep4102_1

Klabbers, J. H. G. (2000). Learning as acquisition and learning as interaction. *Simulation & Gaming, 31*(3), 380–406. doi:10.1177/104687810003100304

Knowles, M. S. (1984). *Andragogy in action*. San Francisco: Jossey-Bass.

Koedinger, K. R., Anderson, J. R., Hadley, W. H., & Mark, M. A. (1997). Intelligent tutoring goes to school in the big city. *Journal of Artificial Intelligence in Education, 8*, 30–43.

Kort, B., Reilly, R., & Picard, R. W. (2001). An affective model of interplay between emotions and learning: Reengineering educational pedagogy—building a learning companion. In *Proceedings of the International Conference on Advanced Learning Technologies (ICALT 2001)*.

Koster, R. (2005). *A theory of fun for game design*. Scottsdale, AZ: Paraglyph Press.

Kozma, R. B. (1994). Will media influence learning? Reframing the debate. *Educational Technology Research and Development, 42*(2), 7–19. doi:10.1007/BF02299087

Krathwohl, D. R. (2002). A revision of Bloom's taxonomy: An overview. *Theory into Practice, 41*(4), 212–218. doi:10.1207/s15430421tip4104_2

Kulhavy, R. W. (1977). Feedback in written instruction. *Review of Educational Research, 47*, 211–232.

Kulhavy, R. W., & Stock, W. A. (1989). Feedback in written instruction: The place of response certitude. *Educational Psychology Review, 1*(4), 279–308. doi:10.1007/BF01320096

Kurtz, K. J., Miao, C.-H., & Gentner, D. (2001). Learning by analogical bootstrapping. *Journal of the Learning Sciences, 10*(4), 417–446. doi:10.1207/S15327809JLS1004new_2

Kuutti, K. (1995). Work processes: Scenarios as a preliminary vocabulary. In Carroll, J. M. (Ed.), *Scenario-based design: Envisioning work and technology in system development* (pp. 19–36). New York: John Wiley and Sons.

Laboratory of Comparative Human Cognition. (1982). A model system for the study of learning difficulties. *Quarterly Newsletter of the Laboratory of Comparative Human Cognition, 4*, 39–66.

Lakoff, G., & Johnson, M. (1980). *Metaphors we live by*. Chicago, IL: University of Chicago Press.

Lakoff, G., & Johnson, M. (1999). *Philosophy in the flesh: The embodied mind and its challenge to Western thought*. New York: Basic Books.

Land, S., & Hannafin, M. (2000). Student-centered learning environments. In Jonassen, D. H., & Land, S. (Eds.), *Theoretical foundations of learning environments*. Mahwah, NJ: Lawrence Erlbaum Associates.

Lane, H. C., Core, M. G., Gomboc, D., Karnavat, A., & Rosenberg, M. (2007). *Intelligent tutoring for interpersonal and intercultural skills.* Interservice/Industry Training, Simulation, and Education Conference (I/ITSEC). November 26–29, Orlando, FL.

Langhoff, S., Cowan-Sharp, J., Dodson, E., Damer, B., Ketner, B., & Reese, D. D. (2009). *Workshop report: Virtual worlds and immersive environments (No. NASA/CP–2009-214598).* Moffett Field, CA: NASA Ames Research Center.

Lantolf, J. P., & Thorne, S. L. (2006). *Sociocultural theory and the genesis of second language development.* Oxford, UK: Oxford University Press.

Larkin, J. H., McDermott, J., Simon, D. P., & Simon, H. A. (1980). Models of competence in solving physics problems. *Cognitive Science: A Multidisciplinary Journal, 4*(4), 317–345.

Lauber, B. A. (1983). *Adolescent video game use.* Unpublished paper, Department of Psychology, University of California, Los Angeles.

Laurel, B. (1993). *Computers as theatre* (2nd ed.). Reading, MA: Addison–Wesley.

Laurel, B., Strickland, R., & Tow, R. (1994). Placeholder: Landscape and Narrative in virtual environments. *ACM SIGGRAPH Computer Graphics, 28*(2), 118 126. doi:10.1145/178951.178967

Lave, J. (1988). *Cognition in practice.* New York: Cambridge University Press. doi:10.1017/CBO9780511609268

Lave, J., & Wenger, E. (1991). *Situated learning: Legitimate peripheral participation.* New York: Cambridge University Press.

Lee, F. K., Sheldon, K. M., & Turban, D. B. (2003). Personality and the goal striving process: The influence of achievement goal patterns, goal level, and mental focus on performance and enjoyment. *The Journal of Applied Psychology, 88,* 256–265. doi:10.1037/0021-9010.88.2.256

Leigh, E. (2003). *A practitioner researcher perspective on facilitating an open, infinite, chaordic simulation.*

Learning to engage with theory while putting myself into practice. Unpublished doctoral dissertation, University of Technology, Sydney.

Lenhart, A., Kahne, J., Middaugh, E., Evans, C., & Vitek, J. (2008). Teens' gaming experiences are diverse and include significant social interaction and civic engagement. *Pew Internet and American Life Project.* Retrieved April 2, 2009, from http://www.pewinternet.org/~/media//Files/Reports/2008/PIP_Teens_Games_and_Civics_Report_FINAL.pdf

Leontiev, A. N. (1978). *Activity, consciousness, and personality.* Englewood Cliffs, NJ: Prentice–Hall.

Leontiev, A. N. (1981). *Problems of the development of the mind.* Moscow: Progress.

Lepper, M. R. (1988). Motivational considerations in the study of instruction. *Cognition and Instruction, 5*(4), 289–309. doi:10.1207/s1532690xci0504_3

Lepper, M. R., & Cordova, D. L. (1992). A desire to be taught: Instructional consequences of intrinsic motivation. *Motivation and Emotion, 16*(3), 187–208. doi:10.1007/BF00991651

Lepper, M. R., & Henderlong, J. (2000). Turning "play" into "work" and "work" into "play": 25 years of research on intrinsic versus extrinsic motivation. In Sansone, C., & Harackiewicz, J. M. (Eds.), *Intrinsic and extrinsic motivation: The search for optimal motivation and performance* (pp. 257–307). San Diego, CA: Academic Press. doi:10.1016/B978-012619070-0/50032-5

Lester, J. C., Converse, S. A., Kahler, S. E., Barlow, S. T., Stone, B. A., & Bhoga, R. S. (1997). The persona effect: Affective impact of animated pedagogical agents. In *Proceedings of 1997 Conference on Human Factors in Computing Systems.* Retrieved from http://www.acm.org/sigchi/chi97/proceedings/paper/jl.htm

Levin, J. A., & Kareev, Y. (1980). Problem solving in everyday situations. *Quarterly Newsletter of the Laboratory of Comparative Human Cognition, 2,* 47–52.

Leyland, B. (1996, 2–4 December). *How can computer games offer deep learning and still be fun?* Paper presented at the ASCILITE 96, Adelaide, South Australia.

Lieberman, D. A. (2006). Can we learn from playing interactive games? In Vorderer, P., & Bryant, J. (Eds.), *Playing video games: Motives, responses, & consequences*. Mahwah, NJ: Lawrence Erlbaum Associates.

Lo, S., Wang, C., & Fang, W. (2005). Physical Interpersonal Relationships and Social Anxiety among Online Game Players. *Cyberpsychology & Behavior, 8*(1), 15–20. doi:10.1089/cpb.2005.8.15

Locatis, C. (in press). Performance, instruction, and technology in health care education. In Reiser, R. A., & Dempsey, J. V. (Eds.), *Trends and issues in instructional design and technology* (3rd ed.). Upper Saddle River, NJ: Merrill Education/Prentice–Hall.

Loughney, P. G. (1990). In the beginning was the word: Six pre-griffith motion picture scenarios. In Elsaesser, T. (Ed.), *Early cinema: space, frame, narrative* (pp. 211–219). London: BFI Publishing.

Low, R. (in press). Examining motivational factors in serious educational games. In Van Eck, R. (Ed.), *Interdisciplinary models and tools for serious games: Emerging concepts and future directions*. Hershey, PA: IGI Global.

Low, R. (in press). Examining motivational factors in serious educational games. In Van Eck, R. (Ed.), *Gaming & cognition: Theories and practice from the learning sciences*. Hershey, PA: IGI Global.

Low, R., & Sweller, J. (2005). The modality principle in multimedia learning. In Mayer, R. E. (Ed.), *The Cambridge handbook of multimedia learning* (pp. 147–158). New York: Cambridge University Press.

Low, R., Jin, P., & Sweller, J. (2010). Learner's cognitive load when using education technology. In Van Eck, R. (Ed.), *Interdisciplinary models and tools for serious games: Emerging concepts and future directions*. Hershey, PA: IGI.

Low, R., Sweller, J., & Jin, P. (in press). Learner's cognitive load when using educational technology. In Van Eck, R. (Ed.), *Gaming & cognition: Theories and practice from the learning sciences*. Hershey, PA: IGI Global.

Lucasfilm Ltd. (2009). *Star Wars Galaxies* [Online game]. Sony Online Entertainment.

Macmillan, R. H. (1955). *An introduction to the theory of control in mechanical engineering*. Cambridge, UK: Cambridge University Press.

Magerko, B., Heeter, C., & Medler, B. (in press). Individual differences in students: How to adapt games for better learning experiences. In Van Eck, R. (Ed.), *Gaming & cognition: Theories and practice from the learning sciences*. Hershey, PA: IGI Global.

Magerko, B., Heeter, C., Medler, B., & Fitzgerald, J. (2008). *Intelligent adaptation of digital game-based learning*. Conference on Future Play: Research, Play, Share. Toronto, ON.

Malone, T. W. (1981). Towards a theory of intrinsically motivating instruction. *Cognitive Science, 5*(4), 333–369.

Malone, T. W., & Lepper, M. R. (1987). Making learning fun: A taxonomy of intrinsic motivations for learning. In R. E. Snow & M. J. Farr (Eds.), Aptitude, learning and instruction. Volume 3: Conative and affective process analysis (pp. 223–253). Hillsdale, NJ: Lawrence Erlbaum Associates.

Maloney, J. H., Peppler, K., Kafai, Y., Resnick, M., & Rusk, N. (2008). Programming by choice: Urban youth learning programming with scratch. In *Proceedings of the 39th SIGCSE technical symposium on computer science education* (pp. 367-371).

Mangels, J. A., Butterfield, B., Lamb, J., Good, C. D., & Dweck, C. S. (2006). Why do beliefs about intelligence influence learning success? A social cognitive neuroscience model. [SCAN]. *Social Cognitive and Affective Neuroscience, 1*(2), 75–86. doi:10.1093/scan/nsl013

Mann, D. (2001). Documenting the effects of instructional technology: A fly-over of policy questions. In Heineke, W. F., & Blasi, L. (Eds.), *Research methods for educational technology: Methods of evaluating educational technology* (Vol. 1, pp. 239–249). Greenwich, CT: Information Age Pub.

Markman, A. B., & Gentner, D. (1993). Splitting the difference: A structural alignment view of similarity. *Journal of Memory and Language*, *32*, 517–535. doi:10.1006/jmla.1993.1027

Marsh, T. (2007). *Informing design and evaluation methodologies for serious games for learning.* Presented at *Learning with Games 2007*. France: Sofia Antipolis.

Marsh, T. (in press). Activity-based scenario design, development and assessment in serious games. In Van Eck, R. (Ed.), *Gaming and cognition: Theories and practice from the learning sciences*. Hershey, PA: IGI Global.

Marzano, R. J. (2001). *Designing a new taxonomy of educational objectives*. Thousand Oaks, CA: Corwin Press.

Massimini, F., Csikszentmihalyi, M., & Delle Fave, A. (1988). Flow and biocultural evolution. In Csikszentmihalyi, M., & Csikszentmihalyi, I. S. (Eds.), *Optimal experience: Psychological studies of flow in consciousness* (pp. 60–81). New York: Cambridge University Press.

Mattel. (1996). *Barbie Fashion Designer*. [Video game].

Maxis. (2003) *SimCity IV* [Computer game]. USA: Electronic Arts.

Mayer, R. E. (1999). *The promise of educational psychology*. Upper Saddle River, NJ: Prentice–Hall.

Mayer, R. E. (2001). *Multimedia learning*. New York: Cambridge University Press.

Mayer, R. E. (2005). Introduction to multimedia learning. In Mayer, R. E. (Ed.), *The Cambridge handbook of multimedia learning* (pp. 1–16). New York: Cambridge University Press.

Mayer, R. E. (2005a). Principles for managing essential processing in multimedia learning: Segmenting, pre-training, and modality principles. In Mayer, R. E. (Ed.), *The Cambridge handbook of multimedia learning* (pp. 169–182). New York: Cambridge University Press.

Mayer, R. E. (2005b). Principles for reducing extraneous processing in multimedia learning: Coherence, signaling, redundancy, spatial contiguity, and temporal contiguity principles. In Mayer, R. E. (Ed.), *The Cambridge handbook of multimedia learning* (pp. 183–200). New York: Cambridge University Press.

Mayer, R. E. (2009). *Multimedia learning* (2nd ed.). Cambridge, UK: Cambridge University Press.

Mayer, R. E., & Anderson, R. (1991). Animations need narrations: An experimental test of a dual-coding hypothesis. *Journal of Educational Psychology*, *83*, 484–490. doi:10.1037/0022-0663.83.4.484

Mayer, R. E., & Moreno, R. (1998). A split-attention effect in multi-media learning: Evidence for dual processing systems in working memory. *Journal of Educational Psychology*, *90*, 312–320. doi:10.1037/0022-0663.90.2.312

Mayer, R. E., & Moreno, R. (2002). Aids to computer-based multimedia learning. *Learning and Instruction*, *12*(1), 107–119. doi:10.1016/S0959-4752(01)00018-4

Mayer, R. E., & Moreno, R. (2003). Nine ways to reduce cognitive load in multimedia learning. *Educational Psychologist*, *38*, 43–52. doi:10.1207/S15326985EP3801_6

Mayer, R. E., Heiser, J., & Lonn, S. (2001). Cognitive constraints on multimedia learning: When presenting more material results in less understanding. *Journal of Educational Psychology*, *93*, 187–198. doi:10.1037/0022-0663.93.1.187

Mayer, R. W. (1999). Designing instruction for constructivist learning. In Reigeluth, C. M. (Ed.), *Instructional design theories and models* (*Vol. 141-159*). Mahwah, NJ: Lawrence Erlbaum Associates.

Mayo, M. J. (2009). Video games: A route to large-scale STEM education? *Science*, *323*(5910), 79–82. doi:10.1126/science.1166900

McClean, P., Johnson, C., Rogers, R., Daniels, L., Reber, J., & Slator, B. (2005). Molecular and cellular biology animations: Development and impact on student learning. *Cell Biology Education*, *4*(2), 169–179. doi:10.1187/cbe.04-07-0047

McClean, P., Saini-Eidukat, B., Schwert, D., Slator, B., & White, A. *(2001). Virtual worlds in large enroll-*

ment biology and geology classes significantly improve authentic learning. In J. A. Chambers (Ed.), Selected Papers from the 12th International Conference on College Teaching and Learning *(ICCTL-01) (pp. 111-118)*. *Jacksonville, FL: Center for the Advancement of Teaching and Learning.*

McClelland, J. L. (2000). Connectionist models of memory. In Tulving, E., & Craik, F. I. M. (Eds.), *The Oxford handbook of memory* (pp. 583–596). New York: Oxford University Press.

McCluhan, M. H. (1964). *Understanding media: The extensions of man.* Cambridge, MA: MIT Press.

McClurg, P. A., & Chaillé, C. (1987). Computer games: Environments for developing spatial cognition? *Journal of Educational Computing Research, 3,* 95–111.

McLuhan, M. (1964). *Understanding media: The extensions of man* (1st ed.). New York: McGraw-Hill.

McQuiggan, S. W., Robison, J. L., & Lester, J. C. (2008). Affective transitions in narrative-centered learning environments. *Proceedings of the Ninth International Conference on Intelligent Tutoring Systems,* 490–499.

Medler, B. (2009.). Using recommendation systems to adapt gameplay. *International Journal of Gaming and Computer-Mediated Simulations.*

Merrill, M. D. (2002). First principles of instruction. *Educational Technology Research and Development, 50*(3), 43–59. doi:10.1007/BF02505024

Miller, G. A. (1956). The magical number seven, plus or minus two: Some limits on our capacity for processing information. *Psychological Review, 63,* 81–97. doi:10.1037/h0043158

Miller, G. A., & Gildea, P. M. (1987). How children learn words. *Scientific American, 257*(3), 94–99.

Miller, R., & Fallad, J. (2005). *Constructivist Theory & Social Constructivism. Unpublished class paper.* University of New Mexico.

Miller, W. (1937). The picture crutch in reading. *Elementary English Review, 14,* 263–264.

Minnesota Educational Computer Consortium. (1988). *Number Munchers* [Computer game]. USA: Minnesota Educational Computer Consortium.

Mishra, P., & Foster, A. (2007). *The claims of games: A comprehensive review and directions for future research.* Paper presented at the Society for Information Technology and Teacher Education International Conference 2007, San Antonio, Texas, USA.

Mitchell, A., & Savill-Smith, C. (2004). *The use of computer and video games for learning.* Retrieved from http://www.lsda.org.uk/files/pdf/1529.pdf

Mitchell, E. (1983, May). *A research agenda for the '80s. Conference on video games and human development.* Cambridge, MA: Harvard Graduate School of Education.

Miyamoto, H., Morimoto, J., Doya, K., & Kawato, M. (2004). Reinforcement learning with via-point representation. *Neural Networks, 17*(3), 299–305. doi:10.1016/j.neunet.2003.11.004

MMOG chart.com. (n.d.). Retrieved from http://MMOGchart.com/

Moerman, M. (1969). A little knowledge. In Tyler, S. A. (Ed.), *Cognitive Anthropology* (pp. 449–469). New York, NY: Holt, Rinehart, and Winston, Inc.

Moreno, R. (2005). Multimedia learning with animated pedagogical agents. In Mayer, R. E. (Ed.), *The Cambridge handbook of multimedia learning* (pp. 507–523). New York: Cambridge University Press.

Moreno, R., & Durán, R. (2004). Do multiple representations need explanations? The role of verbal guidance and individual differences in multimedia mathematics learning. *Journal of Educational Psychology, 96,* 492–503. doi:10.1037/0022-0663.96.3.492

Moreno, R., & Mayer, R. E. (1999). Cognitive principles of multimedia learning: The role of modality and contiguity. *Journal of Educational Psychology, 91,* 358–368. doi:10.1037/0022-0663.91.2.358

Moreno, R., & Mayer, R. E. (2002). Learning science in virtual reality multimedia environments. Role of methods and media. *Journal of Educational Psychology, 94,* 598–610. doi:10.1037/0022-0663.94.3.598

Moreno, R., Mayer, R. E., Spires, H. A., & Lester, J. C. (2001). The case for social agency in computer-based teaching: Do students learn more deeply when they interact with animated pedagogical agents? *Cognition and Instruction, 19,* 177–213. doi:10.1207/S1532690X-CI1902_02

Moreno-Ger, P., Burgos, D., Martínez-Orti, I., Sierra, J. L., & Fernández-Manjón, I. (2008). Educational game design for online education. *Computers in Human Behavior, 24,* 2530–2540. doi:10.1016/j.chb.2008.03.012

Morgan, C., & Cotten, S. R. (2003). The relationship between Internet activities and depressive symptoms in a sample of college freshmen. *Cyberpsychology & Behavior, 6,* 133–143. doi:10.1089/109493103321640329

Morris, B. (1994). *Anthropology of the self: The individual in cultural perspective.* Boulder, CO: Pluto Press.

Morrison, H. J. C. (1931). *The practice of teaching in the secondary schools.* Chicago: University of Chicago Press.

Mousavi, S., Low, R., & Sweller, J. (1995). Reducing cognitive load by mixing auditory and visual presentation modes. Journal of Educational Psychology, 87, 319–334. Paas, F., Van Gerven, P., Tabbers, H. K. (2005). The cognitive aging principle in multimedia learning. In R. E. Mayer (Ed.), The Cambridge handbook of multimedia learning (pp. 339–351). New York: Cambridge University Press.

Murmann, J. P., & Frenken, K. (2006). Toward a systematic framework for research on dominant designs, technological innovations, and industrial change. *Research Policy, 35*(7), 925–952. doi:10.1016/j.respol.2006.04.011

Murray, J. H. (1998). *Hamlet on the holodeck: The future of narrative in cyberspace.* Cambridge, MA: MIT Press.

Mussa-Ivaldi, F. A., & Solla, S. A. (2004). Neural primitives for motion control. *IEEE Journal of Oceanic Engineering, 29*(3), 640–650. doi:10.1109/JOE.2004.833102

Mythic Entertainment. (2009). *Ultima Online* [Online game]. Electronic Arts Inc.

Mythic Entertainment. (2009). *Warhammer Online: Age of Reckoning* [Online game]. Electronic Arts Inc.

Nardi, B. (1992). The Use of Scenarios in Design. *ACM SIGCHI Bulletin. International Perspectives: Some Dialogue on Scenarios, 24*(4), 13–14.

Nardi, B. (1995). Some reflections on scenarios. In Carroll, J. (Ed.), *Scenarios as design representations* (pp. 387–399). London: Academic Press.

Nardi, B. (1996). Activity theory and human-computer interaction. In Nardi, B. (Ed.), *Context and consciousness: Activity theory and human-computer interaction* (pp. 7–16). Cambridge, MA: MIT Press.

National Research Council. (1995). *National Science Education Standards.* Washington, DC: National Academy Press.

NCsoft. (2009). *City of Heroes.* [Computer game].

Negroponte, N. (1970). *The architecture machine.* Cambridge, MA: MIT Press.

Neulight, N., Kafai, Y. B., Kao, L., Foley, B., & Galas, C. (2006). Children's participation in a virtual epidemic in the science classroom: Making connections to natural infectious diseases. *Journal of Science Education and Technology, 16*(1), 47–58. doi:10.1007/s10956-006-9029-z

Neverax. (2009). *Saga of Ryzom.* [Computer game]. Winch Gate Property Limited.

Nintendo. (2001). *Animal Crossing.* [Video game]. Kyoto, Japan: Nintendo.

Norman, D. A. (1993). *Things that make us smart: Defending human attributes in the age of the machine.* Reading, MA: Addison-Wesley Pub.

Norman, G. R., & Schmidt, H. G. (2000). Effectiveness of problem-based learning curricula: Theory, practice and paper darts. *Medical Education, 34*(9), 721–728. doi:10.1046/j.1365-2923.2000.00749.x

Novak, J. D., & Gowin, D. B. (1984). *Learning how to learn*. New York: Cambridge University Press.

O'Brian, M., & Levy, R. (2008). Exploration through virtual reality: Encounters with the target culture. *Canadian Modern Language Review, 64*(4), 663–687. doi:10.3138/cmlr.64.4.663

O'Connor, E. (2009). *Alelo Immersive game process document. Alelo TLT*. LLC.

O'Neil, H. F., Wainess, R., & Baker, E. L. (2005). Classification of learning outcomes: Evidence from the computer games literature. *Curriculum Journal, 16*(4), 455–474. doi:10.1080/09585170500384529

Ohlsson, S. (1992). Information processing explanations of insight and related phenomena. In Keane, M. T., & Gilhooly, K. J. (Eds.), *Advances in the psychology of thinking* (pp. 1–44). London: Harvester–Wheatsheaf.

Okagaki, L., & Frensch, P. A. (1994). Effects of video game playing on measures of spatial performance: Gender effects in late adolescence. *Journal of Applied Developmental Psychology, 15*, 33–58. doi:10.1016/0193-3973(94)90005-1

Okey, J. R., & Jones, M. G. (1990). *Learner decisions and information requirements in computer-based instruction*. Paper presented at the International Conference of the Association for the Development of Computer-Based Instructional Systems

Oliver, M., & Pelletier, C. (2004, July). *Activity theory and learning from digital games: Implications for game design*. Paper presented at the Digital Generations: Children, young people and new media, London.

Ortuno, M. M. (1991). Cross-cultural awareness in the foreign language class: The Kluckhohn model. *Modern Language Journal, 75*(4), 449–460. doi:10.2307/329494

Paas, F., Tuovinen, J. E., Tabbers, H., & van Gerven, P. W. M. (2003). Cognitive load measurement as a means to advance cognitive load theory. *Educational Psychologist, 38*, 63–71. doi:10.1207/S15326985EP3801_8

Pajares, F., Hartley, J., & Valiante, G. (2001). Response format in writing self-efficacy assesment: Greater discrimination increases prediction. *Measurement & Evaluation in Counseling & Development, 33*, 214–221.

Pan, C., & Sullivan, M. (2008). Game-based learning: Guidelines, challenges, recommendations. Presented at annual AETC Convention, October, 2008, Orlando, Florida.

Papert, S. (1980). *Mindstorms: children, computers, and powerful ideas*. New York: Basic Books.

Papert, S. (1993). *The children's machine: Rethinking school in the age of the computer*. New York: Basic Books.

Papert, S. (1996). *The connected family: Bridging the digital generation gap*. Atlanta, GA: Longstreet Press.

Papert, S. (1998). Does easy do it? Children, games, and learning. [Soapbox]. *Game Developers Magazine, 88*.

Park, I., & Hannafin, M. J. (1993). Empirically-based guidelines for the design of interactive multimedia. *Educational Technology Research and Development, 41*(3), 63–85. doi:10.1007/BF02297358

Parker, J. R., & Becker, K. (n.d.). *IEEE game bibliography*. Retrieved from http://www.ucalgary.ca/~jparker/TFGT/publications.html

Parker, J. R., Becker, K., & Sawyer, B. (2008, January). Re-reconsidering research on learning from media: Comments on Richard E. Clark's point of view column on serious games. *Educational Technology Magazine*, 39–43.

Pausch, R., Snoddy, J., Taylor, R., Watson, S., & Haseltine, E. (1996). Disney's *Aladdin*: First steps toward storytelling in virtual reality. In Dodsworth, C. Jr., (Ed.), *Digital illusion: Entertaining the future with high technology* (pp. 357–372). London: Addison–Wesley.

Pearce, J., Ainley, M., & Howard, S. (2005). The ebb and flow of online learning. *Computers in Human Behavior, 21*, 745–771. doi:10.1016/S0747-5632(04)00036-6

Pelletier, C., & Oliver, M. (2006). Learning to play in digital games. *Learning, Media & Technology. Special Issue: Digital Games and Learning, 31*(4), 329–342.

Peris, R., Gimeno, M. A., Ibáñez, I., Ortel, G., Peris, R., Pinazo, D., & Sanchiz, M. (2002). Online chat rooms: Virtual spaces of interaction for socially oriented people. *Cyberpsychology & Behavior, 5*, 43–51. doi:10.1089/109493102753685872

Perkins, D. N., & Unger, C. (1999). Teaching and learning for understanding. In Reigeluth, C. M. (Ed.), *Instructional-design theories and models.* Mahwah, NJ: Lawrence Erlbaum.

Peterson, L., & Peterson, M. J. (1959). Short-term retention of individual verbal items. *Journal of Experimental Psychology, 58*, 193–198. doi:10.1037/h0049234

Phillips, D. C. (1995). The good, the bad, and the ugly: The many faces of constructivism. *Educational Researcher, 24*(7), 5–12.

Piaget, J. (1951). *Play, dreams, and imitation in childhood.* New York: Norton.

Piaget, J. (1985). *The equilibration of cognitive structures: The central problem of intellectual development.* Chicago, IL: University of Chicago Press.

Pivec, M. (2007). Play and learn: Potentials of game-based learning. *British Journal of Educational Technology, 38*(3), 387–393. doi:10.1111/j.1467-8535.2007.00722.x

Pivec, P. (2009). *Game-based learning or game-based teaching?* Research report prepared for the BECTA.

Plass, J. L., & Jones, L. C. (2005). Multimedia learning in second language acquisition. In Mayer, R. (Ed.), *The Cambridge handbook of multimedia learning* (p. 467). New York: Cambridge University Press.

Polanyi, M. (1962). *Personal knowledge: Towards a post-critical philosophy.* London: Routledge.

Pollock, E., Chandler, P., & Sweller, J. (2002). Assimilating complex information. *Learning and Instruction, 12*, 61–86. doi:10.1016/S0959-4752(01)00016-0

Poppendieck, M., & Poppendieck, T. D. (2003). *Lean software development: An agile toolkit.* Boston: Addison-Wesley.

Prensky, M. (2001). *Digital game-based learning.* New York: McGraw-Hill Publishing Company.

Prensky, M. (2001b). Digital Natives, Digital Immigrants. *Horizon, 9*(5). Retrieved from http://www.marcprensky.com/writing/Prensky%20-%20Digital%20Natives,%20Digital%20Immigrants%20-%20Part1.pdf.

Prensky, M. (2001c). Digital Natives, Digital Immigrants, Part II: Do They Really Think Differently? *Horizon, 9*(6), 1–6. Retrieved from http://www.marcprensky.com/writing/Prensky%20-%20Digital%20Natives,%20Digital%20Immigrants%20-%20Part2.pdf. doi:10.1108/10748120110424843

Prensky, M. (2006). *Don't Bother Me Mom I'm Learning!* St. Paul, MN: Continuum.

Price, C. B. (2008). Unreal PowerPoint: Immersing PowerPoint presentations in a virtual computer game engine world. *Computers in Human Behavior, 24*, 2486–2495. doi:10.1016/j.chb.2008.03.009

Principe, J. C., Euliano, N. R., & Lefebvre, W. C. (2000). *Neural and adaptive systems: Fundamentals through simulations.* New York: John Wiley & Sons, Inc.

Quilici, J. L., & Mayer, R. E. (1996). Role of examples in how students learn to categorize statistics word problems. *Journal of Educational Psychology, 88*, 144–161. doi:10.1037/0022-0663.88.1.144

Quinn, C. N. (2005). *Engaging learning: Designing e-learning simulation games.* Hoboken, NJ: Pfeiffer.

Raybourn, E. M. (2007). Applying simulation experience design methods to creating serious game-based adaptive training systems. *Interacting with Computers, 19*, 206–214. doi:10.1016/j.intcom.2006.08.001

Reder, L., & Anderson, J. R. (1980). A comparison of texts and their summaries: Memorial consequences. *Journal of Verbal Learning and Verbal Behavior, 19*, 121–134. doi:10.1016/S0022-5371(80)90122-X

Reder, L., & Anderson, J. R. (1982). Effects of spacing and embellishment on memory for main points of a text. *Memory & Cognition, 10*, 97–102.

RedOctane. (2005). *Guitar Hero* [Video game]. Mountain View, CA: RedOctane.

Reed, S. K. (2006). Cognitive architectures for multimedia learning. *Educational Psychologist, 41*, 87–98. doi:10.1207/s15326985ep4102_2

Reese, D. D. (2003a). *Metaphor and content: An embodied paradigm for learning.* Unpublished dissertation, Virginia Polytechnic Institute and State University, Blacksburg, VA.

Reese, D. D. (2003b). Trees of knowledge: Changing mental models through metaphorical episodes and concept maps. In Griffin, R. E., Williams, V. S., & Lee, J. (Eds.), *Turning trees: Selected readings* (pp. 205–214). Loretto, PA: International Visual Literacy Association.

Reese, D. D. (2006a). *Foundations of serious games design and assessment (No. COTF/LVP/Sep-2006).* Wheeling, WV: Center for Educational Technologies, Wheeling Jesuit University.

Reese, D. D. (2006b). *Inspiration Brief 3: Enhancing perceived challenge/skill and achievement (DiSC 2005)* (No. COTF/B3/Mar-2006). Wheeling, WV: Center for Educational Technologies, Wheeling Jesuit University.

Reese, D. D. (2007). First steps and beyond: Serious games as preparation for future learning. *Journal of Educational Multimedia and Hypermedia, 16*, 283–300.

Reese, D. D. (2007b, April). *Increasing flow during middle school science with the e-Mission live simulation and the DiSC argumentation tool.* Roundtable presented at the American Educational Research Association, Chicago.

Reese, D. D. (2008). Engineering instructional metaphors within virtual environments to enhance visualization. In Gilbert, J. K., Nakhleh, M., & Reiner, M. (Eds.), *Visualization: Theory and practice in science education* (pp. 133–153). New York: Springer. doi:10.1007/978-1-4020-5267-5_7

Reese, D. D. (2009a, October 27-31). *Replication supports flowometer: Advancing cyberlearning through game-based assessment technologies.* Paper presented at the 2009 International Conference of the Association for Educational Communications and Technology, Louisville, KY.

Reese, D. D. (2009b). Structure mapping theory as a formalism for instructional game design and assessment. In D. Gentner, K. Holyoak, & B. Kokinov (Eds.), *Proceedings of the 2nd International Analogy Conference* (pp. 394–403). Sofia, Bulgaria: New Bulgarian University Press.

Reese, D. D. (in press). Games to evoke and assess readiness to learn conceptual knowledge. In Van Eck, R. (Ed.), *Gaming & cognition: Theories and prctice from the learning sciences.* Hershey, PA: IGI Global.

Reese, D. D., & Coffield, J. (2005). Just-in-time conceptual scaffolding: Engineering sound instructional metaphors. *International Journal of Technology, Knowledge, and Society, 1*(4), 183–198.

Reese, D. D., & McFarland, L. (2006). *Inspiration brief 2: The DiSC and RoboKids tools and labs (design and testing) (No. COTF/B2/Jan-2006).* Wheeling, WV: Center for Educational Technologies, Wheeling Jesuit University.

Reese, D. D., & Tabachnick, B. G. (2010). *The moment of learning: Quantitative analysis of exemplar gameplay supports CyGaMEs approach to embedded assessment [structured abstract].* Paper to be presented at the Society for Research on Educational Effectiveness 2010 Annual Research Conference, Washington, DC. Retrieved from http://www.sree.org/conferences/2010/program/abstracts/191.pdf

Reese, D. D., Diehl, V. A., & Lurquin, J. L. (2009, May). *Metaphor enhanced instructional video game causes conceptual gains in lunar science knowledge.* Poster presented at the Association for Psychological Science 21st Annual Convention, San Francisco.

Reese, D. D., Kim, B., Palak, D., Smith, J., & Howard, B. (2005). *Inspiration brief 1: Defining inspiration, the Inspiration Challenge, and the informal event (concept paper) (No. COTF/IB1/6-2005).* Wheeling, WV: Wheeling Jesuit University.

Rehak, B. (2003). Playing at being: Psychoanalysis and the avatar. In Wolf, M., & Perron, B. (Eds.), *The video game theory reader.* London: Routledge.

Reigeluth, C. M. (1994). *The imperative for systemic change. Systemic change in education* (pp. 3–11). Englewood Cliffs, NJ: Educational Technology Publications.

Reigeluth, C. M. (Ed.). (1999). *Instructional-design theories and models* (*Vol. II*). Mahwah, NJ: Lawrence Erlbaum Associates.

Reigeluth, C. M., & Frick, T. W. (1999). Formative research: A methodology for creating and improving design theories. In Reigeluth, C. M. (Ed.), *Instructional-design theories and models: A new paradigm of instructional theory* (*Vol. 2*, pp. 633–651). Mahwah, NJ: Lawrence Erlbaum Associates.

Reigeluth, C. M., & Stein, F. S. (1983). The Elaboration Theory of Instruction. In Reigeluth, C. M. (Ed.), *Instructional-Design Theories and Models: An Overview of Their Current Status* (*Vol. 1*, pp. 335–381). Hillsdale, N.J.: Erlbaum.

Reigler, A. (2003). Whose anticipations? In Butz, M. V., Sigaud, O., & Gerard, P. (Eds.), *Anticipatory behavior in adaptive learning systems*. Berlin: Springer.

Renkl, A. (2005). The worked-out examples principle in multimedia learning. In Mayer, R. E. (Ed.), *The Cambridge handbook of multimedia learning* (pp. 229–246). New York: Cambridge University Press.

Renkl, A., & Atkinson, R. K. (2003). Structuring the transition from example study to problem solving in cognitive skills acquisition: A cognitive load perspective. *Educational Psychologist, 38*, 15–22. doi:10.1207/S15326985EP3801_3

Renkl, A., Atkinson, R. K., Maier, U. H., & Staley, R. (2002). From example study to problem solving: Smooth transitions help learning. *Journal of Experimental Education, 70*, 293–315. doi:10.1080/00220970209599510

Resnick, M. (2004). Edutainment? No Thanks. I Prefer Playful Learning. *Associazione Civita Report on Edutainment*. Retrieved from http://www.parents-choice.org/full_abstract.cfm?art_id=172&the_page=consider_this

Ribbit's Big Splash, (2009). [computer software]Mobile, AL: Educational Concepts.

Rice, J. W. (2007). Assessing higher order thinking in video games. *Journal of Technology and Teacher Education, 15*(1), 87–100.

Rieber, L. P. (1996). Seriously considering play: Designing interactive learning environments based on the blending of microworlds, simulations, and games. *Educational Technology Research and Development, 44*(2), 43–58. doi:10.1007/BF02300540

Rieber, L. P. (2005). Multimedia Learning in Games, Simulations, and Microworlds. In Mayer, R. E. (Ed.), *The Cambridge Handbook of Multimedia Learning* (pp. 549–567). Cambridge, MA: Cambridge University Press.

Rieber, L. P., Davis, J., Matzko, M., & Grant, M. (2001, April 10–14). *Children as multimedia critics: Middle school students' motivation for and critical analysis of educational multimedia designed by other children*. Paper presented at the What We Know and How We Know It, Seattle, WA. Rieber, L. P., & Matzko, M. J. (2001). Serious design for serious play in physics. *Educational Technology, 41*(1), 14–24.

Riegle, R., & Matejka, W. (2006). *Dying to learn: Instructional design and MMORPGs*. 21st Annual Conference on Distance Teaching and Learning. Retrieved from http://people.coe.ilstu.edu/rpriegle/mmorpg/index.htm

Rilstone, A. (1994). Role playing games: An overview. *Inter*Action, 1*. Retrieved from http://www.rpg.net/oracle/essays/rpgoverview.html

Rogers, E. M. (1962). *The diffusion of innovations*. Glencoe, IL: The Free Press of Glencoe.

Rogers, E. M., & Shoemaker, F. F. (1971). *Communication of innovations: A cross-cultural approach*. New York: The Free Press.

Rogers, P. C., Hsueh, S. L., & Gibbons, A. S. (2005). *The generative aspect of design theory*. Paper presented at the Fifth IEEE International Conference on Advanced Learning Technologies (ICALT'05).

Rollings, A., & Adams, E. (2003). *Andrew Rollings and Ernest Adams on game design.* Thousand Oaks, CA: New Riders Publishing.

Rosas, R., Nussbaum, M., Cumsille, P., Marianov, V., Correa, M. n., & Flores, P. (2003). Beyond Nintendo: Design and assessment of educational video games for first and second grade students. *Computers & Education, 40*(1), 71. doi:10.1016/S0360-1315(02)00099-4

Rosen, R. (1985). *Anticipatory systems: Philosophical, Mathematical and methodological foundations.* New York: Pergamon Press.

Rosen, R. (2000). *Essays on life itself.* New York: Columbia University Press.

Rosenfeld, S. B. (1982, June). *Informal learning and computers.* Position paper prepared for the Atari Institute for Education-Action Research.

Rosson, M. B., & Carroll, J. M. (1995). Narrowing the specification-implementation gap in scenario-based design. In Carroll, J. M. (Ed.), *Designing interaction: Psychology at the human-computer interface* (pp. 247–278). New York: Cambridge University Press.

Rosson, M. B., & Carroll, J. M. (2002a). Scenario-based design. In Jacko, J., & Sears, A. (Eds.), *The human-computer interaction handbook: Fundamentals, evolving technologies and emerging applications* (pp. 1032–1050). Mahwah, NJ: Lawrence Erlbaum Associates.

Rosson, M. B., & Carroll, J. M. (2002b). *Usability engineering: Scenario-based development of human-computer interaction.* San Francisco: Morgan Kaufmann.

Roth, W. M. (2001). Situating cognition. *Journal of the Learning Sciences, 10*(1/2), 27–61. doi:10.1207/S15327809JLS10-1-2_4

Rourke, A., & Sweller, J. (2009). The worked-example effect using ill-defined problems: Learning to recognise designers' styles. *Learning and Instruction, 19*, 185–199. doi:10.1016/j.learninstruc.2008.03.006

Rouse, R. (2005). *Game design: Theory & practice.* Plano, TX: Wordware Publishing, Inc.

Rovai, A. P. (2007). Facilitating online discussions effectively. *The Internet and Higher Education, 10*(1), 77–88. doi:10.1016/j.iheduc.2006.10.001

Rubin, J. (1994). *Handbook of usability testing: How to plan, design, and conduct effective tests.* Chichester, UK: John Wiley and Sons.

Ruiz, S., York, A., Truong, H., Tarr, A., Keating, N., Stein, M., et al. (2006). *Darfur is Dying.* Thesis Project. Retrieved from http://interactive.usc.edu/projects/games/20070125-darfur_is_.php

Rumzan, I. (2002). Research report. [Review of the article Building an Educational Adventure Game: Theory, Design and Lessons, by Amory (2001)]. *Canadian Journal of Learning and Technology, 28*(3), 143–144.

Rutter, J., & Bryce, J. (n.d.). *Digiplay initiative.* Retrieved from http://digiplay.info/

Saini-Eidukat, B., Schwert, D. P., & Slator, B. M. (2001). Geology explorer: Virtual geologic mapping and interpretation. *Journal of Computers and Geosciences, 27*(4).

Salen, K. (2007). Gaming literacy studies: A game design study in action. *Journal of Educational Media and Hypermedia, 16*(3), 301–322.

Salen, K. (2007). Toward an ecology of gaming. In Salen, K. (Ed.), *The ecology of games: Connecting youth, games, and learning* (pp. 1–20). Cambridge, MA: MIT Press.

Salen, K., & Zimmerman, E. (2004). *Rules of play: Game design fundamentals.* Cambridge, MA: MIT Press.

Salisbury, D. F. (1988). Effect drill and practice strategies. In Jonassen, D. H. (Ed.), *Instructional designs for microcomputer courseware* (pp. 103–124). Mahwah, NJ: Lawrence Erlbaum.

Salisbury, D. F., & Klein, J. D. (1988). A comparison of a microcomputer progressive state drill and flashcards for learning paired associates. *Journal of Computer-Based Instruction, 15*(4), 136–143.

Salomon, G. (1979). *Interaction of media, cognition, and learning.* San Francisco: Jossey-Bass.

Sandberg, I. W., Lo, J. T., Fancourt, C. L., Principe, J. C., Katagiri, S., & Haykin, S. (2001). *Nonlinear dynamical systems: Feedforward neural network perspectives.* New York: John Wiley & Sons, Inc.

Sandford, R., Ulicsak, M., Facer, K., & Rudd, T. (2006). *Teaching with games: Using commercial off-the-shelf computer games in formal education.* Bristol, UK: FutureLab. Retreived from http://www.futurelab.org.uk/projects/teaching-with-games/research/final-report

Santiago, R. S., & Okey, J. R. (1990). *The effects of advisement and locus of control on achievement in learner-controlled instruction.* Paper presented at the 32nd international conference of the Association for the Development of Computer-based Instructional Systems, San Diego, California, October 29-November 1, 1990.

Savery, J. R. (2006). Overview of problem based learning: Definitions and distinctions. *Interdisciplinary Journal of Problem Based Learning, 1*(1), 9–20.

Savery, J. R., & Duffy, T. M. (1995). Problem based learning: An instructional model and its constructivist framework. *Educational Technology, 35,* 31–38.

Sawyer, B. (2003). Serious games: Improving public policy through game-based learning and simulation. *Woodrow Wilson International Center for Scholars.* Retreived from http://wwics.si.edu/foresight/index.htm

Sawyer, B. (2006). *Serious games.* Retrieved from http://www.seriousgames.org./index.html

Schaal, S. (1999). Is imitation learning the route to humanoid robots? *Trends in Cognitive Sciences, 3*(6), 233–242. doi:10.1016/S1364-6613(99)01327-3

Schaal, S. (2003). Computational approaches to motor learning by imitation. *Philosophical Transactions of the Royal Society of London. Series B, Biological Sciences, 358*(1431), 537–547. doi:10.1098/rstb.2002.1258

Schaal, S. (2006). Dynamic movement primitives: A framework for motor control in humans and humanoid robotics. In Kimura, H., Tsuchiya, K., Ishiguro, A., & Witte, H. (Eds.), *Adaptive Motion of Animals and Machines* (pp. 261–280). Tokyo: Springer. doi:10.1007/4-431-31381-8_23

Schack, T. (2004). The cognitive architecture of complex movement. *International Journal of Sport and Exercise Psychology, 2,* 403–438.

Schank, R. C. (1998). *Inside multi-media case based instruction.* Mahwah, NJ: Lawrence Erlbaum Associates.

Schank, R. C. (1999). *Dynamic Memory Revisited.* New York: Cambridge University Press. doi:10.1017/CBO9780511527920

Schank, R. C. (2004). *Making minds less well educated than our own.* Mahwah, NJ: Lawrence Erlbaum Associates, Inc.

Schank, R. C., Berman, T. R., & Macpherson, K. A. (1999). Learning by doing. In Reigeluth, C. M. (Ed.), *Instructional-design theories and models.* Mahwah, NJ: Lawrence Erlbaum.

Schank, R. C., Fano, A., Bell, B., & Jona, M. (1994). The design of goal based scenarios. *Journal of the Learning Sciences, 3*(4), 305–345. doi:10.1207/s15327809jls0304_2

Schell, J. (2008). *The art of game design: A book of lenses.* New York: Elsevier.

Schilling-Estes. (1998). Investigating 'self-conscious' speech: The performance register in Ocracoke English. *Language in Society, 27,* 53–83.

Schmidt, R. A., & Lee, T. D. (2005). *Motor control and learning: A behavioral emphasis* (4th ed.). Champaign, IL: Human Kinetics.

Schön, D. A. (1988). Designing: Rules, types and worlds. *Design Studies, 9*(3), 181–190. doi:10.1016/0142-694X(88)90047-6

Schrader, P., & McCreery, M. (2007). The acquisition of skill and expertise in massively multiplayer online games. *Educational Technology Research and Development, 56*(5), 557–574. doi:10.1007/s11423-007-9055-4

Schrage, M. (2000). *Serious play: How the world's best companies simulate to innovate*. Boston: Harvard Business School Press.

Schroeder, R. (Ed.). (2002). *The social life of avatars: Presence and interaction in shared virtual environments*. London: Springer-Verlag.

Schuerman, R. L., & Peck, K. L. (1991). Pull-down menus, menu design, and usage patterns in computer-assisted instruction. *Journal of Computer-Based Instruction, 18*, 93–98.

Schwartz, D. L., & Bransford, J. D. (1998). A time for telling. *Cognition and Instruction, 16*(4), 475–522. doi:10.1207/s1532690xci1604_4

Schwartz, D. L., & Martin, T. (2004). Inventing to prepare for future learning: The hidden efficiency of encouraging original student production in statistics instruction. *Cognition and Instruction, 22*(2), 129–184. doi:10.1207/s1532690xci2202_1

Schwartz, D. L., Bransford, J. D., & Sears, D. (2005). Efficiency and innovation in transfer. In Mestre, J. P. (Ed.), *Transfer of learning from a modern multidisciplinary perspective* (pp. 1–51). Greenwich, CT: Information Age.

Scribner, S., & Cole, M. (1981). *The psychology of literacy*. Cambridge, MA: Harvard University Press.

Seels, B., & Richey, R. (1994). *Instructional technology: The definition and domains of the field*. Washington, DC: Association for Educational Communications and Technology.

Seidler, R. D., Noll, D. C., & Thiers, G. (2004). Feedforward and feedback processes in motor control. *NeuroImage, 22*, 1775–1783. doi:10.1016/j.neuroimage.2004.05.003

Seldin, T. (2008). *Montessori 101: Some basic information that every Montessori parent should know*. Retrieved June 11, 2008, from http://www.montessori.org/sitefiles/Montessori_101_nonprintable.pdf

Sengers, P. (2004). Schizophrenia and narrative in artificial agents. In Wardrip-Fruin, N., & Harrigan, P. (Eds.), *First person: New media as story, performance, and game* (pp. 95–116). Cambridge, MA: MIT Press.

Serious Games Initiative. (2010). Retrieved on January 14, 2010, from http://www.seriousgames.org/about2.html

Shaffer, D. (2005). *Epistemic games*. Retrieved from http://www.innovateonline.info/index.php?view=article&id=79

Shaffer, D. W. (2006). *How computer games help children learn*. New York: Palgrave MacMillan. doi:10.1057/9780230601994

Shaffer, D. W., Squire, K. R., Halverson, R., & Gee, J. P. (2004). *Video games and the future of learning*. Madison, WI: University of Wisconsin-Madison, Academic Advanced Distributed Learning Co-Laboratory.

Sharritt, M. J. (in press). Evaluating video game design and interactivity. In Eck, R. V. (Ed.), *Interdisciplinary models and tools for serious games: Emerging concepts and future directions*. Hershey, PA: IGI Global.

Shaw, E., Johnson, W. L., & Ganeshan, R. (1999). *Pedagogical agents on the Web*. Retrieved from http://www.isi.edu/isd/ADE/papers/agents99/agents99.htm

Shearer, J. L., Kulakowski, B. T., & Gardner, J. F. (1997). *Dynamic modeling and control of engineering systems*. Upper Saddle River, NJ: Prentice Hall.

Sherlock, L. M. (2007). When social networking meets online games: The activity system of grouping in *World of Warcraft*. In *Proceedings of the 25th annual ACM international conference on Design of communication* (pp. 14–20).

Sigil. (2009). *Vanguard Saga of Heroes*. [Computer game]. Sony Online Entertainment.

Silber, K. H. (2007). A principle-based model of instructional design: A new way of thinking about and teaching ID. *Educational Technology*, (September-October): 5–19.

Silvern, S. B., Williamson, P. A., & Countermine, T. A. (1983a). *Video game playing and aggression in young children*. Paper presented to the American Educational Research Association, Montreal.

Silvern, S. B., Williamson, P. A., & Countermine, T. A. (1983b). *Video game play and social behavior: Preliminary findings.* Paper presented at the International Conference on Play and Play Environments.

Simon, H. A. (1996). *The sciences of the artificial.* Cambridge, MA: MIT Press.

Simon, H., & Gilmartin, K. (1973). A simulation of memory for chess positions. *Cognitive Psychology, 5,* 29–46. doi:10.1016/0010-0285(73)90024-8

Simon, M. A. (1990). Invariants of human behavior. *Annual Review of Psychology, 41,* 1–19. doi:10.1146/annurev. ps.41.020190.000245

Simpson, J. A., & Weiner, E. S. C. (Eds.). (1989). *Oxford English Dictionary* (2nd ed.). Oxford, UK: Clarendon Press.

SimulLearn. (2006). Independent research from corporate, academic, and military institutions on the effectiveness of SimuLearn's *Virtual Leader.* Retrieved from http://www.simulearn.net/pdf/practiceware_works.pdf

Singer, J. L., & Singer, D. G. (1981). *Television, imagination and aggression: A study of preschoolers.* Hillsdale, NJ: Erlbaum.

Skyttner, L. (2005). *General systems theory: Problems, perspectives, practice* (2nd ed.). Singapore: World Scientific Publishing Co Inc.

Slater, M., & Wilbur, S. (1997). A framework for immersive virtual environments (FIVE)—Speculations on the role of presence in virtual environments. *Presence (Cambridge, Mass.), 6*(6), 603–616.

Slator, B. M., Beckwith, R., Brandt, L., Chaput, H., Clark, J. T., & Daniels, L. M. (2006). *Electric worlds in the classroom: Teaching and learning with role-based computer games.* New York: Teachers College Press.

Slator, B. M., Chaput, H., Cosmano, R., Dischinger, B., Imdieke, C., & Vender, B. (2006). A multi-user desktop virtual environment for teaching shop-keeping to children. *Virtual Reality Journal, 9,* 49–56. doi:10.1007/s10055-005-0003-5

Slator, B. M., Clark, J. T., Landrum, J., III, Bergstrom, A., Hawley, J., Johnston, E., & Fisher, S. *(2001). Teaching with immersive virtual archaeology. In* Proceedings of the 7th International Conference on Virtual Systems and Multimedia *(VSMM-2001), Berkeley, CA, Oct. 25-27.*

Slator, B. M., Daniels, L. M., Saini-Eidukat, B., Schwert, D. P., Borchert, O., Hokanson, G., & Beckwith, R. T. *(2003). Software tutors for scaffolding on Planet Oit. In* Proceedings of the 3rd IEEE International Conference on Advanced Learning Technologies *(ICALT) (pp. 398-399). Athens, Greece, July 9-11.*

Slator, B., Dong, A., Erickson, K., Flaskerud, D., Halvorson, J., Myronovych, O., et al. (2005). Comparing two immersive virtual environments for education. In Proceedings of E-Learn 2005, Vancouver, Canada, October 24-28.

Sloane, F. (2006). Normal and design sciences in education: Why both are necessary. In Van den Akker, J., Gravemeijer, K., McKenney, S., & Nieveen, N. (Eds.), *Educational design research: the design, development and evaluation of programs, processes, and products* (p. 163). London: Routledge.

Smith, G. H. (1972). Like-A-Fishhook Village and Fort Berthold, Garrison Reservoir North Dakota. Anthropological Papers 2. Washington, DC: National Park Service, US Department of the Interior.

Smith, J. (2008). Facebook to blame for friendship addiction. *Therapy Today, 19*(9), 10–11.

Smith, P. L., & Ragan, T. J. (2005). *Instructional design* (3rd ed.). Hoboken, NJ: John Wiley & Sons.

Smyth, P. (2007). Beyond self-selection in video game play: An experimental examination of the consequences of massively multiplayer online role-playing game play. *Cyberpsychology & Behavior, 10*(7), 32–39.

Sonstroem, E. (2006). Do you really want a revolution? Cybertheory meets real-life pedagogical practice in Franken MOO and the conventional literature classroom. *College Literature, 33*(3), 148–170. doi:10.1353/lit.2006.0044

Sony Online Entertainment. (2009). *Everquest.* [Computer game].

Sony. (2006). *FlOw.* [Computer software]. Japan: Sony.

Sosnik, R., Hauptmann, B., Karni, A., & Flash, T. (2004). When practice leads to co-articulation: The evolution of geometrically defined movement primitives. *Experimental Brain Research, 156*(4), 422–438. doi:10.1007/s00221-003-1799-4

Sousa, D. (2005). *How the brain learns.* Thousand Oaks, CA: Corwin Press.

Spindler, G. (1955). *Sociocultural and psychological processes in Menomini acculturation. Culture and Society #5.* Berkeley, CA: University of California Press.

Spiro, R. J., & Jehng, J. C. (1990). Cognitive flexibility and hypertext: Theory and technology for the nonlinear and multidimensional traversal of complex subject matter. In Nix, D., & Spiro, R. J. (Eds.), *Cognition, education, and multimedia: Exploring ideas in high technology* (pp. 163–205). Hillsdale, NJ: Lawrence Erlbaum.

Spiro, R. J., Collins, B. P., Thota, J. J., & Feltovich, P. J. (2003). Cognitive flexibility theory: Hypermedia for complex learning, adaptive knowledge application, and experience acceleration. *Educational Technology, 43*(5), 5–10.

Squire, K. (2002). Cultural framing of computer games. *The international journal of computer game research.* Retrieved February 2003, from http://www.gamestudies.org/0102/squire/

Squire, K. (2002). Cultural framing of computer/video games. *Game Studies, 2*(1).

Squire, K. (2003). *Replaying history: Learning world history through playing Civilization III.* Unpublished dissertation, Indiana University.

Squire, K. (2005). *Game-based learning: Present and future state of the field.* Research paper presented at the e-learning CONSORTIUM.

Squire, K. D. (2005). Changing the game: What happens when videogames enter the classroom? *Innovate, 1*, 6.

Squire, K., & Gaydos, M. (in press). Citizen science: Designing a game for the 21st century. In Eck, R. V. (Ed.), *Interdisciplinary models and tools for serious games: Emerging concepts and future directions.* Hershey, PA: IGI Global.

Srivastava, J., Williams, D., Contractor, N., & Poole, S. (2009, February 12-16 22). *The Virtual World Exploratorium Project.* American Association for the Advancement of Science (AAAS) Conference, Chicago, Illinois.

Sriwatanakul, K., Kelvie, W., Lasagna, L., Calimlim, J. F., Weis, O. F., & Mehta, G. (1983). Visual analogue scales: Measurement of subjective phenomena. *Clinical Pharmacology and Therapeutics, 34*(2), 234–239.

Steinkuehler, C. (2004) Learning in massively multiplayer online games. In Y. Kafai, W. Sandoval, N. Enyedy, A. Nixon, & F. Herrera (Eds.), *Proceedings of the sixth ICLS.* Mahwah, NJ: Erlbaum, 521–528.

Steinkuehler, C. (2005). *Cognition and learning in massively multiplayer online games: A critical approach.* (Unpublished dissertation.) University of Wisconsin, Madison WI.

Steinkuehler, C. A. (2004). *Learning in massively multiplayer online games.* Paper presented at the International Conference on Learning Sciences, Santa Monica, CA.

Steinkuehler, C. A. (2006). Why Game (Culture) Studies Now? *Games and Culture, 1*(1), 97–102. doi:10.1177/1555412005281911

Steinkuehler, C., & Duncan, S. (2008). Scientific habits of mind in virtual worlds. *Journal of Science Education and Technology, 17*(6), 530–543. doi:10.1007/s10956-008-9120-8

Subrahmanyam, K., & Greenfield, P. M. (1994). Effect of video game practice on spatial skills in girls and boys. *Journal of Applied Developmental Psychology, 15*, 13–32. doi:10.1016/0193-3973(94)90004-3

Subrahmanyam, K., & Greenfield, P. M. (1999). Computer games for girls: What makes them play? In Cassell, J., & Jenkins, H. (Eds.), *Barbie to Mortal Kombat: Gender and computer games* (pp. 46–71). Cambridge, MA: MIT Press.

Suits, B. (1978). *The grasshopper: Games, life, and utopia.* Ontario, CA: University of Toronto Press.

Sutton-Smith, B. (1997). *The ambiguity of play.* Cambridge, MA: Harvard University Press.

Svensson, P. (2003). Virtual worlds as arenas for language learning. *Language learning online: Towards best practice, 10*(1), 123–142.

Swan, R. H. (2005, October 2005). *Design structures for intrinsic motivation.* Paper presented at the The Interservice/Industry Training, Simulation & Education Conference (I/ITSEC) Orlando, FL.

Swan, R. H. (2008). *Deriving operational principles for the design of engaging learning experiences.* Unpublished dissertation, Brigham Young University, Provo, UT.

Sweller, J. (1994). Cognitive load theory, learning difficulty, and instructional design. *Learning and Instruction, 4*, 295–312. doi:10.1016/0959-4752(94)90003-5

Sweller, J. (1999). *Instructional design in technical areas.* Camberwell, Victoria, Australia: Australian Council for Educational Research.

Sweller, J. (2003). Evolution of human cognitive architecture. In Ross, B. (Ed.), *The psychology of learning and motivation* (*Vol. 43*, pp. 215–266). San Diego: Academic Press.

Sweller, J. (2004). Instructional design consequences of an analogy between evolution by natural selection and human cognitive architecture. *Instructional Science, 32*, 9–31. doi:10.1023/B:TRUC.0000021808.72598.4d

Sweller, J. (2008). Instructional implications of David Geary's evolutionary educational psychology. *Educational Psychologist, 43*, 214–216. doi:10.1080/00461520802392208

Sweller, J. (2009). Cognitive bases of human creativity. *Educational Psychology Review, 21*, 11–19. doi:10.1007/s10648-008-9091-6

Sweller, J., & Chandler, P. (1994). Why some material is difficult to learn. *Cognition and Instruction, 12*, 185–233. doi:10.1207/s1532690xci1203_1

Sweller, J., & Cooper, G. (1985). The use of worked examples as a substitute for problem solving in learning algebra. *Cognition and Instruction, 2*, 59–89. doi:10.1207/s1532690xci0201_3

Sweller, J., & Sweller, S. (2006). Natural information processing systems. *Evolutionary Psychology, 4*, 434–458.

Sykora, J., & Birkner, J. (1982). *The video master's guide to Pac-Man.* New York: Bantam.

Taba, H. (1962). *Curriculum development: Theory and practice.* New York: Harcourt, Brace & World.

Tarmizi, R., & Sweller, J. (1988). Guidance during mathematical problem solving. *Journal of Educational Psychology, 80*, 424–436. doi:10.1037/0022-0663.80.4.424

Tennyson, R. D. (1980). Instructional Control Strategies and Content Structure as Design Variables in Concept Acquisition Using Computer-Based Instruction. *Journal of Educational Psychology, 72*(4), 525–532. doi:10.1037/0022-0663.72.4.525

Tessmer, M. (1993). *Planning and conducting formative evaluation.* London: Kogan Page Limited.

Tettegah, S. (2007). Pre-service teachers, victim empathy, and problem solving using animated narrative vignettes. *Technology, Instruction. Cognition and Learning, 5*, 41–68.

Tettegah, S., & Anderson, C. (2007). Pre-service teachers' empathy and cognitions: Statistical analysis of text data by graphical models. *Contemporary Educational Psychology, 32*, 48–82. doi:10.1016/j.cedpsych.2006.10.010

Tettegah, S., & Neville, H. (2007). Empathy among Black youth: Simulating race-related aggression in the classroom. *Scientia Paedagogica Experimentalis, XLIV, 1*, 33–48.

The Longman Dictionary of Contemporary English Online. (n.d.). Retrieved from http://www.ldoceonline.com/

Thomas, J., Bol, L., Warkentin, R., Wilson, M., Strage, A., & Rohwer, W. (2006). Interrelationships among students' study activities, self-concept of academic ability, and achievement as a function of characteristics of high-school biology courses. *Applied Cognitive Psychology*, *7*(6), 499–532. doi:10.1002/acp.2350070605

Thorndike, E. L., & Woodworth, R. S. (1901). The influence of improvement in one mental function upon the efficiency of other functions. *Psychological Review*, *9*, 374–382.

Tindall-Ford, S., Chandler, P., & Sweller, J. (1997). When two sensory modes are better than one. *Journal of Experimental Psychology. Applied*, *3*, 257–287. doi:10.1037/1076-898X.3.4.257

Tobias, S., & Fletcher, J. D. (2007). What research has to say about designing computer games for learning. *Educational Technology*, (September–October): 20–29.

Tripp, S. D., & Bichelmeyer, B. (1990). Rapid prototyping: An alternative instructional design strategy. *Educational Technology Research and Development*, *38*(1), 31–44. doi:10.1007/BF02298246

Tuovinen, J., & Sweller, J. (1999). A comparison of cognitive load associated with discovery learning and worked examples. *Journal of Educational Psychology*, *91*, 334–341. doi:10.1037/0022-0663.91.2.334

Turkle, S. (1995). *Life on the screen: Identity in the age of the Internet*. New York: Simon & Schuster.

Turner, V. (1987). *The anthropology of performance*. New York: PAJ Publications.

Um, E., Song, H., & Plass, J. L. (2007). *The effect of positive emotions on multimedia learning*. Paper presented at the World Conference on Educational Multimedia, Hypermedia & Telecommunications (ED-MEDIA 2007) in Vancouver, Canada, June 25–29, 2007.

Valente, A., Johnson, W. L., Wertheim, S., Barrett, K., Flowers, M., & LaBore, K. (2009). *A dynamic methodology for developing situated culture training content*. *Alelo TLT*. LLC.

Van Aken, J. E. (2004). Management research based on the paradigm of the design sciences: The quest for field-tested and grounded technological rules. *Journal of Management Studies*, *41*(2), 219–246. doi:10.1111/j.1467-6486.2004.00430.x

Van Eck, R. (2006). Building artificially intelligent learning games. In Gibson, D., Aldrich, C., & Prensky, M. (Eds.), *Games and simulations in online learning research & development frameworks*. Hershey, PA: Idea Group.

Van Eck, R. (2006). Digital game-based learning: It's not just the digital natives who are restless. *EDUCAUSE Review*, *41*, 16–30.

Van Eck, R. (2006). Using games to promote girls' positive attitudes toward technology. *Innovate Journal of Online Education*, *2*(3).

Van Eck, R. (2007). Six ideas in search of a discipline. In Shelton, B., & Wiley, D. (Eds.), *The design and use of simulation computer games in education*. Rotterdam, The Netherlands: Sense Publishing.

Van Eck, R. (2007). Six ideas in search of a discipline. In Spector, M., Seel, N., & Morgan, K. (Eds.), *Educational design and use of computer simulation games*. The Netherlands: Sense Publishing.

Van Eck, R. (2007a). Building intelligent learning games. In Gibson, D., Aldrich, C., & Prensky, M. (Eds.), *Games and simulations in online learning research & development frameworks*. Hershey, PA: Idea Group.

Van Eck, R. (2008). COTS in the Classroom: A teachers guide to integrating commercial off- the-shelf (COTS) games. In Ferdig, R. (Ed.), *Handbook of research on effective electronic gaming in education*. Hershey, PA: Idea Group.

Van Eck, R., & Dempsey, J. (2002). The effect of competition and contextualized advisement on the transfer of mathematics skills in a computer-based instructional simulation game. *Educational Technology Research and Development*, *50*(3), 23–41. doi:10.1007/BF02505023

Van Gerven, P. W. M., Paas, F. G. W. C., Van Merriënboer, J. J. G., & Schmidt, H. G. (2000). Cognitive Load Theory and the acquisition of complex cognitive skills in the elderly: Towards an integrative framework. *Educational Gerontology, 26*, 503–521. doi:10.1080/03601270050133874

van Gerven, P. W. M., Paas, F., van Merriënboer, J. J. G., & Schmidt, H. G. (2006). Modality and variability as factors in training the elderly. *Applied Cognitive Psychology, 20*, 311–320. doi:10.1002/acp.1247

van Gog, T., Ericsson, K., Rikers, R., & Paas, F. (2005). Instructional design for advanced learners: Establishing connections between the theoretical frameworks of cognitive load and deliberate practice. *Educational Technology Research and Development, 53*(3), 73–81. doi:10.1007/BF02504799

Van Merriënboer, J. J. G., & de Croock, M. B. M. (1992). Strategies for computer-based programming instruction: Program completion vs. program generation. *Journal of Educational Computing Research, 8*, 365–394.

van Merriënboer, J. J. G., Clark, R. E., & de Croock, M. B. M. (2002). Blueprints for complex learning: The 4C/ID-model. *Educational Technology Research and Development, 50*, 39–64. doi:10.1007/BF02504993

van Merriënboer, J., & Ayres, P. (2005). Research on cognitive load theory and its design implications for e-learning. *Educational Technology Research and Development, 53*(3), 5–13. doi:10.1007/BF02504793

VanLehn, K. (2006). The behavior of tutoring systems. *International Journal of Artificial Intelligence in Education, 16*(3), 227–265.

Veletsianos, G., & Miller, C. (2008). Conversing with pedagogical agents: A phenomenological exploration of interacting with digital entities. *British Journal of Educational Technology, 39*(6), 969–986. doi:10.1111/j.1467-8535.2007.00797.x

Vilhjalmsson, H., Merchant, C., & Samtani, P. (2007). Social puppets: Towards modular social animation for agents and avatars. *Lecture Notes in Computer Science, 4564*, 192. doi:10.1007/978-3-540-73257-0_22

Vincenti, W. G. (1990). *What engineers know and how they know it: analytical studies from aeronautical history.* Baltimore: Johns Hopkins University Press.

Vogel, J. J., Vogel, D. S., Cannon-Bowers, J., Bowers, C. A., Muse, K., & Wright, M. (2006). Computer games and interactive simulations for learning: A meta-analysis. *Journal of Educational Computing Research, 34*, 229–243. doi:10.2190/FLHV-K4WA-WPVQ-H0YM

Vygotsky, L. S. (1978). *Mind in society.* Cambridge, MA: Harvard University Press.

Vygotsky, L. S. (1986). *Thought and language.* Cambridge, MA: MIT Press.

Vygotsky, L. S., & Cole, M. (1977). *Mind in society: The development of higher psychological processes.* Cambridge, MA: Harvard University Press.

Waelder, P. (2006). *Bruised and happy: The addicted painstation players.* Paper presented at the medi@terra, September 27–October 1, 2006, Athens Greece.

Wagner, M. (2008). *Massively multiplayer online role-playing games as constructivist learning environments in K-12 education: A Delphi study* (Doctoral thesis.) Retrieved from http://edtechlife.com/?page_id=2008

Wang, N., & Johnson, W. L. (2008). The politeness effect in an intelligent foreign language tutoring system. *Lecture Notes in Computer Science, 5091*, 270–280. doi:10.1007/978-3-540-69132-7_31

Wanner, E. (1982, October). Computer time: The electronic Boogey-man. *Psychology Today*, 8–11.

Ward, M., & Sweller, J. (1990). Structuring effective worked examples. *Cognition and Instruction, 7*, 1–39. doi:10.1207/s1532690xci0701_1

Watson, W. R. (2007). *Formative research on an instructional design theory for educational video games.* Unpublished doctoral dissertation, Indiana University.

Wauters, R. (2008, October 29). *World of Warcraft* to surpass 11 million subscribers. *New York Times.*

Waxman, C., Lin, M., & Michko, G. (2003). *A meta-analysis of the effectiveness of teaching and learning with technology on student outcomes.* Naperville, IL: Learning Point Associates.

Wei, J. (2006). The role of everyday users in MMORPGs. *Driftreality*. Retrieved on August 28, 2007, from http://www.driftreality.com/london/mmorpgs.users.pdf

Weininger, M., & Shield, L. (2003). Promoting oral production in a written channel: An investigation of learner language MOO. *Computer Assisted Language Learning, 16*(4), 329–349. doi:10.1076/call.16.4.329.23414

Wenger, E. (1998). *Communities of practice: Learning, meaning, and identity*. New York: Cambridge University Press.

Wertheimer, M. (1945). *Productive thinking*. New York: Harper and Row.

Wertsch, J. V., Del Río, P., & Alvarez, A. (1995). Sociocultural studies: History, action, and mediation. In Wertsch, J. V., Del Río, P., & Alvarez, A. (Eds.), *Sociocultural studies of mind* (pp. 1–34). Cambridge, UK: Cambridge University Press.

West, C. K., Farmer, J. A., & Wolff, P. M. (1991). *Instructional design: Implications from cognitive science*. Englewood Cliffs, NJ: Prentice Hall.

Westrom, L. E., & Shaban, A. (1992). Intrinsic motivation in microcomputer games. *Journal of Research on Computing in Education, 24*(4), 433–445.

Wewers, M. E., & Lowe, N. K. (1990). A critical review of visual analogue scales in the measurement of clinical phenomena. *Research in Nursing & Health, 13*(4), 227–236. doi:10.1002/nur.4770130405

White, B. (2004). Making evidence-based medicine doable in everyday practice. *Family Practice Management, 11*(2), 51–58.

White, B. Y. (1984). Designing computer games to help physics students understand Newton's Laws of Motion. *Cognition and Instruction, 1*(1), 69. doi:10.1207/s1532690xci0101_4

Whitten, J. L., Bentley, L. D., & Dittman, K. (1989). *Systems analysis and design methods* (2nd ed.). Homewood, IL: Irwin.

Williams, A. M. (1999). *Visual perception and action in sport*. London: Spon Press.

Wilson, B. G. (1995). *Situated instructional design: Blurring the distinctions between theory and practice, design and implementation, curriculum and instruction*. Paper presented at the Association for Educational Communications and Technology, Anaheim, CA.

Wilson, D. (1992). Computer games: Academic obstacle or free-speech? *The Chronicle of Higher Education*, (November): 18.

Winn, B., & Heeter, C. (2007). Resolving conflicts in educational game design through playtesting. *Innovate Journal of Online Education, 3*(2).

Winn, J., & Heeter, C. (2009). Gaming, gender, and time: Who makes time to play? *Journal of Sex Roles, 61*(1–2), 1–13. doi:10.1007/s11199-009-9595-7

Winograd, T., & Flores, F. (1986). *Understanding computers and cognition: A new foundation for design*. Norwood, NJ: Ablex Publishing Corporation.

Wispé, L. (1987). History of the concept of empathy. In Eisenberg, N., & Strayer, J. (Eds.), *Empathy and its development*. Cambridge, UK: Cambridge University Press.

Wittgenstein, L. (1973). *Philosophical investigations: The English text of the* (3rd ed.). New York: Macmillan.

Wolcott, H. F. (1985). On ethnographic intent. *Educational Administration Quarterly, 21*(3), 187–203. doi:10.1177/0013161X85021003004

Wolcott, H. F. (1991). Propriospect and the acquisition of culture. *Anthropology & Education Quarterly, 22*(3), 251–273. doi:10.1525/aeq.1991.22.3.05x1052l

Wong Fillmore, L. (1991). Second-language learning in children: A model of language learning in social context. In Bialystok, E. (Ed.), *Language processing in bilingual children* (pp. 49–69). Cambridge, UK: Cambridge University Press. doi:10.1017/CBO9780511620652.005

WoW Web Stats. (n.d.). Retrieved February 20, 2009, from http://wowwebstats.com/

Wright, W. (2003). Forward. In *Freeman, D. Creating emotion in games: The craft and art of emotioneering*. Indianapolis, IN: New Riders Games.

Wright, W. (2004). Pop quiz with Will Wright, Education Arcade. Los Angeles: E3.

Wright, W. (2004). *Sculpting possibility space*. Paper presented at the Accelerating Change 2004: Physical Space, Virtual Space, and Interface conference (keynote address). Retrieved June 16, 2006, from http://cdn.itconversations.com/ITC.AC2004-WillWright-2004.11.07.mp3

Wright, W. (2006). Dream machines. *Wired, 14*(4). Retrieved from http://www.wired.com/wired/archive/14.04/wright.html

Wu, S. (2008). *Reducing unproductive learning activities in serious games for second language acquisition*. CA, USA: University of Southern California.

MMORPG. *com*. (n.d.). Retrieved from http://mmorpg.com/gamelist.cfm

Yang, H., Wu, C., & Wang, K. (2007). An empirical analysis of online game service satisfaction and loyalty. *Expert Systems with Applications, 36*(2), 1816–1825. doi:10.1016/j.eswa.2007.12.005

Yee, N. (2005). The psychology of MMORPGs: Emotional investment, motivations, relationships, and problematic usage. In Schroeder, R., & Axelsson, A. (Eds.), *Social life of avatars II*. London: Springer-Verlag.

Yee, N. (2006). Motivations of play in online games. *Cyberpsychology & Behavior, 9*(6), 772–775. doi:10.1089/cpb.2006.9.772

Yee, N. (2006). The demographics, motivations and derived experiences of users of massively-multiuser online graphical environments. *Presence (Cambridge, Mass.)*, 309–329. doi:10.1162/pres.15.3.309

Yee, N. (2008). Maps of digital desires: Exploring the topography of gender and play in online games. In Kafai, Y., Heeter, C., Denner, J., & Sun, J. (Eds.), *Beyond Barbie and Mortal Kombat: New perspectives in gender and gaming*. Cambridge, MA: MIT Press.

Yeung, A. S., Jin, P., & Sweller, J. (1998). Cognitive load and learner expertise: Split-attention and redundancy effects in reading with explanatory notes. *Contemporary Educational Psychology, 23*, 1–21. doi:10.1006/ceps.1997.0951

Zeelenberg, M. (1999). Anticipated regret, expected feedback and behavioral decision making. *Journal of Behavioral Decision Making, 12*(2). doi: Document ID: 349484671

Zhang, Q., & Lin, H. (2005). Worked example learning about the rules of the four fundamental Admixture operations of arithmetic. *Acta Psychologica Sinica, 37*, 784–790.

Zimmer, C. (2008, September 2). Gaming evolves. *The New York Times*. Retrieved from http://www.nytimes.com/2008/09/02/science/02spor.html?_r=1&8dpc&oref=slogin

Zyda, M. (2005). From visual simulation to virtual reality to games. *IEEE Computer, 38*(9), 25–32.

Zyda, M. (2007). Creating a science of games. *Communications of the ACM, 50*(7), 27–29.

About the Contributors

Richard Van Eck is Associate Professor and Graduate Director of the Instructional Design & Technology program at the University of North Dakota (idt.und.edu). He has an M.A. in Creative Writing from the University of North Dakota and a Ph.D. in instructional design and development from the University of South Alabama. He was the Media Arts and Communication director at Cochise College, an assistant professor and member of the Institute for Intelligent Systems at the University of Memphis, and served on the board of directors for the North American Simulation and Gaming Association from 2006–2009. He has published and presented extensively in the field of digital game-based learning and has created six original games for learning. He is currently conducting research on visual accommodation and EEG during videogame play, and developing a game on scientific problem for middle school students. In addition to his work in serious games, he has also published and presented on intelligent tutoring systems, pedagogical agents, authoring tools, and gender and technology. He currently lives in North Dakota with his wife Sandra, their two dogs and three cats.

* * *

Amy Adcock teaches courses in Instructional Design & Technology at Old Dominion University in Norfolk, Virginia. She obtained her Doctor of Education degree in Instructional Design & Technology from the University of Memphis in 2004. Her research interests include development and practical uses of multimedia learning environments, the use of instructional games and simulations for educational purposes, and exploring the links between cognitive psychology and instructional design. Amy is President-elect of the Design and Development Division of AECT and Managing Editor of the Technology, Instruction, Cognition and Learning journal.

Bodi Anderson received his B.A. in Japanese linguistics from the University of Arizona in 1992 and his M.A. in Applied Linguistics/TESOL from Northern Arizona University in 2002. He has taught at many universities in Japan, most notably in the science department of Kwansei Gakuin Univeristy and lived there a total of nine years before returning to the United States. He is currently a doctoral candidate in the Educational Technology program at Northern Arizona University. His current research interests include corpus-based examination of linguistic features of interactions in massive multiplayer online role playing games (MMORPGS), using MMORPGs to support learning, and the role of culture in distance education settings. Bodi and his wife Ayaka are currently expecting their first child come October and Bodi hopes his son will appreciate a father who encourages his child to play video games as a means to learn.

Kerrin Barrett has over 20 years varied experience in designing, developing, and implementing courses for a wide variety of audiences in the public, private, and international sectors. In 2008, she obtained her Ph.D. from the University of New Mexico in Organizational Learning and Instructional Technology, with a research focus at the intersection of distance education, culture and language learning. She holds an Ed.M. in Technology in Education from the Harvard Graduate School of Education. Throughout Dr. Barrett's career she has collaborated closely with customers to design innovative courses that leverage technology while considering culture and issues of access. Dr. Barrett has broad experience in instructional design and in the integration of technology into education projects that span cultures. Since 1999, Dr. Barrett has focused her applied research on online course design that leverages synchronous communication for language and culture learning. Currently, Dr. Barrett is Director of the Content Design and Development team at Alelo.

Katrin Becker has taught Computer Science at the post-secondary level for 30 years. She holds a PhD in Educational Technology with a focus on instructional game design. She's been using digital games to teach programming since 1998 and taught one of the first Digital Game Based Learning courses for an Education faculty. She has recently developed a new approach to the study of game design called Game Ethology that approaches the analysis of interactive software by combining software ethology and ethological techniques.

Lee Belfore is an Associate Professor in the Department of Electrical and Computer Engineering at Old Dominion University. His research interests include virtual reality, medical modeling and simulation, game based learning, and web based simulation. Dr. Belfore received his BS in Electrical Engineering from Virginia Tech in 1982, his MSE in Electrical Engineering/Computer Science from Princeton University in 1983, and his Ph.D. in Electrical Engineering from The University of Virginia in 1990. Dr. Belfore is a Licensed Professional Engineer in the State of Virginia.

Otto Borchert was born in Valley City, North Dakota and raised in various locales throughout the tri-state area. He graduated with a Bachelors in Computer Science with a minor in Psychology from North Dakota State University in 2001. He continued on to graduate work at NDSU with Dr. Brian M. Slator as his advisor and completed the Masters degree in 2008 resulting in the thesis "Computer Supported Collaborative Learning in an Online Multiplayer Game." He is currently a Ph.D. candidate and research technician at NDSU. His research interests include computer supported collaborative learning, immersive virtual environments for education, computer science education, networks and network security, and microcomputer graphics.

Lisa Kaye Brandt Originally an OS/MVS IBM Assembler Language Systems Programmer in the 1980s, Dr. Brandt turned to Cultural Anthropology in the 1990s (U. Minnesota). Her research is at the intersection of conflict & change, sociocultural evolution & resource management, and language, learning, cognition & identity. She has taught and worked in academia, tribal communities, business, museums, and social theatre. She is Research Affiliate for North Dakota State University – Sociology-Anthropology Department.

Dennis Charsky is an assistant professor of instructional design and technology in the Department of Strategic Communication at Ithaca College, USA. Dennis teaches courses at the undergraduate and graduate level on instructional design, visual design and development, interactive media, virtual teams, eLearning, and serious games. His research interests include the effective integration of technology into training and instructional environments, innovative instructional strategies for eLearning, and the design of serious games. Dennis is also a part of Ithaca Content Architecture & Design (ICAD), www. icadmedia.com, a consulting firm specializing in instructional design, content architecture, and online learning design and development. Recently, Dennis was the lead designer for two online courses; human resources strategy and talent management.

J.V. Dempsey is a Professor of Instructional Design at the University of South Alabama. He is co-editor of the award-winning *Trends and Issues in Instructional Design and Technology*. He has conducted research and written extensively in a number of areas including digital games and the application of new technologies to learning. He may be reached at jdempsey@usouthal.edu.

Eric John Gutierrez was born in the state of Washington. With a father in the Air Force he had little time to grow up there. He actually spent most of his time growing up across various countries and states; including: Germany, Italy, Colorado and Arizona. Eric Gutierrez graduated high school in May of 2007 in Tucson, Arizona and was accepted to Northern Arizona University in Flagstaff, Arizona. Eric is currently a junior at NAU studying Mathematics Education Secondary Education. He spent his most recent summer months in Fargo, North Dakota studying Immersive Virtual Environments along with Dr. Slator and the computer science dept.

Patricia Greenfield Distinguished Professor of Psychology at UCLA and Director of the Children's Digital Media Center, Los Angeles, is an expert on cognition, culture, and human development. She is the author of *Mind and Media: The Effects of Television, Video Games, and Computers* (1984), subsequently translated into nine languages; coeditor of *Effects of Interactive Entertainment Technologies on Development* (1994); coeditor of *Children, Adolescents, and the Internet: A New Field of Inquiry in Developmental Psychology* (2006); and coeditor of *Social Networking on the Internet: Developmental Implications* (2008). In January 2009, her article, "Technology and Informal Education: What is Taught, What is Learned," appeared in a special issue of *Science* on technology and education. Her empirical research on the developmental implications of interactive media has included action video games, massive multiplayer online role-playing games, teen chat rooms, and social networking sites.

Carrie Heeter is a Professor in the Department of Telecommunication, Information Studies, and Media at Michigan State University, Creative Director of Virtual University Design and Technology, and a Principal in the GEL (Games for Entertainment and Learning) Lab. She co-founded and teaches in the MSU serious game design M.A. specialization. Heeter co-edited the recent book, *Beyond Barbie and Mortal Kombat: New perspectives in gender and gaming*, and is creator and curator of investiGaming. com, an online gateway to academic and industry research about gender and gaming. She designs and studies meaningful applications of emerging media. Over the last two decades her interactive designs have won more than 50 awards including Discover Magazine's software innovation of the year. Current work includes creating and studying games to exercise and enhance cognitive functions, constructing ways to measure fun in games, and inventing a new subgenre tentatively called deliberative decision games.

Guy Hokanson was born and raised in Fargo, North Dakota and the surrounding lake country. He graduated from North Dakota State University in 2000 with a Bachelors degree in Computer Science. He is currently a Research Technician for the Computer Science Department at North Dakota State University, and Programmer/Analyst for the NDSU Center for Science and Mathematics where he works on the development and implementation of a number of virtual learning environments. He is also in the Masters program at NDSU where his research interests include immersive virtual environments for education and expert tools for content creation.

Wen-Hao David Huang is an Assistant Professor of E-Learning in the Department of Human Resource Education at University of Illinois at Urbana-Champaign. His academic background, consisting of material science & engineering, educational technology, and executive business administration, has enabled him to conduct interdisciplinary projects for instructional and research purposes for years. Dr. Huang currently teaches Learning Technologies and Instructional Design in the context of human resource development and E-Learning. His research interests include (1) design of game-based learning environments, (2) design and evaluation of E-Learning systems for adult learners, (3) Web 2.0 emerging technologies and their impact on teaching and learning, (4) measurement and manipulation of cognitive load in multimedia learning environment.

Putai Jin is a Senior Lecturer at the University of New South Wales. His research interests are self-regulated learning and research methods in psychology and education.

Lewis Johnson co-founded Alelo while he was director of the Center for Advanced Research in Technology for Education (CARTE) at the Information Sciences Institute of the University of Southern California, where he was the principal investigator of the original Tactical Language project. He is currently Chief Scientist and President of Alelo, where he leads several research projects investigating the rapid acquisition of proficiency in language and culture. He also continues to be active in research focusing on the successful adoption of interactive learning environments and in the field of artificial intelligence. His work on Tactical Language won DARPA's Significant Technical Achievement Award in 2005. Dr. Johnson is past president of the International Artificial Intelligence in Education Society, and past chair of the ACM Special Interest Group for Artificial Intelligence. He holds a B.A. in linguistics from Princeton University and a Ph.D. in computer science from Yale University.

Renae Low is a Senior Lecturer at the University of New South Wales. Her research interest is in educational psychology for learning and teaching.

Brian Magerko is an Assistant Professor of Digital Media in the School of Literature, Communication, and Culture at the Georgia Institute of Technology. He is director of the Adaptive Digital Media (ADAM) Lab, which explores how to use artificial intelligence to create digital media experiences that tailor themselves to the individuals that use them, and a principal member of the Experimental Game Lab. Dr. Magerko has published numerous articles myriad serious games projects that employ artificial intelligence to adapt narrative and learning content to individual players. He teaches in the Computational Media program, a joint offering between the College of Computing and Digital Media, and in the Digital Media graduate program.

Tim Marsh is currently Assistant Professor at the National University of Singapore (NUS). His Ph.D is in Computer Science specializing in Human-Computer Interaction (HCI) from the HCI Group, University of York, UK, MSc in Computer Graphics & Visualization, and BSc (HONS) in Information Technology. Tim's interdisciplinary research interests are in evaluation, design and development of interactive digital media, simulation, games and serious games. His research in gaming focuses on film informing design for experiential and contemplative gameplay, and development of continuous and unobtrusive approach to analyze player's behavior and experience. He currently teaches graduate modules in serious games and human-computer interaction. Previously he's held positions at the University of Southern California (USC), Los Angeles and at Eindhoven University of Technology, The Netherlands. He's served as reviewer and as organizing committee member of numerous publications and conferences including ACM SIGGRAPH and currently serves as Secretary of IFIP on 'Entertainment Computing'.

Ben Medler is a Ph.D. student at the Georgia Institute of Technology. His research revolves around how players differentiate from one another and what that means for game design and game playing itself. In pursuit of his research, Ben is building game metric/analytic tools in order to collect player gameplay data, which is used to learn about each player's differences by analyzing their gameplay habits. This data can be analyzed through various data mining, statistical, and sociological methods in an attempt to understand player differences and how they can be leveraged in games. In parallel, Ben is researching the ethics behind gathering player gameplay data; looking for best practices that will give players their privacy but allow game designers to use player differences in their game's design.

Gary R. Morrison is a professor and graduate program director in the instructional design and technology program at Old Dominion University. His research focuses on cognitive load theory, instructional strategies, K-12 technology integration, and distance education. He is author of two books: Morrison, Ross, & Kemp's *Designing Effective Instruction* (5th Edition) and Morrison & Lowther's *Integrating Computer Technology into the Classroom* (4th Edition). He has written over 25 book chapters and over 35 articles on instructional design and educational technology. Gary is the editor of the *Journal of Computing in Higher Education* and is on the editorial boards of *Computers in Human Behavior,* and *Quarterly Review of Distance Education.* He has worked as instructional designer for three Fortune 500 companies and the University of Mid-America. Gary is a past president of Association for Educational Communication and Technology's (AECT) Research and Theory Division and Design, Development Division, and Distance Learning Division.

Brian M. Slator was raised in Minnesota and graduated with a Bachelors in Computer Science (with a second major in English), from the University of Wisconsin - La Crosse in 1983. He attended graduate school at New Mexico State University where he studied with Yorick Wilks and received a PhD in Computer Science in 1988. After serving six years as a research scientist at the Institute for the Learning Sciences at Northwestern University he joined the Computer Science department at North Dakota State University in 1996 where he is currently a professor and engaged in research dealing with learning in role-based simulations.

Debbie Denise Reese is Senior Educational Researcher at the Wheeling Jesuit University Center for Educational Technologies® and NASA-sponsored Classroom of the Future™ (COTF) in Wheeling, WV. An instructional theorist, Reese applies cognitive science theory to the design of learning environments and technology tools. She is PI for the NSF-funded CyGaMEs project studying design, learning, and assessment via game-based technologies and applied cognitive science analogical reasoning theory. Reese developed the CyGaMEs approach as lead COTF researcher and project manager supporting NASA eEducation's initiative to study learning and assessment within game-based environments. Reese has lead COTF design and research teams in development and study of technology tools for enhancing self-efficacy, identity, and argumentation. She also conducts evaluation and needs assessment research. She is part of the COTF team producing *MoonWorld,* a 3D, persistent, virtual world simulation for introductory lunar science field work opening in Second Life in late 2009.

Richard Swan has worked in the field of instructional design and instructional technology for the past fifteen years. He currently works as a Teaching & Learning Consultant for the Center for Teaching & Learning at Brigham Young University. Richard has been a member of the development team for several nationally-published instructional products including the Virtual ChemLab Series which was awarded the 2008 Pirelli award. Richard was also name one of the "Top 100 Media Producers" in 2002 by AV Video Multimedia Producer. He received his doctorate in Instructional Psychology and Technology; his research interests include learning theory, design theory, engagement, and the role of agency in learning.

John Sweller is an Emeritus Professor of Education at the University of New South Wales. His research is associated with cognitive load theory. The theory is a contributor to both research and debate on issues associated with human cognition, its links to evolution by natural selection, and the instructional design consequences that follow.

Sharon Tettegah is an Associate Professor in the Department of Curriculum and Instruction, at the University of Illinois, Urbana Champaign. Dr. Tettegah holds a doctorate degree in Educational Psychology, and also degrees in Curriculum and Supervision and Philosophy. In addition, she holds an appointment at the Beckman Institute where she is currently in the Division of Biotechnology, Cognitive Neuroscience Group. Her research focuses on the use of technologies to enhance teaching and learning with an emphasis on simulations and empathy.

Bradley Vender was born and raised in Bismarck, North Dakota. He moved to Fargo to attend college at North Dakota State University (NDSU) and has graduated twice from that institution with first a Bachelors in Computer Science in 1998 and then a Masters in Computer Science in 2004 from that institution. While studying at NDSU, he first encountered text based multi-user environment servers such as LPMud, MUSH and others before meeting Dr. Brian M. Slator and joining Dr. Slator's research projects. He is currently a research technician at NDSU, and the focus of his work there has been part of the development of the Virtual Cell and other environments as part of Dr. Slator's research group at NDSU.

Ginger S. Watson is an Associate Professor of Instructional Design & Technology in the Darden College of Education with a joint appointment at the Virginia Modeling, Analysis, and Simulation Center at Old Dominion University. She completed her Ph.D. at the University of Iowa in 1998 during which she received a number of awards including a Link Foundation Fellowship in Advanced Simulation and Training. She has 19 years experience in simulator research and development, including 15 years in senior and chief scientist positions. Her research interests include performance, cognition, and learning in simulation, gaming, and virtual environments. The backbone of this research is the use of measures to assess attention, immersion, and cognitive processing. She is an associate editor of the Journal of Computing in Higher Education.

Index

Symbols

3D worlds 284, 300
4 Cs in learner motivation 289

A

academic disciplines 55, 56, 70, 72
achievement-focused education 260
Achievement goal orientation 260, 262
Achiever 260, 263, 264, 265, 266, 268,
    270, 271, 272, 273
action 221, 222
active principle
    108, 111, 120, 121, 124, 128
activity-based scenario approach
    219, 220, 221, 222
activity-objective 222
activity theory 213, 215, 216, 217, 219,
    221, 222, 223
ADDIE 290
ad-hoc games 214
ad hoc language 216
ADP 328, 329
ADP to ATP 328
adventure serious games 193, 197, 198, 201,
    203, 205, 206
AI 197, 294, 295, 301
alternate reality 115, 116, 120
alternate reality games (ARGs) 172
analogical reasoning theory 228, 229
anchored instruction
    189, 191, 196, 197, 198, 202
anticipatory systems 121, 122
archaeologist's logbook 326
artificial neural networks 122
assessment 213, 214, 217

Associative 158, 159, 160, 162
ATP 328, 329, 330
authentic consequences 116, 117, 118, 120
Automatic 158, 159, 160, 161, 162
avatar 58, 59, 60, 61, 62, 64, 66, 67, 68,
    77, 79, 201, 202, 203, 204

B

behaviorist learning theory 170
biological evolution 171, 172
biologically primary knowledge 171
biologically secondary knowledge 171
Blackwood 331
Blackwood project 331

C

case-based reasoning 192
challenge 283, 287, 289, 290, 291
challenges 137, 138, 139
childhood education 55
closed system 172
cognition 152, 155, 158, 159, 160, 162,
    165, 167, 282, 283, 284, 291, 306,
    308, 311
Cognition and Technology Group at Vanderbilt
    University (CTGV) 196, 197
cognitive abilities 181
Cognitive Apprenticeship (CA) 191, 195,
    196, 198, 199, 206, 207, 208, 210,
    211
cognitive architecture 169, 170, 171, 174,
    180, 181, 185
cognitive artifacts 313
cognitive capacity
    137, 141, 143, 144, 145, 146